LETTERS OF
LOUIS MACNEICE

by Louis MacNeice

SELECTED POEMS (edited by Michael Longley)
COLLECTED POEMS (edited by Peter McDonald)
THE STRINGS ARE FALSE

LETTERS FROM ICELAND
with W. H. Auden

LETTERS OF
Louis MacNeice

Edited by
JONATHAN ALLISON

faber and faber

First published in 2010
by Faber and Faber Limited
Bloomsbury House,
74–77 Great Russell Street,
London WC1B 3DA

Typeset by Donald Sommerville
Printed in England by CPI Mackays, Chatham

A CIP record for this book
is available from the British Library

ISBN 9787–0–571–22441–8

2 4 6 8 10 9 7 5 3 1

To Corinna MacNeice
and
In Memory of Dan MacNeice (1934–2009)

Contents

Plates

Editor's Introduction

This volume contains an annotated selection of the letters of Louis MacNeice written over a period of nearly fifty years, from the year of his mother's death in 1914 to shortly before his own death in early September 1963. The first letters are written in the style of a young boy and his final letters were scribbled while lying in bed, before being admitted to St Leonard's hospital in Shoreditch, days before his death. In between are the letters of a life lived fully, with passion and intellectual candour. The book includes selections from sequences of letters to those who were close to the author, including his father (John Frederick MacNeice) and stepmother (Beatrice MacNeice), his first wife, Mary Beazley, and his second wife, the singer Hedli Anderson. Most of his family letters date from schooldays at Sherborne Prep and Marlborough, and from his time at Oxford. They are mainly addressed to his stepmother (though it was assumed that his father would read them), but he addressed a significant number of letters to his father only. There are several long sequences to his friends Anthony Blunt, John Hilton, E. R. Dodds and Mrs. A. E. (Betty) Dodds, and to the American author Eleanor Clark, with whom he had an affair in 1939–41. With the exception of the Dodds letters, which span a longer period, in each case these sequences are restricted to particular periods of his life: for example letters to Blunt and Hilton were written during school holidays and after they all went to university; the last letter to Blunt reproduced in this volume was written in 1936, just hours before MacNeice's departure for Iceland. And although there is a letter to Hilton dated 1963, the vast majority of the Hilton letters were written during the late 1920s and early 1930s. I have reprinted almost fifty letters to T. S. Eliot, for so many years MacNeice's editor at Faber, to whom he first wrote in April 1932.

If these ten sequences form in one sense the core of the volume, there are shorter groups of letters, many of them very important, such as those to his children Dan and Corinna, those to colleagues in the BBC – especially Laurence Gilliam and W. R. Rodgers – and small clusters of letters to his lovers Nancy Coldstream (in the 1930s) and Mary Wimbush (in the 1960s). Among letters to his editors, the Eliot sequence is by far the largest group, although he wrote regularly during the last years of his life to

Charles Monteith at Faber. Much earlier, he wrote during the 1930s to Geoffrey Grigson (editor of the important journal *New Verse*) and to John Lehmann who edited *New Writing* in the thirties and *London Magazine* in the fifties. There are letters to editors at Heinemann (Rupert Hart-Davis), Knopf (Philip Vaudrin) and Random House (Bennet Cerf), and at the *New Statesman* (John Freeman, Kingsley Martin and Karl Miller) and the *Observer* (Terry Kilmartin). There is a surprising approach made to Graham Greene, at one time editor of the short-lived *Night and Day*. One may assume there are more like these in the files of various journals and newspapers, which have not yet come to light. MacNeice's letters to editors tend to be businesslike and rather brief, although they reveal something about his work at particular moments in his career. They also say something about his sense of the relationship between writing and money. He was very far from being insistent on this issue but he could be quick to ask for an advance as the occasion demanded. Inevitably, there were proposals to editors that never came to fruition, such as his study of Latin humour (*The Roman Smile*), or his plan to write a book about teaching Classics in Britain, or a children's story about 'the goats of Croaghan' on Achill island, and there are proposals that had to be declined, for instance his suggestion in 1961 that Faber publish a book of poems about places. He wrote often about his volume of prose memoirs which he had contracted to finish, at one point tentatively titled *Plaudits & Aspersions, or Blessings & Curses*, a version of which appeared posthumously as *The Strings Are False*, edited by E. R. Dodds.

Apart from visiting the obvious archives in search of letters I have written to many libraries and individuals. Nevertheless, gaps remain. Auden kept very few letters of any kind, so apparently none from that important friendship have survived, although I have taken the liberty of reprinting MacNeice's public letter to Auden published in *New Verse* and, in an appendix, Auden's sole extant letter to MacNeice. During the thirties, MacNeice occasionally mentioned Stephen Spender and Christopher Isherwood but no letters have surfaced. In Belfast, I was unable to find in the obvious places any correspondence with his close friends George and Mercy MacCann, although the Bodleian holds enough MacCann letters to indicate that letters were certainly exchanged. I have found no letters to relations outside the immediate family circle. Nor have I found evidence of correspondence with contacts in India and Ghana, despite the author's travel to those countries. Other 'missing persons' include his close friend at Marlborough and Oxford, Graham Shepard; the German scholar Ernest Stahl, with whom he translated Goethe's *Faust*; his former teacher Clifford

Canning; and professional contacts such as Reggie Smith and Jack Dillon in the BBC.

The earliest letters are written from the Rectory at Carrickfergus and addressed to his father, away on business – on one occasion apparently in Scotland ('are there fish in the Firth of Forth?'). These letters are simple and descriptive of a boy's daily activities: reading the Bible, playing in the garden, going for walks, doing his schoolwork, strictly supervised by his governess Miss McCready. He was an observant child, and these letters capture the smallness of the boy's world, circumscribed by the Rectory, the cinderpath, the secret hiding places in the garden and beyond that the Lough with its view of distant sails. From an early age, he was intrigued by riddles and word-play, and in writing simple poems which he would send to his sister. They suggest an early interest in rhyme and a feel for rhythm, with a sense of the comic and absurd ('A great old Kangaroo / Used to tease poor Bamboo'). In another poem, the emphasis is on wildness and the wilderness: 'The Cliffs are high / Against the sky / In a wild country.' He ends with the enquiry 'Do you like it[?]' He is something of a performer.

MacNeice went to Sherborne Preparatory School at the age of ten, in November 1917 (his departure had been delayed by illness) and he attended the school until the summer of 1921. He sent a great many letters to his parents from there, written mandatorily on Sunday afternoons and hence sometimes striking a more dutiful than joyful note. They remain, however, an invaluable record of his childhood and youth, his experience of school and of the daily life that shaped him. The early letters from school are mostly addressed to his father, although some are addressed to both father and stepmother ('Daddie and Madre'); he starts writing exclusively to 'Madre' after about May 1918. They convey an impression of the narrowness of the school's world and of its petty hierarchies. It was clearly a competitive environment academically, and the form ranking was allocated weekly and duly reported home. As in most prep schools at the time, games were extremely important, and it was here that MacNeice developed a lifelong enthusiasm for rugby. At Sherborne Prep nature study and country walks were an important part of the curriculum, owing chiefly to the evidently benign influence of the headmaster Littleton Powys. Nature study encompassed lepidoptery, fossil-collecting and the study of local flora, and there are many excited references to these weekly expeditions and the discoveries they involved. In a letter of 1918 MacNeice includes a list of activities unique to the summer term which include 'caterpillars, butterflies, cricket' and 'collecting flowers' (19 May). Although limited by the constraints of school life, the Sherborne letters offer an interesting portrait of the artist as a young boy. Chatty, detailed, comically digressive, they obsessively register sports and exam results. There is pride and enthusiasm when the author scores a try, its description enhanced with a diagram and plan of the pitch. He writes about his reading – mainly the novels of Scott and Stevenson, his taste for whom was fed by gifts of bound volumes from his stepmother's sister, Eva Greer, who lived with the 'folk poetess' Gertrude Hind at Glassdrumman, Co. Down. His grandiloquent thank-you letters to Aunt Eva are cast in a high style, which he perhaps thought appropriate for the friend of a poet, even a 'folk-poet'.

While at Sherborne, MacNeice was very conscious of his Irishness, and of his being one of the few pupils who had to cross the Irish Sea at the beginning and end of every term. The travel arrangements via Kingstown, Holyhead and Euston (a journey sometimes completed with his sister) are rehearsed with great regularity and detail, and the sojourn occasionally sketched or mapped on the margins of the page. He tries to assess the accent of a temporary master from Galway, one Mr Maguire (later skewered in *The Strings Are False*, 1965). All of this he is acutely sensitive to, since his father is after all an Ulster clergyman with a southern accent. One of his teachers is a Mr Lindsay from Portadown, an avid supporter of the Orange Order; a letter written in spring 1918 concludes rather ominously (one might say very skilfully) with an account of Mr Lindsay's estimation of recent British administrators in Ireland: 'One day in Arith Mr. Lindsay started making a kind of lecture about England sending silly people to take care of Ireland. He said it was just the same as if a new headmaster came to the Prep., and somebody flung a pellet at him and it hit his eye and he rubbed his eye and didn't say "who flung that pellet?" then' (17 March 1918).

He went on to Marlborough College in September 1921, where he celebrated his fourteenth birthday. There he remained until 1926, when he obtained a Postmastership (scholarship) at Merton College, Oxford. Letters home from Marlborough suggest a big change from Sherborne Prep, as he adjusts to the demands of a much larger and grander school, with a new vocabulary to master ('condescend the jam' for 'can you send – or please pass – the jam'). He is introduced to waterfagging and milkfagging and 'basements': a prefect's punishment which involved the mounting of many stairs. He was at first in 'A' House, where his form master was Clifford Canning (who remained a lifelong friend), but in his second year he was promoted to 'C' House and to the Classical Fifth. Here he came to know John Betjeman but his great friend was Graham Shepard, with whom he remained close until Shepard's untimely death in 1943. In the Lower Classical Sixth he met Anthony Blunt, who is first mentioned in a letter of June 1924 ('Blunt says Switzerland is very beautiful in parts but not as much as the Downs'). Blunt's opinions on Switzerland and much else clearly exerted a considerable influence over young MacNeice during the following years. Together they went for walks to Martinsell or to Barbury Camp. They collected flowers to arrange in their rooms, and travelled to Bath and to Malmesbury together. They displayed prints of Cézanne and other post-Impressionists which they borrowed or purchased at Zwemmer's art bookshop on the Charing Cross Road. Feeling embattled against the hearty ethos of the school and the hidebound traditionalism of its official culture, they enthusiastically supported modern art as an aspect of intellectual revolt, and their relationship with the art teacher, Christopher Hughes, was particularly heated. He disliked everything after the Pre-Raphaelites, an attitude which Blunt and MacNeice deplored. Together they attended meetings of the Anonymous Society, where Blunt presented papers on cubism and MacNeice spoke about Norse sagas and 'the mailed fist of common sense'. They painted still lives and considered painting frescoes on their study walls. Blunt showed MacNeice books about Byzantine art and 'Negro Sculpture'. Both sons of bishops, they were horrified by their friend Fortie Ross's decision to join the Church. They supported with enthusiasm the school's aesthete magazine, *The Heretick*, whose motto was 'Upon Philistia Will I Triumph' and which Blunt considered a way 'to express our disapproval of the Establishment generally, of the more out-of-date and pedantic masters'. Despite the throwaway intellectualism of much of the correspondence with Blunt, there is also a good deal of playfulness, whimsy and frivolity here, and a lot of posturing. It suggests the influence of Brideshead and of what MacNeice calls 'the Child Cult', but partly it is a Bloomsburyish mockery of Bloomsbury and the Sitwells. MacNeice's other great friend at this time was John Hilton, also in 'C' House and also with strong aesthetic leanings. Much of what we know about MacNeice at the time comes from Hilton's vivid memoir published as an appendix to *The Strings Are False*. MacNeice was delighted by his new friend, who 'took up the Child Cult with alacrity'. Letters to Hilton, which begin during the summer holidays after leaving Marlborough, seem more relaxed and playful, less striving after effect than letters to Blunt, but in many ways strike a similar note. In the first letter to Hilton, in summer 1926, his tone is buoyant and self-consciously whimsical; having read the plays of J. M.

Synge, he parodies stage Irish ('Synge-song') dialect: 'We will make lots of money for it's the great tongue I have.' And yet he warns Hilton against the mystique of Ireland – 'Ireland is a good place but you mustn't be sentimental.' (As he would later write in *Autumn Journal*, being Irish 'gives us a hold on the sentimental English / As members of a world that never was'.)

In his first weeks at Oxford he fraternises with other old Marlburians and satisfies himself that their rooms are not better than his. In an early letter from Merton, he tells Blunt – who has gone to King's College, Cambridge – that he has decorated his room with yellow chrysanthemums, has just seen a performance of *Hedda Gabler* and has recently written 'a perfect Eliotesque'. The poetry of T. S. Eliot looms large on the horizon in these years, and by contrast Osbert Sitwell (a previous favourite) seems like 'a female underdone Eliot'. He informs his parents that the dons are unimpressive ('like vegetables') and his fellow students at Merton are dull. However, his world is expanding and he walks with John Hilton to Thame to see the celebrated innkeeper John Fothergill; he has attended a performance of Stravinsky and is reading Dostoevsky and Joyce. In Hilary term 1927 his letters are peppered with references to Woolf, Eliot and Joyce and he takes to carrying an ashplant in honour of Stephen Dedalus. He reads D. H. Lawrence's *Twilight in Italy* and is writing an essay on Joyce and modern poetry. In *The Strings Are False*, MacNeice writes of Marlborough that 'all the older boys had their mild homosexual romances – an occasion for *billets* and giggling and elaborately engineered rendezvous'. Evidence of these can be found in passing references to Blunt's crushes on people called 'John' or 'Edward', and MacNeice's letters from Oxford to Basil Barr.

Meanwhile, he tells Blunt (29 March) that he and Hilton have discovered T. S. Eliot's walk at Oxford, 'where four gasometers stand over the Isis', which provides an occasion for quoting from *The Waste Land*. In the same letter he unveils a comic genealogy in which he figures himself as the son of Don Quixote and Queen Victoria and as descendant of St Brandon and the playboy of the western world. He tends to associate the Victorians with the Rectory and particularly with his stepmother, so he takes the trouble to remind her on 27 June that abstractions should be avoided at all costs since 'the Victorians fed on abstractions and were sick'. This may be why he is reluctant to visit home, for 'I do not want the North Ireland [*sic*] melancholy to get its teeth into me'. One way of evading the limitations of home and the singular, inherited self is to imagine personhood as multiple or various. After all, 'One is like a fountain – always spouting in the same shape but formed of always different water drops.' He relishes the fact that many people have attributed foreign nationalities to him (including, strangely enough, Indian, Spanish and Japanese) and he concludes: 'I must be very polyglot.' But the obvious way to escape the staidness of home is to get the boat to France with John Hilton, which he does after writing several urgent and finally persuasive letters to his parents to request permission to do so.

At the beginning of 1929, he has apparently become secretly engaged to Mary Beazley although this is not announced to his parents (nor indeed to his friends) until he sends a telegram to the Rectory in March, explaining that he has been arrested for drunkenness and taken in hand by the college authorities but adding reassuringly that he is engaged to be married. When he relates the story to Blunt, he is emboldened to say of Mary that 'she doesn't like you and I gather you don't like her, which is very bad taste on both sides'. It's very flip, of course, but a rift seems to develop at this stage between the two friends. No letter has surfaced in which conclusive reasons are given, although MacNeice's letters to Blunt were in the latter's care, and presented at last to King's College, Cambridge. (There is no record, incidentally, of any correspondence between MacNeice and Blunt on the subject of the Soviet Union or suggestion that MacNeice knew anything about Blunt's activities as a spy.) 'On Tuesday I go to Iceland and that will be the end of an epoch,' writes MacNeice on that summer morning of 1936. Whether the coolness between them was more on one side or mutual, it seems clear that the next epoch for MacNeice was not one that would include Anthony Blunt.

MacNeice's first letter to E. R. Dodds (28 May 1930), written just two months before his marriage to Mary Beazley and his move to Birmingham, effectively closes one era in his life (his undergraduate years) and heralds a new one. It also announces the beginning of a new friendship. He remained at Birmingham University in the Department of Classics, chaired by Dodds, until his move to Bedford College for Women, in London, in autumn 1936. At that time Dodds, too, moved – to Oxford, to take up the Regius Chair of Greek. Dodds had liked the younger man from the time he interviewed him for the Birmingham job in 1930, and during their time together there they became close friends. Since they were both liberal Irish Protestants with roots in the north (Dodds was born in Banbridge and had been a pupil at Campbell College, Belfast), they could perhaps understand each other's background more readily than any of their English friends could. In one of his last letters to Dodds MacNeice remarks: 'I wish one could either <u>live</u> in Ireland or <u>feel oneself</u> in England. It must be one of them ould antinomies' (31 July 1945). It was a predicament the elder man would have understood, and the reference to Yeats's 'antinomies' harked back to the trip the two had made together to see Yeats in Rathfarnham in September 1934. The letters to Dodds (and occasional letters also to his wife, Betty) constitute one of the great sequences in the MacNeice correspondence, spanning a fairly long stretch of time, but mainly concentrated in the years 1939–42, between the outbreak of war and the author's marriage to Hedli Anderson. There is a flurry of letters to the Doddses in 1936 concerning the Group Theatre production of MacNeice's translation of *The Agamemnon*, and then very little until the longer sequence beginning in 1939. After the outbreak of war, MacNeice tries to work out how precisely he feels about his position in regard to the conflict. He writes to Dodds on 24 September that he is 'communing with my conscience' on the issue – should he join the war effort, or not? On 13 October he believes he might have 'come to some decision about the war'. Feeling alienated from the Conservative government, he is reluctant to fight for what he considers to be, in effect, their war. A month later, however, he seems to have changed his mind, and is resigned to things: 'It does however seem to be <u>clear</u> that, in this choice of evils, Mr. Chamberlain's England is preferable to Nazi Germany (& anyhow it won't if people have any sense, remain Mr. C's England). I find it natural to remain agin the Government but in this case it seems quite feasible to be agin the govmt. & still support the war' (19 November).

Meanwhile, he has been offered a temporary lectureship at Cornell University, in upstate New York, for the spring semester of 1940, a position which would give him the opportunity to renew his relationship with Eleanor Clark, with whom he had fallen madly in love the previous April during a lecture tour in the United States. On the other hand, he was also waiting to hear the result of his application for a Chair at Trinity College Dublin, to which he had been invited to apply. When he learned on 8 December that the position had gone to H. O. White, he felt the decision had been made for him and he resolved to sail for New York in the new year. Throughout this period of emotional turmoil Dodds remains a sympathetic listener and sounding board for MacNeice, and a steady adviser. Despite maintaining a lovesick correspondence with Clark at this time, MacNeice is involved with several other women, including Margaret Gardiner in London and Eileen Phillips in Dublin, and remains emotionally tied to Nancy Coldstream, with whom he had begun a passionate affair in 1937 when they went to the Hebrides to research the travel book *I Crossed the Minch*. On several occasions Dodds rebukes the younger man for his apparently cavalier attitude to romance, reminding him of the 'responsibilities' that must attend 'polygamy'. 'I am tired to death of polygamy,' snaps the poet: 'I should like to live somewhere monogamously & work eight hours every day' (6 November). Dodds would remain a loyal friend to MacNeice over the years, and wrote a testimonial in support of his application to the BBC in May 1941. He became the poet's literary executor in 1940, a position he held for most of his life.

The letters to Eliot run from 1932 to 1963 and are almost exclusively concerned with publishing and business matters, to do with *Criterion* and Faber. His first letters are formal and tentative and there is a comic start to the correspondence when he forgets to include a cover letter with poems he sends to Eliot. Those early poems were published as *Blind Fireworks* by Gollancz in 1929, although Eliot almost immediately offered to publish some poems in *Criterion*, and soon invited MacNeice to review for the journal. There are no heart-revealing intimacies in this correspondence; the relationship is cordial but businesslike. In his first approach he apologises for what might be construed as incoherence in his poetry, and he claims to be part of 'no particular school'. He publishes four poems in the *Criterion* of January 1924, and soon is making plans to submit his next manuscript, which became *Poems* (1935). After this, Eliot seems amenable to most of what MacNeice proposes and there is discussion of the publication of *The Agamemnon* and 'the Iceland book'. MacNeice apologises (again) for agreeing with Longmans to publish *I Crossed the Minch* without Eliot's permission. Eliot recommends MacNeice for the job at Bedford College and also, at MacNeice's request, helps to set up the lecture series in America in spring 1939 by writing to friends at Wellesley and Harvard. MacNeice often excuses himself for breaking deadlines, frequently citing overwork as his reason, but remains quite prolific in these years and becomes fairly shrewd about the marketplace and the publishing trade. He is conscious of the 'wartime mood' of his volume *Plant and Phantom* and presses to have it published before the war ends. Occasionally he provides fastidiously detailed notes on his work, as when he gives the place and time of composition of each poem in *Plant and Phantom* (24 September 1940). To avoid a logjam of books he asks Eliot not to follow *Christopher Columbus* too soon with another book, lest it diminish sales of both (24 November 1943). He knows the power of advertising and generally is keen to supply his editor with information about each volume 'in case that will help you with a blurb'.

His relationship with Eleanor Clark began towards the end of his lecture tour in America in the spring of 1939, when he met her in New York. He fell in love with her almost immediately and began a lengthy correspondence seemingly minutes after the *Queen Mary* pulled out from New York Harbor. The voyage back to England took seven days, so he had ample time to write and to add to what he had written, producing in effect the longest letter of his career, reprinted here in its entirety (21 April 1939). Letters to Clark vary in tone from amorous and occasionally rhapsodic to philosophical, gossipy, petulant and near-despairing. At times they can be very needy. They paint a vivid picture of what MacNeice was thinking at the time *Autumn Journal* was published and during the first two years of the war; as with his letters to Dodds, MacNeice is working out his ideas about Britain vis-à-vis America, about the war, about literature, and about politics more generally. He promises to return and his opportunity to do so arrives in the form of a job at Cornell in 1940. (It emerges that Clark's sister, Eunice Jessup, played no small part in arranging the job.) Clark, who had recently been closely involved with Trotskyites in New York (and had been married to the Czech secretary of Trotsky, Jan Frankl), had grown disillusioned, while still believing in some kind of 'revolution'. MacNeice, while broadly sympathetic to the left, and a friend to committed *Partisan Reviewers* such as Selden Rodman and Fred Dupee, remained deeply sceptical about the Trotskyite factions in both New York and London. He was ordered by the British government to return home by the end of June 1940 for wartime duties. His departure delayed by a severe case of peritonitis, he left in November, returning to London with the view that to stay in America was escapist. To his parents he wrote, 'For the last 4 months all my friends over there (both American & British) had been trying to persuade me to change my mind about coming back. However I thought I was missing History' (16 December 1940). The experience of wartime London would come to affect him deeply and his acute awareness of the differences between the American and British perceptions of war became a significant factor in his relationship with Clark. The correspondence continued somewhat fitfully for another year or so, but came to a close with his letter of 9 July 1942, announcing his marriage to Hedli Anderson.

Upon his return to London in the autumn of 1940, MacNeice lodged with Rupert Doone at 34 Wharton Street, where many of his wartime letters were written, reflecting first-hand experience of the German air raids. Often in these letters he interrupts his own narrative to mention in parentheses the sounds of guns or aircraft ('Planes & gunfire overhead as I am writing this', 15 March 1941), or reach for grandiloquent similes to convey his impressions: 'Last raid we had here was extremely noisy – from the AA barrage, not from bombs: a noise like the collision of half a dozen oceans' (3 April). He mentions to Clark the bombing on 20 March of Plymouth (where his sister is then living) and of the terrible raid of 16 April, 'The Biggest Raid Ever': 'The town next morning was incredible. & now it looks more or less normal again – seems to have an extraordinary second wind . . . Some of the fires were staggeringly beautiful in the time before the sun while the moon was still there. I could tell you a lot more about that raid but I have a feeling you may not want to hear about it. Here of course it's an unavoidable topic' (20 April). He joined the BBC in January as a freelance writer, and as a full staff member at the end of May; in this capacity he was responsible for a number of wartime scripts such as the propaganda series *The Stones Cry Out* and *Black Gallery*.

Meanwhile, his son Dan, seven years old in 1941, had been evacuated to Ireland, initially domiciled in Belfast with his grandparents, then briefly in Killyleagh with the family of a Church of Ireland minister, Reverend Mann (there were fears of bombs over Belfast) and finally at Ashfield Lodge, Cootehill, County Cavan, where he stayed with the family of Major and Diana Clements (a step-cousin of MacNeice). Mary MacNeice had left Louis in November 1935 and emigrated with Charles Katzman to America, where they farmed poultry in New Jersey. Dan is a constant concern, and in all his letters to Mary, particularly during wartime, MacNeice has to reassure her that her son is safe and well: 'I had a letter from Dan . . . & also from Elizabeth who is in Belfast & says everything is very quiet & peaceful there & that Dan is flourishing' (28 Oct. 1940). The correspondence with Mary begins on 10 November 1936 (a week after their divorce and almost a year after their separation) and continues through 1950 and after. No letters survive from the period before their divorce. In his last letter to Blunt, in August 1936, he sums up his feelings about the ruined marriage: 'Perhaps being married to M. was a sort of prolonged childhood – many toys, much comfort, painted furniture, running one's hand over materials, hand to mouth idyl [*sic*] as all idylls are. But it went on too long & the habit is hard to break' (3 August 1936). Nonetheless, MacNeice's letters to Mary are mostly affectionate and he is never less than cordial to Charles Katzman, to whom he regularly sends regards or fond wishes. After some time elapses he feels relieved, or says he does, by the divorce, and Mary's occasional overtures to him to reconsider are swiftly rebuffed.

Mary's mother was evidently a difficult woman, who was not supportive of the marriage at the outset and who then tried to retrieve it after the separation. She was insistent that she should continue to see her grandson after Mary's departure, much to the annoyance and eventual distress of MacNeice and his family. Ultimately, MacNeice had to intervene to prevent her attempts to sustain the affections of the infant Dan and, fuelled by exaggerated fears of a Lady Astor-style kidnapping, he finally prohibited her gift-giving and barred her visits.

MacNeice did a great deal of travel during the decade or so after the war, including several demanding foreign assignments with the BBC, beginning with a trip to India in August 1947, where he went with Jack Dillon and Wynford Vaughan Thomas to cover partition and the handover of power. Other foreign destinations while working for the BBC around this time include the Sudan (1955), Gold Coast (Ghana) (1956), and India (again), Singapore and Kuala Lumpur (1957). In 1950, he spent a year with his second wife Hedli Anderson in Greece, where he served as director of the British Institute in Athens, and in 1953 and again in 1954 they went together to America. Alone he visited South Africa in 1959, to give a lecture series at the University of Cape Town and at Witwatersrand. During his travels alone or with the BBC he wrote regularly and often to Hedli at home. While in India in 1947 he kept a diary for part of the time, but the main record of his work there may be found in the great sequence of nineteen letters which he wrote to Hedli between 10 August and 27 October of that year. After writing his first two letters he seems to become aware suddenly of their usefulness as a personal record of his experiences, and asks Hedli to keep them together 'as they will remind me of things & so far I haven't had time to keep a diary' (19 August). The sequence begins in Delhi, where MacNeice attends the midnight session of the Constituent Assembly, when Indian independence was officially declared. He describes the independence ceremony at the Red Fort with upwards of 300,000 people in attendance, and refers to meetings with many top military and political figures, including Prime Minister Nehru, Timbyi (Secretary of the Constitutional Assembly), Field Marshal Cariappa (first Indian Chief of Staff), Sir George Cunningham (Governor of the NW Frontier Province), and the eccentric industrialist Dalmia (the 'Henry Ford of India'), the head of the Indian Cow Protection League, whom he interviewed. He meets various artists and authors, including Chaman Lall ('a pal of Huxley's at Oxford'), the Indian poet Saroyini Naidu and members of the Progressive Writers League. The letters are racy and detailed, and the variety and incongruity of what he sees there is sometimes played for comic effect.

The ampersand is pervasive in all of MacNeice's correspondence, used as a breathless connective and often extending a sentence, detail upon detail, to double or treble its conventional capacity. With all the Indian letters, as with later letters to Hedli from Khartoum, Ghana and Kuala Lumpur, one is struck by the vivid impressions of people and places which illustrate the general narrative or what in a letter from Ghana he calls 'my chronicle'. Indeed, so precise and acute are his descriptions that it is sometimes hard to appreciate the vast distances travelled, and the considerable amount of journalistic and recording work that has been accomplished. In India, for instance, within a period of two months the crew visited Delhi, Agra, Bombay, Benares, Hyderabad, Lucknow, Madras, Trichinopoly and Cape Comorin in the south. In Ghana too he would face a busy schedule as described in a long, detailed sentence in a letter of 18 October 1956:

> On Friday I am to go to a Farm Festival, which sounds great fun, & on Monday 22nd shall be trekking off with a nice young bearded Australian for about a week, first west along the coast, then onto Asharith. Then back to Accra, then onto the Northern Territories (the most primitive part). Then Accra again, then to Togoland. Then Accra for a final round-up, then home. Have to see gold mines, hospitals, medical field units, cocoa groves, a new harbour, a new bridge, various old castles, the fishing industry, the timber trade, a furniture shop, a veterinary farm, & lots of jolly chiefs & London University graduates.

One of MacNeice's last business letters to T. S. Eliot is dated April 1960, when he discusses a possible title (*The Wiper and Other Poems*) for the volume which became *Solstices* (1961). After that point, correspondence regarding his publications at Faber was handled by Charles Monteith, with whom he discusses his *Collected Poems* (published in 1966) and his final volume of poems, *The Burning Perch* (initially mooted titles for which were *Round the Corner* and *Pyres and Bellbuoys*). Other than in this and similar letters to Monteith or to Eliot, MacNeice seldom discusses his poetry directly in critical terms. The letter was a social or business forum and had more to do with friendship or reportage than with working out ideas about art and authorship. Very occasionally he does send poems with a letter, as when he delivers 'Happy Families' to his friend John Hilton, but more usually he sends them to wife or lover, as with 'Trilogy for X' to Nancy Coldstream in spring 1938 (unpublished letter, Ms Bodleian), 'Cradle Song', posted to Eleanor Clark in October 1940, 'Solitary Travel' and 'Half Truth from Cape Town' sent to Hedli in 1959, or 'Good Dream' to Mary Wimbush in 1960. Quite often he tells friends about poems he has recently written, but never in detail. There are exceptions, such as his open letter to Auden (*New Verse*) where he writes as a critic, but that was written for a public forum. Similarly, his statement on *Autumn Journal* sent to Eliot is intended as a public pronouncement, possibly to be plundered by the publisher for blurb material. Even as undergraduate editor of *Oxford Poetry* he would mention poems, but keep critical commentary to a minimum: 'I think yr poem is very pretty – in technique & imagery (here speaks the pedant), though without that compact pregnancy of phrase which I especially look for. Oh, it's calculus that word is it? I've only just been able to make it out. Yes I think that's a delightful phrase. & your alliteration is very nice. Only perhaps it is all a little facile' (To John Hilton, summer 1928). In his sprawling letters to Clark he will occasionally allude to poems he has been writing, as when in the middle of an outburst about the war (he feels like running away to Mexico) he mentions 'a new kind of poem': 'I am rather pleased, darling, because I am writing a new kind of poem; there are going to be 50 of them, called Novelettes – very bleak, very simple, very objective, all in the 3rd person' (2 July 1939). He is upset by a critic's remark, but concedes the point: 'Read a review of my Poems in Time the other day, said I had a "flaccid heart". It ain't true but I know what they mean. If I survive this mess, it (heart) will be what it wouldn't have been otherwise – but, all the same, what it was to have been from the start' (6 August 1941).

In 1960 MacNeice began an affair with the actress Mary Wimbush and left Hedli, who subsequently opened a restaurant in Kinsale, Co. Cork. Two brief letters to Wimbush from a small number which are known to have survived are reprinted here. In the final years of his life he also wrote affectionate letters to his son Dan. He writes in April 1961 that he has not heard from him 'for a very long time indeed'. Clearly there is an effort at rapprochement on MacNeice's part, following the difficulties of nine years before, when Dan had left England to live with his mother in America. His father had refused consent but Dan's solicitor argued successfully that MacNeice had contravened the terms of his legal guardianship by removing his son during the war from the United Kingdom, to the neutral Republic of Ireland. About a year prior to Dan's permanent emigration at the end of 1953, and before the solicitor's battle over the travel visa had begun, MacNeice sent the most honest and revealing letter he would ever write to his son, dated 30 August 1952. As evidenced in some of his letters to Eleanor Clark in 1939–40, his letter to Anthony Blunt of 3 August 1936 and his letter of Autumn 1929 to John Hilton (regarding his relationship with his father and brother), moments of emotional crisis involving those who are closest to him elicit the most candid, heartfelt and often searing confessions. When his daughter Corinna leaves home and goes to the Slade College of Art in 1961 he begins to write to her as an adult as he had seldom done before. These letters are warm and gossipy ('Sark was great fun but strenuous; the cliff paths gave me Charwomen's Ankles. And nobody ever seems to go to bed there; there is a midget millionaire (c. 4 ft 6?) who will buy anyone champagne at sight'), and sometimes very practical ('Would you by the way like that old grey carpet of mine laid down in your room? There's nowhere else to put it & it would warm your room up for the winter'). He announces that he is going out for a drink with Ken Tynan or to drink champagne with T. S. Eliot, or that he has just joined 'the new club called The Establishment, to be run by the four Beyond the Fringe boys'. But he sometimes strikes a very paternal note, advising her to wear a crash helmet if she is travelling by scooter. He complains about his workload ('Astrology is weighing heavily on me,' referring to a long-commissioned book he was then reluctantly completing). His last letter to Corinna is dated 20 August, about a week before he was admitted to St Leonard's Hospital. He apologises for his 'straggly handwriting' and is in bed 'with a mystery temperature'. He lists the books he has been reading and declares his intention of visiting a Henry Moore and Francis Bacon exhibition when he recovers. He has had to cancel his trip to Ireland, where he had hopes of meeting the MacCanns in Belfast and Richard Murphy in Cleggan, but it seems to have cheered him slightly that his daughter had been to the Puck Fair in Kerry, as he mentions to Monteith in what seems to be his final letter, written two days before his admission to hospital. He asks Monteith if his radio play *Persons from Porlock* might be published. If so, he says, 'I'll get it in shape for you.'

Jonathan Allison,
Lexington, Kentucky, 2010

Note on the Text

At Sherborne Prep, MacNeice usually gave his address on the top right-hand side as 'Sherborne' or 'Acreman House', or sometimes both, followed by the date. At Marlborough, he gave the address as 'A House [later C House] / Marlborough College', or abbreviated to 'Marl. Coll.') and as a senior pupil he sometimes used Marlborough ('C' House) letterhead paper. At Oxford he often used Merton College letterhead although his very first letter from university was scrawled, with an apology, on cheap paper in pencil. Throughout his life, he usually but not invariably recorded the address and date (not always the year) of origin on top of the letter. Very occasionally, he wrote on picture postcards. All BBC correspondence and much of his personal correspondence while on duty for the BBC (especially abroad) was typed or written on letterhead, occasionally deleted in ink and replaced with a residential address. The poet wrote on letterhead also from Birmingham University; Bedford College, London; Telluride Association, Cornell University; The British Institute, Athens; University of Cape Town; The South Africa Broadcasting Corporation; 'The Character of Ireland' (book project with letterhead); The Cunard White Star (Liverpool), and from various hotels here and there, including The Belvedere Hotel in Dublin, The Lamb in Burford and The Vineyard Hotel in Cape Town.

Letters have been reproduced in this volume with a regularised format for the date and origin, regardless of where the inscription was made on the original document. Paragraphs following the opening salutation have been uniformly indented, as have the position and spacing of the final valediction. Missing punctuation has been added in square brackets only where necessary to avoid ambiguity. I have used [sic] occasionally to eliminate doubt, but to avoid its overuse I have in many instances left MacNeice's original spelling and syntax unremarked.

Most letters were dated by the author or can otherwise be dated by the postmark on the envelope. Dating has been regularised to day, month and year (where known), although MacNeice dated his letters in a variety of ways. Where I am certain of a date (or part thereof) absent from the letter or envelope, I have placed it in square brackets. Speculative dates are similarly bracketed, with a question mark added. Such speculations are based on all the evidence available at present, though I cannot guarantee their complete accuracy. The dating of some of the earliest letters in the volume follows lengthy deliberation with the late Daniel MacNeice, their guardian until his death.

I have not included in this volume details of ink or paper, or notes on the physical condition of the letters. Apart from business letters typed on BBC letterhead paper, most of MacNeice's letters were written in fountain pen with black or blue ink, although there is at least one letter to Anthony Blunt which was urgently penned in the small hours of the morning in garish green. Sometimes his letters home from Oxford were inscribed in scarlet ink. A number of shorter notes were scrawled in pencil. The vast majority of these letters were signed by MacNeice, although I have transcribed a small number from unsigned carbon copies held in the Bodleian Library.

I have personally transcribed almost all of the letters printed here, although I thank Pipit Godefroy and Morgan Richardson for typing a very small number of them. Several letters to Nancy Coldstream reprinted here were transcribed under the direction of Jon Stallworthy at Oxford University and I thank Professor Stallworthy for the use of them. I have checked all letters against originals or against vivid reproductions. In the very few instances where obscurity remains, I have put 'illegible' within square brackets.

An effort has been made to keep annotation to a minimum, recording only what is necessary to convey the immediate context of individual letters. Biographical information is noted at the first mention of each individual, and the information is restricted, except in unusual cases, to dates of birth (and death, if known or applicable), education, career, publications and marriages. Fuller entries have been provided for major figures in the correspondence. Very occasionally it has not been possible to identify positively an individual mentioned.

There are good bibliographical precedents for using endnotes or even brief headnotes as opposed to footnotes in a volume such as this, but after much deliberation the publishers and I decided for the reader's convenience to display all relevant information at the foot of the page. Apart from the archival repositories and library holdings listed in detail in acknowledgements below, and the published works of Louis MacNeice including *Collected Poems* 1966 and 2007; *The Strings Are False*; *Selected Literary Criticism*; *Selected Prose*; *Selected Plays*; and other volumes (see Bibliography for details), I have relied heavily on the following sources for annotating letters: *Dictionary of National Biography*; *Marlborough*

College Register (9th and 11th edns); *New York Times*; *Sherborne Prep Register* (manuscript); *The Times*; *Who's Who*; *Who Was Who*; and works by C. M. Armitage and Neil Clark, Miranda Carter, Edward Mendelson, Jon Stallworthy and John Sutherland. (See List of Abbreviations for details.) Personal correspondence is listed in footnotes, as are other sources (all published in London unless otherwise stated).

This volume represents only a fraction of the extant letters of Louis MacNeice, and there is certainly enough material for a further volume. All letters here are reproduced in their entirety and all ellipses in the letters are MacNeice's.

Acknowledgements

I wish to express my gratitude to the late Dan MacNeice and his wife Charlotte and son Adam for their unfailing assistance and hospitality. Dan patiently read the typescript in its entirety, gave me a great deal of information about his father and his family, and saved me from many errors. I am also deeply indebted to Corinna MacNeice for her encouragement and assistance. Many thanks to Jon Stallworthy, former Trustee of the Estate of Louis MacNeice, for help and advice at every stage, and for his hospitality at Wolfson College, Oxford. This volume could not have been completed without his support and encouragement from the beginning. Paul Keegan at Faber and Faber read the typescript carefully and was an exemplary editor in every respect. Also at Faber, I am very grateful to Katherine Armstrong, to project editor Anne Owen, to my copyeditor, Trevor Horwood, and typesetter, Donald Sommerville. I wish to thank Bruce Hunter of David Higham Associates for his support and advice. I owe a further debt of gratitude to Terence Brown and David Fitzpatrick for reading a draft of the typescript and providing helpful commentary.

For information, advice and hospitality I wish to thank George Bornstein, Aileen Christiansen, Cairns Craig, Patrick Crotty, Frank Doering and Wallis Miller, Roy Foster, Jack and Marie-Claude Gillespie, Seamus and Marie Heaney, John and Christine Kelly, Máire Ni Choisain and Cormac O'Grada, Bernard O'Donoghue, Nicholas Roe, Daniel Rowland, Ronald Schuchard, John T. Shawcross, Nicholas and Lotte Spice, John Thompson, Helen Vendler, the late George Watson and Jo Watson. For responding to specific enquiries I am grateful to Marigold Atkey, Matthew Bailey, Hilary Benn MP, Melissa Benn, the late Tristram Cary, Neil Corcoran, Anne Margaret Daniel, Dick Decamp, Charles Drazin, Christopher Fauske, Katherine Firth, Jennifer FitzGerald, Kit Fryatt, Matthew Giancarlo, Gerry Harrison, Joseph R. Jones, Rev. Dr Simon Jones, John Kerrigan, Una Lappin, Edna Longley, Joan McBreen, Sam McCready, Peter McDonald, Michael Makin, Stella Mew, Karl Miller, Alastair Minnis, John Mullaney, Richard Murphy, James G. Nelson, Patricia O'Higgin, Christopher Reid, John Rickard, Noel Russell, Martin Saffer, Ian Sansom, Nann du Sautoy, Ian White and Henry Woudhuysen.

Amy Clark and Andrew Hippisley kindly translated several Greek phrases in MacNeice's letters. For information about Sherborne Preparatory School I am grateful to Mary Lindsay, Robin Lindsay (formerly headmaster), Peter Tait (the current headmaster), and Lucie Dillistone, school archivist. Edward Mendelson and Nicholas Jenkins kindly answered questions about the life and work of W. H. Auden. I am grateful to Rosanna Warren for sharing information about her mother, Eleanor Clark. For information about Adrian Green-Armytage, thanks to Stephen Green-Armytage and Janet Kovesi Watt. My thanks to Bruce Arnold, Annie Johnston, Frances Suzman Jowell and Simon Kingston for allowing me to reprint letters in their private collections. For various kinds of assistance and hospitality I thank Chris Agee, Richard Angelo, Edward and Kate Baker, Jim and Martha Birchfield, David Boal, Rev. Paul Bosch, Rachel Buxton, Steven Halliwell, Steve and Dani Hart, Peter Kalliney, Michael and Rosaleen Keohane, Kevin Kiernan, Michael Kinghan and Claire Stentiford, Frank and Catherina McDonnell, Nick and Emily Martin, John Meehan and Rosanna Trainor, Roger and Geri O'Kelly, Jeff Peters and Kristen Seymour, Andrew and Sally Roberts, John Stewart, Max Wright, Arthur Wrobel, Tom and Fiona Young. It also gives me great pleasure to acknowledge the help I received from my parents, Anne Allison and the late Victor Allison, and from my sister Heather Jackson.

Many thanks to the following librarians and archivists for their generous assistance, without which none of this would have been possible: Colin Harris, Judith Priestman and Paul Cartwright of the Department of Special Collections & Western Manuscripts, Bodleian Library, Oxford; Patricia McGuire of Modern Archives, King's College, Cambridge; Robert Brown, the Faber Archivist, his predecessor Victor Gray, and their assistants at Faber archives, John Porter and Barbara Strong; Erin O'Neill and the staff of the BBC Written Archives, Caversham, Reading; Helen Rankin, former Curator of Carrickfergus Museum & Civic Centre; Declan Kiely, Robert H. Taylor Curator of Literary & Historical Manuscripts, Morgan Library, New York; the staff of the National Library of Scotland and of the Public Record Office of Northern Ireland. I am indebted to the following librarians and archivists who located and in some cases reproduced manuscripts, typescripts or photographs: Patricia J. Albright, Archives Librarian, Mount Holyoke College; Wendy Anthony, Archivist, Special Collections, Lucy Scribner Library, Skidmore College, and her assistant Julia Dauer; Ellen Baer, Director of the Telluride Association, Cornell University; Michael Basinski, Poetry Collection, SUNY Buffalo; Philippa Bassett, Senior Archivist, Special Collections, University of Birmingham;

Judy Burg, University Archivist, Hull History Centre; Ann E. Butler, Fales Library & Special Collections, New York University; Lorna Cahill, Royal Holloway College, London; Marc Carlson, Librarian of Special Collections & University Archives, MacFarlin Library, University of Tulsa; Nicholas Clark, Curator, Britten-Pears Library, Aldeburgh; Lea Cline, Richard Workman and Daniele Sigler, Harry Ransom Center, University of Texas at Austin; Laurie Deredita, Special Collections Librarian, Connecticut College; Randall Ericson, Couper Librarian, Special Collections & Archives, Hamilton College; Sarah George and Chris Sheppard, Special Collections, Brotherton Library, University of Leeds; Isaac Gewirtz, Curator, and Philip Milito, Berg Collection, New York Public Library; Susan Halpert, Houghton Library, Harvard University; Eileen M. Heeran and Eleanor Brown, Karl A. Kroch Library, Cornell University; Jonathan Jeffrey, Kentucky Library & Museum, Western Kentucky University; Francis Jones, Broadcast Archivist, BBC Northern Ireland Community Archive, Ulster Folk & Transport Museum; Nancy Kuhl, Curator for Poetry, Collection of American Literature, Beinecke Library, Yale University; Abby Lester, College Archivist, Sarah Lawrence College Archives; Avice-Claire McGovern, National Library of Ireland; Nancy Magnuson, College Librarian, Goucher College, Baltimore; Jane Maxwell and Caoimhe Ní Ghormáin, Manuscripts Department, Trinity College Library, Dublin; Dan Mitchell, Special Collections, Library Services, University College London; Ian Montgomery, Public Record Office of Northern Ireland; Mary Ann O'Kane, Royal Northern College of Music, Manchester; Heather Peacock, Brynmor Jones Library, University of Hull; Sarah Prescott, Archives & Records, King's College London; Meg Sherry Rich and Anna Lee Pauls, Rare Books & Special Collections, Princeton University Library; Nicole Robinson, Lily Collections, University of Indiana Libraries; Dean M. Rogers, Vassar College Library; Ruth R. Rogers, Special Collections Librarian, Margaret Clapp Library, Wellesley College; Valerie Sallis and Ann Skiold, Bird Library, Syracuse University; Kathy Shoemaker, Special Collections, Robert W. Woodruff Library, Emory University; Sandra Stelts, Curator of Rare Books & Manuscripts, and Tim Babcock, The Pennsylvania State University Library; Wilma R. Slaight and Ian Graham, Wellesley College Archives; Morgan Swan, Beinecke Rare Book & Manuscript Library, Yale University Library; Melissa Tacke, Project Archivist, Bennington College; Lorett Treese and Marianne Hansen, Bryn Mawr College Library; and staff at the Special Collections, University of Delaware, and Department of Manuscripts & Records, National Library of Wales, Aberystwyth. I am also pleased to acknowledge those librarians who answered queries, including Kathryn L. Beam, Special Collections Library, University of Michigan; John M. Bennett, Ohio State University Libraries; Delinda Buie, Special Collections, University of Louisville; Richard Childs, County Archivist, West Sussex Record Office; Amanda Jones, Archivist, Borthwick Institute for Archives, University of York; Peter Rawson, Archivist, Hotchkiss School; Terry Rogers, Archivist, Marlborough College; Sara-Mae Tuson, editor, *London Magazine*; and staff of Bancroft Library, Berkeley, California, and Stanford University Library. Furthermore, I wish to acknowledge the generous assistance of James Birchfield, Curator of Rare Books, and Bill Marshall, Curator of Manuscripts, at Special Collections, Margaret King Library; Shawn Livingstone of the Reference Department, W. T. Young Library, and staff of the Inter-Library Loan Department, all at the University of Kentucky.

In preparing this edition, I am indebted to the authorised biographer of the poet, Jon Stallworthy, to the poet's bibliographers, C. M. Armitage and Neil Clark, and to previous editors of MacNeice, namely E. R. Dodds, Alan Heuser, Michael Longley, and Peter McDonald. I am grateful to Edna Longley and the organising committee of the Louis MacNeice Centenary Conference at Queen's University, Belfast, for inviting me to participate in that gathering. I thank John Frow, Susan Manning, Charles Withers and Anthea Taylor for their hospitality at the Institute for Advanced Studies in the Humanities, University of Edinburgh, where I began work on this volume. Thanks to the following at the University of Kentucky who assisted at an early stage with fact-checking and research: Scott Engholm, Pipit Godefroy, Dax Jennings, Katherine Osborne, George Phillips and Morgan Richardson. I am grateful to my colleagues in the English Department of the University of Kentucky for their assistance and to Tom Clayton, Department Chair, and his predecessor Ellen Rosenman, for assistance and support. It is my pleasure to acknowledge the support of Steven L. Hoch, former Dean of the College of Arts & Sciences; Phil Harling, former Interim Dean of the College of Arts & Sciences; Leonidas Bachas, former Associate Dean for Research & Academic Programs; and staff of the Office of the Vice-President for Research, all at the University of Kentucky. Finally, deepest and most heartfelt thanks to my wife Anna and to our sons Victor and Philip Allison.

unpublished letters and documents, including illustrations by the author. The locations of letters printed are given in the provenance line above each letter and in the Bibliography of Primary Sources on pages 723–6, which also includes a complete list of titles published by Louis MacNeice.

For permission to reprint material from other letters and diaries, acknowledgements are due to the following: the Estate of W. H. Auden for Auden's letter to FLM (21 January 1945) and for his inscription on a postcard to E. R. Dodds (22 August 1936); the BBC for extracts from material held at the BBC Written Archives Centre, Caversham Park; Faber and Faber Ltd and Mrs Valerie Eliot for quotations from letters by T. S. Eliot; the Estate of Dorinda Greer and PRONI for a brief extract from her diary; the John Hewitt Estate for a brief extract from a letter to FLM (28 July 1939); the Society of Authors on behalf of the Philip Larkin Estate for a brief extract from a letter to Kingsley Amis; Corinna MacNeice for brief extracts from letters by John Frederick MacNeice, Mary MacNeice, and Elizabeth Nicholson; Rosanna Warren and the Estate of Eleanor Clark for brief extracts from letters by Eleanor Clark and from one letter by Mrs Phelps Clark.

For permission to reprint material held in libraries, acknowledgements are due to the following: BBC Written Archives Centre, Caversham (MacNeice Papers); The Beinecke Rare Book and Manuscript Library, Yale University (Eleanor Clark Papers: YCAL MSS 315); The Berg Collection, New York Public Library (Berg Coll. MSS MacNeice); Special Collections, Birmingham University; The Bodleian Library, The University of Oxford (MacNeice uncatalogued papers; MacNeice: Jon Stallworthy Working Papers; MS Don.c.153/1); The British Library (Letter to John Betjeman, Add.71646); Butler Library, Columbia University (Spec. Ms Coll. Random House); Special Collections, University of Delaware Library (John Malcolm Brinnin Papers: Ms coll. no. 103); Faber Archive; Hull History Centre, Hull University Archives (Larkin DPL2/3/64); King's College Archive Centre, Cambridge (Papers Relating to Louis MacNeice: GBR/0272/PP/FLM); Leeds University Library, Brotherton Collection (MS 20c Silkin); The Pierpont Morgan Library, New York (Letter to Geoffrey Grigson: LHMS; MA 5157); National Library of Scotland (Hector MacIver Papers: MS 26276-77); Rare Books and Manuscripts, Special Collections Library, The Pennsylvania State University Libraries (Letters to Marguerite Caetani); Department of Rare Books and Special Collections, Princeton University Library (Allen Tate Papers: Co106 29/9); The Deputy Keeper of the Records, Public Record Office of Northern Ireland (W. R. Rodgers Papers; Greer, Lowry and Alexander Papers); Sarah Lawrence

College Archives (MacNeice file); The Poetry Collection of the University Libraries, State University of New York at Buffalo (Letter to WHA, 1937); University of Sussex (New Statesman Archive: Coll. SxMs60); Harry Ransom Center, University of Texas (Louis MacNeice, Geoffrey Grigson, Knopf Inc. and John Lehmann Collections); Trinity College, Dublin (H. O. White, TCD 3777/68; Denis Johnston, TCD 10066/290/1529, 1543); Wellesley College Library, Special Collections (Letter of TSE to Elizabeth Manwaring); Robert Woodruff Library, Emory University (Louis MacNeice: MS coll. no. 948).

For permission to reprint extracts from private letters to the editor, acknowledgements are due to the following: the late Tristram Cary, Lucie Dilliston, Frances Suzman Jowell, Mary Lindsay, Corinna MacNeice, the late Dan MacNeice, Peter Tait, and Janet Kovesi Watt.

For permission to reprint material from other sources, acknowledgements are due to the following: the Anthony Blunt Estate for brief extracts from 'From Bloomsbury to Marxism' (*Studio International*, vol. 186, November 1973); Miranda Carter for brief extracts from *Anthony Blunt: His Lives*; the John Hilton Estate for brief extracts from 'Louis MacNeice at Marlborough and Oxford' and remarks in pencil on various letters in the Bodleian Library; Robin Lindsay and Sherborne Preparatory School for brief extracts from *Sherborne Prep Register*; the Society of Authors on behalf of the Compton Mackenzie Estate for a brief extract from *My Life and Times*; the late Dan MacNeice and Carrickfergus Museum for brief extracts from 'Biographical Sketch of Louis's First Wife' and 'Louis' son'; Richard Murphy and Maggs Bros. for his inscription in a volume from his library, reproduced in Maggs Bros. Catalogue; Corinna MacNeice for Elizabeth Nicholson's 'Characters Connected to Sherborne School' (published as Appendix 1 in this volume) and an extract from 'Trees Were Green' (in *TWA*).

For permission to reproduce illustrative material, acknowledgements are due to the following: the Keeper of Western Manuscripts, Bodleian Library, for sketches from letter of Louis MacNeice to Eleanor Clark (13 Feb. 1940); the Estate of Louis MacNeice for all other illustrations and images from letters of Louis MacNeice; Corinna MacNeice and the Carrickfergus Museum for photographs of MacNeice family members (plates 1–7, 10, 12, 14, 18, 20 and 24); Hulton Archive/Getty Images for photograph of Anthony Blunt et al. (plate 8; photograph by Lytton Strachey); archives of King's College, Cambridge, for photograph of Mary MacNeice (plate 9); the Britten-Pears Foundation for photograph of Hedli Anderson (plate 11), © reserved (as we have been unable to ascertain who holds copyright for this photograph); the Center for Creative Photography, University of Arizona Foundation for photograph of Hedli Anderson (1953) by Rollie McKenna (plate 13), © Rosalie Thorne McKenna Foundation; Special Collections, The Pennsylvania State University Libraries for photograph of Louis MacNeice (March 1939) (plate 15); private collection of Corinna MacNeice for photograph of Louis MacNeice (plate 16), taken by Howard Coster, © National Portrait Gallery, London; Kentucky Library and Museum, Western Kentucky University, for photograph of Eleanor Clark (c.1939) (plate 17); the Estate of Douglas Glass for photograph of Dan MacNeice (1945) (plate 19); the Senior Common Room, Christ Church, Oxford, for photograph of E. R. Dodds (plate 21); the Faber and Faber archive for photograph of Charles Monteith (plate 22); the National Portrait Gallery, London, for photograph of the Faber poets (photograph by Mark Gerson) (plate 23); the Estate of Lotte Meitner-Graf for photograph of Louis MacNeice (1954) (plate 25), © reserved (as we have been unable to ascertain who holds copyright for this photograph).

The editor and publishers have made every effort to trace owners of copyright material. They apologise if any person or source has been overlooked in these acknowledgements, and they would be grateful to be informed of oversights.

Abbreviations

AB	Anthony Blunt
AT	Allen Tate
BB	Basil Barr
BC	Bennet Cerf
BCM	Brigid Corinna MacNeice
CM	Charles Monteith
DM	Daniel MacNeice
EC	Eleanor Clark
EM/EN	Elizabeth Nicholson (née MacNeice)
ERD	E. R. Dodds
FLM	Frederick Louis MacNeice
FSJ	Frances Suzman Jowell
GBM	Georgina Beatrice MacNeice
JB	John Boyd
JF	John Freeman
JL	John Lehmann
JFM	John Frederick MacNeice
JH	John Hilton
LG	Laurence Gilliam
MM	Mary MacNeice (née Ezra)
RD	Rupert Doone
RM	Richard Murphy
TMG	Thomas MacGregor Greer
TSE	T. S. Eliot
WB	Wilfrid Blunt
WHA	W. H. Auden
WRR	W. R. Rodgers

PUBLICATIONS

Armitage	C. M. Armitage and Neil Clark, *A Bibliography of the Works of Louis MacNeice*, Edmonton: University of Alberta Press, 1973
AJ	*Autumn Journal*, Faber and Faber 1939

AS	*Autumn Sequel: A Rhetorical Poem in XXVI Cantos*, Faber and Faber 1954
BF	*Blind Fireworks*, Gollancz, 1929
BP	*The Burning Perch*, Faber and Faber 1963
Carter	Miranda Carter, *Anthony Blunt: His Lives*, Macmillan, 2001
Coulton	Barbara Coulton, *Louis MacNeice in the BBC*, Faber and Faber, 1980
CP66	*Collected Poems*, ed. E. R. Dodds, Faber and Faber, 1966
CP07	*Collected Poems*, ed. Peter McDonald, Faber and Faber, 2007
DNB	*Dictionary of National Biography*, Oxford University Press, various years
EC	*The Earth Compels*, Faber and Faber 1938
HS	*Holes in the Sky*, Faber and Faber 1948
LI	*Letters from Iceland*, Faber and Faber 1938
LM	*London Magazine*
Mendelson	*The Complete Works of W. H. Auden*, ed. Edward Mendelson, 5 vols, Princeton University Press, 1986–
MP	*Modern Poetry: A Personal Essay*, Oxford University Press, 1938
NS	*New Statesman and Nation*, later *New Statesman*
NV	*New Verse*
PP	*Plant and Phantom*, Faber and Faber, 1941
PR	*Partisan Review*
RW	*Roundabout Way*, Putnams, 1934
SAF	*The Strings Are False: An Unfinished Autobiography*, ed. E. R. Dodds, Faber and Faber, 1965
SLC	*Selected Literary Criticism*, ed. Alan Heuser, Oxford University Press, 1987
SP	*Selected Prose*, ed. Alan Heuser, Oxford: Clarendon, 1990
Stallworthy	Jon Stallworthy, *Louis MacNeice*, Faber and Faber, 1995
Sutherland	John Sutherland, *Stephen Spender: The Authorized Biography*, Viking, 2004
TBO	*Ten Burnt Offerings*, Faber and Faber, 1953
TWA	*Time Was Away: The World of Louis MacNeice*, ed. Terence Brown & Alec Reid, Dublin: Dolmen Press, 1974

AIR	All India Radio
ARCA	Associate of the Royal College of Architects
ARCM	Associate of the Royal College of Musicians
ARIBA	Associate of the Royal Institute of British Architects
BBC	British Broadcasting Corporation
BEF	British Expeditionary Force
BM	British Museum
BRA	Belfast Royal Academy
CBE	Commander of the British Empire
CCNY	City College of New York
CIE	Companion of the Order of the Indian Empire
CMG	Companion of the Order of St Michael and St George
CPM	Colonial Police Medal for Gallantry
DBE	Dame of the British Empire
DD	Doctor of Divinity
DSO	Distinguished Service Order
FBA	Fellow of the British Academy
FIL	Association of Writers for Intellectual Liberty
FRCO	Fellow of the Royal College of Organists
FRCS	Fellow of the Royal College of Surgeons
FRIBA	Fellow of the Royal Institute of British Architects
FRS	Fellow of the Royal Society
FRSA	Fellow of the Royal Society of Arts
FRSL	Fellow of the Royal Society of Literature
FSA	Fellow of the Society of Architects
GBE	(Knight or Dame) Grand Cross of the British Empire
GCMG	(Knight) Grand Cross of the Order of St Michael and St George
GS	Grammar School
HO	Holy Orders
HRC, Texas	Harry Ransom Center, University of Texas at Austin
HS	High School
ICS	Indian Civil Service
JP	Justice of the Peace
KCIE	Knight Commander of the Order of the Indian Empire
KCL	King's College, London
LLD	Doctor of Laws
LRCP	Licentiate of the Royal College of Physicians
LSE	London School of Economics

M.C.	Military Cross
MC	Marlborough College
MP	Member of Parliament
MRCS	Member of the Royal College of Surgeons
MRIA	Member of the Royal Irish Academy
OAM	Medal of the Order of Australia
O.M.	Order of Merit
OM	Old Marlburian
OTC	Officer Training Corps
OUP	Oxford University Press
OUDS	Oxford University Dramatic Society
PRA	President of the Royal Academy
PRONI	Public Records Office, Northern Ireland
QUB	Queen's University, Belfast
RA	Royal Academy, or Royal Artillery
RAMC	Royal Army Medical Corps
RBAI	Royal Belfast Academical Institution
RCM	Royal College of Music
RFH	Royal Festival Hall
RGA	Royal Garrison Artillery
RIAM	Royal Irish Academy of Music
RIR	Royal Irish Regiment
RSA	Royal Society of Antiquaries, Royal Society of Arts, or Royal Scottish Academy
RUR	Royal Ulster Rifles
SHAEF	Supreme Headquarters of the Allied Expeditionary Force
TCD	Trinity College, Dublin
TCL	Trinity College of Music, London
TD	Territorial Decoration
UCL	University College London
V&A	Victoria and Albert Museum

Chronology

1921   January: back to Sherborne, now under influence of 'aesthetic' master, Mr Hemsted; February: school celebrates centenary of Keats; July: confrontation with two masters (Powys and Lindsay) over the Orange Order; September: enters Marlborough College

1922   19 January: visits London Zoo with Aunt Eva; March: reads letters of Charles Lamb; September: enters Classical Fifth

1923   May: cycles to Avebury with friends; August: reading Robert Louis Stevenson; moves into 'Upper School'. Newcomers include John Betjeman and Graham Shepard; September: moves into Lower Classical Sixth, taught by A. R. Gidney (friends include Fortie Ross, Anthony Blunt)

1924   February: writes letter in verse to stepmother; 29 March: school magazine *The Heretick* appears; May: takes photos of bird's nest; 6 July: in a letter home he signs himself for the first time 'Louis'; summer holiday in Sheep Haven Bay, Donegal (first extended visit to the west of Ireland); autumn: shares study with Fortie Ross (Reckitts in *The Strings Are False*)

1925   March: reading *Jude the Obscure*; May and October: articles in the *Marlburian*; December: sits examinations in Oxford for Post-mastership scholarship at Merton

1926   May: cycles to Avebury with Anthony Blunt and John Hilton; summer in Ireland: visits Dublin Art Galleries; 15 October: enters Merton College; Christmas: before coming home, visits Hiltons in Aylesbury, and the Blunts

1927   Letters to Basil Barr; June: meets Mrs Beazley at Moore Crosthwaite's party; July: visits Paris with Hilton; September: MacNeice family visit west of Ireland; Christmas: in Carrickfergus; starts writing a novel about Blunt

1928   Summer: gets a First in Mods and is reintroduced to the Beazleys; cruise to Norway with his father; September: Hilton visits Carrick-fergus; 18 October: Elizabeth marries John Nicholson in Carrickfergus; late October: crashes car while driving to Cambridge to see Blunt, injuring passengers Crosthwaite and Green-Armytage; Gollancz agree to publish *Blind Fireworks*; December: becomes secretly engaged to Mary Ezra

1929   Arrested for drunk and disorderly behaviour; 14 February telegram home announces his engagement to Mary; parents visit Oxford; 18 March: *Blind Fireworks* published; summer: with Mary and the MacNeices to Achill; to St Tropez with the Beazleys

1930   April: interviewed for job in Birmingham; 21 June: marries Mary

Beazley in Oxford Town Hall Register Office, thence to the Lamb Hotel, Burford, and honeymoon in the Cotswolds; July: is awarded a First in Greats; 30 September: he and Mary move to Philip Sergeant Florence's flat in Selly Park, Birmingham

1931   Completes novel *Roundabout Way*

1932   *Roundabout Way* published (pseud. Louis Malone); first letter to T. S. Eliot

1933   Offers himself as reviewer for the *Criterion* to Eliot; writes scathingly about W. H. Auden's 'communism' to Blunt; writes poems 'To a Communist' and 'Birmingham'

1934   15 May: birth of Dan MacNeice

1935   10 February: father enthroned at St Anne's Cathedral, Belfast; September: *Poems* published; November: Mary leaves him for Charles Katzman

1936   *Agamemnon of Aeschylus* published; Easter: to Spain with Blunt; 4 August: departs for Iceland with Auden (and group from Bryanston); takes lectureship at Bedford College and moves to 4A Keats Grove, Hampstead, with Dan and nurse; November: divorce from Mary finalised; Group Theatre performs *Agamemnon*

1937   Begins affair with Nancy Coldstream; *Out of the Picture* and *Letters from Iceland* published; April and July: two visits to the Hebrides

1938   Meets George MacCann in Mullan's bookshop, Belfast; *I Crossed the Minch* and *The Earth Compels* published; 1 October: Hitler occupies the Sudetenland; 14 October: asks Eliot to help arrange lectures in the USA for spring 1939; November: *Modern Poetry: A Personal Essay* and *Zoo* published; December: visits Spain

1939   2 February: sends *Autumn Journal* to Eliot; March: commissioned by OUP to write a study of Yeats; March–April: lecture tour in USA; meets Eleanor Clark at *Partisan Review* party; 21 April: returns to England on *Queen Mary*; 18 May: *Autumn Journal* published; May–June: invited to teach at Cornell in 1940 and invited to apply for Chair of English at Trinity College, Dublin

1940   14 January: writes to Dodds as literary executor on Cunard White Star letterhead from the waiting room in Liverpool; February– March: American lecture tour, while based at Cornell; 16–17 July: suffering from peritonitis and hospitalised in Portsmouth, NH; recuperates in Maine; 3 September: an 'air ace' flies him to the Clark home at Southover Farm; October: visits Katzman's farm at Egg Harbor; stays with Auden at 7 Middagh

Street; November: returns to England; *The Last Ditch* and *Selected Poems* published

1941 15 February: has his first radio script broadcast on the BBC's *Word from America*; visits Dan at Cootehill, Co. Cavan; sends five 'London Letters' to periodical *Common Sense*, describing effects of war; April: article 'Biggest Raid Ever' (*Picture Post*); 30 May: signs permanent contract with the BBC Features department; 20–29 June: he and Jack Dillon are reprimanded for misbehaviour on board HMS *Chelsea*

1942 February: *Poems, 1925–40* published (NY); April: *Poetry of W. B. Yeats* and *Plant and Phantom* published; 14 April: death of father; returns home for funeral; proposes marriage to Hedli Anderson; they marry 1 July and honeymoon in Ireland; introduced to Jack Yeats in Dublin by John Betjeman; 12 October: *Christopher Columbus* broadcast

1943 January: moves to 10 Wellington Place, London NW8 (near Lord's cricket ground); Dan stays, en route to boarding school; 5 July: birth of Brigid Corinna MacNeice; 20 September: Graham Shepard lost at sea; writes 'The Casualty'

1944 March: *Christopher Columbus: A Radio Play* published; December: *Springboard* published with a print run of 7,000, the largest to date

1945 Easter with stepmother in Carrickfergus; to London with Dan, en route for Downs School; 8 May: VE Day; July: writes to Dodds, 'I wish one could either <u>live</u> in Ireland or <u>feel oneself</u> in England'; 31 July: Features becomes separate department in the BBC

1946 March: moves with Hedli to Tilty (Essex); 1 June: W. R. Rodgers joins Features; July: holiday at Brissago, Switzerland; rents flat at 33 Cheyne Walk; 29 September: inauguration of BBC Third Programme; 17 November: Hedli recital at Wigmore Hall

1947 March: Lord Mountbatten becomes Viceroy of India; April: Hedli and children to parents in Brissago (he follows, via Norway and Denmark); 6 August: flies to Delhi via Cairo, Karachi; 15 August: Indian partition; 25 August: departs Delhi for Peshawar, via Lahore and Sheikhupura; Khyber Pass, then (2 September) to Kashmir; 13–23 September: Lahore, Delhi, Calcutta; 4 October: Lucknow; sends Hedli a poem, 'Letter from India'; 8 October: Delhi, Hyderabad; 21 October: Madras, Trichinopoly, Maduraj, Trivandrum on Cape Comorin; November: moves to 52 Canonbury Park South

1948 13 March: *India at First Sight* broadcast; May: *Holes in the Sky* published; July: reports a long day out with Dylan Thomas; August: holiday on Sark, with Mervyn Peake; 17 September: attends Yeats's reinterment at Drumcliff

1949 1 April: given leave by BBC to translate *Faust* (broadcast 30 October); September: *Collected Poems, 1925–1948* published

1950 1 January: arrives Athens as director of British Institute (eighteen months' leave from BBC); meets Patrick Leigh Fermor, Kevin Andrews, Moore Crosthwaite (old Oxford friend); Easter: Dan MacNeice flies out; they stay on Hydra with the Leigh Fermors; 6 June: lectures at Patras; pilgrimage to Missolonghi; 4 December: lectures at Istanbul

1951 Spring: Dodds visits Athens; expedition to Crete; July: Laurence Gilliam visits Athens; September: returns to England, via Venice; September–November: *Ten Burnt Offerings* broadcast on BBC; *Faust* published

1952 March: signs doomed contract for *The Character of Ireland*; June: Dan passes O-levels in London and spends summer with mother in Egg Harbor; July: Louis and Hedli rent 2 Clarence Terrace (Elizabeth Bowen's house); obtains two months' leave (without pay)

1953 26 February–5 March: voyage to New York; 5 March: start of American tour; spends two weeks in New York with Ruthven Todd; 17 March: visits Denis and Betty Johnston; 22 March: Harvard; 6, 8 April: Minnesota and Chicago; 13 April: solo performance by Hedli in New York; 19, 24 April: double act in Washington, DC and Connecticut College; 28 April–4 May: to England, spending time with John and Eileen Berryman; May: Dan returns to England but avoids FLM, who refuses consent to his return to USA; August: decides to write a sequel to *Autumn Journal*; 19 October: visits Davin in Oxford, Dodds in Old Marston; they dine at Christ Church (see *Autumn Sequel*, XII–XIII); 24 November: attends funeral of Dylan Thomas at Laugharne; 9 December: final meeting with Dan before he departs for USA

1954 May: BBC broadcast of *Autumn Sequel*; 27 September: boards *Queen Mary* for America; visiting lectureship at Sarah Lawrence College, New York; directs student production of *Hippolytus*; 12 November: *Autumn Sequel* published

1955 February: tour of the Nile and northern Sudan; to Alexandria and Athens; April: to Edinburgh to meet Sam Wells; tells Wells he thinks he (FLM) is 'finished as a poet'; spring: Hedli discovers his affair with Cécile Chevreau; 29 July: family holidays in Dorset; September: Edinburgh Festival; 21 October: to Karachi to record Christmas programme; writes 'Return to Lahore'; visits Delhi, Madras and Ceylon

1956   8 April: death of Georgina MacNeice (funeral 13 April); writes 'Death of an Old Lady'; August: completes *Visitations*; commissioned by BBC to write film script about independence of Gold Coast as Ghana; 13 October–16 November: visits Gold Coast and Togoland

1957   22 February: *Birth of Ghana* broadcast; March: *Freedom for Ghana* (film) released to coincide with Ghanaian independence; 10 May: *Visitations* published; July: receives honorary DLitt at Queen's University, Belfast; October–18 November: third visit to the Far East researching *The Commonwealth Remembers* (India, Singapore, Kuala Lumpur, Malacca, Ceylon; nine letters to Hedli in October); Christmas: Isle of Wight at Prospect Cottage, bought from J. B. Priestley and Jaquetta Hawkes

1958   Awarded CBE; six-month course on television production inspires him to write the play *One for the Grave* (not performed until 1966); Anthony Thwaite joins Features

1959   13 February: *Eighty-Five Poems* published; August–September: lectures at Cape Town and Johannesburg; sends poems to Hedli from South Africa ('Half Truth from Cape Town', 'Solitary Travel')

1960   January: attends performance in Belfast of Sam Thompson's *Over the Bridge*; begins affair with Mary Wimbush; September: marriage breaks up

1961   February: records LP of his poetry; March: *Solstices* published; early autumn: car crash while driving with Mary Wimbush; requests a divorce but Hedli refuses

1962   June: in Dublin for Bloomsday, with Dominic Behan and others; tours the west of Ireland in August with Corinna; visits Richard Murphy in Cleggan; 22 August: delivers lecture ('Is Yeats a Good Model?') at Yeats Summer School, Sligo; 26 September: attends party for Eliot's birthday; moves to Aldbury (Herts) with Mary Wimbush

1963   February–May: delivers Clark Lectures, Cambridge; July: records 'Childhood Memories' for John Boyd, BBC; 7 August: while in Yorkshire, records cave sound-effects for *Persons from Porlock*; contracts a cold which turns into pneumonia; 20 August: confined to bed with 'mystery temperature'; 27 August: admitted to St Leonard's Hospital, Shoreditch; 30 August: *Persons from Porlock* broadcast; 3 September: death of FLM; 7 September: funeral at St John's Wood Church; 13 September: *The Burning Perch* published; 17 October: Memorial Service, Church of All Souls, Langham Place

LETTERS OF
LOUIS MACNEICE

1914

TO *John Frederick MacNeice*[1]   MS Bodleian

Sunday evening [1914]   [The Rectory, Carrickfergus,
                                      hereafter Carrickfergus]

My Dear Dad

We are all well, and were at church this morning. It was so warm and I had my summer coat on. We had tea outside on Saturday. I made a flag for Willie on Friday.[2] Mrs MacCaughlin did not come but she sent Willie a Union Jack.[3] Willie made a birthday sermon. I am out without a coat now. I read eight chapters of Job and some out of St. Matthew.

Miss Cready says my writing is very bad.[4] On Saturday I climbed up a tree and got very dirty. I had a bath. Today Willie was in the garden and went through the hedge and climbed up on the palings. We found him

---

1 – Rt Rev. John Frederick MacNeice, DD (1866–1942), born on the island of Omey, nr Clifden, Co. Galway. Educ. TCD; deacon 1895, priest 1897; curate, Cappoquin, Co. Waterford 1895–9; Holy Trinity Church, Belfast 1899–1900; curate, then incumbent, St Clement's Church, Belfast 1901–3; incumbent, Trinity Church, Belfast 1903–8; incumbent, St Nicholas's Church, Carrickfergus 1908–31; precentor and canon of Connor Cathedral 1921–6; Archdeacon of Connor 1926–31; canon of St Patrick's Cathedral, Dublin 1930; Bishop of Cashel and Waterford 1931–4; Bishop of Down, Connor and Dromore 1934–42. Author of *Carrickfergus and its Contacts: Some Chapters in the History of Ulster* (London and Belfast, 1928); *Reunion: The Open Door. A Call from Ireland* (Belfast, 1930); *The Church of Ireland in Belfast: Its Growth, Condition, Needs* (Belfast, 1931); *Spiritual Rebirth or World Revolution: Essays and Addresses* (Dublin, 1932); *Some Northern Churchmen and Some Notes on the Church in Belfast* (Belfast, 1934); *Our First Loyalty* (Belfast, 1937); various pamphlets. M. (1) Lily Clesham, 25 June 1902 (d. 18 Dec. 1914); (2) Georgina Beatrice ('Bea') Greer (1874–1956), 19 April 1917.
2 – William Lindsay MacNeice (1905–68), author's brother. He was born with Down's syndrome; in September 1916 he was sent to a special institution in Stirlingshire, where he remained for some years.
3 – Mrs McCaughen, Windmill House, Belfast Road, Carrickfergus, friend of Georgina Beatrice MacNeice. The McCaughens were among the very few parishioners who came to pay their respects to the MacNeice household at Governor's Walk after the controversial appointment of JFM to the post of incumbent at St Nicholas's Church, Carrickfergus in 1908 (Stallworthy, 19). Elizabeth Nicholson later described a 'Miss McCaughen' of Windmill House as a 'v. old & much-attached family friend – our earliest living friend' (EN, Names of family and friends [1964], *Faber archive, Monteith file*).
4 – Miss McCready (also Miss Cready, Miss Mac, Miss MacC), children's nurse. She is Miss Craig in *The Strings Are False: An Unfinished Autobiography* (1965) (*SAF*).

stuck there. I read some Genesis. We got appledumpling [*sic*] for dinner today. On Saturday morning I was awake at six but this morning I was awake after eight. Miss Mac made Elsie sleep in the room with me when you are away.[1] Elsie did not want to write. Elsie and Willie send their love. There was a young clergyman.

From Freddie
With love

TO *John Frederick MacNeice* MS Bodleian

Tuesday evening [1914?] [Carrickfergus]

My dear Dad

I got ten for conduct this morning.

The kitten is alright and so are Frisk and Mons.

We gathered some of the apples this morning.

This evening Miss Cready took Willie and I to Miss Greenaway's with your letter. We went there by Sinderpath and went up the mill road.[2] When we came to a door in a wall we met a little girl. Miss Cready asked her where Miss Greenaway lived she said, in there.

So Miss Cready knocked at the door several times but nobody came.

Then Miss Cready was going away when suddenly a woman came to the door and opened it to let the little girl in, then Miss Cready went back and asked if Miss Greenaway was in. She said she was in, then Miss Cready gave the letter to her to give to her.

We went home by Loves Lonley, and it began to rain on North road; we went to shelter in the hedge, when the rain had stopped we went home.[3]

1 – Elsie (also 'Eek' and later 'Equator'): FLM's sister, Caroline Elizabeth MacNeice (24 April 1903–1981), the first child of John Frederick MacNeice and Lilly MacNeice (née Clesham). Educ. Sherborne School for Girls, St Hugh's College, Oxford, and Charing Cross Hospital Medical School. She married John Nicholson (later Sir John Nicholson, FRCS) on 18 Oct. 1928. See her memoir, 'Trees Were Green', in *Time Was Away: The World of Louis MacNeice*, ed. Terence Brown & Alec Reid (*TWA*) (Dublin, 1974), 11–20. Her notes on persons in the letters and her letter to FLM concerning their Sligo relatives are presented in the appendices to this volume.

2 – Mill Road, Carrickfergus. The path beside the railway line, near the Rectory, was scattered with cinders from the passing steam engines. 'We called it the Cinder Path because it was made of cinders, it put your teeth on edge to walk on it' (*SAF*, 49). Cf. 'Nature Notes': 'They brightened the cinderpath of my childhood' ('Dandelions', *Solstices*, CP07, 548).

3 – Loves Loanen runs from the Barn Flax Mills to the North Road, near the Rectory. Cf. 'I was walking with Miss Hewitt along Love's Loney (which in English is Lovers' Lane)', *SAF*, 61. EN wrote: 'The North Road on which the Rectory stood climbed steadily upwards into a country of low hills and small farms' (*TWA*, 12). See also 'Landscapes', *SAF*, 218.

I wrote all this myself.

Is Elsie well. Are there any fish in the Firth of Forth. Last night did you see us at the holly bush outside the side-door, Willie and me waved our white hats to you.

I was in three trees gathering apples this morning.

With love

From Freddie

TO *John Frederick MacNeice* MS Bodleian

Thursday afternoon [1914]   [Carrickfergus]

My dear Dad

We went for a walk yesterday evening and got thirty-two black-berries.[1]

I got ten for conduct at lessons.

We are going for a walk this evening.

We are sending you some of the photographs Miss Gorman took of us. Elsie had to be cut out of one because she was too bad.

Frisk, Mons, and Anwill, are all right.

I am writing this at the desk in the schoolroom.

Anwill was in the kitchen today and was hopping and jumping about.

We are all well.

With Love

From Freddie

PS Miss Cready is sending Elsie a photograph of her sitting on the bank she is better in it. It is in the parcel.

TO *Elizabeth MacNeice* MS Bodleian

Monday morning [1914]   [Carrickfergus]

My dear Elsie

Do you like Rosnowlagh is it any bigger than Bonnybefore, is it as nice as Whitehead or Blackhead, have you found any fossils yet.[2] On Saturday,

---

1 – 'In the afternoon when it was not raining too hard . . . we would walk with Miss Craig up the road up the hill behind our house to a point called Mile Bush and back again' (*SAF*, 45).

2 – EM was staying at Coolmore House, Rossnowlagh, a seaside resort in Co. Donegal. Bonnybefore was a small townland near the Rectory in Carrickfergus. Whitehead and Blackhead are also near Carrickfergus.

Annie cleaned out the yard-tank, she had a bath, underneath with the tap pouring water into it, Annie stood on a chair and bailed out the water with a bucket, she got a dirty cup out once.[1]

In the evening, after tea, Archie came to the door when he was going home although it was rainy, and said he had cut the tops of the beans of [*sic*], because the black flies were on them, and he meant to to [*sic*] burn them.[2]

Miss Cready said she is going to make us do some lessons today, she says this letter will do for the writing; but I don't think its very good.

Does every person you meet say "Good morning" to you. Do you remember that piece of poetry I made up about –

> A great old kangaroo
> Used to tease poor Bamboo
> And he used to cry gue gue.

Well I have put some more lines to that[.] I shall put it all on the next page.

> A great old kangaroo
> Used to tease poor Bamboo
> And he used to cry gue gue
> At last an old wombat
> Joined in the combat
> He was sleepy as though it was night
> And always spoke right
> And never was blight
> Though he joined in the fight

Do you like it as well as the other ones[?][3]

---

1 – Annie, the cook at the Rectory, was 'a buxom rosy girl' from the Clogher Valley, Co. Tyrone, known locally for her crochet work and her storytelling (*SAF*, 41). She is the 'Catholic farmer's daughter from Fivemiletown' in *Autumn Sequel* (*AS*, XVII, CP07, 447).
2 – Archibald White (b.1854), gardener and labourer, 'in whose presence everything was merry' (*SAF*, 47). FLM later wrote: 'he was ideal company for someone about the age of 5, 6, or 7', from 'Autobiographical Talk: Childhood Memories', BBC, 1963; repr. *Selected Prose*, ed. Alan Heuser (Oxford, 1990) (*SP*), 269. White lived with his wife Margaret in the Scotch Quarter, Carrickfergus, but was originally from Co. Londonderry/Derry (Census of Ireland, 1911): in 'The Gardener' the old man's soul went out 'To find the Walls of Derry' (*The Last Ditch*; *Plant and Phantom*; CP07, 190; 696).
3 – EN recalled: 'He always wrote poetry from the time that he could write at all. He began writing it when he was about seven' (typescript, 'Louis MacNeice: A Radio Portrait', broadcast 7 Sept. 1966. *PRONI D2833/D/5/21*).

We are all well, except Mons, for I think she is not very well though she was very frisky last night. A few moments ago Miss Cready came in and said this letter would do for all the lessons, I was rather surprised.

With love from Freddie

PS We were at church yesterday Chippie and Miss Higgin were there.[1] In the evening there was thunder, lightning and rain and I saw a flash of lightning when I was beside the fender.

Every night the rooster crows every night [*sic*] since you left[.] Annie thinks he must be lonely without you.

[*adult hand, not JFM*] We are thinking of plucking him & sending him down for your dinner some day, but if we do you would need to boil him well . . . Willie wants to know if you would like some gooseberries.

1 – The Higgins were a Church of Ireland family who lived locally at Rosganna, Kilroot, Co. Antrim. In 1911, two Miss Higgins lived there, namely Lucy Chippendall (age fifty-five) and Margaret (age forty). Also living there were the head of the family, Frances Higgin (age eighty-two, widow of the late William Higgin) and her two grandsons, Thomas Chippendall Lewin ('Chippie'?) (b.1908) and William Patrick Lewin (b.1903) (Census of Ireland, 1911). The two small boys were the children of Major A. C. Lewin DSO (Connaught Rangers) and Nora Constance Lewin (née Higgin, m.1900), whose family home was Cloghans House, nr Tuam, Co. Mayo. Apparently the Lewins were staying in Rosganna in the absence of one or both parents. In light of new evidence uncovered by Professor David Fitzpatrick, most scholars who have considered the issue, including the authorised biographer of the poet, Professor Jon Stallworthy, now accept that the 1911 letter from Cloghans to 'Elsie' (EM), previously attributed to FLM, was in fact written by a young Lewin, presumably William Patrick (cf. Stallworthy, 30–2). My thanks to David Fitzpatrick, Jon Stallworthy, Edward Mendelson and Judith Priestman for throwing light on this matter.

1915

TO *Elizabeth MacNeice*   MS Dan MacNeice

Saturday 23 October [1915]   [Carrickfergus]

My dear Elsie

I got your letter, and we are glad that you are well and seeing so many nice places. It is a very wet day here. There has [*sic*] been girls round here selling red cross flags. Willie and I are sending you ours. There is a fire in the schoolroom today. It is very wintry looking outside as most of the leaves are off the trees, and there is one tree with only two leaves on it. We are all well. Annie was in Belfast on Wednesday afternoon, and I was out for a walk with Dad. We have the flowerbeds nearly all fixed up in the garden. Miss MacC hopes you will do your best when sewing to do as much as you can when you are at it and try and do it well. Did you learn any more swimming. As you corrected my letter now we will correct yours. Both Thanksgiving and imaginary were wrong. You had no k in Thanks-giving and no r in imaginary.

I am sending you a little poem in this letter with the flags. I am giving you some riddles the answers are on the other side.

(1) Spell Blackwater with three letters. (2) Make one word of the following letters. Edarnow, (3) Spell ['']broken down ditch' with three letters.

(1) Ink (2) The letters transposed will make <u>One. Word</u> (3) Gap.

I have made another piece of poetry. It is.

> The water sound
> Gurgles and bubbles around
>   In a wild country
> The Cliffs are high
> Against the sky
> In a wild country
> The Suns great ray
> Makes hot the traveller[']s way
> In a wild country.
>   — —

8

Do you like it.

With Love from Freddie

Saturday
23rd October
My Dear Elsie

I got your letter, and we are glad that you are well and seeing so many nice places. It is a very wet day here. There has been girls round here selling red cross flags. Willie and I are sending you ours. There is a fire in the schoolroom today. It is very wintry looking outside as most of the

(1) Ink (2) The letters transposed will make One. Word (3) Gap.

I have made another piece of poetry. It is.

The water sound
Gurgles and bubbles and
In a wild country
The Cliffs are high
Against the sky
In a wild country
The Suns great ray
Makes hot the travellers way
In a wild country.
Do you like it.
With Love from Freddie.

1916

John Frederick MacNeice   MS Bodleian

28 April [1916]   Carrickfergus

My dear Daddie

We are all well. I think Lincoln and Durham are very nice books.[1] Thank you for them. There are two parcels for you. One came from Belfast and the other came from Dublin. Miss Heward gave the letters to Mr. [sic] Birney.[2] I thought Miss Gorman was coming here today so I waited in Elsie's Forest and in the lookout and up trees.[3]

When Elsie and I made the dugout we dug in different places; so I am going to make a tunnel from my place to Elsie's place.

Archie sowed some peas and potatoes yesterday. Miss Heward bought peas, beans and leeks. Yesterday Jack ran into a field and chased some cows.

I climbed up a tree today. It is called the rigging and I climbed it before Elsie did. I used to get up by a branch like a ladder but Archie cut it down so now I get up another way. It has two bells in it but they are broken.

Jack's house had got hardly any straw in it one night but there was an old bat there. I gave him a sack to lie on.

When I was waiting for Miss Gorman today, I walked through Elsie's Forest. The dugout is in the corner and the chestnut tree and the place with sticks round it are near it. Then there is a place called the Great Central Hall with the reservoir in one corner. A passage goes from it to the stockade with the rigging tree in it. Below the stockade there is a hall place with nettles in it, and a passage goes from it to our new tree.

1 – Presumably JFM had sent home books on the cathedral cities.
2 – Edith Georgina Heward (b.1876) (Miss Hewitt in *SAF*) replaced Miss McCready in the household in March 1916. An Englishwoman, she seemed to the children much more tolerant than her predecessor (*SAF*, 56). She had previously been housekeeper for a widower and his young son at 6 Osborne Park, Belfast (Census of Ireland, 1911). Mrs Birney lived at Ardnamara, Larne Road, Carrickfergus. Elizabeth Nicholson later described her as 'our governess – Louis' first teacher' (EN, Names of family and friends [1964], *Faber archive, Monteith file*).
3 – 'I quickly gave names to every corner of the garden; every little clump of shrubbery was given its special name' (FLM, 'Autobiographical Talk: Childhood Memories', BBC, 1963; repr. *SP*, 268).

Once we saw Archie in the park.

Frisk has not stolen very much but once she got on the table and eat [*sic*] some potatoes but they were meant for her.

Jenny spring cleaned the old schoolroom and I took down the pictures and pulled out the nails. Jenny wanted to burn the pictures but I do not think Miss Heward did.

I wrote a thing about Spring in my book.[1]

With love
From Freddie

1 – FLM kept a regular diary from late 1915 or early 1916, and he made note of seven diaries up to 1921: '(1) tiny one destroyed by Miss McCready, (2) black one (time of Miss Heward), (3) green one 1919, (4) red one 1918, (5) red one 1919, (6) blue one 1920, (7) blue one 1921.' ('List of old diaries', 1921 Diary, *Ms Bodleian, Ms MacNeice, Box 57*). Miss McCready had destroyed his first diary because she thought it would spoil his handwriting, but Miss Heward was more lenient in this and in other respects (*SAF*, 58–9).

1917

TO *John Frederick MacNeice*   MS Dan MacNeice

Sunday [26 November 1917]   Acreman House, Sherborne, Dorset[1]
                                   [hereafter Sherborne]

My dear Daddie

We had a match with Keary's yesterday and won by one point – Stallard was going to get a try and he was just being collared when he kicked a drop-goal.[2] Thanks awfully for the chessmen.

[caption] While Britain's heroic armies fight ashore, Britain's ships keep ward and watch upon the water. Silent but mighty defenders of the sanctity of the Empire's island SILENT MIGHT home and guardians of her commerce on the boundless deep. Ever on the alert, ever eager for action, yet patiently waiting untiringly WATCHING[.] WELL MAY THE BRITISH EMPIRE be proud of her sons of the sea.

----

1 – When FLM went to Sherborne Prep for the third (autumn) term 1917 there were sixty-three pupils in attendance, including forty-six boarders. The number rose and fell over the years, but the school never had more than seventy-five boys registered during his time there. Headmaster Littleton Powys led a staff in 1917 of four assistant masters: F. R. Lindsay (Mr Cameron in *SAF*), J. C. G. Ferguson, Miss A. Langdon and Miss L. M. Whitehouse, who left at the end of 1917 and was replaced by Gordon P. Desages (*Sherborne Prep Register*).

2 – There were two Stallard brothers, one of whom, Hyla ('Henry') Bristow Stallard (1901–73), MRCS, LRCP, became an eminent ophthalmologist. Educ. Sherborne Prep, Sherborne School, Gonville and Caius, Cambridge, and St Barts 1922–5. Olympic bronze medallist 1924. Cf. Elizabeth Nicholson: 'There were several brothers & I think they all became fairly renowned athletes' (Appendix 1).

Mr. Powys gave everybody a card like this.[1]

Please send an old dictionary here. It has not got a cover and it is about this thick [*indicates size*] and has got things about Diana and things like that in the back and it is inside the press.

There are only 2 more weeks and five days till we come home.

We played 'kick and rush' yesterday, its not as nice as ordinary footer and you cannot get trys and there is not any scrum.[2]

With love from Freddie

TO *John Frederick MacNeice* MS Dan MacNeice

2 December [1917]   Sherborne

My dear Daddic

Sometimes a sergeant comes here and teaches us fire practice like this

[*sketch*]

You slide down inside this. Yesterday we watched Downside playing with big school.[3] When we came back we played kick and rush – Downside won. Geog. is about China now. Once we learned a song called 'Oh to be in England.'[4] It is this

> Oh to be in England
> Now that April's there
> And whoever wakes in England
> Sees some morning unaware
> That the lowest boughs and the brushwood sheaf
> Round the elmtree bole are in tiny leaf
> And the chaffinch sings on the orchard bough
> In England now

1 – Littleton C. Powys (1874–1955), headmaster of Sherborne Prep School 1905–23. He was the second of eleven siblings, including the authors John Cowper, Llewelyn and Theodore Powys. Educ. Sherborne Prep, Sherborne (1st XV, 1st XI) and Corpus Christi, Cambridge. Author of *The Joy of It* (1937) and *Still the Joy of It* (1956). His advocacy of country walks, natural history and the collection of fossils helped to shape the values of the school. He is Owen in *AS* and was inspiration for the figure in 'The Kingdom' (II). Cf. 'Auden and MacNeice: Their Last Will and Testament': 'Item to Littleton Powys more and more / I leave my admiration and all the choice / Flowers and birds that grace our English shore' in *Letters from Iceland* (I.I), CP07, 740. Cf. also *SAF*, 64–5, 69, 74, 221, and see Appendix 1 of this volume.
2 – 'A wild game of football with scarcely a rule' (Powys, *The Joy of It*, 177).
3 – Downside School, Radstock, Bath. 'Big school' is Sherborne.
4 – Robert Browning, 'Oh, to be in England'.

Mr Powys has finished 'Francis Cludd'. He used to read it to us before prep. There is a poem here called 'The Vulgar Boy'.[1] History is Edward III now. I played chess with Tory Major the other day.[2] He kept bringing his queen down and getting in front of my king and checkmating me. At drawing last time we drew a shell like this

[sketch]

before that we drew a cross like this

[sketch]

Miss Whitehouse said she would give a Chinese penny to anybody who found a picture.[3] Baldwin found it. Mr Powys gave us apples yesterday We saw a picture here of a new kind of zeppelin like this. Its very large.[4]

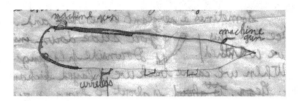

With love from Freddie

1 – 'The Vulgar Little Boy' or 'Misadventures at Margate: A Legend of Jarvis's Jetty', by Rev. Richard Harris Barham (pseud. Thomas Ingoldsby) (1788–1845), *The Ingoldsby Legends, or, Mirth and Marvels*, 2nd series (1864).
2 – Fellow boarders mentioned include the brothers S. and G. Tory and C. Baldwin.
3 – Miss Whitehouse was replaced in the following term by Mr Desages, who had been discharged from the army (*Sherborne Prep Register*).
4 – Zeppelins were in the news: for example there had been a raid in Yorkshire in Aug. 1917 and nine civilians were killed by a Zeppelin attack on south London on 19 Oct. See 'Zeppelin Victims', *The Times*, 26 Oct. 1917, 3. Although German Zeppelin raids had been regular occurrences since the bombing of Antwerp in Aug. 1914, and of Yarmouth and King's Lynn in Jan. 1915, the first British Zeppelin had its trial flight in London on 6 Dec. 1917. See 'British "Zeppelin". A Flight Over London', *The Times*, 7 Dec. 1917, 9. News of this imminent event may have circulated in the school the previous weekend.

1918

TO *Georgina Beatrice MacNeice*[1]   MS Dan MacNeice

17 March [1918]   Sherborne

My dear Madre

Last Sunday I went out with Holloway.[2] We wanted to go to the Haunted Tower but we did not know where it was.[3] We only knew that we had to go to Lovers' Grove first.[4] After a while we saw Hesse and his father in front, because his father had come to see him. They were going to the Haunted Tower too but they did not know where it was either. We knew there was a windmill near it. Hesse's father looked about a lot and suddenly he saw a thing like this

We went across some mud too [*sic*] it and when we got there we found it used to be a church but that the church part had got knocked down. We went inside and we found alot [*sic*] of people had carved their names there we went up a ladder but Hesse's father would not let him come up. When we got up we saw a bell hanging above us with a bit of rope some big school boys had tied on. We found that there used to be three bells but there are only two now.

1 – FLM's stepmother ('Bea') (1874–1956), second daughter of Thomas Greer of Sea Park, Carrickfergus. M. John Frederick MacNeice, 19 April 1917.
2 – Pupils mentioned in this letter for the first time include P. Holloway, J. Hesse, L. Balding and G. Jones (all boarders). Cf. 'And we had our makebelieve, we had our mock / Freedom in walks by twos and threes on Sunday' (*Autumn Journal* (*AJ*) X, CP07, 123).
3 – Possibly Sherborne Old Castle.
4 – Lovers' Grove, a walk through the woods on Plum Pudding Hill, southwest of Sherborne.

On Wednesday Mr. Hudson read out drawing marks for the submarine.[1] Everybody got much more than they generally do.

On Thursday there was a match between Prep. and School House. Prep. won 21–1.

On Friday there was no Prep. because the gas was bad. I think we rolled the cricket field in the evening.

On Saturday I played draughts with Balding. We had half of Jones's cake. Jones is always having enormous cake. Its sixteen days till the end of term I think. I have got one or two pots of jam left.

Thanks awfully for shamrocks and ball.[2] We have only got four more exercises in the Latin book.

One day in Arith Mr. Lindsay started making a kind of lecture about England sending silly people to take care of Ireland.[3] He said it was just the same as if a new headmaster came to the Prep., and somebody flung a pellet at him and it hit his eye and he rubbed his eye and didn't say 'who flung that pellet?' then.

From F.

1 – Since 1917, when German U-boat attacks on Allied shipping began in earnest, more than 1,400 British ships had been sunk by mine or torpedo, including merchant vessels, fishing craft and seven hospital ships. Twenty-eight merchant ships had been sunk by German submarines in the week ending 23 March. 'Heavier Losses by Submarine and Mine', *The Times*, 28 March 1918, 5.

2 – GBM usually sent him shamrocks for St Patrick's Day.

3 – Frederick R. Lindsay (1886–1972) (Mr Cameron in *SAF*), educ. TCD (MA, external student). Lindsay was from a Unionist background in Portadown, one of thirteen children of Richard and Susan Lindsay. (His younger brother, Eric Mervyn Lindsay, was an eminent astronomer and director of the Armagh observatory.) Littleton Powys sold Sherborne Prep to F. R. Lindsay and the Rev. A. W. Hooper in 1923, who took over as joint headmasters; in 1929 Lindsay bought Hooper's share of the school, becoming sole proprietor and head (see EN in Appendix 1). Lindsay's daughter Mary (b.1926) and son Robin (b.1928) both attended Sherborne Prep: Mary Lindsay was the school's only girl pupil. Robin Lindsay later became headmaster of the school (Mary became a psychiatrist). In his notes for first term 1918 Powys records F. R. Lindsay's departure for Ireland: 'Mr Lindsay decided to leave so as to be ordained in Ireland. His departure will be a great loss to us. He has been a most helpful and loyal master. His influence both in school and out has been splendid' (*Sherborne Prep Register*). Lindsay returned to the school the following year, but was never 'ordained'.

TO *Georgina Beatrice MacNeice*   MS Dan MacNeice

5 May [1918]   Sherborne

I saw some guns in the train. When I got here they were mowing.[1] I wrestled with several people.[2] Milford is head.[3] I am still in no 1. Bastin is a prefect. New heads of dormitory are Tory ma = no 10 Baldwin = no. 3 Dawkins <u>is</u> brainy, he's got into Form II. The new master is called Mr MacGuire I do not know how you spell it. He's Irish. His accent is Dublin and Belfast mixed together.[4]

The other day we did something in the Upper and found the table covered with books, gym shoes and a pair of shoes. We told him Mr Linsey [*sic*] used to fling shoes out of the window. The other day we dragged a thing like this across the cricket field to make the grass stick up.

[*diagram*] (much bigger)

Yesterday we went to the Prairie.[5] It was awfully hot.

Today we had porridge, salt (I had none), milk, bread, butter, jam, sugar, tea. Yesterday we had a kind of curry soup I got into top Latin division in third form. Some people have not come back because of chickenpox.

There is a book called Gradatim with things in it you've got to translate. We're doing 29. It's called 'Cruel Frederick'[6] He used to tear up Flies' wings and pierce ants bodies with needles and beat his dog. At last the dog

1 – During the war years, pupils helped with mowing and rolling the cricket ground (Powys, *The Joy of It*, 195).
2 – The school register for second term of 1918 indicates that FLM was by now 4' 6⅞" tall and weighed 5 stone, 2½ oz (Sherborne archivist, private correspondence, 2008). Cf. 'And four foot six was gone / And we found it was time to be leaving' (*AJ*, X; CP07, 123).
3 – Pupils mentioned here for the first time include M. Milford, D. Bastin, C. Baldwin and H. Dawkins.
4 – I. J. Maguire, 'Scholar of Galway University, Ireland', who left for health reasons the following year (*Sherborne Prep Register*). FLM later recalls: 'Mr Cameron left us for a while and in his place we had a master from Galway – seedy, embittered, with a powerful brogue, a bad cough and always the same suit' (*SAF*, 74).
5 – The Prairie: 'a tract of wild country above the Honeycombe Woods' (Powys, *The Joy of It*, 193).
6 – 'Fredericus, puer crudelis, non amavit animalia', from 'Stories for Translation', No. 29, in H. R. Heatley and H. N. Kingdon, *Gradatim: An Easy Latin Translation Book for Beginners* (1890).

bit him and his father said 'Why, at length, you have neglected my counsel.'
Some people caught butterflies yesterday.[1]

F.

(I'll write longer one next time)

TO *John Frederick MacNeice*   MS Dan MacNeice

19 May [1918]   Sherborne

My dear Daddie
     Harker came the other day.[2] He's got rather a queer face rather like this.

[sketch]

The other day we went for a walk and I got caterpillars for Jones. I got
about 16. There are piles here! Dyball got about 22 the other day. They
were all grasseggers except one that was a magpie. Some people say that
'Grasseggers are not grasseggers!' and are drinkers!
     People do not care about magpies much. My one was about this long
___. I've got 3 large fossils for you. We had sausages today and jam Tory's
got a jampot here that's about 10 times as big as a 3 pd. one.
     Williams has left!!
     Places to find caterpillars grasseggers (or drinkers!) = grass or nettles
     Magpies = (very common) currant bushes
     oakeggers = oak (rather rare)
     red soldiers = rhubarb
     wooly bears = I'm not sure[3]

---

1 – Powys notes, second term, 1918: 'Great interest was taken in butterfly collecting: for
which the weather was most propitious – Holt took 7 different kinds of fritillaries' (*Sherborne
Prep Register*). The current school archivist notes: 'Keeping caterpillars and breeding
butterflies and moths from them was a popular hobby taken to almost competitive levels.'
Oliver Holt later became a naturalist, writer and illustrator, author of *Piper's Hill: Memories
of a Country Childhood* (Yeovil, 1992). Powys described Holt as 'one of the best boy
naturalists I ever knew', and published a list of fifty-five birds Holt had sighted in the school
grounds (*Still the Joy of It*, 169, 190).
2 – Pupils mentioned here for the first time include E. Harker, L. Dyball, R. Forshaw, J. Bailey,
L. Weall, H. Gretton, O. Holt (or G. Holt), C. O. Adams and H. Williams.
3 – Caterpillars of the grass eggar moth (*Lasiocampa trifolii*), apparently confused with those
of the drinker moth (*Euthrix potatoria*); the magpie moth (*Abraxas grossulariata*); the oak
eggar moth (*Lasiocampa quercus*); possibly the common red soldier beetle (*Rhagonycha
fulva*), whose larvae resemble small caterpillars; and the 'woolly bear' caterpillars of the
garden tiger moth (*Arctia caja*). 'Sometimes contact with "woolly bears" caused the boys
violent urticaria and Powys had to ban their collection for a while' (Sherborne archivist).

There's a nest in a tree here (covered with ivy) in a hole in the ivy. Yesterday we heard that in the big game one side made 117. Stallard made 49.

We're having lots of queer things this term = curried eggs, some kind of pie, eggs and ham, a rhubarb pudding!! Forshaw's just got 10 magpies on raspberry bushes.

They're humming a tune. I think it may be 'this day—'

Last Sunday I went out with Dawkins and Bailey to a place where there are a lot of trenches.

Today I'm going out with Dawkins[.] Hesse wanted too!! [*sic*]

I clean boots on Wednesday now with Weall, Gretton, Holt & Adams

The other day I filled some inkpots with the can and they overflowed! We had a very small week's order last week for we had hardly any marks. I was sixth.

It's nearly quarter term somebody said.

[*Thumbnail sketches of ball hitting stumps, caterpillars etc.*]

Things in Summer Term different from other terms :
  (1)   caterpillars
  (2)   butterflies
  (3)   cricket
  (4)   changing stockings on Monday
  (5)   collecting flowers
  (6)   going out after tea
  (7)   no gas
  (8)   bats
  (9)   balls
  (10) nets

From F.

TO *John Frederick MacNeice*   MS Dan MacNeice

10 June [1918]   Sherborne

My dear Daddie

The clergyman came here on Monday and gave a kind of lecture, it was awfully nice but he was rather tantalising for he said he'd stop as he was sure we were longing to get our other joys (we weren't).

In a game the other day I was point and caught Holloway but Holloway had his revenge and caught me when he was wicket.[1] We are having a match with no. 3. We have not finished yet. They were in first.

Sides	
No I	No 3
Milford	Baldwin
Me	Tory II
Day II	Dawkins
Day I	Beadon II[2]
Clarke	Hesse

Baldwin got 0 and was stumped by Milford[.] Milford bowled Tory with about [*illegible*] I bowled Dawkins with (I've forgotten) (Dawkins said it was an impossible ball to hit for it pitched in his block and bounced on the top of his wicket.

BAD REPORTS OF THE
GIRL'S SCHOOL
(1) When they're playing cricket they lift their bats above their heads, keep them their [*sic*] for a few minutes and then hit their toe
(2) They run away from the ball
(3) They call each other by their Christian names which is a very bad thing to do

—-|—-

It is Holloway's birthday. I am going out with Holborrow and Brown.

I am called a poke.[3] Tory I says I bowl miles better over than under and do leg-breaks.

No I order.
(1) Milford
(2) Me
(3) Day I Day II Clarke

---

1 – Powys notes for second term 1918: 'There was however plenty of keenness about cricket and there was plenty of promise for the next season' (*Sherborne Prep Register*).
2 – Pupils mentioned here for the first time include E. Beadon, E. Clarke, P. Day, B. Day, D. Holborow, and the dayboy W. Brown. The Clarke boy was Edward Clarke (1908–88), educ. Sherborne School, King's College London, Lincoln's Inn; he took Silk in 1960.
3 – An over-cautious batsman.

Last Sunday we went to a wood We i.e. Day II Clarke and I. Here we met Forshaw and Day I. Forshaw was up a tree and we were looking at a frog in a stream Suddenly a keeper came and turned us out. Then we went into another stream with a hedge over it where there were queer animals.

Everybody's getting pink-eye[.] Day I has.

From F.

P.S. I've made a magic pot out of a jam pot with bits of paper rolled up inside it. You take one bit and read what's written on it.

The Girl's school are very disagreeable. They come about disturbing Quarry Wood on Sunday which is our place.[1] I saw a few Sundays ago an Ealhstan person which shows they are the worst house.[2] As well as that I heard that they dared to go past our yard on our path.

Have you let Frisk live in the house yet?[3]

Has Mick Mac Methuselah started purring yet?

Wilcox was top in halfterm's order. I was 3rd. Beadon I was top of 4th
Holt II = 5th   Holt I = 2nd   Knight = 1st

The Girls' School
at Cricket.

1 – Quarry Wood: on the way to Bradford Abbas, southwest of Sherborne. The old road to this village was within easy access of the Prep.

2 – Ealhstan: Elizabeth's House at Sherborne School for Girls.

3 – His cat Frisk became a character in FLM's childish fantasy. See his eighty-five lines of verse, 'The Lay of Solus': 'I come from the land & the country of Frisk / Where the food is good & the air is brisk. / Far better than this little country of France, / Where horrible French cats gaze at me askance . . .' Red Diary, 3 Aug. 1919 (*Ms Bodleian, Ms Res, Box 57*).

TO *Georgina Beatrice MacNeice*   MS Dan MacNeice

(near half time) [September 1918]   Sherborne

My dear Madre

Can I have the blue Atlas book please?

We had a match against Rosse's yesterday but were beaten.

Prep. things

Antediluvian rubbish (which is a name for some people)

'Bone' which was a name for an old iron dumbbell which Bailey had

Crossyards (a game)[1]

'Cormorant' name for an imaginary ship of the 2nd table

'Beggo Shabbemando V' name for one of Dormy no 1 mascots

'Ebrah's'[2] & 'Anti Ebrahs' (which have stopped now)

'Golliwog' which is a name for Bailey when he's up a certain tree

Oxford v Cambridge (game)[3]

Stags (game)

'Snails' (cabbage sometimes, always cauliflour)

'pig's slosh' a kind of jelly, ham & fat mixed up

Prep. fish (have not had it much this term)

'Fleas in the bolster' a pudding[4]

I cannot remember any more

We are having a 'detective story' competition in no 1 now.

I got a try the other day like this.

[*diagram of rugby pitch*]

X start
= touch
—-- carried by me
. . . by other people

1 – 'The object of this game was to cross the yard from one end to the other without being touched by players in the centre' (Powys, *The Joy of It*, 177).
2 – Rituals performed on new boys in the lavatory with soap and brushes. See next letter.
3 – Football played with a tennis ball.
4 – Suet pudding with caraway seeds: 'modern juvenile palates would not tolerate it' (Sherborne archivist).

22 September [1918] /   Sherborne
['4th Term' *in mother's hand*]

My dear Madre

I thought my box had got lost but it hadn't. Wilcox, Walker, Carey, me, Laws and Powys have been moved up to the second. We had sausages and marrow jam for breakfast. I am not quite sure of the newbugs.[1] I am going to give Day I a 'Hesse' walk today. Yesterday we played Rugger. I was centre forward.

PRIVATE

We had an 'Ebrah' rag last night before reading. We tortured some people with soap, brushes, water, towels etc in the lav.

Forshaw came back yesterday ee! / The dormy is the same. There is a new bug called Alderton who goes back to Ireland by Kingston.[2] My desk is overcrowded with new books. One of them is Palgrave's Golden Treasury. I'll tell you about Day's walk afterwards. There is a new French mistress called Miss Howells.[3] "Whittingdale!["] Has come to the Prep!!![4]

Do <u>you like these</u> names

Baily – Grin, Smilyface etc.   I want to arrange my desk a bit now.
Alderton – Artichoke   This is not the end.
Baker – Mecchano   It will be continued next Sunday. F.
Dawkins – brainy
Day mi – squeak
Day I – you, fag
Me – they
Harker – Ohman

1 – Newbugs were new boys. Pupils mentioned here for the first time include two dayboys, C. Wilcox and K. Carey, and boarders P. Laws, T. Powys, E. Alderton, H. Baker, E. Harker, R. Gell, E. Beadon, R. Beadon, R. Rickett, R. Thomson, W. Forward and L. Weall.
2 – The Holyhead–Kingstown (Dun Laoghaire) ferry.
3 – F. G. Howells was a graduate of University College, Aberystwyth, but did not stay long at the Prep: 'Miss Howells was very painstaking but had no real knowledge of her subject and it was obvious that the French of the school would suffer unless it was taken by some more competent person' (*Sherborne Prep Register*).
4 – R. G. Whittingdale (dayboy) and E. Alderton (boarder) were both registered in third term, 1918 (*Sherborne Prep Register*). The reason for the author's excitement is unclear.

Gell – Jellyfish
Beadon – Joe
Forshaw – Fallshort
Beadon II – Tuppeny
Rickett – Ginger
Jones – Johnny
Stallard – Mouse
Thomson – Tommy
Forward – Willie
Tory I – (occasionally farmer), Sambo I
Tory II – Sambo II
Weall – Weallybus
Clarke – (old one-dog)
I cant remember any more now

We did ambulance work the other day.
    Learnt
    large arm sling
    small arm sling
    broad bandage
    small bandage
    triangular bandage

[*Two sets of initials*]

Which of these is mine & whose is the other?

[17 November 1918]   Sherborne

My dear Madre

I made an awful mess of last letter by mistake. Will you tell Equator I am terribly busy but may write to her on Wednesday

MONDAY[1]	Monday	Tuesday	Thursday
In the middle of «news» & just heard Mrs. Powys come in and said that the Big School had hoisted a flag & sung the National Anthem[.] MacCarthy I.[2] was sent out to discover what had happened. While he was away an aeroplane went up	with a flag on it. We had a kind of service in the Lower, most of it singing Half hol. & got a free — Concert in the dining hall (Of course all the flags were stuck about everywhere & the big flag was hoisted on the road) We yelled	I came as usual as it was wet Wednesday Fireworks instead of Prep. Glorious! Thursday Scouting half hol. We had to find Mr. Ferguson.[3] We were divided into 3 parts. We were given letters and had to open	them at a certain place to find out directions[.] We went through tons of mud Friday I've forgotten[.] I know it was something exciting Saturday Cake pudding[.] Watched a Big School match v Downside[.] D.S. won

I do not know what has happened but I had got an enormous lot to tell & it has all disappeared.

The proportion is not very good in this

1–Monday 11 Nov. 1918: 'In my fourth term at Sherborne the incredible happened. Armistice in Europe, gala in Sherborne' (*SAF*, 71). The layout of this letter is a throwback to the tabulation of mock news FLM had practised at home a couple of years earlier, when he divided sheets into columns (*SAF*, 58).

2–There were three MacCarthys at the school: one D. MacCarthy, a Dermod and a Justin.

3–J. C. G. Ferguson left for Oxford in second term 1919. Powys later remembered him as a keen lepidopterist, very popular with the pupils (*The Joy of It*, 191).

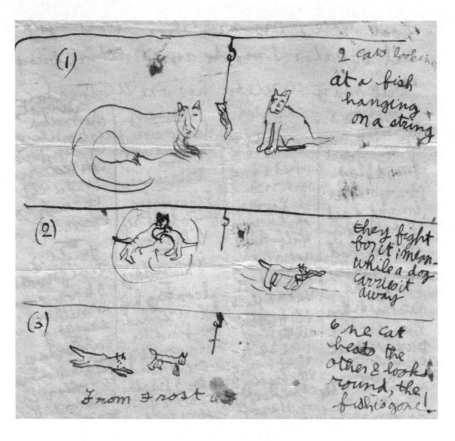

[(1) 2 cats looking at a fish hanging on a string

(2) They fight for it; meanwhile a dog carries it away

(3) One cat beats the other & looks round, the fish is gone!]

1919

TO *Georgina Beatrice MacNeice*   MS Dan MacNeice

2 February [1919]   Sherborne

My dear Madre

Mr Bloy came on Thursday.[1] I did Kim's game and compass on Thursday.[2] We had a footer game yesterday. I am sure there is something I want to tell you that I have forgotten. Day I has been drawing a picture of a new kind of aeroplane with sleeping places in it. Did I tell you in my last letter about the Stoat. There is snow today. We saw a small deer running about near us the other day. I think it's awfully annoying whenever there is warm water for a bath the bath is nearly empty and whenever the water is cold it is nearly full.

Are you going to have a leg of mutton and milk pudding and some other one today?

I have got a new New Zealand stamp.[3] Mr Powys told us there was a poem by Rudyard Kipling in the paper the other day addressed to naval officers going to Cambridge.[4]

1 – C. R. Bloy had studied at the Sorbonne and at Hanover, and was employed to teach French. Powys records in his notes on first term 1919 that they were 'very fortunate in securing the services of Mr Bloy, who has been a master at Newton for ten years and had considerable knowledge of the teaching of French on the direct method' (*Sherborne Prep Register*). The current headmaster writes: '[Bloy] reputedly upheld standards in French, staged a well-attended play, and was also a good cricketer and coach' (Peter Tait, private correspondence, 2008). Bloy also encouraged FLM's astronomical interests. Red Diary, 3 Feb. 1919 reads: 'Star lecture by Mr Bloy. I said Sirius was bright yellow instead of bluish green' (*Ms Bodleian, Ms Res, Box 57*).
2 – For the rules of 'Compass' and Kim's game (a memory game) see next letter.
3 – Possibly the NZ Government Life Insurance stamp, issued in 1919. New Zealand was in the news at this time since the All Blacks were on a tour of Great Britain as from January (for the first time in thirteen years). New Zealand won the first Imperial Services Rugby Tournament in April.
4 – 'The Scholars', *Daily Telegraph*, 29 Jan. 1919; repr. Rudyard Kipling, *Songs of the Sea* (1927).

[caption] I've just got a bit of cardboard and blotting paper.

[bell]'s going

[no signature]

TO *Georgina Beatrice MacNeice*   MS Dan MacNeice

9 February [1919]   Sherborne

My dear Madre
   The rollbooks have come out –

Form II	Kim's game is there are 24 articles on a
1. Stallard	table. You can look at them for 1
2. Walker	minute and then you have to write
3. Whitely	down over 16 of them.
4. (They spell my name wrong)	
5. Weall	Compass is you have to draw a
6. Pritchard	compass putting the 16 chief points in
Carey[1]	
Willcox	Hesse has got mumps. Last Monday I
Laws	got 44 with sacks
K.C. I	Tuesday = Day I's birthday, he got a
Powys I	huge cake and a knife. We watched a
Holborow	big School v. Blundell's match.
Adams	Wednesday = Tory I's birthday. [They]
Harker I	gave our table cake. I learnt Morse this
	way. The ink strokes are important

1 –Kenneth Moir Carey (1908–79) (later Rt Rev.), educ. Sherborne Prep and MC 1922–7 (Captain VIII, 1925–7); Exeter College, Oxford; Westcott House, Cambridge; HO 1932.

[A = · –   D = – · ·   H = · · · ·
B = – · · ·   E = ·   I = · ·
C = – · – ·   F = · · – ·   I will not go any further now.]

Thursday = I was in big game. Doughnuts.
Friday = My 2nd pot of jam
Saturday = Walk. Pickwick Papers. Choc. C.[1]

Did you ever read a poem called – lexanders · · – · · · · – st by Dryden.[2] Of course he did not write the title like that. Fugard, Daunt and Kellock got prizes in the Big School last term.[3]

There are prizes for collections of pressed wild flowers, greatest no. of flowers found in bloom for first time, best collection of butterflies or fossils. I am going to do fossils.[4]

There are signs of the bell going to ring so I think I better stop.

· · – ·

1 – FLM's Red Diary (1919) indicates that he thought a great deal about food at school. On Saturday 8 Feb. he wrote: 'we had a splendid chocolate cake but not much bread. I felt more ravenous than usual'. He even dreamed about food: 'I dreamt about pork, scouts being drilled, the king, hitting people on the head with books, and sliding down ropes' (Ms Bodleian, Ms Res, Box 57).
2 – On St Cecilia's Day (22 Nov.), Powys would read to the assembled school Dryden's 'Alexander's Feast: or, The Power of Music: an Ode in Honour of St Cecilia's Day' (SAF, 74).
3 – T. C. W. C. Fugard (later Teape-Fugard) (b. 1904), educ. Sherborne School 1918–23, Balliol College, Oxford; L. H. G. Daunt (b. 1904), educ. Sherborne School 1918–22, Trinity College, Oxford; J. G. Kellock (b. 1904), educ. Sherborne School 1918–22, St John's College, Cambridge.
4 – 'Because the other boys seemed so far ahead with butterflies and birds' eggs, I chose to collect fossils' (SAF, 69).

TO *Georgina Beatrice MacNeice*   MS Dan MacNeice

16 February [1919]   Sherborne

My dear Madre

It is roumoured [*sic*] we will all have mumps in a few days.[1]

I was in the 2nd game yesterday. I do not like it so much now after being in the 1st game. My leg got rather twisted about in the beginning of the game.

Have you ever read a book called 'Quentin Durward' by Scott.[2] I have started to read it.

<u>Last Week</u>

<u>Monday</u> = Went to ice near Oborne

Tuesday = Went to ice at Lenty.[3]

When we were coming back I fell on some thin ice and stuck my hand through it.

Swetenham (day b). had gone to Oborne where he got up to his neck in water.

Wednesday = We did scouting. One party under Mr. Ferguson tried to discover the place where our outposts were. We were arranged rather like this   [*diagram*]

I was an outpost.

Thursday = A lot of people passed their ambulance. I learnt

— —   — — —   · — ·   · · ·   ·   [*Morse*]

Friday = <u>Game</u>

My locker is arranged like this   [*diagram of locker*]

1 – 'Got mumps before I could write this but have forgotten it now. Very unfortunate. I lost diaries and notebooks when I got it. Mumps, bumps, lumps, humps, umphs etc.' (Red Diary, 20 Feb. 1919, entered in page for 10 Feb., *Ms Bodleian, Ms Res, Box 57*). In his term report, Powys records: 'Our games were interfered with and so was our work by mumps, brought back by Hesse. So as to prevent the disease from spreading throughout the land we prolonged the term until the 23rd of April and began the next term on the 21st of May. No boy developed mumps after leaving here. Mrs Powys had the disease in town' (*Sherborne Prep Register*).
2 – Sir Walter Scott, *Quentin Durward* (1823).
3 – Oborne lies northeast of Sherborne, near Milborne Port. Lenthay ('Lenty') is 'a suburb on the west side of Sherborne on the other side of the A352 (north–south road to Dorchester) built around the old cemetery; it was fields then and is now a post-Great War housing estate. I don't know of any pond which could have ice on it, but could he have been talking about Silverlake, which is a little further west?' (Dr Mary Lindsay, private correspondence, 2008).

This is supposed to be Day I   [*diagram*]

Have you ever told a person to spell Con stan ti no ple in syllables

[Contents of Pockets, Scout Diary, Old green notebook *deleted*]
—

We got Day I to say the Siam national anthem yesterday 'O wha ta na Siam' that is 'O what an ass I am'

If you want a person to say 13 and they are to try not to say it, a good way is to get them to say 14. Then you will pretend they said it and they will say no, that 13 was the number.

Some people had got jampots lined with paper coloured like jam but when you took the cover off a long snaky thing jumped out.

[no signature]

TO *Georgina Beatrice MacNeice*   MS Dan MacNeice

Wednesday [February 1919]   Sherborne

My dear Madre

I am better now. I was 2nd in half term's order but probably will be lower at the end of the term because of mumps.[1]

I practised writing by holding a pencil in my mouth.

I have got enough money thanks.

I am not awfully keen on piano. The only kind of things I like on it are very warlike, loud, things[.] I think the things that are in those book[s], without any words are awful.

I am sleeping in no 1 now. It is turned into a mump dormy. but although I am alright I have to sleep there . . .

We had soup and mincy, half curry stuff for dinner today.

I had my jam yesterday.

There is not much to write now.

I shall write a bigger letter on Sunday.

FROST[2]

1 – FLM had the usual range of ailments for a child of his generation, including chicken pox (1910), croup (1910–11?), whooping cough (1912), measles (1914), German measles (1917) and mumps (1919). JFM, personal notes, *Ms Bodleian, Ms Don, c. 197*.
2 – Occasionally he would sign off as 'Frost' for some reason.

It was in a quite modern year,
That, in an aeroplane
An enterprising pioneer
Set out to study Spain:
When he came near Gibraltar
He made a great nosedive
It is well he did not falter
For he saw a huge beehive
The bees came out around him
He started back for home
He flew so fast we found him
Next day at the aerodrome

16 March [1919]   Sherborne

My dear Madre

I am in no 3 now. The other occupants of it are Gretton (head) Tory II, Baker II, Powys II and Clarke. No 1 is used for a mump dormy.

—

We had a game yesterday. It was not much good and the Other Side easily won. Day I and I are going out together today. Day I was writing some things which were meant to be worldfamous though one of them was meant to be for babies!

The stone here is very good for cutting.

I had more of my jam yesterday.

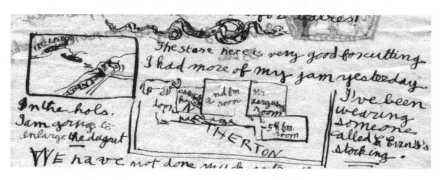

[I've been wearing someone called Evans's stocking.]

[In the hols.
I am going to
enlarge the dugout]
We have not done much extra this week. I paid my scouts sub yesterday
1/0.
Stallard has got mumps

In ambulance Mr. F. read to us about bleeding
and the way to stop it.[1] We also did head
bandage and collarbone.

I wish I'd got more to write.
　　Are the rats in the garden still?
　　Dawkins played chess with me last week, he won.
　　I wish there could be an aeroplane carrying letters from you to us.
　　There may be a passenger aeroplane or airship going from England to
Ireland soon.
　　Next term there are going to be a lot of new nets. There is also going to
be an old Y.M.C.A. hut for playing games in.
　　I'm sure the bell's going to ring now.

P.S. I'm sure something interesting will happen today. I am going to
ornament lock Bell.

---

1 – J. C. G. Ferguson. See FLM to GBM, 17 Nov. 1918, n. 3, p. 25.

My dear Madre

I am in no 3. now. The other occupants of it are Gretton (head) Tory II, Baker II, Pownys II and Clarke. No 1 is used for a mump dormy.

We had a game yesterday. It was not much good and the Other Side easily won. Day I and I are going out together today. Day I was writing some things which were meant to be worldfamous though one of them was meant to be for boleros!

The store here is very good for cutting. I had more of my jam yesterday

In the hols. I am going to enlarge the dugout

I've been wearing someone called Evans's stocking.

WE have not done much extra this week

In ambulance Me II read to us about bleeding and the way to stop it. We also did head bandage and collarbone

I paid my scout sub yesterday 1/0.

Stallard has got mumps now

I wish I'd got more to write. Are the rats in the garden still?

TO *Georgina Beatrice MacNeice*   MS Dan MacNeice

13 April [1919]   Sherborne

My dear Madre

Only one more Sunday![1] We have started shooting again now. I got 35 without sacks. No 2 has turned into a proper dormy. Again.

Did you hear of that aeroplane that did the record going from ___ to Paris. The pilot was an old Prep. boy.[2]

I've got a good idea[:] Eek can build a tree hut now if she has nothing to do.

Noone else has got mumps. Mr Powys says it is dying a natural death.

What is Eek doing? If there are any books she wants to read please make her read them <u>now</u> so that she will not want to do it when I come back.

People practised cricket with an old bat and some balls last week.

I saw some slowworms last Sunday. The upper Paddock is nearly all mown now.[3]

The most interesting animals I have seen this term are stoats, hedgehogs, slowworms, tadpoles and deer.

I wish there was something to write. I can see Ealhstan through the window. It seems awfully queer.[4] [*image overleaf of Carrickfergus*]

1 – Term would end on 23 April.
2 – Presumably a solo flight; however, the first London–Paris passenger service commenced in Jan. 1918, and had received since then a great deal of attention in the press ('London–Paris Air Service', *The Times*, 20 Jan. 1918, 8).
3 – The Upper Paddock was a playing field.
4 – 'Queer' because he can see his sister's House (Ealhstan) but, as seems clear, she is at home in Carrickfergus.

TO *Georgina Beatrice MacNeice*   MS Dan MacNeice

18 April [1919]   Sherborne

My dear Madre

Mrs. Powys is in London and has got mumps.

We had some term's orders the other day. I am 2nd in Geog. and 3rd in History.[1]

Does Eek know about the burglars in the girls' school. I think it was Wingfield (if that is Miss Mason's house) which they went to. They tried to get some of the cups.

The upper Paddock is nearly finished now. We are going to get primroses today. I must count my fossils soon[.] Day I has 69.

The ceiling in the lav. is coming down again. People were hitting balls up there. The other day the floor was covered with plaster.

Mr. Lindsay is rather anxious to do maths. with me in the train.

How long will Eek be able to stay after I have come back?

All sorts of exciting things are going to happen now.

I EXPECT I shall write another letter on Sunday

1 – There were seventeen boys in Form II; the final order for summer term 1919 indicated that FLM was first in Mathematics (although 'did very poorly in the Examination'), second in Geography, fourth in History and sixth in French. Powys wrote that he had made 'good progress' in Latin, 'a promising beginning' in Greek, and in Poetry he was 'Good' (summer term report, *MacNeice papers, HRC, Texas*).

New checkmate

B = Bishop N = white
K = king   P = black
C= castle   black wins

1920

TO *Georgina Beatrice MacNeice* MS Dan MacNeice

Postmark 21 January 1920   [postcard]

My dear Madre

I cannot get a pen yet. Very good crossing. Train to Euston late so missed train to Sherborne. Next train at 5.[1] Stopped at nearly every station so was late. Mr. Powys met me at Sherborne. Had a bath. Could not eat all your provisions in train. In London I forgot to give Robert the letter till after he had sent the telegram.[2] At Fleetwood discovered that McCammonds were in 1st class carriage so had to go in 3rd class one by myself. Saw stars from train to Sherborne.[3] My box is alright. It is coming up to the Prep. this morning. I arrived at the Prep. last night after lights out. Am in same dormy. Train to Euston arrived at 2.45. Tongue for lunch   Freddie

TO *Georgina Beatrice MacNeice* MS Dan MacNeice

25 January [1920]   Sherborne

My dear Madre

The boy who called me 'Horse' is Rickman.[4] He is almost hidden behind Mr. Bloy.

I have still got the same bottom locker.

I have used one pot of jam already.

1 – From Euston he had to make his way to Waterloo for the Sherborne train.
2 – Robert Milliken, manager of the Greer household staff at Seapark. He sometimes shepherded FLM and EM to trains en route to their schools in England. Cf. Appendix 1 to this volume.
3 – In recalling this a long time afterwards, FLM gets the year wrong: 'In January 1921 I found myself wonderfully alone in an empty carriage in a rocking train in the night between Waterloo and Sherborne. Stars on each side of me; I ran from side to side of the carriage checking the constellations . . .' (*SAF*, 78). Cf. 'Star-gazer' in *The Burning Perch* (*BP*), CP07, 607.
4 – Pupils mentioned here for the first time include S. R. Rickman, E. Tisdall, Dawkins II (C. Dawkins), W. Warren, C. King, R. P. Roney-Dougall, Richard Best and R. M. Rickett (Head of School).

Can I have another pair of white footer pants please as I have only got two, one of which is required for gym. Also can I have one of the Shakespeares please as Tisdall & co. have chosen me to be in The Merchant of Venice at the end of the term.[1]

I got your letter before breakfast this morning. Best got two Irish newspapers.[2]

Yesterday we saw the 'old moon in the new moon's arms'.[3]

I got two tries yesterday in the 2nd game.

Rickett has lent me an astronomical book.

While the dancers had dancing yesterday I played draughts with Thomson.

Dawkins II and Warren are newboys. They are always getting where they are not wanted.

King is in infection and is not allowed to be with us.

Roney-Dougall & Adams are the new no. sevenists. I have not had any drawing yet although the other day we were questioned about it at dinner.

I am going out with Day I today as Eek is not allowed to see me yet.

There is a collection for the Yeatman Hospital (Sherborne) today.

Mr. Green has left Sherborne.

I am in the 4th form room now.

Freddie

P.S. We can see Pegasus & Andromeda from the dormy window when we go up to bed.

---

1 – Of this all-pupil production Powys wrote: 'It is true that at the end of term I noticed that the members of the theatrical company were with one or two exceptions at the bottom of their forms; but I made excuse for them, feeling that they had of their own free will learnt something which would probably serve them better in life than an inferior knowledge of Latin verbs' (*The Joy of It*, 179).

2 – Richard Samuel Bevington Best was son of the Rt Hon. Richard Best (1869–1939), Lord Justice of Appeal of the Supreme Court of Northern Ireland 1925–39, Attorney-General Northern Ireland 1921–5 and MP for Armagh 1921–5. The Bests had lived in Dublin until 1921, when they moved to Belfast. FLM later knew Best at Oxford, where he was at Christ Church. (He was called to the Bar by Lincoln's Inn in 1933.) See Appendix 1 and cf. 'Auden and MacNeice: Their Last Will and Testament': 'To the barrister, Richard Best, to wear on walks / A speckled boater' (*LI*, CP07, 743).

3 – Known as 'earthshine', when light is reflected from the new moon's night side. Cf. Coleridge's 'Dejection: an Ode': 'I see the old Moon in her lap, foretelling / The coming-on of rain and squally blast.' The poem's epigraph is from 'The Ballad of Sir Patrick Spens': 'Late, late yestreen I saw the new Moon, / With the old moon in her arms.'

TO *Georgina Beatrice MacNeice*   MS Dan MacNeice

1 February [1920]   Sherborne

My dear Madre

Last night I saw a good many stars and Jupiter. I also saw Sirius. Rickett is more interested in planets than fixed stars. Have you looked him up yet in the photograph. He has red hair.

Thanks awfully about the Merchant of Venice. I am going to be Gratiano.

I had drawing on Tuesday and Friday. On Tuesday we had it in the drawing house but on Wednesday the Big School got some disease so on Friday we had it up at the Prep. I am copying one of Day I's 'hunt postcards'.

We have to have service at the Prep. today because of the Big School disease. We are not wearing Etons.

I have discovered a lot of chemical experiments in Rickett's astronomical book which is called Starland and is by Sir Robert Ball.[1] Laws reads astronomical books I think.

One day last week, Thursday I think, we shot. I got about 32 without sacks.

Baldwin not Balding, when he was addressing his letter this morning, was rather absent-minded and so he put Acreman House, Sherborne on it.

I have still got the six pencils and about six pens.

The new curate preached last Sunday. He used a lot of words like 'skimpy'.

The blue spots on this page have just come from Laws's fountain pen.

                    Freddie

TO *Georgina Beatrice MacNeice*   MS Dan MacNeice

7 March 1920   Sherborne

My dear Madre

Thanks awfully for the cakes. We had the ginger ones on Friday. I am using the box for fossils. I have about eight fossil boxes.

I am going out with Eek today.

---

1 – Robert S. Ball (1840–1913), *Star-land. Being talks with young people about the wonders of the heavens* (1889). Cf. 'Fascinating little book that is of Sir Robert Ball's' (James Joyce, *Ulysses*, Paris, 1922, ch. 8).

I am reading a book now called The Outline of History by H. G. Wells.[1]
The Kings I mean are the Sherborne-Scotch Kings.
I think Sept. 1921 is about right.[2]
I do not think I want anything much except my stamp album. It would be rather useful as I have a good many stamps to put in.
On Wednesday we had a fancy dress competition. I was a prehistoric man.[3]
On Monday I got my first try in big game.
The bell for services about to go, I think.

Freddie

TO *Georgina Beatrice MacNeice*　　　　MS Dan MacNeice

[5 December 1920]　　　　　Sherborne

My dear Madre
I have only got a bit of a pen to write with. I will say what happened from when I left Sherborne on Monday. I changed at Templecombe. It was very dull there. I arrived at Bath alright and met Aunt Eva and Miss Hind.[4] We went to their house & had dinner. I went to bed fairly soon and had a bath. Next morning we went to see the Roman Baths & the Abbey. There were only two old baths we could get close to. Miss Hind was afraid we would fall down some holes but we didn't. The Abbey is very nice. Down the front of the tower are two carved stone ladders with stone angels on them. We also saw a museum and the Avon. Then we went in the train to Marlborough. We got out at a funny little station and drove down to the

1 – Published 1919.
2 – The proposed date of FLM's entry to Marlborough College.
3 – Littleton Powys wrote to JFM at this time: 'Freddie is doing well here in every way & is obviously happy. He is full of interest in everything so his life is never dull. You would have laughed to have seen his get up at our Fancy Dress ball. He posed as a prehistoric man and he was really excellent & by general accord won the first prize. There was more originality about his costume than was the case in any of the others.' Powys to JFM, 9 March 1920 (*Ms Dan MacNeice*). He had actually rolled in the mud 'to add, as he put it, verisimilitude to his get up' (Oliver Holt, *Three Sherborne Memoirs*, 12–13, qtd in Stallworthy, 66).
4 – Eva Mildred Greer, sister of FLM's stepmother, lived in Glassdrumman, Annalong, Co. Down, with her friend, the author Gertrude Hind (pseud. Elizabeth Shane, 1877–1951), whom FLM unfailingly dubs 'the folk poetess'. Together they spent part of each year in Bath. As this letter indicates, Eva and Miss Hind accompanied FLM to Marlborough for his scholarship examination (see Appendix 1). Writing in 1928, JH noted there was by that time ill feeling between Miss Hind and FLM: 'We had tea with another Aunt who lives in the most beautiful garden in Ulster with a famous poetess Miss Hine [*sic*], writing as Elizabeth Shane, who is antipathetic towards Louis' (*SAF*, 269).

Ailesbury Arms Hotel. It wasn't particularly nice. Then we walked along a very wide street, went to the right of St. Peter's Church, turned to the right and came into the midst of hundreds of red brick school houses, including the gymnasium where we had the exam. Then it started to rain, so we returned to the hotel and sat in the smoking room with hundreds of clergymen and boys. We sat there till dinnertime. Next day exams started. 9-30 Latin Translation with dictionaries. Quite nice. 'Greek' without dictionaries. Horrid. Latin Prose + dicts. Quite nice. Afternoon. English. ½ hour for tea at shop, much frequented by school. Latin & Greek grammar. Not very nice. Thursday had to get up about 6-15 for geometry. Then 1 hr. for breakfast. Will continue in a letter tomorrow.

Freddie

1921

TO *Georgina Beatrice MacNeice* MS Dan MacNeice

[5 March 1921]   Sherborne

My dear Madre

This is quite a nice day. Warm. Tomorrow the C.E.E. begins.[1] The proper candidates are N. R. D. Holborow, R. S. B. Best, Holloway. I am getting quite used to Common Entrance now. I am lending Carey some of my brownish wallpaper. The locker is glorious. The books are all on the shelf which is going to be padded.

I am awfully sorry I haven't written. This is break.[2] Saturday. I got your letter yesterday but there was no time to write as it was 4 o'clock. We have been having the Common Entrance so not having done my letter on Sunday I hadn't a chance for ages. I got out my writing pad on Thursday and a bell went. I haven't done my diary for over a week now.

I got 639 in the Common Entrance (max. = 775)[3] and was top in Latin Grammar & Comp., English Comp. & Literature, Geography, Scripture and French Comp. Also in total by four marks. We did the Greek Grammar paper today.

Common Entrance Examination
Marks

Subject	Place	Max	Marks
Latin Trans.	3	100	87
Latin Comp.	1	100	86
Eng. Grammar	6	50	46
Eng. Lit.	1	50	48
Geography	1	50	35

1 – Common entrance examination, administered in the final year of prep school to assess the preparedness of pupils for a public school of their choice.

2 – 'Life was now largely dominated by the names of local institutions. "Break" for instance. Break meant the quarter of an hour in the middle of the morning when we could go into the yard and play games, but the word "Break" itself was something irrefrangible, magical. To have the word "Break" on your tongue gave you an advantage over the ignorant masses, over the People at Home' (*SAF*, 67).

3 – FLM's table is inconsistent with this sentence (and incorrectly added). The marks given total 674 out of a possible 755.

History	3	50	33
Arithmetic	5	75	70
Algebra	9	50	22
Geometry	2	50	45
Scripture	1	50	45
French Dict.	3	30	23
French Trans.	5	50 (?)	42
French Gram. & Comp.	1	–	57
Greek Trans.		50 (?)	35
Greek Grammar		–	–
(Total – Greek)	1	775	637

There is a match v. Connaught House, Weymouth today at 2-30. I am not playing but am about 1st sub. to the team.

The Wednesday before last we had a celebration in the Tower as it was a hundred years since the death of Keats.[1] Mr. King from the Big School came up and recited 'La Belle Dame Sans Merci'.[2] Mr. Hemstead [sic] gave a lecture:[3] Mr. Powys read 'Fancy': Carey I, the boy that is going to Marlborough, recited 'the Ode to Autumn'.

1 – 23 February.

2 – Presumably the Rev. H. R. King, the school chaplain.

3 – Edward Charles Edmund Hemsted (b.Italy, 1898), educ. Lancing 1913–16; lieutenant, acting captain, S. Notts. Hussars, 17th Division HQ Staff; served in France. St John's College, Oxford (distinction, final hons, School of Law) 1920. Teacher, Sherborne Preparatory School 1921; assistant headmaster, Le Lycée d'Anvers 1922; librarian at Toynbee Hall and editor of *Toynbee Book Review* 1923; Professor of English, Imperial Naval College, Etajima, Japan 1924; Raffles College, Singapore 1925; Malayan Education Service 1925; principal, Bareilly College, University of Allahabad 1927; member of University of Agra Senate 1928. Published several novels under the nom de plume 'Edward Charles' (hence, presumably, his sobriquet in *SAF*) and wrote a controversial, explicitly illustrated treatise on human sexuality, *The Sexual Impulse* (1935), which was the subject of a prosecution under the Obscenity Laws (cf. Edward Charles [E. C. E. Hemsted], Correspondence 1929–61, *University of Tulsa, McFarlin Library*). Julian Huxley among others spoke in defence of the book. Hemsted wrote a play, *Men's Gods* (1931) and his novels include *Those Thoughtful People* (1930), *Apple Pie Bed* (1931), *Muscara* (1934), *Portrait of the Artist's Children* (1934) and *Idle Hands* (1936). FLM remembers Hemsted as very keen on poetry, the Romantics in particular: 'It was vulgar to admire Kipling' (*MP*, 45) and 'we need not bother with History and Geography; all that really mattered was Keats' (*SAF*, 76). In his notes for third term 1920 (Hemsted's first term at Sherborne) Powys records: 'Mr Hemsted's enthusiasm for Literature was very helpful & his influence in this respect bore good fruit' (*Sherborne Prep Register*). His style of teaching was unusual: 'he treated [the pupils] in what he called his "lectures," as though they were men of his own age . . . using language they could not be expected to understand' (*The Joy of It*, 168).

The next day we had a Prep collection. It was for a 'Keats fund' or something that wanted to buy his old house at Hampstead.

On Sunday I went out with Adams, Dawkins I & Dawkins II to a wood. We picked primroses and on returning to the Prep gave them to Miss Maskell.

. . .

The match is finished now. The Prep. won, 59 points to 3. We have not had tea yet but are expecting an interesting one because of the match.

After tea there is to be a debate down at Netherton – Whether Keats deserves to be called a poet. (It is postponed now)

Holloway has got appendicitis (Is that the right way to spell it) and is at the Yeatman Hospital so we telephoned the results of the match to him.

I am very hungry and it is nearly half-past five.

The locker is in a mess again now.

. . . I had to go away then to congratulate Waller, Best, Holborow, Lean and Dawkins who had got their caps against Weymouth.

We have had the debate (after tea) It was carried by 16 points to 2. (that is – 16 people voted that Keats did not deserve the appellation of poet. The 2 were Carey I and myself) We had it down at Netherton in the Fifth Form Room. Wilcox is president.[1]

. . .

This is Sunday. We have just heard that there is to be a Pigmy match soon. Carey I is captain of the forwards. I am playing. I will stop now. Will try to write another letter during the week. Am going out with Adams today. I must write to Aunt Eva soon as she sent me a March captain today.[2]

Love
from Freddie

P.S. We still have Service in the diningroom as the big school have chickenpox.

1 – Pupils mentioned here for the first time include K. Waller and C. Wilcox.
2 – Unable to trace.

TO *Georgina Beatrice MacNeice*   MS Dan MacNeice

[March 1921]   Sherborne

My dear Madre

Today is Sunday. Fforde and I were going to try to walk to Camelot but Mr. Powys has advised us not to do so.[1] Yesterday we had the debate after tea. The motion was that Astronomy is a better hobby than butterfly collecting – Astronomy lost by 7 to 11. In the afternoon we watched the Big School steeplechase from the railway embankment.

On Monday there was shooting. I only made 20. There has been a shooting comp. lately. The eight's average was at 25 yards – 60.3 and at 50 yds 61.2. Did I say in my last letter that Waller, Holborow, Dawkins, Best & Lean got their caps last match.

On Wednesday there was a game. I got two tries.

On Thursday there was a walk. We went to a place near the Golflinks, whence you had a splendid view and could see Glastonbury Tor, Camelot etc.

It is raining now.

The term will end soon. The French play is on Easter Tuesday.

Mr. Hemstead [*sic*] has put a little bookcase in the upper. In it are books that we can read.

Some of them are – 'Coleridge, Shelley & Keats' (poems)

Johnson's works (vols. VII & VIII)

'On the Art of Reading' (Quiller-Couch)

'On the Art of Writing' (Quiller-Couch)

'Channels of English Literature – Epic & Heroic Poetry' (W. MacNeile)

'Recollections of the lakes' (Thomas de Quincey)

'The Pilgrim's Progress'

'Lyric Masterpieces by Living Authors'

'The Works of E. A. Poe' (Vol II – Tales)

'Selections from Wordsworth' (Adam Fox)

'Verse & Prose in Peace & War' (W. Noel Hodgson)

'Poems of Today'

'History of King Arthur' (Vols I, II, III)

'Essays in Little' (Andrew Lang)

'Dorset Poetry & Poets' (H. Berkeley Lane)

1–James Edmund Fforde (b.1908); educ. Sherborne Prep and MC 1922–6. The site of Camelot was thought to be Cadbury Hill, about six miles from Sherborne. 'From a point within walking distance we could see Glastonbury Tor which someone, possibly our headmaster Littleton Powys, told us was the site of Camelot' (*SAF*, 221).

'Apologie for Poetrie' (Sir Philip Sidney)
'Poetical Works of Keats'
'Speeches on America' (Burke)
'R.L.S.' (Francis Watt)
'The Life of Robert Louis Stevenson' (Graham Balfour)
'Tutorial History of English Literature' (Wyatt)
'Keats' (W. Michael Rossetti)
'Piers Plowman' (W. Langland)
'On University Education' (Cardinal Newman)
'Aytoun's Lays'
'Burke: on peace with the Regicide Directory of France'
'Byron and his Poetry'
'Keats & his Poetry'
'Poets of the Democracy' (G. C. Martin)
'Shelley & his poetry'
'A Child's garden of Verses' (R.L.S.)
'Shelley, Byron & the Bathos' (Trelawny)

I think I shall finish now. Ten people have been elected as a committee for the society etc.

It is still raining and we cannot go out. We have had service in the dining room.

TO *Georgina Beatrice MacNeice*   MS Dan MacNeice

[June 1921]   Sherborne

My dear Madre

I am sorry that I cannot send this off immediately but I have to wait till Eek gives me back the Prep. magazines. I went out with her on Sunday and am going again today.

Fforde has got several Marlborough papers and things which he has been sent, including the Marlburian and a rollbook.[1] No one is allowed the use of the bath till he can swim 25 yds. However, I can swim over 100 yds. as I did my singles on Wednesday. 'Singles' is twice the length of the bath. It was fairly easy.[2] I did 11 times across the day before. Since then I have got new kickers (singles) and have been experimenting with the shute,

---

1–Like FLM and Carey, Fforde had won a scholarship to Marlborough.
2–Powys records in second term 1921: 'The glorious Summer weather – a record in this respect – made bathing most enjoyable. 37 boys had their singles' (*Sherborne Prep Register*).

spring-board and highdive. I am learning to dive and also am beginning to swim on my back. The deep end is 8 ft deep. Yesterday we bombarded Harker in the bath, because he was a water-funk although a single. He was sitting on the chain by the red line and we got in a sort of ambush round about. Then Alderton pushed him in and we all jumped in around him and splashed furiously.

I have just been for a walk with Eek and have procured the Prep. papers. I wrote the thing about fossils in the first mag. but Adams, who was writing it out put in some additional names of extinct animals which rather annoyed me. You will find on the last page of the 2nd mag. a long epistle on photography by Dawkins I. It does not attract me very much but we had to put it in as he had sent in such hundreds of things and we did not wish to disappoint him.

The Prep. news are chiefly done by Oily and the Old Boys by Carey I, and the nature notes by Holt II. The Sports Items are by L. B. Dyball, Captain of Rugby & Cricket, oldest Single, and head of the school. (His spelling has been corrected in most places, I think.) There are a few misprints.

Please do not lose these as copies are scarce, there being only 19 other copies of the 1st mag.[1] We now jelly over 40.

There is still quite a long time before tea. Do you still have strawberries. They are nearly over here. Mr. Powys thinks they will probably stick me in any house they like at Marlborough. The houses have extraordinary names, such as Fleur de Lys.[2]

I must stop now.

Love from Freddie

P.S. I enclose the C.E.E. papers.

---

1 – Few copies of the *Prep News* prepared by FLM's year have survived; there is one copy in HRC, Texas.

2 – The fleur-de-lys was indeed the crest of the senior house C2, but the 'in college senior houses' at Marlborough were B1, B2, B3, C1, C2, C3. 'Out college senior houses' were called Preshute, Cotton, Littlefield and Summerfield. There were also junior houses.

19 September [1921]   A. House, Marlborough College,
['1921 first letter from   Wiltshire [hereafter Marlborough]
  Marlborough' *in Mother's hand*]

My dear Madre,

Thanks for the parcel (& the letters) which arrived yesterday. The one person which knew of it was too much of a detective to think it anything interesting.

I am writing in this pad as it is easier to manage.

Now I will begin an account of my adventures. I went back from the station with another new boy whose mother was in the same carriage as Daddie. He belonged to Mr. Beacher's [sic] landing.[1] I will here tell you what the house is like. At the bottom, i.e. the basement the tuckboxes or as they are called here the blueboxes [sic] are stored. Is truly tremendous. While a small boy and I dragged and shoved it down the stone stairs to the basement, half the house stood at the top and roared. Above the basement is the ground floor. On one side is A1 (belonging to Mr Becher's collection), and the Library. On one side joining it is the workroom (out of bounds). On the other is the Wardrobe. On the side where I am now is A2 our house classroom where are the lockers. I am sharing one with someone I have not yet seen. He has the bottom and I have the top.

(I think it will be alright having my watch here, only newbugs are compelled to tell the time to everyone)

In the middle of A2 is a table out of bounds for newbugs, of whom there are about 28. (Mr. Becher has about 15.)

Then also on our side is the passage that goes out.

Above this is Mr. Becher's landing and the apartment of Mrs. Booth.

Above that is our landing entering Mr. Guillebaud (bo)'s room and dormitories, H, I, J. I am in I, which holds about 16 and has 10 newbugs.[2] There are windows all round. I have 2 newbugs on one side and one on the other.

Yesterday we got up after numerous bells and gongs, Smith, a boy of my exam who has been here 8 terms, I think, waterfagging (i.e. fetching water and filling therewith the 16 basins). Yesterday it was hot but not so today.

---

1 – G. G. Becher, MA. Teacher at MC 1909–45.
2 – Hugh Lea Guillebaud, assistant master at MC 1914–50; housemaster of FLM's house, C3, 1922–7.

Having dressed we descended into A.2 where we were given instructions.

Then off to the hall for breakfast. First there was a sort of brown grain in a porridge plate – we had to go off to get our places in chapel just now – which I did not procure owing to having only half a place. Then I got somebody else's sausage and was given a plate by the porter person, with a large chunk of bread and a roll of butter about 2 ins. long and an inch in diameter. Also I had a sort of round bowl with no handle, into which you pour tea or coffee. The thing that holds the coffee hasn't got a knob on its lid and is so distinguished from the thing that holds the tea.

The hall itself is huge, each house has its own table. The outhouses do not dine here.

Then there was a horrible muddle about my form. In the Provisional House list I was put in 'Remove' which was quite true, only there are four removes. So I was conducted to C. House Porch by Smith who mistook Maurice for MacNeice in Remove B. and as a result I went with another new boy Outram to Remove B classroom, where the form master refused to have me.[1] Then I was given into the charge of another Remove B boy who took me to another form master who had arranged the lists who sent me to Remove A, the form of Mr. Flecker.[2] Well, I stayed the rest of the time with Mr. Flecker who was rather interesting and amusing but last evening when the House List was passed round I found myself on paper in Remove C., Mr. Canning's form.[3] So I asked Mr. Guillebaud who sent me again to C. House Porch with a boy but there we didn't find my name at all. When we got back I returned there with Mr. Guillebaud who came to the conclusion that they had written MacNutt instead of MacNeice in Remove C. So at present I am supposed to be in Remove C. but I rather doubt if I shall stay there. Of course, I haven't had anything to do with Remove D. yet.

At lunch yesterday I had meat, water, and fried potatoes. There was a pudding some sort of relation of plum pudding, but only about five people on our table seemed to get this. Then the porter came and removed the spoons of the rest.

1 – F. H. Outram (1907–72), educ. MC 1921–6; Pembroke College, Cambridge.
2 – H. L. O. Flecker (1896–1958), MA, CBE, brother of the poet James Elroy Flecker. Educ. Dean Close School and Brasenose College, Oxford. Army commission 1914–18. Teacher at MC (in charge of the Classical Sixth) 1921–7. Headmaster of Berkhamsted School 1927–30 and of Christ's Hospital 1930–55; subsequently principal of Lawrence College, Murree Hills, Pakistan.
3 – Rev. Clifford Brooke Canning (1882–1957). Educ. Clifton; Oriel College, Oxford; assistant master, MC, 1906–10; housemaster 1910–27; housemaster of C3 1914–22; HO 1923; headmaster at Canford School, Wimborne, Dorset 1928–47.

Yesterday I also got a Psalter and a book of rules[.] On Tuesday the hymnbooks are coming.

For a long time yesterday afternoon house and court were out of bounds, during which time I discovered the swimming bath and watched people playing fives in which they used their hands covered with gloves. The bath is a funny winding thing, only 7 ft. deep at the deepest.

Last night we had reading prep. and supper in hall, which consisted of a biscuit and a lump of cheese. The dormitory rules were read out by Greene.[1] Noone is allowed to bar (rag) and everyone has to sing a song before yesterday week.

Today for breakfast we had things like dead leaves in a porridge plate, and coffee, and a sort of little potted meat pie and bread and butter. It will be time for chapel soon so I will stop.

Freddie

TO *Georgina Beatrice MacNeice*   MS Dan MacNeice

9 October [1921]   Marlborough

My dear Madre

This nib is very bad so I have to write upside down.

Today, Sunday, has been quite eventful[.] In the morning, I still had to wear an Eton collar. I went for a short walk with Crichton and got a good view of Savernake Forest.[2] After that I went to the reading room for the first time and studied an old book about Marlborough.[3] There seem to be quite a lot of antiquities about here, among which are the Devil's Den, The Mound and Avebury Temple. Next Sunday I am going to see the Devil's Den. It is a Druidical erection.[4]

After that there was chapel. Then I went round the Museum. Among other things it contains fossils, minerals, birds, a stuffed leopard, the skin of an armadillo, two mummy cases, skeletons of man & orangutan? ashy Koalas from Australia, things that look like Teddy Bears, fishes, jellyfishes,

1-N. D. G. Greene (b.1906), educ. MC 1920-5.
2-J. H. L. Crichton (b.1908), educ. MC 1921-6. Savernake is a private estate of over 4,500 acres in Wiltshire, between Marlborough and Hungerford, and is one of the oldest forests in England.
3-Probably James Waylen, *History Military and Municipal, of the Town of Marlborough* (1854).
4-'There was an allegedly Druidic mound which had been brought up to date by an eighteenth-century countess who had carved a spiral pathway round it and added a couple of grottoes' (*SAF*, 86).

snakes – cobra & ringsnake, tortoises, lizards, sharks.

Then there was dinner. At 2-15 I went with Crichton to Savernake Forest for first time. There we went up the 'Grand Avenue' which goes through the Forest perfectly straight for four miles. In the middle of this is the 'Eight Walks'. They aren't much more than tracks.

We then went to a Keeper's Cottage where we obtained water & directions. The lady there said we could get back on abc side by way [sic] which goes through a beech copse. Then we could get onto Salisbury Road. We went off happily but on rearriving at Eight Walks discovered that a,b,c all went through beech copses. We took c. We saw two little deer looking at us. Further on we got a surprise. We suddenly saw a little way off a huge giant looking at us. He soon turned out to be the trunk of a tree which had fallen down.

We did, all added up, about 8½ miles.

Thanks awfully for the apples and bananas. In your next letter could you enclose a few stamps please. I must write to Aunt Eva about her biscuits. I am getting behindhand with my letters as so many are arriving.

The sports were finished Friday and yesterday[.] You ought to arrange about my house soon. If poss. Canning's. If not Boughey's.

Did you know that the origin of Marlborough is Merlinburg after Merlin.

I am thinking of joining the N.H.S.[1]

I will try to describe my masters to you now.

(1) Mr. Canning. – Fairly ordinary – keeps good order – no signs of temper.

(2) <u>Mr. Flecker</u> – rather mad. Makes you sit in wastepaper basket & such things.

(3) <u>Mr. Boughey</u> keeps good order. Has a funny little sort of looking-down-upon-victims grin.[2]

---

1 – Natural History Society.

2 – C. L. F. Boughey, MA (1887–1934), educ. MC 1900–5; Trinity College, Cambridge. Taught at Uppingham and St Edmund's, Canterbury. Grenadier Guards 1914–18. Assistant master at MC 1919–27 (commander, OTC); headmaster of Sherborne 1928–33. Wrote (with J. W. Ivimey; see FLM to GBM, 5 Nov. 1921, n. 1, p. 56) a comic opera, *The Headmistress*, performed at the school in May 1923.

(4) Mr. Burgess.[1] Cannot keep order well. Gets rather muddled in his
     speech. He said the other day 'Of course you can go on for ever
     but it would take you rather a long time.'
New Chapel list came into force tonight. See plan below

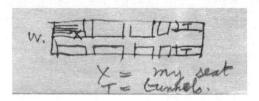

I am getting very sleepy. It is nearly 9-20. Eek will be distressed about
my bedtime here.

I think I will stop now.
Love, Freddie

P.S. I give below a list of chief houses.

Patteson's		Outhouses
Boughey's		Cotton House
Canning's		Littlefield
Gidney's		Preshute
Robertson's		
Turner's		

Why have you got such a bad opinion of 'K—shs'.[2] They are most
important. Of course they haven't died out. How could you carry books
without them?

Go into the upper floor of Head's and you'll see they haven't died out.
Shoals of them. All the colours in the rainbow, also variegated. Come into
court and you'll see lots lying about.

1 – Oliver Ireland Burgess, MA (d.1930), exhibitioner, Trinity College Cambridge. Teacher at
MC 1920–30.
2 – Kishes: schoolbags.

TO *Georgina Beatrice MacNeice*   MS Dan MacNeice

Saturday Night / Reading Prep.   Marlborough
[5 November 1921]

My dear Madre

The other pad is running out so I am using this one. I shall be able to write more to Aunt Eva, now she's gone to Bath. It's so hard to say something new when you're both in the same house.

I have had no more souptickets.[1] You do get a ticket, beautifully made out, with spaces for name of boy, form and name of house master and 'work to be done'.

There are a few Irish boys in the house but I don't think any of them go to Ireland: anyway I couldn't go with them.

As this is Saturday there is burring in dormitory tonight. You leap about on beds – there is no need for distress as they are absolute springless – do dormitories, have tugs of war, fight, do anything you like.

I was reading an old book about M.C. today in the Memorial Reading Room. Before C House was an Inn it seems to have been Lord Hertford's mansion. There is rather a delightful picture of it and what is now the court with a silly little thing like a top upside down for the mound.

Did you know about the 'Great Rebellion' in 1851, when the school revolted on Guy Fawke's Day and spent the night smashing windows and sending off fireworks, which were forbidden. It was most exciting and the then Master resigned after that term and was succeeded by Bishop Cotton.[2] I'm sure you've heard of Bishop Cotton. He is most famous here and there is a large picture of him in Hall, between Dean Farrar and someone else. Cotton House is called after him.

Does Daddie remember about the great space in the middle of A House[?] Long ago, when College started they used to wrap boys up in blankets and hang them over the edge.

I don't think I've told you about the A House Wail. I don't know much about it myself as I've never heard it but lots of people have. It is a most horrid sound caused partly by the mound on a windy night.

Do you know the A House colours – blue and red. The crest, of course, is a crossmoline. Canning's is a mitre. Mr. Guillebaud will probably get Canning's when Mr Canning stops being a house master. Last Sunday

---

1 – 'Souptickets' were presented to pupils for misconduct.
2 – George Edward Lynch Cotton (1813–66), Bishop of Calcutta. Educ. Westminster and Trinity College, Cambridge. Master of MC 1852–8.

instead of reading Prep. I went to the Bradleian where Mr. Ivemy [*sic*] talked about Mozart and played a few things.[1]

There was a match today v the Harlequins 'A' team. The school lost.

Is it you or only Eek that is interested in North. If so, he has been playing for the XV lately and is noted for the enormous size of his legs.[2]

I am beginning to know a few of the ties and caps etc. It is horribly confusing. There are ties for every possible thing. Abell has so many that he has one for nearly every day of the week.[3] On Sunday prefects wear White ties. There are rumours about a Marlburian tie that can be worn in hols. Is my fountain pen any good?

[*diagram of a house crest*]

I'll be able to continue this tomorrow. I'm afraid Adams will be getting rather annoyed as his letter has not arrived yet though I have written a large part of it.

Can you tell me if Ealhstan is prospering under Eek's rule. She hasn't written for quite a long time. Of course I've only written one to her two letters. Mine was the last though.

I am doing Ovid-Fasti VI (i.e. June) now with Mr. Boughey.

When you come here sometime there will be lots of things I can show you:- [all sorts of *deleted*] several classrooms but not labs.

Museum
Art room(?)
Bath
Upper School (if I'm in it then?)
Bradleian
Memorial Reading Room.
A House.

The Gym (where there was an exhibition of pictures on Monday & Tuesday. Miss Norwood paints rather well).[4]

1–J. W. Ivimey (1868–1961), DMus., FRCO, ARCM. Herne Bay College and exhibitioner of the Guildhall School of Music. Teacher at MC 1919–33. Organist, director of music, composer and author.

2–R. E. G. North (1904–52); MC 1918–23; prefect, 1st XV 1922; University College Oxford, and BBC.

3 – G. E. B. Abell (1904–89), OBE, CIE, KCIE. Educ. MC 1918–23; 1st XI; captain of rugby, hockey (MC and Oxford); senior prefect 1922. Scholar, Corpus Christi College, Oxford. A triple-blue at Oxford, Abell was an all-round sportsman and later an administrator in the ICS (Punjab 1928), where he became private secretary to the Viceroy (Viscount Wavell and then Lord Mountbatten).

4–Daughter of Cyril Norwood, headmaster ('Master') at MC 1916–25.

The Chapel.   Gamesfields

Hall.   Also outside of many other buildings:- Music School, C,B,&
F Houses and some outhouses.

I told you the S.O.B.s (Boston Hill) among the Outhouse corresponded
to A House in Incollege houses.[1] However they are very inferior to us.
They wear black games jerseys.

Please don't try to make me have a Cardigan jacket. Only prefects and
such people have them. Also I can't button my coat as I used to, as that was
the mark of a mighty man.

I went to the rackets courts the other day, not to play, of course, but to
look on, which you can do from a very narrow gallery.

The school were beaten by Balliol College (Oxford) on Monday. Balliol
College seems a favourite place for Marlburians.

The school motto is 'Virtute, studio . . .[']

The bell ought to go soon. I don't think I shall go to Hall to partake of
Hallers and 'College runabout' (i.e. cheese)

Sunday Morning

We made a terrific row last night. We got permission to 'sing' in chorus in
dormitory, which is generally forbidden.

It rained hard last night and came into the dormitory.

I was in Savernake Forest again the other day on a sweat to Keeper's. It
was raining.[2] The forest looks awfully nice now, all yellow. The Kennet
which passes through Marlborough is a famous trout stream.

Last Sunday I walked through Preshute & Manton, two villages, with
Crichton.

College cats are amusing. They come everywhere – classroom, Prep.,
Bradleian, chapel. They are rather fond of A house.

So is 'Shag Pat['] (?), the famous dog (?) whose coming was announced
in the Marlburian. He is a queer black creature.

Library (A House, of course) is open today and I am going to get a book
out, as well as returning one by Robert Louis Stevenson.[3]

1 – S.O.B.s: small out-boarders (SOB houses include Priory, Barton Hill and Upcot).
2 – 'On days too wet for games we were sent running over these downs with a time limit out
and back; if you were late either way you were caned but, once you got used to this strenuous
effort, it was exhilarating' (*SAF*, 86).
3 – In 1921 FLM read *Kidnapped*, *The Merry Men*, *The Master of Ballantrae* and *Catriona*.
('Books Read', Memoranda, April 1921, Diary, *Ms Bodleian*, *Ms MacNeice Box 57*.) He
later thanks Aunt Eva for a gift of volumes by Stevenson (below, 31 Aug. 1923). Reading in
1921 also included Malory, *Antony and Cleopatra* and *The Faerie Queene*, Edgar Rice
Burroughs, Storer Clouston, Wilkie Collins, S. R. Crockett, Charles Kingsley, Andrew Lang,
Edgar Allan Poe, and Charles Reade ('Books Read').

Shredded wheat and eggs for breakfast this morning. Shredded wheat is the thing that looks like a roll of dead twigs.

I don't know if I'm going out with Crichton today. After Chapel I'm 1st going to Library and then to the Museum, probably. It is now 9-20.

A few people in A. house are having [a] bolly (Marlburian name for pudding) eating competition. The record is 5 helpings by Brightman.[1] The 'Bolly' (in comps) is generally a sort of tart. 'College Bolly' is some sort of relation to plum pudding.

Have you ever heard of A. H. Beasly [sic]. He was an O.M. (I think) and a house master and wrote poetry etc.[2] As a result there is a Memorial bookcase for him in the Mem. Reading Room. His writings, however, don't attract me particularly.

We have an advantage over Eek, as we have fires in A. House. Pipes are only good to sit on and they are always going wrong. You can sit in front of fires and toast bread and chestnuts at them. They also light up the room and look more cheerful.

Of course you have to do firefagging two days a term. I have one more day of it.

I shall bring my k—sh back next hols. in my brewbox.[3]

At the end of the term I don't think you had better write to Mr. Guillebaud much. There are still 5 or 6 more weeks though.

I think I shall go to the reading room now and make further investigations on the 'History of Marlborough College'.[4] That is if I can get a seat, or in college language, rush a bin.

I have discovered it is raining so am not going across court.

I think the 'Marlburian' will be coming out again soon.

I have discovered a great advantage over Eton, which you can tell Uncle Mac.[5] In winter they play some extraordinary game, which noone else can

---

1 – Geoffrey Brightman (b.1908), educ. MC 1921–6; St John's College, Cambridge.

2 – A. H. Beesley (d.1909), scholar and poet. Educ. Wadham College, Oxford (MA 1864); MC 1863–5; housemaster (Summerfield) 1875–85.

3 – A tuckbox.

4 – Probably *A History of Marlborough College During Fifty Years, from Its Foundation to the Present Time*, by A. G. Bradley, A. Champneys and J. W. Baines (1893).

5 – FLM's stepuncle, Thomas MacGregor Greer (1869–1941), JP, of Tullylagan, Tullahogue, Co. Tyrone, and Seapark, Carrickfergus. (Seapark was the setting for the poem, 'Soap Suds', *BP*, *CP07*, 577.) The Greers were a prominent (lapsed) Quaker family with long associations with the linen trade. Thomas was educ. Eton and Trinity Hall, Cambridge. M. (1892) Dorinda Florence Lowry (1869–1930) of Rochdale, Co. Tyrone; they had two daughters: Gladys Sylvia (b.1896) and Margaret (Betty) (1897–1953). Cf. Appendix 1 to this volume. During the Home Rule Crisis, TMG was actively involved in recruitment efforts in Antrim for the 36th (Ulster) Division, for which he received personal thanks from Edward Carson

understand.[1] As a result they can't play any other school in it, and don't even know if they're good at [sic].

I think it is noisier than the Prep. here. Of course, the Prep. squeals were more treble. Last night we simply howled, over a hundred of us, for 'Door' for Hall (teatime).

There are three chairs in our landing classroom, none of which can be sat in by newbugs. We can sometimes manage to sit on boxes before the fire however but generally I sit on my k—sh or on the edge of Mr. Guillebaud's little dais.

If you are sending any more things, could you send some tooth paste (Kolynos I usually have) too, as my toothpaste has disappeared and I don't know where or how to get any more here.

It is fairly cold this morning, not as cold as it is sometimes though. The other day the roof of hall was white with frost. It's a pity Carey isn't a clergyman's son as then he could come up for the exam. in December and I could show him about. I don't know when the Common Entrance is. He ought to pass it. I shall be furious if he is put above me though. If I get back early next term I ought to be able to meet him. Of course, he may not come to A. House. He might go to Barton Hill or even to a superior house, both of which would be very annoying. If he went to Canning's, for instance, he would actually be allowed to wear coloured socks and such things, before I would. You see, when you have been 5 terms in Upper School (i.e. a senior house) you can do that.

Next summer term I shall be able to set basements. I will give Carey and Fforde lots of them. It consists of going up and down the basement steps.

I shall be able to sit at 'Third Termers' then, if I'm still in A. House. I might even do that next term if there were few 3rd termers.

The next thing that happens is Chapel. I don't know who is preaching. The Master, the Rev. de Candole and the Bishop of Madras have preached, among others.[2] The Master hasn't got a house, as I expect you've noticed by my lists.

---

in a letter of 12 July 1916 (*PRONI, TMG Papers, D4121/C*). He was a prominent figure in the Larne gun-running incident of 24 April 1914. Cf. Appendix 1, p. 716, n. 2, re. Dorinda Greer's Diary, April 1914.

1 – A variant of Eton Fives.

2 – 'The Master': Cyril Norwood (1875–1956) MA, Hon DLitt (Bristol); master and headmaster MC 1916–25. Formerly teacher at Leeds GS 1901–6 and headmaster Bristol GS 1906–16. Educ. Merchant Taylors' and St John's College, Oxford. Headmaster of Harrow 1926–34. Knighted 1938. Cf. 'Auden and MacNeice: Their Last Will and Testament': 'And to Dr Cyril Norwood a new spitoon' (*LI, CP07, 735*). Rt Rev. H. H. V de Candole (1895–1971), MA, teacher at MC 1917–23. HO 1920.

The present bursar is supposed to be most efficient.[1] They are very fond of the word 'efficient' here.

If it goes on raining we will probably be allowed to stay in the house this afternoon.

Is the kitten still in high spirits or is it getting lazy? I should imagine it would want to come into the house a good deal if the weather's like it is here.

We had a most miserable sweat to First Post on Wednesday. We returned like drowned rats. It was horribly wet.

I have a most beautiful house jersey, red and blue stripes, more startling than the Prep. one. It will fade though. Canning's colours are 'majenta' (is that the way you spell it? I heard Mr. Guillebaud say it) and white. They faid horrible though to a sort of 'bad pear colour'.

We haven't much of a view from the window of this room. On one side is the Mound rising straight up, only a few yards away. On the other is the brick wall of Hall and some trees attached to the mound[.] I shall bring my M.C. hymnbook back next hols. It has music in it.

How are the practices getting on? I suppose my 'hole' is filled up in the garden. If not I suppose it is full of water. I must bring a 'bats fives ball' back to play with in the yard. They are made like very tiny fives balls and only cost 3d.

I think it is awfully unfair. Mr. Becher's classroom has all the lists of A. House people who have won A. House things graved on beautiful wooden tablets and we have none. Of course it is a little bigger, as we have the passage on our side: we all have prayers there. They also have a delightful picture of M.C. crests.

I am running out of things to say now. Could you tell me what my halfterm report looked like? About how big was the sheet of paper? As big as Eek's or as small as the Prep. ones?

I think I shall stop now.

Much love from Freddie

P.S. The college cats are all either black or black and white.

---

1 – John Archibald Davenport, bursar MC 1920–38.

TO *Georgina Beatrice MacNeice*   MS Dan MacNeice

20 November [1921]   Marlborough

My dear Madre

Thanks awfully for the 2s/6d & the fountain pen. I will try to return the Stylo. I haven't a good envelope for it though. I got some quince jam yesterday.

No, the work here is quite easy, not much harder, if at all, than the Prep.

Mr. Guillebaud has rather a bad opinion of my punctuality etc. It (his opinion) started from my not having a tiepin. I was then made to get an order for a tiepin. There followed a long series of adventures, concerning the tiepin, which rather annoyed Mr. Guillebaud. Also I missed Call once or twice. There is no call now.

Yesterday was an eventful day. In the afternoon there was a match v Clifton, which we lost 24pts–18pts. Clifton have beaten Cheltenham however, so we may beat Ch. Also. (On Wednesday Howard and Dearman went to Clifton and smashed them at rackets.[1]) After the match I shared a 3d loaf with Brightman. We made toast at h. classroom fire and afterwards covered it with quince and marmalade. (I must put in now, as I may forget, 'please don't buy or send me another rug.') After our 'brew' I read 'Nicholas Nickleby' till Hall.[2] After Hall and in Reading Prep. I read more N.N. After reading Prep. we had an 'A' house singsong in the Bradleian. After that we went to bed.

On Friday we had to write a fragment of a play in blank verse for Mr. Canning. The subject was any bit of History from the time of Alfred the Great to the time of Edward I. I did something about Harold Hardrada.[3]

On Monday we had a half in honour of Capt. James Duck, the new Mayor, who owns the famous shop.

1–A. S. Howard (1903–52); educ. MC 1917–22 (racquets 1921–2); Clare College, Cambridge. E. A. Dearman (b.1904), educ. MC 1918–22 (1st XI 1921–2, racquets 1922); Caius College, Cambridge.
2–Cf. Diary, 17 Nov.: 'Read Nicholas Nickleby too absorbedly & as a consequence upon looking up found it was almost exactly 5-15. Seizing my 'Kish' I made for soup. The stairs were unusually quiet & at the top I was confronted by a closed door. Trembling I opened it. Mr Gaul would not allow my entrance. Having given up my name & that of H.L.O.F. I was turned away to continue N.N.' (*Ms Bodleian, Ms Res, Box 57*).
3–Cf. Diary, 18 Nov.: 'In History Hour wrote fragments of plays (in decasyllabic iambic verse) concerning people in period. I wrote some "magnificent lines" (??????) upon "The Fall of Harold Hardrada". The characters were H.H., Tostig & some Danes. The Danes were rather bloodthirsty people.'

The 'Marlburian' came out on Wednesday. You'll have to endure it next hols as well as the Ealhstan Magazine. It will be 3 to 1 however as there will be 3 nos. of the 'Marlburian'.

It is quite warm again now but it rains quite often.

Of course I take my brewbox back every hols. That is the chief point in it. I am dreading taking this home however. Just about half the size would be nice with the shorter side the longer and the new shorter side ½ the old longer. That is about the size of most boxes. I have never yet seen one as big as mine though I have seen all the A house ones and a good many others.

I think we break up about the 20th but I have lost my school calendar. We go home on a Tuesday, I think, but Irish people can go a day earlier if they like, I think. In ordinary circumstances I'd rather wait as lots of things happen on Tuesdays, but of course if Eek goes on the Monday I'd have to. Of course if I meet Eek at Waterloo on Tuesday she'd probably never catch a glimpse of me and would have to wait till everyone had gone away.

On Friday there was a Newbugs' game as it was Corps day.

I have to write to Aunt Eva after this. She sent me a cake the other day. I must complete my letter to Adams too; and also write to Eek and after that to Fforde whose last letter I did not answer.

So I will stop now.

Freddie

1922

TO *Georgina Beatrice MacNeice*   MS Dan MacNeice

12 March [1922]   Marlborough

My dear Madre

Thanks awfully for the parcel. One from Aunt Eva arrived the day before.

I have quite a lot of things to say:- On Friday there was a ½ 'at the request of Mr. & Mrs. Patteson in honour of their daughter'. As a result I got off Mr. Patteson.[1] I have two 'Swords of Damocles' – for English & Maths.

The stone underneath R. C. Corfield's statue is arising.[2] The memorial garden is being lined with slabs of white stone.

C.P. preached for the first time today.[3]

I have been having a good time in the Memorial Reading Room lately. I generally go there on halves after my brew. I had my first game of chess this term in there. As usual the bell went just before the end. The other day, however, I played him (Outram) again & won. There is always an ancient man in there sitting at a high desk, who looks at you suspiciously when you wander about. His work is to keep order & replace the books – You see, when you have taken out a book, you leave it on the table. The bookcases are lettered (3 letters to a block) up to about Q. There are also the Beesley & the Richardson (Old Dick?) libraries, the former being chiefly poetry & famous literary works, the latter a mixed collection of such books as 'Foxe's Book of Martyrs', 'English Caricaturists', 'A Comic History of Rome', collections of pictures, 'the Ingoldsby Legends'[4] – also

---

1 – Canon Charles Patteson (1891–1958), assistant master, MC 1915–23 (captain of OTC 1914–18; assistant chaplain 1921–3); Hockey international 1920. Educ. MC 1906–11, Pembroke College, Cambridge, HO 1921. Subsequently vicar of South Lambeth, West Dulwich, and then Scarborough; canon of York; chaplain of St Peter's School, York, 1947–56.
2 – Richard Conyngham Corfield (1882–1913); educ. MC 1896–9; police officer in South Africa, Somaliland and Nigeria; killed in action in Somaliland.
3 – Patteson.
4 – *English Caricaturists and Graphic Humorists of the Nineteenth Century*, by Graham Everitt (1886); *The Comic History of Rome*, by Gilbert Abbott à Beckett (1852); *The Ingoldsby Legends, or, Mirth and Marvels*, by Rev. Richard Harris Barham (pseud. Thomas Ingoldsby) (1864).

'Littlefield Annals' (compiled by Richardson himself, who was housemaster of Littlefield). All these books have labels stuck on inside, upon which are Scallop Shells (Littlefield crest). There are some pretty interesting things in shelfs A,B,C – lives of A. C. Hilton,[1] R. C. Corfield,[2] memoirs of Cyril Farrar, a son of Dean Farrar, who (C.F.) was at M.C. for a year but was removed, as he could not be reconciled to the methods of teaching grammar etc.[3]

Yesterday our XI beat some club (Southgate) by 7 goals to 2.

I will have several things to put in the 'Museum', when I return – I've suddenly remembered what you told me about London, which idea is truly 'efficient'. Did I tell you that we had College pancakes on Shrove Tuesday. Just before Hall some lemon-selling men came up, who were instantly overwhelmed.

I must now look up my diary – Nothing very interesting except the fact that I have been having cold baths in the morning lately.

I have a chance of going out of House at the end of next term. I will probably be thrown into whatever place H.L.G.[4] thinks fit.

At house you always ask questions such as 'Which of your masters teaches the best?' This time I have a pretty definite answer, I think, namely 'C.P.' (Mr. Patteson) He is nearly always called 'C.P.' That reminds me that you are very ignorant concerning all our mighty men – Our senior prefect goes by the name of (Hector) Brooke.[5] He is in Littlefield & has been in the 6th for years. The Games Committee (I think that is their name) consists of Abell, Ashfield, Leach, Streatfield [sic], the first three being respectively captains of Rugger, cricket & hockey.[6]

On Friday we beat Clifton at Rackets (here). As the match was at such an awkward time, I could not watch. Our pair – Howard & Dearman. The latter is an XI & XL (?) [sic]

1 – Arthur Clement Hilton (1851–77), clergyman and poet; educ. MC 1864–9; St John's College, Cambridge. Later curate of Sandwich. Author of a book of parodies, *The Light Green* (1872), his collected poems were published posthumously.
2 – Probably H. R. Prevost Battersby, *Richard Corfield of Somaliland* (1914).
3 – Cyril Lytton Farrar (1869–91), at MC Jan.–July 1884. Later employed by Chinese Maritime Customs. Son of F. W. Farrar (1831–1903), dean of Canterbury and master of MC.
4 – H. L. Guillebaud.
5 – Henry Brooke (1903–84), educ. MC 1916–22 (senior prefect); Balliol College, Oxford. Conservative MP for Lewisham (1938–45) and Hampstead (1950–1).
6 – C. R. W. Ashfield (1903–64), educ. MC 1917–22, hockey and cricket XI 1920–2; Robert Leach (b.1903), educ. MC 1916–22; Lincoln College, Oxford; N. R. Streatfeild M.C. (1904–40), educ. MC 1917–21; major in BEF 1939; killed in action at Dunkirk.

Knitted O.M. ties have been produced, costing 3/6. At the end of term, I might get one as a reinforcement. I wish they'd invent an A. House tie. Even Priory have one.[1]

On Monday & Tuesday was C.E.E. H.L.G. corrected the History papers. Fforde got 19 out of 20. I should think Fforde will pass. Mr Guillebaud hadn't anything to do with the Common Entrance before. He says the papers were very boring except one or two. He thinks one boy must have had an interview with his Prep. school master recently. He (the boy) said that 'when Henry VIII wanted to marry 5 (?) wives at once, the Pope said 'he'd had enough of this.'

That reminds me of English – 'Lamb'. His letters are rather interesting. They are to people such as Wordsworth, Coleridge, a man called Manning, Southey. We are just getting on to his writings as 'Elia'.[2]

The pages in my pad have come loose; the result is that, as I write, the page shifts about.

It will be great fun in London. Will we be near the a [sic] museum or the Zoo or something?

How is the kitten. When I was roaming Court in the dark tonight I found something which I thought was a kish but was really a cat.

I wish this wouldn't move; I'm getting annoyed. As it [is] 8.15 (& near Prep. end) I will stop.

Much love Freddie

TO *Georgina Beatrice MacNeice*   MS Dan MacNeice

[Easter 1922]   Marlborough

My dear Madre

Thanks awfully for your letter, which I got today (Saturday) I have got several surprises for you, most of which are nice but one rather Tragic – they are:-

I   I got about the last promo. into the Hundreds & am in Hundred A. There was a muddle about my form, as usual

II   Carey has failed. At least, his name is not included in the list of newbugs.

III   My brewbox locks now. Occasionally it refuses to lock & then I remove the key & try again.

---

1 – A junior house at MC.
2 – Cf. 'And logarithms and Greek and the Essays of Elia' (*AJ*, X, CP07, 124).

IV   I am on <u>Third Tenners</u>.

I forgot to ask definitively last hols. about the O.T.C. I suppose you don't want me to be in it. Of course, they do very little. The advantages are, however, that you needn't play in a newbugs' game once a week (in A House). In a senior house I don't know what you would do (not being in it) as there would probably be noone else. I expect you would go for a sweat.

I don't think it could do me any harm

I've forgotten to tell you about London. I met Aunt Eva but the train was a little late. At first we couldn't find the luggage as it was up in a little place behind the engine. We then, having found the luggage, went to Paddington & put it in the cloakroom. We then went to the Goring Hotel & after that to the Belgravia Restaurant, where we had a funny lunch. Then back to Aunt Eva's Hotel, where Aunt Eva read your letter. I had just put on the clean collar. Then in a taxi to the Zoo (<u>Aunt Eva's idea).</u> We went 1st to the Monkey House (being nearest the entrance) where we saw a glorious Mandrill (the sort you hate). Among other things, we met a rather nice keeper, who brought us behind & up into the back of the Mappin Terraces, & thence into a partition in which there was a black bear, called Winnie, about 14 yrs old. She was very tame & the K. gave me bread to give to her. At the back of the place there was a den with railings across it & behind these railings were Graham's bear & another brown b., looking very pathetic. I hope you won't be annoyed with Aunt Eva for going into this place, as <u>you</u> would probably have wanted to do so.

We also saw lions etc. being fed & were brought by another keeper (also v. nice) into his private place where he had a tame fox in a corner. This we petted.

Below is a list of a few animals that I saw & remember more distinctly –

Lion	sealion	antelopes etc.
Tiger	gulls etc.	black swans
Jaguar	ostrich	elephant
Leopard ([*illegible*]).	rhea	rhinoceros
Mandrill	snakes etc.	hippopotamus (1 baby)
Bonnet macaque	(including pyths	giraffe
wanderoo	& boa)	tapir
chimpanzee	alligator	parrots
orangutan	crocodile	cockatoos
dingo	tortoises	parakeets etc.
hyaena	(1 of which 200 yrs)	llamas

wolf	bear, brown	camels
jackal	" black	dromedaries
fox	" <u>polar</u>	
hogs, etc.	(1 brown one	
	held its forefeet when	
	man wished to photog.)	

I have to stop now (Monday) Mr. Brentnall has my form.[1] Please answer about O.T.C.

> Love
> Freddie

TO *Georgina Beatrice MacNeice*   MS Dan MacNeice

[21 May 1922]   Marlborough

My dear Madre

I am awfully sorry about the letter, but I didn't realise it was such a long time, since I had written. This week has been simply tearing. My last letter ought to get to you soon, which will bring my average (1 per week) right. Then this one will arrive on Tuesday or Wednesday. Thanks awfully for the letter. I got the last one off in such a hurry, that I hadn't much time to describe going to Mrs. Wasey's etc.[2] I went on Thursday with Bent; I rode Stuart's bicycle – Stuart is new on our landing.[3] It was a bit small for me but otherwise I got on all right – (I was interrupted then by someone

1–H. C. Brentnall (1875–1955), MA, FSA. Educ. Rugby and Corpus Christi College, Oxford. Assistant master at MC 1903–44, where he taught Geography and other subjects. A dedicated antiquarian, he was co-author (with C. C. Carter) of *The Marlborough Country: Notes Geographical, Historical and Descriptive* (1912); later vice-president and president of the Wiltshire Archaeological & Natural History Society. Author of *Marlborough Official Borough Guide* (1922) and (with J. R. Taylor and G. C. Turner) a 'revised and continued' *History of Marlborough College* (see FLM to GBM, 5 Nov. 1921, n. 4, p. 58). Co-authored with C. C. Carter *Man the World Over*, 2 vols (1938, 1939).
2–Mrs G. K. Wasey (née Godfrey) (1869–1947) lived at Leigh Hill House, Savernake Forest, near Marlborough, and hosted many tennis parties for Marlborough pupils. Her sister (Mary Rose Bintley) was a parishioner at Carrickfergus (see Appendix 1). Sidney Wasey wrote to GBM: 'Frederick (who tells me he is now called Louis!), has now got so big that he generally has to play with people who have not attained to the Sixth (with a very large S!), & look up [to] him with some awe in consequence, but he does not seem to mind playing with these inferior beings so that is all right! – we look upon him now as an old friend' (S. Wasey to GBM, 30 May 1926, *Ms Dan MacNeice*, 2/2). Two of her own sons had died, one in the First World War.
3–W. E. L. Bent (b.1907), educ. MC 1921–5; N. L. Stuart (1908–69), educ. MC 1922–6, Jesus College, Cambridge.

shaking me by the neck – Just at present it is rather unsuitable for writing – While I was saying that Haldane came and blew a horn in my ears – Then I had to room-fag.) At first we went past the place, which is called Leigh Hill, and descended a huge hill. At the bottom Bent went to a house, where there was a baby with measles or some disease like that, and asked if they had heard of L.H., which he pronounced 'Lee Hill'. (Mrs. W. had said that it was written 'Leigh' & pronounced 'Lie' but I got a little muddled and came to the conclusion that it was written 'Lie' & pronounced 'Lee'.) Anyway the woman said she didn't know anything about it. ∴ we went on. I asked a boy we met, who asked if we meant 'Loi Hill'. We said yes, whereupon he instructed us to go back, up the hill. We did so and discovered the house (about 4 miles from Marlborough). We began tennis almost immediately. One of the people was v. good, going by Carrickfergus play. They both served overarm. I had quite a lot of luck in my serves, which seemed to have improved. We had tea in the house, which was rather pretty-looking. After tea we were shown some birds' nests, on which Mrs. Wasey seems rather keen. Then we had 2 or 3 more sets. Just after 6.0 P.M. we started for home, and raced back. Bent's bicycle had a puncture from the start. We got back just in time – before Shepherd had shut the gates.

On Friday night there was a sort of concert by some wandering people – quite good. Yesterday I managed to make 27 on 4th. ∴ my present av. is 11.66 recurring.

Today I met Carey after chapel. We are going for an expedition tomorrow, taking eatables. I have been doing some St. Luke this morning.

I think I may have told you about the mice here. There is one especially illfated brew-locker, which belongs to Money.[1] The other day he found 2 in it, and they ate a corner off his Bible in trying to get in. They also devoured part of the cork of a lemonade bottle. He has constructed a delightful mouse trap out of a biscuit tin, with a hole in the top. Plan:-

[diagram of a lid with a hole in the top]

The lid has a round hole in the middle covered with paper, which has 2 crossing slits. At the X is put a bait. The mouse is supposed to go for the bait and fall into the tin. In this way it will be taken alive.

---

1 – T. D. F. Money (b.1907), educ. MC 1921–6, Caius College, Cambridge. Later, as a medical doctor, he founded a leper settlement in Nigeria. Retd 1977. Cf. FLM to AB, 13 Sept. 1926, n. 4, p. 118.

I have just been out for my Sunday walk. It is simply boiling. Erith and I lay in the shade in Treacle Bolly.[1] After reading prep. We go to H.C.B. Then to Chapel. Then Hall. Hall reminds me of the change in 'Hallers'. Last term they used to be made exclusively by Huntley & Palmer's. This term some have appeared made both by Macfarlane Lang & Peek Frean. All three sorts are the same size & very like each other but the Peek Frean ones are burnt and the Macfarlane Lang are a little superior. You might be interested to know the food today:- 'Breakfast': grapenuts and boiled eggs. Midday Hall:- Ham and rhubarb tart.

I suppose someone will start sleeping in my room soon and muddle up the fossils. I have got one fossil this term – a sort of sea-urchin but it is rather too hot to go hunting. Tomorrow we are going to the forest, which will not be very suitable for them.

My fortnightly orders are Form = 5th; Greek = 4th; Latin = 1st; Maths = 8th.

On the morning of the day on which we go away, Mr. Canning is going to have his wedding in Chapel. Anyone who likes can wait a few hours extra for it. I am thinking of staying, if it would give no trouble. Eek might be interested. I don't know if he's going to leave after that. I can't imagine a wedding in Chapel very well.

This fortnight I have done my record average:- 4.5. My previous ones were 8.25 10.00 9.5 5.5 9.25 5.75 8.25. And (2nd term) 5.0 5.75 9.00 13.75 7.5.

I hope the last letter arrived all right. I will try to write about Wednesday. Thank Eek for her letter. Tell her an O.M. tie is (I think) like this. [*diagram*] [*diagram*] represents dark blue; [*diagram*] = red   blank = white. It goes alternately thus – dark blue – white – red – white – dark blue – white – red.

I hope the kitten is well. As Eek is at home, I don't suppose you allow it in the house much.

When I have finished this, I must write my diary. I have not much time on other days but it is fairly easy, if you attack it in this manner. Last Sunday, of course, I went for a walk to Treacle Bolly. The Rev. Young-husband[2] preached. (The one word you heard all the time was 'Indian'. He had an awful (London?) accent.) I put down in the diary the brief facts, which I talk about at leisure afterwards. Then for the weekdays. On halves

---

1 – E. J. Erith (b.1907), educ. MC 1921–4. Treacle Bolly: tree-lined footpath near MC. Heavy college puddings were known as 'bolly' but the place was reputedly named in memory of a local miller's horse.
2 – Rev. Oswald Younghusband (1874?–1943), educ. Trinity College, Oxford; founder of Younghusband Collegiate Hostel, Lahore.

games. For them I can look up my 'bathing statistics' in my notebook and work backwards. Thursday, of course, was an exception and sticks in my mind. Fagdays are harder – on Monday I 'netfagged'. On Wednesday I ought to have had nets but it rained.

You can't imagine how hot it is in classroom. I am only wearing a shirt and coat but I feel like lying down in a cold bath.

I expect you would like to know about tennis here. It is only a very secondary affair and what I have seen of it, does not look very good. Of course, only the sort of middle-people were playing. There are about 8 school courts, that I have seen. They are on one bit of Level Broadleaze, the rugger match ground, which is better than you would expect.

I am very glad Lazarus, one of the new prefects, did not arrive at Mrs. Wasey's, when I was there.[1] She had given him a sort of indefinite invitation.

Sometime this term I am going to try to go to Silbury Hill. There is an archaeologist's tunnel in it, that you can crawl into. It is a huge mound, twice as high as the Marlborough Mound, and, as it is, artificial. Another place I want to visit is Avebury Temple, a place like Stonehenge. Only about seven stones are left now. The others were used for building London (?) bridge.[2] I think I shall stop now; so I shall be able to get this off tonight. Will write soon. Could you send me an envelope again, please.

Much love
Freddie

TO *Georgina Beatrice MacNeice*   MS Dan MacNeice

24 September [1922]   Marlborough

My dear Madre

I have arrived here all right: I had an awfully interesting time in London with Robert[3] – Lower: Guildhall (museum etc): I also ascended a tower in a street, that commemorated the Fire of London, I think, while Robert did something below. It only took 10 mins. up & down. When I arrived here I discovered Fforde (our landing) and Firth (the other).[4] I also found that

1 – G. L. Lazarus (b.1904); educ. MC 1918–22, prefect; Caius College, Cambridge.
2 – Silbury, near Avebury, is considered the largest man-made mound in Europe. The village of Avebury rests on the site of a late Neolithic monument, circa 2000 BC. FLM visited both places for the first time in the spring of the following year. See FLM to GBM, 6 May 1923, p. 80.
3 – Robert Milliken. See FLM to GBM, 21 Jan. 1920, n. 2, p. 39.
4 – Presumably Horace W. Firth (b.1910), educ. MC 1922–7.

I was a teamaker and ∴ in library; also that I am in I dormitory, which is the largest.

Yesterday began with the usual long space, during which you wait for your brewbox. I met Carey, who has been promoted into the Shell (Firth's form). The unfortunate Fforde is in the Lower Fourth. I am in the Classical Vth and went to Mr. Emery in the morning.¹ We work in a most splendid classroom, with gilt writing round the walls: I only remember bits of it – 'Hoc conclave alumni gratissimi ornandum curaverunt' ['Grateful former pupils have taken care to decorate this room'] or something like that. Mr. Emery himself was rather exciting. He thinks that variety is very necessary at our stage & ∴ we are to have 4 hrs a week 'Science' from Mr. Smith as a sort of rest.² We are also going to Mr. Turner or rather he is coming to us 3 hrs a week – Eng. Lit. & Vergil.³ Mr. E. says he believes in soaking boys in Vergil. Yesterday we received two books (both quite large & fat) namely Oman's History of Greece & the Masters of Eng. Lit. (S. Grayson?)⁴ Mr. Emery was very horrified when he discovered that only 3 of us learnt music. We are going to do Hecuba (Euripides) in Greek & New Testament on Sundays.

Stewart is out of house! He was new last term! The reason is that few other people wished to go to Patteson's.

—

We began our term's hymns with 'Courage, Brother'.⁵
Latin – Pro Roscio
Paradise Lost: Book I
'Science' – Mr. Smith's Elements of Nat. Sc.

—

As I am late I must send this off now. Very busy all today. Much love.

Freddie

1 – C. A. Emery (1873–1931), educ. MC 1887–92, King's College, Cambridge. Assistant master MC 1899–1930.
2 – Rev. W. B. Smith, BSc (assistant master MC 1918–36), author of *Elements of Natural Science*, 2 vols (1921–3).
3 – George Charlewood Turner (1891–1967), M.C., MA, CMG. Educ. MC 1904–10, Magdalen College, Oxford. 47th London and 23rd London Regt. 1914–18. Teacher MC 1919–26 (commander of OTC); headmaster 1926–39. Principal Makerere College, Uganda, 1939–46; headmaster Charterhouse 1947–52.
4 – Stephen Gwynn, *Masters of English Literature* (1904); Charles Oman, *A History of Greece from the earliest times to the death of Alexander the Great* (1890).
5 – 'Courage, Brother, Do Not Stumble' by Norman Macleod (1857), music by Arthur Sullivan.

TO *Georgina Beatrice MacNeice*   MS Dan MacNeice

5 November [1922]   Marlborough

My dear Madre

Thanks awfully for the photograph. I don't think many people are untidy in it and, anyhow, we were changed.

The last part of this week has been quite eventful. On Thursday I had my first 'hot brew' of the term with Brightman. We had bacon, chipped potatoes, cocoa, cake etc. There was also a match on Thursday V Oxford 'A'. They won.

Yesterday I went out to lunch with Colyer and Johnson.[1] We had a very good time and had pancake things for pudding. After that I watched the match V Harlequins 'A.' They won. Then Wood, who had just had a birthday, gave a great brew to all Library + Worsley and Barr (12 people). We were all employed in getting it ready. I did some toast, which was rather dull. We each had one sausage, one rasher of bacon, some chipped potatoes, some bread and toast, biscuits and an apple. After hall I played 4 games of draughts, which I won.

We have been doing quite interesting things in Science lately. Last Monday when we went down to our hut-place (it is a 'temporary' lab. and is miles away beyond the bathing-place) we discovered a limelight lantern (magic lantern) seated on the table. This was to demonstrate uses of Oxygen – there was to assist the lantern to work, a large cylinder of Oxygen, which, according to Mr. Smith, if knocked about violently would blow up the lab. He then proceeded to operate with the internal arrangements of the lantern and to burn iron etc. in the flame and after a long time, spent in getting things ready and explaining, he got to the actual point of putting the slide in, which process he explained with great care. He then put the slide in

When it did focus, we discovered that it was a drawing of Ionic columns by Mr. Smith. The alternative slide showed two hippopotami at the zoo, which was succeeded by the Ionic columns and so on.

Yesterday morning most of Mr. Smith's experiments didn't succeed but they took up so much time that we didn't have our fortnightly paper.

We have stopped doing 'Hecuba' in Greek now and are going to start some Thucydides next week (if the books have arrived).[2]

1–Pupils mentioned here for the first time include A. G. B. Colyer (b.1907), educ. MC 1921–5; M. T. G. Wood (2 Nov. 1907–1943), educ. MC 1922–5; T. C. Worsley (b.1907), educ. MC 1921–6; St John's College, Cambridge. George Basil Thomas Barr (1909?–67): see 12 Jan. 1927, n. 2, p. 143.
2–Euripides, *Hecuba*; Thucydides, *Peloponnesian War*.

I'm going to the Memorial Reading-room now – till Chapel.

There is at present an exhibition of paintings etc. in the Gym. They are rather good, I think.

I forgot to say that one of your last letters came in rather a roundabout way (via Marlborough Street College, Dublin). You didn't put 'England' on it.

Much love
Freddie

TO *Georgina Beatrice MacNeice* MS Dan MacNeice

3 December [1922] Marlborough

My dear Madre

I got your letter yesterday. I don't think I'll be very tired when I get home – I think I can remember another sale on the day I returned, in which I connected all the gasbrackets with strings of coloured paper. It was in the Parochial Hall.

I can't get orders for things now. (They stopped yesterday) but I could buy a hat, if it was necessary, at the same time as the tie. The special gets to Paddington at 10.17 officially. I think the idea about the Hotel is good. Do I put my luggage in a cloakroom in that case?

Exams start in a week's time so I shall be very busy revising etc. this week. On Thursday Mr. Emery was very enthusiastic about the discovery in the valley of the Kings of the tomb of King Tu-tum-kar-men (I'm not quite sure how to spell it) and read us a long extract from the Times about it.[1] He has a sort of forlorn hope that some lost Greek documents may be found among the papyri. Have you been in the Valley of the Kings?

Yesterday we beat Cheltenham 6 pts to 3. On Thursday (?) there is the landing match. Our captain Smith (who has been called 'Chula' after a monkey in the London Illustrated News, which we get in Library) has gone to 'Sanny', which is rather a handicap.[2]

The College cats have been becoming very intrusive lately. There was a tabby one in Library last night that landed in through the window, and a black and white one appeared in house this morning.

1 – See 'Three Chambers Discovered at Thebes' and 'Importance of New Discoveries', *The Times*, 30 Nov. 1922, 13f., and 1 Dec. 1922, 13f.
2 – H. H. Smith (1905–91), educ. MC 1919–23; 1st XV 1921–2; 1st XI 1922–3. See 'The Gorilla as a London Pet: The Civilising of Chula', *Illustrated London News*, 18 Nov. 1922.

Next term I shall have 4 places to do prep. in – Upper School, Memorial Reading Room, Adderley Library or Vth classroom & sometimes Guillebaud's house class room. I have never been in Adderley and only in C3 house class room once. It is rather an exciting place and has a very good library according to Jefferies.[1] Guillebaud's ought to get the Bell Trophy for the most intellectual house this year.[2] They have got most of the prizes so far.

Tuesday [5th] – I am sorry I cannot say any more but I must stop now

Much love
Freddie

1 – A. P. Jefferies (1904–56), educ. MC 1921–5; University of Paris; Intelligence Corps 1943; SHAEF 1944–5.
2 – Bell Trophy, 'won by the house which obtains most distinction in Scholarships, Prizes, &c.' (*Marlborough College Register*, 986). In 1922, the trophy was won by Littlefield House, but Guillebaud's C3 received the prize for 1923–4.

1923

TO *Georgina Beatrice MacNeice*   MS Dan MacNeice

27 January [1923]   Marlborough

My dear Madre

I have just got your letter and will begin by answering any questions in it. My rug has made an enormous difference in my warmth and I am now almost too warm as I don't wake up till the bell goes, so I certainly don't want another one. I was not invited to sit in the chair, which was rather disappointing though, of course, it is more to your credit if you are left alone. As regards the milk jugs and mugs, they were all put in House Classroom except 4. 2 were put in the Museum block for Barrows[1] (We are not meant to go up to the Museum studies) and 2 were put in Ranken to study. Ranken, as I hope you know, is head of house. His study is a queer narrow place but very comfortable-looking. I went there again today with 4 eggs and ½ lb. of lard for Rotherham. Captains and people like that can send us down the town to get things for them. They are quite nice, however, and don't force you, if you have something important to do. There is one other prefect in house besides Ranken and Barrows. He is a new one and his name is Barlow. He is very musical and tested our voices for some house singing thing. Of course, I was not very successful. We went into Mr. Guillebaud's room, where he was playing the piano, one by one. When my turn came and he struck a note, I made a sort of grunt. I was so dissatisfied with this attempt that I made no more sounds, as he went on striking notes. Then he said 'Can't you get the note?' and I said 'No' whereupon he said 'All right. You may go now.'

Among other interesting experiences was the weighing the other night. The machine was brought into dormitory and we got on, in turn. I don't think it was very accurate. I was 7' 1 [sic].

I haven't yet told you about 2nd Prep. in House Classroom. The superior people walk about and cook and eat. There is one large, heavy clumsy-

---

1–Pupils referred to for the first time here include W. L. Barrows (1905–76), educ. MC 1919–23, prefect; K. F. F. Ranken (b.1904), educ. MC 1918–23, prefect; T. A. Rotheram (b.1905), educ. MC 1919–23; H. A. N. Barlow (b.1905), educ. MC 1918–24, senior prefect 1923; A. I. Roach (1905–34), educ. MC 1919–23; K. W. Y. Fison (1905–43), educ. MC 1919–24.

looking person named Roach, who seems to spend his time eating. There is also a person in our dormitory, a sort of official, who takes our 'Allows.', named Fison. He also supervises our 'pull-throughs'

The Upper School gramophone is at present performing. I have just finished a chapter of Greek History – about the rise of Pericles. By the way we have got our Homers and are going to start off on the first book of the Iliad next week. This week we have been doing Virgil with Mr. Emery. We are starting in the latter part of the Vth book and our chief object is the VIth book. We are also finishing the Hecuba that we left off last term. We are going to do Cicero's De Senectute and Xenophon's Memorabilia, I think, later.

It seems a very long time since the beginning of the term. I have been going 'sweats' practically every day, not slothful sweats like the A. House ones but ones in which you simply have to run hard all the time. I feel as if my muscles ought to be beautifully developed

Sunday: Last night I was 'had out' of bed for the 1st time. There is a custom of upsetting people's beds. They have to be put right again within 2 mins. It is really quite amusing. There are two ways of 'turfing' someone's bed, which are best explained by diagrams –

[*diagram of beds being upended*]

As I was not expecting it my things got in rather a muddle.

The other day I went to 'Adderley' (the famous library) and spent over an hour there. I had never been there before and was greatly excited. It contains all sorts of books, including a good many German ones. Yesterday afternoon I went to the Memorial Reading Room and read some of Addison's essays.

I have discovered that Mr. J. Barcroft is lecturing some boys this term on 'Scenes in the Andes' or something like that.[1] I think I must go to it.

The book of Mr. Emery's is a small, dull, brown schoolish-looking book. It may be in the desk.

I am getting quite used to Upper School now. There is always a terrific row before prep. starts and just at the beginning of prep. in the evening, we have to go round and 'scavenge' (i.e. pick up bits of paper etc).

I have seen very little of the College cats so far. They don't seem to frequent house much. I <u>did</u> meet one in Court the other day – a fat black animal – but it was very sulky and didn't seem to like me.

---

1 – Prof. Sir Joseph Barcroft, FRS (1872–1947), a medical expert on the consumption of oxygen at high altitudes. His son Henry was a pupil at the school.

We have changed our science lab. with Mr. Smith. Our new abode is very plain but has clean, new desks etc.

In Morning Chapel today I got quite startled, as I suddenly thought I saw Eek walk in. It was really some unknown person wearing a red hat like hers, whose face I did not see.

This morning I went round the museum with Carey and Fforde.[1] Carey is always very supercilious in the Museum. He insisted on saying that a stuffed Polar bear was one of the woolly toys, children buy in shops. It really <u>did</u> look rather like that.

That reminds me – There were some rather good drawings and photographs of the contents of Tutankhamen's tomb in some illustrated papers (L. Illust. News etc.) that I was looking at today.[2] There were also some 'Ethiopian discoveries'.

I have got to get through an enormous amount of diary-work soon so I think I will stop now.

Much love
Freddie

TO *Elizabeth MacNeice*   MS Dan MacNeice

6 May [1923]   Marlborough

My dear Eek

I am awfully sorry as regards that telegram. Breakfast at Lime St. removed it from my mind and it did not return there to till [*sic*] I excavated it from my pocket about 1.30. However, I expect and hope you let the 'Princ.' realise that it was my fault. She probably already imagines what my ora (do you spell it like that?) is like.

(Num) Did you go down to Magdalen on May morning or did the alarum clock fail in its duty? Also are you going to send me a Terminal Diary. Leach, as I suppose you realize, played in the Freshers' Match and wasn't much of a success (at least, as far as the scores in the paper go).

1 – Both fellow pupils of FLM at Sherborne Prep. On Carcy see FLM to GBM, 9 Feb. 1919, n. 1, p. 28 and on Fforde FLM to GBM, Mar. 1921, n. 1, p. 47.
2 – The discovery of the tomb of Tutankhamen was generally in the news: articles appeared in *The Times* in Nov. and Dec. 1922 and throughout Jan. 1923. See, for example, 'The Egyptian Find: Sketches Made in the Tomb' (*The Times*, 2 Jan. 1923, 14). FLM is probably referring to photographs in the 20 Jan. issue of *Illustrated London News*, including images of the Camel Corps guarding the tomb against raiders, and of Howard Carter and Mr Callender carrying a jewellery casket. Excitement would continue when a special Egypt number of the *Illustrated London News* appeared on 24 Feb. (too late to be the issue referred to in this letter).

Now, for some moral advice. I sincerely hope that you are not expending your latent energy in the insidious and deteriorating sports of canoeing, rowing, bathing, tennis, cricket, cocoaparties and such like. Nor that you are wearing away the fibrous cerebral muscles while allowing the hours of midnight to give place to those of dawn. Nor that you are missing Chapels, lectures and other such necessities. Nor that you are turning into a brawny unintellectual athlete. Nor that you are developing into an intellectual unbrawny sage. Nor that you are becoming in any way Oxonianly disagreeable. Nor that you are attending too much to the culinary lure. Nor that you are surrendering your room to Untidiness, and the other vices. Nor, and lastly, that you are wasting the unforgiving minutes in that malicious and unnecessary and wholly vicious practice of idle loitering and conversing. (P.S. nor bicycling.)

The weather here (these words are necessary appurtenances to every self-respecting letter) has been glorious of late though there have been occasional showers. I have been for two 'bike' rides, have not fagged once and have had no games. I am in a new dormitory, which to Madre's horror is a sort of attic in the roof. Its captains are Ranken and Rotherham.

Prizeday is on Friday 29th. 'The Head Mistress' is acted on Friday & Saturday evenings.[1] Come down & brew me.

Bathing has not started yet but we despairingly hope that it will soon. When I return for the vac. I trust that you will be able to swim at least half a mile and will have acquired the best fancy strokes. While I am deprived of the cooling effect of the bathing place I am consoling myself with ices – a habit I am sure <u>you</u> have not taken up.

Meanwhile – good luck. Remember the Terminal Diary: also a letter – don't drown yourself or anyone else of your wretched collection just yet – or poison yourself with any fearful concoctions.

Much love and contempt
Fredericus

P.S. What about the canoe?

---

1 – The comic opera by Boughey and Ivimey; see FLM to GBM, 9 Oct. 1921, n. 2, p. 53.

6 May [1923]   Marlborough

Prizeday is on 29th June (i.e. Friday) & Commem. on Sunday following, 'Head Mistress' acted Friday & Sat. evenings

My dear Madre

I did send a postcard after all but it may have been slightly illegible. Also I wrote my letter last Sunday & stamped it up on Monday. Then I thought I had posted it until I found it in my pocket on Tuesday evening.

First of all, before I describe the events of the week, I must ask if you can send me 'The Hundred Best Latin Poems', a little pink papercovered book, which I took down to the drawingroom towards the end of last holiday and left in the piano.[1] Whether it is still there or has returned to my room (in which case it will probably be in the press) I am not sure. I have now discovered that a tennis-racket would be extremely useful: however, I suppose it could not be sent safely or easily. At any rate, when Ross' one arrives I shall be able to borrow it.[2]

The Griffin is getting on beautifully: I think I must get a padlock for him as it is the custom for the Upper School 'bloods' to ride any bicycles they find round Upper School before evening prep. This is not exactly good for the bicycles as the riders spend their time crashing into each other and into desks etc. I have been for two proper rides so far – one on Tuesday and one yesterday. On Tuesday I felt rather stranded as most of house were playing in a game, when W. P. T. Roberts arrived and proposed a ride to Silbury Hill.[3] Before starting off we prepared ourselves for the journey by partaking of some jelly, which Roberts had in his brewbox. Silbury Hill is about 7 miles away and is a common resort in the summer term. As I had never before had a 'bike' I had never before seen this erection.

On Tuesday we had not time to go to the top, though we examined the door at the beginning of a tunnel once used for excavation purposes. Sad to relate, the door was locked. I don't think the excavators found anything of worth inside although they penetrated to the centre. There were two

---

1 – *The Hundred Best Poems (Lyrical) in the Latin Language* by J. W. Mackail (1905, repr. 1920).
2 – Fortescue ('Fortie') Eric Vesey Ross (1907–96), educ. MC 1921–5; Magdalene College and Ridley Hall, Cambridge; HO 1934; m. (1937) Joy Wigram. A clergyman's son, he is Reckitts in *SAF*, 93–6.
3 – William Paul Temple Roberts (b.1907), educ. MC 1921–5. Career soldier, rising to the rank of colonel in 1950.

notice boards opposite the road warning wayfarers not to deface this monument. People have been in the habit of riding down the hill but I am not going to take part in this amusement. You may not understand these remarks if you do not realise that Silbury Hill is a prehistoric artificial mound, far larger than the Mound behind A House.

On Thursday I net fagged for two hours and a quarter. Yesterday the Griffin, Carey and I rode to Avebury which is fairly near Silbury. There we saw the remains of the Avebury Temple which is of the Stonehenge species. Unfortunately it has suffered owing to the Medieval lack of building material and only a few large stones now remain. The Roman Circle (if that is the right name) is still visible. It is a long high bank running in a circle – Carey, I am afraid, was not much impressed by it. The part of the country around the Bath Road is, I should think, of considerable archaeological interest, as it is full of tumuli as well as containing Silburry [*sic*], Avebury and the Devil's Den.

We have started Oedipus Coloneus in form and have done the first 100 lines or so pretty thoroughly. I find it (so far) rather harder than the Euripides we did, but I expect it will grow easier.

Brightman & I bought a 6d cake yesterday which we are going to eat today also some buns & the apricot jam / with love Freddie

TO *Eva Mildred Greer*   MS Dan MacNeice

31 August 1923   Carrickfergus

My dear Aunt Eva

Thanks awfully for the R.L.S.'s. Eek and I got a terrific (though pleasing) shock when we opened the parcel, which did not look as if it contained books. Eek immediately declared her intention of using them as tools to deafen our ears. She started off on Dr. Jekyll & Mr. Hyde directly after tea and waxed wroth when I suggested that I should continue it on my own. Her wroth, however, was ineffectual and I finished the story after church.

The arrival of the volumes was very opportune as the weather that day was of an even more depressing nature than usual and our attempts to postpone melancholy by arraying ourselves in curious and outlandish costumes could not have lasted much longer (although they were not too bad attempts. Madre had followed the examples of those who advertise and had evolved into a giant: Eek, with her usual dignity, was affected by little evolution – merely becoming the Royal Chemist of the King of Siam, arrayed in cap & gown.)

Yesterday the rest of the family went to Belfast – a folly which I wisely shunned, and there visited a flower-show. They returned with a portrait attachment for me and my last lot of photos – two of which are of Carrickfergus, the remainder being of portions of Nendrum Monastery and Strangford Lough.[1] While they were away I read bits of 'Memories & Portraits' & later on the beginning of 'Travels with a Donkey'.[2]

The whole tribe of Stevenson now occupies part of the shelf of honour having expelled thence the Everyman books with the result that all the books in that shelf (except 'Ancient Greece') can claim to be either written by or written about famous men of letters.

As regards photos. my book now contains exactly 50 not yet unfortunately very varied. I hope, however, to get some good ones at Ballycastle, provided that the sun ever comes out there at all. The scenes of my photographic efforts are generally Carrickfergus – there are also several Scotland, Marlborough, some Gobbins, Brown's Bay (Island Magee), Island Mahee (Nendrum Abbey).[3]

A funny coincidence connected with the Stevensons is the fact that I spent several hours last Sunday reading 'Robert Louis Stevenson's Edingburgh [sic] Days' by E. Blantyre Simpson.[4] This made me slightly more fitted to receive them into the library.

It is almost unnecessary to remark that we have not been engaged in any 'Outdoor Sports' of late. Every morning I go up to Mr. Wellington's rabbits and that is about the only interesting out of doors happening. Mrs. Johns's children's Tennis Tournament that was going to take place tomorrow has been postponed to the following Saturday.[5] The lawn, needless to relate, has been neglected for some time . . .

The cats on the other hand are improving physically – Grin took the part of a young Snow-tiger on Wednesday being produced from the folds of the robe of an Indian dispensing chemist and given to a visitor suffering from influenza to be boiled as a remedy.

She thoroughly enjoyed her role of 'snow-tiger' until her dance with the chemist which unluckily filled her with excessive terror so that she fled

1 – Nendrum monastic site, associated with St Patrick, at Mahee Island, Co. Down.
2 – R. L. Stevenson, *Memories and Portraits* (1887), *Travels with a Donkey in the Cevennes* (1878).
3 – The Gobbins cliffs, featuring a spectacular cliff path, at Islandmagee, Co. Antrim.
4 – Published 1898.
5 – The Johns family were parishioners at St Nicholas's Church, Carrickfergus, who lived at Joymount House (now Carrickfergus Public Library) (Helen Rankin, private correspondence, 2008). Cf. Appendix 1. Tyndall Johns was a solicitor. He and his wife had three daughters and a son (Census of Ireland, 1911).

downstairs and up the side door in her desire to escape. I expect she thought we were all minions.

A few days ago Madre indulged in a picture-hanging – which, to my great joy, consisted partly in embellishing my room. I have now nine pictures hanging on the walls and one placed on the mantel-piece as well as numerous minor pictures. Lately she has been occupied in resuscitating the cleanliness of the drawing-room, a process which involves the removal of carpet, most of the furniture, books and innumerable magazines.

We are beginning to stick some of your photos. into Madre's photo book but have not got very far as yet.

Yesterday, as a result of the drawingroom cleaning, Archie beat the carpet and while I was assisting in hoisting it on a rope, announced that he had a present for us. This consisted of two broken china dogs and some dolls' plates (I think) excavated from the henyard last year and stowed away in a little pot.

These curiosities 'reminiscent of antiquity' were, according to Archie's orders, to be shown 'to the mistress'. This would be dangerous for them but it was effected without their destroyal. Eek, having regarded them with interest, said that they must be very old but she thought that she could just remember them.

I suppose you heard about the Rugby Match, which was a great triumph. Abell has been playing for Worcestershire occasionally since then and will appear I expect in the county averages. On one occasion, he made 50.[1] He is expected to get a 'rugger' blue for Oxford next term. He also belongs to Blackheath 'rugger' club. I have been working out roughly the batting averages of the XI from the 'Marlburians' these holidays. Abell is top with (as I work it out) an average over 40. He made three centuries, the biggest being 156. Lord made two centuries, his highest score being 135.[2] Several others came near their 100's, the captain once making 82 not out & someone else 91.

Madre & I have been making an acrostic for you but it is not much good. If we can find it I expect we will send it to you.

Today is up to the usual standard of badness and I shall probably spend the afternoon continuing 'Travels with a Donkey' – that is, unless Eek

---

1 – On Abell, see FLM to GBM, 5 Nov. 1921, n. 3, p. 56. A right-hand batsman, Abell played for Oxford 1924–7, Worcestershire 1923–39, MCC 1935–9, Europeans (India) 1928–30 and Northern India 1934–5, 1941–2. Cf. 'Oxford at Lord's. The Wicket-Keeping of Mr Abell' (*The Times*, 26 June 1924, 7); 'Worcestershire Gain an Advantage. G. E. B. Abell's Big Score' (*The Times*, 18 July 1935, 6).

2 – Reginald Arthur Lord (1905–97), educ. MC 1919–23 (1st XI 1922–3, right-hand bat), St John's College, Oxford (1st XI 1924–6); RAF 1940–5.

insists on reading it aloud – which is always possible. As she has abundance of Botany to do she has less time to spare for reasonable books than formerly. The other day I procured for her some splendid water, which disclosed when examined beneath the microscope, many weird beasts and plants. The distinction was rather hard to draw for the uninitiated. It was my wish to get some of the mosses etc from St Bride's Well, which had excited the attention of Miss Loader but when I went into the field where the well was wont to be I was amazed and horrified to find it was no longer. Eek shared my grief but Madre took the news with inappropriate indifference.

The sun is beginning to come out: if it continues in this good work I shall take a series of portraits of the family with my new attachment. They will probably be hopeless failures.

Much love Freddie

P.S. Have you been to Rathlin yet?[1]

TO *Georgina Beatrice MacNeice*   MS Dan MacNeice

7 October [1923]   Marlborough

My dear Madre

I am writing in the 'Brad' which is now my fixed abode till I get a study or into classroom. It is rather a contrast to Upper School as access is easy either to a fire or a store and prep. is not such a solemn performance. Being in the Sixth I can get bread and butter at supper time when other people merely have 'Hallers' and cheese: this is the only privilege that I have used so far. It supplies you with food for second prep. as you take great lumps and portions of loaves plus butter back with you to the Brad., where you make toast. There is moreover a table you can play ping-pong on, though rather small.

On the first Monday of term there was a Sixth meeting in 'Reader'. Fine for nonattendance was 2/- so I attended with great punctuality. Previously I had to

[page missing]

Yesterday we wrote an essay on Poetry: at tea we received Marlburians. I forgot to tell you that there are two new windows in Chapel, one being a Bell memorial (I am writing like this as my nib is broken).

---

1 – Rathlin Island, Co. Antrim. 'Rathlin, where Bruce had watched the spider, was cut off from the mainland by a notorious sea and its people were entitled to be primitive' ('Landscapes', *SAF*, 225).

At present our chief interest is centred in the Sports, which we have hopes of winning. On Saturday we have a history paper. In Thucydides we have been picking out bits about the siege of Plataea. In private tu. with Mr. Flecker (Herodotus) we did an absurd description of some people who lived in a lake the other day. Their houses were supported on piles and there were trapdoors on the floor: through these trapdoors they used to let down baskets and pull them up in a few minutes full of fish! Moreover they kept their horses and cattle in the lakehouses and fed THEM on fish! Their babies had to be secured by ropes to prevent them falling down the trapdoors!

On Tuesday I played in a team against A. House: we won 36–0 being much heavier than they were.

The weather is wet and horrible at present. On the coldest day this term we had a fearful sweat to Martinsell in icy rain coming down with fury all the time. Yesterday I did good time (for me) to Rockley and back but hurt my toe.[1]

In the sports Ross is running in an underage half mile: he is rather worried about it.

Betjemann [sic] was 2nd in Buchanan Reading Prize: I heard his voice through Adderley door: it was very dramatic[2]

I am going to do Prep. now – a horrid little book on Greek Accents so

Much love
Freddie

TO *Georgina Beatrice MacNeice*   MS Dan MacNeice

4 December [1923]   Marlborough

My dear Madre

We are just becoming unfrozen which means that my epistolatory [sic] talent has fewer impediments in its path. On Saturday I received 'By Bog and Sea in Donegal' from Miss Hind; it seemed very 'superior' to have a book sent to one by its author although as being presented with Mr.

---

1 – Martinsell Hill, Wiltshire. To Rockley and back was approx. 4 miles.
2 – John Betjeman (1906–84), poet and broadcaster. Educ. MC 1920–5; Magdalen College, Oxford (rusticated). Prep school teacher, private secretary to Sir Horace Plunkett, architecture and film critic. British press attaché to High Commission, Dublin, 1941–3, then at 'P' Branch, Bath (secret department). Queen's Medal for Poetry, CBE 1960, knighted 1969, Poet Laureate 1972–84. His many books include *Ghastly Good Taste* (1933), *New Bats in Old Belfries* (1945), *A Few Late Chrysanthemums* (1954), *Collected Poems* (1958), *Summoned by Bells* (1960), *High and Low* (1966), *A Nip in the Air* (1974), *Uncollected Poems* (1982).

Smith's 'Elements of Natural Science' might be reckoned as an exactly similar incident. As regards the contents of the former I like in particular the poem about Cathal O'Flynn and another one about a boy in bed.[1]

Today we played Clifton here, a match that needs as historian the saddest of the Muses(!) We got five tries; so did Clifton. They converted three of theirs; we failed to convert one. On Saturday we are playing Cheltenham away, which I expect to have an even more tragic result, as they are reputed to be better than Clifton.

Last week I played fives twice and partook in an atrocious steeplechase on Friday: we ran miles into unexplored regions, which might judging by their temperature have been Arctic.

I am going to get the History of M.C. (your birthday-present) soon and bring it home in triumph – also a goodly stock of College Christmas cards.[2]

I am absolutely overwhelmed with work now so I must stop.

Much love

Freddie

TO *Eva Mildred Greer* MS Dan MacNeice

26 December [1923] Carrickfergus

My dear Aunt Eva

Thanks awfully for the watch AND the books AND the calendar which are all super excellent. The shock involved in their discovery was, though pleasant, terrific. I had not previously any Kipling and so am especially elated at getting some. I greatly admire the cage of the watch, which I think ought to prove efficient. The watch itself is 'superb'!

The proceedings today have seemed somewhat of a bathos after yesterday but Madre is, I think, rather relieved. Mrs Bailie, the new cook came through with flying colours. We expected her to hash up something but everything seemed all right, though the mincepies were a bit fragile. We had a pretty festive dinner; Madre produced two candelabra (or something like that) which greatly embellished the table in company with the cut glass vases and bowl that have lately been presented to her. The turkey was

---

1 – Elizabeth Shane (Gertrude Hind), *By Bog and Sea in Donegal* (1923). Cathal O'Flynn is the protagonist of 'The Owld Man's Talk' (27). See 'The Wee Boy in Bed' (57). Shane's other publications include *Tales of the Donegal Coast and Islands* (1921), *Piper's Tunes* (1927) and *Collected Poems*, 2 vols (1945).
2 – Possibly the revised *History of Marlborough College* (see FLM to GBM, Easter 1922, n. 1, p. 67).

(I should think) bigger than usual and the plum puddings though not home-made, might have been considerably worse.

Willie had rather an exciting experience this morning, being awakened about 5.0 A.M. by Grin leaping upon his bed. Grin then proceeded to meander through the house shrieking in a heart-rending manner until she brought me to such a pitch of 'wakefulness' that I got up to come to her assistance. I found her huddled up at the top of the stairs lamenting and put her outside the hall door.

Eek and I went to Seapark today and played various dangerous games in the dark.[1] It was quite good fun and a welcome change from 'Twenty Things' which we generally play when we go there.

Madre and Daddie gave me a new bookcase for Christmas, one that you can hang on the wall. The Stevensons fit into the top shelf very well giving it an aristocratic effect. I think I am going to put it on the press in my room.

There doesn't seem to have been much breathing space yet since we came home but as the new housemaid has arrived and Christmas is over things ought to improve.

Madre has refused the Johns's invitation for Saturday week, saying that we are too busy. We have been trying to think of something to prevent us accepting it but could find nothing more expedient.

The house has been ringing lately with would-be musical sounds coming from Willie's musical box and singing top and sundry whistles of an inferior sort that we have collected from crackers. We have been twice visited by 'itinerant singers' – once by four boys in horrible masks, whose role was chiefly comic and once by the Salvation Army who sang hymns.[2]

The cats, instead of moving in a silent and cat-like fashion, are now accustomed to gallop along like elephants, so they are always appearing at inopportune moments and getting in the way and are rapidly ceasing to pay the house and its inmates the respect due to them.

I must now stop, apologising for atrocious writing etc, etc.

Much love
Freddie

1 – Seapark, home of FLM's stepuncle, Thomas MacGregor Greer. See FLM to GBM, 5 Nov. 1921, n. 5, p. 58.
2 – The comic boys in masks were presumably Christmas mummers.

1924

TO *Georgina Beatrice MacNeice*   MS Dan MacNeice

6 February [1924]   Marlborough

Drina, will you please excuse me
(Though I fear you may refuse me)
That the writing of this letter
Is not earlier, is not better
On the score of punctuality
From this far-remote locality,
Where the dry and mouldering fishes
Lie like mummies in their dishes,
And the puddings and the pies
Are of most tremendous size
And the mud abounds in oceans
(Contrary to modern notions
Of the healthy and hygienic)
And the literature Hellenic
Is the subject of perusal
Questions, answers and refusal –

To return to my beginning,
'Tis a certain case of sinning
That the letter meant for Sunday,
Should not start for home on Monday,
Nor on Tuesday but should linger
(While the writer sucks his finger
In his terrible forebodin')
Till the day assigned to Wodin –
O ye villains, O ye heroes,
Rangit-Singhis,[1] Neptunes, Neroes,

---

1 – Rangit Singh (1780–1839) was the first Maharajah of the Punjab, but possibly a reference to K. S. Ranjitsinhji (1872–1933), famous Indian cricketer, who played for Cambridge, Sussex and England.

Big men, small men, horse-men, car-men
Since the days of Tutank-amen
Was there any reason
In the most tempestuous season
For this literary treason,
For this base procrastination;
Oh ye pens of every station,
Oh ye inkpots, oh ye inks,
Reds and purples, greens and pinks,
At the thought of such a crime
Pens are sticks, and ink is slime,
To imagine that a lad
Should become so very bad,
[Should *deleted*] As to hesitate and falter
(Like a monkey at Gibraltar
When about to leap the strait)
As to send his letter late –
See the fate that lies in store
Where the Future oceans roar,
See a squadron of police,
Coats all blue and heads all grease,
Come to seize and justly rate
Him who sent his letter late.
See them put him in the stocks
And lock him up with many locks,
See the carrots hurtle round,
Ounce on ounce and pound on pound –
Tearful picture, cease the tale
Loose the lock and ope the gaol,
Let him write a hundred lines
Saying "The accepted signs["]
Of a lad who shirks his letter
(One who should by rights know better)

Are a weakness for his meat,
Salt and sugar, sour and sweet,
Prunes and pancakes, peaches, plums,
All that from the baker's comes;
Also an unlucky yearning
For extraordinary learning,

Curious things in curious books,
How an armadillo looks
When it meets a brontosaurus,
How the men who were before us
Hewed utensils out of flints
And made their patients granite splints –
And whereas the aforesaid boy
Finds the aforesaid give him joy,
He will send his letter late
Written in an awful state,
I am sure you will agree
This is just the case with me;
Now to come to the point and leave a
Mere digression, from Aunt Eva
Will you send the wondrous book –
Willy-nilly, hook or crook,
As for William will you say
I'm coming back on a Wednes-day,
I'm coming to open the avenue gate,
Be it dark, be it light, be it soon, be it late,
Be it late, be it soon, be it dark, be it light
I'm coming for certain. Goodbye for the night.

TO *Eva Mildred Greer*   MS Dan MacNeice

20 February [1924]   Marlborough

My dear Aunt Eva

I am horribly repentant and tremblingly sorry for being so late in writing. Thanks awfully for the book which is really efficient. The reason for my tardiness is superabundance of work, as we have just had a prize exam.

Today we had quite an energetic sweat, also one yesterday. It has been fairly cold lately and snowed a little yesterday, when I got some muffins, which are very comforting. Some unfortunate people in house have just been forbidden to eat them, as they are bad for their training (This is the Steeplechase term).

We had three weeks of rugger at the beginning of term and managed to win a cup. Now we are playing hockey. We had a good chance of being Cockhouse but one of our best people has just got measles. As for rugger this year's Oxford hockey captain is an O.M.

Tonight I am going to a lantern lecture on the Sun and Stars – that is if I do not feel too heavily encumbered by work. We are doing a Greek play, composed mostly of (1) ridiculous exclamations of sorrow, (2) of proper names. It is our second this term and we are going to do a third. We are reading for English 'The Life and Death of Jason' by Morris, which is largely composed of such words as 'natheless', 'adown' and 'anear'.[1]

I am playing in House fives competition, singles and doubles. In the singles I am doomed to be 'lashed' but in the doubles our opponents are really bad.

Thursday morning.

Today is a half (ordinary) and we hope there may be an extra one tomorrow in honour of a baby of one of the masters.

Thanks awfully for the reptile numbers of the animal thing. I liked the flying-dragon arrangement in one of them.

I must [go] now to work at the Greek Play.

Much love
Freddie

P.S. The watch is going well.

TO *Georgina Beatrice MacNeice*　　　　　　MS Dan MacNeice

11 May [1924]　　　　　　　　　Marlborough

My dear Madre

To begin with business. Vinny's trousers (at least one species, which Ross is getting) cost 32/6. It sounds rather expensive but I don't know 'de rebus his' [*sic*]. I expect there may be some cheaper. Moreover, could you look in my little bookcase and send me a 'Sophocles' that you may find there – a maroon, coloured book.

The next chapter is on work. The following books we have got new this term – (You needn't read this if you don't want to.) Cicero, de amicitia; Apology of Socrates (Plato); First Philippic & Three Olynthiacs (Demosthenes). We are still reading Das Gespensterschiff[2] in German.

Now we proceed to the history of the week. On Monday Ross and I went for a short 'bike'-ride in spite of a high wind. I think my 'bike' has got a slow puncture.

---

1 – William Morris, *The Life and Death of Jason* (1867), a poem in heroic couplets.
2 – Wilhelm Hauff (1802–27), *Das Gespensterschiff* [*The Phantom Ship*].

On Tuesday we played 'squash' in the fives-courts – a game with tennis rackets and a soft ball as I have explained to you before.

On Wednesday we did the same.

On Thursday we had our first game of tennis. I had four sets as I played a second hour. The court was not bad but there was a very strong wind.

Yesterday we had a sweat – a fairly easy one – as it rained all day.

Today is finer but not too good. Ross and I went for a short walk before Chapel. We succeeded in finding three empty nests and one swallow's one containing three or four eggs on the outside of a garden wall. This last I photographed with help of portrait attachment but whether the nest will come into the photo. or the photo. will come out at all, I am doubtful. You see, I had to hold the Kodak above my head, although I was standing on an old grass-collector (of mowing machine) that we borrowed for the purpose from a shed nearby.[1]

I forgot to say that Shepard and I had some tea yesterday – tea, Nestle's milk, lady cake, four buns.[2] We are turned out of Brad. at half-past five every Thursday & Saturday now for an hour, to allow the Musical Society to practise.

We spent some time yesterday rubbing black marks off the Brad. wall (the result of cricket with a soft ball) about which Mr. Ransome was rather worried.[3]

I have a pretty miserable bed after all – the same one I had my first term; but of course, its draughty position is rather an advantage in the summer – not that it has been very hot so far.

I have got my 'Shakespeare' from the book-office. It is not a bad one. Much love.

Freddie

1 – FLM received a Kodak camera 'around my fifteenth birthday' for use during summer holidays in Scotland (SAF, 224).

2 – Graham Howard Shepard (1907–43), educ. MC 1921–6; Lincoln College, Oxford. FLM describes Shepard at school in SAF as 'a surprising blend of precocious wordly-wiseness and faunal innocence' (87). A naval officer during the war, Shepard was lost at sea on board HMS Polyanthus on 20 Sept. 1943. He is the subject of 'The Casualty (in memoriam G.H.S.)' in Springboard, CP07, 237 and is Gavin in AS. Cf. 'Auden and MacNeice: Their Last Will and Testament': 'And Graham Shepard shall have my two cider-mugs, / My thirty rose-trees and, if he likes, my hat' (LI, CP07, 739).

3 – H. A. V. Ransom, MA, taught at MC 1915–28 and was the Adderley Librarian 1927–46.

TO *Georgina Beatrice MacNeice*   MS Dan MacNeice

10 June [1924]   Marlborough

My dear Madre –

Sorry – it seems such a short time since my last. The weather is very hot and nothing much happens. Ross and I had a Cherry Jelly on Sunday. We drink no tea nowadays but only lemonade made from powder. I went to Mrs. Wasey's on the 2nd with Bennitt and had some quite good tennis.[1] There was a strange person there called Lady Rosemary Bruce – a warning to one not to belong to the nobility. We are going again next Saturday. Very jolly for Eek going to Switzerland. Blunt says Switzerland is very beautiful in parts but not as much as the Downs.[2] I can quite believe it. But Eek does not go to look at things, does she? Only to eat and drink and perspire on the perpendicular. Still it is only proper to return to the primitive after Schools.

Bathing has not as yet begun but I hope it will today. That reminds me – I am not sure whether you sent Mr. G. my bathing leave. To make sure you had better write something at the end of your next letter saying you wish me to bathe.

I wrote a letter to Daddie all about architecture. Thank Aunt Eva very much for the cutting she sent me. Yes; the polyanther flourished. We have been having some rhododendrons of late to adorn the room. At present we have rhododendrons, may and buttercups. Blunt got some gorgeous azaleas out in the Forest but they are over now. The rhododendrons grow out on the downs by a copse – also some broom & of course lots of gorse –

[letter incomplete]

1 – A. J. Bennitt (1907–61), educ. MC 1921–6, Clare College, Cambridge. HO 1930.
2 – Anthony Frederick Blunt (1907–83), art historian and spy. Educ. MC 1921–6, Trinity College, Cambridge. Member of Cambridge Apostles; Fellow of Trinity 1932–7. Art critic for *Spectator* 1933–8. Appointed director of Courtauld Institute 1947 and Professor of History of Art, University of London. Knighted 1956; Légion d'honneur 1958. Retd 1974 and five years later stripped of his knighthood and his honorary fellowship at Trinity after Prime Minister Margaret Thatcher revealed to the House of Commons that he had been a spy. Author of *Artistic Theory in Italy, 1450–1600* (1940), *Art and Architecture in France, 1500–1700* (1953) and *Poussin* (1967). FLM and he were close friends at MC, and FLM later wrote: 'In my own house the dominant intellectual was Anthony Blunt, who had a precocious knowledge of art and an habitual contempt for conservative authorities' (*SAF*, 95). AB recalled: 'my closest friend and the strongest and most important figure in the school at that time was [FLM], who was already a person of extraordinary vivacity, imaginative force, brilliance and charm' ('From Bloomsbury to Marxism', *Studio International*, Nov. 1973, 164). Cf. 'Auden and MacNeice: Their Last Will and Testament': 'Item I leave my old friend Anthony Blunt / A copy of Marx and £1000 a year / And the picture of Love Locked Out by Holman Hunt' (*LI*, CP07, 739). He is Hilary in *AS*.

TO *Georgina Beatrice MacNeice*   MS Dan MacNeice

29 June [1924]   Marlborough

My dear Madre,

I hope you will excuse my not having written lately on taking into consideration the festivities and general turmoil of this week, which included the commencement of bathing, a visit to Mrs. Wasey, a horrible House Squad competition, Prize Day and the Day After.

First I will tell you the tale of Mrs. Wasey. Ross and Shepard and I arrived there about 3.35 on Tuesday and played a set immediately – two sets rather, with a captain from Boughey's by name Drummond Hay, who arrived with his people in a car and was not changed.[1] Then I sat out, ie. played croquet on a very sporting course of their's – up hill and down dale and over flower-beds. Thereafter we had tea, which was really good and finished up with the strawberries and cream, the acme of delight. After some more sets and having lost a ball (infandum) we had two glasses of lemonade each and returned home, reaching Gates at 7.10, ie. 10 minutes after our leave permitted.

On Thursday I went to Sixth Bathing and invented a new way of swimming, very indolent but rather liable to discomfort when someone else splashes the water. To describe it – you lie on your back hunched up with your knees near your face, and only your toes and a small portion of your visage round about your nose, showing above the water; then you push your hands gently forward palms foremost and so progress backwards, not moving your legs at all.

Friday being Prize Day, we had to wear stiff collars. Early School was the only period. At Prize Giving in the afternoon I was presented with sham prizes, my real ones being at home. I think that part of the proceedings was rather a farce. The Master's speech was as humorous and Upper School as hot as usual. On being released Ross and Hamilton and I did what was quite unique and played tennis.[2] Unfortunately we had to change back again for Evening Chapel and ices in Hall, after which we played more tennis till it became too dark. On Thursday, I forgot to say, the 'Marlburian' and a second number of the 'Heretick' came out. As for the last named, boys in Newman's of the ultra-athletic non-anything else creed,

---

1–J. W. E. Drummond-Hay (b.1906), educ. MC 1919–24.
2–James Alexander Stewart ('Alistair') Hamilton (b.1908), educ. MC 1921–6 and Trinity College, Oxford. Formerly a pupil at Clifton College (1918–21), Hamilton joined the Anonymous Society at MC and was a friend of FLM's at Oxford (*SAF*, 267, 270).

stole the proofs and altering passages in an absurd fashion, sent them down to the printer so causing some trouble.[1]

'Anent' the ices they had as concomitant abundant and excellent cake, of which I managed four slices. We are hoping to have the remains of it today.

Yesterday evening we saw the 'Mikado' in the gym; it was far and away the best performance I have seen here, Turner being especially good. We got out roundabout 11.0 p.m.

A man called Phelips preached in Chapel today. He is an O.M.[2]

I shall certainly have early dips in Donegal if the shore outside the house is not too stony.[3] I hope Eek will too, but I have my doubts.

Shepard has now got a wonderful syphon, which makes any liquid you put into it full of carbon dioxide so that it 'fizzes' furiously. Ross holds the opinion that it is bad for you but so far it has not had any serious effects on me. That reminds me that I have long been intending to dispel the illusion that seems to have gotten hold on you, that absence of a letter implies that I am ill. The case is really quite the contrary. As soon as I become ill you will be plagued with communications, you may be assured.

The College rose to the occasion at Hall today and swamped us with cake. Ross and I had five and a half slices each. The result is my brain is too crushed to continue this letter any further, for which many apologies and much love, <u>Freddie</u>.

1 – *The Heretick* was an alternative school magazine, planned, in the words of Blunt, 'to express our disapproval of the Establishment generally, of the more out-of-date and pedantic masters' ('From Bloomsbury to Marxism', 164). JH remembered the cover tauntingly featured an image of 'a lumpish hockey player being inveigled by fauns and the motto "Upon Philistia will I Triumph"' (*SAF*, App. B, 242).
2 – Rev. Arthur Henry Phelips (1875–1960), educ. MC 1889–93; Hertford College, Oxford; HO 1899; successively vicar of Wythall, Pershore, Dudley and Wimbledon; honorary canon of Worcester and canon of Pershore. M. (1958) Phyllis Andrews.
3 – During July the MacNeice family took a holiday at Ballymore, nr Dunfanaghy, Co. Donegal (see next letter).

TO *Fortescue Eric Vesey Ross*[1]   MS Dan MacNeice

July [1924]   Farragh, Ballymore, Donegal

My very esteemed Ross,

(it being always best to begin with business), I have been given a teaset (consisting of a milkjug, a cake-plate 6 cups & saucers & 6 plates matching) and so a superabundance of crockery seems imminent. It is journeying in company with a library in an immense box (the pristine concomitant of my travels) which happens to be keyless. (N.B. you will stand by when it arrives to help in heaving it upstairs.)

Secondly anent our coming to this place:- On Monday about 9.45 we left home in the car – we being five persons including Harry and a lot of bags, boxes and loose appurtenances (e.g. a kitten).[2] When we had gone a mile along the Belfast road we smelt a smell of awful import and found the break [*sic*] was on fire. (That was because my sister had forgotten to take it off and it had been braking all the way.) When it had recovered under the refrigerating influence of oil we took up the thread of our journey and went on without any more interesting interruptions till lunch time, when the kitten ate several meat sandwiches and followed us about the road. After that we got upon a road like the worst ones in Pilgrims' Progress – full of gins and snares and broken down bridges. The first broken down bridge was a mass of stones and rubble about 4 ft wide with a deep black boghole on one side, whence a black stream flowed under.

It was moreover tilted at an appreciable angle. Here we all got out even unto the kitten while Harry steered the car across (though it did its best not to come, slipping back etc). On arriving at Omagh we disposed of the kitten. Just before Lifford we crossed the Border and had an interview with a Customs official, a pleasant and unofficious person.

On getting to Ballymore, which is a vague quantity, we found great difficulty in finding Farragh (our house) It is reached by a long lane – hilly, muddy, in parts under water, and full of fearful turns. It faces a little bay (a bit of Sheephaven) and behind it the ground ascends so you seem fairly well shut off from people in general, excepting the neighbouring habitations.

Farragh is not a proper cottage at all. It has an upstairs, a slate roof and a drawing room and a dining-room apart from the kitchen. A redeeming

---

1 – See FLM to GBM, 6 May 1923, n. 2, p. 79.
2 – Harry: the family chauffeur.

attribute is its lack of a bathroom. There is one round flat thing to wash in to be handed round among the inhabitants.

[no signature]

TO *Georgina Beatrice MacNeice*   MS Dan MacNeice

24 November [1924]   Marlborough

My dear Madre

My epistolary idleness is pricking my conscience and driving my pen on an apologetic course. (Yet I wrote a letter to Eek a fortnight ago which is my ultima Thule, last word and X.Y.Z. in letter-writing, so my lapse is that I was so overcome by writing two letters on one Sunday that on the next I had to write more to keep the average right.)

Anent that suit I have inquired at Russel's (Head's being full) and learned the rough facts of the case. The price sounds pretty stupendous (but you will be able to judge) – about 6 guineas. They gave me two samples which I am sending you. If you thought good, I daresay I could beat the price down a bit. This would probably be easier at Head's, Head being at times rather lenient, I believe.

Ross and I had a fire in a frying pan the other day. (It sounds rather like a storm in a teacup.) We were frying bread in margarine and the latter suddenly blazed up with a roar. The atmosphere in the study was almost asphyxiating for a couple of hours afterwards.

Otherwise we have had a mild and pleasant time lately. I have to write an account for the Marlburian of a miniature concert (wholly by boys) lately given in the Bradleian! I am going to consult a musician on the subject. The songs are not so bad but the pianoforte solos, string quartettes and the like are quite beyond me.

I have on my table a collection of exports from the homecountry – the ink-pot bear, the elephant, the 'Ould Ireland's Native Shamrock' inkpot, photos of Grin and Astragalus (and incidentally YOU in the latter). On the wall I have an inspiring picture – all my own work – of a turreted palace – red and yellow and white – under a yellow moon in a deep blue sky.[1] It is a little unsymmetrical, but the colours are cheering.

1 – See JH's remark about MacNeice's paintings, in 1925, that he 'turns out about one a day' (*SAF*, 246). Cf. Katherine Firth, 'Five Adolescent Paintings by Louis F. MacNeice', *Notes and Queries* 55.4, Dec 2008, 514–15.

Last Friday week I went to an Anonymous Society paper on Egyptian Art. I am going to produce one myself (Me miserum) near the end of the term on 'Northern Fairy Tales & Sagas' (or something to that effect).[1]

On last Thursday Blunt and I walked (in flannels) to Barbury Camp and were not back till 6.15 in starless darkness. Barbury Camp is a Roman structure, circular with a fine, double vallum and splendidly placed. King Athelstan (?) fought a decisive battle near it as his headquarters against the Danes.[2]

This letter though not long is 2 times longer than last week's so I think it should do – Much Love,

Frederick L.

TO *Georgina Beatrice MacNeice*   MS Dan MacNeice

2 December [1924]   Marlborough

My dear Madre,

Thanks awfully for the magnificent microcosm of confectionery. We have been feeding on it hard today. It is our cornucopia. I am feeling fairly pleased with life at present – housematch yesterday, and one tomorrow, a game for ourselves today and abundance of victuals. A boy read a paper to the Literary Society the other day on Wordsworth; mine to the Anonymous Soc. has been postponed till next term so you can help me to compose it in the holidays. For private reading I am doing the 'Ion' (Plato) on the subject of poetry. The main argument (so far) is that poets are out of their wits or inspired when in the act of composing. It solves a lot of problems, I think.

It is now 9.5. We have been having fried bread. We no longer turn the flame up to the full and so avoid a conflagration. We also had a 'lady-cake' today.

My table is crowded with old and dusty tomes anent Iceland, Teutonic Tales, Burnt Njal, Mythology of the Aryan Nations etc. They emanate a pleasant though musty atmosphere of erudition. They are propped up on one side by the big Liddell and Scott and on the other by the elephant, representing the West and East, or intellect and muscle, if you prefer it.

---

1 – Anthony Blunt formed the Anonymous Society with the support of Clifford Canning: 'so called because the art master, whose outlook was different, objected to its being called the Arts Society' (*SAF*, 242). FLM claims he read a paper on Norse Mythology to Anthony Blunt's society in autumn 1924 (*SAF*, 95).

2 – Barbury Camp is about five miles northwest of Marlborough.

Rain has come at last in plenty. It has set my watch going, which had temporarily stopped. It is a temperamental watch and subject to moods.

Next holidays I am going to make a systematic exploration of all second-hand bookshops in the neighbourhood. On the way home, too, I must drop in to the Old Curiosity Shop man at Birmingham, if I can find my way thither.

|| Morpheus calls me, so ||
Much love
and thanks
from one who is
smothered in a
deluge of cakes*
Frederick L.

*(I couldn't find the long adjective.)

TO *Georgina Beatrice MacNeice*   MS Dan MacNeice

[22 March 1925]   Marlborough

My dear Madre,

I shall arrive home in all probability on Tuesday week. You will find out all about it from what the College send you. Not that there is much to find. I am feeling a yearning for a second-hand bookshop and shall stop in Birmingham for that purpose, I expect. Coming here I picked up a splendid little book in Birmingham – 'History of the Seven Champions of Christendom. From Harris's Juvenile Library at the Corner of St. Paul's Church Yard, London' and on the back cover 'This, and every useful and entertaining publication for Young Minds, printed for J. Harris, may be had at the principal booksellers and toy-warehouses in the WORLD.'[1]

Date 1804. A jolly frontispiece showing St George finding his two Moorish servants methodically and neatly torn to pieces by two Lions.

The whole thing is a masterpiece. The Young Minds must have loved it. Every incident however appalling is described in such a majestic and superior manner. E.g. when St. Dennis of France on eating of a mulberry tree was transformed into a stag 'This strange metamorphosis filled him with great anxiety . . . But, whilst he was musing on this surprising event . . .'

The narrative never loses control; it sees everything with the eye of a mathematician and records it in its own charming and aristocratic jargon. It never misses the chance of shoving in an epithet, generally an otiose one. A hermit addresses St. George whom he meets by the wayside with a pretty, impromptu piece of journalese, e.g. 'To elude this tremendous scourge, parents have hitherto sacrificed their darling children, and brothers have yielded up their beloved sisters with pangs of unutterable anguish, but now the insatiable monster has devoured all the virgins of Egypt, except the king's daughter, and even she is to be sacrificed to the fiery dragon tomorrow. Under these desperate circumstances, the king has made

1 – *History of the Seven Champions of Christendom* by Richard Johnson (1573–1659?), new edn, 'carefully revised and corrected' (1804).

proclamation, that if any valiant knight will undertake to combat with the fiery dragon and kill him, his bravery shall not only be publicly acknowledged, but he shall also receive the princess royal in marriage, and shall be invested, on the present king's decease, with the sovereignty of Egypt.

St. George listened attentively to this affecting story . . .'

The poor hermit must have become hoarse. The whole book sustains this standard: it is very entertaining.

We had Shepard to tea the other day & had scrambled eggs and chocolate roll. Three daffodils which we dug up in the West Woods are just out. It is our intent always to have some flowers now to make up for having no sun. I have read fairly lately a most terrible book, 'Jude the Obscure'.[1] Has Eek read it?

> Much love to all.
> Hoping to see
> You soon
> F.
> L.

TO *John Frederick MacNeice*   MS Dan MacNeice

3 June [1925]   Marlborough

My dear Daddie,

I am awfully glad to hear you are going on a sea-trip. It should be very warm down there now, I imagine. I only wish I could get on the sea a bit. Not that this place is not very beautiful – in parts – this term. I have gone a few long bicycle rides and found one superbly situated village called Aldbourne with a very fine church.[2] Some day I am going to Malmesbury to see the Abbey, where there are some wonderful Saxon sculptures.[3] We are to have a whole-holiday on June 17th as a reward for having got 29 scholarships and exhibitions.[4] Yesterday I went to Mrs. Wasey for the first time this term; she was in very good form.

---

1 – By Thomas Hardy (1895).
2 – Church of St Michael, Aldbourne, recorded in Domesday Book and restored in the 1860s.
3 – Malmesbury, a twelfth-century abbey in Wiltshire, on the site of a seventh-century monastery. John Hilton had an uncle living in Malmesbury.
4 – Specifically, scholarships to Oxford and Cambridge colleges.

The opening of the Hall last Saturday week was, I thought, a little dull, but we had a very good concert in the evening.[1] At the actual opening the school was all crowded into the ambulatory at the back where it stood throughout the proceedings. The other day I visited a colony of wild rhododendrons by a copse on the downs and brought back some of their flowers and some broom for the study.

At one little church we visited this term we found an owl nesting in the belfry with four eggs.

She flew out of the window as we came in. We hope to go there again soon to see the owlets.

In several of the churches round here there is a peculiar and rather attractive sort of arch. It is half-way between Norman and Gothic – almost flat at the top, with working only on the inside which is broad and flat – e.g.

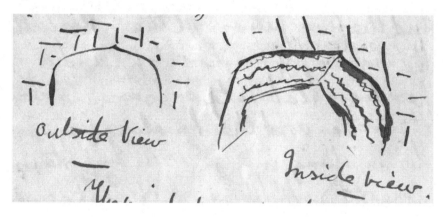

The inside view is out of perspective but it is only to show you how the 3 lines of ornament run down the inside of the arch.

In the church at Aldborne [sic] there are some very interesting monuments, one long slab with a figure of a monk on it of the fifteenth century, I think, several old brasses and two Elizabethan monuments. I now realise that there was a definite style in Elizabethan monuments for these two are very like the Chichester memorial at home on a smaller

1 – Memorial Hall, designed by William Newton FRIBA (OM), who won a competition between Old Marlburian architects for best design. Dedicated to the memory of the 749 OMs who fell in the Great War – with 'Remember' in scarlet letters on the lintel – the Hall was opened by the Duke of Connaught on 23 May 1925. Cf. 'Marlborough Memorial Hall' and 'Marlborough War Memorial', *The Times*, 11 and 23 May 1925.

scale.[1] There are the two round arches in the middle, and the two pillars at the sides with the narrow pyramids on top, and a peculiar elaborate excrescence above the arches and the kneeling figures diminishing in size as in importance. One of the Aldborne ones has also the coat of arms up above. The other is painted the most atrocious colours but has a special attraction for me because of the two brothers in the arches. Of these one reached the eighties and the other the nineties and their figures are very fat and impressive and one has a beautiful Assyrian beard.

My letter seems to have become very architectural, or perhaps, to speak more truly, archaeological. I must write an hortative address to Eek soon as I believe her Schools are at the end of the month. As for me I am reading for the higher Certificate some books of Tacitus about Vitellius and Vespasian and also the 'Oedipus at Colonus'. I had read part of this latter before, but like it better now, though I imagine one cannot fully appreciate Sophocles till one is a good deal older. Besides he was so old himself when he wrote this play – eighty-something.

I hope Willie's back is better. I suppose he enjoys this warm weather. As a matter of fact it only began with us yesterday.

Thanks awfully for your letter. I am glad Miss Higgin is taking the kitten.

Hoping you will have a splendid time –

Much love
Fred<u>die L.</u>

TO *Georgina Beatrice MacNeice*   MS Dan MacNeice

3 July [1925]   Marlborough

My dear Madre,

I am sorry this letter is a little late but I have been thinking out a question which is really rather important, though superficially trivial. I have just read a life of the painter Van Gogh, which makes it seem almost absurd but when I return to cold calculation I remember that I am not a Van Gogh and that conventions must be complied with.[2] The public schools are a mass of conventions, most of which are local and ephemeral. One that is, I am afraid, rather more lasting is that which concerns dress. In the term-time

1–Marble and alabaster burial vault of the Chichester family (1614), St Nicholas's Church, Carrickfergus. Cf. FLM's poem 'Carrickfergus' in *The Earth Compels* (EC), CP07, 55.
2–Possibly *The Tragic Life of Vincent van Gogh* by Louis Piérard, trans. Herbert Garland (1925).

provided one shows a modicum of tidiness, it does not really matter very much, but it is in the holidays (foolishly enough) that the public schools desire that one shall seem moderately well-dressed. By 'well-dressed' it means that one should have one suit which fits properly, i.e. which is tailor-made. Well, this has never really affected me, as living in Ireland I have every holidays regularly, practically escaped from the public schools and only returned to their sphere on the first day of each term. But henceforward my escape will be less and less sure for these reasons.[1] Next term I shall probably be a captain and captains are more bound by this law than anyone else while more subject to curious eyes; if one does not appear on public occasions in a tailor-made suit, one is regarded by the less reasonable half of the community as a half-wit and by the more reasonable half as an object of pity, which is still worse – and in either case where is one's authority? Of course, one can escape this if one can only manage never to appear on public occasions. This I have so far done more or less successfully as my only 'public occasions' have been departing and arriving. Departing I have gone a day early and escaped with speed while everyone else is in school and arriving I have arrived late at night and got into bed with such alacrity that I have escaped notice. But even this is very difficult and a great strain and this term it will be quite impossible as after Camp most of us, including myself, will return to Marlborough before going home. Not only this but, supposing anyone ever asks me to stay with them, which in the case of Ross or Blunt or Shepard is quite possible, I shall of necessity refuse. But, worst of all, next term, I presume, I shall go up to Oxford for the best part of a week for a scholarship exam. For these exams one always goes in one's holiday suits and where am I then? For noone could pretend that my brown suit serviceable as it is, fits me very well. Besides the trousers are now almost too short for me. Nor would I dare to go through London going home, for London on such days (as I know from experience) is thronged with Marlburians. And if Mr. Guillebaud ever proposed to take me (as the senior classical boy in house, which I shall be next term) to a Greek play at Oxford or anything of the sort I should either refuse or go with misery. Lastly, if as I understand, we are going to spend next holidays in Scotland, especially if in Edinburgh, it

1 – 'During term we wore uniform black but at the end of term we were allowed to wear ordinary suits to go home in. At the end of term accordingly everyone was jealously competitive and those boys were despised whose clothes were not well cut. As for the boys who went home in their school clothes – of whom I was one, for I was ashamed to ask my family for a decent suit – they were almost pariahs' (*SAF*, 81).

is more than probable we shall meet a Marlburian. Such a meeting, or indeed the expectation of one, will keep me in a constant state of suspense.

Now I come to my practical proposal. I feel that it is rather awful, after letting you get me my brown suit at Christmas now to come and demand of you another suit of nearly twice the price. Having thought of any other source of money I have finally decided that you are the only one; but realising that six guineas is an immense price and that you are probably at the moment spending a fair sum on Eek (going to Switzerland) not to speak of Willie, my proposal is this. Do not this year give me any birthday or Christmas presents. We will say that that amounts to £2 of the sum. I do not suppose that you have any money put down to my name anywhere or anyhow though if you have, I should advise using that. If not I find I am still £4 to the bad. This I am afraid, I cannot account for; I could make the rather far-fetched suggestion that having won a prize worth £4 last term to be spent entirely on books, and my property going up £4 off my own bat, so to speak, £4 from you would return me to my former condition. But that is a quibble. That, however, £4 will not be wasted, I think I can freely assert. For apart from the intrinsic value of the suit it will enable me to move freely about on holiday occasions and remove a great deal of discomfort. I admit I am weak to bow to the dictates of fashion but who is not? Even the car at home is due to the same impulse (for equally good engines are obtainable with less beautiful bodies). I can only deduce the worth of money by the comparative method; if it is worth spending £3–10 on learning to drive a car, which I could have learned nearly as well as [sic] home, is it not worth spending £4 (accounting rather presumptuously for the rest in accordance with my suggestion) on something which will be much more used by me, which will be much more use to me and as well as giving pleasure will remove discomfort.

I know it seems absurd to spend more trouble or money than necessary on the dress of such an one as myself, yet I would suggest that I am not usually extravagant with clothes and that I might easily, I imagine, have caused greater additional expenditure while I have been here than I now ask.

Hoping you will not be very annoyed I ask you please to comply with this, silly and surprising and petty though it appear, for otherwise I shall have continually to engage in a course of slinking elusion and avoidance of any kind. A new suit adequately made would last me for at least two years and the brown will be very serviceable as a second best. I might even use the coat instead of a sports coat (it would do very well) and that would cut off another £2 or so for I believe you were intending to get me a sports coat. And the brown trousers if worn often would save grey flannel trousers.

Horrible letter this is! It has frightened me very much to write it but it is better to try one's luck than to continue groping in discontentment.

I am afraid there is too much ego in my cosmos. I suppose Daddie is home now and Eek starting for Switzerland. I trust you are all very well. I shall write a respectable letter soon but this has been too overcoming –
Much love, Freddie

TO *John Frederick and Georgina Beatrice MacNeice*
MS Dan MacNeice

Friday [November/December 1925] Marlborough

My dear Daddie & Madre,

Sorry this is written on foolscap. Thanks awfully for the money; though I shall not spend it all, I think.

I shall be in Oxford till at least Thursday night, as there are 6 papers at least, & not more than 2 papers a day.

I have no need of clothing as I have not yet used up my resources. Everything is covered with snow.

Mr. Head, I am afraid, does not do things like that but we can consider it with due attention at the beginning of the holidays.

I am looking forward to seeing Oxford: I hear there is a Tintoretto on the altarpiece of Merton chapel which is not a Tintoretto, if one looks at it long enough.[1]

I suppose Eek will leave Oxford before I do, but as there are some other people with me I shall not be forlorn.
Much love
F. Louis M.

1 – Behind the altar in Merton chapel there is indeed a Crucifixion of the Venetian school, which was wrongly attributed to Tintoretto (Rev. Dr Simon Jones, private correspondence, 2007).

1926

24 January [1926]   Marlborough

My dear Madre,

I am here safely after a very interesting experience all due to the absurd arrangement of trains at Birmingham. There are two trains leaving the same platform both for Cheltenham – one at 5.28 P.M. and one at 5.35. Rushing down at 5.30 I saw a train leaving the station and leaped in. Later I discovered that it took an hour longer than the later train to reach Cheltenham. I reached Cheltenham at 7.30. The train for Marlboro' had left at 7.10. The porter said I could get a connection at Gloucester. I went on. There was no connection. I returned and spent the night in a Cheltenham waiting room with a good fire and a Shelley.

I arrived at Marlboro' in time for lunch yesterday. Noone minded a scrap.

Did William play my game any more? Knocking things, preferably people, down is one of the primal instincts.

We are thinking of painting frescoes in our study. Blunt has brought back some cheese (Norwegian). Cheese after all is one of the primal virtues.

I picked up some Serbian fairy tales in Birmingham. They are awfully jolly.

Much love
F. Louis M.

TO *John Frederick and Georgina Beatrice MacNeice*

MS Dan MacNeice

[After 25 January 1926]   Marlborough

My dear Daddie and Madre,

I am very sorry you have been so worried about my adventure. After all it WAS rather a record. I expect noone else has ever read the Prometheus Unbound at midnight in a station waiting room.[1]

Talking of the Master, we were discussing him with Dr. Ivimey in Hall, who said he thought the Master's chief characteristic was aversion to rules. The Master apparently said 'Make a rule and you invite people to break it' which is very true.

It is great fun this term. I am going for private tuition (Homer) to Mr. Brown, the trains and chocolate maniac. He used to be a Fellow somewhere. His classroom is hung with Railway Posters.[2]

Yesterday I went for a ghastly sweat. Just when we were out on the open downs a hail-storm came on.[3]

Tomorrow night Mr. Hughes will read his paper on Art to the Anonymous society.[4] Mr. Gidney is coming, so it will be very tense.[5]

Last night we had a perfervid meal with two youths – porridge, Kraft cheese and coffee. Bagallay [*sic*] is not living in our study after all. He came to tea today.[6]

In school we are doing Tacitus, Statius and Euripides (Electra). Instead of the master we have Mr. Audemars,[7] a silly man though not bad at classics and quite polite. We have just done a delightful mock poem by

1 – Cf. previous letter. FLM later recalled: '[*Prometheus Unbound*] was one of my sacred books – along with the *Golden Ass* of Apuleius and Dasent's translation of *Burnt Njal* and of course *Morte D'Arthur* – and I felt uplifted, reformist, anarchist, escapist simultaneously, as I listened to the goods trains grunting on their sordid errands and swilled the rhythms of Shelley, the sweet champagne of his wishful thinking and schoolboy anger, his Utopias of amethyst and starlight, and I thought how wonderful to miss one's connections; soon I shall miss them all the time' (*SAF*, 98).
2 – A. C. B. Brown, teacher at MC 1908–42; editor of classical texts. Fellow of St John's College, Oxford. 'On half-holidays he would go by train to Bristol and back for the mere pleasure of train-riding, all the way stuffing himself with chocolates' (*SAF*, 90).
3 – 'I liked it even when it hailed – hard clean hail whipping the throat and the ears and not a bit of shelter within a mile' (*SAF*, 86).
4 – Christopher Wyndham Hughes, Art master at MC 1920–46.
5 – A. R. Gidney, BA, educ. Haileybury and Corpus Christi College, Oxford. Teacher at MC 1907–46.
6 – E. P. B. Baggallay (1907–52), educ. MC 1920–6; Brasenose College, Oxford.
7 – L. F. R. Audemars, MA, teacher at MC 1924–54.

Statius on a parrot. It would go splendidly into Heroic Couplets. I must try that some day.

Blunt has brought back some really interesting new books – in particular two large ones on Negro Sculpture and Byzantine Art.[1] I have never seen anything like the negro things. As Blunt says, their artists think in three dimensions.

By the way (excuse irrelevance) à propos of dimensions Blunt thinks that he, in his scholarship, was first only in alphabetical order. The four-dimensional boy, of whom I have told you, who lives at Marlborough and is a genius, beat him. So, at least, Blunt says. The top of our form failed to get a scholarship at New College. For all that people are, as usual, thrilled about our scholarships. An article in one paper, written by a man who had collected statistics, says 'Marlborough is not a public school, it is a miracle.' I should not say so much myself, yet I think it is less cruel to people with minds than any other public school. There is so little cramming. Harrow did not raise one scholarship. We have now over twenty. The Master will have a hard job at Harrow. As Ivimey says, it is no good trying to make it into a Marlborough.[2]

Blunt has been made a prefect which is a great thing. There are so few prefects with any intelligence. He caused quite a stir at the Sixth meeting on Monday by proposing the 'Apollo' for the Sixth papers.[3] Blackburne the most notable 'Lobber' was furious.[4] That an Art Journal should be taken in by the Sixth seemed to him horrible.

I intend to read the Aeneid through this term, leaving out Bks I, II, III, V & VI, which I have done before. I am now half-way through Bk IV and think it superb. I also propose a course of Ibsen. I must write a paper for the Anonymous but am not yet sure of the subject. With Mr. Gidney we are to read Raleigh's 'Wordsworth'.[5]

Hockey is a distressing game. When I was playing today someone let fly and the ball hit me with considerable force in the front of my neck. Very disturbing.

1 – Probably *Primitive Negro Sculpture* by Paul Guillaume and Thomas Munro (1926) and either *Byzantine Art* by Hayford Peirce and Royall Tyler (1926) or the V&A's *Picture Book of Byzantine Art* (1926).
2 – After nine years at MC, Cyril Norwood became headmaster of Harrow in 1926.
3 – *Apollo: A Journal of the Arts*, edited by R. Sydney Glover, first appeared in Jan. 1925.
4 – K. W. Blackburne, GCMG, GBE (1907–80), educ. MC 1921–6; Clare College, Cambridge. Joined Colonial Service 1930; Governor of the Leeward Isles 1950 and Governor-in-Chief of Jamaica 1957–63. He was presumably the unlikely 'tone-deaf' author of the pop parody 'Yes, we are aesthetic', to whom John Hilton refers in *SAF*, App. B, 244.
5 – Walter Raleigh, *Wordsworth* (1903).

The weather here is horrid but quite warm. Whatever you do, do not send me any more vests! The ones I have are mainly an additional incumbrance in getting up.

Spencer has just been showing me how to make paper boats. I think we must get a fleet and sail them down Treacle Bolly – a reminiscence of early romance.

I hope you all flourish. Give William my love. We found a strange cat in our study today. Blunt was horrified.

And do not imagine me at a loose end here for I am very far from it – besides converse with people like Mr. Sargeant [*sic*] is so edifying.[1]

Much love, F. Louis M.

TO *Georgina Beatrice MacNeice*   MS Dan MacNeice

14 March [1926]   Marlborough

My dear Madre

I am glad you enjoyed your time here. I see Archdeacon Brett is down here today (Confirmation Sunday). Yesterday was gorgeously vernal. I & Hamilton went to tea with Sargeant. Sargeant was anxious to know if people in Ireland really spoke like the characters in the Playboy of the Western World. He thought 'their' languages very fine and imaginative.

I wrote a 'poem' to the arch-Philistine here yesterday and someone rashly delivered it. It began 'O infinitesimal Calculus' and was all but unintelligible but the recipient managed to find a great number of veiled insults in it which I had never thought of![2]

The other evening we went down to Canning's and read a miscellany of fairy stories.

---

1 – George Montague Sargeaunt, MA (1883–1934), educ. Shrewsbury and Gonville and Caius College, Cambridge. Teacher at MC 1914–34; OTC 1914–18. Author of *Classical Studies* (1929), *The Classical Spirit* (1936). 'He was aloof and austerely Olympian, had a private religion of his own founded on ancient Stoicism. He had once been a housemaster but had resigned because he refused to give religious instruction to the boys in his house who were about to be confirmed' (*SAF*, 91). Another former pupil and obituarist wrote: 'Few have the opportunity of being taught by such a one before they reach Oxford or Cambridge. He had that unconcealable feeling for scholarship which can transform a boy's mind. Without it the mere aggregation of knowledge earned no praise from him' (obituary, *The Times*, 9 Nov. 1934, 19).
2 – Cf. 'Auden and MacNeice: Their Last Will and Testament': 'Item to J. R. Hilton a Work of Art / And a dream of the infinitesimal calculus / Bolstered on apples in an apple-cart' (*LI*, CP07, 740).

I bought a beautiful slice of cheese the other day – orange and red – not that it tasted very good. Blunt has been painting a still life. Hoping you are all well

Much love

F. Louis MacNeice

TO *Georgina Beatrice MacNeice* MS Dan MacNeice

Sunday [Easter term 1926]   Marlborough

My dear Madre,

Mr. Turner has been appointed master – a remarkably good though unexpected choice. He had already refused Clifton. He will be very successful, I imagine, being cultured, attractive, tactful and strict. He is very short – considerably shorter than myself – but also very good-looking. He is only about 35, which is very young for a head-master. Not being married he will be somewhat desolate in the Lodge. He was Senior Prefect here. He is the first O.M. and also the first assistant Master (that is direct) to be made Master. Colonel Wall was lamenting to us in school that he had never beaten him when he was in his house.[1]

Mr. and Mrs. Canning came to tea last Tuesday. I was all but late, being lost in the mist on the downs.

Tuesday.

I have just got your letter. It is very strange that you did not receive my last one. It was quite a good one too, I think.

Yes I should like you to come down here, but it would be best for the day, I think, this term. The only advantage, otherwise, would be breakfast. All the morning is occupied, and you would have to be indoors most of the time.

The steeplechase is tomorrow fortnight. The week-end before that we are arranging the print exhibition. Mr. Canning is very thrilled over it.

I hope your holiday is a success. It will be a great relief, I imagine, escaping from William's voice for a little.

The weather here is moderately bad but not excruciating. I am now going to get on with a thesis I am writing – I am at the moment dealing with ballad poetry.

---

1 – Arthur Henry Wall, MA (d.1944), educ. Trinity College, Cambridge. Teacher at MC 1896–1930. Commander OTC 1907–19, Lt. Col., TD, Home Despatches twice. Author of *A Concise French Grammar* and *A French Primer* (both 1901).

Mr. Fry is unable to come down to lecture on Art this term, but we are having an exhibition of prints in about a fortnight's time.[1] A large print arrived the other day, which Blunt has bought for himself – a garden by Van Gogh, with flower-beds radiating from a rich blue pond, two great trees swirling up out of the picture on either side, and a sort of verandah on the right with yellow arches and a cool shade within.[2]

Quite a sensation has been caused here by another picture by the same man reproduced in the February 'Apollo' – equally dynamic – of a cypress tree and layers of ground swirling down to the left, with a bright chaotic band of corn in the fore-ground.[3] Several unexpected people have admired it very much, have even ordered copies of the 'Apollo'; several others have fumed over it, muttering 'treacle-tart' etc.

On Monday week we had a debate 'That the Victorians were greater than ourselves' which I (you will be surprised and, I expect, pleased to hear) proposed. The attendance was very bad and the speeches worse but we won, surprisingly enough, by 19 votes to 15 or 16.

The opposition were particularly futile, the sum of their arguments being that as the Victorians flourished in 1870 and not in 1925, therefore they were inferior to ourselves. The stuffed humming birds etc. brought some relief but on the whole it was a very poor debate.

I must now write so much love,

F. Louis M.
[*flourish*]

TO *Georgina Beatrice MacNeice*   MS Dan MacNeice

Sunday ? [*sic*] [13 May 1926]   Marlborough

My dear Madre,

I have not written for a shocking time and lots of things have happened. Firstly, this is a very bad business about Camp. I am, you see, already

---

1 – Roger Fry (1866–1934), critic and painter, who was influential on FLM and his circle. Cf. 'what we really hoped for was "experience". Pater once more, but backed up by Roger Fry' (*SAF*, 234). AB recalls 'we were inspired by the writings of Roger Fry and Clive Bell' ('From Bloomsbury to Marxism', 165).
2 – *Le Jardin de la Maison de Santé a Arles* (1889).
3 – *Landscape with Cypress Trees* (1889), reproduced in *Apollo* 3, 14 Feb. 1926, opposite p. 94. FLM would have read the accompanying article by J. B. Manson, who wrote of Van Gogh: 'Vitality is the first essential of a work of art, and no picture in existence – not excepting El Greco's – possesses more of that quality than his 'Landscape with Cypress Trees' – a picture which has almost more vitality than life itself' ('The Courtauld Collection', 95).

enmeshed[.] If I have to go, however, I think you can still leap off quite unfettered, as, if it is anywhither in the British Isles I can come to you direct. This might even be better than going home first. I am also a little more reconciled to camp as it is a certain prolongation of the Term and my last chance of communing with all these frightful people.

Secondly the American (Mr. Waring) is a charming man.[1] We have had several meals with him. He has prophesied journalism for both Blunt and me.

Did I tell you we had a reading of vernal poetry at the Cannings'? Since then we have had an evening of modern music (illustrated by Dr. Goard[2]), and on Tuesday Waring is to read a paper – on Sentimentality.

On Wednesday (the Whole Holiday) I went to Bath and got a Pickering (miniature edition of Catullus, Tibullus, Propertius – marvellous print). It was a wet afternoon: we visited the Roman baths & Anthony was profoundly bored

We have been once to Mrs. Wasey's. Fine afternoon. Most of the term has been wet. Bathing has not yet started. I am writing a series of articles on Marlborough in the Marlburian. The first one was on A. House.[3]

I have heard from Shepard. He is learning French at Tours – sounds a dull place.

Oh – at the vernal evening Dr. Goard scored rather a coup by reading a passage from Dante, giving, as he said, a certain aspect of spring. It sounded all very charming – roses, roses all the way – but when we asked for a translation – hail, snow, the ground emitting a putrid smell and the cries of the damned (from the Inferno). He also recited a vernal verse from the Fascist anthem.

Anthony is getting up another exhibition of Prints – and some originals (with luck) – the last nail in poor Hughes' coffin. He (Anthony) has written an article 'De Cubismo' for the Marlburian declaring the point of modern art.

1 – J. F. Waring (1902–72), educ. Yale (BA 1923) and Cambridge. After teaching at MC he moved to the Salisbury School, Salisbury, CT, and taught for many years at Western Reserve Academy, Hudson, OH. John Hilton recalled: 'The Principles of Literary Criticism [I. A. Richards] probably came in with a delightful American master, temporarily attached for our last term, J. Frederick Waring (what's become of him?)' (SAF, App. B, 244).

2 – Arthur Kenneth Goard, MA, PhD, educ. Exeter School and Trinity College, Cambridge. Lieutenant RGA 1916–18. Science master at MC 1925–52. Author of Five Years of Cambridge Music (1924) and of Chemistry textbooks.

3 – FLM contributed four items to the 26 May 1926 issue of the Marlburian: 'Gardener Melancholy', 'Moon-fishery: A Dialogue', 'Apollo on the Old Bath Road I' and 'Miss Ambergris and King Perhaps'.

My word – I have been writing badly! (A boy from the Prep. has got the top Foundation Scholarship – very brilliant for the Prep.)

I hear from White[1] that Daddie made a stupendous speech at the Synod. White I have decided is really very nice – with a very developed sense of humour. He made a brilliant speech at the Debating Society the other night. I merely recited a home-made Limerick which fell flat. We have had lots of azaleas in study lately but have just got rid of them. Now only have some rhododendrons.

I have gone in for three prizes; don't expect to get any of them. It is very trying. I wore my home-made tie on the Whole Holiday. People were duly impressed.

Mr. Waring thinks we are unjust to Mr. G. There is something in it.

We are going to tea with Alastair (Hamilton) today. Our Christian names have extended somewhat e.g.

Alastair 2 (MacDonald): Basil (Barr): John (Hilton): Guy (Lambert).[2]

Love to ALL

F. Louis MacNeice

TO *Georgina Beatrice MacNeice*   MS Dan MacNeice

Thursday [20 May 1926]   Marlborough

My dear Madre,

Excuse me writing on this.[3] It seems quite some time since I wrote last. I got two of your letters, for which many thanks.

Re kittens, one must be called Old Foss after Mr. Lear's famous cat. The other two might perhaps be called Barocco and Rokoko (Anthony read a paper on these last night.) But cats have little interest in architecture, so perhaps Rodillardus and Chat Botté would be more appropriate – though French is so difficult to pronounce. Other charming names that occur to me are Malinn, Fanfreluche, Cydalise, Poll Troy, Dobbin, Queen Anne, Pactolus, Parthenon, Laidronette, Midas, Oenone, Quangle Wangle (Mr.

1–George Kirkpatrick White (1908–93), educ. MC 1922–7; Balliol College, Oxford (son of Rev. N. J. D. White, Dublin).
2–Alastair MacDonald (1908–95), educ. MC 1921–6; Gonville and Caius College, Cambridge. Later an associate and friend of AB at Cambridge (Carter, 46–7). Basil Barr: see FLM to BB, 12 Jan. 1927, n. 2, p. 143. John Hilton: see FLM to JH, Summer 1926, n. 2, p. 116. Guy Raymond Lambert (b.1907), educ, MC 1921–6; Pembroke College, Cambridge; RA 1930; rose to the rank of Lt. Col.
3–Modest paper from a jotter, lined on one side.

Lear again), Amanda, Passionata and Perhaps. You may select from these – but remember Old Foss.

Mrs. Wasey next Saturday. It was very wet till this week so I have not played any tennis yet. I am writing a prize essay at present on Doric architecture, with the Calton Hill, Edinburgh, for an exordium – that abortive Parthenon that must be the furthest effort of the Greek revival.[1] Revivals are never any good. In Oxford, apparently, the Gothic revival nearly ran into the end of original Gothic, as Oxford went on building in Gothic throughout the centuries.

We had a good meeting last night at the Cannings' – the second this term. The first was a paper on Modern Music by MacDonald[2] when Dr. Goard got worked up and played some Stravinsky, which was very thrilling – Dr. Goard with his pipe in his mouth swaying at the piano and Canning leaping about behind him dementedly with an electric lamp. We nearly ran into Canning bicycling down a precipitous hill the other day – We had been getting wild apple-blossom at Martinsell. As Anthony says, this really is the most beautiful country in the world. You should see the view from Martinsell. There was a cuckoo performing all the time we looked at it.

The study is pretty floral at the moment – tulips, lilac, blue-bells, apple-blossom and narcissi.

If I had been at Oxford this term I should probably have rushed off to Hull to unlade fish. It would have been most amusing. I'm afraid I should not have been competent to drive a lorry – or even a train.[3] I wonder if Best ever got to Paris. Shepard is back from Italy – at home; but he may be going to France. He was running some show, I hear, during the strike. Masters here did night-duty in a canteen for lorry drivers – even Sargeant.

Hoping you all are well, with love to William – Have you been to the Synod yet,

Much love
Louis

1 – Cf. 'Auden and MacNeice: Their Last Will and Testament': '. . . item, the Parthenon / On the Calton Hill to Basil de Selincourt' (*LI*, CP07, 735).
2 – Alastair Macdonald; see previous letter.
3 – A reference to the General Strike of 1926, which involved over two and a half million workers and lasted nine days from 4 May, when workers in printing, transport, iron and steel, gas, electricity and building were called out; on 11 May a second wave of workers went on strike, particularly engineers and shipbuilders. Many miners stayed out for half the year. FLM wrote: 'It was in this summer of 1926 that the English General Strike occurred and was broken. The most publicized blacklegs were the undergraduates of Oxford and Cambridge who regarded the strike as the occasion for a spree' (*SAF*, 101). Cf. AB: 'the general strike in 1926, my last term at school, was treated very largely as a sort of joke' ('From Bloomsbury to Marxism', 166).

TO *Georgina Beatrice MacNeice*   MS Dan MacNeice

Sunday [27 June 1926]   Marlborough

My dear Madre,

You are nearly as bad a correspondent as I am! (Unless of course, my last letter, addressed by Blunt, did not arrive.)

We had a splendid night last week at Canning's – climbed about in the roof-tops and on a great tree over the river – quite mad – and read stories by one Lord Dunsany.[1]

Friday was Prize Day. Today (Commemoration Sunday) Anthony and I to lunch with Hilton and out in his car to see his uncle beyond Malmesbury.

We had to start back very soon after arriving, gulping down a hurried tea. Splendid day, clear sky and the downs.

The last 'Marlburian' caused a sensation – two articles by Anthony and a literary one – in defence of vers libre – by Hilton. I merely continued my series on Marlboro' including our Classroom Captain.[2] He considers it not true to life.

George (the Master) made a very good first speech on Prize Day commending Blunt's propaganda of Modern Art.[3] Guillebaud was enraged. He has been rampant lately – looking forward, however, to next term when he shall have no more 'long-haired aesthetes' and 'intellectual snobbery'.

Waring has gone for good. Very pathetic. He read a good paper on Sentimentality just before leaving. The most broad-minded person I ever met, favouring at the same time the Royal Academy and Picasso, Blunt and Mr. Guillebaud. He has a very attractive mouth. Is going to conduct a public school for plutocrats in U.S.A. (a rotten job).

We sent in some paintings for the School's Prize-Day exhibition. Hughes was furious. He turned [down] nearly all of them after a violent argument with Canning and Mrs. [*sic*]

1 – Edward Plunkett, 18th Baron Dunsany (1878–1957), Anglo-Irish playwright, influenced at an early stage by the 'Celtic Twilight'. Educ. Eton and Sandhurst; Coldstream Guards (Transvaal); captain, 5th Inniskilling Fusiliers 1914–16. Byron Professor of English Literature, University of Athens 1940–1, FRSL, MRIA, Hon DLitt (TCD, 1940). Author of fantasy novels such as *The Gods of Pegana* (1905), *A Book of Wonder* (1912), *The Blessing of Pan* (1927), and other works. His plays proved very popular and were staged at the Abbey Theatre, Dublin, as well as in England and America.

2 – FLM contributed 'Apollo on the Old Bath Road II–V' to the 23 June 1926 issue of the *Marlburian*.

3 – George Turner. See FLM to GBM, Easter term 1926, p. 110, and 24 Sept. 1922, n. 3, p. 71.

There is probably not going to be any Camp. I should like there[fore], possibly, to return through London (staying, perhaps, a night or two with Anthony) to see the new rooms at the Tate.[1] Mrs Blunt who was down here lately, is slightly reconciled to me. I went to lunch with her.

Mrs Wasey was charmed with your letter. We were pigs there. Hot day. Bathing has started.

Much Love
Louis

TO *John Hilton*[2]   MS Bodleian

Summer 1926   Carrickfergus

Good afternoon my Child[.] I have just written to Anthony. No I don't dress respectably with the Curate.[3] Why on earth do you go to dances? Will you run a paper with me at Oxford to be called the Oxford Farrago. It would be a good show with a coloured cover. You could design that.[4] There is a Degas tree behind our house now; & what fun for you in Yorkshire. When I was with the Curate in an hotel I used to play the first line of 'Hark the Herald Angels Sing' repeated ad infinitum on the piano with one finger.[5] Wasn't it clever? But the Curate didn't like it & played bits of Lilac Time.[6] I chased a pig for a mile along the road the other day

1 – On 26 June the King, accompanied by the Queen, opened the Modern Foreign and John Singer Sargent Galleries extension in the new wing of the Tate Gallery (*The Times*, 28 June 1926, 18).

2 – John Robert Hilton (1908–94), educ. MC (1921–6), Corpus Christi College, Oxford and Bartlett School of Architecture, UCL. ARIBA. Director of Antiquities in Cyprus 1934–6, architect 1936–41, captain, Royal Engineers 1941–5; Foreign Office (Istanbul, Athens). Author of memoir on FLM (appended to *SAF*), 1965. His father, Oscar Hildesheim MD, changed the family name to Hilton in 1916. He is Stretton in *AS*. FLM wrote of Hilton: 'He was good at mathematics and endowed with some horse sense but was willing to be seduced into fantasy and took up the child-cult with alacrity' (*SAF*, 99). On the 'child-cult' see FLM to GBM, [May 1927], n. 1, p. 166.

3 – JFM's curate at Carrickfergus in 1923 was apparently Rev. H. Wellington, succeeded by Rev. W. J. Parr (1926–30) (Helen Rankin, private correspondence, 2008). The previous curate at Carrickfergus had been Rev. Bloomer (1918–22).

4 – JH wrote: 'I did a design or two but that was about as far as the Farrago got' (*SAF*, App. B, 257).

5 – Cf. *AJ*, XX: 'A week to Christmas – hark the herald angels.' And *SAF*: 'Hark the lying angels sing, Every man's birth might be a Messiah's but is it?' (36).

6 – Popular operetta, first staged in London in 1922. See 'Day of Renewal' III: 'And being forty / Was an arm sore from the needle, a Tom Collins / In the garden of Faletti's with Lilac Time / Tinkling between the massacres . . .', from *Ten Burnt Offerings* (*TBO*), CP07, 353.

in our stupid car. Ireland is a good place but you mustn't be sentimental there for there are lots of little shops with bogwood toy harps & Connemara marble pigs & other knickknacks.[1] If you like I'll walk home with you at the end of next term. We will make lots of money for it's the great tongue I have.[2] I made a shop-woman here fall in love with me the other day by telling her that Sarsparilla (that's an Irish mineral water) was good for rheumatic cats. I argued modern art for hours yesterday with a clever woman. I got bored in the end and went to Church. Before going to Ireland read all J. M. Synge's plays. It's a jolly photo but very inferior. I must get another. It does not bring out his spiritual element. He is rather Kubla Khan – also Christabel & the Eve of St. Agnes & Sir Galahad (not Tennyson though) & perhaps a little The Witch of Atlas though not so aloof.[3] Still he is aloof, sitting in Marlborough 'on a hill retired' while all those dull people grovel in the plain and wear their own College Caps with the pride of respectability My brain is a little sterile today so excuse this vapid letter. I am getting worse and worse at golf.[4] The Spartans were wise. I wrote a lot of amorous verse on getting home but am now past the milking season. None of the blotting paper here ever blots – like the Marlborough College arrangements for putting down the wisdom of Solomon – to replace it by the wisdom of Dr. Arnold. I hope you flourish and Southcombe – must he not be nearly ripe for the Textile Goods Factory?[5] So yrs in the saints bless you and give you daily stirabout.

Louis M.

TO *Anthony Blunt*   MS Cambridge

Postmark 13 September 1926   Carrickfergus

My dear Anthony,

Yes, do send it. Thanks awfully for catering so well for my artistic self which is mouldering here among the cabbages & well-intentioned people.

---

1 – FLM later counts among his earliest memories of Dublin 'some little black bog-oak pigs in a window of knick-knacks' (*SAF*, 222). Cf. '. . . a shopwindow with little souvenirs of bogoak and Connemara marble . . .' FLM, 'Under the Sugar Loaf', in *SP*, 250.
2 – According to JH, they walked the fifty miles to Northwood, but 'we made no money' (*SAF*, 258).
3 – 'Anthony told me I must beware of the influence of Tennyson (*SAF*, 100). Cf. AB: 'Tennyson was the great bugbear' ('From Bloomsbury to Marxism', 165).
4 – Hilton recalled: 'Having refused to play backyard cricket I allowed Louis to teach me golf' (*SAF*, 255).
5 – Hector George Southcombe (1907–95), educ. MC 1921–6; Clare College, Cambridge.

Did I ever tell you C.T. sent me a large photograph of himself?[1]

. . . excoriating . . . [*sic*]

Now about Ross. He has just written to me after a year & it is very distressing. <u>Don't tell anyone this.</u> He has been 'converted.' He seems so emotional about it that I am afraid he will get a lot of shocks – for he never was long-sighted. He is going into the church & ended with an appeal to me. I told him what I thought of the church – but not what I thought of his conversion.[2] He is very sincere. But after the first attempt to convert him he had recourse to a friend – as a matter of fact, as he says, to Hopkins![3] God! To think of Hopkins helping to mould anyone's destiny & advising anyone to forsake the world & fight the good fight! The best people are always the blindest – to believe in Money[4] & Hopkins as spiritual beacons! It revolts one's stomach.

I shouldn't mind – I should be rather pleased if he'd been converted to an intelligent Christianity, like Canning's, but this is obviously the cheap though, doubtless, earnest rant of a weak-minded sentimentalist. At least I think it is. Perhaps I'm a fool & damned.

I got a letter from Canning today. He hasn't yet sent me his photo. He is ramping in a place with chocolate & magenta cliffs & a bottle green sea. It sounds Ugh.

Malory's Morte D'Arthur is the greatest English novel. Keats is the greatest English poet. There is one thing than these more desirable.[5] Our garden was wonderful one night. I wrote blank verse about it –

1 – Charles Thurstan Edward-Collins (b.1910), educ. MC 1924–8, 1st XV 1928. Lt. Central India Horse 1933; Lt. Col. 1944; Brigadier 1952. See FLM to AB, 14 Oct. and 3 Nov. 1926, and to JH, Jan. 1927, pp. 129, 136 and 141.

2 – FLM describes his growing resentment for the religiosity of Ross, depicted as Reckitts, in *SAF*, 93–4.

3 – A. L. E. Hopkins (b.1906), educ. MC 1920–5, Jesus College, Cambridge; HO 1930; vicar of St Luke's, Wimbledon; then Kew, High Wycombe and Folkestone, then rural dean of Elham 1970.

4 – T. D. F. Money. See FLM to GBM, 21 May 1922, n. 1, p. 68. Money had a bed beside AB in C3 and he recalls his neighbour's artistic enthusiasms: 'In the time between going to bed and the prefects coming up to turn the lights out, Blunt would talk to me about the French Impressionists, and bring out postcards to show. And he would talk about Clive Bell and Significant Form' (Carter, 26).

5 – He would later attribute his interest in both Malory and Keats to Mr Hemsted's influence at Sherborne (Mr Charles in *SAF*): 'I had read Malory's *Morte D'Arthur* sitting in a windowseat and reading with such concentration that my hair stuck to the paint of the woodwork' (*SAF*, 77). Cf. FLM, 'Sir Thomas Malory', in D. Verschoyle (ed.), *The English Novelists: A Survey of the Novel by Twenty Contemporary Novelists* (1936).

'The garden tonight is all Renoir & Keats
In the mouth melting to forgetfulness
   . . . . .   [*sic*]
   . . .   & bonfire smoke
Covers the garden with a dreamful blue'

With more about fusing oneself through a cigarette into the garden &
being stranded in the sunset. I am cracked and stuck with Seccotine.
Seccotine sticks everything – beasts & sheep & horses & chariots & slaves
& souls of men. Cracked or rather unhealthy as Keats said in the Preface
to Endymion, between a boy & a man.[1] Then one becomes healthy like
Swinburne in his middle age going for walks regularly with one's food
rationed.

I hope you are merry in Italy & getting things done. For me I am already
nearly a respectable Briton with a character unstained by emotion –
'But that was in another country
& besides . . .' [*sic*][2]
You are really rather sublime. I can imagine you preaching to a spell-
bound Cambridge Anonymous Society. I hear, too, you are getting up an
exhibition for Basil. Such are the world's protagonists who get things done.
I expect I shall leap in on you – on your family sometime if I don't die of
my own company. Write & tell me about Ross. I think of getting the
Village Way but am waiting to see if I can rise instead to the sunflowers –
tho' I don't know if they'll last. I should get that Matisse only I am afraid
it is ephemeral. You could only get it out in spring.

              Yrs
              F. Louis MacNeice

---

1 – 'The imagination of a boy is healthy, and the mature imagination of a man is healthy; but
there is a space of life between, in which the soul is in a ferment, the character undecided, the
way of life uncertain, the ambition thick-sighted: thence proceeds mawkishness, and all the
thousand bitters which those men I speak of must necessarily taste in going over the following
pages' (Keats, Preface, 'Endymion', 1818).
2 – Barabas in Marlowe's *The Jew of Malta*, IV: 'Fornication? but that was in another
country: / And besides, the wench is dead.'

TO *Anthony Blunt*   MS Cambridge

Postmark 25 September 1926   Hotel Carrig-na-cule, Portstewart[1]

My dear Anthony,

Thanks awfully for yr postcards & letter. I am having a golfing holiday
with the curate as the result of the Charwoman's Shadow where the
magician decides boarhunting to be the surest way to happiness & the best
philosophy.[2] It is a good book & the last chapter – 'The End of the Golden
Age' – is just like me, only refined. I have also read 'Tess' for the first time.[3]
Is not this one of the least happy endings in Hardy. Tess is impressive but
very melo [*sic*]. Last night at the pictures with the curate aforesaid it struck
me that that these types of film with interrogation marks etc. flying about
& views of one's thoughts & impressions is the real prelude of an arty
cinema. Jolly for you seeing so much Giotto. I am in a sad state over art
and am all for flux as opposed to hard lines etc – only an aberration, I
think.[4] I saw some interesting stuff in Dublin – six Poussin. One (marriage
of Peleus & Thetis) rather like that print, like golden tea without milk.[5]

A Greco of Vision of St. Francis all slate blue with white streaks splashed
with yellow & framed very suitably in darker slate blue & v. tarnished
gilt.[6] A decorative group by Giovanni Battista Piazzetta which rather
fascinated me – very sensuous very lush, very Susie.[7] An intensely
melodramatic landscape by Magnasco.[8] A bit off an altar by Fra Angelico
with two saints standing on a biscuit surrounded by a ring of fire like red

1 – Seaside resort, Co. Londonderry/Derry. For FLM's early childhood memories of a visit
there see *SAF*, 38–9.
2 – Lord Dunsany, *The Charwoman's Shadow* (1926). Hilton recalled FLM introducing his
friends to 'the cult of James Stephens and Dunsany' (*SAF*, 244).
3 – Thomas Hardy, *Tess of the D'Urbervilles* (1891).
4 – 'Flux' is one of the keywords in FLM's early criticism; he admired Joyce, Lawrence and
Woolf, 'who give you the flux but serve it on golden platters. We considered them good
because they were the acolytes of Flux' (*SAF*, 118–19).
5 – The Poussin collection in Dublin includes *The Marriage of Peleus and Thetis*, *Acis and
Galatea*, *The Lamentation over the Dead Christ* and three paintings bequeathed by Sir Hugh
Lane: *The Youthful Romulus*, *Pluto and Proserpine*, *A Bacchante and Satyr*. See T. Bodkin,
'Nicholas Poussin in the National Gallery, Dublin', *Burlington Magazine*, 60, 349 (April
1932), 174–5. AB was interested in Poussin and would later write a catalogue raisonné (1966)
and an authoritative monograph on the subject (1967).
6 – El Greco (1541–1614). AB recalled, 'We were greatly encouraged in our admiration for
El Greco by the fact that Cézanne had admired him so much, and that gave him a sort of
cachet that we could accept' ('From Bloomsbury to Marxism', 165).
7 – Cf. 'They'd invented girl's names for each other: MacNeice was "Susie", Blunt was
"Antonia"' (Carter, 48).
8 – Giovanni Battista Piazzetta (1682–1754); Alessandro Magnasco (1667–1749).

strings of seaweed or an anemone or starfish with a red king up above.[1] An Andrea di Giusto, v. symmetrical & v. crude but not bad & one of the saints had his hat lying on the ground, a runcible one and bright vermillion.[2] I wondered what would happen when it clashed – in 2 senses – with his halo which was rather a solid one like Mr. Audemars, not pre-Raphaelite like yr. post-test match one. I believe that the music of the spheres is caused by the halos of the chief saints turning round like gramophone records. That's why it's so discordant.

Did you see about Lord Wavertree?[3] Christopher Hughes has obtained his photo in a gunmetal locket.[4] I have not worn a collar or tie since Sunday. Golf is (as I play it) a delightfully abandoned game – over the hills & far away.[5] Only I hate replacing divots. It is like apologising to one's parents. I met a boy vaguely like C.T. today, a faint travesty. He is coming to play golf with me tomorrow morning. I am still averse to women except an Indian woman of about 80 I saw in Dublin & promptly fell in love with. I saw White in that place looking very nice & young, also met Waller in a bookshop.[6] Have begun to wear an old hat of my father's.

> O plus 4 ghosts O swaggart shades
> Who bluster heavenwards with yr passes
> While yr 1st cousins sink to hell.
> You will recline on pampas grasses
> & they in meads of asphodel.

I have to restrain myself so much. Today I all but said to the curate 'Lord teach us how to putt' but stopped in time.

1 – A very colourful description of Fra Angelico's *San Marco Altarpiece: Cosmas and Damian Are to Be Burnt Alive*, *c.*1439–42.
2 – Andrea di Giusto (*c.*1400–1450), Florentine.
3 – William Hall-Walker (1856–1933), the 1st Lord Wavertree, had criticised two Epstein sculptures on the occasion of opening an exhibition at the Liverpool gallery: 'Poor fellow, I have no doubt he has done his best, but after all, many other very poor artists could have done much better if they had done their worst.' Wavertree, whose father had donated to the city of Liverpool the Walker Art Gallery, later apologised for his remarks after Epstein threatened to withdraw his sculptures. (See 'Lord Wavertree and Mr Epstein', and 'Epstein Sculptures in Liverpool', *The Times*, 22 Sept., 14; 23 Sept., 10.) Cf. AB's remarks about Epstein's relief of Rima in Hyde Park: 'we had to stand up and defend it because it was Modern Art' ('From Bloomsbury to Marxism', 165).
4 – Christopher Wyndham Hughes, Art master at MC 1920–46.
5 – 'To me there was nothing incompatible between this most bourgeois of games and my romantic feelings for the desolate, the primitive, the antiquated' ('Landscapes', *SAF*, 226).
6 – John Patrick Waller (1909–34), educ. MC 1923–7; Trinity Hall, Cambridge.

My people think I'm an imbecile.

Ross wrote to me again an impressively forgiving & sincere letter. Only he told me to go & hear Dr. Richardson.[1] Richardson is a name I would never believe any good of. Trams are very like dogs aren't they tugging at their leashes? What about your Swiss hyacinths? By the way I met someone who thought you were like Apollo. I'm sure you'll bear Cambridge all right. I imagine you could bear most things like Atlas. That Rokoko garden is jolly. The cherubs in my Poussin had little blue wings rather like it. I really believe I haven't any emotions at all. I'm like the people in the Charwoman's Shadow who sold their shadows to the magician & he gave one of them a false one instead that always stayed 5 ft. long. The real ones went off at the magician's command to hobnob with demons or plumb the depths of space. I have no poetry left in me – only rhetoric & tricks of technique.

You must have filled up with petrol in Italy. You are lucky. In a few months you'll be able to use it – tranquillity recollected in emotion.[2]

I'm tired of theories. It will be some time before I read another 'aesthetic'. Theories are the combination of abstractions & an abstraction is the rough & ready term that covers a lot of individual concretes. It saves time but it doesn't lead anywhere. To talk about the man-in-the-street is easy but doesn't give you any information about the men in the street. As J. B. Priestley (I think) says through the mouth of the Village Idiot, I don't know the man in the street, I know Poussin & I know Mantegna & a gt. number of artists but I don't know THE ARTIST. Jesus we know & Paul we know but who are ye? I don't believe in pure form.[3] I don't believe in pure anything. Anything pure is an abstraction. All concretes are adulterated.

1 – Fortie Ross. 'Dr Richardson' is untraced.

2 – Reversal of Wordsworth's 'emotion recollected in tranquility'.

3 – Clive Bell's doctrine of pure or 'significant' form, as explored in his volume, *Art* (1914), had been influential on FLM and his circle: 'Even before leaving Marlborough we had swallowed Significant Form' ('Landscapes', *SAF*, 234). FLM's comments above, however, mark a moment of departure from agreement with Blunt and greater sympathy with Shepard: 'Graham Shepard was suspicious of Anthony's aestheticism and rarely attended the meetings of our society. He did not prefer Things to People and thought that Pure Form was nonsense' (*SAF*, 98). AB recalls that he [Blunt] 'believed without any qualification in Pure Form. In fact it was really the only thing in art that we did believe in' ('From Bloomsbury to Marxism', 165). By the mid-thirties however, pure form 'went by the board, totally' (ibid., 167). Cf. 'Auden and MacNeice: Their Last Will and Testament': 'A pure form, very pure, / We leave Clive Bell' (*LI*, CP07, 738).

Sorry to rave. I wish you dreams of Edward's eyes. I am afraid they're not pure anything either. Only space is pure and isn't it dull, except from the edge. The shore of the sea is far jollier than the middle.

> 'Look not on the infinite wave
> Dream not of the siren Cave
> Nor hear the cold wind in the tree
> Sign of worlds we cannot see?[']

———

I wonder how Basil will prosper next term.[1] Colwin seems to have been very [prosperous *deleted*] amorous lately.[2]

I expect I shall leap in & see you. I have taken to eating in the streets. I tried to see Juno & the Paycock in Dublin but couldn't.[3] I am hoping to write a paper on Christina Georgina Rossetti, Francis Thompson etc. I think the Prince's Progress (C.G.R.) is good.[4] By the way women specialise in disappointment – C.G.R. & Edith & Elizabeth Barrett Browning.

> The glass is going down. The sun
> Is going down. The forecasts say
> It will be warm with frequent showers
> We ramble down the showery hours
> & amble up & down the day.
> Mary will wear her black galoshes
> & splash the puddles on the town,
> & soon in fleets of macintoshes[5]
> The rain is coming down. The frown
> Is coming down of heaven showing
> A wet night coming, the glass is going
> Down, the sun is going down.[6]

———

1 – Basil Barr. See FLM to BB, 12 Jan. 1927, n. 2, p. 143.
2 – Colwin is untraced.
3 – Sean O'Casey, *Juno and the Paycock*, first performed at the Abbey Theatre in 1924; published (with *The Shadow of a Gunman*) in *Two Plays*, 1925.
4 – Christina Rossetti, *Goblin Market, The Prince's Progress and Other Poems* (1913); Francis Thompson (1859–1907), author of *The Hound of Heaven* (1893).
5 – *Sic.*
6 – 'Glass Falling', published with minor changes in *Blind Fireworks* (*BF*) (1929), CP07, 638.

Thanks awfully for introducing me to Art.
    The saints send you what you want.

                                            Louis MacNeice

TO *Anthony Blunt*   MS Cambridge

2nd [2 October 1926]   Carrickfergus

My dear Child,
    Thanks awfully for your lavish letters. I should love to come and see
you but I can't yet. This island is so distant. I am glad you liked 'Crime &
Punishment'. Is it Marmeladoff (?) who is such a sympathetic character?[1]
Thanks for yr list of books. I should like that fascinating 'Ancient
Mariner', also Meirgraefe's Cezanne, if you can get them? That Puget is
ripping.[2] I have just been very moved by the Elizabethan monument in our
church viewed by oil lamp, the gas having run out & my family trying to
follow the Creator's precedent & 'there was light' but not much.[3] The
monument's a beautiful autumnal yellow, mildly sentimental like Walter
Pater. By the way I looked in a glass yesterday & saw myself with a parody
of the Gioconda smile.[4] I was pained. Disgusting ink our family own – like
spinach. Yesterday evening I felt just like that desperate afternoon at the
end of last term when I had a nightmare in the study & you dragged me
away to play tennis.
    My Roger Fry & Milton arrived from Marlborough. Some splendid
trees in our garden now, just like the ones Midas touched. I am beginning
to collect children's drawings. One splendid concept of a cow, a great
towering cylinder with saucer eyes interlocking and two little legs. Also a
cat all whiskers & claws (5 legs) like a centipede & several houses all
windows, with front door & backdoor alongside each other. Crashaw
seems good. Have you seen any good editions of him?[5] This room is
crawling with heat. My imitation C.T. was a failure. I am having C.T. to
tea next term in Basil's study. I want another photo as I feel this one is

1–Semyon Zakharovich Marmeladov, father of Sonya and Polina Marmeladova, is a
harmless drunk who befriends Raskolnikov in *Crime and Punishment*.
2–Julius Meier-Graefe (1867–1935), art critic, author of *Cézanne* (1927); Pierre Puget
(1620–94), French painter and sculptor.
3–See FLM to JFM, 3 June 1925, n. 1, p. 102.
4–The Mona Lisa's smile was the subject of a famous passage in *Studies in the History of the
Renaissance* (1873) by Walter Pater (1839–94).
5–Richard Crashaw (1612/13–49), seven of whose poems FLM would have read in his
beloved *Oxford Book of English Verse: 1250–1900* (ed. A. Quiller-Couch, 1906).

inadequate. I have been painting an old croquet set here. The balls are to have a second coat of spots & ringstripes. Talking of clergymen's daughters it is a good link between religion & the man in the street. I am becoming profane rapidly – probably the thought of Hopkins.[1] I suppose I am feeling Baroque.[2] At least the last Sunday I was in church I was planning a new pulpit & reading desk facing each other with a backward surge of concave white marble ending in a curled crest with – [*sic*] I had another idea of electric signs in churches e.g. the Ten Commandments in shifting colours. The other day I was sitting under an umbrella & notice[d] that the raindrops on it were just like hanging gas lamps, diaphanous above & opaque below. Eternity must be like sitting under an umbrella and not daring to move because one is sitting on the only dry patch. I think I shall go about the country like the man in 'Tess' painting up warning signs e.g. '& there was death in the Pot' outside public houses. We have a cemetery beside our garden. (Cemetery has an appropriate sound value like 'calamitous'.) Our gardener cut the hedge there lately leaving a great wave to hide the obelisk whom he used to call 'the bad man', but he is not hidden & still peers over – polished grey granite after a wicked life.[3] Our cat had a kitten lately. This new regard for unity leads me to believe in the great advance of feline eugenics. I read J. B. S. Haldane's 'Daedalus' against the beginning of this creation. It was read to the 'Hereticks' at Cambridge.[4] Mr. Lear seems to have heralded Gertrude Stein in the choruses of 'Mr. & Mrs Spikky Sparrow'.[5] Sorry to be so incoherent but the time dropped an hour in the middle. I hope you have by now seen Edward. Give him my love and a dose of Marchand's Aspidistra to be taken after each meal, preferably administered by another person than the patient. You could make an excellent Doctor to Deficient Aesthetic Sensibilities, with a Rokoko scroll instead of a brass plate. Sorry, I mean Uneducated Sensibilities. Our mistake was at the Priory sometimes to defend modern

1 – See his views on fellow pupil A. L. E. Hopkins in his letter to AB of 13 Sept. 1926, p. 118.
2 – '"Baroque" was still a magic word, though all we could find in Oxford was the porch of St Mary's with its barley-sugar pillars . . .' ('Landscapes', *SAF*, 234). On his generation's interest in the Baroque, see AB, 'From Bloomsbury to Marxism', 165.
3 – 'Each spring when he cut the hedge between the garden and the cemetery a polished granite obelisk would reappear looking over at us. Then Archie would shake his fist, say "Thon's a bad ould fella"' (*SAF*, 48).
4 – *Daedalus; or, Science and The Future; A Paper Read to the Heretics, Cambridge, on February 4th, 1926.*
5 – AB recalls: 'We read Gertrude Stein, though we had a slight suspicion even at the time that she was not as good as we pretended to think; but she was admirable to read up and down the dormitories to exasperate our neighbours' ('From Bloomsbury to Marxism', 165). The chorus of Edward Lear's poem reads: 'Twikky wikky wikky wee'.

paintings as mere patterns. It is only a half defence. A pattern is often emotionless. I often see possibilities of excellent patterns but if I had the ability to put them down I shld not consider myself a great artist. Christopher Hughes has bought a parrot educated in a respectable art school to keep him accurate in his maxims now he has noone much to practise them on. I wonder if Basil has hung his Matisse. I am really cheered with the Montagne Ste Victoire.[1] He is uniquely satisfying, like the earlier books of Paradise Lost. I should think his little sensation is one of the most crushing replies to the Ruskinian Fallacy.

I am already beginning my vigil for the spring. Then I should like to run away and sit on some promontory in the south among the ruins of disgusting prosperous civilizations & there salute those peculiar influences again with the Pervigilium.[2] At the moment, excepting the last verse, it seems a thing of the past. 'The swansong of a materialistic hedonism' I read of it in some history. Reading Francis Thompson on Shelley I realised the great illogicality of 'Adonais'.[3] That Shelley as a Pantheist shld be so disloyal to his Pantheistic theory of redistribution of one's personality among the elements is cheering. (Also Sir Thomas Browne.) If you read 'Adonais' you will see that he begins with his theory & ends in contradiction. I have decided I don't want to be fused into stones and stars and things. If I held together it might be amusing (& wld explain Dryads etc) but to run away from oneself like quicksilver is disgusting. And how is your toy? I am thinking of getting a wooden dog on wheels to draw about after me at Oxford. He will sit in my room in front of a bowl marked DOG and listen to me reading sonorously. If the strike continues I am thinking of painting myself a fire with solid rolling flames & blue depths between them to get up in my grate and blow upon with bellows.[4] I am not looking forward especially to Oxford except in that I will have a room where I can rant to myself & shut myself off from the absurd & pusillanimous world. I am enclosing 2/- in some form or other. Don't spend it all on Art. As my father said once in a sermon, there are other things in

1 – Paul Cézanne, *La Montagne St Victoire* (1887). 'On top of this bookshelf we had some photographs of pictures by Picasso and a small coloured print of Cézanne's inevitable Montagne St Victoire' (*SAF*, 97).
2 – 'Vigil of Venus', Latin poem, second or third century AD. Hilton wrote: 'There was a reading of vernal and amorous poetry when Louis declaimed the *Pervigilium Veneris* with harsh resonance and a percussive menace in the refrain that was almost a threat' (*SAF*, 244).
3 – Francis Thompson, *Shelley* (1909).
4 – The General Strike had taken place during nine days in May 1926, but the dispute in the coal industry continued and by October many miners had been on strike for well over twenty weeks. Cf. 'Coal Dispute. Big Return to Work', *The Times*, 20 Oct. 1926, 16.

the world besides football and pictures. Thinking the other day that the dark was the colour of blue plums & this an original thought I decided that it was an unconscious crib from 'the stars were like prunes', for the sky at night is just that colour & texture but it is shown up & emphasised by stars. 'The huntsmen are up in Persia' so goodnight[1]

Yrs

F. Louis MacNeice

P.S. Sunday. Wrote a bit of Vers Libre today called 'MacNeice prays to his Deity'. Very pithy. Have been reading some more Morte D'Arthur about Sir Percivale riding on a black horse which was a fiend and ran away into the sea & the waters 'brent' after him. It is jolly stuff – no abstractions & very few adjectives. One's own supplied adjectives are naturally more appropriate. 'Les sanglots longs' is how just right.[2] We have a telephone now. If only I were a spiritualist I would ring up Moses.

I am sending your dog an A.A.[3] badge for his birthday and your family much love. Shall see you soon I expect. The evenings are getting shorter now – or is it longer.

Yrs
but I've signed
myself already

[*pencil*] That professor in the hat was like a Hans Andersen troll.

TO *Anthony Blunt*　　　　　　　　　　　　　　　MS Cambridge

14 October 1926　　　　　　　　Carrickfergus

My dear Anthony,

I hope you prosper at that place. I haven't got to mine yet.[4] Have had a desperate time at home. There was a week of sickly, clammy heat (but no rain) with no sunlight, though you could hear the sun shambling behind the clouds, and no moonlight or starlight, only the sound of leaves falling. Then I got a cold and the rain came very dynamic with the wind [whipping

1 – Sir Thomas Browne: 'The Huntsmen are up in America, and they are already past their first sleep in Persia', from 'The Garden of Cyrus' (1658).
2 – 'Les sanglots longs / Des violins / De l'Automne / Blessent mon Coeur / D'une langueur / Monotone' (Paul Verlaine, 'Chanson d'Automne').
3 – Automobile Association.
4 – University.

deleted] trundling the leaves up the avenue but I sat in the house looking unpleasant and feeling fogged. I painted two texts for my bedroom (the traditional ones – Pactolus & kitchen garden) very neatly executed with beautiful placid amber spangled over the blue, and a fine horizon of cauliflowers in the other. They tried a horrible spray (called Flypic) in my bedroom on the flies (and all their fragrant corpses lined my bed). [']As flies to wanton boys are we to the gods.'[1] And one can smell the celestial Flypic in the better churches. But at present I am rather impressed with God. Do you know a line of Yeats – 'And God stands winding his lonely horn'?[2] You find him in a valley sitting on a rock with his hair long and still like icicles and his eyelids half closed like Buddha. And covered with bracken a few yards away is a granite sphinx of the first Egyptians. There is a little park here for the town which was very thrilling some time ago – painted and unreal and no longer ancillary to human recreation but in itself an entity. Beyond it a bleaching factory with a red chimney and domed roofs of corrugated iron & gabled roofs of glass (very Rousseau)[3] and to the left the railway line with telegraph posts – the lines smooth like shot silk and the insulators clear against the sky like dominoes. And plain wooden benches unpainted unsat-on.

I got a letter from John Hilton. It will be very jolly having him next door at Oxford? I am broke but if you send me those books I shall be able to embezzle some money for you. The furniture of my Oxford rooms belongs, I hear, to the College, which prevents me selling them & getting kitchen chairs. I saw our kitchen chairs in the sun after washing & they were v. beautiful. I also saw some deck chairs lately, in rich oranges & green, which were attractive. I am not going to M.C. before Oxford, am feeling too incompetent. Last night wrote a pretty-pretty little poem called 'Whistler Blue'! –

> Little memories rouse & ripple
> The fishes that tipple the flat ragout,
> Little sighs from the sleepers
> Drop like water the night through,
> A little smile smiles the moon
> Stooping to tie her silver shoe.

1 – *King Lear*, IV.i, 37–8.
2 – 'Into the Twilight', *The Wind Among the Reeds* (1899).
3 – Henri Rousseau (1844–1910), painter of the modern primitive school.

The 2nd line is an auto-plagiarism. I am longing to get away from here – even to face the educated beef and cultured inanity of Oxford. Oh, these dear, good, patient people! They are having a Harvest Thanksgiving this week. I offered to scheme for them the whole decoration of the church but they thought my taste too vulgar. I proposed blazing the Chancel with the various yellow flowers still extant but they prefer bracken & pampas grass & perhaps a few Michaelmas daisies. I must visit the Ashmolean with care. By the way Graham Shepard is at Oxford (Lincoln). I wrote to him at the beginning of August but he never replied (contrary to his custom) so I expect he was shocked by my revelations about C.T. (Thurstan, I mean). I hope you saw Edward. He is so responsive. The viscous rain is dripping down & I have lost my T. S. Eliot. But this morning I saw the most gorgeous Pratts van newly painted an emotional green spangled with letters like flaming yellow chrysanthemums, and vermilion wheels. This is healthy but lately my taste has experienced the strangest aberrations and I have liked the most Victorian things. At the moment I am whistling 'For all the Saints'.[1]

Not animula vagula blandula[2]
But practical sensible methodical
You have paid your penny & chosen
Duty consistency stupidity.

But I am tired of grieving against people. They are all so nice & funny – except perhaps Bennitt.[3] He is already fading in my mind but will recur probably when I am middle-aged, as some sort of mania rolling up the oesophagus.

'This is I who leer obscenely in a green latrine.' Don't you think this a pretty line – also a lot of atmosphere? // The Sitwells correspond to the Rossetti family.[4] I opened a ripping book in a bkshop some time ago called 'The Healthy Citizen' or 'Mens Sana in Corpore Sano' or one of those other alluring titles.[5] There was a chapter called 'Art', containing words like this. 'It has been for some time generally recognised that for an artist

1 – 'All the Saints', by William How (1864), music by Ralph Vaughan Williams.
2 – 'Animula, vagula, blandula': a poem addressed to the departing soul written by the emperor Hadrian on his deathbed; it is also thought to resemble a Latin children's nursery rhyme.
3 – A. J. Bennitt: see FLM to GBM, 10 June 1924, n. 1, p. 92.
4 – Dame Edith Sitwell (1887–1964), Osbert Sitwell (1892–1969), Sacheverell Sitwell (1897–1988).
5 – Mens sana in corpore sano is the slogan of Sir Randall Belcher's campaign for moral purity in Roundabout Way (RW) (6). Cf. 'Auden and MacNeice: Their Last Will and Testament': 'We leave a mens sana qui mal y pense / To the Public Schools of England . . .' (LI, CP07, 735).

to attain the highest standard in his calling a moderate knowledge of anatomy and physiology is necessary. In these more advanced days the ambitious artist will be sure to add to his repertory a similar knowledge of Geology & Botany.' Oh, and remember to put on thicker vests for the winter. Hannibal the Great repented this omission when prostrated on the Alps

> Yours with love
> & in hope of better things
> trusting you stand firm
> in the face of temptation
> (unless it has an infectious cold)
> Louis

[P.S.] I reread last night Walter Pater's Essay on 'Style'.[1] It is really very good. Incidentally it calls Blake [']an instance of preponderating soul embarrassed, at a loss, in an era of preponderating mind'. It makes some very Roger Fry remarks – only so much better expressed. And have you read any Flaubert?

TO *Georgina Beatrice MacNeice*   MS Dan MacNeice

[18 October 1926]   Merton College, Oxford /
                                  '1st from Oxford'
                                  [*red pencil; mother's hand?*]

My dear Drina,
    Excuse pencil. (I have no ink yet.) Am writing in my room, a spacious place with 2 windows, green panelled, 3 tables (one longish one with leaves), 2 pots of yellow chrysanthemums, a writing desk, a hanging bookcase (longish) and a cupboard with bookshelves. Spent a fortune on utensils etc. yesterday. Will tell you details when I have completed my purchases. An efficient and humorous scout.[2] Friday was ghastly wet. I met John Hilton & had tea with Richard Best who has dreary palatial rooms in Tom Quad.[3] Had breakfast yesterday with John Hilton & he had lunch with me. It being Saturday we were extravagant & had beef and apple tart. (Usual thing is bread & cheese.) Dinner in Hall – 3 courses

1 – *Appreciations, with an Essay on Style* (1889).
2 – 'My scout had never compromised with the twentieth century. He was a tiny man designed by George Cruikshank, with a long ratlike moustache . . .' ('Landscapes', *SAF*, 232).
3 – Richard Best; see FLM to GBM, 25 Jan. 1920, n. 4, p. 39.

– scrambled eggs etc: meat, sweet. Saw Bell. He is sharing rooms in Oriel with his cousin & Mynors (Oriel).[1] Shepard, Hilton & I are running a communal fire in the evenings turn about – Friday Hilton, yesterday I, tonight Shepard (Lincoln). Hilton is just across Merton St. in an annex to Corpus. He came up on Thursday. Had tea with Hamilton (Trinity) today. They nearly all have smaller rooms than mine but warmer. My windows look out on a tennis court, lawns & elms. My tutor has schemed for me 13 lectures a week, also given me already a Latin prose. I will have a tutorial with him every Saturday. He is very jolly, goodlooking, whitish hair & 3 prints of Vermeer in his room. Of course, they are very popular here. Mynors is very sceptical about people at Oxford. He says (like Elizabeth) that none of them are normal, also that they are all hideous & nearly all stupid. In particular he disapproves of his college. Also he is very contemptuous of Marlborough. I may get down there on O.M. Club day.[2] On Nov. 1st am going to hear Paderewski.[3] Aunt Eva gave me £1 before I left! (I took care not to tell you then, fearing your wrath at my wickedness in being given it.) I have my floreate handkerchief out on a little table.

My books from M.C. arrived safely. Am to be admitted of College tomorrow morning, & matriculated on Wednesday. Have bought a cap & gown. J.C.R. meeting tonight after Hall. 30 Chapels a term (Sundays excluded) or roll calls necessary (Chapel at 8.A.M.). Lectures 10, 11, 12 tomorrow. I shall miss my bicycle. I hope the Harvest Festival was a success. But my poor windows! How is Aunt Eva? This is not a bad place. Very quaint though & some terrible people. I actually visited a new person – name Lauriel from Shrewsbury. Quite nice but dull, & listened to me talking. Bought a new tie at [Woolworth?]

Much love
Will write again – in ink
Louis M.

1 – Thomas (Tom) Halliday Baskerville Mynors (b.1907), educ. MC 1921–5; Oriel College, Oxford.
2 – The celebrated pianist Ignacy Jan Paderewski (1860–1941) was made an Honorary Doctor of Music at Cambridge on 29 October, during his English provincial concert tour, which closed in Oxford.

TO *Anthony Blunt* MS Cambridge

Postmark 23 October 1926   Merton College, Oxford

But my dear Anthony

You must not become an hypochondriac. Universities are really rather amusing. I have got some grand yellow chrysanthemums in my chaste green room and tonight I went to Hedda Gabler by the Oxford Players. I am now feeling pretty stupid and the fire is all but out and all the other postmasters of this year are vile – so stupid – while those of earlier years are aesthetes with a slight gift for obscenity but pretty deplorable . . .[1] Still . . . And I went to see your Harrison man and borrowed 'Before the Bombardment' from him – the peculiar dreamy triviality of spinsterdom.[2] It is the only thing to write about in so decadent an age. Decadence is the boredom of civilisation – the Alexandrians and Silver Romans. Then comes the sea of barbarism. Our symptoms are clear. We could produce Petronius or Apollonius (possibly?) or Apuleius but Aeschylus for example?[3] . . . we are far too sophisticated. Sophistication is the dung of wisdom. Literary sophistication is the worst. What fun to eat grass with the better class human beef. I hope to follow the Christ Church Beagles. Nice and brutal and invigorating. There is a fine hall in Queen's – gold and white barrel vaulted with large gilt–framed portraits.[4] I have seen Mynors. He is deplorably sane and superficial. Also Glennie who is so big that you never know if you are addressing his front or back.[5] Also Bell who lives with a religious cousin.[6] Also Alastair H. (I went to the pictures with him & a friend of his from Clifton![7] We think of getting down to Marlboro' for the Clifton match.) By the way I want (& Shepard & Mynors & Hilton ditto) to get up to London to see the Rousseau exhibition.[8] How lucky & unsophisticated HE was. I am reading Shepard 'the Charwoman's

1 – FLM was a 'postmaster' (a scholar of Merton College who is supported on the foundation).
2 – Osbert Sitwell, *Before the Bombardment* (1926).
3 – Hilton recalled: 'Louis introduced us to Apuleius' (*SAF*, App. B, 244). See FLM's introduction to *The Golden Ass of Apuleius*, trans. W. Addington (1946); repr. *Selected Literary Criticism*, ed. Alan Heuser (Oxford, 1987) (*SLC*), 127–31.
4 – Queen's College, Oxford.
5 – Ian Herbert Campbell Glennie (b.1906), educ. MC 1920–5; Oriel College, Oxford. RAF 1940–5.
6 – Christopher Bell (b.1907), educ. MC 1920–5; Oriel College, Oxford. Colonial Education Service, N. Rhodesia 1931.
7 – James Alexander Stewart Hamilton, see FLM to GBM, 29 June 1924, n. 2, p. 93.
8 – Rousseau Exhibition, Lefèvre Galleries, King Street, St James's, sw1, 25–29 Oct., 1–8 Nov. 1926.

Shadow'. Hilton has found a fellow scholar who thinks 'Antic Hay' the most brilliant book he has read.[1] And I shave in cold water every morning. Give my love to Michael.[2] I wrote a perfect Eliotesque before leaving home (my only one) with a sort of refrain booming among knick knacks & yellow lace curtains – 'Where shall I go Maria, where shall I go?'[3] My brain is quite dry tonight – dry rot. Today I spent thus – morning to dreary lectures, an old vegetable cleric flapping a beard that had gone to seed, afternoon walked with Shepard along an endless suburban road – oh such arty houses with curtains to match the slates – tea in my rooms – sodden toast and crumpets, then Charwoman's Shadow aloud to Shepard, then after a visit to latrines, to find Mynors constructed in my room like the latest War Memorial, then letters to my sister etc., then a hearty dinner, then Hedda Gabler, then a Latin prose then this. Now I shall go to bed in my scarf and a bath towel (clothing being insufficient). I borrowed for matriculation an unique white tie from Hilton which I borrowed at the last moment and was so large that it stood out almost the width of my body like cat's whiskers. I put a ginger cat in Hilton's room the other day which he turned out fearing the wrath of his scout. His scout turned ME out the other night when I went in late – though I told him time was relative. To be tastefully inane, inanely obscene and obscenely tasteful is the whole duty of an aesthete. I'm sure that is nonsense (it is too late at night to make epigrams) but it goes in a circle like the moon last night in the Oxford haze surrounded by wheels of divers colours – very regular and a little ugly like a multicoloured blazer. But very sentimental. It is so late that the minutes are petrifying into little stalagmites on the mantelpiece and the silence is crackling and the embers in the fire only retain a stiff smile to be polite. Their flaming petulance is over and now Requiescant in the dustbin. Yet still they may line the paths of a garden. Our England is . . . [sic]

And I wish Osbert Sitwell wouldn't push in so much figure. It is not a riot of figure only a full market, not a Bacchanal but a Vintner's. Too laboured too clever. And the boredom etc. in Before the Bombardment is that of a female Underdone Eliot. This is probably incoherent. My word I am tired.

Yrs. Louis

1 – Aldous Huxley, *Antic Hay* (1923).
2 – Michael Robertson (b.1908), educ. MC 1921–6 (senior prefect; 1st XV, 1924–5; 1st XI, 1926; Hockey XI, 1925–6); Trinity College, Cambridge; Lincoln's Inn. Of his schoolboy crush on Robertson, AB later recalled him as 'enchanting, highly intellectual and good at games' (AB interviewed by Jon Stallworthy, qtd Carter, 40).
3 – Cf. 'What shall I do now? What shall I do?' (*The Waste Land*, II, 131).

TO *John Frederick and Georgina Beatrice MacNeice*

MS Dan MacNeice

[23 October 1926]   Merton College, Oxford

My dear Daddie & Drina

I am writing this in our J.C.R. I progress favourably – though my Tutor was quite worried with my Latin Prose this morning. I finished it after going to 'Hedda Gabler' the other night, which perhaps accounts for it.

I went to breakfast the other day with Holt, a man from the Prep. Quite nice though dull.

I went to the Holywell music room the other night – String sestets & quartet – Brahms, Haydn and Schönberg.

Am going to tea with a man at Balliol today, an O.M.

My lectures on the whole have been pretty deadly – old dons like vegetables. One of the better ones is in the hall of Queen's – a very fine hall, barrelvaulted, white and gilt with gilt-framed portraits.

I have been having scanty lunches but good breakfasts. Dinners have 3 courses, usu. scrambled eggs, steak and cold fruit (tinned, I think) with a solid pudding as alternative. Hamilton has a friend from Clifton and we think of getting down to M.C. for the Clifton match.

My other postmasters are so dull. There is one freshman (a commoner at the bottom of the list called Small) who must be 40 or over. I think he was probably a Commercial Traveller in his youth.

My tutor is estimable. He said this morning that if postmasters didn't get 2nd in Honour Mods., one called in the hangman. It's a bad lookout. I have lots of books to get.

The undergraduates are terrible. I pity Elizabeth living with them.

I am thinking of playing rugger after all. It is so unhealthy here to take no exercise. Continual haze, giving very romantic moons.

Prince Chichibu has taken up residence in Magdalen![1]

Yrs with Love

Louis M.

Thanks awfully for yr letters.

---

1 – Prince Chichibu of Japan (1902–53), member of the Imperial Japanese family, entered Magdalen College in the autumn of 1926, but left the following year, on the death of his father.

TO *Elizabeth MacNeice*   MS Dan MacNeice

Postmark 3 November 1926   Merton College, Oxford

My dear Elizabeth

I'm so glad you're coming down this week-end. What would you like to do? Nothing too formal. I hear the family en masse intends to come and live here for a few weeks later on. I went to lunch with Mr. Nicholson and H. W. Davies on Sunday.[1] Quite nice. And do you know Miss Wingate? I had a ghastly time last Sunday week. Miss W. has a Freshman cousin in Merton who lives next door to me and her legate seeing MACNEICE CARPENTER on the board in our passage thought it was a double name and left a note in MY room inviting me to tea with himself, a Mr. Moore on Sunday. I went and oh it was ghastly. They all seemed out to convert.[2] Anyhow I gave them a nasty shock by appearing instead of dear Carpenter.

I hope you flourish. What time will you come here?

etc etc.

Louis M.

TO *Anthony Blunt*   MS Cambridge

Postmark 3 November 1926   Merton College, Oxford

My dear Anthony,

I'm sorry to have been rather stupid the other night. I hope you gathered I was not coming to London. I was dazed by your appearance. I'm afraid Mynors, too, was rather silly. I hope you did not go away enraged with us. But your appearance was so meteoric.[3]

I'm sorry John was unresponsive but (not to be an emotional pander) I will say that I think he is quite hopeless – and secondly that I don't think him worth hoping for. And I don't see anything but mutual loss in the continuation of this affection – except a little emotion which might be called Platonic. Edward is far superior in every way and Michael, I should say, is superior to Edward. I think the only satisfactory end for a violent

1–H. W. (Hugh) Davies (b.1905) of C3 House, MC, later an Oxford friend of John Nicholson's at New College. He was John's best man at his wedding (see Illustrations); see also Appendix 1.
2–FLM later recalled the incident in *SAF*: 'Arriving at the unknown house I found myself in the midst of Plymouth Brethren . . . The room was full of cake-stands and suspense' (107).
3–AB had visited FLM at Merton unannounced, having returned crestfallen from a weekend at MC, where he had declared his affections to a boy ('John') but was rebuffed (cf. Carter, 46). AB prohibited quotation from this letter during his lifetime.

affection is a break. The present position of Basil and Colwin seems to me – possibly Platonic from Basil's standpoint, but what about Colwin? It must knock him out of his proper course. Noone ever seems to consider the position of the object. I admit he may often enjoy it but it is an enjoyment essentially detrimental.

I am afraid this is a brutal letter, especially considering C.T. But I think he too would be better if not subjected to this admiration. (I still believe in the ideal mutual affection but I have never yet seen two people capable of it.)

I hope you flourish. Give my love to Michael. I'm sorry to be a didactic & moralising pig.

Yrs.
Louis M.

TO *Anthony Blunt* MS Cambridge

Postmark 17 November 1926   Merton College, Oxford

My dear Anthony

Good Afternoon, I hope you flourish and take enough exercise and go to bed in good time. I do.

Have just got & read 'All Summer in a Day'.[1] He is much better than Osbert, & has not his cheap cynicism. 'Before the Bombardment' is trying – laughter tinkling among the cups. I have hopes of getting a few books free by reviewing for the 'Cherwell'.[2]

Think of going to the Marlborough Downs tomorrow with Shepherd [*sic*] to flaunt our gowns in the wind. Have you got Roger Fry's new book.[3]

And Oxford Poetry is bad. And a man read a paper at our College the other night on 'Donne the First of the Moderns' in which he would compare Donne to Rupert Brooke. & then they discussed what a 'modern' was, the only pithy remarks being by the Editor of the Outlook viz. that the last century had given up religion & we were giving up the Intellect & returning to the 5 senses.[4]

1–Sacheverell Sitwell, *All Summer in a Day: An Autobiographical Fantasia* (1926).
2–Cf. his review of James Stephens and Edwin Muir in *Cherwell* (Oxford University magazine), 11 Dec. 1926, 329.
3–Probably *Vision and Design*, or *Transformations: Critical & Speculative Essays on Art*, both published in 1926. His study of Cézanne appeared the following year.
4–Graham Greene was then editor of the *Oxford Outlook*, which Beverley Nichols had founded.

I spoke at a College debate the other night against the Censorship of the Press.

> 'There was an old lady called Dahlia
> Who censored the press of Australia
> She turned all the nudes
> To commendable prudes
> & a roaring success to a failure.'

Then my sister came down & I was going to a dance with her to support John Hilton who would not go alone but I pretended to be drunk so he did.[1]

Am going to hear René Creod (a Surréaliste) on Monday.

The Ashmolean has a grand collection of Pre-Raphaelites – Watts, Watts, Watts and the holy Seraphim[.][2] The Mene Mene of religious art.

Am going to tea with Baggallay today. He has two white mice – Polyphiloprogenitive.[3]

Went with Bowle last week to Lener String Quartet – some delightful Mozart.[4]

I must make a pilgrimage to see Robert Graves some time. He lives in some little cottage near here.

Walked with John Hilton one Sunday to a village called Thame. Had lunch at an Inn run by an old Oxonian, a friend of Augustus John & very Johnesque hair and tie with brass buckles on his shoes.[5]

1 – JH tells his side of the story in a letter of November 1926: 'On Saturday I was suddenly roped in to take Miss MacNeice to a dance, her partner having failed and Louis being unable to dance . . . I then thought myself very clever to discover, by one or two minute signs, that he was drunk. He said he was ill and sent me off with a note to his sister, alone in the dark. It turned out that it was all a brilliant bit of acting on his part, to get off the dance. I have hardly forgiven him' (repr. SAF, App. B, 260).

2 – The Ashmolean houses a significant collection of paintings by George Frederick Watts (1817–1904).

3 – A fashionable coterie allusion to the first line of T. S. Eliot's 'Mr Eliot's Sunday Morning Service' (1920), a word Eliot coined to mean 'highly productive of offspring' (like mice). FLM writes elsewhere (SAF, 233) about his generation's fascination with Eliot, particularly with The Waste Land. (Cf. Anthony Blanche intoning The Waste Land through a microphone in Brideshead Revisited.)

4 – Hungarian quartet, founded in 1918 by Jeno Léner, popular in London in the twenties and thirties. John Edward Bowle, educ. MC 1919–24; Balliol College, Oxford. With Betjeman and Ben Bonas he founded the Heretick (SAF, 242).

5 – John Fothergill (1876–1957) ran the Spreadeagle in Thame, Oxfordshire, and was the author of An Innkeeper's Diary (1931). Cf. 'Auden and MacNeice: Their Last Will and Testament': 'And to John Fothergill a Corner House in Heaven' (LI, CP07, 736).

Donne's sermons are much better Stein than Stein.[1]

I hope you are not becoming sane – like John Hilton & Thomas Mynors – Aurea mediocritas[,] such a golden sanity but My God.[2]

Commend me to Michael, Alastair & Andrew

Yrs F L

Louis M.

TO *Anthony Blunt*

Postmark 6 December 1926   Merton College, Oxford

My dear Anthony

Thanks awfully. Would you like to receive me on this day week? Everything is rather muddled and I have promised everyone in Oxford to go to the Zoo with them and I want to see several exhibitions. I met some men from your College here one Saturday and talked to them kindly. I am having a sort of reading in my room next Wednesday evening – very heterogeneous, I imagine. I spent all yesterday in a check rug before the fire trying to make a poem coherent which I wrote at 12.30 the night before. Thomas Mynors thinks all my stuff charlatanism, which is annoying. I am walking home with John Hilton in the night. I am a little sad about my ties, most of which were destroyed in a raid.[3] I am going to carry a flask of pepper about with me and then go into Hertford.[4] Hertford, apparently, have vowed a vow to debag me if I enter their gates, having once seen me with Shepard, going to visit Harding. I am now reviewing a book by Edwin Muir called 'Transition' – essays on Contemp. Lit. eg. James Joyce, D. H. Lawrence, Virginia Woolf, Aldous Huxley, T. S. Eliot, Edith Sitwell, Robert Graves.[5] Mynors says it is a bloody book but it is really rather good. Shepard has got hold of a copy of 'Ulysses' which I am about to read.[6] Mr. Muir [*sic*] is mad on it. He puts Aldous Huxley in his proper place by

1 – On Donne, cf. *SAF*: 'But Graham and I went back to Donne's sermons, pretending they had nothing to do with religion; it was just all style – and death' ('Landscapes', 233).

2 – Golden Mean (Horace).

3 – JH recalls the attack: 'People in Louis's college made a bonfire of some of his prettiest ties (one with small parrots among jungle flowers); and I was threatened with possible removal of my side-whiskers' (*SAF*, 251). FLM seems in retrospect to have had mixed feelings about it: 'I was indignant but at the same time recognized that this was another good step down the ladder. One's self respect must go' (*SAF*, 104).

4 – Hertford College, Oxford.

5 – FLM's review of *Transition* appeared in *Cherwell*, 18 (11 Dec. 1926), 329.

6 – JH: 'Ulysses burst on us during this year' (*SAF*, 252).

ascribing his popularity to the popular matter of his ideas. The distinctive factors of the lost seem to be the realisation of what was unconscious, the exaltation of the senses[,] instincts and physiological functions. Exeunt intellect, God and one increasing purpose.

I went to an astonishing play by Strindberg at the Playhouse – 'The Spook Sonata'.[1] I think it was great part irrelevant vulgar mystery and green lights on middle class faces but I only came in the middle and could not judge of the coherence of the whole. I have been reading 'The Brothers Karamazov'. There is a precious little boy in there who is just like us, picks up the fag-ends of a dozen of the latest ideas and says [*illegible*] Look at me smoking.[2]

And how is Alastair M?[3] There is noone here beautiful at all. John Hilton is excited over a little boy in his College who has a little picture (Church Almanac Style) of a girl-angel in his bed-room. Quite a pleasant boy but so methodical, so moral, so scrupulous, so simple.

Did I tell you how Shepard and I went down to M.C. Got out of bus at Oglume St Andrews and went up that lane towards Old Eagle.[4] As we crossed the ridge we heard Lowers and Thirds being played. And then little boys draggling along the road at 1st Post Cotton House having a scrum practice. They all disentangled themselves and stood up to watch us – the Man with the Bad Shadow idea.[5] Then through Barton Bottom and up to peer in at the playing fields. This made Shepard nearly vomit and he refused to go any further. I said I wanted to see Basil & at last we compromised, Shepard to go to Town Hall to wait for bus and I to go very hurriedly to see Basil. But we missed the Bus & had Basil to tea in town. Saw noone else interesting. Rain falling all the time and noone to be seen – all of them brewing in back-yards and basements, I suppose. Went to see Canning; Enid had been ill a fortnight and Canning was all in black and less fluent than usual.[6] He told me that I was very strong, awfully strong, extraordinarily strong and must play lots of football and gave me poems (vile things) by a friend of Aileen, to criticise and a copy of Chelsea Buns,

1 – J. B. Fagan's production of Strindberg's *Ghost Sonata* (1907), presented as *The Spook Sonata* in the Oxford Playhouse in 1926, later moved to the Globe Theatre, London, where it was reviewed by *The Times*, 15 June 1927, 14.

2 – Kolya Krasotkin, precocious and wayward character in the 'Boys' section of the novel.

3 – Alastair Macdonald; see FLM to GBM, 13 May 1926, n. 2, p. 113.

4 – Old Eagle Inn, also known as the St John's Arms, at Rockley, near Marlborough. This was his old cross-country ('sweats') route.

5 – A reference to the man who sold his shadow in *The Charwoman's Shadow* by Dunsany.

6 – Clifford Canning, FLM's form master at MC, and his wife.

whose owner he had forgotten & which I left behind in the train.[1] I met Shepard at the station. He had run away down the High St. when I went in to Canning.

I nearly came down to see you for Relay Races but was too much a pauper.

Canning was very worried about your hatred of Cambridge, and wouldn't believe me when I told him it was probably somewhat exaggerated.

Burrell[2] is flourishing socially, in the O.U.D.S. et cetera, and his white mice though they smell. Shepard is going down to M.C. next week-end. I wanted John Hilton to go there before walking home but he won't. If, however, YOU came down here next Saturday you could collect John H. & me (& Alastair H.) and take us there by force. Alastair is going anyhow. Instead of you going the week after, which is a foolish time. Anyhow you can do both. Because that is the ideal idea – lots of solacing & suitable O.M.s to support one and before the term has accelerated to a scramble for labels and packing straw. And if you don't come I shall have to walk back with John Hilton on Saturday, instead of Sunday night to Monday, which would be much better.

I hear (J. G. C. Spencer wrote to Shepard) that you have become quite sane.[3] Cheering from Mynors. That is very sad. Because I know what Spencer's idea of sanity is. However he's such a dolt, I expect it's untrue. Alastair H. is well and looking charming. I have relapsed into my aloof skepticism [sic] like Gallio[4] and the Cupids pass me by on the other side – I read the lesson in chapel this morning and was suddenly obsessed with an Irish pronunciation of certain words. Dreadful.

Your brother was down here but I was out, very sorry.

Hope you come; anyhow may I come to the mountain.

Yrs.

Louis M.

1 – Noël Coward, *Chelsea Buns* (1925).
2 – Burrell is untraced.
3 – John Gray Churchill Spencer (1907–77), educ. Marlborough 1920–6; Magdalene College, Cambridge; London Hospital.
4 – Gallio, Roman proconsul, AD 52. See Acts 18: 12–17.

1927

TO *John Hilton*   MS Bodleian

January 1927   [Merton College, Oxford]

My dear John,

And how are you? I suppose your brothers are now at home. I was very disappointed in your house – not at all properly suburban.[1] Have you seen Anthony lately? He is going to burn his books. He was down at M.C. the weekend I was there and we ate our dinners in the dark with Canning who had been sinning against the Holy Ghost and blowing his nose on horseback in pink silk pyjamas near Brown's Copse and Mrs. Brown who was surprised. I have been reading 'Daphnis & Chloe' (Abbey Classics) & writing Conventional Serenades.[2] In London I got the Cezanne Still Life & a booklet by D. H. Lawrence – 'Glad Ghosts' – good.[3] Charles was looking charming. He does not live at Farnborough (only was staying there) a great relief because it is so foul & military. He lives in the remote interior of Cornwall in a dark glade shining like the moon through trees or white feet on the sand when the dark sea throws itself up after them and the bits of sand scuttle away and progress becomes retrograde.[4] He was dressed very nicely but wearing very jolly very vagabond shoes because he was (I suppose) going to wear brown tomorrow and his usual black were packed. He still has a delightful appetite. He is not at Big Fire, which is good, and

1 – The Hiltons lived in Northwood, Middlesex. JH's younger brothers were Roger and Michael: Roger Hilton (1912–75), painter, educ. Bishop's Stortford College and the Slade. Commandos 1939–40 (POW); UNESCO prize 1964; CBE 1968. Michael Hilton (1913–2001), educ. MC 1926–30; RA 1939; Intelligence Corps 1941–5. Later diplomatic correspondent and leader writer with the *Daily Telegraph*.
2 – Longus, *Daphnis and Chloe*, trans. George Thornley, intro. George Saintsbury (1923).
3 – D. H. Lawrence, *Glad Ghosts* (1926). FLM and AB admired the work of Cézanne. FLM recalled: 'Cézanne, of course, was the touchstone' ('Landscapes', *SAF*, 234); AB wrote: 'Modern Art in 1923 meant Cézanne first and the other Post-Impressionists, who were still regarded in this country as dangerous revolutionaries' ('From Bloomsbury to Marxism', 165). Cf.: 'Admire Flaubert, Cézanne – the tortured artists', 'Eclogue from Iceland', *EC*, CP07, 76. They bought their prints of Cézanne and others from Zwemmer's bookshop on the Charing Cross Road. Cf. 'Zwemmer's' in G. Grigson, *Recollections* (1984), 38–42.
4 – The Edward-Collins family home was near Bodmin, Cornwall.

he dislikes all the new boys in our house, which is good taste.[1] He did not get an Upper but he may be going to play against Clifton Colts next term. He said Stenning had been painting some very good things lately.[2] We sat on a Sofa in the Castle & Ball.[3] But now in Cornwall he walks down the forest avenue approaching his house swinging a lantern, eclipsed at each step by himself, while evergreens crane down at him until he goes into the great portico and the bang of the door leaves silence and darkness.

To return to prose & stupid people like you & me, why should expression of one's likes be a pose and conforming to an arbitrary fashion be natural? And when the devil will people realise that all art MUST be artificial? As if one could produce a poem in the same spontaneous way as a belch.

Yrs.
<u>Louis M.</u>

TO *Anthony Blunt*   MS Cambridge

Postmark 9 January 1927   Merton College, Oxford

My dear Anthony,

Will you come over here any time after you go down and we can put you up? That will be delightful.

Give my love to Michael and Alastair M. I am sorry Michael is going out.

We stay up about a fortnight longer, you see.

I am hopefully beginning the Golden Bough so as to hinge on to the tradition.[4]

What fun selling your soul to those millionaires in Italy.[5]

Art begins and ends in the Phallos. If you are discreet you will get out halfway in this circular tour. The flesh catcalls on the roof.

---

1 – Big Fire, gathering of senior boys at large fireplace in Upper School: 'The group who monopolised the biggest of the two fires which alone provided any heat, was known as Big Fire, like some gang of Indian braves' (T. Hinde, *Paths of Progress: A History of Marlborough College*, 1992, 135). Cf. FLM's memories of Big Fire in *SAF*, 83–4.

2 – Presumably Alexander Dives Stenning (b.1911), educ. MC 1924–9; New College, Oxford.

3 – The Castle and Ball, High Street, Marlborough.

4 – J. G. Frazer, *The Golden Bough* (1890–1915), which T. S. Eliot had invoked in *The Waste Land*.

5 – Blunt had arranged to tutor the sons of French art dealer René Gimpel at Lake Como in summer 1927. In the end he resented the position since 'he was treated like a servant' (Carter, 50).

John Bowle gave me a heart to heart talk the other night and has now, I opine, consigned me to Limbo and Coventry.

Graham and I are producing 'Troilus and Cressida' in modern dress next term.

I am half-asleep. The original 'Anatea' is marrying a man called Mr. Cree.

What do you think of Wyndham Lewis' onslaught on the moderns? He will try to build a wall between the idea (or spirit) and the form – as in the book on Shakespeare, i.e. between Craftsman and Creator. It is obvious that any idea in a new dress must produce a new effect. Ideas are all very much the same in the nude.

But he is very brilliant. That is what suggested 'Troilus and Cressida' (the 'Lion & the Fox' I mean).[1] If you will base your judgment of Shakespeare on the Merchant of Venice . . .

I hear Guillebaud is marrying. I am sending him an Epithalamion, including a few practical hints.

So come here and bring with you the Elixir Vitae or, failing that, Mortis[.] So saying he rubbed the stone and the genie appeared weeping tears like sawdust –

Yrs with love – Louis M.

TO *Basil Barr*[2]   MS Emory

Postmark 12 January 1927   Carrickfergus

My dear Basil

Thanks so much for your letter. I was sorry not to see you before going but I left rather hectically after a breakfast of ambrosia and nectar – although I was feeling so ill after a night on the Downs that I couldn't feel

1–Wyndham Lewis, *The Lion and the Fox: The Role of the Hero in the Plays of Shakespeare* (1927).
2–George Basil Thomas Barr (1909? 67), educ. Marlborough 1922–7; Clare College, Cambridge; CBE 1961. Alastair Macdonald recalled: '[Blunt] was friendly with a boy called Basil Barr (later referred to by MacNeice in letters to Blunt as "beautiful Basil"), who was very homosexual, but I don't think he had a crush on him', qtd Carter, 41). Barr read Law at Clare and went to Gray's Inn in 1931, later serving in both the Army and RAF (Legal Adviser's Department 1941–5). His obituarist ('C.S.K.B.') described Barr as 'both an individualist and a conformist. As individualist, he was erudite on unusual subjects like pre-Conquest English history and water colours of the eighteenth and nineteenth centuries. As conformist, he lived a life of public and private service. He was a shy man, but he could be vastly amusing when in the mood' (*The Times*, 24 Jan. 1967, 14). This letter was addressed to Barr at Ormiston, Kirknewton, Midlothian, Scotland.

anything, which was all to the good as eating is an irreverent action and one has to look at one's plate.[1] I am so relieved he doesn't live at Farnborough which he detests.[2] He asked me if he could see me again that term which I thought delightful – I was almost persuaded to stay but my people were ramping. What rather bowled me over was that on bidding me farewell on the High St. he raised his cap, which annoyed me very much but I couldn't reprove him by the time I recovered from the shock and as it was Dr. Knight was looking on rather grimly.[3]

Yes, a very nice little boy in Priory – name Enid (i.e. in their play) but I don't know his real name – a little disappointing in real life.[4] By the way I wrote some rather derivative amorous verses the other day –

'The sea now hoary with desire
Yet follows feet that walk the beach
The sensuous plumes of brine as fire
But cannot reach beyond their reach
Will amor'd Neptune never tire . . .'
    et cetera.

Colwin's is rather a Madonna blue, I think, serene like evening.

I have just read Yeats' 'Autobiographies'.[5] Quite a lot about Oscar Wilde. I still admire Wilde very much though they must have been a trying circle e.g. Ernest Dowson was just a fag-end of drunkenness.[6] And Yeats, of course, believes in ghosts. The World was not made by Aldous Huxley. You must remember this. Dreadful little intellectual frothing away & showing off so nicely.

I had a letter from Ross today first since last vacation. He seems to think you are a pantheist I don't know what he thinks I am – something between an esoteric Buddhist and a Presbyterian.

How brave of you to go to a wedding, especially a family one. But then you are rather social. Next term I am expecting an eremite life, semi-nude with a great fire and beer and my new Zwemmer print of Cezanne Still Life

1 – Possibly he is referring to his visit the previous month with GS to MC, as described in letter of 6 Dec. 1926 to AB, when they had tea with Barr.
2 – The 'Charles' referred to in the previous letter to Hilton.
3 – Dr William A. Knight, senior Science master at MC 1919–30.
4 – Priory, a junior house at MC.
5 – He reviewed *Autobiographies* in *Cherwell*, 29 Jan. 1927, 28.
6 – Cf. Gabriel Crash's protest in *RW*: 'I'd rather have a soul than a character any day. Look at Ernest Dowson. Look at Lionel Johnson. They were better men than you but—' (70).

and myself lying on cushions before the fire utterly impracticable [*sic*] and the smoke curling itself into Venuses and Adonises and other people. If I had a car I should come down and bring you & Colwin & C.T. to tea in my room and I would play my toy musical box; it only has one tune – some sort of Hymenaeal.

I am thinking of writing a Pastoral mask bringing in all my favourite lyrics and getting people to act it somewhere on a dewy lawn with artificial stylised flocks and skilled persons playing Pan-pipes. We might do it in the arena at Martinsell towards the end of next term. I would bring down my people and you could lead out the few enlightened or delightful Marlburians and when it was over we would climb to the top and lead a rout about the trees & then lie down gasping looking over the plain & refresh ourselves with wine. Each person would wear a great bunch of appropriate flowers and hold a peeled wand in his hand with a few of the same flowers tied round it. It would be a very hot day with noise like drums in the distance yet the air would be fresh.

It is splendid about your dormitory. Have you read 'Glad Ghosts' by D. H. Lawrence? Also you must read 'Daphnis & Chloe' by Longus (Abbey Classics). They are both appropriate.

All my poetry this vacation has been amorous except some stanzas about Hell:-

> 'Thin filaments of wind we gather
> like the spray from falling water,
> the drops from Charon's oars patter
> with a flaccid vapid pother,
> like pale lamps we wave & gutter.
>
> We have no longer lovers now
> from Saturday to Saturday,[1]
> frayed black velvet is the sky
> & wax flowers in endless row
> tell us there is nothing new.
>
> Gray [*sic*] vistas of suburban meadows
> where the rivers drag their shallows
> but now no river-god now follows

1 – Cf. 'To click the bonds of business / From Saturday to Saturday.' From 'Candle Poems', *BF* (1929); repr. as 'Candles', CP07, 637.

any lady of the shadows,
calm they lie on flaxen pillows.[']

———

I have given up being discontented with life although I am. After all there are all the things that melt in the mouth. And there are one's immortal mind & immortal body (both immortal in the same way, melting in the mouth) to be satisfied, walking about like lions searching for unicorns. Sometimes one sees the tip of the horn like a star above the woods and then one tosses back one's mane and runs like fire, leaving a track of sparks like a comet and the unicorn glances between tree-trunks and slips round the horizon. Or one comes upon him standing by a lake and then he plunges into the reflected foliage, there is a chaos in the craters and then there are the reflections again but he is hidden behind them, ensconced in a Mystical Fourth Dimension.

Did you get your scholarship[?]

If not I presume you will get one at Oxford. Do try.

I am going to start an Enthusiastic Society, a reaction to all the typical Oxford cynicism and superior boredom. It will be a Society without theories, the only premise being 'Coronemus nos rosis antequam marcescant'[1]

Richard I don't believe in although I once fell in love with him myself for about 3 days. Which I consider depraved in myself. Besides A.A.W.W. defiling the waters. Although apart from taste I don't damn W.W. For which forgive me. I'm sure he is frightful to live with. <u>And the brother.</u>[2]

Phoenix & The turtle Fled
In a Mutual Flame from Hence.[3]

I have only just found that that is a really good poem. I should like to see the Phoenix and its resurrection – in a Druid clearing in the woods – 'feathers green across Casbeen'.[4] The union of two flames is the completest

---

1 – Thomas Jordan (1612–85), 'Coronemus nos Rosis antequam marcescant' ('Let us drink and be merry' etc.), in Quiller-Couch, *Oxford Book of English Verse: 1250–1900*.

2 – A. A. Wynne Wilson (1908–38), educ. MC 1923–7. His brother, C. B. Wynne Wilson (b.1912), also attended MC 1926–8.

3 – Shakespeare, 'The Phoenix and Turtle', ll. 23–4.

4 – 'By feathers green, across Casbeen / The pilgrims track the Phoenix flown', from 'The Phoenix' by A. Christopher Benson (1862–1925), in Quiller-Couch, *Oxford Book of English Verse: 1250–1900*.

of unions; their wedding bed is also the altar of cremation and in smoke they are not divided.

I have again renounced women (Mary Shepard being wrapt in oblivion) but I fear it may not last.[1]

I am very eager to read 'Mrs. Dalloway' by Virginia Woolf.[2] I have read some wonderful extracts from it, strange rhythms and an exquisite correlation of sensations. She must be a good Modern, I think, but Aldous Huxley is 'dust a little gilt'.[3] I am going to visit Robert Graves next term & get him to write a preface to one of my books.[4] He is Irish. As Oscar Wilde said 'We Irish are too poetical to be poets; we are a nation of brilliant failures, but we are the greatest talkers since the Greeks.'[5]

Sorry to be pouring out all this stuff on you. I want to go to a wake. My father says that at a wake there is a basket of new clay pipes on the right of the door and each man takes one as he enters, which he fills from a great plate of tobacco on the chest of the corpse who is laid out in the middle. Then the professional mourning women intone a dirge and suddenly break off to talk gossip while in another room the men drink poteen. Imagine that sometimes in the small hours the corpse too feels thirsty and sitting up calls for a glass. All the house begins to sway to the rhythm of the keening while strange people outside press their hairy faces against the window. When I have a tomb it will be a large and broad one with ancestral portraits on the walls so that when I feel inclined I can take a walk round and talk to them for company – no, not ancestors I think. And next term I am going to claim acquaintance with my Merton ghost, who is at present rather vague though I often see him at the window griping at the pane. I feel he is a dead immoralist.

I told Charles I wasn't coming to M.C. any more but I expect I shall. The College is so sordid, all the black puppets trolling round with their kishes. Still it is worth it. Don't you think Charles was looking very beautiful at the end of last term[?] I wish his photograph did him justice.

Anthony & I have become very avuncular to each other of late – Mutual Correction League and Wipe Your Shoes on the Mat Dear.[6] Every one

1 – Mary Eleanor Jessy Shepard (1909–2000), artist and illustrator, sister of Graham; m. (1937) Edmund Knox.
2 – Published 1925.
3 – Shakespeare, *Troilus and Cressida* (III.iii): 'And give to dust, that is a little gilt, / More laud than gilt o'er-dusted.'
4 – See FLM to AB, 17 Nov. 1926: 'I must make a pilgrimage to see Robert Graves some time.'
5 – Wilde's remark qtd in W. B. Yeats, *Autobiographies:* 'The Trembling of the Veil', Book I, x.
6 – For example, cf. FLM to AB, 3 Nov. 1926.

corrects me so much that there is hardly any of me left. E.g. Guillebaud didn't say anything at M.C. but he grinned at me like the Holy Ghost and even Canning gave me a long lecture before I left. I hope you don't take up the habit. You have been very good so far. Forgive this trash & give my love to Colwin while you can take some for yourself

Yrs. Louis M.

TO *Georgina Beatrice MacNeice*　　　　　MS Dan MacNeice

[7 February 1927]　　　　　Merton College, Oxford

My dear Drina

It was with the greatest pain that I realised how long it was since my last letter. Fifteen and six the Pullover cost, a jolly one of a plain colour somewhere between yellow and terra-cotta. There was some snow here but now it is just plain Oxford. I went to breakfast with Richard Best and a bad poet yesterday, very good for eating and not bad conversation. I am writing an obscure paper for the Bodley Club (this College's Literary Society). I have more interesting lectures this term e.g. Cyril Bailey who is prominent & has a sense of humour.[1] One of my lecturers suddenly stopped me in the street & exhorted me to play in an University Tennis Tournament. I then recognised him as the don who was staying at Marlborough at the end of the summer. It was too late to go in for the tournament. I have yet played no tennis – nor anything else. Thanks so much for the groceries. I have discovered the values of coffee as an antidote to sleep – but you should drink it in bowlfuls. I have bought a lamp-shade (apparently orange) for my room.

My Scout hid the black table cloth behind the bookcase. I don't think he likes my pictures.[2]

1 – Cyril Bailey (1871–1957), CBE, classical scholar. Educ. St Paul's School and Balliol College, Oxford. As FLM implies, Bailey's lectures were popular. According to his obituarist, 'His lectures were exhaustively prepared and admirably delivered, and he was second to none as a teacher of Latin and Greek composition. At the same time he was preparing and publishing works connected with the subjects of his special studies – Lucretius, Epicurus, and the Religion of the Romans' (*The Times*, 6 Dec. 1957, 13). A former colleague of Bailey's commented on his famed sense of humour: 'All this simple humour preserved his high seriousness from any touch of the high-faluting, and allayed the natural alarm of young philistines finding themselves upon the threshold of the Arts' ('L.E.J.', *The Times*, 12 Dec. 1957, 16).
2 – 'When [my scout] was reproaching me, for my taste in pictures . . . he would edge to the door for his curtain line and then slam it behind him' ('Landscapes', *SAF*, 232). Cf. 'When he told a story he closed the door on you to clinch it' (*RW*, 91).

148

How good that Harry has repaired the musical boxes. You should put one at the end of the Broad Walk at Sea-Park and then track it down the vista on a day of white clouds and infant bees. Or you could Hunt the Slipper with them through all the 'gardens & gallant walks';[1] the notes would come trickling through the leaves and flowing down the steps by the conservatory where they would lose themselves in a wide estuary of air. Then you might put one in the greenery where it could fight with the water-music (for you would turn on the fountain) and you could see the greenish drops of water falling twined with the pinker drops of music like a varied neck-lace [sic].

Or again place them at the far end of the lawn where their sound would be like a fire through an inverted telescope. Or on the bridge to the Bathing Box where their notes would be now submerged in brine, now would raise their heads dripping and sleek between the waves like a boat rising and falling. And the sound would be like the bells of a sunk ship or the sirens of a liner a mile below the Atlantic.[2] But it should be a still day, else the wind like an eagle would seize them up like victims and their reddened feathers would fall here and there about the house.

Alastair Hamilton and a friend of his are trying to borrow a baby Austin for next Saturday, that we may all three go down to Marlborough to inspirit the people there.

At the Bodley Club the other night a young clergyman read a paper on 'The Poetry of the Opposition' which turned out to be mostly Blake, Byron and Shelley.

My room reminds me of the remark of the painter Gauguin (the man who ran away to Tahiti) – 'If you want to express green-ness, a metre of green is more green than a centi-metre.' Or as Andrew Marvell says, 'annihilating all that's made to a green thought in a green shade'.[3] Thus it is that I anticipate the spring but hang behind the summer unless I shall heap the room with flowers so that the painted wood of the panels will preen itself on its blossoms. In the summer I shall make the fireplace as a silvan altar, great festoons of furze and bloom.

1 – From 'New Jerusalem': 'Thy gardens and thy gallant walks / Continually are green' (anon., *Song of Mary the Mother of Christ*, 1601), in Quiller-Couch, *Oxford Book of English Verse: 1250–1900*, 91–2.
2 – Presumably he has in mind the *Titanic*, which he watched with his father leaving Belfast Lough ('Autobiographical Talk: Childhood Memories', BBC, 1963; repr. *SP*, 271; Stallworthy, 32). The image of the sunken bell resurfaces in *Autumn Journal*: 'Though yet her name keeps ringing like a bell / In an under-water belfry', *AJ*, XVI, CP07, 139.
3 – From Andrew Marvell, 'Thoughts in a Garden', in Quiller-Couch, *Oxford Book of English Verse: 1250–1900*, 390–2.

In the Ashmolean there is a jolly picture of Venice by Canaletto, in the middle a block of buildings and on either side two water vistas with the gondoliers poling.[1] The smell of flowers might draw one into the picture when one would drift down the smooth canal, chequered with shadows, the perspective would expand, one would drift and turn the corner.

There is a Stag Hunt in the Forest by Night attributed to Uccello where the grey-hounds go prancing in the most joyous curves, farther and smaller between the trees, followed by the hunters in vermilion coats.[2] // Love to All   Louis

TO *Anthony Blunt*   MS Cambridge

Postmark 7 February 1927   Merton College, Oxford

My dear Anthony

I have just written a very rhapsodic letter to my people all about musical-boxes in the Sacheverell[3] style and perspectives of Canaletto, so you will have to be content with prosaics.

I am reading D. H. Lawrence 'Twilight in Italy' – our vegetable aspects,[4] which is apposite to a paper I am writing called 'Joyce and Modern Poetry'.

I saw Betjeman in his lodgings the other morning. Wonderful room, dark panelling and lit by candles. Tangerines and gin and ginger beer and a printed book on flowers illustrated on every other page by a pressed flower neatly inserted, horrid corpses but very comic. They had all but inserted a heading into the 'Cherwell' saying 'Bishop Opens St. Mary the Virgin's Organ'.

I met an Anglo-Catholic Jew the other day who the day before had gone up to town to see a black-bearded saint off to India.[5]

John Hilton is distressed because you have given him up.

I have borrowed what promises to be an interesting book on Art from Alastair by George (?) Cox called 'Art for Amateurs' or something horrid like that.[6]

1 – Giovanni Antonio Canal detto Il Canaletto (1697–1768).
2 – Uccello (1397–1475), *The Hunt in the Forest*.
3 – Sitwell.
4 – A book of travel essays published in 1916.
5 – Cf. FLM to GBM, 25 Feb. 1927. He puts this more offensively in his memoirs: 'There were many Anglo-Catholics. One of these was a tall, gross young man with a sweeping Jewish nose, rich wet lips and a wish to convert people' (*SAF*, 107).
6 – George J. Cox, *Art, for Amateurs and Students* (1926).

The only thing that is not truth is verisimilitude. See 'Tiger, Tiger burning bright'.[1]

The fire is so hot that I can't think.

Alastair & a friend of his are trying to borrow a baby Austin for next Saturday that we may go again to the house of the damned.

A friend of John's saw us at Twickenham & thought you were my brother!!

What of the Ancient Mariner?

I have a toy musical-box which I play at night. Like a bath-tap.

As Mme. Blavatsky warned one of her disciples I am hearing the divine spark within me snore.[2] So farewell with lullaby.

Love to W.L., Alastair & Michael.[3]

Yrs in the peace of the Lord
<u>Louis Sanctus</u>

TO *Georgina Beatrice MacNeice*　　　　MS Dan MacNeice

[25 February 1927]　　　　　　Merton College, Oxford

My dear Drina

Of course Elizabeth would choose the one weekend when I was really engaged. Anthony is coming down to stay with a man in Balliol. But I expect John will do his bit.[4] I went to tea with him last week – He was in great form.

One Mr. Schiff and I are starting a society which shall not be a society. He is a most remarkable man – a Jew, an Anglo-Catholic, is going out to India, wears ugly plus-fours, is always trying to express himself in verse & is very susceptible to music.[5]

I went to a delightful concert the other night, archaic instruments – harpsichord, lute, viols, recorders and a spinet. A lute is so beautiful in shape like a split melon water-dropping. But a harpsichord is the most wonderful in tone. An old man in black with a gaudy tie and long white

1 – William Blake, 'The Tyger'.
2 – Cf. W. B. Yeats, *Autobiographies*: 'There was a woman who talked perpetually of "the divine spark" within her, until Madame Blavatsky stopped her with, "Yes, my dear, you have a divine spark within you and if you are not very careful you will hear it snore"' (157). Cf. 'Bagpipe Music' (1937), CP07, 95.
3 – Alastair Macdonald and Michael Robertson; 'WL' is unidentified.
4 – Nicholson, presumably.
5 – Possibly Sydney Alfred Schiff (pseud. Stephen Hudson) (1868–1944), novelist, Proust translator and patron of the arts. See also FLM to AB, 7 Feb. 1927.

hair, very foreign was running the show. He made me think of monkeys with green eyes, like the sun through leaves, collecting jangling coins in deep bass dishes, the coins falling from shuttered windows in a southern street.

John H. & I went for a walk the other day (I have bought a beautiful ash-plant with a great knob).[1] Dreadful country this is, hung under a wet blanket – and we had decayed tongue in an Inn.

I anticipated spring the other day. It was great but now it is gone again in the wet –

> 'A great while ago the world began
> With heigho the wind & the rain
> but that's all one, our play is done,
> & we'll strive to please you every day.'[2]

Last week I went to 'King Lear' – the O.U.D.S., a wonderful Russian setting.

I met John Fothergill the Hotel Keeper at Thame & friend of Augustus John, the other day – with buckles on his shoes, a tie of many colours and a black hat perched on top of his weird black hair.[3]

What am I to do with Elizabeth & Anthony?

They are rowing bumping races here this week. My place is at the moment Head of the River, so I am not its only distinction.

Well,

> I hope you are all well
> and love to William
> Louis M.

Dreadful place, dreadful rain and Spring still procrastinates – in some far arbour . . .

---

1 – JH wrote: 'About this time he acquired a large knobbed ash walking-stick which was sometimes a danger to passers-by. It became invested with the qualities of Stephen Dedalus's ashplant' (*SAF*, 252).

2 – Shakespeare, *Twelfth Night* (V.i), 'When that I was and a little tiny boy.'

3 – Cf. Hilton's account of this journey to Fothergill's Inn in Thame, Oxfordshire (*SAF*, App. B, 258).

TO *Georgina Beatrice MacNeice*   MS Dan MacNeice

14 March [1927]   Merton College, Oxford

My dear Drina,

Thanks so much for the groceries which are invaluable. (It is a long time since I have written as you may have noticed.)

Expect me home on Tuesday 22nd.

Here life is placid. Our college were head of the River.

Graham may be coming over to Ireland towards the end of April to stay with some people at Ballymoney and we hope to go for a ramp 'on wet roads where men walk'.[1]

You might start us off in the Austin, pick Graham up at Ballymoney and drop us penniless on a rocky coast. Then over the hills and far away.

I shall have to look pretty hard these 'holidays' (one must not become too varsity and talk about 'vacs.' – vile jargon) for I am to be examined on four Greek plays at the beginning of next term.

> John Hilton and I intend to hire a canoe
> to race up water alleys
> under willows and pile
> the poop with fruit –
> reciting to the trees like
> Troubadors while even
> cracked pianos jangling
> in the distance are tuned
> by the alchemy of summer
> to a shower of sleepy gold.
> Then borne Ophelia-like we
> drift to slumber, dissolve
> into the waters as ripples
> drown the sun's reflection.

> Much love to all
> <u>Louis M.</u>

1 – W. B. Yeats, 'The Happy Townland'. Ballymoney (where Shepard was visiting) lies forty miles northwest of Carrickfergus.

[Hilary term 1927]   Merton College, Oxford

Basil my love

Hidden in the deeps of time like an over-rippled moon's reflection, I come again to plumb your dolorous waters and with a silken net to fish you out of slumber.

Next weekend I am coming to your town with a red-haired man and the redhaired man will stay and admire the Burne Joneses in the Chapel.[2]

Anthony was down here this term staying with John Bowle. We spurned the scum of Oxford and all the broken fountains spouted, spurning up in a silver tinkling spear that drew from the clouds a vermeil blush.

So now will you come and wander downsward.

Let the galled jade wince and Guillebaud flee.[3] Hold the fort for I am coming.[4]

Holla ye pampered jades of Asia[5] –
Out of the night of
Oxford epigrams . . .

> Love to you with tulips
> Love to you with nightingales
> Love to you with crocuses
> Golden cars of Proserpine;
> Upon the hills of Crete
> the Kourētes[6] clang their
> cymbals to hide the infant
> cries of Jews and harbinger
> the spring, vernal eternal,
> eternal vernal,

Love to you with pregnant buds. Yrs.
Louis M.

1 – The letter was addressed to Barr at C House, Marlborough College.
2 – Edward Burne-Jones designed the 'Scholars' Window' on the south side of Marlborough College Chapel, which portrays the boys Samuel and Timothy. Cf. 'Oh, I was forgetting chapel. Yes, come on. It's full of Burne-Jones and William Morris' (*RW*, 100).
3 – 'Let the galled jade wince, our withers are unwrung', *Hamlet* III.ii.
4 – Attributed to General Sherman, but also a hymn by Philip Bliss.
5 – Marlowe, *Tamburlaine*, part 2, IV.iv.1–2. (FLM had recently reviewed *Christopher Marlowe* by Una Ellis-Fermor, in *Cherwell*, 19 Feb. 1927.) Cf. his memory of drinking at the Ritz on the occasion of Reggie Smith's wedding in 1938: 'None of us had been in the Ritz before and we felt like Tamburlaine – "Holla, ye pampered jades . . ."' (*SAF*, 210).
6 – The nine dancers who venerate the goddess Rhea.

TO *Anthony Blunt* MS Cambridge

Postmark 29 March 1927 Carrickfergus

My dear Anthony,

Just go and change your shoes, I know what these walking-tours are and it accounts for a great deal of rheumatism and ungodliness in later life. I myself went down to Marlboro' with a red-haired man and we slept in the topmost shed on Broadleaze where by night the dons were heaving like many-breasted Cybele. So at 3.0 a.m. we walked in the forest where all the trees were dripping lugubriously and the white rumps of the deer walked away like ghosts. Canning invited me to M.C. by canoe so next term I shall plough up the Kennet pushed by waternymphs and eating grapes – 'supine on the floor of a narrow canoe'.[1] We discovered T. S. Eliot's walk at Oxford, where four gasometers stand over the Isis – 'the river sweats oil and tar'.[2] There we shall paddle next term with a large musical box playing silly polkas – 'This music stole by me upon the waters' – but at the moment I am working as it is called; for at the end of last term my tutor told me he would give me collections at the beginning of next – on 4 Greek plays (the hardest in the language), 16 books of Homer and 16 speeches of Cicero – none of which I have read. My last tutorial was altogether unfortunate. He said 'You have been doing Cicero this term?' (lectures or something) so I said yes. He said 'Did you do the so & so' so I said 'No' very promptly, when he said 'Did you do so & so?' so I said 'No' more promptly but he then said 'Did you do the so & so?' I then thought for a long time, all in a muck of sweat and eventually said 'Well as a matter of fact, I didn't go to any lectures because the man was so dreadful.' This was received rather badly and at my donrag he told the Warden that with hard work I might attain the standard of a postmaster.

Basil is going to stay with you or by proxy with your people.

I have been having such curious dreams, visions and phantasmania lately. e.g. At the end of last term I dreamt (it really was the most disgusting experience of my life) that I married the anglo-Catholic Jew who had somehow assumed femininity.[3] Ugh. Then I saw a witch in a blue robe

---

1 – This and the following quotations are from 'The Fire Sermon', section three of *The Waste Land*.

2 – '[We] used to paddle along the evil-smelling canal through the slums or up the Isis past the gas drums' (*SAF*, 108). Cf. 'Our first summer term we shared a hired canoe and, partly because of *The Waste Land*, spent whole afternoons or even mornings paddling beneath the gas works' ('Landscapes', *SAF*, 233).

3 – See FLM to GBM, 25 Feb. 1927, p. 151.

who vanished and yesterday I saw the three Fates wheeling the Future in a perambulator and King Solomon weighing himself on a penny-in-the-slot machine. Then the Court Jester came in and gave the machine a lozenge whereupon it began to purr and revolved its dial round and round very fast. Then a drunk man came out of a cinema that was underwater and embracing a pillarbox began to kiss it but all his kisses turned into letters edged with broad black bands of mourning which shot down its mouth. All the time a submarine carillon was sounding in the cinema.

I have decided to be a tennis-blue next term. I am going to achieve this by winning the University Tournament. I am going to achieve this by exploiting a red handkerchief and quotations from 'Ulysses.'

I have just discovered my pedigree

Concobhar MacNessa = Clytemnestra   Hamlet = Katherine of Aragon
                | |
           St. Brandon   Playboy of the Western World
                | |
         Stephen Dedalus   Bishop Heber
                | |
          Don Quixote   =   Queen Victoria
                                 |
                              Myself.

This is not an allegory – only a matter of lefthanded alliances and because I am feeling silly after the Oresteia – 'You don't see them you don't but I see them.'

I have latterly read 'Mrs. Dalloway' (V. Woolf) – superb – and as being a one-day novel with similar interweavings of subjective & objective to Ulysses interesting comparison, punctuated by the striking clocks – 'the leaden circles dissolved in air'.[1]

'Drop drop drop drop for nature's pride is now a withered daffodil[']'[2] but I was shocked by the following – 'In this roaring moon of daffodil and crocus' from Tennyson – Sonnet to usher in the 20th century – o this grotesque burlesque modernity.[3]

I am going to take up the cinema – unique powers of the combination of the latitudinal assault of painting with the longitudinal of music.

1 – Woolf, *Mrs Dalloway*, 186.
2 – 'Drop drop drop drop / Since nature's pride is now a withered daffodil': Ben Jonson, *Cynthia's Revels*, I.i.
3 – Tennyson, from 'Prefatory Sonnet' (1877), in *Ballads and Other Poems* (1880).

I am also going to start a new dynasty of the Sublimated Senses or Ruskin Revised. The Prince of Wales will declare open the first Phallic Procession to the accompaniment of massed bands and followed by an instructive lantern lecture.

I am afraid this is all stuff. It is the influence of homelife and archdeaconal telepathy. I am so afraid, incidentally, that my thoughts are becoming obvious to others; it must be so bad for their nerves.

To return to M.C. we went to Martinsell and the redhaired man received it with the most abject Philistinism. It was a very beautiful day

I saw C.T. from a window but I did not go to see him because I have left the world damn it.

The redhaired man and I met Andrews in court in the dark.[1] I said 'How is the Literary Society' to which he replied in a burst of confidence and saliva that it was Getting On Very Well in the Same Old Way.

I have run sterile; my Castalian fount is just dribbling over a beard of weed. I hope to clear my system by a surge of tragicomedia. Anyhow Spring ought to do something.

The cymbals of the Kourētes at the rebirth of my Zeus will deafen the Old Saturn that sits in my brain glowering while from his mouth flow reams of newspaper – Click Click Click.

> Dance we over heaven wonderingly
> Culling white starlight,
> Tomorrow falls the shadow
> From death the broken statue
> But dance dance dance
> Till Summer dolorously languorously
> Pulls the cords of slumber
> And folds her drove of sheep.

When I die I am becoming a woodpigeon and you are becoming a Hoopoe and Alastair Hamilton is becoming a canary. He will be in a Gothic cage before the Cherubim and you will flaunt along the walls of heaven and I will sit on a lot of old sticks making an occasional apophthegm. Graham Shepard will be an obscene parrot sitting on the Devil's shoulder.

1 – J. L. Andrews (1893–1968), MA; assistant master at MC 1923–7.

But for the moment let us crown our heads in camellias and go to see the phonofilm of this world joining hilariously in the final chorus – 'This is the Way the World Ends'.[1]

For a picture of the Zeit Geist see the woman leaning chin on hand in Picasso. She is getting us; we are sucked in among the drowned men making nets and wicker baskets – St. Satan's Home for the Drowned where these unfortunately disabled persons are enabled by kind attendance and sympathetic instruction at the same time to further the one decreasing purpose and to pay their own way – in fact to make good. The Old Saturn, Old Adam, has a reeking fancy. But Zeus will grow and straddle across the world and, a Blakian [sic] colossus, will toss that old disease to chaos – 'in huggermugger to inter him'.[2] This is our Indian dream on our way to the steep of Montmorency – see Keats.[3] See an early poem by me on the City of God –

> 'a ceaseless cataract of atoms churning . . . [sic]
> a million whirling spinning wheels of flowing gossamer
> a million hammers jangling on the anvils of the sky
> the crisp chip of chisels and the murmuring of saws
> and the flowing ripple of water from a thousand taps
> with the champ of griffin horses with their hoods in sacks of hay
> and sawdust flitting to & fro in newborn fragrancy.
> But not the same for all-flooding over weedy rocks
> a green sea singing like a dream & on the shore
> fair round pebbles with eggy speckles ½ transparent
> and dark sodden tangles of odorous wrack.'

A good poem but my critical faculty has gone up in smoke. How is yr brother?

Will you come for a ramp with me this summer? I am already due to ramp with lots of people but they don't matter.

I want to get away from the family and the Zeit Geist and the Old Saturn and the stinking picture palace. I don't want to marry a pillar-box. If I stay here all the time the Fates will wheel perambulators containing turnips heads in white and pink ribbons. I want to 'cuff the thunder with one

1 – T. S. Eliot, from the final stanza of 'The Hollow Men' (1925).
2 – 'We have done but greenly in hugger-mugger to inter him', *Hamlet* IV.v.
3 – 'Stop and consider! life is but a day; / A fragile dew-drop on its perilous way / From a tree's summit; a poor Indian's sleep / While his boat hastens to the monstrous steep / Of Montmorenci', Keats, 'Sleep and Poetry', ll. 85–9. The falls of Montmorenci are in Quebec.

hand'. Anywhere you like. D. H. Lawrence says you should always go South or West.

Yrs. till all the sots go dry
Louis M.

TO *Anthony Blunt* MS Cambridge

Postmark 5 April 1927   Carrickfergus

My dear Anthony,

We clowns shall skip through the hoops of the seven sphears [*sic*] and sway by our toes upon the balls of heaven. But what you and Brentnall were discussing about people and things is all stuff for as long as these are distinct they are unrealised.[1] A cypress tree is so much muck till it is ordered in the mind and man qua man is a stranded colour with no other to give it bearing. God is Nature (God the Father) receiving apotheosis from the individual Mind (God the Son) which is infused and stimulated by the blasts of the universal mind (God the Holy Ghost). The individual mind that has such powers is a Christ. Blake was the only Christ of Anglo-Saxonry, whipping Sir Joshua Reynolds out of the Temple.

Thanks so much for your letters.

→ S.W. 'We left behind the painted boy.'

I have been very pained by exploring my father's library. It is nothing but sex and Commentaries on the Second book of Kings.

All the people here are so many devout prisoners, phantoms chained to earth by clerical collars. One day there will be a volcanic snap and they will float away like bells borne out to sea.

In the New Jerusalem what will happen when the sea suddenly vanishes? All the drowned sailors will be revealed lying on a muddy strand playing on octopuses for bag-pipes and sporting with the SeaKing's daughters.[2] Yesterday I wrote a funeral song for a drowned sailor – 'They use his bones for dumbbells beneath the cliffs of Dover.'

I hear that sometime I may edit one of the Oxford papers. I shall then blow seven blasts as I walk round Oxford and the walls will fall flat – proctors will howl there and satirists will dance there.

1–H. C. Brentnall (assistant master at MC, 1903–44), see FLM to GBM, Easter 1922, n. 1, p. 67.
2–In 'Our God Bogus' FLM described the modern world as 'a blankness of mud below us and the danger of drowning and the nearness of octopuses', *Sir Galahad*, 2 (14 May 1929), 3–4.

I don't know why I am writing all this, throwing the sand against the wind. Out of your mouth there comes a great Boreas scouring the earth to a perfect nudity. When I write my first futurist play I shall have you, a κωφὸν πρόσωπον[1] walking in & out of rooms, and whenever you appear everything will blow off the tables and fly out of the window and the hair of the other characters will run desperately away from you.

I am endeavouring to arrange a parochial show to welcome in Spring but the curate is very suspicious.[2] He is to play vernal music (selected by me) against a background, painted by me, of angular lambs gambolling upon an undulating meadow under a trellis work of bells, flowers, stars and fruit. I am to declaim a prologue, various poems and an epilogue. Some real lambs (if too troublesome, they can be first asphyxiated and propped up) are to be exhibited and my father can give a short biblical talk on the subject.

Graham is in Languedoc, a mystical country, Land of Beulah. But talking of Cambridge I have some sort of uncle who lives near there.[3] I expect he is a clergyman which most of this family seems to be, excluding paupers, poets, lunatics and criminals.

I go to Oxford on Thurs. 27th

How nice that you should have been to see the horses. I saw some on the field near Broadleaze at five or so in the morning looming in the mist all taut and rugged and massive like the Mountain of Stones where you must not look behind you.

I am reading Aeschylus, Homer, Sophocles, Tchekov, Julian Huxley, McDougall, T. R. Glover, and Dean Inge.[4]

1 – 'Mute character'; the orthography is FLM's.
2 – Possibly Rev. W. J. Parr of Carrickfergus (cf. FLM to JH, Summer 1926, n. 3, p. 116).
3 – FLM's uncle was Rev. Herbert Henry Howell MacNeice, youngest brother of John Frederick MacNeice. Vicar of Melbourn and co-author, with William M. Palmer, of *Melbourn, Cambridgeshire*, etc. (1925). See Appendix 1.
4 – William McDougall (1871–1938), psychologist, author of *An Outline of Abnormal Psychology* (1926) and other works; T. R. Glover (1869–1943), classical scholar and historian, author of *Herodotus* (1924), *Democracy in the Ancient World* (1927) and other works; Rev. William Ralph Inge (1860–1954), dean of St Paul's (known as 'the gloomy dean'), author of *Society in Rome under the Caesars* (1907), *Lay Thoughts of a Dean* (1926), *Wit and wisdom of Dean Inge* (1927) and many other works. On Huxley, see next letter.

I have written a semi-automatic story 'The Twilight of the Gods', staged in Oxford, featuring the Murder of Balder contemporaneous with the discovery by Dr. Faustus of a new word in the lexicon.[1]

With apologies for writing so soon
Yrs. Louis

TO *Elizabeth MacNeice* MS Dan MacNeice

25 April 1927   4, Oxford & Cambridge Mansions,
                                        Marylebone, London NW

My dear Elizabeth,

Having at last discovered some ink which is not water and a pen which is intact I wish you all the appropriate things. You seem to have been having a very merry time – though last night I dreamed of you, very lugubrious and academic. I trust John's car has survived your minis-trations.[2] I have just taken our machine to the north coast and back with some family trepidation, but nothing worse than a dented mud-guard and a puncture.

The latest horror is that Margaret Johns is being installed at the Shamrock Tea Rooms. So passes the glory of Oxford. Mrs. Johns achieved a great sun-burst at Easter with a combination of pink primulas and daffodils on the Pulpit.[3] One of the Bintley children is staying with her and has mumps – the sine qua non of such sojourning.[4]

Are you coming up to that place next term or is the new firm too grim? I hear someone saw you walking down the Broad. As for that book of Tottenham's I have asked for it.

We have acquired instead of Harry a very stupid and large boy with a red face who is much loved by the family for his honest geniality.[5] He has just discovered that to start the car it is not necessary to turn on the inside light; he announced this to us all with great éclat.

1 – The Wagnerian title 'The Twilight of the Gods' was also given to a poem published in *BF* (CP07, 647–9). Balder the Beautiful, son of the Norse god Odin, was murdered by a mistletoe thrown at him by his brother Hod, who believed Balder was immune to all harm. Hod's hand was guided by the trickster Loki.

2 – John Nicholson, Elizabeth's fiancé.

3 – Margaret Johns (b.1909) was the second youngest of four children at Joymount House, Carrickfergus. See FLM to Eva Greer, 31 Aug. 1923, n. 5, p. 81.

4 – John and Mary Rose Bintley were parishoners at Carrickfergus. They had two children (Census of Ireland, 1911). Cf. FLM to GBM, 21 May 1922, n. 2, p. 67.

5 – Presumably 'David', whom EN describes pithily in the last sentence of Appendix 1 as 'a rather dumb boy who drove the car'.

Archie has reappeared like Adonis and is in great form – physical and vocal. He ran through a series of songs the other day – a sort of Musical Changes or whatever the name is – beginning with some ancient ballad about the Merchants of London Town going to Church, and via some Orange Anthems to 'There is a Happy Land', and thence to 'The Cat sat by the Barndoor'. He remarked to me the other night, speaking of the moon, that for other lamps one had to pay, for gas and oil and all the rest but no man ever paid for that lamp; and that if anyone tried to interfere with it they'd fall flat just like that.[1] Which I told to Graham Shepard who is staying at Ballymoney and he declared pagan. I met Graham on Monday and went as far as Ballymoney station with him. He disliked the people's voices but was evidently feeling romantick as he wanted a copy of the 'Pervigilium Veneris'.

I got Miss Hind's virulent verses and returned them with interest. I hear she is bringing out another book.[2]

The family are a little bewildered by my wilful schemes for the Summer Holidays – viz (a) to go with Anthony South and West to France, Spain or Morocco there to slough civilisation, (b) to go with Graham Shepard to the Latin Quarter in Paris, (c) to go with John Hilton for five weeks' harvesting in the middle of Canada, (d) to go with a lot of Oxford decadents to a Camp for Miners, (e) to go slumming with Mr. Schiff, a Roman-Catholic Jew.[3]

I had quite a pleasant time at the end of last term when I took a red-haired man for the week-end to Marlboro' and we slept in a half-open shed at the top of the playing-fields. Noone wanted us and it was cold but we walked in the forest at 3.30 in the morning with the trees dripping and the whites of the deer gleaming.

Next term I think of forming a society for My Education, formed of Theosophists, Scientists, Poets and Artists. By the way some time I hope to edit the 'Cherwell', when Graham and I will mop up Oxford.[4]

1 – Cf. 'And sometimes he would point at the sky and say "I believe in the Good Fella Up There," or point at the thin moon that appeared in the sky before twilight and say "Thon's the Good Fella's Lamp"' (SAF, 48).
2 – Elizabeth Shane (Gertrude Hind), whose chief publication in 1927 was *Piper's Tunes*. Others include *By Bog and Sea in Donegal* (1923), *Tales of the Donegal Coast and Islands* (1921), *Warming the Bed Pan* (play, 1933), and *Collected Poems*, 2 vols (1945).
3 – See FLM to GBM, 25 Feb. 1927, n. 5, p. 151.
4 – FLM had published several poems and prose pieces in *Cherwell* in 1926 and in 1927 he contributed several essays and book reviews, including reviews of Yeats (29 Jan.), Hugh MacDiarmid (5 March) and an essay on American Universities (25 June).

I hear Mrs. Johns with seven worse than herself descended on you at two in the morning, plundering the larders and giving Miss Tottenham hystericks. And what DID you talk about? Also Betty[1] was most entertained by your Hospital but Drina thought it was very morbid and not what SHE would have been entertained by when she was that age.

I have taken the book, which you offered me, by Julian Huxley, rather liking it though I object to the shoddiness though not to the principle of his sonnets.[2] What I mean is I approve of science bursting into poetry but I disapprove of it coming out all over a rash of doggerel. Also I don't see how you can cut out your stuff ready and paste it on so neatly as a preface just like a stamp-album – and a true poet cannot be a true philatelist.

I will now stop as I am all over tar from changing a wheel today between Ballymoney and Ballymena. The family thermometer was sadly deciduous for a little.

Next time I go to Belfast I shall probably send you some second-hand literature for your birthday – I forget the exact date – so do not be surprised at anything.[3]

I am in a dreadful state over my Collections next week on Everything that Ever was Written. I shall try a few nights with Liddell & Scott under my pillow and round my neck a locket with a picture of Homer cut out of a Royal Academy catalogue.[4] However I shall probably be rusticated – to cool retreats and rural lawns where I shall learn to play the lute.

> [*in pencil*] I have forgot to post this
>> So much Love
>> Louis

TO *Georgina Beatrice MacNeice*   MS Dan MacNeice

1 May 1927   Merton College, Oxford

My dear Drina.

I am here safely and have finished, I am glad to say, my Collections. John and I have been out in our canoe without mishap. The weather is

---

1 – FLM's step-cousin Margaret Elizabeth MacGregor Greer.
2 – Julian S. Huxley (1887–1975) won the Newdigate Prize in Oxford for his poem 'Holyrood' and some years after this letter was written he published *The Captive Shrew and other Poems of a biologist* (1932). His recent publications were *Essays in Popular Science* (1926) and *Religion Without Revelation* (1927).
3 – Elizabeth's birthday was 24 April.
4 – *Greek-English Lexicon*, comp. H. G. Liddell and R. Scott.

delightful, though not very hot, and the trees are half feather, half water. I have in my room cowslips and wall-flowers and yellow tulips and it is all very odorous. This morning I heard in the distance (6 a.m.) the chant on Magdalen Tower, followed by extraordinary joyous bells.

I think of going to-night to St. Aldate's to hear Dean Inge on 'Is there a God?' Prof. W. Brown is giving a lecture on 29th on Religion and Science.

I have met Richard Best who had a great time without many mishaps – except walking over a fifteen-foot drop at Monte Carlo. They stayed a week in Florence.

Graham, I think, will return tomorrow – sunburnt after Ireland.

I suppose Uncle Mac is back by now.[1]

The College Gardens are fascinating outside my window. Everything is fairly well out. I expect some tennis tomorrow.

John thinks his brothers may be poets. The youngest one has advanced from bottom of the school to 3rd from bottom. He has, acc. to John, lots of enthusiasms but no vitality. He is quite confident that he will be a millionaire.[2] John has, he says, two uncles in Toronto – one a doctor and one selling picture-postcards.

Tomorrow my Tutor is going to heap luminous coals on my head. But the yellow tulips are turning gracefully downwards into a Rokoko fountain so – though I would not be guilty of saying Beauty is Truth – I am quite contented.

> I send you love and wish
> you sunshine
> Louis

TO *Georgina Beatrice MacNeice*   MS Dan MacNeice

[May 1927]   Merton College, Oxford

My dear Drina

I call that an ungrateful remark about the stamps but I am trying to live up to it. This, if my memory holds, is Number Three.

I have now got some scarlet daisies with yellow middles and have evolved an entirely new theory about Virgil. Graham and I think of going down to Guildford at the end of the term in a punt.

1 – Thomas MacGregor Greer; see FLM to GBM, 5 Nov. 1921, n. 5, p. 58.
2 – Neither of his brothers Roger and Michael became a poet or a millionaire: see FLM to JH, Jan. 1927, n. 1, p. 141.

Elizabeth is here at the moment. Graham and I found her sitting on the river-bank on Saturday.

John H. and I went to hear Magdalen Choir sing in their cloisters yesterday evening.

I am thinking of getting Mr. Blackwell to publish an anthology of short prose-pieces by undergraduates.

I have just read a most illuminating book on Shakespeare, clearing away a lot of critical rubbish.

Anthony is getting a job as tutor in Italy for August which he describes as a menagerie but 'highly lucrative'.

I went to lunch with John N. the other Sunday and he told me of the exploits of his youth – e.g. electioneering and escaping the proctors.

If you listen very carefully you can hear a noise like a train going on all the time – 'Qūi‾te time' at ni‾ghttime' to cūt short' Kirkshaw.' I have written a little fantasia on this, blending it with my Virgil myth and atavism.

I got a letter from Daddie the other day 'for which relief much thanks'.[1] He was just going to the wild west like Saint Brandan, sailing into the sun.

I am also thinking of writing an historical thesis on 'The Pathetic Young Man' from Orestes through Hamlet and the Romantics and Tchekov etc. to the very latest specimens.

Sorry, I am being rather highbrow. Yes, I have ordered a new suit and bought various rags to cover myself. I shall probably be insolvent and hanged on the Martyrs' Memorial amid universal cheers.

I have booked another room for next term – immediately above mine but larger and panelled with the most revolting sham-graining. Still it has windows on both sides – a large one unto the Quad and two smaller unto the gardens (with the fire-place between them).

Graham cheered when he discovered about Miss Hind and Ernest H.

John's brother (the Marlboro' one)[2] sent him a letter the other day addressed –

Corpus Christi College

Cambridge

Herts.

which I thought distinctly brilliant. John was a little pained.

I am having a great number of afternoon teas viz – being both prodigal and priggish – though perhaps it is because I frequently cut Hall.

1 – Francisco, in *Hamlet*, I.i.8–10.
2 – Michael Hilton.

I have played a fair few games of tennis; my hand has worn away in three places.

So Elizabeth is going home. Here begins a new epoch – blare of trumpets – miniature Millennium etc. etc.

Oxford in Summer is a vast cucumber-sandwich – a layer of river-life and watery poetry between two great slices of soggy heat and sentimental athleticism.

I began writing a thesis the other day on 'Unconscious Humour and Great Unconscious Humorists' but finding that there was nothing or nobody outside that category, I desisted.

I am reading now a brilliant attack on the Child Cult of today (e.g. Peter Pan, Charlie Chaplin etc. etc). by an advocate of a return to the Intellect (a very rare person in these days of flux and popularised, misinterpreted Relativity-Theory).[1]

I am almost due for a Tutorial so goodbye – Love to All –

<u>Louis</u>

---

1 – 'We used the fashionable phrases of the highbrow twenties . . . and practised the fashionable child-cult' (*SAF*, 97). FLM wrote in 'Our God Bogus' (*Sir Galahad*, 2): 'Mr Hilton . . . says we are not to go back to the child and the primitive.' Cf. AB: 'we found the child cult a very useful way of exasperating the other boys in the school, which was one of our main ambitions' ('From Bloomsbury to Marxism', 164–5).

TO *Adrian Green-Armytage*[1]   MS Emory

[1927?]   Carrickfergus

My dear Adrian,

Wie geht es?[2] And could you either send me something <u>new,</u> or else last term's paper if you don't mind my extracting from it? And are there any books you would like to review? I shall be greatly grateful for any assistance you give me in my arduous . . .

Oh yes is it merely the text of the Ethics?[3] Or also the meaning?

I am become an optimist. Like Cratinus I have put away the Bottle for the Muse.[4]

I hope you are well and it is fine. We are all well and the cats are well. It is fine here too. I am planting sweet peas in my garden. My garden looks like this

[*Square diagram*]

I hope your friend Hugh is well. We are all very well here, thank you, and the cats are fine.

Miss Stein is well too, thank you, and Uncle Joyce is making puns in the jakes.[5]

Yes, I think it is a nice world. The sun is shining over here. Have you got a nice sun which shines too? Our sun is round but Uncle Joyce is going to take the step-ladder some day and make it what he calls rhomboid.

1 – Adrian Howell North Green-Armytage (1908–71), educ. Downside and Merton College, Oxford. He served in the Royal Navy during the war and later worked in Bristol as a stockbroker. An expert on the New Testament, he is the author of two books on the Evangelists: *John Who Saw* (1952), and *A Portrait of St Luke* (1955). See also his *Bristol Zoo, 1835–1965* (Bristol, 1964) and *Taking Stock: Collected Writings of A. H. N. Green-Armytage*, selected and ed. by Janet Kovesi Watt (Claremont, W. Aus., 2001). FLM wrote: 'I now had a new friend, Adrian, who was indolent and pliable and willing to abet my career of minor anarchism' (*SAF*, 113). Cf. 'Auden and MacNeice: Their Last Will and Testament': 'Item I leave to my old friend Adrian / Green Armitage [*sic*] who now is a stockbroker, / A jolly life as an English gentleman' (*LI*, CP07, 741). JH wrote: 'Louis's closest friend in Merton, Adrian Green-Armytage, was a charming, elegant, slender, gentle person who went about for a time in a cloak; a cousin of Graham Greene's' (*SAF*, App. B, 252). He was not in fact a cousin of Graham Greene's, though his first cousin, Vivien Dayrell-Browning, was married to Greene. Of his cloak, his daughter wrote: 'The cloak was made for him when he broke an arm or a collar-bone and had to wear a sling. He amused himself by having it in tweed, which puzzled people, since tweed was normally worn by the "hearties" and a cloak was the sort of garment an "aesthete" would wear. I gathered that he was a good customer of his tailor' (Janet Kovesi Watt, private correspondence, 2007).

2 – 'How are things?'

3 – Aristotle, *Nicomachean Ethics*.

4 – Cratinus (*c*.520–423 BC), Greek comic poet, author of *The Bottle*.

5 – Jakes: lavatory. Cf. Joyce, *Ulysses*, 4.494: 'He kicked open the crazy door of the jakes.'

Goodbye now and I hope you are reading a lot of Hegel.[1] I have not come on to him yet but my teacher says I shall be able to try three syllable words soon but not surds until the weather is warmer.

I am planting broad beans in my mind. My mind looks like this –

[Square diagram]

Love Ever
<u>Louis</u>

TO *Georgina Beatrice MacNeice*   MS Dan MacNeice

[11 June 1927]   Merton College, Oxford

My dear Madre,

Yet once more I write from the ruins of Carthage.[2] I am staying up here (probably) for a few days after term to see Graham act in the 'Tempest' and generally amuse him in his spare time. After that Graham and I had thought of going to his home in a punt. [']Apres ca le deluge' . . .[3]

Anthony is coming up here this week so we can make fuller arrangements.

One must beat things into shape; one must twist and hew and steal and borrow and maim and paint and cement and solder till the irrelevance of nature is distorted into order and an artificial harmony is produced which is more real than an unharmonious reality. For 'Beauty' etc. etc. are only generalisations and conventions – which are proper to the intellect. Yet we do not as yet intend to give up the intellect. It may be a fraud but as I said, an harmonious fraud is more true than the truth. In this sense a character like Hamlet is truer than anyone you may meet in the street.

I think it still holds good that nature imitates art. 'Humanity' is a work of art. That is all that distinguishes it from the rest of the physical world. It is the great fraud & the great triumph of the physical world. All the rest is 'natural'.

1 – Green-Armytage and FLM were both taught by Geoffrey R. G. Mure (1893–1979) at Merton, 'one of Oxford's few remaining neo-Hegelians' (*SAF*, 125). Cf. 'Auden and MacNeice: Their Last Will and Testament': 'The marriage of universals to Geoffrey Mure . . .' (*LI*, CP07, 737; a reference to Mure's 'The Marriage of Universals', *Journal of Philosophical Studies*, 1928. See note on Mure in Mendelson, vol. I, 789).
2 – On the eve of their departure from MC, FLM and AB proclaimed 'Ruins of Carthage' as they smashed a tea-set in their study. (Cf. FLM to GBM, July 1926, qtd in Stallworthy, 105, and *SAF*, 101).
3 – Adapted from 'Après moi, le déluge', a phrase attributed to Louis XV.

So much for 'Today's Great Thoughts'. I hope you are all well and still cheating the animals (see Above). Homo sum – a magnificent imposter –[1] Lots of <u>Love, Louis</u>. [MacNeice *deleted*]

TO *Georgina Beatrice MacNeice*   MS Dan MacNeice

[27 June 1927]   The Corner House, Northwood,
                                  Middlesex

My dear Madre,

I left that place as it was a bore and am staying with John. I saw Elizabeth yesterday. She thinks she is ploughing in her exam. I told her that her growing dislike of work was a very healthy sign. It is ridiculous for girls of that age to cram.

I don't think I shall come home yet – especially as you are coming over soon, and I do not want the North Ireland melancholy to get its teeth into me.

Anthony came up and stayed with me and then with John in Oxford. He is in good form. We are going to the Russian Ballet with him tomorrow.[2] The point is that the Victorians fed on abstractions and were sick.[3] We have returned to the concrete and so laid ourselves open to the charge of triviality. But we can build art out of those tangible odds and ends. The day of the chameleon who feeds on air is over.[4] Ordinary man is more like an ostrich. He thrives on broken glass and rusty nails. I have just read a brilliant novel – 'To the Lighthouse,' by Virginia Woolf – illustrating this.[5]

I saw the O.U.D.S. 'Tempest.' Graham was very good in his little part as Boatswain.

1 – 'Homo sum' was the title of an early poem, published in *BF* (CP07, 629).
2 – Diaghilev's Russian Ballet was performing a six-week season at the Princes Theatre, beginning on 13 June, with performances at 8.45 each evening. The season included music by Prokofiev, Satie and Stravinsky, and set designs by Matisse and Braque. On the night of 27 June, Stravinsky came in person to conduct three ballets: *Petrushka*, *Pulcinella* and *The Firebird*. 'M. Stravinsky was called before the curtain many times.' See 'Russian Ballet. M. Stravinsky's Visit', *The Times*, 28 June, 14 and other articles under the header 'The Russian Ballet' on 6 June, 8; 14 June, 14; 15 June, 14; 21 June, 9. Cf. Blunt's remark: 'about 1925–6, we were beginning to know about the Russian Ballet and came to love Stravinsky' ('From Bloomsbury to Marxism', 166).
3 – 'My stepmother was viciously Victorian. I was emulating Anthony's antagonism to the generation of our parents' (*SAF*, 96).
4 – Sir Thomas Browne, *Vulgar Errors*, III, xxi: 'Concerning the Chameleon, there generally passeth an opinion that it liveth only upon air.'
5 – *To the Lighthouse* (1927).

It is ridiculous to say 'I am not interested in art, I am not interested in poetry, I am interested in humanity.' These things are the largest of the rare pegs on which one can hang one's ideas of humanity. They are the most truthful means of communication between people – excepting a very rare mystical sympathy.

Dean Inge goes off the rails when he comes to discuss art and poetry.[1] He says that any poetry which does not scan or any painting which is not strictly 'true to nature' is the result of mere slackness. He has just not troubled to attempt to sympathise with the artist or poet. He is taking his criteria ready-made on moralistic premises and the fallacious assumption that description is identical with representation.

Art which is merely 'true to nature' is merely sensational, only fit for the movies. We want not sensation, but emotion, which will not show what is only momentary and haphazard, but will connect momentary sensations with the past and future, welding the whole into a <u>scheme</u>, an epitome of the universe.

After all you cannot say what is anything's real shape or colour; they change continually. Your mind must catch this changing Proteus and COMPEL him into shape.

Well, to return to 'plans,' (a word which is properly tabu) – after John I go to Graham and then John suggested I should go to France with him but I don't know what you think about that or how or when or where. Still it would be certainly most instructive, delightful and entertaining. As someone said to me the other day – what I want is a great deal more experience and a great deal less theory. The reorientation which one gets through contact with strange peoples is among the most important experiences.[2]

I have been set quantities of work for the vacation. If I do it all I shall vanish in smoke – beautiful spirals of thin blue filaments – the sacrifice which is the prologue to every beauty.

Yrs. with love

Louis M.

[*flourish*]

1 – FLM had planned to attend a talk by Inge on 1 May (FLM to GBM, 1 May 1927). Cf. 'Auden and MacNeice: Their Last Will and Testament': 'Item, we leave to that old diehard Inge / A little Christian joy . . .' (*LI*, CP07, 733).

2 – 'I had never been abroad (my family were as unwilling to send me abroad as they were to allow my sister to go to dances), so that, when I went to Paris in the summer of 1927 with John Hilton, I went there in a bubble of naïve expectations' (*SAF*, 110).

TO *Georgina Beatrice MacNeice*   MS Dan MacNeice

30 June 1927   The Corner House, Northwood,
                                Middlesex

[*Scrawled on envelope in red pencil:*
'Prance to France we'll pay expense Peremere']

My dear Drina,

Here we are again – John is playing Nursery Rhymes on the piano – . . .
about the Paris business. Anthony has suggested himself coming too which,
of course, would be an excellent safe-guard as he knows the place upside
down. I find that if I get a passport I shall need your written consent; and
must also know the <u>date</u> and <u>locality</u> of Daddie's birth.[1] As for your
consent, of course, I should not presume to take it for granted – but, as I
said, one needs this reorientation, also Paris is today the vortex of art.

Anthony went up north for the Eclipse.

I saw Elizabeth on Tuesday and gave her a print for her last Birthday. I
had lunch in her Hospital Refectory and saw Robert Graves' sister.[2]

I saw three Art Exhibitions, the Russian Ballet, and went to the National
Gallery again.

I saw John N. with Elizabeth. He seemed in very good form.

John's 2nd brother came home for an eclipse holiday and we drove him
back to Bishop's Stortford last night.[3]

Elizabeth, I suppose, will go to Betty's wedding with you. But for myself –
'far from the madding crowd's ignoble strife.'[4]

It is good Uncle Mac getting a house in Belfast within reach of the
human telephone.

I hope Daddie enjoyed his time in the West. One should always go south
and west (according to D. H. Lawrence).

I gather Uncle Herbert lives out this way.[5] I should like to go and see
him.

---

1 – British passport. He later took an Irish passport on the outbreak of war, issued on 4 Sept.
1939.
2 – EM studied medicine at Charing Cross Hospital Medical School. Robert Graves's sister
was Dr Rosaleen Graves (later Rosaleen Cooper), also a student at Charing Cross.
3 – Roger Hilton.
4 – FLM quoted Gray's 'Elegy Written in a Country Churchyard' to excuse himself from
attendance at the wedding on 27 July of his step-cousin Margaret Elizabeth MacGregor
(Betty) Greer of Seapark (Co Antrim) to Major A. E. Percival at Brompton Parish Church (cf.
'Marriages', *The Times*, 30 July 1927, 1).
5 – On Uncle Herbert (Rev. H. H. H. MacNeice) see FLM to AB, 5 April 1927, n. 3, p. 160.

Anthony only got a Second in his Schools; he is going to drop Maths. and do Modern languages. John H., as I think I said, is dropping maths. to do Modern Greats (Economics & Philosophy), and his ridiculous College is taking away his Scholarship. They do not approve of that school, which has not yet had time to accumulate the Oxford dust.

I trust Daddie is better. It is the unhealthy climate. Still, it is not as bad as Oxford. That was why they put a University there – so that noone should ever be able to use their wits enough to refute their professors. Oh, the man who lectured on Aristotle's Poetics! His words just clacked from his mouth as if he was a typewriter but a little less musical. Most academic great men are all piecrust and no plums.

How is Mrs. Hind's new book? I shall have to publish something soon.

I am having some things in this year's Oxford poetry.[1] In a few years I imagine I shall have gradually stopped writing verse. This is because my verse and prose are becoming more and more like each other and they promise a most remarkable compound. You see, some time ago my prose was intellectual and crisp and my verse sensuous and florid (all according to established regulations) but now my prose is becoming more sensuous and my verse more intellectual. These combined will form a sponge to soak in quantities of experience.

One sits on top of the pyramid of oneself – a mass of experience ending in the sharp apex of the present moment. Above are the jangling planets pealing from their belfry. One's past self is buried in state in the inner chamber sealed behind granite doors with a few tapes of memory burning.

One is like a fountain – always spouting in the same shape but formed of always different water drops. Now suppose someone turns off the fountain; it is not. Turn it on again and it exists again (the same fountain). Where has it been in between?

I must really be very polyglot; John and I were counting up yesterday the racial qualities which people claim to have found in me:-

American	Indian
French	Japanese
Spanish[2]	Negro

---

1 – His poems in *Oxford Poetry 1927* (ed. W. H. Auden and Cecil Day-Lewis) include 'Harvest Thanksgiving' and 'The Tournament'.
2 – FLM when young cultivated a myth of 'Spanish blood', passed through the Clesham family line. Many years later, his sister Elizabeth wrote to him: 'Incidentally, you remember how we used to jest years ago about "Spanish blood in the West of Ireland" based mainly on our looks & as I thought, purely a figment of our imagination. So I was surprised when my cousin

Italian   (Russian?)
Jewish   German.

This heterogeneity is very painful. I expect to fall to pieces like a jigsaw.

Well, I hope the garden is full of milk and honey and William is sufficiently restrained and all the birds are jargoning,

With Much Love

Louis

TO *John Frederick and Georgina Beatrice MacNeice*

MS Dan MacNeice

[1 July 1927]   The Corner House, Northwood, Middlesex

My dear Daddie and Madre,

I am sorry you disapprove of the France business so I will just explain it a little more.[1] John and I (and possibly Anthony & Graham) only intended to go for a short time and only to Paris or the extreme north. This would not be expensive and we should have returned before the end of July[.] I should not therefore have been away from home longer than I was last year (at M.C. and Camp). You will then have me during August, September and half October which I am sure will be as much as you can manage[.] So much for my Absence from Home. Now for my Presence Abroad. (1) Madre herself suggested this a little time ago – quite vehemently. (2) All the obvious advantages – picking up bits of the language, imbibing the culture etc. etc. (3) Catching up with other people's minds who have in the intellectual race got an unfair start through the stimulus given by a foreign country. (4) Suitable people (viz. John and Anthony) to go with. N.B. these may not occur again. (5) Such experiences are much more potent if they happen before the great spurt of development in oneself is finished. (cf. the stock remark that everyone is a genius about this age; and genius means the power to devour and digest experience.) (6) Something to cheer me up before I start grinding and cramming. (It is

---

Willie told me that the two daughters of my grandfather's nephew, old Major Clesham (now dead), told him that there really is a legend of a Spanish ancestor in the Cleshams! So there perhaps you explain your black hair & both our elegant profiles!' (EN to FLM, 23 March 1950, *Ms Bodleian, Ms Res, c. 587*).

1 – Cf. 'It was only after I had written several letters of pompous and dishonest argument that I obtained the money from them to pay for my first visit to France' ('Landscapes', *SAF*, 235).

much easier to work when one has had enough new experience to last one for some time. I have had little desire to work lately merely because I have had nothing else to do. (7) And (this is far the most important, as I said before), REORIENTATION – getting one out of the rut before one sets in it for ever. The walls (like the story in Edgar Allan Poe) are always coming closer and closer with a monotonous babble of Cockney and an unbroken glare of British faces.[1] (Not that these are at all bad, but one cannot judge their good till one has something else to judge them by. As even Rudyard Kipling (was it?) said – 'What do they know of England who only England know?'[2]

Hence I feel myself at a disadvantage compared with people like Anthony – not because they can lard their speech with tags of French but because I feel their outlook is necessarily broader; compared with them I am a gaping provincial or a self-opinionated Cockney.

So much for my side of the case, now for your side.

These, I surmise, are more or less your reasons against it:-

(1)   Louis is too young.
(2)   Louis ought to be at home, making himself useful in his charming way.
(3)   Louis will be wasting his time; Louis never wastes his time at home.
(4)   Louis will be wasting money; Louis has no idea of the value of money.
(5)   Louis ought to have someone competent to go with him; John Hilton is not forty-five therefore John Hilton is not competent.
(6)   Paris is a wicked city. Louis is so impressionable that he will certainly become wicked, too, if he goes there.
(7)   Louis is self-centred.
(8)   Louis will be sea-sick crossing the channel.
(9)   Louis will lose everything en route.
(10) Louis is mad.

Q.E.D.

I am now tired of talking about that.

I should like to see Spring Hill very much some time.[3]

1–Edgar Allan Poe, *The Pit and the Pendulum* (1842).
2–Rudyard Kipling, 'The English Flag' (1891).
3–Springhill, Moneymore, nr Magherafelt, Co. Londonderry/Derry, was the seat of the Lenox-Conynghams and the home of Mina Lenox-Conyngham (née Lowry), whose sister Dorinda Florence Lowry had married Thomas MacGregor Greer. The house was acquired by the National Trust in 1958.

Yes, I will drive you to Armagh like a shot.

I am ready for the West of Ireland. It would be splendid. John Hilton would like to go there.

As for my career, Anthony apparently discussed it with a master at Marlboro' the other day and they agreed that it was obvious that I should write. This, of course, many people have said of me before.[1] Of course, it is a rotten career financially and I suppose one should begin by doing something else.

Anthony was down staying with Canning lately. Mrs. Norwood and her daughters were down there too.[2] Guillebaud is engaged. The whole lot had the most hilarious time-free fights every day. Anthony had never had such an experience.

Yes, David, I fear, is a dolt.[3]

It is raining here very hard. Quite King Lear. I hope it is better with you.

Elizabeth seems very contented. She is out of the whirl pool.

Richard Best, I have decided, is really rather a bore. He maps things out too much. He worships the complacent Law-and-Order of the commercial plutocrat. But he is quite pleasant.

Anthony is wavering in his decision to be a schoolmaster. I expect his tutoring in Italy will finish that off (– although he gets £4 a week plus expenses).

I am terrified of meeting Mrs. Johns again. What is to be done?

To return to my career, I suppose the best thing to do is to 'go through the mill' – garrets and Grub St. and all that.

By the way Graham has got a job on the 'Illustrated London News' for part of the vac. (This is a secret.)

I am going down to Graham for a few days soon to discuss our play next term. Graham and John are painting the scenery.

All the students in Elizabeth's Hospital looked the same. I pity tomorrow's invalids.

Well, I shall write again soon and I hope you will not call me home too urgently (for, after all, I see much more of you now than when at Marlboro') but I shall soon come home 'piping down the valleys wild'[4] with lots of love, Louis.

1 – The American schoolmaster Frederick Waring had suggested both he and AB would go into journalism, which may not be quite what he has in mind here.
2 – Wife of Cyril Norwood, headmaster ('Master') of MC.
3 – The new family driver referred to earlier.
4 – William Blake, from 'Introduction' to Songs of Innocence (1789).

TO *John Frederick and Georgina Beatrice MacNeice*

MS Dan MacNeice

[July 1927]   The Corner House, Northwood,
                                               Middlesex

My dear Daddie & Madre,

'For this relief much thanks'.[1] We shall get off the mark as soon as possible and load our minds with pollen of wisdom.

I have not been with the Hiltons all this time as John went up to Oxford for an exam. Meanwhile I went to Graham. On the way I tracked down Elizabeth who was watching an exhibition of fencing with John N.

Graham and I slept again in our small hut by the tennis court. But yesterday came the great thrill. I was on the way back here and was walking through London with Anthony when someone hailed us from behind. It was Waring who had come over from America the day before.

We had tea with him. He finds the boys at this school in America distressingly orthodox after us.[2] He was in good spirits but rather lean. We went to the Royal Academy. It is becoming slightly modernistic.

John and his father and I went for a moonlight walk last night to a neighbouring lake – with nightjars and other birds calling and the old dog panting like a steam-engine. It does not get much exercise.

Mr. Shepard told us the most wonderful stories about his five maiden aunts who live together. Their names were Emily, Alicia, Fanny, Annie and something else and they were superlatively decorous.

Anthony's Schools were only his first part, corresponding to my Honour Mods next March. You see, really grave schools have <u>two</u> Honours Exams. John has been doing the first part of the Maths. School (but, as I said, is now changing to Modern Greats – philosophy etc. A vast parcel of philosophy has arrived for him from Blackwell's).

Language is at first a help but at last a hindrance. When you first name a dog a 'dog', it helps you to get at its entity but in a little time the word 'dog' becomes a cliché and helps little towards the visualisation of dog. The essence of dog is lost while the symbol remains.

This is why there must always be a renovation of language. Words, metaphors, constructions, aphorisms, all become dead soon after becoming current. This is the dilemma – on the one side the language of a literary clique, upsetting by its novelty; on the other that of popular tradition, whose triteness leads to atrophy.

1 – Francisco, in *Hamlet* I.i.8–10. FLM is thanking his parents for permission to go to France.
2 – J. F. Waring; see FLM to GBM, 13 May 1926, n. 1, p. 112.

The Shepards' new house is well underway – a chaos of foundations. We saw it in the dark. Mr. Shepard did the designs which were revised by an architect.[1] He is having a splendid studio at the top of the house, reached by an outside stair-case – and with numerous windows.

I will try Uncle Herbert and the Cottinghams (if time).[2] With many thanks and much love. Louis.

TO *Hilda Violet Blunt*[3]   MS Cambridge

[3? December 1927]   Carrickfergus

Dear Mrs. Blunt,

I hope you are having better weather than this place for it sleets or snows all the time and everyone attributes it to me.

I had a dreadful time after I left you as the Liverpool train was full of middle-aged Lancashire men who were carousing and talking in accents in memory of something or other. Meanwhile I hope you enjoyed the show you were going to, though it was rather a pity not to be in at the death of the House of Commons, for one so rarely has an opportunity of seeing men like that – I mean politicians – under the influence of the passions. At least I only once went to the House of Commons and then they were all asleep except one bovine old man who was reading aloud some regulations.

I suppose Wilfrid has now come home. I hope he did not get into a row because my paper went on so long. Haileybury suggested to me that rows must always be very welcome to the authorities – as a reaction to the stolid ugliness of the Chapel.

Anthony's farewell to Canning must have been very pathetic. Canning's departure from Marlborough is rather an Armageddon.[4] You feel it is the end of Marlborough. Still I suppose Anthony can always stay with Sargeant if he wants to roam about the Downs.[5]

1–E. H. Shepard (1879–1976), book illustrator (well-known for his illustrations of Pooh).
2–Uncle Herbert lived in Cambridgeshire. The Cottinghams were relations of the Greers: Mary Cottingham ('Cousin Pixie'), was the first cousin of FLM'S stepmother. She lived in Harrow, although her family, the Bowen-Colthursts, were from Co. Cork. She had two children, Teddy and Myrtle. EN wrote: 'Her mother was a half-sister of Thomas Greer & on the other side she was a cousin of Elizabeth Bowen.' Cf. Appendix 1.
3–Hilda Violet Blunt (1880–1969), wife of Rev. (Arthur) Stanley Vaughan Blunt (1870–1929), and mother of Anthony, Christopher and Wilfrid.
4–Clifford Canning moved in 1927 to Canford School, Dorset.
5–G. M. Sargeaunt who taught at MC 1914–34. See FLM to parents, [after 25 Jan. 1926], n. 1, p. 109.

I look back regretfully on your dog. Irish dogs always have such muddy paws. Besides they are never very intelligent and even lack the proverbial Irish wit. But your dog has a subtle and almost insidious intelligence and to renew acquaintance with him is always to me a spiritual renovation and revigoration [*sic*] of the intellect. Incidentally it was awfully charming of you to put me up as I hove in suddenly out of the void. By the way there is apparently at the moment a new comet as my father is always looking out for it. Unfortunately as it is raining he never sees it.[1]

I hope you will have, or are having or have had (in the case of Irish postal offices one can never be sure of one's tenses) an excellent Christmas (I don't think Christmas post-cards ever use the epithet 'excellent' but they are afraid of Latin: and it is much the most comprehensive epithet, as well as having an air of a practical reality which is often, I think, absent from such terms as MERRYE). oh yes, and an excellent new year (parentheses had nearly left this strand in oblivion – so that the world would have come to an end on the 31st of December).

. . . Yrs. Sincerely
<u>Louis MacNeice</u>

TO *Hilda Violet Blunt* MS Cambridge

[December 1927]   Carrickfergus

Dear Mrs. Blunt,

I am now arrived in this country and find it, as usual, wet. Also foggy. This is made up for by the fact that I have at last come into a real bedroom, having spent the last few vacations among boxes and abandoned furniture. To signify my joy I have placed a copper lustre jug in the middle of the mantelpiece and flanked it by Blake postcards.

I have just tried my musical-box again but it sounds very effete after yours; being very, very slow and rheumatic. So I have shut the door on it and left it talking to itself; I fear it is in its dotage.

I suppose Wilfrid is home now. I wish he would make me some soup-plates; I was much impressed by the ambiguous service he gave you. I suppose, really, coffee . . . [*sic*]

1 – The comet known as Skjellerup (or 1927*k*) was expected in the northern hemisphere on 19 Dec. but no sightings were reported in the British Isles. An Australian observed it on 3 Dec. (the putative date of this letter) and excitement slowly gathered among British and Irish stargazers during that month. 'A Comet Expected', and 'The Comet', *The Times*, 16 and 20 Dec. 1927.

Give my love to James; not that I suppose he will be very interested in such a gift. He probably hates me for eating his biscuits. You may tell him that I will never do so again without his leave.

I hope you got all the cards you wanted at the British Museum. I think they are delightful and have almost decided not to send any of mine to anyone. But I expect altruism will win in the end. I should have got duplicates.

Christmas here is distinctly imminent; with all its parochial concomitants by which the family are much harassed. The queue of beggars has not yet started but I expect it will soon.

I hope Anthony is enjoying himself with Canning and not going in for too much break-neck riding. Also that his paper was a success; I should have liked to hear it and observe its effects on the boys.

The family are calling me all over the house; I don't know what they want. I must, therefore, end this letter with many hopes that the weather in London is more pleasant than the weather here, and that you will have a perfect Christmas, also with an acknowledgement of the very delightful time I had staying with you; it is a good thing one does not have to make out receipts for such pleasures as they would be so difficult to estimate. And I have not got a good head for more than small calculations.

The family say that if I sit any longer in this room I shall die of cold. So perhaps I had better go away. Of course it may be too late already, in which case Moriturus te saluto,

Yrs sincerely
Louis MacNeice

TO *Anthony Blunt*   MS Cambridge

Postmark 31 December 1927   Carrickfergus

My dear Anthony

Thank you so much for your card and for sending my toothbrush. I am busy writing a novel featuring you etc.[1] I hope to get it done properly after

---

1 – Possibly an early draft of *RW*, in which Blunt was a model for the character Hogley, although other references in this letter – to the novel beginning 'in the cradle' or the first sentence ('Doors closing in the distance' – which is not the first sentence of *RW*) suggest this may be one of several novels FLM began to write but did not publish, and probably did not complete. FLM claims he wrote *RW* in 1930 ('I wrote it 2 years ago': FLM to AB, Oct. 1932). In a later letter (6 April? 1932), he refers to two unpublished titles, 'Going Out & C.I.' and 'Your Esteemed Order'.

Mods. and finished in the summer but a few tentative scraps now are helpful.[1] It begins in my cradle. I began writing it, like Plato, when I had thought of my first sentence. I had some difficulty explaining it to my people. They said 'But have you got a plot?' and I said 'No but I have the first sentence.' It is 'Doors closing in the distance, was all he could remember, and the light beneath them.' I meant to write to you or yr brother or dog or someone to thank you for putting me up at Haileybro', Marlboro' etc. I hope y'are going to read yr. dialogue, or at any rate one of you a paper to my College.[2] Please preserve or send back my MSS, in particular, 'Adam's Legacy'.[3] Give my love to Canning & Michael & Edward & John & all the rest of the Elect.[4] I hope you don't mind but I am giving you dark hair & some athletic prowess in my novel. That story of mine you have may come in useful for adaptation so please preserve, if you've not already destroyed it. I have shaken off the dust of the old School and am never going down there again till I am on the Ministry of Works & Pipes. I have been feeling very amorous lately (having bought some crimson pyjamas) but vainly so. By the way I don't think the concluding figure of that story is to be applied physically but that may be a side to it. I am pretty wretched here. The family is just like a bad Tchekov play. But today I played golf with the Curate again.[5] I think I am corrupting him. But the ground was rather too hard. Very chilling. It is now half past eleven o'clock. I don't mean that. I think your conversation's become just horrid. Noone talks like that over here. A very charming woman I know has just produced a tract on the Poisoning of our Youth by Modern Literature. But I do think you're divan [sic]. But if one keeps seeing through things one never sees into them. Too, too gnomic. Yes, you are first seen playing stump cricket at my preparatory school. I am also making yr. father die some time ago & I think you die too – drowning but not Via Reggio. Still I think you turn up again at the last moment & upset all the mourners. If you had dark hair you wld look slightly like John but you haven't got his figure. Yes of course it was malicious really. But there was no reason for it. For then it wldn't have been malice. Or spite if you prefer it. But I

1 – 'Our classical course took four years and was divided into two parts, each terminating in an examination – "Honour Mods." and "Greats" respectively' (*SAF*, 102).
2 – Wilfred Blunt taught at Haileybury, 1923–38.
3 – Published in *BF*, but dropped from *Collected Poems, 1925–1948*.
4 – Clifford Canning; Michael Robertson; John Hilton. Edward (unidentified) is often mentioned in the letters, in relation to AB.
5 – Presumably the curate with whom he played golf at Portstewart in 1926 (FLM to AB, 25 Sept. 1926).

suppose the reason is that you are so tall. I hate all tall people. How are yr brothers pots. I should like two great pots to stand like idols on the mantelpiece. I gave no Christmas presents. But you have a conscience. You all have consciences & you all are respectable & industrious. It is very strange. I think I cld turn and live with god. When with a small g you see he counts as an animal & shall so be classed in my natural history. I am just panickt over my exam. If I get a 4th I shall go to Canada & write my novel in a log hut. This letter is very egotistical. This is natural because I am using the first personal pronoun as always ∴ always egotistical except in my written works where I use the seventh. To continue in the first I have got diphtheria & a touch of Synizesis so – no not really; I hope you haven't. Your name is Carteson. Give my love to all yr. brothers and parents and to Alastair and Alastare and John and all the blessed.[1] Did you see C.T. again? But I hate all tall people. The brute in this room is going to strike midnight – consummation . . . homo tristis? I hope you were unscathed the rest of time at Marlbro', me the cockatrice having gone. Tell me if you're giving anything to Canning. Do hurry up and grow your hair. Oh give my love to Graham.[2] Graham is an entity. Why was Canning lecturing to yr father's curate? I got a Christmas card (Magdalen [sic] Coll. Cantab. Very natty) from Ross – saying – 'What are you going to do in life?'[3] I thought of sending a telegram saying RUT but perhaps not. Oh dear, I shan't be able to have a bath tonight. My father reads the Bible in his Bath. The Romans read the Ars Amatoria.[4] But then they did not go in for enamel.

[Stylised line drawing of man dancing or otherwise stepping out]

Yrs with love. Louis

1 – Wilfrid Blunt (see next letter) and Christopher Blunt (1904–87); Alastair Macdonald, Alastair Hamilton, John Hilton.
2 – Graham Shepard.
3 – Fortie Ross entered Magdalene in 1925.
4 – Ovid, Ars Amatoria.

1928

TO *Wilfrid Blunt*[1]   MS Cambridge

Postmark 23 January 1928   Merton College, Oxford

Dear Wilfrid,

You are coming to read a paper with Anthony aren't you? On the 3rd, 4th, 5th, 6th or 7th Friday from now.[2] If a dialogue is impracticable you might read short amoebean rhapsodies (which need not then be relevant to each other) – so that all you have to do is each to write a series of idyllic outbursts or satirical observations and then read them out in turn with appropriate flourishes. My college is frightfully ignorant so practically anything would be to them a surprising revelation so you need not trouble to produce anything very recondite. And if you're very busy you can use some of your old papers. I am writing to Anthony about this. I will put you both up and get all sorts of people from other colleges to yr paper so it will be all very amusing and instructive so that's that. Gardens would be charming. Your man Levens seems rather nervous.[3] He admires you all very much. He & Morgan etc. are very keen on your coming.[4] If you like I will write to your headmaster about it. I enjoyed Hailybro so much last term. I hope you are equalling the Sungs, Tungs etc. Not forgetting the Divine Potter. Anyhow youre coming Thanks so much

Yrs sincerely

Louis MacNeice

1 – Wilfrid Jasper Walter Blunt (1901–87), ARCA; educ. MC 1914–20; Worcester College, Oxford 1920–1, Atelier Moderne, Paris 1921–2, Royal College of Art 1922–3. Taught at Haileybury 1923–38 and was later Drawing master at Eton. Cf. 'Auden and MacNeice: Their Last Will and Testament': 'Item to Wilfrid Blunt a pretty piece / Of the best rococo and a crimson shirt . . .' (*LI*, CP07, 740).

2 – They soon finalise an arrangement that Wilfrid and Anthony should come to Oxford on Friday 24 Feb.

3 – R. G. C. Levens (1901–76) had recently moved to Merton from Haileybury where he had taught from 1924 to 1927, hence would have already known Wilfrid. He was educated at Rugby and Balliol College, Oxford, and had recently been appointed Classical Tutor and Fellow of Merton College.

4 – E. G. T. (Guy) Morgan, junior to FLM at Merton College. He was later a journalist and author.

TO *Anthony Blunt*

MS Cambridge

[after 23 January 1928]   Merton College, Oxford

My dear Anthony

I have writ to your brother. You are to come up here on the 3rd, 4th 5th 6th or 7th Friday from this week (inclusive). And you needn't contrive a proper dialogue (as I imagine you wont be able to confer beforehand) but rather I suggest that you each compose a series of short lyrical, idyllic or satiric effusions on Life, Art etc. which you can then declaim in turn & my college will be frightfully pleased. I will put you (both) up & it will be all very charming. So I shall expect you as I am sure you can both get away which is all that is necessary as all or any of your words will be manna to my ignorant fellow students. Write soon. I am decaying. Yrs with love

L.

Dying, Egypt, dying[1]

TO *John Betjeman*

MS British Library

[February 1928]   Merton College, Oxford

Dear Betjeman,

Anthony and Wilfrid Blunt are coming down to my College next week to read papers to a stupid College Society. If you would like to come we should be immensely pleased. [They *deleted*] Anthony is reading on Brueghel – in my room on Friday (24th) at 8.15. I think it will be amusing and the society is quite harmless. I heard you have become an Old-Boy.

Yours sincerely
L. MacNeice

TO *Wilfrid Blunt*

MS Cambridge

[February 1928]   Merton College, Oxford

Dear Wilfrid

I'm frightfully glad & immensely honoured you are coming. I am putting you up in the College but then you are being led as a beast to Levens. We are collecting quite a pretty, I think, meeting on Friday.[2] Don't mind being

---

1–Mark Antony, *Antony and Cleopatra*, IV.xv; adapted in 'Sunlight on the Garden' (1937), CP07, 57.
2–Friday 24 Feb.

bitter or outrageous or witty or clever or romantic or anything. They need it all. Your programme before Levens[.] Betjemann [*sic*] is giving us dinner on Friday & yre coming to lunch with me on [Wednesday *deleted*] Saturday. So looking forward frightfully to yr Epiphany

Yrs
Louis

TO *Anthony Blunt*   MS Cambridge

Postmark 15 February 1928   [Merton College, Oxford]

[scrawled in pencil:
'presumably this letter was addressed to Wilfred Blunt']

My dear Anthony

Sorry to keep writing to you like this but Levens has just come round. He wants yr brother to stay on as his guest after Friday but you are both to belong to me for Friday night. So you had better stay with me till Sunday or Monday. So you needn't come up early on Friday if you don't want to (Levens says yr brother cant get away in time). & we can have the amusing lunch on Saturday.

I am feeling frightfully dishonoured as having been kicked out of Balliol last night by a drunken monster. I am still thinking what to do about it. It was very difficult being kicked out with dignity & I don't think I achieved it; still I think he must have looked more ridiculous than I did; he was a bloody man like a prize fighter, in a highly coloured waistcoat. If I can find out his name I shall go round & interview him in his soberer moments. The world is really not a safe place for me.

Its rather a bore about Levens but he seems to want to do his bit; I suppose yr brother can survive it.

The O.U.D.S. starts today – Graham's got quite a good part as a scurfy old man.

Have just read such a bad novel by Ernest Hemingway one of those tiresome Parisian Americans.[1]

So come for as long as you like

Yrswithlove
<u>L.</u>

---

1 – Possibly *The Sun Also Rises* (1926), published in London as *Fiesta* in 1927.

TO *Anthony Blunt*   MS Cambridge

Postmark 29 February 1928   Merton College, Oxford

My dear Anthony

Sorry to be writing again but am so desolated. Stuck once more among all the mudfaced abortions & cyphers & dullards & frogspawn – Might God engulf them in a yawning nullity. But God is in a bad way himself – it's all up with God (ha! ha!) only the mastheads showing of the foundering bloody armada of the stars.

> 'But I beneath a rougher sea
> Am whelm'd in deeper gulfs than he'[1]

My love to Michael & Alastair & Basil & Adonis & Attis & Osiris & Hyacinthus & Prometheus & Ganymede and my hatred to the commissionaires of Heaven & the Dons of the Universe & the sweating purple militia of the Elemental Powers. And may their voices become a little toothy crack & a rusty tap dripping. And may the brine anointed hungry-breasted Venus breathe you full of a roar of life for ever (that you may swivel the mountains with yr thumb & spatter the seas with yr heel) and why in the name of G? didn't you come to Oxford?[2]

TO *John Frederick and Georgina Beatrice MacNeice*
MS Dan MacNeice

[7 March 1928]   Merton College Oxford

My dear Daddie & Madre,

Thank you so much for your letters. The sea voyage is a great idea.[3] But as for grinders they delight not me.[4] Besides Mods begins this Thursday so we are in the very extreme of hopelessness. But I don't take these things too

---

1 – Mr Ramsay in Woolf's *To the Lighthouse* repeatedly mutters these lines from William Cowper, 'The Castaway' (1799).
2 – Whereas this might suggest AB did not come to Oxford on the agreed date (24 Feb.), a letter to FLM's parents indicates that the Blunt brothers came and that Anthony gave a paper (see next letter). It seems more likely that he means 'come to Oxford to study, instead of going to Cambridge University'.
3 – FLM agreed to accompany his father on a cruise to Norway, which he later recalled as 'a huge boat packed with middle-aged Americans and with English spinsters who were blowing their savings' (*SAF*, 116).
4 – 'Man delights not me, no nor women neither' (*Hamlet*, II.ii).

185

seriously. The rest of the world, if they like, may faint and have nervous break-downs but it seems to me all rather trivial. Now the Blunts were much more instructive though Anthony's paper was far too technical for everyone. But Wilfrid was very entertaining. Anthony is going to Vienna this vac. (to improve his German) & Wilfrid is going to the Sahara. (And Crosthwaite is going to Egypt to stay with his people.) I don't think Graham is coming over to Ireland. They are shifting house. Give my love to Elizabeth. I am bringing her a horse (which I have detained some time on my mantelpiece). I hear Belfast has been presented with quantities of Lavery.[1] So ends Belfast. I went for a walk the other day (first exercise this term). Am growing fat & sinking rapidly. Was photographed yesterday (as you insisted on it) – before my hair is entirely white or I am killed by the Philistines. The men at my table eat more & more potatoes in Hall. They think I am frightfully affected because I rarely eat more than three. I hope you are all in high health.

Yrs with Love
L.

TO *Georgina Beatrice MacNeice*   MS Dan MacNeice

[29 April 1928]   Merton College, Oxford

Dear Madre,

I fear this is as usual late – due to the plenitude of events. However I have already written to Melbourne [*sic*].[2] It was very pleasant there, except that I first mistook a man with a red beard for Uncle H. I think his garden etc. are charming. N.B. His hair is <u>not</u> snow-white; that is a myth[.] Desmond & Dan look very well. I went with Uncle H. to Royston heath, a pleasant place with even a wind on it. I went up to Cambridge with him in a bus after lunch on Wednesday. There it was delightful – but too many Old Marlburians. Wednesday night I stayed in Trinity, Thursday in the Lion Hotel. I met a friend of Anthony's who had frescoed his entire bed-room with pictures of the fall of Adam & Eve etc – done in distemper. I saw

1 – Sir John Lavery (1856–1941) donated a group of paintings worth £25,000 to the new Art Gallery in Belfast. Lavery wrote to the mayor: 'I would much like to be represented, and with that object in view I beg to offer you, as a free gift to my native city, a small collection of my pictures, dating from 1884 to the present time, which include some Ulster personalities.' Cf, 'Pictures for Belfast Art Gallery. Sir John Lavery's Gift', *The Times*, 11 Feb. 1928, 8.
2 – Melbourn (Cambridgeshire), the home of FLM's Uncle Herbert. See FLM to AB, 5 April 1927, n. 3, p. 160.

Michael Robertson a good deal & Basil Barr & was much pleased by the view of King's from the river. But there is no room in the streets & too many young men about. On Thursday night we saw Ibsen's 'Pretenders' at a very remarkable Cambridge theatre (the Festival T).[1]

Elizabeth, of course, came round on Saturday before I was (properly) up. She seems in good form & my scout was pleased to see her again. A man (presumably a lab. boy) told him the other day of her proficiency in the labs. My scout told Graham that cleverness runs in families like wooden legs.[2] He nearly had sent me a wire & was very moved over my first.

Someone was talking . . . [*page missing*]

Today I had Graham & John H. & John's younger brother (the moody one) to tea & afterwards we made a steeplechase course down the back stairs, up the front etc. with sofas & chairs for obstacles.

Crosthwaite is back from Egypt with very farouche sidewhiskers (nearly down to his jaw). Thank you for the letter. Love. Louis.

TO *Wilfrid Blunt*   MS Cambridge

[1928]   Merton College, Oxford

Dear Wilfrid

This is my 5th letter today so please pardon its aridity. I am a monster arent I, never yet having returned yr invaluable paper. But it has only just occurred to me that you are not still in the desert eating your last date while you watch your bones slowly wearing through your toes – your whole body approximating to a skeleton, flesh being very out at elbows. Till at last you would die without noticing it & the wind wld blow the sand in at your eye-holes and thus make an hour-glass of yr remains, a sad warning to future artistic temperaments and overventurous adventurers. I am just going to the other extreme viz the Arctic, where the ice will encase me like a transparent sarcophagus for the Americans of 1000 yrs hence to come & hiccough over, saying with due admiration & some little concern 'These be they before us weren'.

---

1 – The Cambridge Festival Theatre was a venue for the leading avant-garde dramatists of the day.
2 – '[My scout] was full of aphorisms, "Brains runs in a family like wooden legs, sir"' (*SAF*, 232).

Dear me I am babbling.
Babble babble
Boil & gabble
Be kind to God & worship the rabble.

Give my love to Carrington, the cleverest chap I ever met, and put a shilling for my sake in the Barnardo's Box on the altar of yr chapel; which shilling I will refund later – D.V. Cast your bread upon the altars.

Ach ach ach, it hurts . . . what . . . my conscience. So I must conclude hurriedly this letter for evil communications . . . I hope yr paper is intact. A million thanks & apologies Yrs Louis.

TO *Anthony Blunt*   MS Cambridge

Postmark 4 June 1928   Merton College, Oxford

My dear Anthony,

You to Alastare, Michael to John, Alaster M. to me – delightful – as long as you like.[1] Come soon as I am rather lost, everything being so impalpable. There is an old don lives in his dotage across the quad, white hair back bowed, imbecile. On a morning after I get up & look out of the window. The 1st thing I see is the old don taking down a gt book from his book case, laying it laboriously on the table, gazing at its cover & then putting it back again laboriously. You have to be artificial but not superficial necessarily. But I'm stuck on the surface. You have to create yr own world (see Schopenhauer) but my creation never gets further than a little daub with lipstick, bloody 2nd rate futile pompous decoration.[2] One must be deliberate but deliberate mudflies are a bathos. The best thing to do is to soak up a lot of externals. At the moment I'm just too damnedly aloof weaving it all out of my inside like a spider, getting emptier & emptier & selfconscious all the time, saying to myself this is a pretty histrionic & when I see all you dear people I don't conceive of you as real live entities, I just look at you shuffling in & out behind the footlights & I yawn or clap or throw some cheap confetti & say to myself 'That's quite amusing in its way but there doesn't seem much plot in it.' & when I see you in particular I say 'Here we are again, old curtain's gone up, what shall I say next?['] Or else be the silent man mystifying the auditors? Then I

1 – Presumably Alastair Hamilton, Michael Robertson, John Hilton, Alastair Macdonald.
2 – He saw Schopenhauer as a philosopher of free will: 'Hence Schopenhauer's view of the Will as determinist tyranny and his opposition to it of *Vorstellung*, the freedom which is freedom from the Will and from narrow personality' (*SAF*, 32).

come back here again & the old don is taking down another bk from the case. Then I think how good it wld be to be a mystic (ie. not an actor, everyone else is an actor) & be fused with the universe, but of course I shant be. I shall sit here selling words to friends. You all thing [*sic*] it's v. surprising I shd be able to write my delightful little phantasies. It's not surprising in the least. 'Genius' is the last resort. If you are destitute of all the usual things, if you can't sing or dance or play or run or paint, if you havent got a body worth trundling in a dungcart & you havent got beauty & you havent got money & you havent possible relations or environment or prospects & you live in a sort of din of silence & are out of gear with the dear bloody little rectory & the dear bloody little College, then it's not surprising you shd be able to write. It's the inevitable result of a chain of trivial prosy circumstances. & all the kind appreciative people stand around & say 'How does he manage to think of the things?' & 'How brilliant that is!' when it's only an assumed brilliance put on to keep out the urinating rain. But I don't know that I shall keep it out much longer. I shall just settle down & become a (success / failure) ie. Make a living & be an utterly revolting spectacle like Rev. Bernard Smith or Harling or Harmer.[1] Or else I shall tope & sleep & glut into oblivion, utterly vacant, a black cat in a dark room seen by a blind man. Well remember to send that Bible & my love to Basil & Michael & Alister & I shall give you a peony to wear if you're good.[2] By the way this is all rather prettily phrased (so natural) isnt it – 'a pretty histrionic.'

Love
<u>Louis</u>

---

1 – MC schoolmasters: Rev. W. B. Smith, BSc (Science teacher, 1918–36); William Francis Harling, BA: commander of the OTC, 1922–51 (2nd Lt. 1924; Capt. 1929; Maj. 1938); John William Harmer, BA (Mathematics teacher, 1924–34).
2 – Presumably Alister Watson (1908–81), educ. Winchester; King's College, Cambridge; Fellow of King's. He was a Cambridge 'Apostle' and a Marxist (Carter, 61).

TO *John Hilton*   MS Bodleian

Summer 1928   Carrickfergus

Dearest John,

I think yr poem is very pretty – in technique & imagery (here speaks the pedant), though without that compact pregnancy of phrase which I especially look for. Oh, it's calculus that word is it?[1] I've only just been able to make it out. Yes I think that's a delightful phrase. & your alliteration is very nice. Only perhaps it is all a little facile. Sorry if that is rude only unlike you I can pass out futile comments by the hour. However enough of that. All that borderland dalliance must have been a charming release (I am sorry I don't dance; but then my uncouthness – aloofness . . .) I wish I could have seen you running & shouting thru the streets. A pumping-shanty for the blood.

No, I don't think I can come to Greece (although of course I might at the last moment) but you can go quite well without me. What absurdity? If not, come over here, wont you.

I leave for Spitz B. tomorrow.[2]

By the way I thought people didn't wear under clothes in Greece? Or do they wear nothing else?

I had only 2 minutes with my publisher having gone to the Earl of Lytton's by mistake.[3] I left him one copy of my poems.

I am in a frightful hurry; give my love to your family.

Well chaps I think there's something to be said for this old Kosmos of ours

Hoping to see you (vel in Hibernia vel in Hellade).[4]

                                    Love Louis

P.S. How much would Greece cost?

1 – He may have been reading Hilton's poem 'The Deserted Astronomer' which includes the lines: 'My planet has smiled at the dust of continuity, / Evaded my axiomatic web, escaped / My tenuous sentimental calculus / And damned and sent me down to celibacy' (*Oxford Poetry*, 1929, 18). Cf.: 'Item to J. R. Hilton a Work of Art / And a dream of the infinitesimal calculus / Bolstered on apples in an apple-cart' (*LI*, CP07, 740). FLM also used the phrase 'infinitesimal calculus' in a poem which he wrote at MC (cf. FLM to GBM, 14 March 1926, p. 109).
2 – The Norwegian cruise was headed for Spitzbergen.
3 – His publisher was Victor Gollancz (1893–1967). Right Hon. Sir Neville Stephen Lytton, 3rd Earl of Lytton (1879–1951), was a painter.
4 – 'Either in Ireland or in Greece.' Cf. FLM to JH, telegram, 26 July 1928: 'Greece scrapped try Ireland' (*Ms Bodleian, Ms Don, c. 153/1*).

TO *Anthony Blunt*   MS Cambridge

Postmark 21 July 1928   Royal Mail Steam Packet Company

My dear Anthony,

   I am nearly home from Kuchenwanderung which is a relief though it
has been an interesting study in Poldy Bloom & the American Girl.[1] But
the friends [?] & things are some of them rapturous & Spitzbergen was v.
impressive, black & white peaks like skeletons with glaciers in between.
Also we got into a fascinating ice-floe – blue underneath the water. My
novel is just setting in its mould; I know more or less how to finish it off.
But old God wont it be ghastly transcribing it into legibility (I am writing
this nasty script partly because my pen is bad & partly because I am
impeded by a stiff shirt; Kuchenwanderers make a gt point of dressing for
dinner (see the 1st story in Triple Fuge).)[2] Yes there are over 200 Americans
on this boat. I have decided not to become quite ordinary after all, my
apotheosis of the common man having fallen through; so far I agree with
Nietzsche. Also Sprach Z. is exciting poetry. But I feel I am setting in my
mould too so want you to start educating me again. I don't know what my
fate is for rest of vac. There is a faint chance of going to Greece with the
Beazleys.[3] If not I hope to see you in Ireland (by the way Ireland has nearly
twice as large a population as Norway; it really is just like Norse fairy
stories, you wander for miles & miles & the 1st house you see you enter,
the odds being it belongs to a troll[)]. Have been re-reading Brand & Peer
Gynt with enjoyment. Am going to shove a little play (as a nightmare) into
my novel on End of the World. I think there will be 3 nightmares running
& have been adding some more infancy. & a lot more of Panyard. & am
tempering Carteson with a little ironic treatment.[4] Have you looked at my
poems yet? Mal de mer perhaps? But you asked for it. For them. Wld you
like walking tour in West of Ireland. All bogs & bare rocks & breakers. I
hear Guy Morgan powdered himself ALL over on his last meeting with
Alastare H.[5] H.W. C.3. is best man at my sister's wedding in Oct.[6] I don't

---

1 – *Küchenwanderung*: an outing for the retired and elderly, with a focus on dining.
2 – Osbert Sitwell, *Triple Fugue* (1924, 1927).
3 – Mary's parents: Lady Beazley and Prof. J. D. ('Jackie') Beazley (1885–1970), Lincoln
Professor of Classical Archaeology at Oxford 1925–56, who lived at 100 Holywell. FLM
did not accompany them to Greece. For longer note on Lady Beazley see FLM to her,
[June/July? 1929], n. 2, p. 206.
4 – Neither Panyard nor Carteson appeared in his published novel.
5 – Alastair Hamilton.
6 – H. W. (Hugh) Davies (1905–67?) of C3 House, MC 1919-23, later an Oxford friend of
John Nicholson's at New College (see wedding photograph). He later became an eminent

know what is to be done about it my father being so temperance & I shall want to get drunk. Each to his pleasure intox. & cop. Have you married Aileen N. yet? She shd. have a hat grafted on; or else have an injection of Umbrella Bird.[1] Such a dainty little plaster frieze above me of dolphins & boys; the dolphins have curiously boring tails. I was sorry to hear yr father's etymological expedition was not a success. But it was v. clever of Mr Paisan[?] to catch an owl in his butterfly net. John H. sent me a pleasing poem the other day. Oh yes & I saw the Midnight sun. It is rather dreadful having no night. I worship Night; there I am agst. Nietzsche. & I cant abide blonde beasts & husky Uebermensch. But tonight the sun actually set & for the 1st time for ages a moon, thin white curd. You hear people taking photographs all day long here. Only they ruin most of the films by untoward salivation. Too much longitude & no latitude, that is our tragedy. No I am not being personal. Is yr brother engaged yet? But all the old women here are a shape like Australia.

What about that Breughel essay? Shall we write a dialogue & read it at M.C. to Goard's people?[2] & wld you like to act my playlet on the End of the World, there is only one character that counts & I want yr help for the décor which is simple but must be v. subtly done. Only 3 characters altogether – the King of the World (a dingy person) that's for you, & a waiter & an Irish fruit girl (I cld be that if necessary). Oh yes & as a sort of Epilogue God but only his voice, speaking out of a grandfather clock, all except dial being wrapped in a curtain on which is written 'A & Θ'. The dial snaps back leaving a black pit out of which voice comes, 1st voice, then laugh.

Goodbye, I'm going to post this in Molde tomorrow. Beautifully wild sea to bathe in West of Ireland. Might go to Aran Islands like Synge. & eat lobsters & salmon all the time.[3]

> Ardet amor pectore
> Nullo frigens frigare . . .[4]
> Louis

—

radiologist (Exhibitioner, King's College Hospital; lecturer in Radiology, University of London; National Hospital, Queens Square; President, British Institute of Radiology 1949). Cf. Appendix 1.

1–The Umbrella Bird elevates a crest which lies above the bill, rising umbrella-like above the head.

2–Dr A. K. Goard, Science master at MC (see FLM to GBM, 13 and 20 May 1926, pp. 112, 114), attended the Anonymous Society. See *SAF*, 244.

3–J. M. Synge (1871–1909) first visited the Aran Islands in May 1898, returning each summer for the next four years. His *The Aran Islands* was published in 1907.

4–From 'Importuna Veneri' by Walter de Châtillon (twelfth century): 'Such love is in my breast that I / When the winter is most frigid, fry.'

Postmark 3 August 1928   Carrickfergus

Dear Anthony,

Can you come here any time about beginning of September? (John H. is coming some time then.) My American friend has politely returned my poems, thinking they wld. take better in England. So you can show them to Rylands.[1] I am going to write a preface.[2]

We may be taking the car to the south during latter part of this month so might be able to pick you up on way back. John is among the collieries trying to look like the god Vulcan in Elegy on Dead F. I am having 2 or 3 things in next Oxford Poetry.[3] My novel nears a close but revising & rewriting it will be ghastly. & I have to read up all last term's philosophy & history. How are the Waterfords? I am pregnant with a paper to be called 'Programme for the New Romantics' involving a comparison of Shelley & Nietzsche & a deification of laughter. I am so tired, you see, of all this scientific approach to reality; nothing but books & microscopes & scalpels & Dean Inge. Heraclitus was much better who said fire was the primary substance.[4] Laughter is the fire rioting & flapping. & it goes upwards all the time instead of burrowing. It will be a great lark seeing you. I have got a photograph for Canning.

I hope you enjoy Waterford. I have lost my voice to the family's surprise. Only a little whispering noise comes out like a breeze creeping through a scullery. You will have to go to Church if you come here. However my father is quite an impressive performance.

Goodbye now. With my sincere regards

Louis

1 – G. H. W. ('Dadie') Rylands (1902–99), Fellow of King's, close associate of AB and fellow Cambridge 'Apostle'. He was a friend of the Woolfs and other figures in Bloomsbury.
2 – *BF* contained a 'Foreword' by FLM.
3 – 'Reading by Candle-light', 'Glass Falling', 'Happy Families', 'Impermanent Creativeness', in *Oxford Poetry 1928*, ed. Clere Parsons, 30–5.
4 – Cf. *SAF*, 96, 109: 'For Heraclitus recognised the flux – and one has to do that to be modern.' Many years later he would write 'Variations on Heraclitus', *Solstices*, CP07, 560.

TO *Anthony Blunt* MS Cambridge

[22 August 1928] Carrickfergus

Dear Anthony,

Do come on Friday 31st if you can; (there probably won't be anyone but my father about for a few days). I'm afraid this place is probably inferior to Waterford & trust you wont be too ghastly bored. I am half asleep, it being very late; I have been beginning an anthology of VIth century prose in an exercise book.

My next book will be called A Baedeker's Guide to Purgatory; I am looking forward to writing it but must finish the wretched novel first.

The family are quite cheered about you coming as the only topic for a month has been my sister's impending wedding, which is not really very remarkable.[1]

Do tell me when you arrive in Belfast & I'll try to meet you. I'm afraid when you're here the family won't entrust me with the car for solitary ramps as they think I'm reckless[2] & also the principle of the thing – Indulging the Youth of the Nation.

I hope you're enjoying Lady Goff etc. & have not crashed too much in yr German. Are you bringing Also Sprach Z. with you as I want to get some of the phrases in German?

I hope John H. will turn up sometime.[3] By the way you will have to go to church on Sundays. I wrote such a good sermon for my novel the other day – by Carteson's father.

Poor John. I'm afraid I cant take philosophy seriously yet, being still obsessed by my own little games of stitching words together. Really to be a philosopher you have to really doubt everything & I only pretend to doubt.

It is bound to rain all the time you are here. I have a very nice Contemplation Cave for you in the face of a hill overlooking the Lough if you feel eremite.

I am considering a pamphlet 'The Beauty in Guffaws.' But as for yr

1–The wedding ceremony took place on 18 October at the Parish Church, Carrickfergus, conducted by the father of the bride, assisted by the bride's uncle, Rev. Herbert MacNeice, Vicar of Melbourn, Cambs. ('Marriages', *The Times*, 3 Nov. 1928, 1).

2–See his description of a near collision with 'a curious cart' in the next letter.

3–He wrote to Hilton around this time encouraging him to come to Carrickfergus, promising 'to console you & Anthony because you'll need it in this rainy hell', and again at the end of August, stating 'my people can stand you for an indefinite length of time. "Yonder all before us lie / Deserts of vast eternity"' (FLM to JH, [Summer 1928] and 31 Aug., *Ms Bodleian, Ms Don, c. 153/3*).

paper I wrote a pretty little poem this morning (which you may have) – first this vac. I'm afraid my poytry days are over. Poor boy, I always thought he was a fake, hadn't got the figure for a poyt somehow. But will do all right in the Union – the County one. Oh dear Im so sleepy

Goodnight (I'm longing to see you)

Louis

TO *John Hilton*   MS Bodleian

['Autumn 1928' pencil   Carrickfergus
in Hilton's hand]

Dear John,

I write to you in a state of surprise that I am not in pieces. Driving along tonight in the dark & finding I cld not see the speedometer, my usual criterion, I commended myself to the Deity & went 'flat out' (a phrase I learned from Anthony). So coming round a corner in this manner I saw before me a curious cart in the middle of the road, which concluding to be coming towards me I tried to pass on the left. It, however, going away from me drew in to the left so that I had to tug the wheel round & swirled toward the right-hand edge, & then tugging it back from the hedge we skidded with a great rocking swoop back towards the cart and missed it by about two inches. My latest idea for my novel is an appreciation of Edith Sitwell written by Walter Pater. Cld you ask Moore where he hired his wedding garment?[1] & tell me soon? Also have you asked him about his sister's typographical potentialities?[2]

The family think you have a very nice character.

How is the Old Adam? Give him my love & Give Old Moore of Maudlin Alley my love also – what is left.[3] (Being rather doughy it is not so apt to fall into crumbs.[)] But remind Old Dives (alias Adam) what is in store for him on the other side of the Gulf which beat Miss Gleitze. And

1 – Ponsonby Moore Crosthwaite (educ. Rugby and Corpus Christi College, Oxford), joined the Diplomatic Service in 1932. FLM met Mary Ezra and Mrs Beazley at a luncheon given by Crosthwaite at his rooms in Corpus. Hilton later recalled: 'In Corpus Moore Crosthwaite, heading decisively for the Foreign Office . . . was keenly interested in architecture and interior decoration' (*SAF*, App. B, 253). Cf. 'Auden and MacNeice: Their Last Will and Testament': 'Item to Moore Crosthwaite a concrete house / Built by Gropius' (*LI*, CP07, 740).
2 – Crosthwaite's sister Alexie was Victor Gollancz's secretary. She typed the manuscript of *BF* (FLM to GBM, 1 Dec. 1928, p. 200–1). Cf. next two letters and March 1929, p. 203–4.
3 – FLM mentions an 'Old Moore' in his autobiography, an undergraduate who was Plymouth Brethren, but this was presumably someone else (*SAF*, 107).

tell Old Lazarus (alias Ponsonby)[1] that as far as his sores are concerned –
no, perhaps you had better not tell him, but if you ask yr dear papa, I have
no doubt he will undertake in yr behalf, this delicate & knowledgeable
task. Well, boys, (yes, quite right Prebendary MacNeice calling) I must be
going along now my bed has been long expecting me. So my love to the
whole Blind Cats & Lost Souls Reformatory. I hear Dives has brought an
opulent car. I am sorry for that. Let him revel in his wickedness as he will,
but I warrant Master Hilton, there will be some pretty picking for me &
my down-trod fellows of the nuts that fall from the rich man's table. It is
well known, says Prof. Gilb. Murray B.A., that screws & small tappets
were often distributed among the guests at the higher-class Roman
weddings – see Cat. 'Concubine, nuces da.'[2]

Madame La Comtesse de Pilkington is lodges [*sic*] here at the moment.[3]
Every night we play Fantan loo and faro, or sometimes pam for a change,
while my father & the bishop sit happily in the corner with their
snuffboxes out and their gouty legs (2 per bishop, 1 per arch deacon)
propped up in the commode.

> However however however
> however, how how how, ever ever
> ever Yrs Louis

TO *Alexie Crosthwaite*[4]   MS Texas

[Autumn 1928]   [Oxford]

Dear Miss Crosthwaite,
Moore tells me I can send this stuff to you so I hope you don't mind.
Also could you possibly type out the foreword enclosed? I am sorry to be
so irruptive and it is frightfully kind of you to godmotherise this garbage.
I don't in the least expect Mr. G. to have anything to do with it but it
relieves my conscience considerably to feel that I have made some sort of
effort to get things published. Like educating one's children.
I hear the O.U.D.S. ball was most amusing. I have been thinking ever
since how extraordinarily Egyptian Moore is. I expect you are all

---

1–Presumably Ponsonby Moore Crosthwaite.
2–Gilbert Murray (1866–1957), Regius Professor of Greek at Oxford (predecessor of
Dodds). 'Give nuts, beloved slave' (Catullus 61, 131). Cf. FLM's review of Murray's
Aeschylus, *SLC*, 7–9.
3–Mary Pilkington, sometimes called 'Pilk', friend of Elizabeth MacNeice and a bridesmaid
at her wedding.
4–See previous letter.

descended from Akhenaten somehow or other & so should by rights spend your time writing hymns to the sun.[1]

Please don't show these to Mr. G. if it will reflect on your sanity. I must go out with John Hilton now to watch a tennis tournament.

Yours sincerely

Louis MacNeice

TO *Alexie Crosthwaite* MS Texas

5.30 a.m., Tuesday [1928]   Merton College, Oxford

Dear Alexie:

I am always a little shy about sending copies of this, especially to you as it seems somewhat coals to Newcastle; but I remembered such a good quotation for you in my bath yesterday, so I hope you don't mind. It is from Ennius ('the father of Roman poetry') – hence its rather primitive metre.[2]

I put the time of day so ostentatiously at the top of this because I am enjoying myself intensely, having just finished a philosophy essay. And there is a pleasing fog oozing over the garden from the Meadows. Also woodpigeons. About 6.30 I think of going out & rousing Moore to walk with me. Do you think he will mind much?

Moore is too flourishing, is he not, after Sicily? Miranti-chromatic.

As for the novel do you think you could tell Mr. Gollancz that I am failing daily [& that I should like to have a novel *deleted*]

. . . As time grows late & there might be a Second Coming or anything . . . [*sic*]

Such a strange man appeared in my room yesterday. I thought he was a secret service agent but he was really a German (?) baron who was studying the development of English Literature & had known Lenin at Geneva.[3]

My poems, it seems, are the fashion with the Colonials of this University. I expect to make a living by being an itinerant rhapsodist round the outposts of Empire.

---

1 – Pharaoh, 18th Dynasty. Cf. 'King Akhenaton attempted to overthrow the long-established polytheism and substitute a monotheistic sun-worship' (*Astrology*, 46).
2 – Quintus Ennius (239–169 BC).
3 – The German was very persistent and '[f]or months we were unable to get rid of him . . .' (*SAF*, 120).

Birds are making such a noise & there seems to be a sun imminent. I am terrified that my scout may appear any moment and eye me for not being in bed. Especially as the room is in a mess, there having been a Poetry Society in it last night.

I hope you have a delightful time abroad (? . . . I can't remember more precisely)

I remain ever

Yours sincerely
<u>Louis MacNeice</u>

TO *John Hilton* MS Bodleian

[1928?] [Merton College, Oxford?]

Dear John, Thank you so much. I liked yr letter. I am feeling too ill to write you a letter so I send you a copy of a poem. Here beginneth . . .

HAPPY FAMILIES.[1]

The room is all a stupid quietness
Cajoled only by the fire's caress
We loll severally about and sit
Severally and do our business severally
For there's a little bit for everybody
But that's not all there is to it.

Crusted in sandstone, while the wooden clock
Places two doctor fingers on his mouth
We seem fossils in rock
Or leaves turned mummies in drouth
And garnered into a mouldy shrubbery corner
Where the wind has done with us. When we are old
The gardener will use us for leaf mould.
Dutifully sitting on chair, lying on sofa.
Standing on hearthrug here we are again.
John caught the bus, Joshua caught the train
& I took a taxi so we all got somewhere.
None deserted, noone was a loafer,

1 – Draft of version published in *BF*, CP07, 626–7. No substantive changes.

Nobody disgraced us. Luckily for us
Noone put his foot in it or missed the bus,
But the wind is a beggar and always
Raps at the front door back door side door
In spite of the neat placard which says
'No hawkers here' he knocks the more.
He blows loose paper into petulance
& ruffles the brazier's fiery hair. And once
He caught me suddenly surreptitiously
& heft me out of my shell. We'll pass that over
& forget about it & quietly sit
Knitting close, sitting close under cover.
Snuff out the candle for the cap, I think,
Seems to fit, excellently fit.
Te saluto – in a fraction, half a wink.
But that's not all there is to it.

———————————————————

P.S. I have just been rereading 'Timon of Athens'. I hate yr out & out cynics
who go on & on like Babel. But he put a roof on his misanthropy – a
perfect pediment –

'Timon hath built his everlasting mansion
Upon the beached verge of the salt flood.'[1]

Give yr brothers my love

Yrs . . . 'nor custom stale . . .'[2]
L.

TO *Georgina Beatrice MacNeice*   MS Dan MacNeice

[12 November 1928]   Merton College, Oxford

My dear Madre,
It is ages since I have written. How is William? Over here it rains but I
expect you are more fortunate. I am very busy. Today I have written 2

1–*Timon of Athens*, V.i.215–16: 'Timon hath made his everlasting mansion / Upon the
beached verge of the salt flood . . .'
2–*Antony and Cleopatra*, II.ii: 'Age cannot wither her, nor custom stale / Her infinite
variety . . .'

reviews & have still to write 2 essays. Yesterday week I had M. Johns to tea, having met her unexpectedly the day before.[1] I also got an invitation from Mrs. J. but think I shall rather stay with Anthony. Next year Moore and Adrian & Dickie & I are all going to live together in a house called Balliol Hall in St. Giles – charming rooms free from the usual garbage.[2] John & Graham are going down. I read a paper in Oriel this week on 'Policemen.' Are you yet recovered? I'm more or less. Have you heard from Elizabeth? I am in a dilemma between 2 publishers.[3] I have to write an essay today comparing the Greek, French (or is it Roman?) and English law-courts. I don't know anything about Law (of any sort). I think it stands or sinks on the same level as Cross-word puzzles. Canning hove in on Saturday morning (going to preach at a prep. school) and completely frozen and starved.[4] I have met such a comic lot of Marlburian decadents (freshmen) who paint their eyebrows etc. The poor Beazleys have no servants[;] some go up sometimes to hew wood & draw water for them. Anthony's paper has come out – disappointing. We had a High Tea the other day – winkles & passionfruit & mangoes & chicken. & the other night I played charades (!) with the Dons (some of them; not the bicentenarians). Moreover I am getting very corpulent so that I can hardly carry myself. And there have been some fogs. Which is all there is to say at the moment.

Love Louis

Except that there are more fogs in the immediate future.

TO *Georgina Beatrice MacNeice*   MS Dan MacNeice

[1 December 1928]   Merton College, Oxford

Dear Madre,
    It is long, I fear, since I have written to you though I have been doing plenty of writing – copying out this wretched novel. I shall have to make up in philosophy etc. next vac. I had lunch with the Beazleys today; Moore was there also. Moore's sister (being his private secretary) gave my poems

---

1 – Margaret Johns.
2 – FLM spent the 1929–30 academic year at 26 St Giles, Oxford, a University boarding house, once the home of the Dragon School. The row of houses comprising 24–29 St Giles was demolished in 1964.
3 – He eventually showed the novel he was then writing to both Gollancz and Heinemann.
4 – Clifford Canning was now at Canford School.

(45 in number) to Gollancz some time ago but Gollancz has been ill so they have not yet been rejected.

I am half asleep, I hope you are twice as much and having a good rest.

Thank you for the photos, which I shall return; I'm afraid I don't like them much.

I went to the Oxford Old Marlburian dinner (so patriotic!); my word what speeches – too long-winded for anything. But George Turner sang one of his best folk-songs.[1]

How is William? ⎫
How is David?[2] ⎬ Neither starved, I trust
                  ⎭

Poor car, having its mudguards etc. hurt.

A young man came round this morning and asked me to join in the creation of an Oxford University Poetry club (the first of its kind – with various lofty aims).

No, I shan't come home till after Nan's wedding;[3] shall stay with Anthony, I think.

I hope Daddie is in the height of good form.

I have some wonderful pink chrysanthemums in my room, very old and languorous. Have you any flowers in the house?

But I shall come home some time; do not be worried.

Graham is working so hard; but Adrian and I have been eating oysters. I told you, I think, how Adrian & Moore & Dickie & I (& possibly John H.) are all going to live together next year in such charming lodgings in St. Giles!

And thank you so much for the tea which everyone pronounces excellent. I told you, did I, I had Margaret Johns to tea? (But that was a good time ago; I must really improve my correspondence).

Now I am going to bed; love to all (with expectations of a speedy meeting),

Louis

1 – On Turner, the headmaster ('Master') at MC, see FLM to GBM, 24 Sept. 1922, n. 3, p. 71.
2 – That is, his brother Willie and David the family driver.
3 – Nan, sister of Margaret Johns of Carrickfergus.

1929

TO *Anthony Blunt* MS Cambridge

March [1929] Merton College, Oxford

Dear Anthony,

'Blind Fireworks' comes out on March 18th. Cld you possibly out of the bounty of yr heart beat up one or two Cambridge book-sellers & get them to <u>stock</u> it in large numbers as such 'display' is all-important? I shall be deeply grateful.

Oh yes. My people have come & gone. I sent them a telegram, you see (to anticipate the dons) which ran as follows – 'Expect dons letter detailing childish outburst merely emotional crisis finding melodramatic outlet am now well out of it and engaged to be married gaudeamus love Louis.'[1] Which was telephoned home from the post-office & taken down by a menial because my S.-mother couldn't hear, & the menial kept bursting into laughter at the strange words (DONS came out BONS) & my Step-mother grew progressively horrified as she watched the writing-pad.[2] So I asked John to send them a re-assuring telegram & he sent them 'Can vouch for Louis' rationality judgment excellent' but it came out NATIONALITY & as it was merely signed 'John' they thought it came from Nonesuch run mad.[3] So late one evening I got a wire saying they were arriving next morning, which they did. & I got my sister & Nonesuch up to meet them which caused a diversion. & John H. was frightfully good & generally soothed them. So that after a few interviews & remarks about God & prayers they went away again.

---

1 – FLM had been arrested for drunk and disorderly behaviour after a boisterous lunch party at Merton College. The police arrest was reported to the College, then by the Warden to the student's father. FLM recalls the incident in *SAF*, 121; cf. Stallworthy, 127–8. (The telegram, dated 14 Feb. 1929, is at HRC, Texas.) FLM had evidently become engaged to Mary the previous December, but the couple had kept it a close secret. Two days after receiving the telegram, JFM wrote to Hilton: 'it was good of you to wire. But how could you think I could approve Louis' choice? It is a terrible disappointment. It promises to bring nothing but misery. I think it is shamefully wrong of Mrs Beazley, that is if she had reason to anticipate an engagement' (16 Feb. 1929, unpublished letter, *Ms Bodleian*).
2 – His stepmother was slightly deaf.
3 – John Nicholson.

. . . yes, Mary Ezra.[1] She doesn't like you & I gather you don't like her. Which is very bad taste on both sides. We are going to live in a garret.

Yes, my family had an alarm about synagogues.

<u>But on no account tell anyone anything about this</u> as the ground is full of mines.

& it is not all for effect as you might think. (having a well trained mind *deleted*)

My author's copies may come any minute; I will send you one.[2]

Give my love to Michael & the others.[3]

In Nomine Domini

Love Ever

<u>Louis</u>

TO *Alexie Crosthwaite*   MS Texas

[March 1929]   Merton College, Oxford

Dear Alexie,

Thank you so much for your letter. As for book-sellers I tried a few (Blackwell's, the Davenant and W. H. Smith) but they were rather snubbing and seemed to know about it already. There was a suggestion that Gollancz should send a card or something round to them all saying he was ready to supply them with it. Blackwell's, Parker's & Thornton's are, I think, the most hopeful ones.

Anthony is doing a little boosting in Cambridge.[4]

I am sorry it is not coming out till 18th as the Oxford Term ends on Saturday 16th & most people will have gone down by then. However . . . [*sic*]

1–Giovanna Marie Thérèse Babette ('Mary') Ezra (1908–91), daughter of a stockbroker's clerk, David Ezra (killed in action, 1918); and Marie Bloomfield, educ. local schools and School of Agriculture, Oxford (no degree). Her stepfather was Professor J. D. Beazley (see FLM to AB, 21 July 1928, n. 3, p. 191). At Oxford, she was drawn to 'dancing, tennis playing, and punting on the Cherwell' rather than to academic pursuits, though was well read in ancient and modern literature and 'knew vast stretches of Shakespeare's plays by heart, merely from having read them without obligation' (Dan MacNeice, 'Biographical sketch of Louis' first wife', *Ms Carrickfergus Museum*). Married FLM 21 June 1930; separated 1935; divorced 1936. She appears as Esther in *AS*.
2–Of *BF*.
3–Michael Robertson.
4–FLM approached a number of Oxford bookshops to encourage them to sell *Blind Fireworks*.

I got my author's copies & had great difficulty in giving them to the right people. However . . . [*sic*]

Moore seems in very good form. They had a Bump Supper the other night & the president gave them all soup at U.O.P.M. which Moore, being his right-hand man, ladled out to all the little boys with alacrity, accuracy and the true Dickens spirit.[1]

I also heard him (Moore) read a paper the other night – enunciation perfect and content instructive.

I think 'Blind Fireworks' is very pleasingly brought out & it is much admired by the young men here for its chaste elegance. It is so much better than the Hogarth people would have done it.

I must return now to my breakfast. I apologise for my writing but it is the result of having a bath.

I feel you are entirely responsible for the production of this book for which I am very grateful in a gaping sort of way like a little girl whose (fairy) godmother suddenly produces a golden pumpkin etc. It is rather a joke, I think, being an author.

I hope you are prosperous. I suppose Mr. Gollancz hasn't read my novel yet? I am expecting him to reject it but what I <u>shall</u> dislike will be if it is classed as an 'Adolescent Novel'.

There is a slight fog here obtruding the mind. I hope it is better in London.

Yrs sincerely
Louis MacNeice

TO *Anthony Blunt*   MS Cambridge

Postmark 27 May 1929   Merton College, Oxford

Dear Anthony,

Sorry not to have written before but time scuttles so. I am bloody busy this term but do come over here some time or other. I am sending you a Galahad.[2] I think your article is fairly free of misprints. I corrected l'Infirm (which seemed a little dull) to l'Infini. I have got a shoal of new pomes

---

1 – A bump supper is given to celebrate the success of a college boat in a rowing event. I have been unable to ascertain the meaning of 'U.O.P.M.'.

2 – JH writes: 'In this Easter term of 1929 another event was the appearance of the first number of a magazine called Sir Galahad with whose engendering and further care Louis had a good deal to do.' JH designed the cover (*SAF*, 257).

[*sic*] for next spring. Give my love to Michael & the VIII.[1] & could you ask Canning to have my book read in the forms in Canford? I am rather upset by hearing that Humbert Wolfe recommended my poem to Gollancz.[2] This is like Ellis Waterhouse's letter to John Bowle in which every sentence began with I.[3] I am glad you like Life: it has its points. The chaps here want to see you much. Is it a good job at the Fitzwilliam: tell me all about it.[4] I am going to be a colonial professor, I expect. My Life hangs on getting a first & at the moment . . . that seems a trifle impossible. Otherwise I am joyous. But there is a widespread conspiracy against us here & they are all so two-faced. So we spend our time in fields.

Love ever;
Louis

TO *John Hilton* MS Bodleian

['?Spring 1929' *Hilton's hand* Carrickfergus
in pencil]

John my Dear,

Thank you so much for your letter – not that I understand it. & Good Luck to your Work. & could you possibly write me an article on the Child Cult?[5] My father says you are a Trump Card.[6] Which is a very sporting expression for him. Or on the Art of the Illustrator? Or on Reciprocity? But I want the Child Cult rather, bringing in the Naïf & All That. I think we shall run Away this summer. The Life of Man being short. And one tires of Intellectual Aphasia & Ask Longer Veda Bread, old Joyce punning down the telephone. & it is a mistake to ascribe one's own Halitosis to the Universe (or the Varse as we call it in our Colloquial way). & when I talk Like this you don't know If i am being Too clever for you or Just A fool. But you wrote Betty good dung yourself in Your last. The cat is on the

1 – Michael Robertson.
2 – Humbert Wolfe (1885–1940), poet and civil servant. Educ. Bradford GS; Wadham College, Oxford.
3 – Ellis Kirkham Waterhouse (1905–85), educ. MC 1919–23; New College, Oxford.
4 – Blunt had applied for a curatorial position at the Fitzwilliam Museum, Cambridge, but his application was unsuccessful. He later applied for the directorship of the museum, again without success (Carter, 69, 181).
5 – On the child cult, see FLM to GBM, [May 1927], n. 1, p. 166.
6 – There had been a brief correspondence between JH and FLM's parents that spring. Thanking him for his letter, GBM wrote, 'I am so thankful that Louis has such a real friend as you' (GBM to JH, 6 March 1929, *Ms Bodleian, Ms. Don, c. 153/3, ff. 76–8*).

mat. Tit for Tat. The mat is on the cat. οἴμοι[1] I too can play the hilton in my turn.

I like you very much though.

& after that

& after

& after

& af

te

R

That,

We shall all have a good time doubtless,

Yours affectionately

Louis

TO *Lady Beazley*[2]   MS Simon Kingston

[June/July? 1929]   Merton College, Oxford

Dear Mrs. Beazley,

A mere detail, but if I must be damned, I should rather be damned on the right evidence. I hear you are very much shocked because I never sent the proofs of 'Sir Galahad' to Anthony.[3]

Anthony sent me his article last vac., having written it [']straight off the reel', without, apparently, any preliminary draft, and in pencil. I had much difficulty in reading it. Anthony said in a later letter that he did not think

---

1 – 'Alas'/'Woe is me'.

2 – Marie Beazley (1885–1967), daughter of London businessman Bernard Bloomfield, widow of David Ezra (killed in action, 1918); subsequently wife (m.1919) of Professor J. D. ('Jackie') Beazley. By repute a rather formidable woman, she spoke several European languages and was an expert photographer. In an otherwise affectionate account, Harold Acton described her as a Cerberus guarding her husband's cloister (*Memoirs of an Aesthete*, 1948, 140). Her obituarist records: 'Strikingly handsome, she ever remained a picturesque figure. Fearless in all her attitudes, she never pretended to conceal her strong likes and dislikes and was the first to admit this' (*The Times*, 6 Dec. 1967). Stallworthy wrote that she 'sailed through life like the well-endowed figurehead of a nineteenth-century clipper, trailing stories as a ship trails seaweed' (116). Her relationships with FLM and JFM, as with her daughter and grandson, eventually became extremely difficult for all concerned. As the letter suggests, she temporarily took AB under her wing, but for FLM this was to be a rehearsal for many further arguments with his future mother-in-law. Cf. 'Auden and MacNeice: Their Last Will and Testament': 'And to the most mischievous woman now alive / We leave a lorry-load of moral mud / And may her Stone Age voodoo never thrive' (*LI*, CP07, 737).

3 – AB had contributed to the second issue of *Sir Galahad* (May 1929).

206

much of it (as far as he could remember its content) and seemed to consider it little more than a piece of hack-writing.

I sent it down to the printers in good time this term but they set up none of the type till some time later and even then left Anthony's article over till the 2nd batch of proofs. This batch reached me only about 5 days (or less) before publication. I thought it too much of a rush to send them to Cambridge and did my best to correct them myself. Anthony's article was full of mistakes (as was to be expected from the illegibility of his MSS.); of the mistakes which survived me one ('national' for 'rational') is certainly heart-breaking; the others are comparatively trifling but I much regret all of them. The whole paper, however, was full of misprints (including an annoying one in my own article); misprints are infuriating but they always occur in Oxford papers, especially if their production is as haphazard as 'Sir Galahad's'.

I apologize for this self-vindicating letter but in literary matters I retain a little conscience; (and though Anthony and I have always treated each other cavalierly, I like him too much to neglect either out of spite or mere laziness his contributions to my paper.).

Yours sincerely
<u>Louis MacNeice</u>

TO *Anthony Blunt* MS Cambridge

Postmark 13 July [1929]   SS *Patriotic* (Belfast Steamship
                                 Company Limited)

Dear Anthony,

I apologise for never having written to you about Marlborough but have been ghastly busy & much pulverised. I hear you were much pained by my treatment of you. Meaning when? Apart from Galahad which was a bad show (though I <u>had hardly</u> any time to send you the proofs).[1] I am sorry if I really have pained you. I conjecture, if I have, that it is either (a) by non-confidence or (b) by general negligence. Well my dear, (a) it has never been my custom to publish private squalors, while as for private delights their bloom is apt to be lost in the transit. & as you were at Cambridge it seemed to me unnecessary to mesh you up in such a very tangled skein. (b) Mrs. B. (I gather) regards me as a friend-forsaker – the sort of man, in fact, who lets everyone down in the long run. I am sorry

1 – See previous letter, to Lady Beazley, written a short time before this.

about this but once she has got hold of the wrong end of the stick, she goes on chawing it. Only I am sorry if I seem to have forsaken you in any way. I think if you knew <u>all</u> the good & bad demons that crowd me, you would not be surprised if I am somewhat abstracted 'Ubi nunc sapientis ossa Merlini?'[1] I don't think I can write out a vindication of myself here (I gather that Mrs. B. has fairly well damned me to you & she always convinces one) but I should like you to take it that I am not entirely selfish (Mrs. B. does not know the facts) & moreover that I am (for once at any rate) not acting which is possibly why there are so many crashes (see Schiller: 'Art is easy, Life is difficult.[']) Oh, & finally that Mary is quite different from what you think & is not to be totted up & analysed & prescribed for like any creature off the streets or tennis-courts. & that we know each other very well indeed so that when these people prophesy, most of their prophecies at any rate are those of mere doctrinaires. When you stayed with me last I rather posed as being in the wrong (that is a disease I have) but I don't think anyone's in the wrong really. & I would readily jump off the Radcliffe Camera if it was going to solve the question but it wouldn't. Whereas if I stay where I am there are very good chances of a better solution.

I write this because I don't want you to dislike me. I am tired, however, of talking & apologies. & apart from Mary I am pretty well tired of things. & anyhow one is so old sometimes that it all seems hoary dither. But I want her much. & the ego wont be denied. No tu-quoque. But do write to me (I am on the bloody boat home at the moment).

Love ever:
<u>Louis</u>

TO *John Hilton*   MS Bodleian

[Autumn 1929]   [Oxford]

Dear John,

Thank you for your letters. You are rather an old truant aren't you? I fear I argued [your *deleted*] one of your points with Mary & she is fed up with you now. She has been in bed nearly all this week with a frightful throat. All due to rows & nerves. My advice to you is keep clear of all Families – they are either swamps (e.g. mine) or geysers (e.g. Mrs B). By the way did I tell you I have worked out that I am really a mistake (i.e. my

---

1 – 'Where now are the bones of wise Merlin?' Motto of the town of Marlborough.

birth ought to have been forbidden);[1] this is the basis for rather a nice & novel snobbery, feeling one has done the Forces of Nature etc.

Yes, we are very sad about the vac but hope to stay with Graham a good part of the time. I am practically banned the [*sic*] house now by Mrs. B. (not but what the big muck has been to all intents & purposes cleared up). She thinks I am totally undesirable. There may be something in this, but of course there are many instances of totally-undesirables being very good people to live with. & after all is your ideal husband a combination of Every-Boy-about-the-House & a prize stallion?

Mary is composing a detective story to be called the Mutton Crushett Mystery. We invented some very good names in the S. of France, also an unprintable song about Auntie.[2]

Did you get your Oxford P.? Your contributions are much approved.[3]

I made a speech at the Old Marlburian dinner the other night, followed by the conciliation with Sandford etc.[4] The man proposing the other toast was in his dotage (being the head of the Bodleian).

Yes I want to go to one of those universities like Leeds or Stellenbosch. Mary is not being given any trousseau, so we shall have the hell of a time (but quite an amusing hell) collecting household furnishings.

My philosophy tutor, it seems, remarked the other day to Jacky that I should probably land myself with a very poor 2nd.[5] This is much more encouraging than anything they said about me before Mods. (Excuse conceit).

I think of writing (in an off moment) a comic historical novel about the Early Roman Empire as a counterblast to the numerous serious ones (e.g. 'Quo Vadis?')[6]

---

1 – FLM's mother believed his difficult birth had been partially responsible for her developing a uterine fibroid: 'I believe that [Louis] had an irrational idea, perhaps only partly conscious, that his birth had caused his mother's later illness and death' (EN, in *TWA*, 16).

2 – FLM and Mary had visited St Tropez in summer 1929.

3 – Hilton published four poems in *Oxford Poetry 1929*, ed. FLM and Stephen Spender, 17–20.

4 – T. C. G. Sandford (1877–1942), educ. MC 1892–6; Keble College, Oxford. Assistant master MC 1902–37.

5 – Geoffrey Mure of Merton, who came to think very highly of his student: he wrote in a testimony the following spring: 'Mr L. MacNeice has been reading Philosophy with me for Lit. Hum. for two years. He has very considerable ability and grasp. He also displays an occasional power of quite brilliant writing which he probably sometimes allows to run away with him. His good Classical Scholarship is attested by his First in Honours Moderations, & shows great hopes of his returning the same class in final schools' (G. Mure, 14 May 1930, MS Bodleian). 'Jacky' was Professor Beazley.

6 – *Quo Vadis: a Narrative of the Time of Nero*, by Henry Sienkiewicz (1896).

I agree with Anaximander that all (specific) existence is an usurpation.[1] God be praised (or perhaps it is flying in the face of God). I then specifically exist. The more specifically the more of an usurper. Come then, let me see what I can lay hands on (the world for an orb & a red-haired paintbrush for a sceptre) . . . and upon a time the Punch & Judy show revolted.

Half these dons are only stamp-lickers anyhow. If I am a don I shall launch all my letters into the void unstamped & God will have to pay the other end.

As for Mrs. B. I ran in & swore at her the other day but it is difficult not to laugh – even though I love Mary much & much [sic]. There is something so crude about Fighting One's Way & Playing the Man.

But of course it would be beyond laughing if one lived with Mrs. B. Mary has much endurance.

When I say 'get away soon' I don't mean till after Greats. As soon as possible then. I must have got a job first.

Oh yes, if we have a daughter we shall call her Ramah. (Mary had a gdmother called Ramah Judah).[2]

By the way if you would really like to put your foot out (as you so quaintly phrased it) you could at the same time help us & (possibly) reconcile yourself with Mary, by writing to my people out of the German distance.[3] I know you don't believe it but they are strangely blind. What I should like you to put across (in your own words) is (a) Mary's extraordinarily sensitive nature. (My people still judge everyone by themselves). (b) the necessity (if either of us is to survive) that we hang on to each other all these vacs. (You see, we can't go to my home because, under present circumstances, it would be more than Mary can stand.) You needn't write any such letter, of course, if you don't like it. But I am sure they can't imagine what a difficult time we have here (& they themselves are to a great extent responsible for it). They are so stogged [sic] in a sort of Christian fatalism that they can't see for example why Mrs B. should get in a state about anything; or why I should not like to go home & spend a quiet 6 weeks with them; or why Mary should not get on all right at her home (being ranted at by a chimera-ridden mother).

What they need is some straight talking to – & by the more people the better (they are apt to look on me as both deluded & a poseur). They need

1 – Anaximander (610–546 BC), pre-Socratic philosopher.
2 – Rama Judah was Mary Ezra's paternal grandmother (m. Ezekiel Elias David Joseph Ezra). Cf. 'Sassoon and Ezra Families', *Ms Dan MacNeice*.
3 – Hilton was in Stuttgart in Nov. 1929. See JH to FLM, 9 Nov. 1929, unpublished, *Ms Bodleian*.

to be woken up to the realisation that they ought to be shivering with excitement at the advent of Mary instead of first shrugging their shoulders & saying it is the Will of God, & then patting themselves & saying, it is the will of God [*sic*], & then (as soon as they themselves are involved in any bother) frowning & writing to Mrs B. that they cannot accept any responsibility for this intimacy! They ought to have it battered into their fatalistic brains that if they can't accept responsibility for Mary they needn't expect me to consider myself under any obligations to <u>them</u> – even if they do open my letters & pay my debts unasked. No, I shouldn't put your finger into this pie if I were you. If you write to them, tell them you have heard from me & you gather from my tone that if I am not humoured, I may sheer off at any minute. & you might imply that if they don't thank God daily for the existence of Mary (instead of disclaiming responsibility!) they are just damned fools & not even good Christians. You might also imply that you needn't be a parish-meeting fan to be truly religious. You might also imply that I have been a long way too filial already & that they may count themselves merely lucky to have seen as much of me all those vacs as they have, & that if they have me alone at home (a) I shall be bloodily gloomy, (b) it will ruin my work & (c) it will make me dislike them. & on the other hand Mary cannot go home with me because of her one & unsurmountable inhibition. So that (seeing I am now well on in years) they must get used to not seeing me for a bit.

Sorry to suggest all this to you. Don't do any of it.

Nor should I write to Mary yet as she is still freshly vexed with you (my fault, I fear, for trying to explain your views on 'marrying'. The real reason of course was our state at the time & you couldn't help it. However lie low as yet).

I am now going to bed.

Love Lou?

Sunday

Anthony is bringing over a hockey-team this week. I trust you are keeping up your Ju Jitsu at the expense of the Continent.[1]

Today is very Sunday, but Mary is a little better.

I hope you are happy. Send me any poems you write.

Yours ever

Louis

1 – Hilton wrote: '[Adrian Green-Armytage] and I later started ju-jitsu lessons together but only got as far as how to release your wrists from holds' (*SAF*, App. B, 252).

TO *John Hilton*   MS Bodleian

[Autumn 1929]   [26 St Giles] Oxford

Dear John:

Many thanks for your charming letter & apologies for delay in answering it. And many wishes for success in all your affairs and affaire. You seemed to wish to be helpful to me (or us) in your last letter, so if you do not mind some sordor & the chance of being put off me for life – here goes: Apologia pro Vita Mea. Only not even an apologia. (You may very possibly think me (a) a swine & (b) dishonest. As for the latter I have always thought of truth as something one constructs, & never seen any need to load my friends with superfluous unpleasantness.)

The crux of the matter is that I have got an idiot brother (a 'Mongol' i.e. non-hereditary). Hence the greater part of my rows with Mrs. B owing to my inefficiency in producing non-hereditary evidence.

I will now start at the beginning: my father was engaged to my mother for God knows how long & it seems to me that when they did marry they made rather a hash of all the more material side of it e.g. not taking proper precautions for child-birth etc. My birth was managed so rottenly that my mother had eventually to have a hysterectomy; after which she was ill off & on till she died for obscure reasons when I was just 7. Even the operation was done in a very crude manner which my sister tells me is now obsolete.

From the age of about 5 or 6 till 8 or 9 my sister & I (& my brother) lived all together at home without being in any way properly looked after; first we had a hopelessly uneducated woman from a farm in Co. Armagh who used to tell my sister how she would soon die because she (i.e. my sister) had so many colds, & what nasty things they would write on her grave-stone.[1] Then we had a worthless zany or two; I think for several years I never had my teeth washed. As for my father he loomed about the house & hardly ever spoke to us. At one time I had to sleep in the same room with him & all night he used to groan & mutter & toss about.

My stepmother appeared when I was about 9.[2] My brother was sent off to an Institute in Scotland & my sister & I were sent to school. As my stepmother's ideas were then wholly quaker, mixed with a naïve & charming innocence & a little snobbery, it was one dotty epoch on top of another. I always remained terrified of my father.

1 – Miss McCready.
2 – JFM married GBM on 19 April 1917, when FLM was aged nine.

Once or twice while I was a little boy my brother was brought from Scotland to stay with us. Each time he seemed to be uglier & more monstrous & on one occasion I had to sleep in the same room for a fortnight; one morning he woke me up by beating me on the face with a shoe.

When I was at Marlborough I had already escaped from the 'fear of God' & the missionary atmosphere & general unwholesomeness. When I was 17, however, owing to a (sentimental &, I think, foolish) proposal of my sister, the family reinstalled my brother at home. In case you don't know what Mongols are like, they are stunted & very ugly but very goodnatured; my brother, for instance, is talking & laughing all day long; he, of course, talks only very imperfectly.

The result of this was that while the rest of the family seemed even to enjoy it (as a Christian burden?) I became in a strange way hollow; I am only filling up again now. My only way out was to imagine it away, when I was not at home.

My family have always been making bloody mistakes; they sent (I am not quite sure of this but deduced it from writings in a margin) my sister to school at the age of 14 without telling her anything about adolescence etc.

Anyhow this is all irrelevant; the summer you stayed with me my brother was away in England.[1] I expected my family to let it out to you; I only objected to talking about it myself.

I seem to be writing this up more morbid than it was. I was really quite merry most of the time. & anyhow I devised an adequate scheme, or rather drift, of life. But then Mary came.

Here I crashed. We hove up to each other on Monday in the last week of the Christmas term & then we hove away again; I felt I was too hollow for anyone to marry. Besides I knew I ought to explain everything first.

On Tuesday, after being very sad and then merrily-&-sadly drunk the night before, I rushed off (after your lunch-party) to the Judge's Lodgings & we got engaged.[2] Then (this is where I really was swinish) I didn't tell Mary anything about my brother. It all seemed a myth anyhow. Besides the world seemed sordid enough (e.g. Nonesuch) to spoil a myth before it spoiled itself.[3]

---

1 – JH visited FLM in Carrickfergus in Sept. 1928. Cf. JH, *SAF*, App. B, 268–9.
2 – They became engaged during the last week of the Christmas term 1928, but kept it secret until the following February.
3 – 'Nonesuch' was his brother-in-law, John Nicholson.

We went to Cambridge the next week end. Then I stayed with you, then with Anthony; while staying with Anthony I went (on the Sunday) up to Oxford & spent the afternoon with Mary & told her nothing; for, just as I thought of unloading it all, she said she had a horror of lunatics.

The next day (Sunday) I wrote her a long letter (from Anthony's house) all about it. Then began the complications which have been going on ever since.

Mary & I love each other very much. If I had been ordinarily practical, or had some more guts, I should have cleared it all up earlier. The stages were:- (Mrs. B., you see, heard from an Oxford doctor that such cases were v. difficult to diagnose etc. & that one should know all about them before thinking of marrying). –

(a) Mary wrote to me saying I must ask my father about it. Which I did & he simply said – non-hereditary; perfectly well established. I communicated this & everyone said all was well & we needn't do any more for the moment. (Of course, if I had had any foresight, I should have done a lot more. Being already thoroughly convinced myself & trusting that my father knew all about it, I didn't do anything.)

(b) I stayed at Hekaton for Mary's birthday. I also stayed a night with my sister & omitted to ask her anything about it. Mrs. B. ramped at me at the end of this week & said it was dishonourable (I think) to stay on with her without clearing up this problem. I said I would write to my sister about it as she & Nonesuch must know, both being doctors.

(c) Easter term: I wrote to my sister asking her about it but without saying anything about Mary. My sister thinking it was mere general inquisitiveness, omitted to answer. After about a fortnight I wrote again telling her about Mary. She had been to Switzerland, which wasted about a week(?) more. In the interim came my drunkenness. Then my sister's letter (which seemed very authoritative) arrived & Mrs. B. seemed fairly well pleased, & generally it seemed that it would suffice. Mary said that Mrs. B. would <u>some</u> time want a certificate. Then my people arrived & distracted everything. Which you remember. Mrs B. was very much shocked that my people when seeing her said nothing about my brother.

All this was, of course, frightfully bad for Mary's nerves, especially when Mrs. B. pointed it up. My only early suggestion, however, of looking up the Scotch place in a directory & writing to it, was promptly quashed.[1] Then my sister's letter created a lull. & then when my family knew about it, I felt everything was more or less clear. I had expected my family to try to blow up the whole thing.

1 – Willie's school in Stirlingshire.

(d) Easter vac was tranquil & about the 1st week of summer term. Then Mrs. B.'s anxiety & anger etc. welled up again & she started nagging Mary. I didn't realise the trouble as I thought it was all settled. Then my people arrived, which was the final blow; as being stogged in Christian ignorance or forgetfulness or carelessness they told Mrs. B. hardly anything & what they did tell her was mainly wrong. She asked Dr. Heaton about it & he said their theories were nonsense. But he said it could be looked into & settled by one Dr. Farquhar Buzzard.[1] So she decided to write to my father & ask him to take my brother to Dr. F.B. at her expense. She told me I could keep out of it as I would do no good. Mrs. B. delayed sending this letter till I was at home for a fortnight in July. My family on receiving it didn't tell me at once; it eventually slipped out & we had some mutual ramps, as my family had no wish to do anything; I persuaded my father (who revealed in the most childish way that lots of specialists knew all about it already) to write to one of them & get some sort of written evidence. When I was back in Oxford before going to Ireland with Mary my father's letter arrived; & he had merely <u>copied</u> out in his own hand some more or less irrelevant remarks of the specialists on Mongolism! Whereupon Mary & I began to swear & say what a knave or fool my father was, while Mrs. B. upped & said that she alone understood him & that he was really a good man who failed to see her point! She would write a very clear & convincing letter which could not fail to elicit the right information.

This arrived when we were all in Achill in August.[2] Mary & I did not know till we got to the South of France (September) whether my father had answered or not. There we found he had not! I thought that perhaps he was waiting till the end of the vac. or had sent it to Oxford. But when Mary & I got to Oxford in October, there was no letter! Then Professor & Mrs. B. came back & there was the Hell of a Ramp. Why had I not written threatening my father?

1–Sir Farquhar Buzzard, 1st baronet (1871–1945), physician. By 1929 Buzzard was very eminent: he was in this year created a baronet and was appointed to the Regius chair of medicine at Oxford. He was physician-extraordinary to King George V. He provided the model for the neurologist in *RW*. FLM skewers him in *SAF*, 128–9. Cf. 'Auden and MacNeice: Their Last Will and Testament': 'Item, to Sir Farquhar Buzzard a raspberry' (*LI*, CP07, 734).
2–'In the summer of 1929 I spent four weeks in the island of Achill and six weeks at St Tropez. The former place was inhabited by stage patriarchs on stage donkeys, the latter by stage Frenchmen who lolled on a stage beach'; 'When I Was Twenty-One: 1928', *The Saturday Book* 21, ed. John Hadfield (1961), 230–9; repr. *SP*, 234.

So I wrote to him saying I would cut myself off if he did not give Mrs. B. what she wanted; after which with some delay he proceeded to produce evidence. Even yet full documentary evidence is not forthcoming! but is at hand.

It is really all right, as I have always known. (a) my brother is a Mongol (as was from the beginning decided by specialists), (b) Mongolism is not hereditary. But Mrs. B. owing to her Jewish passion for health & eugenics has raised such storms etc. that Mary (& herself) have both suffered a good deal. So I feel a swine as being so inefficient. As for Mrs. B. Mary & I do not mind about her any more, having decided that both our families are cracked. (Do you agree?)

Oh yes; Mary dreamed all my first [informing?] letter the morning of its arrival; when she got up there was the letter on the [Hall-]table & inside it what she had been dreaming.

I hope you don't mind my telling you all this. Otherwise Mary & I had a gorgeous vac. – digging up amethysts in Achill & chasing cicales [sic] in St. Tropez. Where we also bathed, the water being velvetly buoyant. Mary is flourishing & looking very 'bewitching' as you once said of her in a letter to me. There is no point in living by oneself. Yet you don't think I will blast her do you? Because I am a creature of not much vitality. Or not enough for her, as she is most alive of anyone.

It is so bloody getting mixed up in sordors & tediums. We hope soon to get away & live more livingly. [sic]

Sorry if this is illegible; I have been up all night & it draws near to breakfast.

Moore is rather nice.[1]

Write to me too.

Mrs. B. thinks we shall get divorced because I am a 'swamp'.

You must build us a house, though.

What fun in Sweden.

You have 4 poems in Oxford P. I expect you will be sent a copy. Adrian & C. Holme are much pleased by 'Cogito Ergo Morior'.[2] So am I.

I depart now, wishing you a good breakfast;

Much love ever,

Don't think me too much of a swine –

Louis

1 – Moore Crosthwaite.
2 – Hilton's poems in *Oxford Poetry 1929* (ed. FLM and Stephen Spender) included 'Cogito ergo morior' (19–20). The issue also carried poems by FLM and Christopher Holme. 'Adrian' was Green-Armytage (*SAF*, 270).

P.S. I don't mind you telling anyone anything in this –
P.P.S. Mary would like it well if you wrote to her.

Prosit.

Note
I am afraid
the contents
are rather
grim

TO *Anthony Blunt*   MS Cambridge

Postmark 23 October 1929   Oxford

Dear Anthony,

A thousand apologies; I trust you have not compromised me with any literary power yet, as the word of God came to me this morning (just as I was going to send the thing to you) telling me to send it to Heinemann instead? The reason for this is that I MUST HAVE MONEY & Adrian's cousin who is now in great favour with Heinemann will give me a boost.[1] They have just published his 1st novel[2] which sold so well that they are now giving him £700 a year merely to write novels (no specified number) for them.

So I hope you will forgive me if I try them, as I owe £70 to my father much against my will (fathers who open letters are anathema don't you think?)

Oh yes, the Old Marlburians want me to make a speech at their dinner. Rehabilitation.

How is the Cambridge verkehrte Welt?[3]

Tell me about your prospects. & may your namesake saint look after you.

Love
Louis

---

1 – Adrian Green-Armytage's cousin Vivien Dayrell-Browning, m. Graham Greene 1927.
2 – Graham Greene, *The Man Within*.
3 – A phrase of Hegel's, from *The Phenomenology of Spirit*, meaning an inverted or topsy-turvy world.

1930

TO *E. R. Dodds*[1]

MS Bodleian

28 May [1930]   Oxford

Dear Professor Dodds,

I must thank you firstly for your hospitality on Monday, secondly for your letter and for Professor Thomson's telegram, and say that I feel very much honoured indeed by your nomination of me for such a responsible post – especially as I have not yet finished my course here. I only hope that as a lecturer I shall be successful in proportion to my keenness.

Professor Thomson told me that the Pass students are 'incredibly bad' and have no knowledge even of the rudiments of Latin. As my two years of Greats work have left me a little 'transcendental', I intend to devote a fair amount of time in this vacation to repairing my groundwork so as to be sure of myself when I start with you.

I am most grateful to you for your financial information, which does not frighten me. And I shall keep June 26th and 28th free for a visit to Birmingham.

As for digs. this raises a difficulty (or facility!) – in that I have some hopes of being married in the immediate future and, if possible, before I come to you in October. This has been for some time in the air and mainly

---

1 – Eric Robertson Dodds (1893–1979), educ. Campbell College, Belfast; University College, Oxford. His appointments included Lecturer in Classics at Reading, Professor of Greek at Birmingham 1924–36 and Regius Professor of Greek at Oxford 1936–60. He appears as Boyce in *AS*. His wife A. E. (Betty) Dodds was on the English faculty at Birmingham University. A renowned expert on Neoplatonism, Dodds's publications include *Journals and Letters of Stephen McKenna* (1936), *Proclus' Elements of Theology* (1933, 1963), Euripides, *Bacchae* (1944, 1960), Plato, *Gorgias* (1959) (all as editor), *The Greeks and the Irrational* (1951), *Pagan and Christian in an Age of Anxiety* (1965) and *The Ancient Concept of Progress* (1973). His memoirs were published as *Missing Persons* (1977). He nominated FLM for a lectureship in Classics at Birmingham in 1930, and they remained lifelong friends. Appointed MacNeice's literary executor, he edited CP66 and *SAF* (1965). Cf. 'Auden and MacNeice: Their Last Will and Testament': 'And Professor Dodds I leave the wind which whips / The Dublin mountains . . .' (*LI*, CP07, 740). The obituarist in *The Times* wrote: 'Rebellious in youth, pacifist, distinctly non-Christian, well to the left politically, Dodds held his opinions not as a party matter but as robust individualist' (19 Nov. 1979). Cf. ERD, 'Louis MacNeice at Birmingham', *TWA*, 35–8.

depends on how much of a joint annual income my fiancée and I discover ourselves to have – apart from what I earn. I think it very probable that we shall find it feasible to get married.

I asked your wife whether the University objected to young lecturers being married, and she told me that they were at first a little taken aback by John Waterhouse producing a wife but that they were reassured when they found that it did not prevent him going about with the under-graduates.[1] In my case (if I get married) I have an exceptional reason for confidence in guaranteeing no disastrous consequences – in that my future wife has been brought up in the family of an Oxford don and is, if anything, only too alive to the necessity both of industry in one's work proper and of phil-undergraduate activity ἐν παρέργῳ.[2] And I feel that, if married, I should prove in general more fit for my work.

As you say in your letter, I shall certainly not bruit about the fact of my nomination but I shall inform the Sheffield people at once. As for Greats I am now in great fear of falling between two stools, being unable to decide what to plump on.

I must end by repeating that I fully realise both the honour you have done me in giving me this job and the responsibility I incur by accepting it.

With kind regards to Mrs. Dodds and yourself –

Yours sincerely

F. L. MacNeice

TO *E. R. Dodds* MS Bodleian

29 July [1930] 35 Craven Hill Gardens,
London W2

Dear Professor Dodds,

Thank you so much for your very welcome telegram. I was very much surprised by my first and attribute it entirely to Heaven.* My viva was curt and all about Sitalces, so that I had no expectations.

---

1 – John Waterhouse, a colleague of Mrs Dodds in the English Department at Birmingham. He used to accompany FLM on walks near Dudley, with his dog: 'Waterhouse had always seemed reserved but he capered about on the lost black hills just as Dodds had capered about on the Dublin mountains' (*SAF*, 149). Cf. 'Auden and MacNeice: Their Last Will and Testament': 'Item to dear John Waterhouse a gymnastic / Exercise before breakfast every day' (*LI*, CP07, 740).
2 – 'Secondarily'/'By the way'.

My wife and I are moving to Oxford for August. I am going to take my degree on August 2nd. We live in hopes of securing the cottage which you so wonderfully discovered for us.[1]

With kindest regards from us both to Mrs. Dodds and yourself –

Yours sincerely
F. L. MacNeice

*and my wife.

TO *Georgina Beatrice MacNeice* MS Dan MacNeice

6 August [1930]   1, Park Terrace, Oxford

Dear Madre,

Many thanks for your letter; I hope you will have a good time in the Wild West.[2] The weather should be somewhat better by then.

As for your questions about my academic expenditures! I have written cheques for them all already; as I had suddenly to pay my battels this must have involved, I fear, somewhat of an overdraft, though I have not yet heard from the bank about it. The items are –

Battels (inclusive of £2 to College on taking my degree) 16-0-4
Fee to the University Chest – 7-10-0
Parliamentary Registration Fee 10-0
Traditional Tip to Stone who
dresses one in one's B.A.
gown & hood   1-0-0
totalling -   25-0-4

As for my gown & hood for the ceremony these were borrowed for the occasion by the porter who will in time get me some new ones at reduced prices. The ordinary prices are pretty high e.g. 54/6 for a hood and round about two guineas for a decent gown.

To turn to the degree-giving itself, I don't expect you would have enjoyed it very much as it was very long and mainly in Latin. Not but what there were great numbers of spectators (in the Sheldonian galleries). Adrian took

1–Highfield Cottage, Selly Park Road, Birmingham. This was part of a large Victorian house, converted into rented flats, which was owned by two Americans, Philip Sargant Florence (a Professor of Commerce at Birmingham University) and his wife Lella (cf. Stallworthy, 144–5).
2–The West of Ireland.

his degree at the same time.[1] We were the only people from Merton excepting a man blind with cataract who was taking his M.A. (One cannot take one's M.A. for 3 years after graduating; otherwise it is merely a matter of money, but I shall have to take it as in an academic career it gives one certain advantages, such as being entitled to examine an Oxford & Cambridge board (School Certificates). (Note: correcting School Certificate papers means a fortnight's exceedingly dreary work in the summer but one raises about £100 from it. While if you examine on the London board, they also pay your fare down firstclass!) But all this profitable but hackish labour is at least three years ahead).

As for Adrian we put him up for Saturday night in a little room at the top of the house; he was much delighted with his meals – we gave him steak and onions for dinner. Mary had been sitting at home all afternoon collecting various articles of food which arrived from time to time from the shops. She had been going to look on in the Sheldonian but actually I think it was just as well she didn't, considering the heat and tediousness aforementioned.

Mary is writing to you at this moment & tells me she is telling you the latest news from Birmingham. We are just wondering whether (a) to be extravagant & (b) whether this extravagance might not prove in the long run to be economy. The £20 extra certainly seems a bit much; I think the American lady in question must have put in quite a number of 'modernisms', as Mrs Dodds foretold. Of course, these might turn out to be the saving of us, but we shall certainly have a careful look at the whole place before we abandon our tenet of £80 (inclusive of rates & taxes) as an outside limit. We are hoping that perhaps Mrs. Florence (the American lady) may come down a little. Of course (in any case) we should probably only feel the strain of paying so much for the 3 years my salary remains the same. After that we should I fancy, be pleased to find ourselves already ensconced there. Because, if we began somewhere else, we should probably (from what I hear of the average run of houses in Birmingham) pretty soon want to move. My own idea is that we should take the cottage right away (that is, if we find it to be as good as its description); but Mary is rather more doubtful – on the financial side.

If we go up to B. to view it we think of going by bus, which is much cheaper; we are always seeing vast de luxe buses passing thither through Oxford.

1 – Adrian Green-Armytage.

We are now going to cook our dinner, so farewell for the present. Mary is become a very good cook & I am reduced to hanging against the doorpost in a helpful attitude. As a matter of fact I usually while she cooks do something on my own such as reading & only go down to the basement to do the more brutish tasks such as stoking the stove. In fact everything goes without any commotion and no one gets indigestion. Hoping you all prosper – Love. Louis.

P.S. Stone deviated so far from his usual morality as to have a small bet with another scout on my getting a 1st! I think this should have counted as a tip from me.

TO *John Hilton*   MS Bodleian

['Summer or autumn 1930'   The University, Edmund Street,
in Hilton's hand]   Birmingham

Dear John

Sorry for the delay but life is too short for tattle. That is if one 'writes' at the same time. Always remember to keep clear of 'writers'. Apart from the inkpot everything is fine. We live in a yellow & pink house done by a couple called Freeman (Frank & Joan). We have a marmalade coloured cat. Mary makes divine curtains & cushions. Also beefsteaks full & bloodily fine. I scuttle about to my classes of stupid but affables. Lots of lovely particulars; I suggest keeping generalisations out of it. Leave that to the Chorus (see the Greek tragedians passion). Thank you much for suggesting a present. An ingenious game like Ludo (which we have) would be not at all unwelcome. Or one of those dart-targets you have in pubs. We have a wonderful big room one could chuck darts in. Or one of those things you roll things into or round or up or down – the high Metaphysicke of the Fair. By the way, we went to St. Giles' fair & there spent all our money. & all that is is fun. I am writing a novel very straightforward about a young man who married a neurologist's daughter;[1] it is a much subtler (I hope) attack than the last. & Baedeker I have discovered in moving house & hope to go on with.[2] Also an epic. & sometime soon, when I have

1 – *RW*.
2 – Cf. 'My next book will be called A Baedeker's Guide to Purgatory', FLM to AB, 22 Aug. 1928, p. 194.

time, I shall have a mass of poems typed & hawk them round (Faber &c)
So save your pocket money

Yours well-wishingly
Louis

1931

TO *Rupert Hart-Davis*[1]   MS Bodleian

22 August [1931]   Highfield Cottage,
                                    28 Selly Park Road, Birmingham
                                    [hereafter Birmingham]

Dear Hart-Davis,

Very many thanks for your letter. I am so glad you found the novel readable. I agree that the title is not much good and will change it if I can think of anything; it seems a hard book to find a title for.

Yes, I should like to send it to Heineman's [*sic*] first and should be very grateful indeed if you could tell me who to send it to etcetera. And thank you so much for offering to read the proofs if they ever come into being.

By the way (as you say you like Bilbatrox) I hope one day to write a novel about North of Ireland clergymen (one of the few subjects I know something about) – mainly hypocrites but one, at least, hopelessly sincere.[2]

With repeated thanks

                                    Yours sincerely
                                    Louis MacNeice

P.S. I hope it is nice all among the fuchsias[3]

---

1 – Rupert Hart-Davis (1907–99), publisher, editor and writer. Educ. Eton and Balliol College, Oxford (no degree). Author of a volume of memoirs, a life of Hugh Walpole, and an edition of Oscar Wilde's letters, he worked at Heinemann in 1929 before becoming a director at Jonathan Cape.

2 – The 'hopelessly sincere' clergyman was his father. The novel is *RW*, published in October 1932 by Putnam, which features a clergyman called Bilbatrox.

3 – The letter was addressed to Rupert Hart-Davis at Dooneen Lodge, Letterfrack, Clifden, Co. Galway.

1932

TO *Anthony Blunt* MS Cambridge

Postmark 24 February 1932   Birmingham

Dear Anthony

Sorry to bother you again. Oh no, dearie, this aint about that novel (I'm sure you must be terribly embarrassed & bored with it by now), this is just another little suggestion about your poor Rylands. Do you think he would possibly like me to do a book in that Hogarth Lecture Series on Latin Humour (& of course the lack of it?)[1] After all you see I <u>am</u> now an academic. & it is rather a good, & not (I think) much touched subject. Not to mention the obvious people like Cicero & Catullus & [Propertius *deleted*] Petronius (!), one could have an amusing & instructive time with the Fathers who herald the peculiarities of modern Christian Humour (Donne Swift etc). Well I daresay this is very cheeky of me, but really I should like to do it very much (& of course it would please the blokes here).

Well goodbye (isn't this bloody weather, as the man said in the Lays of Ancient Rome?)[2]

Your old pal in the Lord
Louis

TO *Anthony Blunt* MS Cambridge

Wednesday [6 April? 1932]   Birmingham

Dear Anthony

Forgive me for answering so promptly. You see, old Shepard is having us all next week from Monday (11th) & I thought perhaps if you could

---

1 – His first mention of a study of Latin humour, which he began but never completed. He refers to it often in letters over the years. The first volume of the Hogarth Lectures on Literature series (by A. T. Quiller-Couch) was published in 1927. Hogarth also produced a series of pamphlets in which lectures were published.

2 – Thomas Babington Macaulay, *Lays of Ancient Rome* (1842). The weather in the Midlands on 24 Feb. 1932 was cloudy and showery, with heaviest rainfall in the south and east. A temperature of 44 °F (7 °C) was recorded in London at 6 p.m.

spare time from the British Museum you might come & see us. As a matter of fact I believe Graham is going to ask you to a party (plus Betjeman et cetera), but anyhow here is a general warning of our imminence.

As to the novel you are, of course, quite right about poor Mrs. Harris & Co. They will all have to go.[1] I have not yet done the rehashing & anyhow I think I had better not give it to the Hogarth at the moment, as my second novel, 'Roundabout Way', which I had given to an agent; has just got itself taken by Putnam's (all along with Marie Stopes).[2] & the contract would, I think, claim the other novel too. So I shall let 'Going out & C.I.' wait until I have finished the austere work I am on at the moment, which will, I think, be called 'Your Esteemed Order'.[3] My apologies. But to turn to Latin Humour, as soon as I have got a scheme, I shall hand it on. I know only too well that there's no money in it, but my reasons are (a) to reassure the folks here that I am not forgetting my classics, & (b) because I think it will be rather fun to treat (sic) that aspect (sic) of Latin Literature (sic). More of which perhaps when we meet.

My love to the World & the Flesh.

Yours L.

P.S. Graham's address is 16D Queen's Gardens, w2.

TO *John Hilton*   MS Bodleian

12 April [1932?]   Birmingham

Dear John

Thank you for your letter but I'm afraid my only advice is not to take any. The tigers of wrath are wiser than the horses of instruction.[4]

And if I were you I should add a drop of Falstaff to my Hamlet.

How did you like Shropshire (if you ever got there, which I doubt)? We voyaged into it the other day in our caah & much enjoyed the view from Clee Hill. Have you ever been to Clun?[5] We want to go there a lot.

---

1 – Presumably characters in one of the works referred to below.
2 – Putnam published the works of the birth control campaigner Marie Stopes (1880–1958), such as *Married Love* (1918), *Radiant Motherhood* (1920), and *Change of Life in Men and Women* (1936).
3 – Neither book appears to have been completed.
4 – William Blake, from *The Marriage of Heaven and Hell*.
5 – Brown Clee Hill is the highest point in Shropshire; Clun is a local village.

We approve of your idea of confluent cars. Sometime in May? I hear from Anthony he thinks of coming to B'ham in the summer. Like a deus ex machina who's missed his cue & is slightly stiff in the joints.

Do you know your prose style is (in parts) suspiciously like Walter Pater?

We have just been planting our five roses; their names are Alberic Barlies & Dorothy Perkins (climbers), & H. E. Richardson & Scarlet Glory & Madame Isaac Periers (who stand on their feet).

We are just going a short pilgrimage ending up with the Merton Gaudy.[1]

Yes Milly's cakes are truly wonderful;[2] Mary makes them too with full artistry, we are eating one at the moment. I'll tell you about your poem sometime, I haven't had time to let it get old yet. I don't think I shall write many more short poems – one has to be rather childish for that, or else very old. Soon I shall be producing magnum opus on the Christian fathers who write a very amusing prose. By the way our Old Friend Augustine always felt ineffectual, rather like you, until he became a saint; you see the moral. But as I said before, for God's sake don't bother about morals or principles. Philosophy should be kept strictly on the mantelpiece.

In my epic the young man is done in through having philosophy in his blood. Mixed up with ballet dancing. Have you read 'Bengal Lancer' – all about Yoga?[3] Why don't you take that up; one of the better things to do is to stand in a river & pull out your long intestine. Only English rivers are very cold.

Well I must stop now (forgive my insensitivity but I'm really not competent to give advice, what I say is Every Boy his Own Redeemer. By the way, surely it's bad to do something merely to escape from 'the intolerable'; one pursuit is worth X escapes?)

Well goodbye for the moment;

See you in Heaven

Love: Louis

1 – Merton College Ball.
2 – Milly was the Beazleys' maid.
3 – Francis Yeats-Brown, *The Lives of a Bengal Lancer* (1930).

TO *T. S. Eliot*[1] Faber archive

19 April [1932]   Birmingham

Dear Mr. Eliot

I met Father D'Arcy last week and he tells me that you have some poems which you received without any letter or explanation and which he thinks are mine.[2] I think this is probable, as I sent you a large number of poems in January with a letter enclosed. The letter must have been lost owing to my use of a double envelope; I must therefore apologise.

As for the poems themselves I think that only a few of them stand on their own merits, but that as a collection and arranged in a certain order they would supplement each other and make an aggregate of some value. Whereas if I chose a dozen individuals, they would remain, perhaps, merely individuals. It seems to me (as far as I can see myself) that I am not sufficiently in a school for my poems to be readily significant; therefore they have to build up their own explanation. This is my apology for what may seem a haphazard mass of indifferent or casual verses.

My hope was that Faber and Faber's might publish the collection in book form.

Yours sincerely,
Louis MacNeice

1 – T. S. Eliot (1888–1965), educ. St Louis, Harvard, Sorbonne, Merton College, Oxford. Lloyd's Bank 1917–25; director Faber and Faber 1925–65. He founded the *Criterion* in 1922. Author of *Prufrock and Other Observations* (1917), *Poems* (1919), *The Waste Land* (1922), *Four Quartets* (1935–42) and many critical works such as *The Sacred Wood: Essays on Poetry and Criticism* (1920), *For Lancelot Andrewes* (1928), *The Idea of a Christian Society* (1940) and *Notes Towards the Definition of Culture* (1948). His plays include *Sweeney Agonistes* (1932), *The Rock* (1934), *Murder in the Cathedral* (1935), *The Family Reunion* (1939), *The Cocktail Party* (1950) and others. Nobel Prize for Literature, O.M. (both 1948). M. (1) Vivien Haigh-Wood (1915, separated 1933; d. 1947), (2) Valerie Fletcher (1957). FLM's correspondence with TSE runs from 19 April 1932 to 12 Aug. 1963.

2 – Martin Cyril D'Arcy (1888–1976), Jesuit and theologian. Lecturer (1927–33) then Master at Campion Hall (1933–45). The foremost Roman Catholic apologist in England during the thirties and after, and a famous influence on Graham Greene and Evelyn Waugh, he was author of *The Nature of Belief* (1931) and other works. FLM wrote of D'Arcy: '. . . he alone among Oxford dons seemed to me to have the glamour that medieval students looked for in their masters. Intellect incarnate in a beautiful head, wavy grey hair and delicate features; a hawk's eyes' (*SAF*, 128). Cf. 'Auden and MacNeice: Their Last Will and Testament': '. . . item to Father / D'Arcy, that dialectical disputer, / We leave St Thomas Aquinas and his paeans' (*LI*, CP07, 743).

P.S. (In case the poems, which Father D'Arcy mentioned, are not mine) the first poem in my collection is called τὸ νῦν and the last 'Neurospastou-menos'.[1]

TO *T. S. Eliot*   Faber archive

16 June [1932]   Birmingham

Dear Mr. Eliot

Very many thanks for your letter; I must apologise for my delay in answering it.

I should very much appreciate the publication of any of my poems in the 'Criterion'.[2] I may be in London towards the end of this month and should be very much pleased if I could discuss this with you.

I should add that I have recently received a suggestion as to the publication of some of these poems as a volume; but this, if decided on, would not, I think, be for some time.

Some of the poems which you have, have already been published in 'This Quarter', 'Oxford Poetry' etc. Of the remainder I should myself propose 'The Green Bird', 'Everyman his own Pygmalion', 'Hustled by Wind' or 'Colonel X speaks from his Coffin'.[3]

Yours sincerely
Louis MacNeice

TO *T. S. Eliot*   Faber archive

8 July [1932]   Birmingham

Dear Mr Eliot

Very many thanks for your letter of July 5th. I regret to say that of the poems, which you have chosen, 'Vitreamque Circen' and 'Belfast' appeared recently in 'This Quarter' (as did also 'Sleep'), while 'Threnody' was in

---

1 – τὸ νῦν = 'Now'/'The present time'; 'Neurospastoumenos', *Oxford Outlook*, Feb. 1930, 421–9; repr. CP07, App. 2, 666.
2 – TSE had written in May, asking FLM to visit him in London, and inviting him to submit poems for the *Criterion* (TSE to FLM, 18 May 1932, *Faber archive*). The journal ran to eighteen volumes (1922–39); the first issue carried *The Waste Land*.
3 – 'Everyman His Own Pygmalion (*Moriturus me saluto*)' appeared in *New Verse* (NV), Jan. 1933, 10–11, repr. CP07, App. 5, 722–3.

'Oxford Poetry 1930'.[1] I believe that poems from 'Oxford Poetry' are sometimes reprinted in periodicals, but as I am not certain either of this or of your own custom in this matter and in case you wish to make another choice, I must add that the following poems in this collection also appeared in 'Oxford Poetry' (1929 and 1930) –
   'Spring Sunshine'
   'Dr Bruno'
   'Cradle Song'
   'Laburnum'[2]
   'Utopia'
   'Hinges'.
I am afraid that if these ten already printed poems and those, which are too long, are excluded, you may not wish to take any of the others. I enclose therefore my latest, though it may seem fatuous to anyone other than myself.

I may be in London on or about July 21st and, if so, shall try to come round to Russell Square on the chance of seeing you.

I must apologise for not having previously mentioned which poems had already been printed.

Yours sincerely
Louis MacNeice

TO *T. S. Eliot* Faber archive

19 July [1932]   The Lamb, Burford, Oxford

Dear Mr. Eliot

I have nothing against your choice of 'The Creditor' and 'Trapeze', and am pleased that you have been able to make a choice after so many eliminations.[3]

---

1 – 'Sleep', 'Belfast' and 'Vitreamque Circen', in *This Quarter*, June 1932, 610–13. 'Threnody', 'Utopia' and 'Hinges kill themselves' in *Oxford Poetry 1930*, ed. S. Spender and B. Spencer, 20–3.
2 – 'Spring Sunshine (April 1929)', 'Address from my death-bed to Dr Bruno, the Concrete Universal (May 1929)', 'Cradle Song (Nov. 1928)', and 'Laburnum (May 1929)', in *Oxford Poetry 1929* (ed. L. MacNeice and S. Spender), 24–9.
3 – 'Two Poems: Trapeze, The Creditor', *Criterion*, 12: 46 (Oct. 1932), 54–5.

I hope to come to London on either Monday (25th) or Tuesday (26th) next; if you could see me on either of these days I should definitely decide to come on that day.

Yours sincerely
Louis MacNeice

P.S. I shall be at the above address till next week.

TO *Anthony Blunt*   MS Cambridge

[October 1932]   Birmingham

Dear Anthony

Herewith my unhappy novel in its goddamned wrapper & full of other people's punctuation.[1] I wrote it 2 years ago & am now not very interested in it, especially (Damn, you got my telegram didn't you? for if not I must congratulate you anew on your fellowship which is really very good you know. Think how proud the fellows in the C3 must be.[2] Are you very rich now? Perhaps you will be able to afford the fare here some day). especially, as I was saying, seeing that it was a negative experiment, an attempt to write a novel according to popular standards 'coherent'. Never mind, I am letting myself go in the next one which will be called 'an Everlasting Cold'.[3] As for derivations in the enclosed. Mary contributed a good bit to the girl, & the Oxford neurological professor gave me the idea for the neurologist,[4] Bilbatrox is Ulster fanaticism multiplied by Inge,[5] Hogley is the Oxford cultured don spiced up with my idea of what you might be like if you were two-dimensional & lived in Oxford (I have made him a little more unpleasant, of course, but just for fun). The other people I cant trace. I am just writing a satirical work in a sort of music hall form. I hope you had a good time in Germany. Peace be with you. Louis.

1 – *RW*.
2 – AB was elected to a Fellowship at King's College, Cambridge. C3 was AB's (and FLM's) House at MC.
3 – Yet another reference to an incomplete novel. Cf. FLM to AB, 31 December 1927, n. 1, p. 179.
4 – The neurological professor on whom Sir Randal Belcher is partly based was Sir Farquhar Buzzard.
5 – Cf.: '. . . he was broad-minded, the Rev. Bilbatrox; like Dean Inge, but a much more telling speaker' (*RW*, 7). FLM tended to say unpleasant things about Inge in letters home (e.g. 27 June 1927, p. 170).

1933

MS Cambridge

TO *Anthony Blunt*

Postmark 19 January 1933   Birmingham

Dear Anthony

The arrival of a funny review from the 'Egyptian Express' reminded me that I owed one to you, so here it is. Change or scrap it as you will. Do you know I fear we shan't be able to come to Wilfrid's Social Evening (even if they would have us) as dear Ellis has 'flu & I have to do all his work & Tuesday is just the worst day, aint that a shame?[1] The animals sent you your umbrella so perhaps you have got it. Betsy is lame & I am having a painful time helping her round in the snow.[2] We embrocate her twice a day.

We think we might come to your city some time towards the end of February when I have a centenary & get off some work (which would enable an easy weekend).

Well goodbye, the gas has been turned off here. Auden turned up again after all & talked a deal of communism.[3] So I dare say you were well out

---

1 – Wilfrid Blunt; Ellis Waterhouse.

2 – FLM makes many passing references to the behaviour of his dogs, but there is in a box in the Bodleian a concentration of dog letters written during the Birmingham period which feature comic mock postcards and letters on Birmingham University letterhead between dogs, as well as many letters pertaining to the breeding and showing of dogs with the Kennel Club and 'Tail Waggers Club' (*Ms Bodleian, MacNeice, Box 13; Ms Res, c. 588*). See also FLM's masterful evocation of dog shows in 'The Kennel Club' (*Ms Tulsa*), written for *Night and Day* (Cf. FLM to G. Greene, 26 Aug. 1937, p. 303).

3 – W. H. Auden (1907–73), poet and writer. Educ. St Edmund's School, Hindhead; Gresham's School, Holt; Christ Church, Oxford. Schoolteacher at Larchfield Academy, Helensburgh, and then the Downs School, Colwall, 1930–5. GPO Film Unit 1935–6. M. (1935) Erika Mann. Became US citizen 1946. Various teaching appointments in America include St Mark's School, Southboro, MA; League of American Writers, New York; New School, New York; University of Michigan; Bennington College; Smith College. His many works include *Poems* (1930), *The Orators* (1932), *The Ascent of F6* (1936), *Letters from Iceland* (with FLM, 1937), *Journey to a War* (1939), *Another Time* (1940), *New Year Letter* (1941), *The Age of Anxiety* (1947), *The Shield of Achilles* (1955), *Collected Shorter Poems* (1966), *Collected Longer Poems* (1968) and, as editor, *The Oxford Book of Light Verse* (1938) and *The Faber Book of Modern American Verse* (1956). Oxford Professor of Poetry 1956–61.

of him.[1] You wouldn't have liked his ears either. He is really a good man though.

Be sure to keep yourself well muffled up this treacherous weather.

Love
Beasts

P.S. You must have left an influence in the bed as Mary has been having extraordinary (oh dear yes) dreams about you ever since.

TO *Geoffrey Grigson*[2]   MS Texas

8 November [1933]   Birmingham

Dear Grigson

Here is that review of Laura Riding. I meant it to be more impartial but found it easier to say what I felt like. I will return your two books separately; many thanks for sending them.

Yours sincerely
Louis MacNeice

TO *John Hilton*   MS Bodleian

11 November 1933   Birmingham

Dear John

Your hat seems to have missed its connection after all but never mind, here it is. The cats & dogs have been using it for their purposes but you won't mind that. We are all very busy here, lots of books in the making, also a baby (booked for May).[3] We find it very thrilling & shall get old Blunt to pour Holy Water (of some sort or other) on it. It is rather good

---

1 – Prior to his conversion to communism in 1935, AB was impatient with political talk. Cf. '. . . I was hurt when Blunt denounced politics as beneath the attention of a civilized person' (*SAF*, 231).

2 – Geoffrey E. H. Grigson (1905–85), author and editor. Educ. St Edmund Hall, Oxford. Renowned for his tough criticism, he was the founding editor of *NV* (1933–9). Cf. 'Auden and MacNeice: Their Last Will and Testament': '. . . to Geoffrey Grigson of *New Verse* / A strop for his sharp tongue before he talks' (*LI*, CP07, 743). This letter is one of the earliest to Grigson, who published FLM's review of Laura Riding's *The Life of the Dead* in NV, Dec. 1933, 18–20. The same issue carried FLM's poem, titled simply 'Poem' (later retitled 'Nature Morte'), ibid., 6–7; *Poems* (1935), CP07, 23.

3 – FLM's son Daniel was born on 15 May 1934.

to be in May I think (such a lot of literature) – like what we got with our new car which is sumptuous in the extreme. I have also got a very smart camera. Well hoping you are both in extremis (the good sort I mean) Love Louis.

TO *John Hilton*   MS Bodleian

[Autumn 1933?]   Birmingham

Dear John

Herewith some little mementoes of your old pals and also to check your growing vanity. How do you go? We go very well and your rug behaves like a saint. We hear that Moore is in this country but I suppose the Censor will soon deport him again.[1] I have just finished my novel (rough draft). It is to be called Anacoluthon.[2] This will make the public think it is an historical romance. Some day I shall write a novel and call it 'A Walking Tour in the Congo' or 'Thrills and Spills in Aeronautics'; but I keep this type of title as a last & mercenary resort.

I am going to send it along to Hart Davis (Heinemanns). Have you read a book called 'The 12 Winded Sky' by an Oxford don.[3] Dodds admires it but I prefer the 17th century. It contains what would make a good text for the Waste Land. I am going soon to write a oneday novel about Birmingham – unity of space too (possibly) as I think of staging it all on the railway station all about 2 families connected by the wife & mother of one charring for the other. Comic relief in daughter of the other affected by 'G.P.'s. Tragedy in suicide of charwoman's husband. Throughout Greek Chorus of posters on the railway hoardings.

Our cat has just become demonstrably male. Sic transit gloria cunni. Robinson has made me a wonderful new bookcase. Billy has written me a letter addressed Proffessor F.L.M. to thank me for getting him through in Greek. Can you tell me how to make a durable bas relief in the kicked in window on the gardenside of our cottage? The other day we went to Dodds' and helped him to drag huge tonweights of limestone across his garden for a rockery. We had a sort of sledge of galvanised iron on which we put one crag at a time and then Dodds & I & his gardener & an old

---

1 – Moore Crosthwaite had entered the Diplomatic Service in 1932, hence his whereabouts was news.
2 – 'Anacoluthon': suggesting a lack of grammatical sequence. In *RW*, Devlin thinks: 'Make life grammatical (nature and life are so bloody anacoluthic)' (15).
3 – Ernest Llewellyn Woodward, *The Twelve-Winded Sky* (1930).

weedy man dragged it by a wire harness along slimy paths & over bridges
– at one point one of the crags fell into a river, whereupon Dodds jumped
in in his army boots & we all began to lever & splash just like in the
Golden Age. Making a rockery is really very epic. Dodds had mapped it
out exactly with all its moraines etc. & all the time Mrs. Dodds' carefully
bred ducks swam up & down beside us quacking derisively. Their dog is
so well-trained that the ducks steal his biscuits & he will not defend
himself. This is the end of my paper so good bye – L.

P.S. I hear Graham was sick all over Heaton.[1]

TO *T. S. Eliot* Faber archive

23 November [1933]   Birmingham

Dear Mr. Eliot

Some time ago you asked me if I would like to do any reviewing for 'The
Criterion'. I should very much like to review, if you approved of the idea
and the book were sent me, my friend Professor Dodds' edition of Proclus
'Elements of Theology' (which came out this summer). I am not an
authority on Neo-Platonism but I think I could give it a fair review as a
non-specialist; and it is, I imagine, well worth reviewing, as Proclus is
almost unknown in English. I suggest this rather timidly as I do not know
if your reviewers are in the habit of asking for particular books![2]

Yours sincerely
Louis MacNeice

1 – JH writes: 'My parents had an old spaniel whom Louis called Henniken-Heaton. There
was a man of that name in my college, but the connection was never clear to me' (*Ms
Bodleian, Ms Don, c. 153/3*). Heaton was the name of one of the doctors Lady Beazley
consulted about the hereditary potential of mongolism. FLM may have mischievously
transferred his name to the Hilton spaniel.

2 – FLM did not in fact review the Proclus, but the Jan. 1934 issue of the *Criterion* carried
four of his poems: 'To a Communist', 'Museums', 'A Contact' and 'Sunday Morning'
(230–1).

[Christmas card with photo of MM and a borzoi]

[Christmas 1933]   [Birmingham]

Dear Anthony: This is a Christmas card. Mary says it is the last time you will see these two girls looking so elegant as they are both going to have litters before you see them next; hers will be in May but Betsy hasn't begun hers yet. We thought May the best month; don't you? Come & see us when you get back. Love, Mary & Louis.

1934

TO *Geoffrey Grigson* MS Berg

24 January [1934]   Birmingham

Dear Grigson

Here is that Christmas Eclogue.[1] I think of sending it also to the 'American Review' who have asked me for some poems for their April number; I hope you don't mind their printing it also, if by any chance you both want it?

Would you by any chance like me to review Yeats' new Collected Poems? I want the book and I think I might manage to be intelligent about it.[2]

Yours sincerely
Louis MacNeice

TO *Anthony Blunt* MS Cambridge

Postmark 3 February 1934   Birmingham

Heilige Stumpf[3]

It was very sweet of you to send me the charming pictures; I am going to try & grow my hair like St. Hubertus; but it is most sad that you cannot come.[4] Next weekend Graham with his wife & sister come so you would have a gay time. Yes, they always want one to have read books. My poems have again been postponed. Eliot wants me to send them back to him for the autumn, if possibly having rearranged them. That was one for me as I

---

1 – 'An Eclogue for Christmas' (written Dec. 1933) was published in *NV*, 8 (April 1934), 3–7, and *American Review*, May 1934. On 7 Jan. 1934 FLM had tentatively asked Grigson if he would be interested in 'An Eclogue for Christmas' : 'it is about 140 lines so I don't suppose it would be any use to you for "New Verse".' With this 7 Jan. letter he submitted 'Birmingham', which was published in *NV* in February (*Ms Texas*).

2 – Grigson asked him to review Edwin Muir instead. (*NV*, June 1934, 18, 20). But see his review of *A Full Moon in March* two years later ('The Newest Yeats', *NV*, Feb.–March 1936, 16).

3 – 'Holy Blunt'.

4 – Hubert (656?–727?), the 'Apostle of the Ardennes', withdrew from court when his wife died giving birth to their son. He devoted himself to hunting, until religious revelation came in the heat of a stag hunt.

had taken great trouble arranging them in their present order. However I am going to scrap some more & see what I can do. He does seem to intend to do them sometime so I think it is better to wait than to take them elsewhere. Also I shall have time to include one or two Eclogues.[1] These I find have great possibilities. There is going to be one all about my education. By the way, did I tell you sometime soon (in the Long Vac. I expect) I shall start writing a sort of limited autobiography, concerned chiefly with the changes in one's taste etc. – all the things one has ever liked & disliked. You will have to come into this of course, so it will be as well if you get yourself still more famous before it is published; then everyone will buy my book as throwing intimate sidelights on Mr. Anthony Blunt. If you like I will let you see the MSS so that you can censor it. In the course of the book I shall show up the Protestant Church, Dr. Norwood, the Ulster Scot & the Oxford Intelligentsia.[2] Also of course myself. This brings my total of books which I want published 1934–5 up to 5:- (1) Poems (2) Novel (3) Play (4) Latin Humour (5) Analytic Autobiography. I have also the most ingenious idea for a new novel but I shan't have the time for that just yet. The Latin Humour book I ought to finish by the end of the Easter vacation. / No, Betsy has not done her act yet, she was always a bit slow in coming to the point. &, by the way, is Michael going to be here again for the Industries Fair? Moore, who has been over here from Coventry, said something about it. He (Moore) with his mother & sister came & gave us a large dinner; it seems that Moore may go to Tokio [sic]. Well if I can't prevail upon you, as your Mama said about her barleywater, I suppose I can't but you needn't come bitching along to me the next time ye have the drouth in the gullet (she went on, breaking into the old Irish lingo of the O'Blounts). Sure an' God be my witness, she said, & Mary & Joseph & Patrick that it's thanks to this barleywater me sons is saved from the priapus & that's the longs & the shorts of it, Glory be to God this day she said, for me son Anthony would be the fearful lecher. Lookin' at all them statues, she said, sure it goes to a feller's head. Not his head, I said. Sure when I say head, said your mama, I'm speakin' honoris causa. Well goodbye & love, Louis.

---

1 – *Poems* (published Sept. 1935), including 'Eclogue for Christmas' and 'Eclogue by a Five-Barred Gate' (CP07, 3–7; 10–14).
2 – Cyril Norwood, headmaster ('Master') at MC, 1916–25. See FLM to GBM, 5 Nov. 1921, n. 2, p. 59.

TO *T. S. Eliot*   Faber archive

2 April [1934]   Birmingham

Dear Mr. Eliot

I don't believe I ever answered your letter about my collection of poems. I have, however, thought over what you said and have cut out a number (mostly earlier ones) and have rearranged the rest. I have lately been writing some longer poems which, for want of a better name, I am calling 'Eclogues'. Two of these, I think, I could put at the beginning of my book. I have also one or two new short poems which I will add and I shall be able to send you the revised collection in the early autumn, as you suggested in your letter. I think that in this form they should make a quite presentable book, and, as most of them will have already been printed in various periodicals, I am rather eager to get them off my hands. I had much rather however they were published by you than by any other firm.

Yours sincerely
Louis MacNeice

TO *John Hilton*   MS Bodleian

12 May 1934   Birmingham

Dear John

Mary is writing to your lady wife in answer to her very kind offer re our baby which has not yet arrived but ought to any time this next week.[1] In the meantime I must tell you about Cyprus[.] A fellow came along to Oxford & asked the Professor (J.D.B.)[2] if he knew of any budding architects, so he, being a man of infinite discrimination, said he knew John Hilton. So the fellow said that was very astonishing because you (J.H). had already written him an application. So the fellow, being much struck by this providential coincidence, asked if you were a very snobbish chap & would only associate with the damned English. But the professor said No, you wld associate with anyone. Then the fellow asked if you & yr wifc wld set yrselves to learn Modern Greek, & they told him that there was nothing the two of you wld like to do more. So the fellow went away full of faith hope & charity, & all you have to do now is confirm these

---

1 – Daniel MacNeice was born in a nursing home on 15 May. ('Births', *The Times*, 19 May 1934, 1). Cf. FLM to JH, 16 May: 'Mary had a little boy yesterday, scarlet as the rose' (*Ms Bodleian, Ms Don, c. 153/3*).
2 – 'Jackie' Beazley.

good impressions. The 2 main pts are to get yourselves up well as Good Mixers & Friends for Modern Gk. & of course throw in a little culture. Cyprus, I shd think, will be just the place for you.[1] If there was a University there I might go there myself but I don't think there is. Our creature is going to be called either

Daniel Padraig

or

Dinah Miriam.

Mary is feeling very merry; not so the Cat. If you wait a little before going to Cyprus you may be able to help with the scenery for my tragic farce in a railway station; there's got to be a tea-urn throws a shadow like Buddha.[2] Love: Louis

P.S. Won't it be just too God All Damn Romantic if you go to Cyprus?

P.S. [*sic*] Hill at the British Museum has something to do with yr job.[3]

TO *John Frederick and Georgina Beatrice MacNeice*
MS Dan MacNeice

16 May [1934]   Birmingham

Dear Daddie & Madre

Many thanks indeed for your wire & letters; you were marvellously quick to get the letters here by breakfast time. I saw Mary & the baby for half an hour yesterday; they both seemed marvellously well. The doctors & co. didn't expect it to be born till the evening, so everyone was pleased. (I had taken M. round to the Home at 8.0) Its head was slightly big which made it harder for Mary, but the Doctor says it has had no bad effects. The baby weighed 6lb 14oz, & has a very lusty voice, lustier than the new baby in Joyce's family had for quite a long time! M. says they didn't have to slap it etc. to make it breathe as it yelled the moment it appeared. It has very large hands. An old lady on the University staff told me this is a sign of strength! It also has black hair all over its head. We are going to call him Daniel.[4] The 2nd name is rather a difficulty; M. wanted something Irish

---

1 – Hilton became Director of Antiquities in Cyprus 1934–6.

2 – *The Station Bell*, set in the waiting room of a Dublin train station.

3 – Sir George Francis Hill (1867–1948), numismatist. Director and Principal Librarian of the British Museum 1931–6. Author of many books on Greek and Roman coins.

4 – Dan MacNeice (1934–2009), educ. Maria Grey Kindergarten, north London 1938–9; Dungannon HS for Girls (as an evacuee), Co. Tyrone 1940–1; governesses, Cootehill,

but we found that the only Irish name we liked was Padraig & people say that would be affected. Nicholas we have dropped as it doesn't fit with Daniel. One of the best candidates for rhythm is Daniel John MacN. & we might possibly choose that. I am going round to see M. at 2.30 today & will write you again soon. We are all very pleased; at least M. & I are: if the baby is, it has a funny way of showing it but I suppose it doesn't know any better! Love Louis

TO *Anthony Blunt* MS Cambridge

Postmark 8 June 1934   Birmingham

Dear Blunt: I haven't really much to say, you know how costive I am when it comes to words, dumb & dominant that's my way. & indeed I am returning to my old athletic sports & have been playing tennis for the 3rd time since 1928. I find a hard court now suits me admirably as you can make the ball bounce over the stop-netting where, there being no Outfield or Longstop in tennis, it cannot possibly be taken. Thank you indeed for the Volksmärchen[1] etc; I find them much more sympathetic than the commentaries on Aristotle, not to mention Emil Ludwig by whom I once for no reason tried to read a life of Goethe.[2] (But the grownup German sentence is quite beyond me.) You will be very sad to hear that I have withdrawn my novel. But not for good. I shall add some bits to it & then publish it when the right people are dead. My family, you see, have behaved so well lately that I feel it wld be a pity to get into a bldy mess with them. But old Eliot has as good as said he will do my poems next January or so.[3] (Though in view of his latest work – apotheosis of C. of E. – he is not so honoured in my sight as he was aforetime.) Graham & I got free tickets to it – it's a sort of pageant play you know – God, it was awful. & the audience so smelly at Sadlers Wells.[4] My play is still unfinished – so

—

Co. Cavan 1941–2; Springfield Grange, Great Missenden, Bucks. 1943–4; Downs School, Colwall, Malvern, Worcs. 1944–8; Bryanston School, Dorset 1948–52; Davies, Laing & Dick, Notting Hill Gate 1952. Permanently residing in America after 1953. National service: US Army, 1955–7; various occupations. M. (1) Janet Glaser (1970), (2) Charlotte Wynia (1983). Children: Jill Ann; Rebecca Louise; Adam. (See 'Louis's Son', MS *Carrickfergus Museum*.)

1 – 'Folk Tales'.
2 – Emil Ludwig (1881–1948), *Goethe: The History of a Man, 1749–1832* (1928).
3 – Faber published *Poems* in Sept. 1935.
4 – T. S. Eliot, *The Rock* (pageant play), produced by E. Martin Browne and performed at Sadler's Wells Theatre, 28 May–9 June 1934.

protean – but I hope it will be done in London by a thing called, I think, the Group Theatre. I am afraid it wouldn't be allowed in the I.F.S. as De Val. wld take it personally.[1] It will look very well on the boards. Altogether this summer I have too much to do. I am writing an article on Modern Poetry for some rotten book[2] & then I want to finish my thesis on Latin Humour; also correcting (hackwork £50) some Northern School Certificate papers! About your professorship I must ask Dodds. You will probably get it as all the old gang are now getting easy jobs – you heard about old Betjeman?[3] I have now been to see Dodds. He says they haven't decided to advertise the job yet, but it is quite likely they will do so this vacation. & he says your best string would probably be the Courtauld people if you could get strong backing from them. My suggestion is you now begin to fish gently for a few testimonials from your friends or at any rate warn them to be ready to say a word for you in the near future. Also this University sets great store by published works so you want to represent yrself as on the brink of bringing out 2 or 3 important opuses. The only sorrow is that you have never practised any of these arts, but I don't suppose they will get anyone who is distinguished both academically & practitionally. Dodds says the only limitation on your purchases is that they must be works done before 1900; but anyhow they hope to get that altered. It would certainly be gratifying if you got the job. Dodds says he doesn't think your youth will matter so much. My family are coming tomorrow for a weekend in B'ham. I told you they have been much humanised by living in the South?[4] But they will, I fear, want the creature to be christened; not that they will get it. & the nurse won't even let them see it having its bath. After old T.S.E. I feel more averse to the Protestant cultus than ever. Anyhow Daniel is a good Papist (& also of course Jewish) name so there's not much taint of old Luther there. What a world. You'll laugh at my play I trust, as in parts it is meant to be funny. There are 2 Carnaval giants (part of the Dictatorial propaganda Corps) who get drunk, still as giants, & chase a girl about with much collision.[5] Very Olympia

1 – References to the Irish Free State and Eamon de Valera. The protagonist of *The Station Bell* (1934) was a female fascist dictator of Ireland. Rupert Doone found the play 'too Irish' and it was never performed at the Group (FLM to RD, 22 July 1935). Cf. 'Auden and MacNeice: Their Last Will and Testament': 'To the Group Theatre that has performed our plays / We leave the proceeds of the Entertainment Tax . . .' (*LI*, CP07, 738).
2 – 'Poetry Today', in G. Grigson (ed.), *The Arts To-Day* (1935), 25–67, repr. *SLC*, 10–44.
3 – In 1934, Betjeman was working for the *Architectural Review* and had been commissioned to publish a series of *Shell Guides* to Britain.
4 – JFM had been Bishop of Cashel and Waterford, 1931–4, before returning to Belfast.
5 – Again, *Station Bell*.

Circus but there's nothing like these old & vulgar tropes. Our landlords have become lower than ever & are now always being sick on the front doorstep. Our cat, however, is handicapped in his amours by wearing a bell on a green collar. Music in Bed? Said the Hon. Belinda Cat, Certainly not, my people were Presbyterians. Then there is Betsy who has turned very thin through eating nothing but cheese & toffee. (Pig, by the way, we haven't got any more.) Later in the summer we are all going to go & live somewhere in the country – possibly in the Shepards' house at Guildford.[1] They have now also got an excellent Georgian house in St. John's Wood. Graham's novel will be out very shortly.[2] I have raked up an old preparatory school pal on the Midland Regional so soon, no dbt, you will hear me broadcasting. & that's about all the news I think; the creature will be old enough to learn nasty noises by the time you return. Love, Louis.[3]

TO *John Hilton*

MS Bodleian

11 June [1934]   Birmingham

[*MM's hand*] Dear Peggy & John,

So many thanks for that sweet little coat. Daniel wears it such a lot, & it suits him beautifully. I know I should have written ages ago, but really what with stuffing herself, & stuffing Daniel, & answering letters, time goes before you can think.

I hope all goes well with you. Are you any nearer to Cyprus?

We are flourishing, only deluged by exam papers. I have the divinest nurse, so life is exceedingly peaceful. Also Daniel is extremely good. He sometimes makes me laugh so much, it really hurts! You will have to see him if you go away – or he will be too big when you come back.

Anthony has sent him some lovely books!

1 – Graham's father, the illustrator E. H. Shepard (1879–1976), well-known for his illustrations of Pooh, lived at Long Meadow, Longdown, Guildford.
2 – *Tea-Tray in the Sky* was published by Arthur Barker in 1934.
3 – The following fragment is a note from Mary to AB, enclosed with the above letter: '. . . from the dark anemone colour they were, through very dark green! to still darker brown – we think. I think he looks very like L. when L. was about two. He is really quite irresistible, & it's lucky that I have a most efficient nurse, because I am sure we should spoil him horribly. I am now running about again, & as good as new. I hope you will come & stay again soon. You won't have to mind Daniel coming through your room at 6 A.M. though, for his early breakfast, if I am still a cow when you come! Now I will hand this over to Louis to continue . . .' (postmark 8 June 1934).

Well – food time once more, so farewell & repeated thanks.

Love

Mary, Louis, & Daniel

[*FLM's hand*] P.S. (from me):- So sorry not to have seen more of you blokes the other day. Did you hear that the Eliot (plus Martin Browne a filthy chap) pageant was muck? Now to cadge a little. I am writing an article to order on Modern Poetry & need books.[1] So could you lend me (or bring, if you come up soon) any of the following? –

E. E. Cummings again; Active Anthology; any of the Imagists; P. Valery; any other modern French stuff; Edgell Rickword; Ronald Bottrall; any of the Georgians; latest Graves; Wilfred Owen; Rupert Brooke; McDiarmid (excepting the Thistle); A.E.; D. H. Lawrence (excepting the Beasts); any work by Empson (a filthy fellow); New Country; Michael Roberts' 'Critique of Poetry'; John Sparrow; any criticism by old Pound; latest Sitwell; Marina & Animula; Hardy; Herbert Read, poetry or criticism; Laura Riding; Time & Western Man; 'The 17th Cent. Background' by Basil Willey; anything you recommend.[2]

Love. Louis X X X X

1 – 'Poetry Today' (see previous letter).
2 – FLM refers in passing to many of the above mentioned, in 'Poetry Today', but describes the *Active Anthology* (ed. E. Pound) as 'instructively bad' (*SLC*, 44); Grigson had reviewed Ronald Bottrall, *Festivals of Fire* (1934) in *NV*, April 1934, and Michael Roberts (ed.), *New Country: Prose and Poetry by various authors* (1933) in *NV*, March 1933. Charles Madge had reviewed Basil Willey's study of the seventeenth century in *NV*, June 1934. Other works mentioned here include Robert Graves, *Poetry, 1930–1933* (1933); T. S. Eliot, 'Marina' and 'Animula' ('Ariel Poems'); Wyndham Lewis, *Time and Western Man* (1928), and Laura Riding, *The Life of the Dead* (1933). FLM wrote of Laura Riding: 'All her previous poetry which I have read seemed to me appallingly bleak and jejune' (*NV*, Dec. 1933, 19) and in 'Poetry Today', he found her 'obsessed by the paradoxes of Nothingness'; both she and Robert Graves 'are both painfully lacking in worldly content' (*SLC*, 19). FLM described the work of Empson and other 'imitators' of Eliot as 'frigid intellectual exercises' (he later reviewed Empson's *Poems* in *NV*, Aug.–Sept. 1935, 17–18). Cf. 'Auden and MacNeice: Their Last Will and Testament': 'A terrible double entendre in metre or in prose / To William Empson' (*LI*, CP07, 743).

TO *T. S. Eliot*   Faber archive

23 July [1934]   Birmingham

Dear Mr. Eliot,

I find I have two reasons for writing to you.

(1) I have a book for review for the Criterion and I find I am expected
to produce a 1000 word review by August 1st.[1] As I am doing some
hack-examining at the moment, I wonder if I could have a few days'
grace, which would enable me to do this more presentably.

(2) I shall have that collection of poems, which I promised to send you,
made up shortly, and will send them along to you in August, if that
suits you. I have cut out a lot of earlier poems; the collection now
totals thirty and includes four fairly long poems. It seems to me to
be fairly homogeneous and I have taken some trouble over the order.

Yours sincerely

Louis MacNeice

TO *John Hilton*   MS Bodleian

Saturday [Summer 1934]   [Birmingham]

Dear John

The chaps here must like you very much to have given you all that extra
time.[2] As for me I so exhausted myself with excitement & waiting for the
telephone at the beginning of the week that I now can't say anything more
at all about it. Talking of philosophy though, I have just been reviewing a
book by old Feldman (did you ever meet him?) for the Criterion. This was
rather embarrassing (1) I didn't want to upset Feldman who is upsetable,
(2) I don't like overdoing the kind stuff in reviews. However I talked about
the Jews. Birmingham by the way is full of Jews. Ladies very handsome &
black. Another philosophical point I have just remembered is that I have
got to read a pseudophilosophic paper here on The Possibility of Literary
Criticism, which you could write for me if you were here. But don't let
that put you off; I am now so autarkic that I wouldn't encroach on
anyone's time for the world. On Wednesday next we are going to 100
Holywell;[3] on Thursday I am going back to B'ham to fetch Betsy & back

---

1–Review of R. V. Feldman, *The Domain of Selfhood*, Criterion 14: 54 (Oct. 1934), 160–3;
repr. *SP*, 8–11.

2 JH had been offered a lectureship at Birmingham University but was awaiting news of a
Colonial Office position in Cyprus as Director of Antiquities. He took the latter.

3–Home of the Beazleys.

the same day. I suppose by the way you wouldn't like to come with me – free drive both ways & I could point out to you that bit of country which you could live in which you don't seem to believe about. Undulating aery ridges & no houses (they won't sell the land); the thing to do would be to let some derelict farmhouse. If you would like this jaunt turn up at 100 Holywell by 11.0 [sic] A.M. or so on Thursday & I'll take you along. We can run Betsy on the wide open spaces on the way back; rather a nice drive by the way. Yes, you could even live on Icknield Street which is a very charming thickly hedged Roman road about 4 ft broad (you can just squeeze a car along it). Talking of scattering oneself it is certainly an important point. With university jobs, of course, one always has the option of going to Chicago or Cairo or somewhere for a change; we shall probably do that some day. Even old Russell went to California for their extra summer term along with his family (a painful bunch) & had picnics with the filmstars.[1] There is a charming man called Stahl going to live up in the Florences' roof who comes from South Africa where we think of going too.[2] The trouble is you get mixed up with politics there (as I suppose you will too in Cyprus); also they are very disgusting to the black students. He (Stahl) has gone back to S.A. for the summer so you see what can be done on the salary (he is a lecturer in German). Old Daniel, whom you ask about, is full of life & has developed a low-caste snigger. We shall have a job [consoling?] him & the black dogs in Oxford, where I hope you & Peggy will come & see us. Someone on the telephone told me that she (your lady wife) was away but do give her my love & regards when she comes back & tell her that if she comes here we shall fit her up with an Afghan. You want one from the north of Afghanistan, I am told, – the darker brand. Then you read the Arabian Nights to it. Betsy is meant to be married in August, I should like her to have 4 puppies but am afraid she will have a dozen or two. I am going to have a new house built for them

1–Bertrand Russell had taught at UCLA after the war. Christopher Isherwood wrote home from California in the 1940s: 'And there are exotic glimpses of Garbo, Krishnamurti, Bertrand Russell and Charlie Chaplin' (qtd in John Lehmann, *Christopher Isherwood*, New York, 1987, 59).
2–Ernst Ludwig Stahl (1902–92), Lecturer in German, Birmingham University, later Reader and then Taylor Professor of German Language and Literature at Oxford. M. (1942) Kathleen Hudson. Author of *Hölderlin's Madness* (1944), *Friedrich Schiller's Drama* (Oxford, 1954) and editor of many volumes, including Goethe's *Werner* and Rilke's *Duino Elegies*. Appears as Aloys in *AS* (XII–XIII). Collaborated with FLM on his translation of Goethe's *Faust*. See 'The *Faust* Translation', *TWA*, 67–72. Cf. 'We had a new friend Ernst, a lecturer in German, who now lived in a flat at the top of our landlady's house. I used to go up there continually and get Ernst to listen to me; he listened just as John Hilton or Graham used to' (*SAF*, 148). Florences' roof: a flat in 'Highfield', Selly Park.

with a change of floors & other hygienic contrivances. Then we shall sell them all for Christmas presents. My play too should be finished soon; it is the most difficult thing I have ever struck. Everything is on several planes at once. I am sending my book of poems back to Eliot soon – having ruthlessly struck out all the halfbaked ones. Total just 30 (including 4 long).[1] Should be quite a good book for once, I think. Which shows that old Eliot is not such a fool, as two years ago no one would have read the good poems for the bad ones. (You know that I long ago disowned 'Blind Fireworks' though there is, I think, just one possible poem in it?) But enough of this. Consider my suggestion about Thursday &, if not, I hope you will be able to do what you like as to these jobs; Will the Colonial have decided by the end of the 10 days? I suppose you have to keep them to it. Love ever L.

TO *John Hilton*   MS Bodleian

Tuesday afternoon [Summer 1934]   Birmingham

Dear John

As it seems impossible to get you on the telephone I am writing you what I think about all this nonsense. I may say that I am by now in a vividly bad temper. Firstly, it was very ill advised of you not to come & see us yesterday when we might have schemed up something.[2] 2dly if you had rung me up early this morning, I would have gone & blarneyed the Vice Chancellor[3] (I had washed my face in advance) & tried to get you a few days' grace (though I don't think they'd have given you beyond the end of this week, if that). But now, you see, the V.C. will have left his office & anyhow I don't know exactly what you want me to say to him as I don't know the latest about old George Hill.[4] All [of] which is deplorable. But it now occurs to me that it was really very Christian of me to be on the point of going & annoying the Vice Chancellor seeing that I have no personal interest whatsoever in getting you to Cyprus, whereas I shall be vastly disappointed if you don't come here. By the way, unless you get definite assurance about Cyprus don't you think it will be tempting

---

1 – *Poems* (1935) comprised thirty-two poems; the '4 long' were 'An Eclogue for Christmas', 'Valediction', 'Eclogue by a Five-Barred Gate' and 'Ode.'
2 – FLM is frustrated that JH seems to have missed his chance of accepting the job at Birmingham.
3 – Charles Grant Robertson (see FLM to him, 1 Oct. 1935, n. 1, p. 256).
4 – Sir George Francis Hill. See FLM to JH, 12 May 1934, n. 3, p. 240.

Providence to turn down this place? However I won't lecture about Birds-in-Hands as I know that would rightly annoy you. But forgive me for mentioning the following pros & cons in case you haven't thought of them. If you come here you will, of course, have less salary than in C. but you will have a job practically assured for life & what is better, 6 months' holiday per year for life, in which time you will be able to have all the exotic adventures you like without tying yourself to a painfully provincial island (so I have been told) where you will have to spend your time being socially tactful & where your children, if you have any, will die of dysentery & from which, when you retire, you will be transferred to Carlisle or somewhere to fiddle with the Roman Wall. & to return to salary – in the already mentioned 6 months holiday it is well possible to make quite a lot more in sidelines (which you needn't tell to the Income Tax) & anyhow 300 goes a very long way here. Then for your work – you would have a very easy time (about half as many lectures as I have for instance) & all they like you to do is occasionally to read a recent book. I believe old Gibson is going to go away soon. Birmingham is now becoming a grand place as there are at least ½ a dozen really good people here (which is more than can be said of almost anywhere). You can have a house out in the fields with a cob & an Afghan & Dodds will be very excited about you. Then when we are tired of midlanding (though the Midlands are excellent for creativity) we will all go & run one of the South African universities & live on fruit & you will also be able to design the new buildings. All this seems to me quite as exciting as Cyprus but then I am prejudiced & I shall really burst into tears if you don't come here because after all you let us down last year. Anyhow <u>IF</u> you can't get a definite promise of Cyprus <u>DO</u> plump for the job here. & I should say turn down Cyprus anyhow. But that is again my self-interest. Last point – surely once you have been a professor it will be easier to rebecome an architect than viceversa. & anyhow an archaeologist isn't an architect (& is perhaps that special sort of archaeologist not slightly bogus?) & who wants to be run by the Colonial Office? Well farewell & good luck. We shll be here a little longer if you want to come up & look for a house. L.

TO *Anthony Blunt*   MS Cambridge

[30 September 1934]   Birmingham

COMMON[1]
COMMON
UNCOMMON
DAMCOMMON
HAMCOMMON
COMMON

Dear Anthony,

Yes, for God's sake do come here. Not but what I'm sick to death of getting you fellows jobs here (see old Hilton on that). Now about your quandaries:- No foreigner (esp. a Jew) would have much of a chance here though it's just possible he might get it if all the other chaps were dumb or mad or something. Dodds says you would be a fool to stand down for Friedlaender; or indeed for anyone.[2] As for old Waterhouse I've told Dodds he's a filthy fellow & we'll hope that will get round. Dodds expects chaps like Herbert Read & Wilenski will be in for it ....[3]

[*MM's hand*] Dear Anthony, Louis says I am to put in a 'spree' here, while he has a rest. Do most certainly get the job here – If only to dissuade the old man from going to Cape Town!! Shall I ask my family to pull strings with K. Clarke?[4] Will you come & see Daniel soon? He is very nice & attractive.

We have also got a bull mastif! [*sic*] She & Betsy had 16 hearts for their dinner to-night. L. says it's a sensual pleasure & not like mathematics to be fascinated by the hearts – but I think I have got it wrong, being rather

1 – This sequence of 'commons' is written sideways in a box drawn in the top margin of the letter.
2 – FLM had encouraged AB to apply for the position of professor at the Barber Institute of Fine Arts at Birmingham University, but AB had enquired if Walter Friedlaender would get the position if he withdrew his application. Walter F. Friedlaender (1873–1966), a Jew, was an authority on Poussin and had recently been ousted from his professorship at Freiburg by the Nazis. AB found this very harrowing since he had only recently visited Friedlaender in Germany, shortly before his expulsion (Carter, 116–17). The successful applicant was the Director of the National Gallery of Ireland, Thomas Bodkin (1887–1961), author of *The Approach to Painting* (1927) and *Hugh Lane and his Pictures* (1935).
3 – Herbert Read (1893–1968), art critic, literary critic and poet. AB had been very disparaging in print of the criticism of Reginald Howard Wilenski (1887–1975): 'Mr Wilenski has clearly attempted the impossible. But he need not have failed so grossly' (*Cambridge Review*, 13 June 1930; qtd in Carter, 91).
4 – Sir Kenneth Clarke (1903–83), art patron and historian.

sleepy – so come along & be professor; & Dan will teach you awful noises.
Love M & D.

. . . P.S. I have taken to rouge & blue eyelids & cardinal nails: having a son
makes one rather frisky I find.

[*FLM's hand*] To return to business – you want both kinds of testimonials;
those from chaps in Museums & Art Galleries are probably the most
important but you must get some from Trinity too, as you will probably
be the only don in the field & they respect academics here. Dodds says
especially important to stress any lecturing on art you've done –
Courtauld lectures & all that.[1] Then it's a great pity you haven't published
any books yet, but if there are any soon to be, you had better make much
of them.[2] A testimonial from Friedlaender would doubtless look
important. The electing body is the University Faculty of Arts; they may
consult outsiders but they themselves make all the decisions. All the same
I should keep in with anyone liable to be consulted. It would certainly be
a nice job for you. They tell me the University won't approach anyone
who don't approach them. There are more nice people here now than
there used to be, not counting our family who are going a trifle goofy. I
have got quantities to do & feel thoroughly idle. I have just been over to
Dublin where Lennox Robinson gave me lunch & listened about my
play.[3] I am now going to do reviews for the Morning Post, which shows
what we all come to. But I want to get all my serious work off my hands
& then take a holiday & get educated. After all if you do nothing but
write & take the dogs for walks you may be benefiting the world & the
dogs but what about your soul? Or as Mrs. John Betjeman says, Are you
interested in culture?[4] I am now going to bed so I hope I've answered
everything. Come up & see us if you want oral information. The nurse is
just going away so M. will be a bit absorbed but we don't mind informal
blokes. Talking of the human race, I don't know about Cambridge but I
came to the conclusion this August staying in Oxford that it would be
fatal to live there. I should really like to live in Dublin. Well damn it, I
must go to bed now. I am sick with sleep ('The Milky Way was nothing
to his spew'). Goodnight, farewell, love, best wishes, we'll do what we
can for you here, & do you pray for our souls. L.

1–Courtauld Institute, University of London.
2–AB's first book was *Artistic Theory in Italy, 1450–1600* (1940).
3–Lennox Robinson (1886–1958), Irish playwright and one of the directors of the Abbey
Theatre. During this trip to Dublin (Sept. 1934) FLM visited Yeats at Rathfarnham with
ERD. Cf. *SAF*, 147.
4–In 1931, JB married Penelope Chetwode (1910–86).

TO *Anthony Blunt*   MS Cambridge

Postmark 17 November 1934   Birmingham

Dear Anthony,

We condole with you more than ever. & now, if I may be selfish, I want to trouble you. (a) I see someone's reviewed Stephen's 'Vienna' in the Spectator, but I should like very well to do either Yeats' 'Collected Plays' shortly coming from Macmillan, or Stephen's critical book (I forget the title) from Cape.[1] & by the way, it might be a good idea for me to review any of the more general classical books which are always coming from the University Presses. (b) As you owe me, if you remember, 30/-, would you like to find me in one of your Cambridge bookshops any of the following & balance it against above – a really handsome copy (preferably 18th century) of Ovid, either complete or Metamorphoses in particular; ditto Virgil (I find at my age I only have a Marlborough Coll. Virgil 2nd hand); ditto Lucan. Don't do this if it is a bore, but only if your impeccable eye happens to light on such while you are digging down to the Folios. The latest news about the Art Chair here is vaguely funny; I will tell you it when they settle the business next week. Dodds regrets that they did not honour you with at least an interview. But he says that they were keenest of all on having someone who had had experience of buying pictures. Which reminds me, if one can really, as you said, get a nice more-or-less Pannini for £10, perhaps you will get me one sometime when I am more in pocket.[2] It would I feel give tone to my classical pretensions – bogusly mellow, or mellowly bogus. If you are in London after term, I shall probably be coming up some time to fish about among some theatrical pals of Stahl's, which being so we might meet & have a mild binge. No, I don't know how long we shall stay in B'ham. I put it at 2–3 years (preferably 2). But where in Hell to go? That is the problem. Oxford (& C. too) would, I agree, be disastrous. A nausea submerges me at the thought of ALL those clever people with their pipes. What is Constable going to do for you?[3] I should like you to get some very swish job & snub the Birmingham bleeders. Old Dan, M. & the four feet send you their love.

L.

1 – Stephen Harold Spender (1909–95). Educ. University College School, London; University College, Oxford. Author of *Twenty Poems* (1930), *Poems* (1933), *The Still Centre* (1939), *Collected Poems, 1928–1953* (1955) and many other works. Memoirs include *World Within World* (1951) and *The Thirties and After* (1978). I. M. Parsons reviewed SS's *Vienna* (1934) in the *Spectator*, 153, 728. The critical book *The Destructive Element* (1935), was forthcoming.
2 – Giovanni Paolo Pannini (1691–1765), Italian painter and architect.
3 – Constable, publisher.

1935

TO *Geoffrey Grigson* MS Texas

6 March [1935]   Birmingham

Dear Grigson,

Thanks for the warning about these Spaniards. I shall try and give them something if I hear from them.

About Hopkins I will (as you suggest it) produce a few stray remarks.[1] I should have liked to know more of his views about Greek metric, but don't know where to look for same. There is not much to go on in the letters.

Yours sincerely
Louis MacNeice

TO *Anthony Blunt* MS Cambridge

11 June [1935]   Birmingham

Dear Anthony

If I may interrupt the even tenor of our correspondence to make you a sound commercial offer, which you with your clerical upbringing should not fail to appreciate, we are taking a large house, plus cow, in the Cotswolds for 5 weeks from beginning of August, & we thought that if you are not abroad all that time we would offer you for a space one of the rooms, just to keep the sulphuretted hydrogen going.[2] People don't like to come back & find the atmosphere too pure. You could also no doubt have a sittingroom of your own for doing your books, as my stepdame wld say, as there seem to be lots of them. It is at a place called Oddington & has

---

1 – See 'A Comment' [on G. M. Hopkins], *NV*, 14 (Hopkins issue), April 1935, where he wrote: 'Hopkins was a poet of many assets, in particular a sharp eye, a precise mind, and an intense religious feeling. It is a pity, therefore, that he should be thought of as primarily a Jesuit, or primarily a metrical experimenter' (26).

2 – 'For August of that year, 1935, we took a large old farmhouse in the Cotswolds, the floors and stairs on a slant and the garden full of stone mushrooms . . .' (*SAF*, 149). Blunt did not come, but guests included Ernst Stahl, John Waterhouse and Tsalic (Charles) Katzman. This was Mary's first introduction to Katzman.

what aspires to be a tennis court with a cowbyre along one sideline & a fountain along the other.[1] Etc. (You needn't come by the way if we have now fallen into the Basil Barr category & you find us good creatures but just too deadly tiresome. Far be it from us to press our leaden company upon anyone.) About your Art – if I remember, you were thinking of some job in Dublin? The headship of the gallery there (which you <u>don't</u>, I take it, want) is being hotly pursued by your old pal Pevsner (with some strong backing) who will be on the rocks otherwise but will very likely get it as they have a weakness for Germans in Ireland.[2] Bodkin, I see, (who has always an eye to the main pipe) is retaining a lectureship or chair or something of Art at T.C.D. So I don't know what other jobs there are there but I thought I would give you this perhaps superfluous information.

Your friends at the Spectator keep sending me the most deadly books but I suppose it is worth the money.[3] Next month I am going to be slavish enough to correct School Certificates. Daniel now says 'bum'; he is self taught.

There is a scheme to do my play at the Westminster Theatre by people called the Group Theatre who are going to have a season there for 6 months from the autumn. They are doing Auden's new one (good stuff). I suppose you don't know a competent musician who would do me an orchestral Irish PotPourri super-imposed (or whatever it is called) on the noises of trains coming & going in a station. The Ould Irish Melodies should, of course, be guyed – they will be the ironic frills or foam on the too-too-real basis of the trains. I haven't the technical talk but you see, no doubt, what I mean?

You might meet Bodkin sometime; he is very sweet &, being elderly, might recommend you as his successor here. Not that we shall, I trust, be here then.

I am just doctoring up my poems to send them back to Faber's for autumn publication. & my bloody little Latin Humour book is finished though it needs rewriting. I have said I will send it to Constable's whom it just about suits (humanism you know – what a disgrace. Which reminds me, you should really borrow from the library a very nice little jeu d'esprit,

1 – Oddington, Gloucestershire.
2 – Sir Nikolaus Pevsner, CBE (1902–83), art historian. He taught at Birkbeck College, London and later at Cambridge, where he was Slade Professor of Art (1949–55). Pevsner never worked in Dublin.
3 – Cf. FLM's reviews in the *Spectator* during 1935, which included: 'Greek Classical Writers', 11 Jan., 58–9; 'Plato on Knowledge', 5 April, 575–6; 'A Brief for Cicero', 26 April, 700; 'Translating Aeschylus', 10 May, 794.

'Homo Sum' by Nancy O'Toole; you would like it. The style is so good). Well that's all the news. I don't know why I waste all these priceless pearls on you because, really, nonexistence is all right when it stays where it belongs (vide Kant) but you want to keep it out of your letters, my boy. Don't you know that informal letterwriting is the only genre in which the English excel. & you are English. Not so me, thank God. I have nothing whatsoever in common with Cowper, Lord Chesterfield or Queen Victoria. But you, my dear, should really pay more attention to these great masters. Would old Vic ever have let me down, had I written to her? No. Why? Because she was a gentleman. That's what it all boils down to. The English (not so, again, the Irish) are no good except when they're gents. Which reminds me, Adrian is getting married this Saturday.[1] He met A. Macdonald the other day in Bristol who was in dread of being sued by a bookie. There is another book which I expect you know but if not, I think it would amuse you – 'Mr. Norris changes Trains' by Isherwood.[2] It is all, nearly all, from the life. Talking of life, my family came to see us the other day. Being all these bishops has made them more material; they could do nothing but tell us how many garages & lavatories they would have in their new house.[3] And every post brings us press-photographs from the step aunt who lives with the Folk Poetess,[4] of them shaking hands with the Duke of Gloucester or presenting the prizes at the Home for Lost Seamen.

Yesterday I went to see Auden teaching his little boys at Malvern, a unique & very impressive spectacle. We took Betsy in the classroom & they all had to spell her. He leaves there at the end of this term to do films with Grierson.[5] & now my good fellow, my old Icarian guest, my dear old urinal-drip, I must make an end. (What – so early in the morning? Yes, even so early. One should be more careful what one takes for breakfast) [T]ell us if you will be seeing us. Yours L.

1 – Adrian Green-Armytage married Elizabeth Lesley Wace (always known as Lesley) on 15 June 1935, at St Mary's Church, Julian Road, Bath. The bride's father was Stephen Wace, a marine officer.
2 – Christopher Isherwood. See FLM to MM, 10 March 1937, n. 1, p. 296.
3 – As Bishop of Down and Connor, JFM now lived in the Bishop's House, Malone Road, Belfast.
4 – Eva Greer and Gertrude Hind (Elizabeth Shane).
5 – WHA was teaching at the Downs School, Colwall, near Malvern. He had arranged to work with Scottish producer John Grierson (1898–1972), who was making documentary films for the GPO Film Unit. Auden collaborated with Grierson and Benjamin Britten on *Coal Face* (1935) and *Night Mail* (1936).

TO *Rupert Doone*[1]   MS Berg

22 July [1935]   Birmingham

Dear Mr. Doone,

Many thanks for your letter. I would have answered before but have been very busy at some hack work.

I had rather expected you would find the Irishness of that play a bit much.[2] Several people have told me to send it to the Gate theatre, Dublin, & I expect I may do that, though I don't know the people there. The Abbey certainly, I fear, seems to be past its prime.

I have another play, planned but not written, which I think might be your type. It will be less of a compromise between two traditions.[3]

Yours sincerely
Louis MacNeice

TO *T. S. Eliot*   Faber archive

15 September [1935]   Birmingham

Dear Mr. Eliot,

I have read through the Solovyev book on Plato, in fact I have written a short notice of it for (of all papers) the Morning Post. I do not think much of it myself but it is perhaps (Platonically) heretical enough to merit a note in The Criterion. It would give the English professionals a laugh anyway.[4]

Yours sincerely
Louis MacNeice

1 – Rupert Doone (1904–66), dancer, choreographer, theatre producer. *Premier Danseur,* Ballets Russes, 1925. Associated with the Repertory company, Festival Theatre, Cambridge, 1930, and founded the Group Theatre, 1932. Later, founded a theatre school at Morley College.
2 – *The Station Bell.*
3 – *The Rising Venus.*
4 – His notice of *Plato* by Vladimir Solovyev appeared in the *Morning Post* on 20 Sept. and another review of the book in the *Spectator* (20 Dec. 1935). He reviewed a good deal of classical literature for the *Spectator* in 1935; see FLM to AB, 11 June 1935, n. 3, p. 253.

TO *Sir Charles Grant Robertson*[1]

MS Birmingham University Library

1 October [1935]   Birmingham

Dear Sir Charles,

   Here is the book; I hope you will like at least some of the things in it. I have crossed out the blurb because it is untrue.[2]

                              Yours sincerely,
                              L. MacNeice

TO *Anthony Blunt*   MS Cambridge

Postmark 10 November 1935   Birmingham

Dear Anthony

   May I come & see you in Cambridge some day? If you are there of course. No one seems to have heard of you this half year. I cadge thus shamelessly because the other day I had a car-smash & when you have had a carsmash you are privileged to trade on your friends for a good 3 month afterwards.[3] One might be dead you see & not be able to sponge any more any more any more. I have decided that I am now of an age to acquire Culture. You must tell me about it. Having done one's little bit of Creation it is now full time (a) for easy hackwork that brings in money (b) for self-education. The motives, like all, are doubtless ulterior. It is time once more to cut out the introspection. Introspection is antipathetic (a) to knowledge (b) to art. You think so, no? The trouble with me is, dearie, (cutting out the introspection, you see, suiting the action to the word, isn't this boring?) that I am all form & no content. Whereas you, dearie, are all

1–Charles Grant Robertson (1869–1948), historian; principal (1920) and vice-chancellor (1927–38) of Birmingham University; later Fellow of All Souls. He wrote a strong testimonial for FLM, recommending him for the BBC, 28 May 1941: 'When I knew him he was very shy & only revealed his true quality when you had got past that barrier. For his gifts are considerable . . . I feel he ought to prove a real acquisition – because he will bring a sensitive & artistic mind to the technique required' (*Ms BBC L1/285/2*).
2–Written on University of Birmingham letterhead, pasted onto inside front cover of *Poems* (1935). The blurb, written by Eliot (and cancelled in this presentation copy), reads as follows: 'After a distinguished reputation while an undergraduate at Oxford, contemporary with Mr Auden, Mr Louis MacNeice has allowed his verse to appear only rarely in periodicals and anthologies. His classical scholarship has informed a genius representative of the spirit of his Northern Ireland. The most original Irish poet of his generation, intensely serious without political enthusiasm, his work is intelligible but unpopular, and has the pride and the modesty of things that endure.'
3–The accident occurred on 11 Oct. 1935. See next letter.

content (& of course your form is quite nice too no doubt). Well I must really get some content. Content is eating & drinking & remembering the names of things. Inventory work or colouring the pictures in the Kindergarten. I'm sorry. This is all what my friend Vilfredo Parreto would call derivations.[1] Smokescreen of words, abstractions, to cover the eternal sponger. If you are at all free any time & you could bear me coming along I will come. Mary alas cant, as Daniel (you remember him) is too rabid to be left for any length of time. A savage child. Will probably grow up a Nazi. Talking of these things I suppose you won't be able to go to Italy for some time. If you go to Spain I will come too.[2] Graham & Anna went to Spain this summer.[3] (I am quite rich these days). Well, love, apologies, all the usual. I am a rugger fan too & am going to go to Dublin to watch a match some time. Be rude if you want to.

Yours ever
Louis

TO *Anthony Blunt* MS Cambridge

Tuesday [19 November 1935][4] Birmingham

Dear Anthony,

Thank you very kindly for the invitation but, alas, I am not sure that I shall be able to come to either of those weekends as I have now sprained my ankle electioneering. However it is possible it may be mended by 30th. I don't mind you working at all, I shall bring some opuses with me as there are always plenty unfinished. The Latin Prof. here has appendicitis so I am doing extra work, doddering round on a stick. If you know of any good sticks in Cambridge, you might buy me one. Oh yes, about the car-smash. On 11th October, I think, a man in a large car hit mine broadside on at a crossroads & threw me to the winds. Our car described a semicircle, mounting pavement, & waltzing round a lamppost, ending up 90 ft from scene of impact, & I & a man who was with me fell out somewhere by the

---

1 – Cf. FLM's review of Vilfredo Pareto, *Mind and Society* (1935): 'Charlatan-Chasing', in *Morning Post*, 15 Nov. 1936, 6.
2 – FLM went with AB to Spain the following Easter.
3 – The Shepards.
4 – Mary went away with Charles Katzman on this day or next. In his divorce petition against her (filed 5 Dec.), FLM alleged that 'from about the 20th day of Nov. 1935 to about the 23rd day of November 1935 at the Grosvenor Hotel Victoria in the County of London the Respondent [Mary] frequently committed adultery with the said Charles Katzman' (*Ms National Archives*).

wayside but the birds of the air did not destroy us. We had a case over it & I had my license endorsed but I will tell you all the details of that later; they throw a devastating sidelight on the workings of the English law. The man is now putting in a claim against me for about £80. He is a garage proprietor. I am not disfigured though I had a very fine forehead for a week or so. This ankle however is far more incapacitating & I am very annoyed as I want to play golf again. I played some this summer with Doc Stahl, the man who used to live in the roof, & found I was very good when exhilarated by the scenery.[1] Cambridge I imagine has a bum course. I have just got Cocteau's illustrations to 'Les Enfants Terribles' which I like very much though I suppose you think them frivolous muck.[2] I like the book too. You too? Yes? No? Did I tell you I am reading 4 novels a week for the Morning Post?[3] It makes me think I could write novels too, so I have written two short stories. I should so like to stop writing. Think of all the things there are to eat & drink, think of all the kitchens, diningrooms, buffets, urinals & beds, & think of all the baths one could be having all day long & all the bath salts – rose, verbena, peau de bougne – & then there are all the things one could be rubbing into one's skin – talc, oil, butter & rouge – & then there are all the good things one could be holding in one's hands – cakes of soap, borzoi's ears, raw herrings under the tap – & then there are all the things one could be letting drop on one's face – sunlight, starlight, syringa meal & rain – & then there are all the things one could be just listening to – – With all which what does one do? One writes. Very very very very pitiable. My father is being blasted again in Ulster. I will tell you more about that great man when I see you. He had to sprinkle earth from the 6 Northern Counties on the coffin of Sir Ed. Carson his lifelong bête noire out of a large gold chalice.[4] That was very hard on him. It is about time someone kicked that bloody corner of the

1 – Cf. 'Auden and MacNeice: Their Last Will and Testament': 'Item my golf clubs to Ernest Ludwig Stahl . . .' (LI, CP07, 739).
2 – Jean Cocteau, Soixante Dessins Pour 'Les Enfants Terribles' (Paris, 1935).
3 – He reviewed fiction for the Morning Post on a weekly basis from Sept. to Nov. 1935. On 3 Dec., his review of Nora Hoult's Holy Ireland and novels by Morna Stuart, R. J. Narayan and John Steinbeck was titled 'Ireland – a Tragic, Realistic Presentation'.
4 – JFM officiated at Carson's funeral in Belfast on 27 Oct. 1935 ('Lord Carson's Funeral. Great Crowds in Belfast', The Times, 28 Oct. 1935, 11). He subsequently objected to the Stormont government's proposal that the Union Jack should fly over Carson's tomb, 'on the ground that the flag should not be brought into political associations' ('Lord Carson's Tomb. Bishop's Objection to Use of Union Jack', The Times, 10 Dec. 1935, 13). The Bishop prevailed. In early 1936, he wrote to his son: 'The Recorder & others stood by me splendidly in all the "flag" business' (JFM to FLM, 24 Feb. 1936, Ms Bodleian). See also Stallworthy, 173–4.

earth up the arse. Next time they have shootings in Belfast I shall go over for copy. I saw Stephen Spender the other day & his soldier boy who was trying to make pastry with nothing but flour & water. I also saw an exhibition of the 7 & 5 (is that right?) but they struck me as quite exceptionally halfbaked – I mean not baked at all.[1] Stephen has a madwoman who writes him loveletters all quotations from Marie Corelli. I have a man in Dewsbury (where's that?) who writes me quizzical poems –

> A bishop's son I hear you are
> But that not proves you great –

I must go & read my four novels now. Do you know any way I could make a lot of money? Never mind. More of this hereafter. Love to the College Cats. I'll try & make the 30th if that stands with you. Yes, Mary & Dan would love to see you here sometime.

Love L.

See note on prev. page!

---

1 – The Seven and Five Abstract Group (so christened in 1935, though originally known as the Seven and Five Society), included Ben Nicholson, Henry Moore and Barbara Hepworth. FLM is describing his reaction to the first British exhibition of all abstract art, at the Zwemmer Gallery in London. Cf. 'Auden and MacNeice: Their Last Will and Testament': 'To the Royal Academy we leave the 7 and 5' (*LI*, CP07, 735).

1936

TO *Geoffrey Grigson*   MS Morgan

[January 1936]   Birmingham

Dear Grigson,
    Here is the Yeats review. Also poem.[1] I don't know if I have got the price of Yeats right?
    I see you are having a great time with St. J. Ervine in the Observer.[2]
                                        Yours sincerely
                                        Louis MacNeice

TO *T. S. Eliot*   Faber archive

15 January [1936]   Birmingham

Dear Mr. Eliot,
    Thank you for your letter. I will try the Longinus if you like.[3]
    Do you mind my consulting you on the following question? For various reasons I should rather like to go to the U.S.A. this summer in my long vacation and I wondered if there was any chance of doing this profitably, or at least less expensively, by means of giving lectures. Either academic lectures, literary lectures, or just lectures. Is there an organisation to which one applies for these purposes? If you could give me any information on

---

1 – 'The Newest Yeats' (*A Full Moon in March*), NV, Feb.–March 1936, 16, and in the same issue, his poem 'Homage to Clichés', 2–4. He later reviewed Yeats's *Dramatis Personae* in *Criterion* (Oct. 1936, 120–2).
2 – See FLM's letter (in reply to Ervine's article, 'Our Peevish Poets' – one of a series of attacks Ervine had launched against Auden, FLM, Day-Lewis and other 'renegade poets'), *Observer*, 2 Feb. 1936, 13. Cf. 'Auden and MacNeice: Their Last Will and Testament': 'Item to St John Ervine, ornament of the nation, / His Ulster accent and les neiges d'antan / And a little, if possible, accurate information' (*LI*, CP07, 742).
3 – FLM, review of Frank Granger, *Longinus on the Sublime*, *Criterion* 15: 61 (July 1936), 697–9.

this subject or refer me to a source of information, I should be extremely grateful.[1]

> Yours sincerely
> Louis MacNeice

TO *Rupert Doone*

8 February [1936]　　　　　　　　Birmingham

Dear Rupert Doone,

Thank you for your letter. I saw the private performance of the Dog and thought it went over well on the whole.[2] Sorry you had to cut the psalm-singing in the operation scene. I thought the Witnesses spoke their verse very well but they say Gyles Isham is not so good.[3]

As for my play I was rather stuck over it but it is now evolving rapidly. I would send you a scheme of it, only it looks rather bare on paper. I should like to meet you some time in London. If I am not up before, I shall definitely be up for the weekend of March 1st and might even have a draft of my play ready by then.[4]

I hear Wystan's new play is going to be all about mountaineering.[5] A grand subject for him.

> Yours sincerely
> Louis MacNeice

TO *Geoffrey Grigson*

MS Berg

25 February [1936]　　　　　　　Birmingham

Dear Grigson,

Do you know of anyone who will pay me any money quickly for anything – reviewing or otherwise? I must have some money as I want to

---

1 – TSE replied on 20 Jan., claiming it was impossible to find lecturing jobs at universities or ladies' clubs during the summer, but that he would make some enquiries (*Faber archive*).

2 – *The Dog Beneath the Skin*, written by Auden and Isherwood, produced by the Group on 30 Jan. 1936 at the Westminster Theatre. Faber published the play much earlier, on 30 May 1935.

3 – Gyles Isham, 12th Bt. (1903–76), actor. Educ. Rugby and Magdalen College, Oxford. President, OUDS, 1925; President, Oxford Union, 1926.

4 – Possibly *The Rising Venus*; see FLM to TSE, 23 June 1936 (*Faber archive*), p. 265.

5 – Auden and Isherwood, *The Ascent of F6*, which was published by Faber in 1936.

go to Spain in a few weeks.[1] Second point, once I have got to Spain, I suppose your Morning Post wouldn't like to pay me for any of those half-witted little articles people are always writing about what they think they see in these places. Say the Seville do at Easter or the Joy in the Face of the Masses as the result of the last election.[2] Sorry to bore you with this.

Yours sincerely
Louis MacNeice

TO *John Frederick and Georgina Beatrice MacNeice*

MS Texas

25 April [1936]   Birmingham

Dear Daddie & Madre,

I am afraid I must return for a moment to the subject which we usually avoid. I had meant to tell you that I was taking divorce proceedings against Mary but had postponed doing so in case an opportunity should arise for me to drop the whole business. The opportunity has not arisen and is now, I think, out of the question.[3] Things on the other hand have moved much quicker than I expected and I was called up to London yesterday where the first part of this business went through successfully (if success is the right word).

I do not know what your views on divorce are but I think you will see that in the peculiar circumstances it is the necessary course, if only to give Mary a chance to re-establish herself. I naturally get the custody of Daniel and it is as well that this too should have been legally decided as Mary would otherwise be quite capable of making trouble over that at some point in the future. Technically it is still for some time open to her to attempt a reconciliation but I do not think that there is any likelihood of her doing this and this is, I think, just as well under the circumstances.

1–FLM had very recently complained to his parents about his impecuniosity. His father sent him £50 but was unable to send more since he was currently paying income tax both to Northern Ireland and to the Irish Free State (JFM to FLM, 24 Feb. 1936, *Ms Bodleian*).

2–FLM went with AB to Spain at Easter 1936 (cf. *SAF*, 158–9). The Spanish general election was held in February 1936. The Berg dated this letter 1934, but it seems very likely to have been written closer to the eve of his departure for Spain. Cf. 'Naomi Mitchison after a fortnight or so in Russia gave a lecture at Birmingham University about the joy in the faces of the masses' (*SAF*, 134).

3–FLM wrote this letter the day after issuance of the decree nisi. The divorce petition had been filed on 5 Dec. 1935 and the cause set down on 8 Jan. 1936; the decree absolute was finalised on 2 Nov. of that year (*Ms National Archives*).

I am sorry on your account that I have been forced to take this step. I do not think, however, that the affair will get the least publicity. It has occurred to me in that respect that it may save you some embarrassment if I don't come over to Belfast for a little time yet; my presence might make people inquisitive?

This is, I think, all I need say on the subject. I very much hope it doesn't upset you but, as I said, it seems to be an inevitable consequence of the situation. I talked about it with Elizabeth and she completely agreed.

I shall be writing again soon. Daniel is very well. Term starts on Tuesday.

love ever, Louis

TO *Anthony Blunt*   MS Cambridge

7 May [1936]   Birmingham

Dear Anthony,

I came back refreshingly jaded from your town. I fear that I enjoyed myself at the expense of all you chaps but never mind, you can do the same on me some day. You see, I am really so much happier when drunk. But I 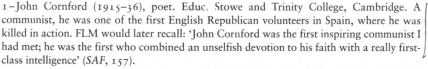 really must congratulate you on your university for producing this Cornford boy because obviously he is the one chap of the whole damn lot of you who is going to be a great man.[1] There is still hope for the human race. As for Guy B. he is quite the nicest of your pals by a long way.[2] We had a puncture on the way back when just inside the Birmingham boundary. Pathetic it was to see us all sitting in the road fiddling with our jacks & things. Guy's communist girl was rather nice I thought but Jewish you know. Cuidado las judias![3] Last night I went to see 'Troilus & Cressida' at Stratford (which usually does its plays lousily, I am told) & do you know it came over damn well & so coherent.[4] Just disproves everything anyone has ever said about it. About your paper I spoke to the

1 – John Cornford (1915–36), poet. Educ. Stowe and Trinity College, Cambridge. A communist, he was one of the first English Republican volunteers in Spain, where he was killed in action. FLM would later recall: 'John Cornford was the first inspiring communist I had met; he was the first who combined an unselfish devotion to his faith with a really first-class intelligence' (*SAF*, 157).
2 – Guy Burgess (1911–63), educ. Eton and Trinity College, Cambridge. Worked for BBC 1936–44 and joined the Foreign Office 1944. As Second Secretary in Washington, he was recalled in 1951 and asked to resign. A Soviet spy, he defected to Russia on 25 May 1951.
3 – He means 'Cuidado con las judias' ('Watch out for Jewish girls.')
4 – Iden Payne's production of *Troilus* was reviewed warmly in *The Times* ('Stratford Festival. "Troilus and Cressida"', 25 April 1936, 10).

head chap & it would be welcomed here with open arms. Tell me more about the slides. Guy thought all the young men in the streets of B'ham were queer. I dare say they are, lucky creatures. Since being back here I have had an almost continuous feeling of exalted irritation. I had another Italian letter from Mrs. B. this morning. If I hadn't thrown them overboard I would send her back a dozen in French. I think of having a Freudian party to celebrate Freud's 80th birthday.[1] Illumination by candle, toy balloons & a nice selection of shoes from lady's six inch heel size 4 to cast off track shoes of famous athletes with the spikes on. Do what you can with cyclamen. Couldn't you get old V.R. to buy it to reduce his weight with if nothing else?[2] (I don't admit that it is a merely decorative work anyway). & now farewell, hoping to see you again soon, at any rate with your paper. (Shall I get all the Left chaps here to come to it?) Personally I am going to read no more papers. I've been born & once is enough (as T.S.E. says). Nothing at all but 3 things. Birth (messy) & copulation (not enough of it) & death (we don't know about that).[3]

Love however, L.

TO *T. S. Eliot*   Faber archive

9 May [1936]   Birmingham

Dear Mr. Eliot,

I am just about to have typed a verse translation which I have done of the Agamemnon. I don't know if you would like to see it in case Faber's might think of publishing it. Various people, including Wystan Auden, have read it or part of it and Rupert Doone may possibly be going to produce it with the Group Theatre but I think he will find it too

1 – On his birthday on 6 May Sigmund Freud was presented with a congratulatory address, organised by a committee including Thomas Mann, H. G. Wells, Virginia Woolf and others ('Professor S. Freud's 80th Birthday. Congratulatory Address from 200 Writers', *The Times*, 5 May 1936, 10).
2 – Victor Rothschild, 3rd Baron Rothschild (1910–90), Labour peer and a friend of Blunt and Burgess while at Trinity College, Cambridge. Cf. 'Auden and MacNeice: Their Last Will and Testament': 'Item I leave . . . to Victor Rothschild the spermatozoa of frogs.' (*LI*, CP07, 739). He was an amateur biologist with a particular interest in fertilisation (Mendelson, vol. I, 791). On this occasion, FLM had attempted in vain to sell a Gordon Herickx sculpture, 'Cyclamen', to the reluctant Rothschild (cf. Stallworthy, 182; Carter, 148).
3 – T. S. Eliot, 'Birth, and copulation and death. / That's all, that's all, that's all, that's all', from 'Fragment of an Agon' (1936).

discouraging. It is practically line for line so it has that over G. Murray anyway.[1]

Yours sincerely
Louis MacNeice

TO *T. S. Eliot*   Faber archive

28 May [1936]   Birmingham

Dear Mr. Eliot,

My translation of the 'Agamemnon' is not quite ready. I gave it to my Greek professor, E. R. Dodds, to vet and he is suggesting certain changes. I hope to have it ready in three or four weeks' time.

A friend of mine is anxious to meet you. His aunt wants to do a production of 'Murder in the Cathedral' in the cathedral of Lahore! I shall probably be in London next week. I wonder if he and I might possibly come round to see you at Russell Square?

I am just applying for a rather absurd job at Bedford College for Women, London – not because I want to teach women but because I should like to live in London.[2] I gave your name to them among others for purposes of reference. I hope you don't mind?

I have a play of my own which I am writing for the Group Theatre. I wonder if you would like to see it also sometime.

Yours sincerely
Louis MacNeice

TO *T. S. Eliot*   Faber archive

23 June [1936]   Birmingham

Dear Mr. Eliot,

Here is my new play, The Rising Venus. I shall be very interested to know what you think of it. Auden liked it very much.

---

1 – *The Agamemnon of Aeschylus*; tr. into English rhyming verse with explanatory notes by Gilbert Murray (1920).
2 – Bedford was the first English college to offer women instruction in Greek. Professor J. M. MacGregor was Chair of Greek until 1936, succeeded by Professor Dorothy Tarrant (1885–1973). R. B. Onians was appointed to the Hildred Carlile Chair of Latin, also in 1936. During the mid-1930s most of the teaching and research staff at Bedford were women.

'Agamemnon' progresses; Dodds has made some very helpful suggestions. I hope to have it ready within a month.

Yours sincerely
Louis MacNeice

P.S. The stage directions in this typescript are possibly a little inadequate. The hoarded oil (v.p. 104) aint an essential, but it's all readable.

FLM

Note on my translation of the Agamemnon of Aeschylus.

This translation was primarily written for the stage. Of the many English translations already existent none of them seems to me to emerge as a live play. I hope that mine reads like a live play; in working to this end I have been prepared to sacrifice the parts to the whole. I have consciously sacrificed two things in the original: the liturgical flavour of the diction and the metrical complexity of the choruses. I have tried to make this translation vigorous, intelligible, and homogeneous. I have avoided on the whole poetic or archaic diction and any diction or rhythm too reminiscent of familiar English models. The dialogue is in an elastic blank verse; the choruses are unrhymed (occasionally they echo the cadences of the original.) The translation is [still *deleted*], I think, closer to the original than many; I first wrote a very literal version, line for line, sometimes word for word, and afterwards modified it with a view to form, intelligibility, and dramatic effect.

Louis MacNeice

TO *T. S. Eliot*   Faber archive

17 July [1936]   Birmingham

Dear Eliot.

Here is Agamemnon. I shall probably want to make a few minor changes but the mass of it, I think, had better stay as it is. I should like to write a short introduction and put in a family tree. For the Group Theatre I am writing an explanatory prologue but I don't fancy that that would improve the book. Rupert Doone, by the way, is anxious that mention shall be made that he and the Group Theatre expect to produce this version.

I don't think I shall be going away now till August 4th. I shall be in London next Tuesday. Would it be possible to see you some time after

5.0 p.m.? Don't bother to answer, as I shall ring up your secretary when I get to London.

In haste,
Yours sincerely
Louis MacNeice

TO *Rupert Doone* MS Berg

23 July [1936]   Birmingham

Dear Rupert,

I would have come today but can't face driving 200 miles in this bloody rain.

I have just got a job in London – same place as the other one but a different job.[1] It's in Regent's Park so I want to live somewhere on edges of same. If you hear of a good flat (not too expensive) anywhere round Regent's Park, you might let me know? I have to start work on October 1st.

About Agamemnon – it is ESSENTIAL to have a really good Clytemnestra. Perhaps you can wangle Flora Robson after all? Some time ago you also mentioned Beatrix Lehmann.[2] Is she still on the cards?

I have been thinking idly about costumes etc. The Greeks themselves on their stage went in for having them as gorgeous as possible; they also used masks, hugely thicksoled shoes to increase height of the main characters, & a thing on top of the head called the <u>onkos</u> for the same reason.[3] Not that I'm suggesting you should do it at all archaeologically. Far from it but I think the production ought to tend towards the statuesque & rather larger-than-life. I think the classical Greek dress (tunic + much much too flowing <u>peplos</u>[4]) ought to be avoided; it is too vague & incoherent. Best to create your own costumes with hints (?) from the Mycenaean age etc. & archaic statues & vase-paintings. e.g. I think you might use the very precise, elaborate coiffures of the archaic period. & Clytemnestra might have a very lofty one. Also I don't think she should have a flowing unbusinesslike dress but a fairly fitting one like some of the goddesses; or possibly a highly flounced skirt like the Cretan snake-priestesses; earrings;

---

1 – Lectureship in Classics, Bedford College for Women.
2 – Dame Flora Robson (1902–84), actress; Beatrix Lehmann (1903–79), sister of John and Rosamund. In the event, Clytemnestra was played by Veronica Turleigh.
3 – High, ornate, traditional head-dress, adding height to the wearer.
4 – Peplos, a traditional garment worn by Greek women.

plenty of colour. Agamemnon might wear a cloak such as some of the Homeric heroes have on the vases – very patterned, all over stars & rosettes. The soldiers should have round shields with lions (not too naturalistic) painted on them; the lion was the trade-mark of the house of Atreus. It would be nice if you could have relief lions on the front of the palace but that, I suppose, would be too difficult. I also think it would be a great thing if one had a drop-curtain with the Family Tree on it & possibly ornamented with a kind of Ancient-Greek pastiche – scenes from the Trojan War etc. etc. Only it would have to be a good artist who did this. If you need any hack-painting (things like shields) I could probably get people to do it for love?

I expect to be in London next week Wednesdayish. Will ring you up. I go away August 4th, return early September.

Yoursever   Louis

TO *Rupert Doone* MS Berg

Friday [1936]   Birmingham

Dear Rupert Doone,

In great haste (having just finished this very rough draft, still full of obscurity & without stage directions) I send it to you so that you may have it for the weekend. I am going abroad next Friday (20th) & should like it back before then.

The trouble with this play is it is so static. & what to do with the choruses? (A lot would have to be cut of course). Wystan believes it could be done however. With really good people for Clytemnestra & Cassandra the audience ought to be held I think. & there <u>must</u> be good people who can speak the choruses.

Yours
Louis MacNeice

P.S. I would write a prologue (a) explaining the necessary previous history, (b) putting across as plainly as possible the Greek ideas on sin etc. Wystan thinks before [the] play started, one might hang up a huge family tree on the curtain!

I imagine you could make up for lack of 'business' by formal marchings & countermarchings & things of the slaves; old men, Ag's soldiers & Aegisthus' guards.

Postmark 3 August 1936   The University, Birmingham

My dear Anthony [green ink],

Thank you for your letter. I can't answer any of that – or didn't you ask it – as I am only writing this, it being 3.0 p.m., as a catharsis & nothing else.[1] You needn't read it. The fact is, dearie, I am feeling sentimental. This don't happen often to me. I told someone the other day that I was sentimental sometimes & they were very surprised & said their opinion of me went up. I have just been up in London. The first night I had to spend on the streets as the hotels were full of Canadians. Then the Shepards too had come back from Canada with personal news – good really but a bit reawakening, & now I have just driven 90 miles home in the middle of the night & this house for the first time ever is entirely empty except for me so I have been playing ancient dance records & walking up & down through all the rooms which are all much too reminiscent so that I am glad to be leaving them. On Tuesday I go to Iceland & that will be the end of an epoch.[2] I still speak individualistically, you see, because the outer world is too bloody chaotic to divide up into epochs or any pattern at all. Now that was an epoch in which I did nothing at all: no go getting, no great works, no development, no self-education, no altruism, no daily grind even. However at the moment (viz. in this mood) I feel it was really very valuable (for me again, dearie, – all this is the most lowgrade individualism) & that with it my day is done & that nothing again will ever have such a definite flavour or such an entirely apposite rhythm. Playing these records (which I am doing as I write) is a stock schoolgirl trick in order to get the associations. However it is about my last chance of retrospective orgy as one needs this bloody house round one. Not like an ordinary house, you see, because we did nearly every bit of it ourselves. (I spent 3 days lately having a holocaust of letters & Mss. Most satis- factory.) The cat has very appositely died too. At least he disappeared, so I suppose he is dead, & I have given all the pigeons to the gardener. M. was very narrow, I suppose, but she was very genuine.[3] Narrow streams, as they say, run deep & have no mud & weeds. We are all so weedy, no? All

---

1 – He means 3.00 a.m. He is writing this early on Monday morning at Highfield Cottage, Selly Park, having just driven from London to Birmingham. He has only a day to prepare for the trip to Iceland on Tuesday.
2 – Departing 4 Aug., arriving at Reykjavik on 9 Aug. He returned mid-Sept. (cf. Stallworthy, 186–91).
3 – Mary Ezra MacNeice.

terribly spread out & dissipated & full of backwashes & contrary eddies. & all terribly desolate. When I get away from this house I am going to make a virtue of desolation. The really desolate chap sees a lot of people & does a lot of things, keeps on the move & always thinks of himself. You watch me. (When one is being sentimental, one is often very bragful at the same time. Do you find that? So it makes me feel very fine to say 'you watch me' though of course there will be nothing to watch. Anyhow there is going to be a war which will wipe us all out.) Perhaps being married to M. was a sort of prolonged childhood – many toys, much comfort, painted furniture, running one's hand over materials, hand to mouth idyl [*sic*] as all idylls are. But it went on too long & the habit is hard to break. Do you remember a jazz song –

> 'I'm bringing him a diamond stone,
> I'll take it back when I go home.'

Significant, I think. Or as Shakespeare said –

> 'I have but had thee as a dream doth flatter,
> In sleep a King but waking no such matter.'[1]

It is essential to find new people. You can't step into the same river twice. & we are all getting so old. 40 years on getting bigger & bigger, as Priapus said. There is such a lot of one's life that is waste products, not even padding. In front of me is a blue teapot with a rubber spout (bought in Charing X Road no doubt) which I got my first term at Oxford. It would give me great pleasure to smash it. Subsidiary to sentimentality (which is regression to adolescence) are Bullingdon violence & schoolboy smut. Thank God for these crumbs –

> Pissing down the valleys wild
> Pissing jugs of pleasant P.[2]

These routine idiocies serve to pass the time. Someday one will go socio-political-minded & run over the time instead of passing it. That's what steam-rollers are for. Remember them chasing you in your dreams when

1 – 'Thus have I had thee, as a dream doth flatter, / In sleep a king, but, waking, no such matter' (Sonnet 87).
2 – Parody of William Blake, 'Introduction' to *Songs of Innocence* (1789).

you were young? Or didn't they? It would be funny to see a lot of steamrollers go Gadarene. Perhaps we shall. Shortly, if I remember the other night correctly, there will be some dawn. Really there is little point in going to bed with no one in it. Besides I may as well get really tired before I go to Iceland & then I can fill in the four days on the boat sleeping. (What fun it is talking about oneself. I don't suppose you have got as far as this.) I may take my dog a dawn-walk; she really ought to appreciate Nature more. Nothing but sleepin' & eatin'. That's what comes of being a County dog. At least I suppose the Grand Dukes were County weren't they? I must buy a cloth cap tomorrow. Auden's parents lent me £25 to go to Iceland last week & it's all but gone. I have sold some wire-netting to a shoemagnate [sic]. He woke me up & asked for it on a morning after. I get night terrors in this house so that will be another blessing. My flat in London is going to be what they call a new synthesis.[1] Synthesis is a bloody word isn't it? Like progress. Progress is a bloody word. Well, here ends the nth jeremiad. See you when I come back from the lavafields.

Love.   Louis

TO *E. R. Dodds*

MS Bodleian

Postmark 22 August   Edinburgh 'Paquebot', Iceland
[postcard]

So sorry Betsy misbehaved. She has often done that shaking-by-the-throat game with Pug & Shepard's poodle but they usually know what to say to make her stop. I expect she will be all right with George. If you hear that she is being difficult, perhaps you could send her to the home at California? Sorry it is all such a trouble. We are just off on ponies round a glacier. Yours ever, Louis MacNeice.

Francis is very well, but still looking for a job. We hope the Iceland book will be a wow.

[signed] Wystan Auden

1 – Cf. FLM, 'Garlon and Galahad': 'Finally he came to the top of Mt. Everest and there sat a bald old man ... "I am just aiming at a new synthesis"' (*Sir Galahad*, 21 Feb. 1929, 15).

TO *Richard de la Mare*[1]   Faber archive

[1936]   17 North Road, Highgate Village,
                                     London NW8
                                     [hereafter 17 North Road]

Dear Mr De la Mare,
   Here are the proofs of my 'Agamemnon'.[2] I hope that I have not kept
them too long but there were one or two points which held me up. I
wonder if it will be possible for me to have a last look at the page proofs?
   It has been pointed out to me that for the convenience of people who can
read the Greek, e.g. under-graduates, this translation would be greatly
improved if some clue were given to the numbering of the lines in the
Greek. The simplest thing would be to do this at the top of each page e.g.
'Agamemnon ll. 872–945' etc. Unfortunately, as those were not page-
proofs, I have been unable to do this but, if it can possibly be done, I
should very much like to have some reference to the numbering put in
before it is published.[3]
   I wonder if the people concerned at Fabers could let me have some
copies of their Autumn list which I could then send round to some
schoolmasters etc. of my acquaintance?
                                     In haste, yours sincerely
                                     Louis MacNeice

TO *T. S. Eliot*   Faber archive

[October 1936]   17 North Road [postcard]

I should like to review for the January Criterion any one of the following
books:-
   'Paideia' by Jaeger (trans. Highet) publ. Blackwell.
   Journals & Letters of Stephen MacKenna ed. E. R. Dodds (Constable).[4]

1–Richard de la Mare (1901–86), educ. Keble College, Oxford. Vice-chairman of the board
of Faber and Faber, then chairman and later president. Author of *A Publisher on Book
Production* (1936). He was the son of Walter de la Mare.
2–*The Agamemnon of Aeschylus* was published by Faber on 29 Oct. 1936 in a run of 2,000
copies. Guy Manton reviewed it very favourably in the *Criterion* (16: 64, April 1937,
528–31).
3–Faber decided against this.
4–FLM reviewed Dodds's edition of MacKenna's *Letters* for the *Morning Post* (4 Dec. 1936,
19).

The Notebooks of G. M. Hopkins ed. House (O.U.P.)[1]
The Years. Virginia Woolf, (Hogarth Press)
Ulysses (the new English edition)
M Poems. A. E. Housman (Cape)[2]
The Collected Poems of Isaac Rosenberg (Chatto & Windus)
The Thought & Character of William James R. B. Perry (O.U.P.)

Yours, Louis MacNeice

TO *John Lehmann*[3]   MS Emory

10 October [1936?]   17 North Road

Dear John Lehmann,
   I am very sorry. I cannot remember getting your letter as to choice of
poems and I particularly do not want 'Mayfly' used – (1) because it was
written over seven years ago, (2) for personal reasons.[4] So I should be
grateful if you could possibly cut it. I can send you a new poem as a
substitute if you like.
   There are 3 long poems (one ready, two in preparation) any of which
you could have for New Writing.

Yours sincerely
Louis MacNeice

1 – Nothing by FLM appears in the Jan. or April 1937 issues. However, his review of Hopkins
appeared in *Criterion* 16: 65 (July 1937), 698–9.
2 – Housman, *More Poems* (1936)
3 – John Frederick Lehmann (1907–87), publisher and author who founded the twice-yearly
journal *New Writing* (later *Penguin New Writing*). He had worked for the Hogarth Press
and FLM had sent him poems in 1932, in the hope that Hogarth might publish them.
Lehmann expressed some interest but nothing came of it. Cf. FLM to JL, 7 May; 17 July
[1932] (*Ms Texas*). Later, Lehmann recalled how his hopes of publishing MacNeice's poems
were dashed by Dorothy Wellesley and Leonard Woolf, who didn't like them. Cf. JL, *Thrown
to the Woolfs* (1978), 34. JL greatly admired what he called FLM's 'effortlessly airborne
songs, with their colloquial freedom and gaiety' (JL, *In My Own Time: Memoirs of a Literary
Life*, 1969, 166).
4 – 'Mayfly' (written 1929–34), CP07, 31. Despite temporary misgivings, the poem was
published in subsequent editions, e.g. *Poems* (1935), *Poems* (1937); *Collected Poems, 1925–
1948* (1949).

[After 13 October 1936]   Bedford College for Women

Dear Mrs. Dodds,

Thank you very much for your letter. I will arrange about cupboard but have not yet mentioned it to Mrs. F. as we are having trouble over money & I did not want to annoy her.[1]

I am not surprised about herself.[2] She thought my family very very immoral. I will explain this to you sometime if it interests you; a long & rather depressing story.

My solicitor tells me the earliest divorce can get through is Nov. 2nd but I hope that week anyway.[3] I am losing my hair every time I put a comb through it; my sister says maybe functional [*sic*].

Cassandra seems good & Clytemnestra though not nearly powerful enough will say her lines well.[4] No Aegisthus yet. Someone (Clyt. actually) suggested me but I think not. Failure about choruses: the singing gents have dropped out & the conductor men are in despair. A pity because I think the music may not be so bad. Latest trouble: Cassandra & sedan chair. Doone wants to shut her up in a sort of portable bathing tent & have her gibbering unseen. I don't like this. Nor does she. Doone says it would be very unusual.

Repertory Welsh girl has come to London & is doing very well in Jane Eyre.[5] I must therefore no doubt go & see that presumably appalling play.

I hope himself had successful lectures. Where is inaugural & can we come to it?[6] When car is working again I will nip it up, but perhaps urgent to wait for the divorce.

1 – Mrs Florence, landlady.

2 – Mrs Beazley.

3 – The divorce was decreed absolute on 2 Nov. See *MacNeice v. MacNeice and Katzman*, 'Probate, Divorce and Admiralty Division', *The Times*, 3 Nov. 1936, 5. Cf. FLM to AB, 19 Nov. 1935, n. 4, p. 257.

4 – Played by Vivienne Bennett and Veronica Turleigh respectively; Robert Speaight played Agamemnon; Aegisthus was eventually played by Guy Spaull. See Michael J. Sidnell, *Dances of Death: The Group Theatre of London in the Thirties* (1984).

5 – Curigwen Lewis acted with the Birmingham Rep and had 'a triumphant West End debut' in *Jane Eyre* (adapted by Helen Jerome), on 13 Oct. ('Jane Eyre in London', *New York Times*, 14 Oct. 1936, 31). However, the reviewer for *The Times* felt that 'without the unrelenting and unwinking passion of the Bronte narrative, the play, though an intelligent handling of the plot, is almost dull. There is neither suspense nor thrill' (14 Oct. 1936, 12). Cf. 'The Theatres: Miss Curigwen Lewis as Jane Eyre', *The Times*, 8 Oct. 1936, 12. See 'Auden and MacNeice: Their Last Will and Testament': 'Item to Curigwen Lewis the Broadway sky / Blazing her name in lights' (*LI*, CP07, 742).

6 – In his Inaugural Lecture at Oxford, 'Humanism and technique in Greek studies', ERD suggested that scholars should 'devote less energy to textual criticism and more to general

Grigson clears out in a fortnight. One Fickling will then distemper main room for me (about £2-10-0). So I hope to be in by end of month.[1] Agamemnon published 29th.

Did I tell you I walked in on drunken party at B'ham, going to bed 4.30 Sunday morning – my last night among the ruins of Carthage, mothballs & ragbags. Mother F.[2] wrote very flattering letter after it saying she was so sad without me & would I pay her £50 to tide her over her low water. So I sent her £25 & a few details of the prices of things I have to leave. That miserable Mr. Williams never sent me the full account.

Next door mad lady in Keats Grove is daughter of bishop & has an aeroplane & a foul mouth. She may not dislike me as much as Grigson as Grigson's brother jilted her or something. When your bath overflows it gets her & she sends back oaths through the floor. Landlord hates her, it seems.

Ellis-Fermor woman was nice; pal of the Abercrombies.[3] I must go home now as it is only 4½ hours before Staff Social & it takes me about that time to get to Highgate & back again,

Yours with best wishes
Louis MacNeice

TO *E. R. Dodds* MS Bodleian

[October 1936]   Bedford College for Women

Dear Professor Dodds,

Postscript to my last. If you really want to join the Group you must do it at once as one has to belong seven days before the performance.[4]

---

interpretation' (*DNB*). It was not well received. Cf. FLM: 'There was a lot of silly opposition to the appointment; it was argued that they ought to have had someone from the spot who had been tutoring in Mods. for decades, that Dodds, who had been editing Proclus, must have forgotten the authors of the syllabus, that Dodds was a radical, a spiritualist, an alien . . . And so on and so on' (*SAF*, 164).

1 – Grigson was living in the flat at 4A Keats Grove, where he edited *NV*; FLM moved in on 6 Nov. (Stallworthy, 197).

2 – Mrs Florence, landlady.

3 – Una Ellis-Fermor (1894–1958), member of the teaching staff in English at Bedford College 1918–58 and from 1947 the Hildred Carlile Professor; she wrote *Christopher Marlowe* (1927) and *The Irish Dramatic Movement* (1939); Lascelles Abercrombie (1881–1938), professor at Leeds, m. (1909) Catherine Gwatkin. Abercrombie was at Bedford 1929–35, before taking a post at Oxford, where he was a Fellow of Merton.

4 – Group theatre production of *Agamemnon*, staged Sundays 1 and 8 Nov. 1936, Westminster Theatre.

Grigson now says he hopes to move on the 2nd, possibly before, so it looks as if I shan't be in Hampstead when you come up. & until he gives me a definite date I can't give notice to my movers.

Some unknown & sinister woman, saying she is from B'ham, has been ringing up the porters here & threatening to waylay me on the way to lectures but we have not made contact yet. I shall be very cross if it is Eva.[1] It seems rather hard that God should have picked out <u>two</u> & + [*sic*] lunatic females to put upon me.

I am going to try & review Mackenna for John O' London's who have a wide circulation.[2] But <u>when</u> is he coming out?

Nonesuch (my brother-in-law) is coming to Ag. (much to my astonishment) so no doubt you will see that pathological specimen. I should like to have a bottle of something for them-as-I-know afterwards but it doesn't seem feasible as I think I shall know the whole audience.

I am doing the Hippolytus with my girls here & would be doing a verse draft of same but think it would be too discouraging when the reviews of Ag. come in.[3] Am doing very little at the moment but have 300 lines of the Iceland Eclogue.[4] Have also written some of the poem on Moving House but it is sorrowful.

I did their bloody menu & tomorrow I go to their bloody dinner. (Mackail & such). The Bedford Coll. people are aimiable [*sic*] but the atmosphere is a cross between a municipal museum & a dentist's waitingroom. Central heating & copies of Punch. It is better however than Highgate & I have come in here to work on my own today. I have a childish phobia that this divorce will never come off. But talking of solicitors Betsy is to be allowed although she weighs over 23 lbs. which is the limit for dog or cat in the lease. There is no linen cupboard. I went to the National Gallery yesterday & paid homage to the Piero della Francesca baptism but no longer seem to like those earlier Italians as I did. Perhaps because they appeal so to the escapist in us. When you come you must see the Ladislas Paris.

I have at last written my little essay for Miss Darbishire.[5] I dare say it is too late to be used. You must excuse me if you meet her. If she doesn't

---

1 – Dan's nurse.

2 – His review appeared not in *John O'London's* but in the *Morning Post* ('Stephen MacKenna: A Writer Who Had the Courage of His Instincts', review of *Journals and Letters of Stephen MacKenna*, ed. E. R. Dodds, *Morning Post*, 4 Dec. 1936, 19).

3 – FLM worked on a translation of the *Hippolytus* which he never completed. He later staged the play at Bedford College and at Sarah Lawrence College, New York.

4 – 'Eclogue from Iceland', *EC*; *Poems* (1937), CP07, 72–87.

5 – 'Subject in Modern Poetry', in Helen Darbishire (ed.), *Essays and Studies*, by members of the English Association, 22 (Dec. 1936), 144–58; repr. *SLC*, 57–74.

have it, I shall use it for my paper in Oxford. I see that Day-Lewis has a new edition of a Hope for Poetry out, with a postscript including remarks about my sardonic-ness.[1] Oxford Book of Modern Verse is going to be out soon too.[2] I hope your Unregius poems are selling well among the dreaming spires. How I hate that town! I fear I shall be rude about it in my English club paper. Give my respects to D'Arcy if you see him. Also to Levens, Mure, Blunden, Isaiah Berlin.[3] I thought that the lastnamed might review Ag. somewhere. When I come to Oxford next you must come & walk in Merton garden. I hope the Clarendon cook will be good,

With best wishes
Yours ever
Louis M.

TO *Mrs E. R. Dodds*   MS Bodleian

[Late October 1936]   Bedford College for Women

Dear Mrs Dodds,

I am so sorry himself has a throat but hope it will be better by Saturday. Yes, I will be ringing you up. Does he eat raw lemons, because they cure a throat in no time? What am I to call him, by the way, if I can't call him Professor? It is a good thing you are seeing Ag. this Sunday as the next time Clytemnestra will probably have to be understudied.[4] The present one is definitely good, I think. I rather think you have to write for your complimentary tickets even though you belong? You write to the Box Office at the Westminster.[5] The murder has been amended & now happens behind a human screen & during a blackout. I have to do the atmospheric voice after all because they all like it (no doubt it has a religious flavour, the episcopal heritage). Costumes (excepting Chorus) are very good.[6] All

---

1 – Cecil Day-Lewis, *A Hope for Poetry*, 3rd edn (April 1936). He describes MacNeice as 'shrewd, fatalistic, a bit of a tough really; an Ulster product' (82).

2 – W. B. Yeats's edition of the *Oxford Book of Modern Verse* (1936).

3 – Father D'Arcy, R. G. C. Levens, Geoffrey Mure, Edmund Blunden (1896–1974), Fellow of Merton 1931; Isaiah Berlin (1909–97), Fellow of All Souls 1932, Fellow in Philosophy, New College, Oxford 1938–50.

4 – Sunday 1 Nov.

5 – It was a Group production, though was performed at the Westminster.

6 – The reviewer ('F.G.') took a dim view of 'the curious spectacle of a chorus dressed in dinner-jackets and coloured goggles', and the entire cast wearing gloves ('did they all bite their fingernails?'). 'The Agamemnon Performed' (*Time & Tide*, 7 Nov. 1936, 1562). The reviewer for *The Times* felt that 'the play is allowed to slip towards bathos' (2 Nov. 1936, 12).

the principals say their lines well but choruses are a bit at sea still. Webster at Manchester wrote to say he has been reviewing Ag. for the Guardian; he likes it. Grigson is moving out on 2nd. Distemper man starts on 3rd. Movers collect stuff on 5th & I get in with the grace of God on 6th.[1] Did you offer loan of some curtains because, if so, they would do for the Nursery temporarily, as when D. comes he will have to have curtains at once? That Bitch[2] has sent me a poem (not by herself; Eliza Cook or some such) called 'The Marriage Vow,' beautifully written out; all the t's crossed with red pencil & ivy leaves drawn between the˙ verses.[3] Must go & do Homer now. Reggie Smith & girls are coming for Ag.[4] Would you like to come to a Group Theatre sherry party on Monday where old Eliot is going to speak; possibly also Yeats.[5]

> In haste,
> Yours
> Louis M.

TO *Mary MacNeice*   MS Bodleian

10 November 1936 ['first letter'   As from 4A Keats Grove, London
in pencil in unknown hand]   NW3 [hereafter 4A Keats Grove]

Darling Mary,

First letter, in haste, having read yours (all of them!) after seeing Humphrey today for the first time.[6] I would have written last week but had

1 – The date appointed for FLM to occupy Grigson's flat.
2 – Mrs Beazley.
3 – Possibly written by Letitia Elizabeth Landon (1802–38).
4 – Reginald (Reggie) Donald Smith (1914–85), radio producer. Educ. King Edward's GS, Aston (schoolfriends include Walter Allen and Henry Reed) and Birmingham University, where he was taught by FLM and ERD; founder of Birmingham University Socialist Society and, recruited in 1938 by Anthony Blunt, a Communist Party member (until 1956). British Council Lecturer in Bucharest before the war and in Alexandria, 1941. Later worked with FLM in BBC Features (1945–54). His British Council years are treated in trilogies written by his wife, Olivia Manning (married 1939). Professor at New University of Ulster 1968–79. See his 'Castle on the Air', *TWA*, 87–95. In *Letters to Iceland*, FLM 'bequeathed' to Reggie (and his then girlfriend, Cicely Russell) a Shropshire pub (*LI*, CP07, 741).
5 – Yeats had had an uneasy relationship with Doone and the Group since the autumn of 1934, when they had expressed an interest in performing his plays. Nothing came of this. Yeats was decidedly unimpressed by the Group's production of the *Agamemnon*, which he attended with ERD. Cf. R. F. Foster, *W. B. Yeats: A Life*, vol. II: *The Arch Poet* (Oxford, 2003), 506–7.
6 – The divorce had been finalised a week earlier, the day after the first performance of *Agamemnon*. Humphrey Thackrah was their solicitor and a personal friend. He was so upset

got such a phobia that I waited for the certificate of divorce & also thought you might have changed your address. This must be short as I have to see a man who is painting my flat. Well first of all I too with all my heart wish you both everything you want & send you all my love as ever. You have had a hell of a time, haven't you? Reading your letters was an alarming experience! And now just one point which they bring up though on the whole I don't want to mention the lady (Lass die alte Hüre [sic] aus dem Spass[1]) you seem to have got the idea that your mother was at B'ham almost daily. Flatly untrue: she came to B'ham about 4, possibly 5 times in all, which I had to tolerate for diplomatic reasons (too long to explain now) & she got damn little change out of anyone when she did come. Admittedly she rang up & wrote a great deal & I saw her 2 or 3 times in Oxford to prevent her coming to B'ham. If you think I was very soft with her, you can ask the Dodds? She probably heard more home-truths from me than from anyone else in her life. But I had to avoid explosions because her situation was so complex especially with Eva[2] about (she was a pretty little legacy!) & Eva too I couldn't explode with or sack, as I wanted to, or she'd have perjured herself to the K.P. in no time. I was proved right over this as your mamma had detectives on to Eva these last weeks grilling her to say I was immoral & I bet she would have if I hadn't gone easy with her.[3] Mad, both of them! You needn't think your mamma's getting any look in now. Only Humphry & the Dodds [sic] think I'd better not tell her the whole story as she might possibly put the public prosecutor on to me for perjury & also make scandals (a) with my family (b) with my bosses. & now, darling, we'll leave this very unpleasant subject, only I just wanted to vindicate myself.

About Dan, he flourishes exceedingly. I am very surprised that you should think I would send him to Ireland without making arrangements. Actually he has had the time of his life there, & there was nowhere else to send him at the moment. He is talking a lot more & very large, takes sizes a year ahead. Very placid & adaptable, & loves dancing on the sofa to the

---

by their divorce that he gave up divorce cases thereafter. Educ. Oxford and Gray's Inn, he served in the army (Durham Light Infantry) in North Africa. He was said to have experienced a religious epiphany in the desert and vowed to join a monastery after the war, which he did. (Dan MacNeice, private correspondence, 2008; Mendelson, vol. I, 792). Cf. 'Auden and MacNeice: Their Last Will and Testament': 'Item to Humphrey Thackrah a flowered silk / Dressing gown and a bottle of Numero Cinq' (LI, CP07, 742).
1 – 'Keep the old whore out of this game'.
2 – Dan's nurse.
3 – Mrs Beazley had recently hired a private detective to investigate FLM.

gramophone. He is coming over to London on Monday. He will have a very good nursery in Hampstead with the nurse sleeping next door. There are some nice people near who have a 2½ year old son, very well fitted up for amusements, whom he is going to play with. Dan is now eating much better though he don't half take his time over it. [*side of page:* The Scotch nurse is EXCELLENT.] Oh lord, I have to go to Hampstead now & see the painter man & also poor Betsy who is tied up to a table leg. Life here is hectic. I will tell you about the plays & things in my next. All great fun so you needn't think I'm sad. Us Irish you know, we never stay down long! Which reminds me – Sir F. Buzzard, poetic justice; his daughter has gone looney & can only remain sane by having a child per year (I have this on medical authority). Many other funny things have happened which I will tell you later. I know lots of nice people in London. The flat, as well as having an excellent gardener, is two minutes' walk from the heath. I moved the rosetrees. Don't bother anything about money; me [*sic*] prospects is better now. Will get you photos of Dan – of course! There is so much to write I just can't cope with it. Expect more. All my love, dearest, you must go right ahead now & make an A1 job of it. Love to K. Did I hear he was playing rugger? I hope so. Yours ever (& as ever) Louis.

TO *Mary MacNeice*   MS Bodleian

10 November [1936] ['second letter']   As from 4A Keats Grove

Dearest Mary,

My first letter today was written in such a hurry after seeing Humphrey that I fear you will find it rather inadequate, so I am sitting up late to write you another. I will be able to tell you all about Dan next week when he comes over. Everyone agrees he is an exceptionally strapping & handsome child & there is no doubt he gets plenty of fun out of life. I think he will like it in Hampstead. His nursery faces south onto the garden & has huge windows (9ft 6" X 10ft 6!) The old chaps in Ireland have been treating him very nicely & sensibly, doing exactly what the Nurse (& I) tell them. They write to say that he now says Goodnight books when he goes to bed. When I took him over to Ireland he saw numbers of crows & other animals all of which he called 'G.G.' indiscriminately. & I also took him to the seashore where there was sand. He had no use for the sublime spectacle of the sea but knew exactly what to do with the sand straightaway, also ran round picking up great trees of wrack & all sorts of other messy objects. He had a very good time in Hitchin while I was in

Ireland & was much loved by Cherry.[1] One of his chief parlour tricks is imitating the noise of a car. He is not at all shy now & made an amazing & amusing contrast in this respect with the little boy next door to the Dodds whom he saw sometimes. The Dodds' doctor, who had a look at him while Dr. Horton was away (only because I was worried about his eating) thought he was a very fine specimen; he said the not chewing was psychological & he would get over it but must not be pressed; & now he has got over it. It was the same doctor who said that he ought to see other children eating, which he did once or twice at the Doddses'. The Dodds' have been awfully nice to him, also to the Nurse who, poor woman, had a rough time with that bitch Eva.[2] Eva, by the way, after leaving my employment wrote frightful letters to the Nurse & also to Elizabeth. Dan is also rather a one for little girls; there was a very nice little girl at the Florences', daughter of a new maid of theirs, whom he used to pursue in the garden & stroke in the most affectionate manner. Mother Florence offered to do all sorts of things for Dan but actually I did not avail myself of this! Edith, I think, was just right for him & all her many sons spent their days conversing with him. I am going to make a sandpit for Dan in the new garden & next summer I think he ought to learn to swim (don't you?) He is really very good company & has now got past the smashing stage. About mid-summer he spent his time throwing gramophone records, vases & the electric clock on the floor. He thought this was the hell of a joke. He also had a rather wearing game where you had to keep the lampshade spinning round incessantly & also keep lifting him up to sock them one (& he is no small weight!) It is a very lucky thing Dan is not a little girl or I should be very sentimental about him. As it is, our relationship is very hearty & sane. I know it must be frightful for you, darling, not having him but I do think that for the moment he is doing very well here & that you can feel quite happy about him. Talking of bringing up children I told your mother more than once that she ought never to have been allowed to do such a thing. But don't let's talk about her. I am afraid that if I see her again (I haven't seen her for months) I may possibly slap her face & be put in quod for assault.

1 – Hitchin (Herts.) was the home of Aunt Edith Burton, née Frizelle (first cousin of FLM), mother of Archie Burton. She was a niece of JFM. Cherry was a 5-year old Old English sheepdog that the MacNeices later inherited (FLM to Mrs E. R. Dodds, 2 May 1937, n. 1, p. 300). Cherry's pedigree form and multiple letters to and 'from' Cherry are in the Tail Waggers Club box at the Bodleian Library (*Ms Bodleian, Ms Res, c. 588*).
2 – Eva clearly had come between FLM and Mrs Beazley.

I have been staying with the Nonesuches for the last month.[1] Pretty appalling but I swallowed my pride & a lot of rather ill-cooked food, thinking that a month's free bed & board might help to balance my budget. You have no idea the bills Eva ran me in for. Also the blessed car, which has taken it into its head to go wrong in all its parts at once. I have, however, been offered £50 for it if I sell it at the end of the year. Which is good, considering it needs new brakes, new tyre, a new dynamo & re-boring! & new batteries. I didn't make a good deal with the Florences because at the critical moment when I was haggling valiantly your mamma sprang her little joke with the detectives & I had to be very careful to keep in well with the Florences.[2] A week before the absolute she sent them a registered letter for Eva (bribery & corruption) asking them to forward it. They got on to Waterhouse who trunk-called me & asked what was to be done.[3] So I said tell the Florences to hunt like mad for Eva's address for a week & then, not finding it, to send it back to your mother. But being the Florences I don't think they've sent it back yet! I will say for Mrs. F. that she got very good at frustrating your mother on the 'phone. So after all I didn't grudge the money lost on the exchange so much. You would have laughed though if you'd seen the letter Mrs. F. wrote me. All flattery on the first page & when you turned over you learnt that she was at very low ebb owing to her charities to refugees from the Canaries & that if I paid the rent it would just waft her out etc. etc. They don't change, do they?[4] You should hear Wystan Auden on these bogus socialists. Wystan is very nice indeed & we had a marvellous time in Iceland. About Easter we bring out a best-selling travel book about it[5]. I will send you a copy; 4 photos of me in it but comics, far from flattering. It was great fun riding the Iceland ponies though some of them are very uncomfortable & one of them had such queer effects on me that for 24 hours I thought I had clap – not that there was any reason why I should have. You wouldn't like Iceland though (too bleak), only you would like their habit on all the farms of giving you're [*sic*] your breakfast in bed (breakfast is mainly cakes, or else cheese). I enjoyed Spain too, & now London.[6] Hampstead is the best part to live,

1 – Following his return from Iceland in mid-September he stayed with his sister Elizabeth and her husband John Nicholson at Highgate, before moving into Keats Grove in early November.
2 – Again, Mrs Beazley's detective.
3 – John Waterhouse, in Birmingham.
4 – '[Mary] was especially suspicious of the Labour Movement because our landlord and landlady, who lived across the yard, were militant socialists and we had to pay them £100 a year rent' (*SAF*, 134).
5 – *LI* (published Aug. 1937).
6 – He had travelled to Spain with AB in March and April of this year.

I think. Stephen Spender is back in London (very nice now; he has become sexually normal) & I am going to a party he is having this Thursday.[1] He still hardly knows the names of the different drinks. Do you like gossip about our mutual acquaintances? You know that Anna is going to have another baby?[2] Anthony is staying in Cambridge but being transferred to King's where he belongs. John Hilton is designer to a paperbag factory in Bristol. John Waterhouse hopes to get his Nisi in November;[3] he is comparatively happy, now. The waiter who was their sole evidence went & died & they had to start all over again. It was very interesting my last few months in B'ham for I got to know some of the students[4] (not my own classical ones though; they kept up their good old tradition of dimness). Two very nice ex-students, living in sin; you saw the man once as Othello. The sort of people who have Midland accents & see the joke against themselves. & completely un-class-conscious, which is rare among such. & such sensational dramas have occurred lately among the B'ham students – elopements & seductions & angry fathers knocking each other down. You wouldn't never have thought they had it in them. Dear me, this is all very trivial but I do like blethering to you because after all I've not been able to do it for a long time. Not that I'm really lonely because I'm so busy – or else so idle in that I waste a lot of time seeing people & talking. A B'ham paper had a little gossip column about Wystan & me the other day & said that I was a mystery man & had 2 borzois with whom I shared my attitude of cautious reserve. Cautious reserve! One certainly needed it. I think, that reminds me, that I deserve credit for my blameless existence & because it could easily have been blameful. I had no idea that when one is not protected by a wife, people are all over one so! By the way, you needn't be frightened of me marrying again. Standards too high altogether; that's your fault! The detectives, it seems, said to Eva 'were you ever alone in the house with Mr. MacN.?['] & Eva, according to herself (it was poor Waterhouse who had to hear all this) said to them 'Mr. MacN. was a nice quiet gentleman & I never felt unsafe when alone in the house with him.' I'm sure she didn't! Not a few jokes in this squalid affair really. The last one

1 – Spender's housewarming party at Queen's Mansions, Thurs. 12 Nov. It was here that Spender met Inez Pearn (a very earnest postgraduate student at Somerville College) and proposed to her the next day. In Sept., Spender had ended his relationship with Tony Hyndman; he married Pearn on 15 Dec. (Cf. Sutherland, 200–2.)
2 – Anna Faith Shepard (née Gibbon), wife of Graham. Their daughter Harriet Minette was born the following spring. See FLM to MM, 7 May 1937, n. 1, p. 301.
3 – Legal prerequisite for divorce.
4 – Students who became friends included Reggie Smith (1914–85) and Walter Allen (1911–95).

was that your mother, also in the week before the absolute, had the nerve to send me a poem called 'The Marriage Vow' (by Eliza Cook or someone though she didn't say it wasn't hers) written out in her best handwriting, all the 't's' crossed with red pencil & ivyleaves drawn in between the verses. How anyone can be so dumb I can't imagine. I suppose she thought: Last chance – I'll get him where he lives. Talking of poetry old Yeats' Oxford Book of 20th Cent Verse is coming out soon with all us chaps in it.[1] We are quite notorious. Graham met Beachcomber the other day & mentioned my name whereupon Beachcomber flared up & said 'Auden! Spender! MacNeice! Beasts! They won't live! Beasts!' Never having met us, of course.[2] I don't think I shall become actively political but I do tend now to sympathise with the communists. (Even old Anthony has gone Marxist![3]) Only I don't believe in bloody revolutions. There is a kind of fascist movement even in the Irish Free State now.[4] I just have a slight awakening of conscience that one ought to do something to try & stem all these bloody things happening in the world & not just lead a pretty little private life like any old Bloomsbury pansy.

The production of my Greek play on the last two Sundays was, in my opinion, a success though they would go & spoil the first programme by a crazy bogus idea of having the chorus in modern dress.[5] They changed it afterwards. It is great fun seeing a production in the making. The actual acting was extremely good, I thought. I will send you one or two cuttings

1 – W. B. Yeats's *Oxford Book*, infamous for its eccentric selections and its exclusion of the poets of the Great War. In his introduction, Yeats wrote: 'MacNeice, the anti-communist, expecting some descent of barbarism next turn of the wheel, contemplates the modern world with even greater horror than the communist Day-Lewis, although with less lyrical beauty. More often I cannot tell whether the poet is communist or anti-communist . . . . Indeed I know of no school where the poets so closely resemble each other.'

2 – John Morton (pseud. Beachcomber) (1893–1979), author of the 'By the Way' column in the *Daily Express* 1924–75. Cf. 'Auden and MacNeice: Their Last Will and Testament': 'And to the Natural History Wing we give / The reviewers on *The Observer*, the whole damn bunch, / And Beachcomber and the beasts that will not live' (*LI*, CP07, 736).

3 – Cf. 'Anthony had now gone Marxist . . . Cambridge was still full of Peter Pans but all the Peter Pans were now talking Marx (Anthony himself was writing Marxist art critiques each week in the *Spectator*, extolling Diego Rivera and deprecating Picasso)' (*SAF*, 156). AB's sympathy for Marxism became increasingly evident at this time, e.g. in his *Spectator* article on Soviet architecture, 27 Sept. 1935.

4 – Army Comrades Association (later the 'National Guard'), commonly called the Blue Shirts, formed in 1932; from July 1933 the movement was led by Eoin O'Duffy, former Garda commissioner. Cf. 'Auden and MacNeice: Their Last Will and Testament': 'And General O'Duffy can take the Harp That Once / Started and somehow was never able to stop' (*LI*, CP07, 735).

5 – *The Times* reviewer complained of 'the grotesque make-up of dinner-jackets and masks' (2 Nov. 1936, 10).

about it. A chap called Ashley Dukes may be going to put it on at a little theatre for a fortnight about Easter.[1] Then I have a new play which the same chaps are going to do in the spring[2] & an old play (the Irish one about seaweed) which I may still launch on the commercial theatre. J.W.'s girl, who is very nice, showed it to some of the influentials.

As for Bedford Coll. it is rather funny; too much floorpolish & central heating but the old ladies on the staff are very amiable, the students are harmless (only one looker in the whole place & she is an Indian & wears a sari) & the refectory is very much better than in Edmund Street;[3] you can get a perfectly good lunch for 8d.

It is nearly 4.0 a.m. now & I must stop or I shall be muzzy when I give back their comps. tomorrow. A cushy job, by the way. I am getting £450 + extras for internal examining (which they didn't give us in B'ham). It goes up to £500 but I shall probably be made simultaneously a lecturer to London University, which means still more money. & then there are the literary oddments so I shall be quite comfortable, especially without Eva. Last year in B'ham I totalled about £600 as came out when I had to do my income tax.

Well, I must go to bed. The other night I dreamt that a bomb had fallen by me & was going to explode in 3 seconds so I jumped out of bed, took the rubber hotwater bottle by its neck & threw it into the neighbour's garden. Embarrassing thing to tell the Nonesuches next morning.[4]

Wystan & I interviewed the press in Iceland & filled half their Sunday newspaper. What really fetched them was W. being son-in-law of Thomas Mann. T.M.'s daughter was going round Europe conducting an anti-Nazi cabaret & Wystan married her to give her British nationality. When she turned up at the station to marry him she jumped out of the train &

1 – Ashley Dukes (1885–1959), playwright and theatre critic, owned the tiny Mercury Theatre (a converted church hall) at Notting Hill and was an exponent of poetic drama. He staged Auden's and Isherwood's *Ascent of F6*; Eliot's *Murder in the Cathedral* played for over 220 nights in 1935. Yeats, who had flirted with the Group Theatre but had his hopes dashed of seeing his plays performed there, referred to him as 'false, fleeting, perjured Ashley' (W. B. Yeats, *Letters*, 1955, 835).
2 – *Out of the Picture* was performed at the Westminster Theatre in Dec. 1937, several months after publication by Faber in June ('The Theatres', *The Times*, 2 Dec. 1937, 12).
3 – Birmingham University.
4 – His sister and brother-in-law, Elizabeth and John Nicholson, with whom he was staying. He gives an account of this story in *SAF*, 165.

embraced the wrong man.[1] I attended a similar marriage in Solihull – very, very funny.[2]

Well, Schlafe, mein Liebe hen, Schlaf Ein, only I don't suppose you have bed at the same time over there.[3] Do you know a poem by Samuel Butler with the refrain 'O God! O Montreal!'[4] I expect you feel like that & what is all this about a fire which Humphrey mentioned?

There. It strikes Four. Betsy is sleeping in my bedroom here & God knows she will be on the bed by now. She stayed with George while I was in Iceland & they fed her on butter & bars of chocolate. George & Young Robinson & old R. of course were the only two decent chaps really.[5] The Maycocks & Mr. Williams washouts. I gave Robinson your white bed for his granddaughter; I hope you approve? What about all your books? Can I send them over? By the way I may come to the States next August– September if I can get some lectures.[6] That book to which I contributed an article when concussed has just had an American edition out.[7]

What a very odd letter I seem to have written instead of talking about all those very serious things. I am sorry, darling, I am not really flippant you know; or, if flippant, not callous. But what can I say about all those things? I mean – you know it all already; what I think & feel. But what is all this nonsense in your letters (a) suggesting that I don't like you as I did & (b) suggesting that you have ruined my life? What b—-ls! Or is it just fishing, sweetest? You know perfectly well (a) that I continue to like you as I did & (b) that you set my life on its feet a long time ago &, like Felix, it has been walking ever since. You've done your bit by me once & for good & I shall always be very, very grateful to you. For not only did you make me extremely happy, not only did I enjoy living with you very much indeed (though, as I now see quite clearly, it had to come to an end & it

1 – Auden's biographer Humphrey Carpenter relays two versions of this story, one in which Erika Mann (1905–69) embraces the wrong man, another in which WHA embraces the wrong woman; neither version was true, however, since 'Auden met Erika Mann a few days before the wedding' (W. H. Auden: A Biography, London/Boston, 1981, 176). Erika Mann (1905–69) was the eldest daughter of Thomas Mann (1875–1955), German novelist and critic of Nazism. She and Auden were married 15 June 1935.
2 – The wedding of John Hampson and Therese Giehse. Cf. Walter Allen's account of this in As I Walked Down New Grub Street (1981), 56–8.
3 – 'Sleep, my darling, sleep' (see 'Cradle Song for Eleanor'), PP, CP07, 209.
4 – 'A Psalm of Montreal', Spectator, 18 May 1878; repr. in W. H. Auden (ed.), Oxford Book of Light Verse (1938).
5 – Robinson, gardener at Highfield, Selly Park.
6 – FLM did not travel to America until the spring of 1939.
7 – FLM contributed 'Sir Thomas Malory' to Derek Verschoyle (ed.), The English Novelists: A Survey of the Novel by Twenty Contemporary Novelists (London/New York, 1936).

was lucky it ended with K. & not some other way) but you stopped me being a sap & that is no small service! So now, my very dear, you must really quit worrying about me or thinking I am sad because I AIN'T. One can't have any one kind of happiness for ever but there are various kinds & I really am feeling alive these days; the important thing, I think, is not so much comfort or contentment as to be functioning vitally. So you'll be doing that over there & I'll be doing that here; yes-no? I like writing to you very much. It's very quaint really that we should have got on because I suppose we are entirely different in our psychological makeup. Them of the woods go back to the woods & them of the sea go back to the sea.

All my love, darling,

& to K. Yours ever, Louis

TO *Mrs E. R. Dodds* MS Bodleian

18 November [1936] 4A Keats Grove

Dear Mrs. Dodds,

I suppose your last letter, received last night, did start where it did, or was there a page missing?

Yes, I heard from Wystan that Fate was after him. He will have fun with it though: We met at a thing called a Poetry Dinner last night, given by the Lyceum Club which turns out to be old women.[1] And all gaga. The one whom I sat next to who was an Honourable kept telling me how she had always liked the Greeks & thought they were dear old boys, especially Pythagoras.

Dan & Nurse arrived successfully & slid into their positions without fuss though Nurse wants to shift things round rather & the measurement & angle problems are most difficult. Your Freda Pal came today; I hardly saw her but she seems to like the idea of wafting us over a week or so. Shops are expensive here. Which reminds me: I still have my B'ham butcher's bill for £23. Dan has lots new words [*sic*] but is crazy for playing [cards *deleted*] cars. Herself has sent us each a guinea for a little present. I hope you will come up sometime soon & make suggestions. Elizabeth is not a very good suggester, as she is so vague. I feel too tired to be very competent myself, which is my own fault no doubt. For the sake of my

---

1 – The Lyceum was established by Constance Smedley (aka 'The Princess') (1876–1941), author and founder of the International Lyceum Clubs for Women Artists and Writers. She helped establish women's clubs across Europe in London, Amsterdam, Berlin, Paris and Florence.

health & hers I am going to take Betsy a daily walk on the Heath which is pleasant but very cold. We are certainly very conveniently situated for we have not only the Heath at our door but also 3 late-open cafés which give you fried eggs if you have forgotten to lay in anything; & a cinema. But our own road is most retired & residential. I am going to stop this now in order to try to review Mackenna.[1] Will be all anacoluthons no doubt.[2] If I were a lady filmstar I should call myself Anna Coluthon, I think. One would have to act spy parts then.

Am glad about G.T. at B.[3] Anthony says he [*arrow pointing at 'G.T.'*] is reviewing my Ag for something. Hope to go up to B'ham on 30th to hear E. M. Forster.

The girls keep asking me for advice about the drammer & to propose the toast of the College at society dinners & to give them lunchhour talks on mod. Poetry. I can't cope. I come to Oxford M 22nd to talk about humanity.

The hell, as Mr. Hemingway says.[4] Paxvobiscum, absit Medusa.[5]

Yours ever,
L.M.

Graves & Riding? [margin annotation]

TO *Mrs E. R. Dodds* MS Bodleian

26 November 1936   4A Keats Grove

Dear Mrs. Dodds,

In haste. Yes, may I stay next Tuesday night after paper? Only I shall have to get back very early next day. But may I come early Tuesday? We heard from Mrs. Cook, who comes no more, that you very kindly want measurements of nursery windows but the point is this: nursery is such a queer colour that I think you ought to see it first or else I ought to see curtain samples. No green or blue I think required. Also I hope no human figures? Dan & Nurse flourish. N. doesn't want daily help because they fuss her; only cleaner once or twice a week. I look forward to when you come to London. Have been rather busy; Mackenna review in M. Post on

1 – FLM, 'Stephen MacKenna: A Writer Who Had the Courage of His Instincts', review of *Journals and Letters of Stephen MacKenna*, ed. E. R. Dodds (*Morning Post*, 4 Dec. 1936, 19).
2 – FLM had playfully suggested 'Anacoluthon' (meaning a lack of grammatical sequence) as title of his early draft novel. See FLM to JH, Autumn 1933, n. 2, p. 234.
3 – Geoffrey Taylor (pseud.), born Geoffrey Phibbs (1900–56), poet and editor.
4 – Cf. FLM's Hemingway parody, which concludes with the words, 'What the hell, he said. What the hell.' From 'Or One Might Write It So', in *I Crossed the Minch* (1938), 184–6.
5 – 'Peace be with you, may there be no Medusa.'

Friday I think.[1] (No one seems to want to review Ag.; all frightened off it.[2])
Dialogue with Doone quite fun; he said the silly things & I was Socrates.
Only he did get so tied up over phrases like a fortiori. Wystan came &
read the Letter to Byron (c.1250 ll.)[3] [V]ery very good. It seems that Yeats
Oxford Book is loony; they haven't sent me a copy, the swine. Herself has
written again; seems cheerier.[4]

                              Yours ever
                              Louis

1 – The review was published in the *Post* on Friday 4 Dec.
2 – The play received a mixed review in *The Times*, 2 Nov. 1936, 12.
3 – 'Letter to Lord Byron'.
4 – Mary, presumably.

1937

TO *Mary MacNeice*   MS Bodleian

10 January [1937]   4A Keats Grove

Darling Mary,

First of all thank you very kindly for the Christmas cable & the charming napkin rings. I hope you got my cable, also the long letter preceding which you oddly didn't seem to have had when you cabled (these posts are beyond me). I would have written soon after Christmas but was taken unwell with a mild variety of 'flu. I trust you are now comfortably in the States & have surmounted these last annoyances. All goes well here. Daniel flourishes & did not catch anything. He had many Christmas presents & we got him a small Xmas tree. The old stepdame sent a large hamper of foods. Also a xylophone for Dan which he likes very much. He is a great one on the music & I am going to get him some nurseryrhyme [*sic*] records when I can find some where the singer is not too unctuous, as they often are. Did I tell you that Wystan Auden said Dan was the bestnatured [*sic*] child he'd ever met? Well, Dan goes well. The other one (that's me) not quite so well because during the vacation (but please don't mention this anywhere!) I had one petite affaire with someone very charming but which came to an end with her suddenly leaving the country.[1] No doubt just as well but I am at the moment feeling very down about it. All very à la Hamlet you know – 'Man delights not me nor woman neither.'[2] And my heart ain't even in my work. However I expect to be meself [*sic*] again in a fortnight. I hope you don't mind my telling you this? It has just occurred to me that one could construct a good practical philosophy out of the following 3 well known sayings (1) Man cannot live by bread alone (Christ) (2) If they haven't got bread, give 'em cake. (Marie Antoinette) (3) You can't have your cake & eat it (English Traditional). Anyhow I am feeling rather wormwood & ashes; quite ludicrous eh? I fear

1 – Leonora Corbett, 'a musical actress, very tall, very blonde, all eye-veils, furs and egotism; dabbled in religion and poetry, mixed her conversation with French and German, and was painted by Royal Academicians' (Ann Thwaite, *A. A. Milne, His Life* (1990), qtd in Stallworthy, 202).
2 – *Hamlet*, II.ii.

I am not one of those people who can keep their physicals disconnected |] ✓
from the rest of them. Much the more comfortable way to be, I'm sure &
by the way I can see that it will be very difficult in future because I'm not
sure that I shall be able to tell you about these things (which I should
instinctively tend to) (1) because that would be partly putting the
responsibility on you (which doesn't seem fair & anyhow I don't think you
would like it), (2) because from my observation of women in general I
foresee that anyone who likes me is likely (however nice they are) to be
extremely jealous of you so that it might even be enough to break up the
whole business if they knew that I wrote to you about them. I'm sorry but
it's your sex, not mine. However enough of this subject & let's see if we
have any news. I have been asked by the Oxford Press to do a book about
Modern Poetry.[1] & I am having my portrait painted by a young man called
Robert Medley.[2] In about a fortnight I am going to the theatre with
Humphrey to see Hamlet.[3] Otherwise there are no great gaieties on. I saw
in the New Year with the Stahls who were in London. The old Doc. got
tipsy again, not having a great head. Mrs. Dodds has sent curtains for the
nursery but they miscalculated the size. She has embroidered animals on
them to my own designing. I have ordered some very refined curtains for
my sitting room. I have not yet finished arranging my books! The long
mirror which used to be in the Cottage bedroom is in my sittingroom [sic]
with a semicircular table in front of it on which I stand my flowers so that
you always get 'em double. I am enclosing some photos which Wystan
took lately of Dan & an extract from a comic Polyfoto which I had done
of me – a year ago.[4] Hollywood, eh? I must stop now & get on with this
Iceland book which is to bring us in a lot of money. I am going to make
enquiries about American lectures some day soon. Goodnight to you now,
all my love as ever & good luck to you both. Have a good time.

L.

P.S. Sorry if this was a little gloomy. Don't worry about it because I shall
probably be as merry as the day is long by the time you get this!

---

1 – *Modern Poetry: A Personal Essay* (*MP*) was published by Oxford University Press in 1938.
2 – Robert Medley (1905–94), painter, designer and founder member of the Group Theatre,
with his partner Rupert Doone. He studied in Paris for two years and did wartime service in
the Middle East. Later taught at the Slade and at Camberwell School of Art. Cf. 'Auden and
MacNeice: Their Last Will and Testament': 'Item, to Robert Medley some cellophane / And
a pack of jokers . . .' (*LI*, CP07, 741).
3 – Tyrone Guthrie's production of *Hamlet* at the Old Vic, starring Laurence Olivier, was
reviewed in *The Times* on 6 Jan. 1937, 10.
4 – Snapshots from a photo kiosk.

TO *T. S. Eliot*   Faber archive

21 January [1937]   4A Keats Grove

Dear Eliot,

Thank you very much for Hopkins.[1]

The Iceland book is nearly ready. Dr. Auden who has the map says that there are three places where Þ (= th) has been printed as P; also one other misprint. If to correct these in the map itself is too expensive we might have a note of Errata somewhere?

Are you using the Icelandic Eclogue for the next Criterion?[2] Because John Lehmann wants something from me and I thought that he might have the Eclogue if you are not using it, provided of course that he prints it before the book itself comes out.

I am thinking of going to America for two or three weeks at Easter.[3] Could you suggest any way by which at that time I could make a little money to balance some of my expenses? Journalism, lectures, anything like that? And is there a possibility of going out as a steward or something of the sort?

Talking of America, is there any more news from Harcourt & Brace who, you said, thought of doing the Agamemnon?[4] And what about 'The Rising Venus'?[5] I am thinking at the moment of expanding it, which I shall have to do soon if the Group Theatre do it this spring, as they still hope to.

                              With apologies for all
                              these questions,
                              Yours sincerely
                              Louis MacNeice

1 – He reviewed the *Note-Books and Papers* of G. M. Hopkins for the July 1937 *Criterion*.
2 – 'Eclogue from Iceland' did not appear in the next *Criterion*. It was published, however, in the Random House *Poems* (1937).
3 – Soon he had changed his mind: see FLM to MM, 10 March 1937, p. 295.
4 – Harcourt, Brace and Co. published an American edition of *The Agamemnon of Aeschylus* on 25 March 1937 (260 copies imported from Faber).
5 – See his letters to TSE, 23 June 1936, p. 265.

TO *T. S. Eliot*   Faber archive

18 February [1937]   4A Keats Grove

Dear Eliot,

I am afraid Curtis Brown's typists are being unexpectedly long with the
Iceland Mss. They have had it over a fortnight though it was, of course,
rather a tough job.

I have been thinking that there ought to be at least one photograph of
Wystan in this book. The man who said he would illustrate the Byron letter
has failed us so I take it that there would be room for another illustration
or two.[1]

I hear from Geoffrey Grigson that Paul Willert who manages the Oxford
University Press in America would like to publish my Poems there.[2] The
idea is that they would buy sheets from you and they suggest that, if you
agree to the idea, you send them out a specimen copy. It seems a good
suggestion to me.

Yours sincerely
Louis MacNeice

TO *Mary MacNeice*   MS Bodleian

10 March [1937]   4A Keats Grove

Darling Mary,

Just had your latest, from March 1st. I haven't written for the simple
reason that I <u>have</u> written several times but torn 'em up because I didn't
think they were nicely put. More on the theme of putting the clock back.
You see, it's bound to sound a little crude & I won't write much about it
now but the fact is that in any relationship (past, present or future)
between 2 chaps there are <u>two</u> people in the question & not one. Well in

---

1 – William Coldstream was supposed to illustrate 'Letter to Lord Byron'. There were no
photos of Auden in *Letters from Iceland* because he took all the photos and omitted to
include himself. The volume includes fifty-one illustrations, mostly photos but also five
historic prints. The photos feature Icelandic farmers, fishermen, haymakers, horses and men
on horseback, and various landscape features, including geysers. There are also seven
diagrams (pie charts, graphs) and a map of Iceland on the endpapers. There are several photos
of FLM, e.g. 'Leaving Hraensef' (opposite 17), 'The Student of Prose and Conduct' (opposite
48) and 'Louis' – supine on grass (opposite 257).
2 – Paul Willert, educ. Eton and Balliol College, Oxford (BA, 1930); vice-president and
manager OUP, New York, 1936–9. *Poems* (1937) was published in New York not by OUP
but by Random House.

this particular question I am very sorry if you really think (but I hope you don't) that it would be a good thing for us ever to join up again because frankly I think it would be hopeless. I cannot imagine enjoying being married again in any case. It's not my métier! But if I did marry I should want to marry someone (1) with a job & (2) not too many nerves & (3) prepared to do the sort of things I like. Which couldn't very well be you, darling. If however you suggest that we should join up again not for ourselves but for Dan, I think it vastly improbable that under those circumstances Dan would benefit from it. Everyone thinks that Dan is all right as he is so I think we had better leave well alone, don't you? He doesn't appear to be either hypersensitive or particularly 'Jewish' so I don't think you need worry that his inherited genius is being frustrated or anything like that. As a matter of fact I think it very wicked to assume that a child is born something very extraordinary & therefore must be treated in an extraordinary way (it's what your mother did with you). What Dan really needs is not any more mothers, fathers, aunts or grandfathers but more children to play with & I'm going to see about that next week when he has had his 3rd & last inoculation for diphtheria. Naturally it's rather bloody for you but it looks as if that bloodiness was predestined. There's nothing to be done about it. I'm very sorry but I didn't arrange the present situation & in fact I think I put up as much opposition as was reasonable. I really changed my attitude after the car smash which must have shaken up my mind as well as my body (!)[1] & it occurred to me that what you were forcing on me against my will might really turn out to be the best thing for me[,] whatever it turned out for you. So it is really a tragicomic paradox if your very temperamental & forceful action has landed you in a mess & me in clover! But I don't see why you should be in a mess. Unless you are a perfectionist (which is a bad thing to be!) it seems to me that living with someone you really like you are miles better off than the majority [of those who are] stuck. To parody a remark of one of your American Presidents (?), you can have everything some of the time & you can have SOME things all of the time but you can't have EVERYTHING ALL of the time.[2] Can you now? What I like is to feel alive. Well, at the moment I feel a lot aliver than I have for many a day & being as selfish as anyone else, I prefer to remain that way. And I just can't see why we can't regard our marriage as a very pleasant & on the whole satisfactory episode which is now finished. If it had gone on from where it was it would

1 – The car crash of 11 Oct. 1935 (cf. letter to AB, 19 Nov. of that year, pp. 257–8).
2 – 'You can fool all the people some of the time, and some of the people all the time, but you cannot fool all the people all the time' (attributed to Abraham Lincoln).

probably have ceased (sooner or later) to be satisfactory; if it started again now it wouldn't have a chance.

I am afraid I shan't be able to come to America this spring after all. No money & not enough time. Also though I should like to see you very much, I think it will be better if I see you later. Also I have been offered money to go to the Hebrides this vacation & write a little book about it. Also I am having a relationship here of a very attractive kind & I do not want to go away & prematurely break it up.[1] Il faut cultiver notre jardin – my garden; nobody else's. Sufficient unto the day is the good thereof[2] & I do not feel enough of a boy scout (not no more!) to go across the world to try & untie anyone's knots (even yours) especially as untying their knots might mean knotting up oneself![3] How nasty all this sounds but it is true & must be said.

About your books I shall certainly sort them out & arrange to have them sent along. It will give me a bit more space as we have too many books here!

Well, I have never said how pleased I am that you have got to New York. I hope K. gets his job & that all goes well.

You have no idea how busy I am at the moment. Like Mother Florence I am trying to do too much.[4]

Result, I go to the movies & forget about it.

The Hebrides idea is a good one though & money for jam. The publishers give me £75 advance & I go up & stay anywhere I like & write chitchat about it. They want the script by the end of August. The Oxford Press want their book by the end of September. Look out for our Iceland book in New York. It is being published by Random House. The Oxford Press in America are going to do my poems there.[5]

---

1 – The book was *I Crossed the Minch* (1938), illus. Nancy Coldstream, with whom he was having the affair. Nancy Culliford Coldstream (née Sharp) (1909–2001), m. (1931) William Coldstream and later lodged in Hampstead with WHA, who introduced her to FLM. She travelled to the Hebrides with FLM while he was writing *Minch*. Their affair lasted less than two years, beginning early 1937; she was the dedicatee of *The Earth Compels* (1938) and later the subject of *Autumn Journal*, IV. She is Jenny in *AS*. Her portrait of FLM (1938) hangs in the National Portrait Gallery. She married Michael Spender in 1943. See FLM's letters to her, 14 April 1940; 16 Aug. 1940; 2 July 1942, pp. 382–3, 399, 444.
2 – Adapted from Matthew 6.34.
3 – Whereas he is, of course, speaking figuratively, FLM had been a Boy Scout at Sherborne Prep. (FLM to GBM, 6 Oct. 1918, unpublished, *Ms Dan MacNeice*; *Sherborne Prep Register*).
4 – Mrs Florence, landlady.
5 – Respectively, *MP*, *LI* and *Poems* (1937), the last published in New York by Random House, not OUP.

Christopher Isherwood (who wrote 'Mr. Norris Changes Trains') is in London now.[1] He is very nice. Wystan is back from Spain; he could not get much to do there.[2] Anna is very well though large![3] I was at their house the other day listening in to a rugger match. But I actually saw a match between England & Ireland at Twickenham. Very exciting: England won by a point.[4] I have a funny date for Coronation day with old Stahl.[5] We are going to the Mayfair in the evening to entertain a bevy of young American girls who will have come over for the occasion.[6] Most instructive, I should think. I met your old friend Cyril Connolly the other day who said cross words about your mother (unsolicited by me). I thought he was rather nice. He asked Christopher & me to his flat in the middle of the night & gave us champagne & his fat American wife cooked us some scrambled eggs.[7] I had a mild party myself some weeks ago, the chief incident being the production by a little Scotsman of the privately printed indecent poems of Burns – very funny.[8] The other day I drove labour voters to the polls in a by-election for North St. Pancras.[9] I got a puncture for my trouble but it was rather fun.

The weather has been filthy & ruined the crocuses in our garden – such as had so far survived Betsy & Dan! Dan went to a birthday party of a little

1 – Christopher Isherwood (1904–86), educ Repton; Corpus Christi College, Cambridge; King's College, Cambridge (1 year). Collaborated with Auden on three plays for the Group Theatre. Emigrated to USA with Auden in 1939, became US citizen in 1946. Author of *Mr Norris Changes Trains* (1935), *Goodbye to Berlin* (1939) and many other works.
2 – WHA went to join the Civil War in Spain in Jan. 1937 intending to drive an ambulance, but instead worked on radio propaganda in Valencia. He returned after a very short stay.
3 – Anna Shepard: cf. 'You know that Anna is going to have another baby?' (FLM to MM, 10 Nov. 1936), p. 283.
4 – On 13 Feb. 1937, Ireland lost at Twickenham, 8–9.
5 – The Coronation of George VI took place on 12 May 1937.
6 – Mayfair Hotel, Stratton St, London W1.
7 – Cyril Connolly (1903–74), educ. Eton and Balliol College, Oxford. Literary editor of the *Observer* 1942–3 and editor of *Horizon* 1939–50. Author of *The Enemies of Promise* (1938) and other works. He married an American, Jean Bakewell, in 1930 (div. 1950). Connolly later remarked '[FLM] had a very good mind and got a Double First I think, and that made him rather intolerant; yes, he could be inclined to make other people feel they hadn't got these Firsts' (typescript, 'Louis MacNeice: A Radio Portrait', broadcast 7 Sept. 1966; *PRONI D2833/D/5/21*).
8 – *The Merry Muses of Caledonia*, first published anonymously, 1799. FLM was shown either the 1911 Burns Federation limited edition or possibly one of over twenty variant reprintings, all dated 1827 (though actually issued in 1872 and thereafter).
9 – By 'the other day' he means Thursday 4 Feb., when the poll was taken for the by-election. The Labour candidate was H. M. Tibbles, who had unsuccessfully contested the seat in 1935, when the Conservative incumbent, Capt. Sir Ian Fraser, was re-elected. The Conservatives won again in 1937, but by only a narrow margin. Cf. 'North St Pancras Election', *The Times*, 7 Jan., 14; 8 Jan., 9; 21 Jan., 9; 5 Feb., 14.

girl last Saturday & made love to her. His energy is appalling! He is eating rather better. Elizabeth came & saw to him for a weekend while the nurse went away for a rest. I fear I must stop now & review some novels (I am on that racket again – for the Spectator).[1] Humphrey had a meal here the other night & was saying what amusing letters you wrote.[2] Well, all love & the best of luck (tell us more about New York)

as ever. L.

TO *T. S. Eliot*

Faber archive

28 March 1937   4A Keats Grove

Dear Eliot,

Thank you for your letter. The report about the Hebrides project is quite true.[3] It did not occur to me till I saw Wystan the other day that there was any question of my having committed a breach of etiquette because the proposal was made to me like this. Curtis Brown[4] wrote and said that there was a publisher (who turned out to be Longmans) who wanted someone to do a book about the Hebrides and that, if I liked, they could get this job for me. So it seemed to me that the choice was not between my doing a Hebrides book for Longmans and doing it for you (or for anyone else) but between Longmans having <u>their</u> book done by me and having it done by someone else. So, as I badly need money and it seemed an easy, if frivolous piece of work, I agreed to do it for them. I am sorry, however, that I did not mention it to you at the time but it really did not occur to me that under the circumstances you would object to my doing this.

Wystan and I have gone carefully into the criticisms of the Iceland book made by your reader. I shall be bringing back the Mss tomorrow and perhaps I could see either you or Mr de la Mare about it?[5] I shall ring up before I come. Wystan has gone back to Birmingham for sometime but I think he has now done his worst with the text so we hope that it will really now be able to go safely to press!

Yours sincerely
Louis MacNeice

1 – FLM's reviews of fiction appeared in the *Spectator* on 19 Feb., 5 March, 19 March and 2 April 1937.
2 – Humphrey Thackrah.
3 – *I Crossed the Minch*. See also 'The Hebrides: A Tripper's Commentary', *Listener* 18: 456 (6 Oct. 1937); repr. in *SP*, 23–8.
4 – Spencer Curtis Brown (1906–80), literary agent, became manager of his father's agency in 1936.
5 – Richard de la Mare. See FLM to him [1936], n. 1, p. 272.

TO *Hector MacIver*[1]   MS National Library of Scotland

31 March [1937]   4A Keats Grove [postcard]

I shall be in Edinburgh this Saturday night on my way to the Hebrides &
should like to see you. Shall probably stay in the Roxburgh Hotel.[2] Could
you let me know here if there is a chance of seeing you Saturday evening
or sometime on Sunday?

Yours ever
Louis MacNeice

TO *Mary MacNeice*   MS Bodleian

19 April [1937]   Barra, the Hebrides[3] [letter card]

Darling Mary,

In great haste just to say all goes well, Dan goes well at home (your
family are in Italy!) I am having a great time here at the expense of Mr.
Longman but am returning home at end of this week. The Hebrides turn
out to be mild & sleepy places, somewhat like Ireland but the people are
much dourer.[4] God knows what I shall find to write about them. I am
coming back in June or July when there will be more doing – herring
fishing etc. I got your last letter. I am not really steely you know but it is
no good vacillating between sentiments. There are too many conflicting
sentiments so it is better to follow the cold light of reason. Will write soon.
Love ever, L.

1 – Hector Morrison MacIver (1911–66), educ. Edinburgh University. A native of Lewis and
a Gaelic speaker, he taught English at the Royal HS, Edinburgh 1948–66 and also worked
for the BBC in Edinburgh. Author of 'The Outer Isles', in G. S. Moncrieff (ed.), *Scottish
Country* (1935). Cf. 'Auden and MacNeice: Their Last Will and Testament': 'Item to . . .
Hector MacIver . . . I leave a keg of whiskey, the sweet deceiver' (*LI*, CP07, 741). He appears
as Calum in *AS*. FLM later wrote a testimonial for MacIver for a fellowship at Oxford (see
FLM to Balliol College, Oxford, 1961, pp. 688–9). Mary MacIver recalled FLM's visits to
Scotland: 'He had a long, pale, Irish-looking witty face . . . very entertaining in a dry,
sophisticated kind of way' (*Pilgrim Souls*, 1990, 154).
2 – Roxburgh Hotel, Charlotte Square.
3 – Barra, southernmost island of the Hebrides.
4 – He elaborates on this theme in 'The Hebrides: A Tripper's Commentary', *Listener* 18: 456
(6 Oct. 1937), repr. in *SP*, 23–8 and in *I Crossed the Minch*.

TO *Mrs E. R. Dodds*   MS Bodleian

2 May [1937]   4A Keats Grove

Dear Mrs. Dodds,

Here is an instalment on my debt to himself. It leaves, I think, £10 owing, which I hope to send along shortly. Term has started here; I got back from the Hebrides a week ago. Disappointing islands but we saw some very fine seals. The collies are nice & much kinder than the Irish ones. The Scotch are a dull race though & have no sense of time which is all right in the Irish but not in Presbyterians.[1] They are also uniformly ugly & generally suffering from depression. The food is bad & drink hard to obtain. Compton Mackenzie whom we saw twice is even more conceited than you would expect. He has 4 Siamese cats sitting on an Aga cooker. The natives of Barra regard him as a God. They say he has to work at night because there are so many things in Barra to distract him during the day, viz. the clouds & the birds. He has just been writing a life of Pericles & offered to show me the proofs but I got out of that.[2] Talking of proofs I have instalments here both of Iceland book & play. Play should be published in either May or June but they want to time it near its production & Rupert who is being very shifty, can't say when he is producing it because he seems to have quarrelled with Ashley Dukes.[3] My garden is rather attractive now; I wish you would both come & see me. By the way would you like himself to be painted by Coldstream who has now stopped doing films & is free to do lots of portraits (being subsidised by Kenneth Clark)?[4] He has just done Isherwood & is doing Stephen, will do me later, also the Duke of Marlborough. Then if you liked to buy it yourselves, it would look very nice in your drawing room. I saw Wystan in B'ham; he is going back to Colwall & was all smiles about it.[5] Dan flourishes. I am going to send him to a very swish nursery school (Maria Grey).[6] Have you heard from Mary? The Nurse has been away most of a

---

1 – 'Yet it must be admitted that the islanders, like the Southern Irish, show a disregard for time and for penny-in-the-slot efficiency', 'The Hebrides: A Tripper's Commentary', *Listener* 18: 456 (6 Oct. 1937); repr. in *SP*, 26.
2 – Sir Edward Montague Anthony Compton Mackenzie (1883–1972), a prolific author, was not Scottish but settled in Barra and built a house there. *Pericles* was published in 1937.
3 – Rupert Doone. *Out of the Picture* was published by Faber in June, and performed in Nov. 1937.
4 – William Coldstream (1908–87), educ. the Slade 1926–9; started a school of drawing in 1937, known as the Euston Road School. Official war artist, 1943; professor and later principal of the Slade 1949–75. Married Nancy Culliford Sharp in 1931 (later divorced).
5 – Auden was teaching at the Downs School.
6 – Maria Grey Nursery School, north London.

week while my bobtail cousin took over.[1] Mrs. B. wrote to me (though she had said she would never write again) to say that her poor old mother was below par & would I send Dan to console her & she would not object, in spite of all, to my even coming myself. This I have not answered. I hear Westminster Abbey is going to fall down on the Coronation. My father is going to be there complete with crozier. I must go now to my Sunday lunch. Do write & tell me things. How is the Home of Lost Tempers? & have you been on the river?

Love to Greg & Them
Yours ever
Louis

TO *Mary MacNeice*   MS Bodleian

7 May [1937]   4A Keats Grove

Darling Mary,

Many thanks for all the gay skyscrapers. I will be sending you a photo of Dan when I have a new one that is good. Dan is full of beans, says sentences now quite well & after the Coronation is going to a lovely nurseryschool near here where he will eat his lunch with all the others.[2] He has a crush on a little girl called Caroline. Edith came here while I was away in the Hebrides. Did you get my letter from Barra by the way? I enjoyed my holiday very much though the Hebrides themselves are no great shakes. No doubt they are better in summer. My friend came with me & did some drawings for the book.[3] We had a very funny time interviewing Compton Mackenzie who is the most conceited man ever. We also did a great deal of walking. Some of the islands are Presbyterian & some Catholic & the contrast is very amusing.[4] Food pretty terrible on the whole. Nice collie dogs, very aimiable [*sic*] & not noisy like the ones in

---

1–Probably 'Aunt Edith' Burton, JFM's niece, daughter of Caroline Matilda Frizelle (née MacNeice). 'Aunt Edith was born in 1883, which would make her somewhat 'bobtailish' to her 1907 first cousin Louis, I suppose . . . hypothetical conflation has just occurred to me: Aunt Edith had an Old English sheepdog, Cherry, whom we later inherited when Edith became too blind to care for it. The breed, if I remember it correctly, is bobtailed and now I'm wondering whether my father unconsciously hoisted this attribute onto his cousin!' (Dan MacNeice, private correspondence, 2007). See FLM to MM, 10 Nov. 1936, note 1, p. 281.
2–Coronation Day, 12 May.
3–Nancy Coldstream.
4–The Hebrides were predominantly Presbyterian, Barra predominantly Roman Catholic.

Ireland. We also saw some simply enormous grey seals sitting on rocks in the sun. London is busy again. When I came back I found that Anna had had a daughter. All very successful; she is to be called Harriet.[1] Anna had a new anaesthetic called peraldahide(?) very good it seems. My flat here is snowed under with proofs – (a) of the Iceland book (b) of my play which is being called 'Out of the Picture'. I will send you a copy. I heard from Random House in New York the other day. They want to do the Poems which Faber's did plus any more written since.[2] Things are looking up on the whole. Only my hair keeps falling out. I went to a very swish hair-dresser the other day & he simply soused me in strong-smelling stuff called MonteCarlo, most embarrassing. Did I tell you I played rugger (!) in March as guest of the Old Boys of King Edward's Grammar School, Aston?[3] I was very proud of myself for lasting the course. I played tennis two days ago but am handicapped now by being shortsighted. Betsy stayed with George while I was away. Stephen's marriage is not going too well, I gather.[4] Do you remember the Florence's pal, Frank Freeman?[5] It seems that he made a great effort to marry Millicent before Paul did.[6] Your mamma's latest wickedness was to tell your grandmother that Dan had been deadly ill but was now out of danger – quite apocryphal (I was rung up by Paul about it & couldn't make out what he was talking about). Faber's were rather cross with me for doing this Hebrides book for Longman's – all to the good though, as they say <u>they</u> will henceforward give me a potboiler whenever I want one.[7] I thought they might pay me to come to America some day. Wystan & Stephen are going over next spring to lecture on Spain. It is good you have got into a flat. Tell me about it. My garden has jonquils & bluebells & there are tulips coming. I will also send you a copy of Letters from Iceland which should be out in June.[8] I am sorry about letters – lack of them I mean – but while in the Hebrides I had no home news at first hand. You would like my new friend very much (she is a great one for dogs & cats & such). You wouldn't have liked my Christmas friend who went to the West Indies.[9] She came back & was difficult but now I see

1 – Harriet Jessie Minette ('Minky') Shepard (later Hunt) was born 22 April 1937 at 5, Melina Place, St John's Wood, London NW8 ('Births', *The Times*, 24 April 1937, 1).
2 – *Poems* (1935); *Poems* (1937). The American edition was longer, including an additional twenty poems.
3 – Reggie Smith's old school.
4 – Spender had married Inez Pearn on 15 Dec. 1936.
5 – Painter and decorator, who worked for the Florences in Birmingham.
6 – Paul Bloomfield, Mary Ezra's youngish uncle on her mother's side.
7 – See FLM to TSE, 28 March 1937, p. 297.
8 – *LI* was published by Faber in July 1937 (and reissued in July 1941).
9 – Presumably Leonora Corbett.

her no more. (She was, however, highly spectacular to look at!) Now I must get on with the daily grind,

Love ever, (& all wishes to C.)
L.

TO *T. S. Eliot*

20 August [1937]   4A Keats Grove

Dear Eliot,

I am afraid this letter will be a series of questions.

(1) Would you like a poem or poems for the next number of the Criterion or am I too late for it?[1]

(2) Would it be possible at the next printing of 'Letters from Iceland' to add my initials (L.M.) in the table of contents after the heading 'Hetty to Nancy'? Several reviewers attributed this to Wystan, which I feel is bad for business as it suggests that I really wrote very little of the book, whereas actually I wrote 40% of the original part.[2]

(3) Is there any news of an American publisher wishing to do 'Out of the Picture'? I think you said that Harcourt Brace were thinking of it.[3]

(4) Wystan is eager that I should revive an earlier play of mine and get the Group Theatre to do it. It is a straight play – a rather farcical satire on dictatorship but with the characters more in the round.[4] There is practically no verse in it but I wondered if you would like to see it with a view to the possibility of publishing it.

(5) I find that I have about fifteen new poems since those in the book you published. Two of these are long (if Eclogue from Iceland is included). I expect to write several more this year and have been wondering if you would like to do a new collection for me in the spring if I had by then got twenty or more together.

I am sorry to launch so many questions on you at once.

Yours sincerely
Louis MacNeice

1 – The next issue of *Criterion*, 16: 66 (Oct. 1937), included Edwin Muir's review of *LI* and *Out of the Picture* (148), but no poems by FLM.
2 – WHA claimed that FLM wrote only 81 of the total 240 pages (*Time and Tide*, 21 Aug. 1937, 1118; qtd in B. C. Bloomfield and Edward Mendelson, *W. H. Auden: A Bibliography, 1924–1969*, 1972, 30–1).
3 – The American edition of *Out of the Picture*, made possible by the importation of 520 copies from Faber, was published by Harcourt, Brace on 24 Feb. 1938.
4 – *The Station Bell*.

TO *Graham Greene*[1]   MS Tulsa

26 August [1937]   4A Keats Grove

Dear Graham Greene,

Thank you very much for your letter. I should like very much to do sporting articles for Night & Day – especially on rugger (which I know something about) but also on dogracing (which I know nothing about) or indeed on almost anything. And by the way would you like a review any time of one of the Championship Dog Shows? I should like to do that.[2]

> In haste,
> Yours very sincerely
> Louis MacNeice

TO *T. S. Eliot*   Faber archive

4 October [1937]   Bishop's House, Malone Road,
                                        Belfast (as from 4A Keats Grove)

Dear Eliot,

Thank you very much for your letter. I am glad to hear that the Poems may soon need reprinting but I am not at all sure that it is a good idea to include my new poems in the book.[3] I now have nearly twenty, including three long ones, which would almost make a new book by themselves.[4] From talking to people I am pretty sure that while many of the people who bought the original volume of 'Poems' would buy an entirely new book, very few of them would buy a new edition of the original book even if it were announced as containing some new poems.

I do not feel like trying a detective story at the moment, but someone has made a suggestion to me which I think rather good. Namely, that I should write a shortish book about my experience of the teaching of the Classics (at two English schools & three universities).[5] Not however in the form of

1–Graham Greene (1904–91), novelist and playwright, educ. Berkhamsted School and Balliol College, Oxford. Greene was literary editor of the fashionable magazine, *Night and Day*, which ran for six months in 1937. He married Vivien Dayrell-Browning in 1927, cousin of FLM's Oxford friend Adrian Green-Armytage.
2–'With the Kennel Club', *Night and Day* 1: 16 (14 Oct. 1937), 40 (autograph manuscript, 'The Kennel Club', *Ms Tulsa*).
3–Faber published a second impression of *Poems* (1935) in Dec. 1937, without additions.
4–The new book was *The Earth Compels* (1938).
5–Unpublished. The five establishments to which he refers are Sherborne Prep, Marlborough, Merton College, Oxford, Birmingham University and Bedford College, London.

a treatise but impressionistically – e.g. presentation of the classroom or lecture room, specimens of Greek & Latin literature <u>as they appear</u> in translationese, some good translations for contrast, the point of the whole thing being to show the very different & distorted ideas people in schools (& universities) get of the 'Classics'. One might have also a few words against pseudo-Hellenism etc. Some of the book could be in verse.

I am over here for the weekend; coming back on Wednesday.

Yours sincerely
Louis MacNeice

TO *W. H. Auden* MS Buffalo[1]

21 October 1937   4A Keats Grove

Dear Wystan,

I have to write you a letter in a great hurry and so it would be out of the question to try to assess your importance. I take it that you are important and, before that, that poetry itself is important. Poets are not legislators (what is an 'unacknowledged legislator' anyway?), but they put facts and feelings in italics, which makes people think about them and such thinking may in the end have an outcome in action.

Poets have different methods of italicisation. What are yours? What is it in your poetry which shakes people up?

It is, I take it, a freshness – sometimes of form, sometimes of content, usually of both. You are very fertile in pregnant and unusual phrases and have an aptitude for stark and compelling texture. With regard to content, the subject-matter of your poems is always interesting and it is a blessing to our generation, though one in the eye for Bloomsbury, that you discharged into poetry the subject-matters of psycho-analysis, politics and economics. Mr. Eliot brought back ideas into poetry but he uses the ideas, say, of anthropology more academically and less humanly than you use Marx or Groddeck.[2] This is because you are always taking sides.

It may be bad taste to take sides but it is more a vital habit than the detachment of the pure aesthete. The taunt of being a schoolboy (which, when in the mood, I should certainly apply myself) is itself a compliment because it implies that you expect the world and yourself to develop. This

---

1–Published as 'Letter to W. H. Auden', *NV*, Nov. 1937, 11–12.

2–Auden was fascinated by the theories of George Groddeck (1866–1934) concerning psychosomatic illness. Cf. FLM to ERD, 22 Nov. [1939], p. 368 and FLM to NC, 15 Feb. 1940, *Ms Bodleian, MacNeice and Nancy Coldstream.*

expectation inevitably seems vulgar to that bevy of second-rate sensitive minds who write in our culture weeklies.

'Other philosophies have described the world; our business is to change it.' Add that if we are not interested in changing it, there is really very little to describe. There is just an assortment of heterogeneous objects to make Pure Form out of.[1]

You go to extremes, of course, but that is all to the good. There is still a place in the sun for the novels of Virginia Woolf, for still-life painting and for the nature lover. But these would probably not survive if you and your like, who have no use for them, did not plump entirely for something different.

Like most poets you are limited. Your poems are strongly physical but not fastidiously physical. This is what I should expect from someone who does not like flowers in his room.[2]

Your return to a versification in more regular stanzas and rhymes is, I think, a very good thing. The simple poem, however, does not always wear too well. At first sight we are very pleased to get the swing of it so easily and understand it so quickly, but after first acquaintance it sometimes grows stale. A. E. Housman, whom I join you in admiring, was a virtuoso who could get away with cliché images and hymn-tune metres, but, as you would, I think, admit, his methods are not suitable to anyone who has a creed which is either profound or elaborate.

I am therefore a little doubtful about your present use of the ballad form. It is very good fun but it does not seem to me to be your *natural* form as I doubt if you can put over what you want to say in it. Of course if you can put over half of what you want to say to a thousand people, that may well be better than putting over two thirds of it to a hundred people. But I hope that you will not start writing down to the crowd for, if you write down far enough, you will have to be careful to give them nothing that they don't know already and then your own end will be defeated. Compromise is necessary here, as always, in poetry.

I think you have shown great sense in not writing 'proletarian' stuff (though some reviewers, who presumably did not read your poems, have accused you of it). You realise that one must write about what one knows. One may not hold the bourgeois creed, but if one knows only bourgeois one must write about them. They all after all contain the germ of their opposite. It is an excellent thing (lie quiet Ezra, Cambridge, Gordon

1–On 'pure form', see FLM to AB, 25 Sept. 1926, n. 3, p. 122.
2–Cf. FLM on WHA: 'He did not seem to *look* at anything, admitted he hated flowers ...' (*SAF*, 114).

Square,[1] with your pure images, pure celebration, pure pattern, your scrap-albums of ornament torn eclectically from history) that you should have written poems about preparatory schools. Some of the Pure Poets maintained that one could make poems out of anything, but on the ground, not that subject was important, but that it didn't matter. You also would admit that anything can go into poetry, but the poet must first be interested in the thing in itself.

As for poetic drama, you are now swinging away from the Queer Play. This, like the formal change in your lyrics, is also a good thing and also has its danger. But the danger is not so great for you as it would be for some. Whatever the shape of your work, it will always have ideas in it. Still, when authors like Denis Johnston, who can write excellent straight plays, feel impelled to go over to crooked plays and 'poetic writing', there must be some good reason for it and it may appear perverse in you to forget your birthright and pass them in the opposite direction to a realism which may not be much more natural to you than poetry is to them.[2]

These are the criticisms which occur to me at the moment. I have no time to expand on your virtues, but I must say that what I especially admire in you is your unflagging curiosity about people and events. Poetry is related to the sermon and you have your penchant for preaching, but it is more closely related to conversation and you, my dear, if any, are a born gossip.[3]

> Yours ever,
> LOUIS MACNEICE

1 – Cf. Ezra Pound, 'Canto 1', 68: 'Lie quiet, Divus'. The Hogarth Press was housed in Gordon Square, home of the Woolfs; also resident in the Square were the Stracheys, Clive Bell and John Maynard Keynes.
2 – Denis Johnston (1901–84), educated Cambridge and Harvard, author of *The Old Lady Says 'No'* (performed at the Gate Theatre, Dublin, 1929), and *The Moon on the Yellow River* (1931).
3 – Cf. WHA, 'In Defence of Gossip', *Listener*, 22 Dec. 1937, 1371–2.

1938

TO *Hector MacIver*   MS National Library of Scotland

20 March 1938   4A Keats Grove

Dear Hector,

In haste. Thank you very much for your letter.[1] My book ought to be out pretty soon (April 4th). I will send you a copy. I'm afraid you won't like it. It is largely chatty, catty or irrelevant.

Two points occur to me. (1) If your family should see it (perhaps they won't) they may be surprised (a) at my illustrator's name,[2] (b) at no mention being made of 'my wife' in the book. If they ask you about this, you might say (a) that she always draws & paints under her maiden name (true anyway) & (b) (also more or less true) that I have 'stylised' the whole narrative: Object Side = Myself plus a couple of fictitious commentators & that therefore I did not (on the subject side) wish to mix up reality & fiction.[3] Or what words you will.

(2) There are several pages about Compton Mackenzie in it. I hope he won't take umbrage at them. If anyone you know sees him, they might tell him that they are meant in a friendly spirit.[4]

1 – Of 6 Feb. 1938, in which MacIver praised FLM's article in the *Listener* ('The Hebrides: A Tripper's Commentary', 6 Oct. 1937, 718–20).
2 – Nancy Coldstream used her maiden name, Sharp. MacIver recalled: 'So much for Louis' visit. More than twenty years after, my family still became virulent when discussing the "immorality" of his visit' (*Pilgrim Souls*, 99).
3 – The fictitious commentators were principally Percevel and Crowder, but also Foot and Head, Guardian Angel and Hetty.
4 – Not quite true. See FLM to Mrs ERD 2 May and to MM 7 May 1937, pp. 299 and 300. Mackenzie would later recall FLM's visit: 'The editor of the chief Opposition paper in Belfast had been on Barra this summer and from him I had heard about the great courage the Bishop of Down had shown in criticizing the behaviour of the Orangemen. So the first thing I said to Louis MacNeice when he arrived with a young woman whose name I have forgotten was to express my admiration for the courageous attitude of his episcopal father. "Oh, I'm not interested in what my father is doing". And as he said this he looked quickly at his young female companion as if for an approving nod. I suppose he was piqued because I did not express my interest in his poetry. As I had never read any of it this was unfortunately beyond me . . . . In a book he wrote called *I Crossed the Minch*, which he seemed to think was a feat of condescension, he wrote with evident disapproval of my wearing a green jumper to match a green tweed suit and went on to talk about the rich white rug in the billiards-room as if it

I have also, by the way, mentioned you once or twice.[1] I hope you don't mind.

My life is very full. I am just moving house. I have a new book of poems coming out in April.[2] Let me know when you come to London.

Yours ever

Louis MacNeice

P.S. Please burn this. (This is not neurotic of me. It's just because I have one or two people about only too eager to blackmail me!)

TO *Mary MacNeice* MS Bodleian

29 April [1938]   As from 16A Primrose Hill Road,
                                   London NW3 [hereafter 16A
                                   Primrose Hill Road].

My dear,

I wrote you half a letter but lost it. I am sorry not to have written for such a time but have been terribly busy – moving house, looking for another house & looking for another factotum. I have parted with the old Nurse because Dan, I think, had rather outgrown her; she was really a small-child expert & very good though she was for that, had served her time, so we parted with mutual respect. I then took Dan over to Ireland where he has been being supervised for the moment by an accredited woman. I hope to get into the above address in about a week & then he will come back. I am just on the point of choosing between two women – an English widow (aet. 37) & an Hungarian girl (aet. 28). I had 83 replies to an advertisement in the Daily Telegraph![3]

The new place is a maisonette overlooking Primrose Hill (very near the Zoo, which I shall join!) with views at the back to Highgate.[4] The only snag is that there is no garden. Nearly all the places with gardens are <u>lower</u>

---

was an ostentatious display of luxury to find across the Minch; it was in fact a cheap Indian rug that cost eight guineas' (Compton Mackenzie, *My Life and Times*, 1963–71, vol. VII). Cf. 'Auden and MacNeice: Their Last Will and Testament': 'Item, to Compton Mackenzie, a sprig of heather' (*LI*, CP07, 737).

1–There are numerous references to MacIver, including 'On Those Islands (A Poem for Hector MacIver)'.

2–He is moving to 16A Primrose Hill; the book is *The Earth Compels*.

3–He employed the Hungarian girl, Sophie Popper.

4–*Zoo*, illus. by Nancy Sharp, was published by Michael Joseph in Nov. 1938.

maisonettes which means that someone has to sleep in the basement. However we are right on Primrose Hill & handy for Regent's Park & still within possible distance of Hampstead Heath. Dan when at school is there from 9 till 4 when he is in the open air most of the time but on the other days he will either go to the parks or play with some friends' children in two gardens in Hampstead. He is having a good time in Ireland though I imagine he plays up the chaps a bit. When he comes back I am going to make a point of taking him out a lot so that the new woman does not get in any way piqued by it as the last one sometimes was. I told you, I think, that some friends of mine drove him & me down to the country where he had a sleep after lunch with a large black-&-white-cat. Which reminds me – I must get a cat to start off the new place properly. I shall now have more room – 5 rooms instead of 4; the last tenants fitted it all up with windowboxes, so I must try & keep that up. Betsy & I are at the moment staying in a Hampstead maisonette lent me by some friends who also left their maid. I am supposed to be finishing a book but can never get much work done when I am alone. The Hebrides book which came out at the beginning of April got a very good press. Incidentally I got £109-18-4 for the first 6 months of the Iceland book. It goes as soon as it comes, of course! My new book of poems is just out too.[1] Term has already started & I am having my sausages-&-mash once more in the Hall of the Thousand Virgins. Which reminds me – I received a wild outpouring yesterday addressed to Wystan & me, denouncing us for immorality & signed 'Isabella Purgola (virgin who may revenge herself on your kind some day)'. Certainly must be a virgin, as Dodds said, who visited me last night.

Your mother tried again! On the last day of last term I was rung up by someone who said Mr. Mavrogordato wanted to see me, so I being a fool, said 'certainly, certainly,' & who should turn up in Bedford but Jack Mavrogordato & your mother behind him.[2] So as I could not have a scene

---

1 – EC.

2 – John George 'Jack' Mavrogordato, CMG (1905–87), educ. Charterhouse, Christ Church and Gray's Inn. Friend of Mrs Beazley, a naturalist, member of the British Ornithological Union and Director of the International Association of Falconry. He had been a pupil of Jacky Beazley, whose wife Marie he described as 'an enchantress, and it was through her that I became very friendly with the family on a social basis, and was a frequent visitor at the lovely old "Judges' Lodgings" in St Giles' (*Behind the Scenes: An Autobiography*, 1982, 35). Dan MacNeice wrote of Mavrogordato: 'he was very close in age to my mother herself, unlike the majority of her Oxford chums who tended to be a full decade older. This would explain how he survived the Great War, when so many of the others didn't: he was too young to serve' [DM, private correspondence, 2007].

in Bedford I put them in the auditorium in a lecture room & myself stood in a point of vantage behind the desk. Whereupon your mother burst into tears, after which she explained that she wanted to buy a house for Dan but this could not be done unless I signed a document. So I said I was signing no documents & after a bit of the usual nonsense they went away with nothing accomplished.

It was a very nice weekend when I took Dan over to Ireland, & we went a drive through County Down which was brimming with gorse. Dan is extremely talkative now but still not awfully interested in books, though he likes Beatrix Potters. Sometimes he & I are going down to stay with the Cannings (you remember?) in Dorset.

I am sorry you have been having colds. I seem to get ailments very little – touching wood – these days. Ditto Dan. O & I forgot, I will do the Polyfoto as soon as Dan comes back.

I wonder if you saw a rugger match. The rugger season was crazy over here – very high scoring (Ireland coming out of it badly!)[1] The charwoman stole my tennis racket, so I am going to stand myself a new one. Am also thinking of joining a squash club, life being so sedentary. I stayed in Oxford last week with the Dodds' & met one of the Merton scouts who said to me 'Ah, things are much more quiet since your time. They think of nothing but their books now.' I have been lent an enormous car (Ford V8) for 3 months.

Well, be happy; love & best wishes to both,

Louis

TO *T. S. Eliot*   Faber archive

14 October [1938]   16A Primrose Hill Road

Dear Eliot,

I find that my Easter term ends March 21st but I think I could get away, if necessary, on March 18th. My summer term begins on April 25th. This would leave me about three weeks in America – roughly, I suppose (?), from March 25th–7th [*sic*] till April 16th–18th. I imagine that my lectures would have to be squeezed in immediately after my arrival or immediately

---

1 – Ireland lost to England at Lansdowne Road, 14–36 (12 Feb.), to Scotland at Murrayfield, 14–23 (26 Feb.), and to Wales at St Helen's, 5–11 (12 March).

before my departure but I don't mind that. I shall be very grateful if you can fix up anything for me with the people over there.[1]

Yours sincerely
Louis MacNeice

TO *T. S. Eliot*   Faber archive

9 November 1938   16A Primrose Hill Road

Dear Eliot,
    Thank you very much for your letter and (still more!) for your sponsorship. I shall write at once to Theodore Spencer and say I am willing to give the lecture at Harvard.[2] I shall also be on for the other places you mention. Four lectures would suit me but I shouldn't object to one or two extra.

Yours sincerely
Louis MacNeice

P.T.O.
[*overleaf*]

This is really a matter for your treasury department but could someone possibly let me have a statement of my royalties etc. which I have received from you during the 1st two Income Tax years i.e. April 1936–April 1938. My Income Tax people are being tiresome and refusing to allow me relief till I give them some more details of my literary income.

1 – In response, Eliot wrote almost immediately to Elizabeth Manwaring, Department of English, Wellesley College, Massachusetts, describing FLM as 'one of the best of our younger poets, whose work is I am sure known to you' (TSE to Elizabeth Manwaring, 18 Oct. 1938, Ms Wellesley).
2 – Spencer wrote (3 Dec.) to invite FLM to stay with him in Cambridge during his visit to Harvard the following spring. Cf. also Spencer to FLM, 22 March 1939 (Ms Bodleian, Ms Res, c. 590, Box 15).

[29?] November 1938   16A Primrose Hill Road

Dear Eliot,
Here are some notes on 'Autumn Journal' for the Spring Catalogue
in haste,
Yourssincerely [*sic*]
Louis MacNeice

<u>Autumn Journal</u>.

A long poem of from 2,000 to 3,000 lines written from August to
December 1938. Not strictly a journal but giving the tenor of my
intellectual & emotional experiences during that period.

It is about nearly everything which from firsthand experience I consider
significant.

It is written in sections averaging about 80 lines in length. This division
gives it a <u>dramatic</u> quality, as different parts of myself (e.g. the anarchist,
the defeatist, the sensual man, the philosopher, the would-be good citizen)
can be given their say in turn.

It contains rapportage [*sic*], metaphysics, ethics, lyrical emotion,
autobiography, nightmare.

There is a constant interrelation of abstract & concrete. Generalisations
are balanced by pictures.

Places presented include Hampshire, Spain, Birmingham, Ireland, & –
especially – London.

It is written throughout in an elastic kind of quatrain. This form (a) gives
the whole poem a formal unity but (b) saves it from monotony by allowing
it a great range of appropriate variations.

The writing is direct; anyone could understand it.

I think this is my best work to date; it is both a panorama and a
confession of faith.

L.M.

5 December [1938]   16A Primrose Hill Road

Dear Eliot,

Thank you for your letter. I am afraid I cannot promise the long poem before the end of the year.[1] There are 1700 lines written but I have several more sections to write. Also I am going abroad for Christmas and I feel that I might be moved, as they say, to write the final section then.

As to the Hippolytus: it is to be ready for the Group Theatre according to schedule by the end of February.[2] I shall translate it roughly on the same principles as the Agamemnon but the choruses will be treated more formally and less literally (this is because Euripides' choruses seem to me less integral to the play). I cannot think of anything to say about it in a blurb unless you say that the Hippolytus is a very actable play & that this is intended to be the most actable version in English.

Tomorrow I am finding out about sailings to America. Perhaps I could come round and discuss the whole American scheme with you again soon?

Yours sincerely

Louis MacNeice

---

1 – *AJ*.

2 – The translation of the *Hippolytus* did not come to fruition.

1939

MS Yale

TO *Eleanor Clark*[1]

Friday [21 April 1939] Cunard White Star /
RMS *Queen Mary*

Darling,

It was simply horrifying not being able to see you on the pier. I don't know what came over me (perhaps it was being up all night but when I got up on deck I expected to see you at once & after two minutes of not being able to find you, I just got panic-stricken & the pier looked like thousands of faces which couldn't be pinned down & I began to think everyone was you but of course they weren't; I dare say I must have looked straight at you some of the time (did I?) but I couldn't see properly, darling, & (which is unusual with me) I couldn't even remember what kind of hat you were wearing. Perhaps it may have been my fault for I still find you hard to recognise in a hat anyway, being chiefly used to you without. Now it is worrying me that you may be thinking that you really can't have anything to do with a man who can't even pick out his love from a crowd of people on a pier. Please don't think that darling. I know it was silly of me to get in a panic but I was so afraid of the boat going before I could see you

---

1–Eleanor Clark (1913–96), author, who grew up in Roxbury, Connecticut. A graduate of Vassar, she moved in circles associated with the left-wing political journal *Partisan Review* and became briefly married to Trotsky's Czech secretary, Jan Frankel (alias John Glenner), who was resident in New York during the thirties (Leon Trotsky Exile papers, *Houghton Library*). She worked briefly as an editor with W. W. Norton, and during the war she worked for the US Office of Strategic Services, Washington DC. A member of The Corporation of Yaddo and a Guggenheim Fellow (1946–7, 1949–50), she published five novels, including *The Bitter Box* (1946), *Baldur's Gate* (1970), *Gloria Mundi* (1979) and *Camping Out* (1986). Her travel books included *Rome and a Villa* (1952) and *The Oysters of Locmariquer* (National Book Award, 1965); a memoir appeared in 1977, *Eyes, Etc.* She married Robert Penn Warren in 1952. Early on, she co-edited with Horace Gregory a selection of new writing, *New Letters in America* (New York, 1937), which carried her short story 'Call Me Comrade' (151–69). FLM met her at a *Partisan Review* party in New York in early April 1939; they began a long-distance affair and a correspondence which ended when he married Hedli Anderson in July 1942. FLM wrote: 'At this time I met someone whom according to fairy story logic I was bound to meet but according to common sense never. A woman who was not a destroyer. Something inside me changed gear, began to run easily on top' (*SAF*, 204). She is Isabel in *AS*.

again. Which – just because of my panic, I suppose . . . it did. Darling, you're not to be cross with me about it. I have been unhappy about it ever since – as if, the moment you crossed the gangway, some bloody Queen Mary spell had come down upon me & bewitched my vision. I hope you got my radiogram. I am thinking about you all the time & hating this Atlantic. I don't think I've ever missed anyone to this extent. Of course, I would rather know you & miss you than not know you & not miss you but it is hell, my love. However I mustn't go lamenting to you. I should like to tell you what lovely times I had in New York with a lovely girl but then you were there, so you know. And it is, as you said, very good indeed to be leaving in the middle (in that sense); but you are not to slide back again, darling. Because we shall be able to have the most wonderful times – lots of them. We could, by the way, have had our bouillon in comfort if you'd stowed away as there is nobody else in my cabin after all. I feel rather sleepy now (I think it is about 5.00) so I shall go & lie in a deckchair. I hope you are not too exhausted, darling, by all this lack of sleep etc. I was worried about you this morning when you felt funny. Darling (that suggests to me), I suppose you were on that pier? Because I'd much rather have the horrible irony of your being there & my being unable to see you than that you should have had to go away because you felt bad. I think it is so good you having gaiety. So few people have both beauty & intelligence & a conscience & gaiety but you seem to, darling. I am too feeble in the head just at the moment to be able to tell you articulately the things I like about you but, putting it shortly, you are, as they say, a revelation to me. The sort of thing (person I mean: forgive me) that I have felt a longing for for a long time without being able to give any conspectus of it; anyhow I never thought I should meet it. Darling, you are quite right about letters. This looks awful, all that I am writing so banal & frigid & inadequate; I want to be able to use my voice to you, darling. Writing is all very well in its way but this is just not its way. All the same, Eleanor darling, you must write me lots & lots of letters; I must have some communication with you. And you're to come over soon, my love, & see if I can recognise you on the other pier. (I think I shall). Now I shall go to that deckchair. On this boat I shall be writing all the one letter so it will no doubt be both long & repetitive. Only you mustn't mind my repeating certain things because they mean such a lot to me; if you were with me, I could repeat them in kisses but, as it is, one's just got to sacrifice all literary standards, darling, in the attempt to remind you of things. The chief things are (a) that I love you & (b) that you have got to love me & (c) that if (a) & (b) are established, ((a) is anyway), things will be lovely & there is nothing really – except in the short run – to be sad about. My love, I will talk about some other things in letters besides you & me (in case that's boring you) but just at the moment it is so on my brain – or heart – that I can't be nice & observational & full of intelligent commentary about this bloody boat which is taking me away from you or about the thoroughly tiresome (until you come) place I am going to. As for New York, I shall always be so sentimental now if I see any pictures of it, that no doubt I shall have to be careful about going to the movies; I mean, one would look rather silly bursting into tears in the middle of a nice, slick comedy just because there was a skyscraper around.

Darling, be happy & keep writing & love me well. Just three precepts (I should like to think they might link up with each other). // Later: Before dinner, darling, I drank two Daiquiris in your honour (not being a drink I should have thought of otherwise). There are not nearly as many people on the boat as when I came over & what there are seem pretty dull. The First Class however runs to Spencer Tracy.[1] Tomorrow I shall start reading & writing. I want you, darling, to send me that list of books you promised. I am appalled to think that I shan't hear from you for, I suppose, about ten days at least & that it will be still longer before we can get to the point of answering each other's letters. Which is all the more reason why you must write often. Talking of writing, I went away without sending the Saturday Review their piece. I suppose, darling, you wouldn't, while you are still there, like to be my literary agent in America (25% commission)? Talking of literature, I don't at all feel like going back & mixing with the old gang in London; I am feeling a nausea for literary sherry parties. (Better Fifty Years of Auden) There are so many things we haven't talked about, darling, but most of them are too elusive, to be treated merely in a letter. There is a noise of pingpong balls going on outside the window & I am filled with a quite unjust hate for my fellow passengers – only because here they all are & you are not. It seems all wrong to me. Darling, that was a very nice & rambling evening we had last night; but it was wicked of them to keep turning us out. I think you are perfect, my love, for spending evenings with: because you are very lovely & very intelligent & very sympathetic & you like to laugh & you are not snobbish or embittered or selfsatisfied or any of the other distressing things one or other of which one seems to find in everyone. Of course you are catty but I rather like

1 – After disembarking on 26 April, Spencer Tracy had some difficulty getting to London. So many people had turned out to see him that he couldn't get out of his train compartment at Waterloo ('News in Brief', *The Times*, 27 April 1939, 14).

that. O hell, darling, now I have to go: fill in some form or other. By the way, you're all wrong about it being bad for one's writing to be practical. At least I can't see why it should be. You will remember to send me your writings, won't you, darling? I suppose it's very bad style (I don't know about prose, you know) to keep saying 'darling' but that's the way I feel, darling. I had better go now. Buenas Noches & much, much love. // Saturday: I stayed in bed till lunch & now feel considerably brighter. They have some photos here of people on the pier seeing us off but I still don't see you anywhere. However I must stop talking about that or I shall be making it into some sort of symbol of failure or evil omen or something else quite irrational. The only point is that you must forgive me for it. Well, darling, I have been thinking about you again (one-track mind I seem to have) & it has been occurring to me (darling, please don't mind me if I seem candid or impertinent or any of those things) that you are almost virginal (this has nothing to do with how many times you have slept with people; nor of course is it an insult) & that therefore we were probably quite right not to sleep together just now because that makes it (a) much more delicate but (b) much fuller of possibilities; when we have a lot of time, it will evolve very naturally – beautifully. All the same I feel very Western Wind about it.[1] And you MUST COME, darling. There shall I be, waiting in the benighted Old World, &, if you don't come, I shall just give up the affections & turn Parisian. One of the first things I shall do in London is clear up the situation with my married friend.[2] Of course, I have been cleaning it up for some time – negatively, by explaining I am no longer in love with her – but I had better now, I think, make it quite positive that I am definitely orientated elsewhere & therefore cannot be banked upon for any relationship out of the ordinary. Talking of personal relationships, darling, there is one thing I want to impress on you: that is that you must never do anything for me out of mere kindly feeling if it is against either your impulses or your better judgement. If for instance you thought of going off with someone else, you mustn't not go merely because you thought it would hurt me (which of course it would); you must only not go if you find that you really don't want to or if you think that you yourself will be happier if you stay with me. Now is that straight? Because however forlorn I should be without you, it would be better than that you should stay with me merely to be kind to me. You must always want something

1 – 'O Western wind, when wilt thou blow / That the small rain down can rain? / Christ, that my love were in my arms . . .' Anon, 16th (?) century, Quiller-Couch, *Oxford Book of English Verse: 1250–1900*, 53.
2 – Nancy Coldstream.

for yourself out of a relationship; even the King of Spain's daughter did, she liked silver nutmegs.[1] Well, darling, you are welcome to all my nutmegs as long as ever you like them (May it be long). My visual memory, darling, is, I am glad to say, proving a little better than my real vision. But now I am not in a panic. In fact (if only I were sure that you wouldn't really vanish) I should be in a state of vast encouragement. Because I shall be able to get on with things quite happily if I know you are going to reappear. You will won't you, my love (I mean – see above – you will because you want to?) Now I must go & read. // 11 p.m. I tried to radio-telephone you tonight but you were out (with your young Irishman? damn him). I shall try again tomorrow; I hope you won't mind. After all what are these modern amenities for? Before dinner I had a drink with one Geoffrey Nares who is a friend of Christopher's & has just driven from California to New York via New Orleans; he is crazy about the South.[2] I have been thinking about this War question. You say quite rightly, darling, that it will be just a dirty war of power politics, so what am I doing in it? All you are interested in is 'The Revolution' & you say that, if one is going to take action, the only thing to do is to foment the revolution directly. But look: if a war with Germany starts, it will be no damn good having an immediate revolution at home or a mutiny at the front. Because that will not (as you suggested) encourage the workers in Germany to revolt. It is much more difficult to revolt if your country is winning a war &, on your plan, Germany would be winning. (In Russia the war on that front was being lost.) Now supposing people just did nothing & let Hitler win? It is perfectly possible for him to Hitlerise the rest of Europe & I do think that Hitler is a worse bargain than Chamberlain (who, God knows, is bad enough). It's no good telling the ordinary people throughout Europe to keep their hands clean of power politics & sit down & let Hitler win until they have the chance of a nice pure revolution of their own – a holy war. Because if Hitler wins Europe, they won't have the chance. The analogy of Russia is misleading. England intervened in Russia after the great war but they couldn't bring it off – partly owing to the spirit of the people but partly owing to geography. No country in Europe has got the Russian

1 – Nursery rhyme: 'I had a little nut-tree, nothing would it bear / But a silver nutmeg and a golden pear; / The King of Spain's daughter came to visit me, / And all was because of my little nut-tree.'
2 – Christopher Isherwood. Geoffrey Owen Nares (1917–42), actor and stage designer, was the younger son of the English actor Owen Nares (1888–1943). Lieutenant Geoffrey Nares died while on active service in Egypt with the 12th Royal Lancers in 1942. Cf. 'Fallen Officers', *The Times*, 31 Aug. 1942, 6.

advantage in geography. It seems to me that the only hope in this war (if it happens) is for the people of England to enter into it on certain terms with the government (i.e. that it shall be terminated as quickly as possible by negotiation & with no Versailles nonsense). This sounds quixotic but it could have been done in the last war. Now it is possible that such an ending to a war would be the end of Hitler. & the end of Hitler would also put a check to the fascist trend in England. A gradual & roundabout way of doing things but you must remember, darling, when you put your money on the lower classes & their <u>internal</u> capacity for revolt, that the English lower classes won't realise that capacity until they are beaten to it from outside. & I still think it preferable (a choice of evils of course) that they should be beaten to it by a war against Hitler (during which their own country will go partly fascist) than by passive assimilation in a completely fascist Europe. Now if I hold this view, darling, i.e. that it is a choice of evils but that the lesser evil may lead indirectly to good, it would not be logical of me to say 'I am going to keep out of things until I can choose some course which is directly & definitely good.' The only logic for me is to go in with it (history after all has been mainly a choice of evils & one can't be Utopian about it).[1] All right, darling, now the next point (I know you will be thinking all this terribly childish & unenlightened & bourgeois but that won't prevent me saying it): on these premises, if I get involved in this impure War, I may as well be involved in it in one of the less impure ways. Now all the men I know are trying to book themselves nice little jobs on the Propaganda Ministry & I could probably trade on my qualifications to do something like that. But if one's going to be defiled, one may as well keep one's mind out of it. ∴ I cannot use my claims to any privileged position as they are all mental claims. ∴ I just have to be fatalist & see what they set me to do. In the course of that, if I think the time has come to be vocal (or if I change my mind about the whole situation), then, if I have the courage (which is problematical) I can start being vocal. Or do you think I am terribly muddled about it? I only wish, darling, you would tell me what <u>you</u> would do if you belonged in England. Not that I think there will be a war this time but I suppose there will be sooner or later. Well, I think that's enough of this as I don't like to make you cross.

I will just start on this page before saying Goodnight (I am afraid this is going to be the hell of a long letter). Tomorrow I think of reading some

1 – 'I had been tormented by the ethical problems of the war . . . I had decided, however, that any choice now was a choice of evils and that it was clear which was the lesser' (*SAF*, 21).

Hawthorne & possibly doing my Greek play, for which today I feel too tired. I believe – to revert – that Christopher & Wystan have both gone quite pacifist. But I can't see, if one wasn't pacifist over Spain or Munich, how one is justified in being pacifist now; I admit the casus belli from now on is bound to be a [*illegible*] one but the implications of such a war are the same, i.e. there is the same chance in a roundabout way of preventing complete fascism all over Europe. But to leave that (once again): if I don't get you by telephone tomorrow, I shall just try you again on Monday (I am terribly obstinate, you know, darling) because I so much want to know how you are & if you've got over your coffee jag. You see, once I've found you're still there when I'm not, I shall find it easier to subsist by letters. By the way, the Queen Mary in future is going to leave on Wednesdays, so if you mark your letters via her & post them on Tuesdays, they will get to me in the quickest possible time. If they are unspecified, the American Post Office like to send them by American boats which are slower. & now goodnight, my love, & sleep well & be happy & remember me in your orisons or whatever revolutionary girls have. Goodnight, darling. //

Sunday: Darling, I have just had my Daiquiri on you; it was much better than a Daiquiri could be. It was lovely hearing you on the phone in spite of the machine being crazy. Now I feel ever so much better & very happy. I can see you when I shut my eyes. Darling, it strikes me this letter must read awfully frigid. – especially all this about wars. They tell me here that noone in England dreams there is going to be a war, so perhaps we had better stop arguing about it until I get better informed (?). But about this letter, I feel anything but frigid, darling, & I do wish I could put it across. Not but what you must know how I feel anyway. I feel utterly in love with you, darling, & so all sorts of clichés keep running to my pen but then I remember you know about literature, so I have to keep them back for fear of offending your taste. However I shall copy out my little poem for you before I finish this; it is a kind of love poem in the third person.[1] I have been reading E. E. Cummings on this boat & find him once again very sympathetic (perhaps more so now, having been to your country). He is sometimes very sentimental but he has got an élan.[2] Darling, if you would

1 – The poem was 'Meeting Point' (*PP*, CP07, 183, 686).
2 – FLM had an ambivalent response to the poetry of Cummings. He reviewed *The Enormous Room* in 1928 (*Oxford Outlook* 10: 47 (Nov.), 171–3), and in 'Our God Bogus' he described him as a 'ragamuffin', though 'there is form in his disintegration' (*Sir Galahad* 2 (14 May 1929), 3–4). He was critical of him in 'Poetry Today', yet considered him 'the best of his group' (*The Arts Today*, ed. G. Grigson, 6 Sept. 1935, 25–67, repr. *SLC*, 10–44).

like that, I shall be seeing John Lehmann when I get back & could tell him to put a story of yours into New Writing.[1] They don't pay awfully well but they have prestige in England. I could also, if you liked, put you on to my English agent. I shall send you my new book from Faber's as soon as I can get a copy.[2] I don't suppose you will like all of it – some of it you will think bourgeois & some Stalinist (or are those the same thing?) & some of it is perhaps distressingly personal. I wrote a lot of it, as I told you, when I was in a very bad way over my old friend.[3] Darling, meeting you is like coming up to light after living in an underground country; there were lots of nice people, difficult people too, down there but the trouble was they were all underground – I mean it was in their system. & there was nobody underground so lovely or charming as you or so exactly what I have always wanted. I had really of course got cynical about what I wanted because of course one can want the moon & I had half thought, as I told you, of settling down underground with the least difficult of the undergrounders. But all that Faute de Mieux policy is now cancelled for good. Even if you were to vanish, darling. For once one has seen the light (as they say) one can't go back. But you are not to vanish. Definitely not. Darling, I am sorry I could not give you anything more permanent than roses. Or perhaps they are? The roses I wrote that poem about – in a window against the snow – always seem to me permanent, so perhaps Friday's could be too?[4] & now, my love, I am still feeling much encouraged; perhaps it will be chronic. I began reading The House of the Seven Gables & will tell you what I think when I have read more of it.[5] I met a nice young man, small dark American called Saffer,[6] who is going to Oxford with some sort of fellowship in Chemistry & who is crazy about Joyce's 'Work in Progress' which he thinks (God help him) is 400 years ahead of its time (or perhaps one should say God help 400 years ahead).[7] He has lent me the Grapes of Wrath which, I hear, has been damned by Christopher.[8] I have read some of that

1–FLM had recently published in John Lehmann's New Writing 'June Thunder' (autumn 1937) and 'Three Poems' (later 'Trilogy for X') (autumn 1938).
2–AJ was published by Faber in May 1939.
3–Nancy Coldstream.
4–'Snow', written in Jan. 1935 (CP07, 24).
5–Nathaniel Hawthorne, The House of Seven Gables (1851).
6–Charles Martin Saffer, Jr. (1914–2004), educ. MIT (PhD 1938); and visiting Research Fellow in Chemistry at Oxford in 1939.
7–'Work in Progress', published in thirteen instalments (1927–9) in the avant-garde literary magazine transition, was part of the evolving text of Finnegans Wake.
8–Isherwood found the novel didactic. Cf. 'Tragedy of Eldorado', Kenyon Review, autumn 1939, 450–3.

(which I like so far) & also done a little work at my Greek play[1]; so you see I am not being too idle. I am missing you very much but I am at the same time very happy. You have such a nice way of speaking, darling, I can hardly wait two months or whatever it is to hear it again. About money, darling, I suggest you come over on a single ticket unless you have plenty to spare. I can always beg or steal you some to go back with – if you must go back. The poem I wrote yesterday, as you will see, is all on the Still Centre theme.[2] I think it so good that you & I shall be able to have still centres. It's what breaks up so many people – that they can't. Perhaps I'm being over-confident about you & me? No doubt we shall have all sorts of set-backs, but I do feel very strongly that we (you & I, I mean) can survive them. Anyhow I'm not going to be <u>under</u>-confident because it isn't every life that one meets someone like you. So, when one does, one must, if one possibly can, cling on to it. Which is what I'm going to do, darling. Of course, if you want to slip me, you can try but the world is not really so big (you might find it difficult?) Well, now I must read some more. Goodbye for the moment, darling; I want it always to be only for the moment. //. Monday, after dinner: Darling, the boat is now rolling a little & I am feeling rather stupid. I spent this afternoon reading the Grapes of Wrath which I must say – pace Christopher – I enjoy. I can see that people might say it is (a) mannered, (b) sentimental, but I do like novels which (a) are informative, & (b) have sympathetic people in them. I get so sick of the sort of realism where the people have to be puppets. When I was going to bed last night, a little redfaced, rawboned, hardbitten man with red ears like pothandles asked me to join him & his friends (who turned out not to be his friends anyway) so we all had some whiskies & they made jokes about an Englishman, a Scotsman & an Irishman. Today I watched a very delightful sunset – the sun like a great bulgy apricot; I had forgotten how quickly it sinks. Someone told me that at sea when the sun sinks, you sometimes see a flash like green lightning run along the horizon; that is something, darling, we must look for. I am anxious now to get off this boat as I want to get on with my various works. A boat is demoralising; I sit in a deckchair & watch the rail come level with the horizon & calculate, supposing I had a gun, which would be the right moment to shoot at the horizon, supposing I wanted to shoot it. Today I have done no Greek play. I keep thinking about you & sometimes it gives me a feeling of inadequacy.

1 – *The Hippolytus*.
2 – 'Meeting Point'. The reference is to Spender's *The Still Centre* (1939), the title of which he later disparages (FLM to EC, 8 May 1939), p. 328.

Because, darling, you are what (to use a very banal phrase) they call a real person & I don't suppose I can claim to be that. Just a few bits of reality, perhaps, clinging round me like burrs. & for this reason it is very arrogant of me to lay claim to you. All the same I do (& perhaps I may get realer in the course of it? I should like to, you know). & now, darling, I am feeling terribly sentimental, so I think I had better go away & read a book. I mustn't be shocking you with block capitals & underlinings; after all I'm not Queen Victoria. But you must just imagine blocks & blocks of capitals all as high as the Empire State building & all, darling, in your honour. Goodnight, darling, sleep well & be happy. // My darling, it is late now but I have just been having alarming thoughts while drinking brandy with a man who talked politics. How long are you intending to come to Europe for? If you mean to go back in the Fall (as they say in your country) I could probably get a job over there for at least a year but I should have to start arranging about it soon. If on the other hand you could stay over for a year, then I could arrange something in America at my leisure & go back with you in 1940. This seems perhaps a better scheme; as long as you were in England you could stay with me (no rent) & – if you wanted – do some temporary work in London. Because, darling, if you suddenly went back in September & I was not prepared, I shouldn't be able to see you for at least six months, probably nine or ten. Which would be terrible. I hope you don't mind my taking it so seriously; you must say if you feel I am suffocating you & if you would prefer a long time by yourself. But if you wouldn't, then, if you could possibly let me know in advance, I could plan things out so that we needn't be very much separated. If you could bear to be 'famished' for about a year from this summer on & it is merely a question of money, you needn't worry about that as there is plenty of money in London. & after that you can get un-famished again & I shall go over & be famished (or see if I shall be) in my turn. (I don't believe America would really famish me too bad). I'm afraid you'll think I'm trying to order your life, darling, but it's only that I feel I can't be separated from you for too long & that therefore I want to be able to do something about it. So perhaps you'll be able to tell me? & now goodnight again, my love. // Tuesday: Today, darling, is much more exhilarating. The sea was deep blue for the first time & whipped with white all over & there is a heavy swell. I have been talking again with the chemist who is going to Oxford. He has never been out of Massachusetts before & is not feeling so good. He neither smokes nor drinks but I am giving him some introductions in Oxford, so no doubt he will become corrupted. I am very angry to discover that the Queen Mary is docking ten days in England, so this letter instead of going back on her will have to go on some slow little boat & by that time you will have forgotten about me (?) The pens have now begun to slide off their racks, so you must forgive my writing. I have been thinking, darling, how fascinating it is that you can look so serious one moment & so gay the next (owing to your eyes, I suppose – which are very beautiful – & the way they are set: also to your mouth which can look rather anxious & then can smile quite widely – I do dislike it when people's mouths are chronically inhibited). I found a review here in an old Spectator of Christopher's & Wystan's book on China. By Evelyn Waugh & entitled 'Mr. Isherwood & Friend.' It was extremely rude to Wystan.[1] Some day someone will have to put Mr. Waugh in his place. There is nothing so bad as some of these arty converts to Roman Catholicism. I don't think I am going to mix much with the literary gangs when I get back. But I must go & see my professor friend in Oxford, Dodds, who is one of my few friends whom I think you would like. He is Irish & goes his own way. He has a very nice & intelligent, if eccentric, wife & they both hate Oxford – which is to their credit. I am getting more & more adverse [*sic*] to England in general; I don't think she'll have my bones. I feel, darling, my sense of balance can't be so bad after all – being able to write with the boat rolling like this. When I get back I shall take up tennis again so as to be nice & fit by the time you arrive. The trouble is that so few people I know are at all good at tennis. I do get tired of moving round in the same circles, darling; I feel the time is nearly ripe for Peru or Java or Glencolumkill.[2] Perhaps now I ought to go & try some Greek play. Goodbye for the moment, darling. // 2.a.m.: Darling, I have been sitting up having drinks with some quite nice but not very enlightened people. Before that I walked round the top deck by myself in the dark, feeling I owned the boat. There was a crescent moon behind us & the hell of a wind & noone at all about; I enjoyed myself very much. The boat is still rolling. I do hope, darling, that you don't regard all this – you & me, I mean – as a joke. Because it isn't. Please, darling, realise that it isn't. I want you so much all the time & I just can't conceive of you disappearing into any Night of After-Being. You are not to disappear, my love, & you are to take care of yourself. (Awfully aunt-like that sounds but you are to all the same). I suppose I must go to bed now – though there doesn't seem so much point in my going to bed by

---

1 – Evelyn Waugh, review of W. H. Auden and Christopher Isherwood, *Journey to a War*, *Spectator*, 162 (24 March 1939), 496, 498; repr. John Haffenden (ed.), *W. H. Auden: The Critical Heritage* (1983), 288–90. See also 'Bloomsbury's Farthest North' (Waugh's review of LI), *Night and Day*, 1 (12 Aug. 1937), 25–6.
2 – Glencolumcille, Co. Donegal.

myself. You are to sleep well, darling & you are to write a lot. I shall finish this letter tomorrow. Then I shall write to you later from London. Goodnight, my love, be happy. //. Wednesday, after lunch: Darling, I got up late & had to pack & now I find this is due to be posted. We have left Cherbourg & are moving along the Channel. I shall just copy out that poem for you. For all I know, it is a bad poem – sentimental or flat or something (I never can judge straight off). Darling, as long as you keep writing to me & don't disappear, I shall be very happy. As I said, don't mind how you write; if you feel gloomy, write gloomy. & remember to send me carbon copies of all your stories. & don't smoke too much (it is a habit of which, as you know, I disapprove). & drink a drink to me once in a while (I shall to you). & don't run away with any wolf in sheep's clothing or for that matter sheep in wolf's clothing. & don't even run away with any paragon – prophet, saint, hero, genius or anything like that (one mustn't run away with people who belong on pedestals). & don't get yourself shut up anywhere; if you have to do that, you must wait till I can join you. & don't forget your Rimbaud when you go to the office. & don't, my darling, fret yourself over any family relationships; remember that they have their fun being martyrs & if you are too nice to them you spoil it all, & don't fret yourself more than necessary about work or rather don't fret yourself about fretting about it, because work involves fretting anyway, & don't, darling, be haunted in any way or sad or remorseful; if you do feel like that, write a story at once but don't let it get you down. & finally, darling, you are to love me a lot – as much as you possibly can. Because you possibly can't as much as I do you, so it is only fair that you should level up as much as possible. Now I must stop, damn it. All my love, darling,

> Yours ever (yes, I know one is
> always using that in letters but in
> this case when I say yours ever, I
> mean yours ever)
> Louis

P.S. Be happy.

2 May [1939]   16A Primrose Hill Road

Darling,

I am writing this in the rather soulless common room in the college where I work.[1] I feel a terribly long way from you & subsist on the hopes of a letter. This is a bloody little country & no one talks about anything except pro & con conscription. When I arrived the sun shone & it was all flowing & flaring with green but since then it has been wet & cold, I have had several painful scenes & been made to feel very conscious of moral irresponsibility etc. You know, darling, I am just a mess of evil appetites & indolences &, if you abandon me, no doubt I shall go down the sink where I belong.[2] I spent the weekend in Oxford with these awfully nice people called Dodds, who gave me some whiskey & a little moral support. Yesterday I went to a sherry party given by a little novelist from the Birmingham slums.[3] There I met John Lehmann who gave me a terribly snob dinner at the Athenaeum. He wants the stuff for the next New Writing in before the end of June, so it would be nice if you could send something along before then. I showed my Dodds friends your story ('Call me Comrade') which they both liked very much indeed.[4] My child is well & very full of himself & we are just about to have a Spanish refugee aged 21 & designs aeroplanes. Miss Popper (the woman who works for me) is crazy on refugees, so she is feeling very uplifted about it. I haven't properly got into my work yet, shall feel much better when I do. I doubt if I shall be able to endure this country for long. Darling, you <u>must</u> come over. For my sake & the gospel's (interpret the gospel how you like). I may not be able to leave London till the middle of July, when I want to go to this place in the South of France; I am sure we could both work there beautifully.[5] (It would be fun to get hold of a car.) O hell, darling, I really oughtn't to be writing to you now, as I feel depressed. I think you are so lovely & there you are miles away where those skyscrapers stick up from the sea like tiny

1–Bedford College for Women.
2–'I found myself back in London with renewed vitality but afraid of imminent disaster. I felt immediate nostalgia for America' (*SAF*, 207).
3–'At this time, 1936, literary London was just beginning to recognise something called the Birmingham school of novelists' (*SAF*, 154). The Birmingham novelists included Walter Allen (1911–95), Walter Brierley (1900–67), Leslie Halward (1905–76) and John Hampson (1901–55).
4–'Call me Comrade', in *New Letters in America*, ed. H. Gregory, E. Clark (New York, 1937), 151–69.
5–He had been to St Tropez with Mary in 1929.

fingers; it makes me very sentimental & lonely. I walked into T. S. Eliot last
night on an underground station. Surprisingly, he seemed to be blind drunk
– rocking on his heels & staring at me vacantly. Eleanor darling, <u>please</u>
write to me or this place will get me down. I have to write to my father
now; he has been ill – heart I think. I love you quite shockingly but, once
I start hearing from you, I expect I shall function better. You might have a
drink on me when you get this (what would you like?) I shall write again
soon & more cheerfully. But <u>you</u> must be cheerful over there, as that is
much more important. I hope you are writing a lot. I had a very depressing
letter this morning from my ex-wife. That is really what is upsetting me –
everyone being so unhappy. There is not, however, I think, going to be a
war – not just yet. I had an argument with Dodds as to how well one could
write outside of one's own country; myself I feel it can be done. Goodbye,
my darling, remember me. All my love & be happy.   Louis.

TO *Eleanor Clark* MS Yale

8 May [1939]   16A Primrose Hill Road

Darling,

I have just had your lovely letter; I am sorry I can't do neat typewritten
letters like that for you. I am feeling much cheered since your letter because
I thought maybe you would never write. On getting home this evening –
before finding your letter – I must say I felt very down. Had been having
a very stupid row with someone & before that was pretty sour anyway; I
can't settle down again here & all one's English contacts seem a little
degrading. You are very fierce about War, darling, aren't you? I expect you
are quite right. However I don't think there'll be one this time. I suddenly
thought the other day what one might do in a War – have some dim little
job at home & spend the rest of the time in underground broadcasting.
No doubt this sounds silly. Throwing the sand against the wind? However,
I have been thinking more about getting a job in America. Only there's no
point in my getting a job in America if you won't want to see me when I'm
there. I should feel awfully silly if I worked all the ominous machinery
necessary to get me there, then darling, you just shut the door on me. But
if you are going back yourself to America this year & if you would like me
to be around, I dare say I could start straight away trying to arrange
something. I am really just sick of this place. I was asked to do television
tonight with a gang of people doing a programme about America. They
wanted me to do some pretty generalisations at the end. However I refused

to do the particular generalisations they wanted, so in the end they said perhaps they had better ask Stephen (Spender). So I said perhaps they had.[1] So Stephen did it (anyway he must have taken up more of the screen). Stephen's new book of poems – just out – turns out, to my disgust, to be called The Still Centre.[2] That little poem I sent you I offered to the literary editor of the Listener (with whom I had tea today) but he would have none of it; said it was slight. I was rather annoyed as he has never returned anything of mine before. However, for all I know (as is the case with some poems which come out of very definite moods) it may be all mood & no poem(?) My long poem is coming out soon; I have just got my presentation copies & will send you one tomorrow. I expect, as I have said already, that some of it may annoy you very much. But perhaps, darling, you could try & imagine yourself in my context (God forbid you will say). Because one can only see the world from where one is in it (perhaps that is a good reason to keep moving) &, if you had been living here darling, for the last few years, I should very much like to know what would be your line on things. & by the way you have still not given me that list of books. If & [scored out] when you are in England, I want you to argue with this man Dodds, whom I mentioned in my last letter, because I rather argued your line against him – just to see – & didn't come out of it very well. I have just been looking at your letter again. Darling, you are not to have such gloomy things in your mind – gangplanks etc. – when you think of me. Darling, why is this summer decisive for you? You are not to go & fail to come over the sea, because that would be very wicked. I liked your dream about bishops. My father, incidentally, has been discovered to have very high blood pressure & has been ordered a rest for six weeks. My father, now I think of it, is a case in point. Here is someone who has plenty of wrong ideas, working through a very distorted medium, & yet being in many ways very useful; & he has done a lot to counterbalance the Orangemen (who, as you probably know, are Ulster's own brand of fascist).[3] Now, if his ideas were less wrong, i.e. if he were less conventionally Christian, he

1–FLM later claims that this event 'brought to the surface a debate going on within myself: was America today preferable to England and, if so, why?' (SAF, 208).
2–Stephen Spender, The Still Centre (1939). The title was Eliot's suggestion (Spender's original title had been 'The Silent Centre'). There was a certain feeling of rivalry between Spender and FLM at this time, Spender's book appearing just prior to publication of AJ. As Sutherland writes: 'It marked Stephen's return to romantic lyricism and re-established him at the age of thirty (with Auden now in exile) as England's leading young poet; a pre-eminence contested only by Louis MacNeice' (245).
3–On FLM's views on this, see 'Northern Ireland and Her People' (c.1941–4), repr. SP, 143–53.

would probably be quite unable to cut any ice in the North of Ireland at all. You may say of course, darling, why want to cut ice in such a place? O hell, darling, I can't start arguing now; it is nearly 2.0 in the morning. Wystan, you see, is all now for the writer (or artist) keeping his hands clean of politics . . . But it's no good discussing these things in letters (another reason for you to come over quickly – save my soul with a few illuminating words?) I am now eating salt biscuits, so no doubt am a little incoherent. My painting friend[1] has been very angry with me for agreeing to sit for a painter who she says (a) is a bad painter, (b) an unpleasant person & (c) – most important – has a wife who has behaved very badly to her. I didn't know – am not sure anyway – about (a) & hadn't thought that the other two mattered so much but it seems that, as usual, I have behaved unethically. As a result my friend & I are now hardly on speaking terms. Everyone here – a terribly petty society I move in, darling – has been complaining to me about Christopher, who left behind him a boy called Jackie whom he had made to give up his job on the understanding that he should learn to become his (Christopher's) secretary.[2] But here the boy is in London being supported by Christopher's friends & no prospect of reunion with Christopher. I don't know, darling, why I tell you this rather dreary gossip. It is not really for its own sake but because it represents a whole little world which I am tired of (not that there's any reason why I should write to you about such little worlds – except that one likes to better one's worlds sometimes). Also perhaps I perversely wish to provoke you, darling. (?) Because if you are going to be truculent to me & suggest I am just a damn bourgeois, I feel like bringing up all my bourgeoisdom on parade & saying just look at them. So don't be truculent, darling. No doubt the truth is not in me but I have a kind of a feeling for it. Just needs watering a little but it doesn't get much of that among most of these people I meet around here. Darling, you are please to love me a lot. It makes me very annoyed to think that you wouldn't love me if I went up a gangplank (not that I am likely to). I have just finished this book called 'I helped to build an Army' by José Martín Blásquez[3] which I found extremely interesting & perfectly sincere. I feel like recommending it to your friend

1 – Nancy Coldstream.
2 – Isherwood.
3 – José Martín Blázquez, *I Helped to Build an Army: Civil War Memoirs of a Spanish Staff Officer* (1939). 'Books such as that by Martin Blazquez . . . made only too clear the self-deception which the Civil War had occasioned in nine minds out of ten' (*SAF*, 197).

Dwight Macdonald[1] who did seem to me, I must admit, to be clean off the map when he talked about Spain. Now one is getting near the edge again. About poetry, I have written quite a little batch of other poems; will send you them when I've checked them properly. You see, I can never tell what they're like for a little time after writing. Eleanor darling, I must go to bed now. I am slightly cross because there are such lots of things I want to say to you & it's no good just in ink across all that water. Darling, do you mean your summer starts on June 11th? That doesn't seem so far away. You must come to England as soon as you can; there is nothing 'rash' about it at all. You must do a lot of work in the meantime but you will also be able to do lots later. Besides there is this place near Nice. Darling, you are not to be dilatory & hang about in America once you are free. & you are to tell me if I am to try to go to America later in the year. Now I must go to bed, damn it (I miss you very much going to bed though technically I suppose one can't miss things one's never had?) Goodnight, darling, please sleep well. // Tuesday: The weather has now changed & has become really May. I have two not awfully appropriate lines running in my head from an early English lyric –

> Through the glass window shines the sun.
> How should I love, & I so young?[2]

I find my week is all booked up with unprofitable dinners & lunches.

This house is just flowing with mice; Miss Popper keeps asking me to get a cat & I keep forgetting & the mice go on for ever. Chattering, chattering as they flow. My little boy has taken to filling the inkpots with cigarette cards. I wish I still had a car. If you will be in England any length of time, I might manage to hire one from one of my friends. I now have to invent an essay about the Greek Spirit or something for my girls to do. After that I must go on translating this play. I have done nothing about Yeats yet. Damn: the (rather arty little) producer who is supposed to be producing my Greek play rang up this moment – very hurt – & I have to go & have lunch

and
Parody

1 – Dwight MacDonald (1906–82), editor, philosopher, radical social critic. Educ. Phillips Exeter and Yale. Edited *Partisan Review* (1937–43) and *Politics* (1944–9); contributed to *Esquire* and the *New Yorker*. Formerly a Trotskyite, later a 'Cold Warrior' in the 1950s. Author of many books, including *Fascism and the American Scene* (1938) and *Memoirs of a Revolutionist* (1960).
2 – Anon, 'The Bride's Song' or 'The Maiden's Song' (British Library: Harley 7578, f. 110): 'And through the glass window shines the sun. / How should I love, and I so young? / The bailey beareth the bell away; / The lily, the rose, the rose I lay.'

with him.[1] So I must stop. Be happy, Eleanor darling, & don't work yourself up to thinking I am some sort of ideological (or unideological) monster. There is always hope for those who are half-damned; the really sunk are the people who think they are saved. Please write to me lots & lots more because it makes me so happy. Goodbye, darling, & all my love.

L.

TO *Eleanor Clark*

MS Yale

14 May [1939]   16A Primrose Hill Road

Darling, my love,

I am just waiting for lunch having come home an hour late. I am feeling rather guilty, as I have done nothing but go out in the evening lately; however this week I am going to reform. (Lunch now.) I am now drinking coffee in my sittingroom – sitting at a sham walnut writing desk & looking out on a green hill. All round me are stacks of bills. I am feeling in moderately good spirits. – except, darling, that I get more & more irritated with the Atlantic. I had lunch with Stephen the other day who had a very superiorish letter from Christopher. Christopher, it seems, has gone completely pacifist but what was irritating was his tone of condescension to all of us (assumed lost souls) over here. Knowing how rude Christopher & Wystan were about America, I feel they can't have it both ways like that. Yesterday I spent hours arguing with someone who felt suicidal; after which I did what I had never done before – came up the Thames on a little steamer from Greenwich to Westminster. Very exciting – all tumbledown wharfs & pyramids of barrels & rusty tugs & tarpaulinised barges. Perhaps you will do that with me sometime? I had a long argument with one of my college girls the other day who seemed to think the Good Life consisted in committees, committees & more committees. England is very like that now. The other night I went to the cinema with my Catalan Nationalist friend. He is very depressed because, although he may wangle it to stay in London indefinitely, there is no prospect of being allowed to work here. Tomorrow my son – Dan – has his fifth birthday. He decided, while I was away, that his mother was a negress because someone had told him that negroes live in America. He has now been advanced to doing carpentry in his school – whatever that means. Now, darling, I think I had better work. You mustn't interrupt me (you do, you know). //. Tuesday:

1 – Rupert Doone.

here I am, darling, sitting on my window again for a morning's work (just a moment, I must change this nib). The weather has gone terribly dreary – grey & wet & – in particular – cold. I have finished my string of evenings out & am prepared to be good. Yesterday I had dinner with a little man – very ugly, like a gargoyle suffering from malnutrition – who a few years ago had a temporary academic job in Iowa. He doesn't think one would be uprooted in America & is very eager to get back there himself; only he finds the Middle West too puritanical.[1] We had a great many drinks & when I got home I lay in bed & wrote some verse – only it came too easy, so there must be something wrong with it. The night before I had dinner with a very different man whom I have known for years, an art-critic, very tall & aesthetic.[2] We had the usual mixture of backbiting & politics-with-soda but I found it very refreshing after the intimate talks about LIFE etc. which I have been forced to have lately with people. Talking of politics, darling, every day something occurs to me which I want to argue with you (this sounds shockingly aggressive) but I feel it is no good until I see you. At the moment I feel a little sour about Trotskyites as some of the London Trotskyites have behaved in a quite extraordinary way over a Spanish refugee who was supposed to stay with me but was quartered with them while I was away. Touchy, offensive & wildly inaccurate. & they all seem to be so smug, darling, (I mean these ones here).[3] There they sit, being all Bohemian & superior, waiting for THE REVOLUTION & sneering at anyone who does anything. I admit that all the Leftist groups in England suffer from superiority complex but the others at any rate don't just live on a would-be astral plane waiting till the stars join them. Which reminds me: I met someone the other day who said 'I hear Wystan has gone to the good.' Which just about covers it. Well, darling, don't be cross with me (re Trotskyites or anything) until you see me; one should never be cross with people at a distance. I try to keep what they call an open mind (or is that just a chimera?) & my open mind tells me that history has always been, &

1 – Unidentified.
2 – Anthony Blunt.
3 – Although briefly married to Trotsky's Czech secretary, EC had partially rejected Trotskyism by the time she met FLM (how committed a Trotskyite she was isn't clear). The depth of her disillusionment is suggested in a letter the following spring: 'Went to a "mass meeting" formalizing the split among the Trotskyites and launching the new party: it was depressing and nostalgic: horrible invective and that crazy courageous smugness those people have. They look at me now as if I were a traitor, or rather with a certain kindness, as if one ceased to be real when one isn't with them anymore, and they are sorry for you' (EC to FLM, April [n.d.] 1940), *Ms Yale*. Cf. FLM's acerbic treatment of New York Trotskyites in *SAF*, 203.

is still bound to be, a series of compromises, & that people who won't compromise are mere Utopians & that people like Dwight Macdonald who say 'Given the revolutionary spirit, everything else follows' are just not realistic. But I can't really follow up this line now, only I rely on you, darling, to discuss it all with me sometime; but you mustn't keep saying everything you disagree with is 'childish' for that is what all the political groups keep saying about each other & it stalemates any discussion from the start. Well, my darling, I must post this as I think it may catch the Queen Mary. You must keep on writing to me for I miss you continually &, if you will only write, it will make ever so much difference. Would you, by the way, be interested in an Anglo-American (mainly literary) quarterly (including a good deal of much-needed rapportage from both sides?) I think of proposing it to Faber's, who some time ago were half on for running a new paper & who have strong American contacts; F. V. Morley is just about to leave England to go back to Harcourt Brace & no doubt they could manage it over there.[1] Which reminds me, darling, I hope you are writing a lot. Will you send me some? &, by the way, as you wouldn't have a hat in America, perhaps you will do me the honour of accepting one from me in London? There are some very nice Susy models about. Darling, you are so lovely to look at, it seems a great waste you should be somewhere out of sight all this time.

> basia mille, darling,
> remember me,
> be happy,
> do lots of work,
> come as soon as you can,
> all my love,
> L.

P.S. Darling, I was just taking this to the post when I found your two Queen Mary letters in the box. Darling, how silly you are. There was nothing to be sorry about in the long letter. I can understand only too well how angry we must all make you & I do apologise for using the phrase 'lower classes' (I didn't know I had; it is of course a cliché here). My chief

---

1 – Frank Vigor Morley (1899–1985), educ. Haverford College and New College, Oxford (Rhodes Scholar, 1919, DPhil 1923), author of *An Analytical Treatment of the 3-Bar Curve* and (with his father, Frank Morley), *Inversive Geometry* (1933). Also *The Wreck of the Active* (1936), *The Life of Samuel Johnson & the Journal of a Tour to the Hebrides with Samuel Johnson* by James Boswell (editor, 1966), *The Long Road West* (1971) and many other books.

objection, darling, to your attack is that it is all very well for you to say that England is doomed but it is not all very well for me (that was why I wouldn't speak on television & Stephen got his five guineas). I admit that England is terribly sick but, if you are part of a place, you don't just wash your hands of it because it is sick. Now, if you will grant that, darling, all I want to ask you, darling, is what your line would be if you lived in such a sick place. By the way, you are overdoing the public school stuff. All the things which I say – tentatively – are said & believed very much more definitely by thousands of people in England who have never seen a public school & possibly never heard of one, e.g. by the out of work miners in South Wales. However, darling, enough of this for the moment. I do see your line & I feel, if I were you, I should probably despise me but you can't expect me to do that, can you? & now, darling, I am horrified to hear about your tooth. But it must be better by now, yes? & about this money question . . . If you can come over here leaving yourself fifty dollars, I am sure it will be possible for you to earn your way while you are here. It seems a terribly long time to have to wait till the fall & then we shouldn't be able to go to the South of France. Now about me: it has occurred to me that I might get some sort of job in America from January on (I could possibly, if I knew at once, arrange it from October on but there is the question of giving notice etc. & it would soon become very difficult). I suggest therefore that you come over as soon as possible in the summer but that you let me know soon when you intend to go back; then I can start arranging about transferring (or don't you want me over there, darling?) The alternatives are (I mean the ones that would fit in with me) (1) that you go back at the end of September, (2) at Christmas, (3) next summer – at any of which times I could probably go back with you, though (1) would need rapid arranging. (4) (but I don't like this because it means such a long wait) you could come over here in September & stay till Christmas or the summer. In any case, once you are here, I feel sure you can raise money (not my money) if you don't mind doing occasional reviewing etc. & if you were going to stay over here for a fair time, i.e. approaching a year, I think – as I suggested before – that you might be able to get a temporary job (if you didn't hate that) in an English publishing house. As I said, Faber's are linked up with Harcourt Brace – in case you know anyone on the latter. I know various publishers here whom, if authorised by you, I might work on a bit. To return to reviewing, I think with very little effort you could make a safe £3 to £4 a week &, if you won't stay in my house, you can still have quite a nice room for that & leave quite a bit over. So you see, darling, this time it is just a choice of simplicities. I shall be seeing Eliot this week

& I might – discreetly – manage to find out from him ways for you to make money here. Yes, darling, of course the Empire State is our building. & now I don't know what you mean about Letters from Iceland: I didn't write any letters in it calling anyone darling except an entirely fictitious piece – a long private joke which you would hate – called 'Hetty to Nancy' in which everyone's sex was inverted – Nancy representing a man we know called Anthony. The fact that later I met & became very intimate with a girl called Nancy is coincidence.[1] Anyhow, darling, I don't advise you to read the Iceland book as it is all playboy stuff & you would dislike it still more than Lions & Shadows.[2] (I told you that I had written lots of junk.) If you would like to read anything else by me, I suggest my translation of the Agamemnon; I am rather proud of some of the choruses. Darling, I am so pleased you have been playing tennis. I haven't started yet as the weather is so filthy & I have to buy a racket. Now I must really post this. It was lovely of you to write me such a long letter; send me some more. Darling, I am just simply & indisputably crazy about you, so you must manage to come over somehow. Tell me what you would prefer – in the way of dates, jobs, occasional work etc. etc. – & then I can apply my brain to it. Awful waste to have my brain here waiting to devise schemes for you if you won't give it anything to work on. Darling, you are to say anything you feel like to me in these letters. Because, as so often, I sympathise with the opposition & anyway, as long as you bother to tell me how awful I am, I shall feel you must be interested in me. Yes, I shall do some of that reading. Now, darling, goodbye (no, it's not unrealistic at all: if a thing's a spade it's a spade & if a thing's enchanted, it's enchanted). O, by the way, about us all being so 'bright', I feel I can claim to be not nearly so bright as Christopher. In fact hardly bright at all. Just dumb but shockingly affectionate. Goodbye, my darling,

L.

TO *Eleanor Clark*   MS Yale

18 May [1939]   16A Primrose Hill Road

Darling,

I am writing to you again although I dare say there is no boat, just because I like writing to you. I am feeling in better spirits because I have

1 – Blunt, of course, and Nancy Coldstream.
2 – Christopher Isherwood, *Lions and Shadows: An Education in the Twenties* (1938).

been working. An unknown man rang up just now to say how much he liked Autumn Journal, which only came out today. Being a flatterable person I was naturally very pleased. Yesterday I got my copy of Partisan Review. For your sake & the gospel's, darling, I read all through Dwight Macdonald's editorial (which, I must say, reads very cogent) & also the attack on Popular Fronts by Sidney Hook.[1] Admittedly you all have a case but it seems to me – in England at any rate – that it is open to criticisms (which I have lately been reading) expressed by Lenin in his book about 'Left-Wing' Communism, e.g. Sidney Hook brings up Kerensky as evidence of the futility of a Popular Front.[2] But Lenin (who after all was in a position to know) maintains that (a) the Kerensky episode was a necessary one & (b) that at that time & for the time being it was the best tactic for the Russian Communists to go in with the Kerenskys (while of course knowing fully how reactionary they were). Applying this to England in 1920 Lenin's line was that the Communists must <u>not</u> take up this pure no-compromise attitude but must be prepared to utilise for their purposes a reactionary parliament & the reactionary trade unions. & I do not see that this line has been disproved. In case you don't believe me I quote Lenin himself: 'It is just because the backward masses of the workers . . . in western Europe are much more strongly imbued with bourgeois democratic & parliamentary prejudices than they are in Russia that it is <u>only</u> within such institutions as bourgeois parliaments that Communists can (& must) wage a long & stubborn struggle . . .'[3] Now the fact is, darling, (when you say that England is doomed) that the trade union system in England is something quite exceptionally well organised & (potentially) powerful. There are two obvious snags about it: its leadership is reactionary & its membership is dumb. It will certainly take a crisis to change that. But such things as the present Popular Front agitation here & the Stafford Cripps split will probably shake up the unions to some extent

1–Dwight MacDonald, 'War and the Intellectuals, Act Two' and Sidney Hook, 'The Anatomy of the Popular Front', *Partisan Review* (*PR*), 6, 3 (Spring 1939), 3–20; 29–45. The issue also carried FLM's 'Autumn Journal, II', Auden's 'William Butler Yeats: 1865–1939, The Public v the later W. B. Yeats' and Delmore Schwarz's essay on Yeats, 'The Poet as Poet'. MacDonald warned of the conquest of socialism by war: 'socialism vanishes, and in its place there appears what can only be called anti-fascist fascism' (11).
2–Sidney Hook (1902–89), New York philosopher; educ. CCNY and Columbia (a pupil of John Dewey); taught Philosophy at New York University (1927–72). A student of Marxism, he broke from communism after 1933, and in 1939 formed the Committee for Cultural Freedom. Remained an opponent of communism throughout the Cold War and was latterly a fixture at the conservative Hoover Institute.
3–From V. I. Lenin, 'Should We Participate in Bourgeois Parliaments?', in *Left-Wing Communism: An Infantile Disorder* (1920).

– discrediting the leaders & putting ideas into the rank-&-file.[1] Now it seems to me that if the people in the unions can really become politically critical – & therefore responsible – in time, England is not doomed. But you can only start them being critical by meeting them halfway (the sort of compromise which Lenin saw to be necessary); you will never jump the English workers over-night bang into hundred-per-cent revolutionaries. & the English Trotskyites who sit by ignoring the technical (& therefore often roundabout) side of politics & keeping their hands pure of degrading contacts, are failing – it seems to me – (a) to dig gradually into the mentality of the workers (which is the only way of bringing to light the capacities they certainly have got) & (b) to utilise the perfectly good instruments provided by the unions etc. As for war, darling, I am not arguing about that now as I can't make up my mind on it. I think of going round sometime soon to talk with John Strachey who lives almost round the corner.[2] You mustn't object to me talking about these things in letters for they are always worrying me, so naturally I tell you about them. Well, darling, soon I have to go down town & see Eliot (I shall see if I can find you a fortune). I heard from Random House today. They want to do Autumn Journal but, very stupidly, they want other poems in with it. However I have got about fifteen which I shall send them. Would you like me to dedicate their volume to you or would that get you in bad in American circles? (Of course, you may hate the long poem. I was thinking to myself how shocked you would be by the bit about the Oxford by-election – also the implications as to Munich which, according to you (?), made no difference one way or the other.[3]) I don't think I shall post this now, darling, but shall see if Eliot tells me anything of any profit. My bitch of an ex-mother in law has been molesting me again with letters & phone calls. People here give me no rest; I don't think I shall stand it long. Also the weather is unspeakable & my dog, after living with me for nearly seven

1 – As chairman of the Socialist League, Stafford Cripps (1889–1952) was at loggerheads with the national executive of the Labour Party, which he considered conservative and reactionary. The Labour Party finally expelled him in early 1939 for proposing a 'popular front' against the war, which would unite elements of the Communist, Liberal and Independent Labour parties.
2 – John Strachey (1901–63), Labour politician and selector for the Left Book Club. Author of *The Coming Struggle for Power* (1935), *Theory and Practice of Socialism* (1937), *Federalism or Socialism?* (1940) and other works.
3 – Chamberlain's pro-appeasement Conservatives won the Oxford by-election in Oct. 1938, despite heavy opposition from the anti-appeasement lobby. The successful candidate was Quintin Hogg (later Lord Hailsham). FLM had played his part by driving anti-Munich voters to the polls (Stallworthy, 231). Cf. *AJ*, XIV.

years, has taken to eating mats. Worst of all, the hot-water machine is ceasing to supply hot baths & I sit shivering in the bath trying to console myself with lily of the valley soap. O, you asked about my house, darling. It is what they call here an upper maisonette – i.e. the two top floors of a four storey house. I have five rooms – two in the roof where Dan & Miss Popper life, & three below – one my bedroom, one my sitting room & one a diningroom. The bedroom has primrose walls & grey woodwork & an enormous bed which is unfortunately pink, having been painted that many years ago by my wife. On the grey mantelpiece is your yellow China horse. The diningroom looks over the roofs of North London & you can nearly always see smoke coming up from the trains. The walls look off-white but are really pink & the woodwork is an almost invisible lavenderish grey; the floor is fine Chinese matting. Sounds very pansy but the rest of it is kitchen furniture (again unfortunately painted) plus a large divan with my dog on it. The sittingroom, where I am now, looks southwest on to a green hill with trees; when it is fine, couples lie on the hill in trances. My desk is in the window & I have some awfully pretentious curtains – red & gold stripes. The walls are white & there is a thick carpet, warm grey. A lot of books on white shelves, an open fire, a large sofa, an armchair, a rockingchair, an ordinary chair & a card table. It is, I think, a very attractive room but I don't (I am continuing this sentence over 24 hours later because I ran out of notepaper, am now in this college) awfully enjoy rooms when I am by myself in them. I am already getting into trouble over Autumn Journal because of the personal references. But that is the trouble with poetry – my kind anyway – that you have to write about what you feel about &, if you have recurrent feelings on any one subject, they have to be expressed – especially in that journal kind of poem. But I do make a point of not giving unnecessary information about other people & of trying to confine my personalities to my own reactions to people. I should have thought that was legitimate. Perhaps, darling, I am an awful cad. But how can I know? Yesterday I had drinks in a pub – called the Friend at Hand – with Eliot.[1] // He becomes slower & slower in conversation & I did not get a great deal out of him. He thinks Autumn J. ought to be published without other poems in America & that, if Random House won't agree, I ought to give it to Harcourt Brace. He thinks my idea of an Anglo-American quarterly a very good one but didn't make any offers. I asked him if someone off an American publishing house could get a temporary job in London. He was vague about this but said the obvious

1 – Friend at Hand, Herbrand Street, near Russell Square, London.

thing to do was to see Morley, who is very well up in these things. Morley will reach New York in July but of course, darling, I am hoping you will have left by then. I had a letter from Selden today asking for a copy of Autumn J. & saying Wystan had left New York for his school in New England & Christopher for California.[1] Fabers are probably going to do my little book (really written years ago) about Latin Humour; I shall write them a new introductory chapter attacking all the forms of classical education in England.[2] My frightful translation is still not finished; whenever I should be doing it, I start reading or thinking or fretting or taking my dog to the public house at the corner – a sombre place where we sit vacantly in the gloom eating potato crisps. Eliot says I could easily get a job in America but the difficulty would be to get back again.[3] However I never think ahead all those ways & anyhow I have a feeling I don't want to be academic forever. If I didn't have a child, of course, I shouldn't have to play so much for safety. I could easily pay my <u>own</u> way without universities. Anyhow, darling, everything will work out. I can't see really why you shouldn't stay in my house in London. Anyhow you could always stay there to start with until – if you were going to be a long while – you had to be independent & working. (There are lots of quite nice rooms available near me.) Well, darling, I think I have to go out now; this seems rather a dry & dim sort of letter when I look back at it. Not that I feel dry or dim at all. It <u>is</u> infuriating not being able to see you. I keep hoping you are having a good time, working a lot & playing tennis – & arranging to come over here. Darling, you are, you know, something quite new in my experience. Of course some things which are new are not particularly good but then there is the other kind which is new partly just because it is so good. Which is your kind, darling. & it is so rare too that people are lovely both inside & out.

> Goodbye, darling,
> be happy,
> all my love
> L.

1 – Cary Selden Rodman (1909–2002), a founding editor of *Common Sense* (NY, 1932–45), 'a magazine of social protest.' M. (1933) Eunice Clark, sister of Eleanor Clark, but by 1939 they were divorced and Eunice had remarried. Rodman's sister Nancy was married to Dwight Macdonald.
2 – The 'study of Latin Humour', *The Roman Smile*, was never published. Indeed, the author's typescript was found gathering dust in his desk drawer at the BBC after his death. See 'List of Personal Possessions belonging to Louis MacNeice' (*BBC, WAC, R71/919/1*).
3 – See TSE to A. Colby Sprague, 8 Nov. 1938, arranging USA lecture tour for FLM (Houghton Library, Harvard, *Ms Am 1691.3*).

TO *John Frederick MacNeice*   MS Bodleian

Thursday [?May–June 1939]   Bedford College for Women

Dear Daddie,

Very pleased to hear from you. I hope you are now feeling a lot better.

About America – I think that a lot of our popular ideas are misconceptions. The Americans, for example, with the exception of the police, are not noticeably less polite than the English; most of them on the contrary seem very friendly and considerate. On the other hand they are not nearly as efficient as one expects; the broadcasting station I went to seemed very slovenly compared with Broadcasting House in London. And outside New York the whole country gives an impression of slovenliness – untidy wooden shacks and an appearance of desultory agriculture. New York of course is a thing on its own, very impressive – the contemporary city – but probably awful to live in. Not quite such a bustle as I expected & much of what there is is probably put on – people in offices all very busy pretending to be busy.

I gave lectures at Harvard, Wellesley (one of the chief women's colleges),[1] Princeton,[2] Hamilton College (a little one by itself in the country) & State College, Pennsylvania (like all state colleges co-educational).[3] I failed – because the air service was cancelled – to keep an

1 – He arrived in New York on 23 March and lectured at Harvard and Wellesley on 11 and 12 April (FLM to Elizabeth Manwaring, 12 March 1939, *Ms Wellesley*). At Wellesley, his hosts included Mary Cross Ewing, Dean of Residence; Lucy Wilson, Dean; Grace E. Hawk and Charles Kerby-Miller from the Department of English, and Theodore Spencer of Harvard University (*Ms Wellesley, Manwaring poetry scrapbook*). Cf. 'Mr MacNeice to Read to College Audience' and 'Author Criticizes New English Verse: Louis MacNeice Describes Own Work and Theories of Contemporaries', *Wellesley College News*, 29 March, 20 April 1939.
2 – Eliot wrote on FLM's behalf to Willard Sharp at Princeton on 2 March 1939 (TSE to Willard Sharp, *Ms Princeton*), and Sharp responded by inviting FLM to give a talk at the Princeton undergraduate club in April, for a fee of $25 (Willard Sharp to FLM, 21 March 1939, *Ms Bodleian, Ms Res, c. 590, Box 15*).
3 – The only photograph available of FLM during the lecture tour was taken at State College (now Penn State) and is reproduced in this volume. 'The first lecture I gave in America was at State College, Pennsylvania . . .' (*SAF*, 202). His Hamilton lecture was reviewed in a campus paper: 'In his analysis of the nature of poetry, the speaker condemned the extremes of the two modern schools of thought on the subject: the one which would make of the poet a propagandist, a mouthpiece for a social creed; and the other, the surrealist school, which would have the poet cut himself off completely from contact with the world. Mr MacNeice chose to accept Matthew Arnold's definition that "Poetry should be a criticism of life"' (*Alumni Review* [Hamilton], 4, 1939, 19). See also 'Louis MacNeice Speaks on Hill', in which MacNeice is dubbed 'one of the better known insurgent penmen of the Left Wing of English poetry' (*Hamilton Life*, 12 April 1939, 1). The American perception of FLM as a communist sympathiser is suggested by EC's report of a conversation with a faculty member at Barnard:

appointment at Bowdoin College, Maine. I also took part with Auden & Isherwood in a talk to the League of American Writers in New York. I made over £80 on lectures & that left me forty odd pounds down! As I only stayed ten days in a hotel & for the rest got hospitality, that gives an idea of the prices. Two or three of my audiences numbered over 300; they seemed, though I say it, pretty appreciative. At Harvard I was made to make gramophone records.

This cousin, Virginia, is a relation of the Howells.[1] She is petite & lively with dark hair & blue eyes & obviously can look after herself very well. She went to college at Vassar which is supposed to be the best women's college.

The food – as perhaps I said – seems to us eccentric. Things like clams are very popular & they tend to dump ice cream on top of all their puddings. Eating in New York is rather hurried – all quick service counters where you have a ticket punched etc. On the other hand their coffee is made very much better than in England.

Of course we get a wrong idea of America over here because the Americans who can afford to come over are not representative. Far from being a frivolous race, they are if anything too serious-minded. And most of them slow in the uptake. But most of them essentially humane & kindly with no intention of throwing up the sponge. You feel a certain warmth in their company which you don't so often get in England. I very much want to get back there & see more of them.

Well, I might come over for a weekend before the end of June.

Love to all,

Louis

'She said "Well, I suppose we do think of him as a Russian envoy." I didn't get it for a minute and finally managed to say "What?!" "Of course we're not feeling much sympathy for Russia these days," says she very calmly, "naturally, if he'd talk about pure poetry . . ." whatever that is. I was furious. However I controlled myself enough to tell her that you were not in the pay of Moscow . . .' (EC to FLM, 23 Feb. 1940, *Ms Yale*).

1 – Elizabeth Nicholson wrote: 'Virginia Howell (Mrs Soskin) is a distant cousin of ours whom Louis knew much better than I do, as I only met her once in New York. But Louis always met her when in the U.S.A. & liked her very much . . . she and her husband who is dead had a publishing firm Howell-Soskin which specialised in children's books & had its offices in New York' (EN to CM, 26 Jan. 1964, *Faber archive, Monteith file*).

TO *Eleanor Clark*   MS Yale

20 June [1939]   16A Primrose Hill Road

Darling,

   Here I am alone in my house guarding my child (who has whooping
cough) feeling terribly for no reason tired & smoking myself silly. I am so
pleased to think of you going off to this [Utopian *deleted*] idyllic-sounding
place in the country where everyone has his own studio;[1] I hope you will
eat lots of cream, darling, & work just the golden mean amount & set
yourself all up rigorous & beautiful. (& I will try to do the same – being
neither at the moment, rather passé styes in my eyes & creakings in my
chest, not to speak of chronic Londonschmerz & my national tendency to
desidia. Darling, I had a batch of letters from you in rapid succession,
which is what I like. Will you send lots more? Don't forget me when you
get among the sumach or whatever it is you have in those parts. Yes, I shall
be over, provided there is no catastrophe here, sometime in September; I
have blackmailed my old ladies into giving me a year's leave of absence.[2]
All against their principles but I suggested that otherwise I would quit.
Isn't it fun? The only thing is I still haven't fixed anything in America.
Wrote to two or three people but haven't had any reply yet. Old Eliot tells
me I shall never get anything so late in the season. Of course I could just
come over like Wystan & trust to luck if it weren't for my child. However
it will all work out; it always does if one wants it to. It's lucky, darling, you
don't think much of my letters as it will keep you with a nice low opinion
of me so that you won't be expecting me to be anything much when I
reappear. (I think so often people colour their conception of one in one's
absence & then what a bathos – thoroughly undistinguished, what you
call average, man stepping off a boat or a train or something probably
with toothache & searching around peevishly for his luggage which he has
mislabelled & no doubt a roaring cold so as to be quite inaudible & ugly
with a swollen face whereupon you would say to yourself Really what had
you been thinking of when there are so many highergrade [*sic*] people
everyday just around the corner?[)] But you see in this case you ought to
be prepared, me writing such poor letters which imply no doubt every kind
of deficiency – not that I really have toothache hardly ever or even mislabel
my luggage but you know what I mean, me being really awfully average
& nothing heaven-inspired about me, & you being such a one for

1 – Yaddo Writers' and Artists' Colony, Saratoga Springs, New York.
2 – Leave of absence from teaching at Bedford College for Women.

inspiration & the volcano type & the geniuses & the men with burning missions & all those other pigs, however my darling this sentence is getting rather mixed up & having said all this I must say that I shall be very angry indeed if you don't like me when you see me again because I know I shall like you so much, of course that is Life as they say but I think it is a bloody bore when one likes someone & someone doesn't like one, so I <u>shall</u> be very angry. Though no doubt polite. Darling, I can't write to you any more of those serious controversial things at the moment. They are always coming up here & I will be discussing them with you some day; it doesn't matter so much, you see, you feeling violent towards me if we're in the same room but I don't like it from a distance. Besides now you know just how perverted (public school, bourgeois, decadent Left et al.) I am, you can't bring it up at me later that I never told you. & as you know, darling, I am always on for seeing the light if you can produce it. But that will be easier (perhaps?) when we are both in the same country. It's awful to be so fluxy as me, you know. The only things I feel definite about are concretish things & what I like to eat or to wear or other people to wear or the sound of a line of verse or how to sleep with people or whether X is nicer company than Y or Z a nicer place than Q. [B]ut when it comes to these awfully complicated international problems where one's never seen X or Y or Q or Z, I feel terribly uncertain. Perhaps you find that very contemptible, darling, but all round one there are these people being so very certain & they all cancel each other out just like the old metaphysicians. Such an odd woman came to see me today, darling (I had never seen her before) – a Russian Jewish journalist from South Africa who in her spare time stagemanages hundreds of Zulus & people doing wardances on the West End stage. She wanted to interview me for something. Says the only thing to do in South Africa is sleep with black people. I gave her some tea but the interview wasn't much of a success as my child got bored with it & he is a genius at sabotage. In a few weeks, darling, I am going over to Belfast to broadcast & shall be there for the twelfth of July. Haven't seen the processions (one of the most extraordinary sights in the world) since I was a little boy;[1] I expect they may have trouble this year. (Two or three years ago the procession ran amok & burned out

1–FLM attended the Orange parades with his father when he was seven and possibly on other occasions. Cf. Collins Paragon Diary, No. 181, Thursday 12th [July 1917]: 'Daddie and I went to North Street and there were flags sticking out of the wall. We went to see Orangemen.' *Ms Bodleian, Ms Res, c. 1051, Box 39.*

some of the Catholic streets.[1]) Tomorrow I am supposed to be going to a dance. I think I shall be well out of this town; I am always hearing now of women just under forty who go round throwing mud at me, me having at some distant time in the past declined their advances. O yes, darling, you mentioned John Davenport. He is one of the most God-awful men in the world – really subhuman.[2] I met him again the other night when I was having an incipient scene with one of the women mentioned (now engaged to Tom Harrison [sic] the Mass Observer).[3] Well, darling, I must go to bed. Was it today you were going to Yaddo? O by the way, darling, when is your birthday?[4] You said July, didn't you? Mine is September. If I were over in time (but I don't suppose I shall be; it is the 12th) I would ask you out to celebrate it & we could have 32 drinks instead of candles (it's a terrible age, isn't it?) In August I shall be staying a bit in Ireland in a house by the sea with my family; will try & get healthy there & write this awful book about Yeats.[5] After that, no more books to order; I am sick of it. Will be sending you some short poems soon. Darling . . . [sic] I was just going to become rather intense then but I think you had better imagine it. (Mr X having thrown his heart on the table, she said 'Can't you do any better than that?' 'I am so sorry' he said, hastily putting it back in his attaché case & offering her a cigarette. 'There are some things which are better concealed' she said, 'especially when they tend to be so noisy!' For his heart had just gone off in the attaché case like an alarm clock. 'It does that,' he said, 'I can't really control it.') Nor can I, you see, darling. However when next I offer you a cigarette, you'll know what it stands for.

---

1 – Presumably the disturbances of 12 July 1935, when two people were shot dead and over forty shot or injured, in riots in the York Street district. Although a curfew order was enforced, seven people were dead within a week. See 'Street Shooting in Belfast', *The Times*, 13 July 1935, 12, and subsequent reports. Cf. 'the noise of shooting / Starting in the evening at eight / In Belfast in the York Street district' (*AJ*, XVI; CP07, 138).

2 – John Davenport (1910–66) was a scriptwriter and critic whose family inheritance allowed him to feel – in direct contrast with FLM – casual about regular employment. After Cambridge, he had worked in Hollywood before returning to England where he lived in a large country house in Bristol; he was variously employed as a teacher (Stowe), writer (BBC) and critic (the *Observer* and other papers). Cf. 'Auden and MacNeice: Their Last Will and Testament': 'And to John Davenport a permanent job to hold' (*LI*, CP07, 743). Davenport co-published with Dylan Thomas *Death of the King's Canary* (1940, published posthumously). He published a review of *SAF* ('Louis', *Spectator*, 26 Nov. 1965, 714–15).

3 – Tom Harrisson (1911–76), anthropologist and founder of Mass Observation (1937) with poet Charles Madge, painter William Coldstream and filmmaker Humphrey Jennings.

4 – Clark's birthday was 6 July (b.1913).

5 – *Poetry of W. B. Yeats* (Oxford, 1941).

344

Goodnight, my darling, forgive the frivolity of this letter (it is rather fun, isn't it, though, the old ladies giving me my freedom?)

all my love, darling,
L

P.S. Darling, you won't get ill again, will you? I get very worried about you.

TO *Eleanor Clark*   MS Yale

27 June [1939]   16A Primrose Hill Road

Darling,

Please forgive this junk I enclose; it is for Vassar or any other academic body who might be interested in me. I dare say it is really too late in the season for me to fix a static job at any one college but they tell me here that I can probably get something itinerant. In any case I shall be coming – even if I have to gamble on fixing something after my arrival. Have burned my boats for a year, you see; they are appointing my substitute in Bedford today.

Darling, I have just had your first letter from Yaddo. Darling, how awful about your temperatures & things; please don't be a martyr to science. You are to be happy in Yaddo & not get any more of these things. Darling (I am just going through your letter) you have got me wrong about normal people; I am all for (moderately) normal people but I don't count salesmen & clerks normal at all: I count myself fairly normal & Wystan (except for sex) & many farmers & doctors. By abnormal I mean undeveloped or blinkered; this applies to most of the literaries [*sic*]. If I were pedantic I should refer you to the Greeks.

Darling, if I failed to fix anything before Christmas, I could always raise money for us to go to Peru or something in the autumn provided we were prepared to write something nominally about it, only that is no doubt prostitution (unless you could do a bulk of genuine prose & I were to just fill in with some genuine poems. I hate this idea of commissioned books but it would be one way of getting there).

It has only just dawned on me why Athens was as she was; there were always a good many more men (citizens) than women.

I have now got so muddled with this letter-writing that I have no idea which letters of mine you are answering etc. I am afraid one or two will have been reaching New York after you have left. Darling, please forgive

me if I am writing rather dim. It is very dimming you being so far away &
I <u>hate</u> thinking of you being ill & what is there I can do about it? O yes,
darling, do tell me when your birthday is & I'll write you a birthday letter
with a picture of candles or roses or something on it.

Am going over to Belfast soon to broadcast about poetry on July 11th
so will see the twelfth processions (did I tell you about them? I think there
may be trouble this year. If so, I shall write an article anti-Orange).

Had lunch with Stephen yesterday who spent time running down
Christopher. What cats we all are (Heaven awaits us full of saucers of milk
– like some sort of super-Automat). My dance last week was not really so
unpleasant. We all drank a great deal & I have the happy delusion that I
can dance when I am drunk. I also went to the Ballet with someone who
never watches anything except Les Sylphides – escape, escape, escape.[1]
Also to hear Eliot reading his poems to a half-baked audience rotten with
money. He reads <u>his own</u> poems very well though awfully tired & unwell-
looking – very much the aged eagle. Did I tell you Morley is working a
conspiracy (this is secret) to effect my secession from Random House to
Harcourt Brace?

After this I must walk through the park to my college & draw my salary
– last till November a year. In any case I doubt if it will cancel my
overdraft. From now on must work hard on Yeats – shall be a little tired
of the phases of the moon by the time I see you.[2] Am going to take my
friend Stahl to Ireland with me in August; we shall both work in separate
rooms & occasionally take to the moors for purgation.[3] He is an authority
on Rilke. I had a silly review the other day (jointly with Stephen), the point
being that Stephen strikes a deep note whereas I am merely concerned with
the daily moods. Not that I disagree with this but I didn't like the slur on
the daily moods, feel they deserve a square deal. Besides anyone can strike
a deep note if they choose to mention nothing but ice & crystal & roses
& Life & Death & Europe. (Stephen can't be in love with anyone without
seeing him poised over Europe. If you knew Tony, you would appreciate

1 – Possibly a source for 'Les Sylphides': 'Life in a day: he took his girl to the ballet; / Being
shortsighted himself could hardly see it –', from 'Novelettes', *New Statesman* (*NS*), 12 Aug.
1939 (*PP*, CP07, 187). Cf. next letter but one. AB blasted 'Les Sylphides' while praising
Stravinsky: 'Needless to say we did not approve of the more romantic ballets such as
Sylphides . . .' ('From Bloomsbury', 166).
2 – Cf. 'Auden and MacNeice: Their Last Will and Testament': 'Item, we leave the phases of
the moon / To Mr Yeats to rock his bardic sleep' (*LI*, CP07, 735).
3 – Stahl was in Ireland with FLM when Germany invaded Poland (*SAF*, 211–12; Stallworthy,
373–7).

this picture.[1] Tony has now got a job – £5 a week & expenses – going round pubs listening to what people say about the beer & reporting it to the brewers.)

Now, darling, I must stop & this has to catch the Queen Mary. Please don't have any more afflictions. I feel like an aunt saying a pint of milk a day & don't go to bed late. I don't really feel like an aunt at all (one has to be homosexual to be aunt-like; Wystan can do it perfectly). But please, my darling, be well & don't fret & don't force things; if you fret, you won't be able to work. Goodbye, darling,

L.

TO *Eleanor Clark*   MS Yale

2 July [1939]   16A Primrose Hill Road

My darling,

How are you in Yaddo & are you fully recovered & gay & sparkling with health? I don't seem to have heard from you for a long time. Really these posts are just bloody. However I got the drawing of you for which many, many thanks; I like it very much. You do look rather serious but then you often do of course. I shall bring it over with me in case you insist on having it back but perhaps she could do another one?

I am in charge of my child for the whole day today. We have just been walking through Regent's Park, looking at llamas on the fringe of the zoo & sitting in a rose-garden. He is taking his whooping cough very lightly & appears in fact very much healthier than I am as I have been struck by a sore throat, aching eyes etc. etc. & generally feel very much below myself. This is not helped by having to read 'A Vision' by Yeats which is enough to send anyone to a sanatorium.[2] Tomorrow I start reading Yeatsiana in the British Museum. I rather like working in the Reading Room there; makes me feel very virtuous & also a citizen of the world, most of the other readers being foreign, every so often I go out & sit among totem poles & pigeons on the colonnade in order to smoke.[3] My term is now over, I have drawn my last salary, & had a substitute appointed for a year.

1 – Tony Hyndman was Stephen Spender's partner for several years prior to Spender's marriage in 1936.
2 – W. B. Yeats, *A Vision* (1925, 2nd edn 1937).
3 – Of the summer of 1939 he recalls: 'The British Museum became a sort of club for us. Ernst and Reggie and Walter Allen and several others were all attending it' (*SAF*, 209). Cf. 'The British Museum Reading Room', *Plant and Phantom* (*PP*), 22, CP07, 172, 690.

Feel very much on the streets. Before coming to America I have to (a) write the Yeats book, (b) finish my Latin Humour book, which Fabers have taken, (c) finish this damned Greek play. Talking of plays I went with my sister the other night to an Irish play, 'Bridgehead', written by an old man, Rutherford Mayne, all about land commissioners (a new kind of hero but the old conflict – duty v. the heart – & duty winning).[1]

Disapproval of my going to America is general. They all say: 'Look at what it has done to Wystan & Christopher.' I haven't mentioned it to my father & step-mother yet, who won't hold with it at all as they think I ought to keep the Atlantic between me & my ex-wife. She is indeed, as I think I told you, very difficult & for that reason I probably couldn't have a job at Princeton as it is too near her. I heard from Harvard the other day. There is a remote possibility of a job there (£600 a year) but depending on the present man leaving (which is possible but improbable). They all work so hard that I am not sure I shouldn't prefer hanging about and living by visiting lectures plus journalism.

My child is now beating on a tympanum. Outside the day is grey & windy. Everyone's fretting about the Danzig crisis.[2] I (who am becoming more immoral every day in these respects) have been wondering how I could run away if they have a war. I suppose if I got to the States they would repatriate me. A decadent young man the other night told me there is someone in Mexico who will harbour us all. I really don't care a bloody damn about Danzig & England isn't any country anyway &, though I do hold that morally the British Government ought to check Hitler, there will be so little morality in it by the end of it that I don't feel very inspired to have my legs shot off to bring about that a Europe which is now say 80% rotten should be 85% rotten, supposing H. is checked, instead of say 89% supposing he isn't. Of course these things are all a question of degree & if I have got the degrees all wrong, I am no doubt being very disgraceful. Anyway I haven't filled in any of the forms which they keep sending me so, if there is a war, I shan't have any nice little cushy pigeonhole for myself, so I shall either have to be completely fatalistic & let them shove me into anything they like or else, as I said, run away. There was an interruption then; 3 men & a dog came to call for a typescript after which Dan & I

1 – Rutherford Mayne was the pseudonym of Samuel J. Waddell (1878–1967), who wrote for the Ulster Literary Theatre. *Bridgehead* was first performed at the Abbey Theatre on 18 June 1934. A television adaptation, directed by Dallas Bower, was broadcast in the UK on 16 July 1939.
2 – Poland refused Hitler's demands to cede Danzig to Germany; Britain and France pledged support to Poland. Hitler's invasion of Poland began on 1 Sept.

had lunch including a potato salad sprinkled thickly with caraway seed (an odd habit of Miss Popper's). I am rather pleased, darling, because I am writing a new kind of poem; there are going to be 50 of them, called Novelettes – very bleak, very simple, very objective, all in the 3rd person.[1] Did I tell you I met Gogarty the other day – the original of Malachi Mulligan in Ulysses but, unfortunately, not so funny; conceited in fact & even a little pompous.[2] I don't know what's wrong with me, darling, but I feel frightfully tired, so shall finish this & go to sleep on the sofa (Dan is having his rest upstairs). It has just dawned on me I shall be seeing you the month after next (that doesn't sound so long). Darling, I love you quite exorbitantly. Please write some more,

be good & do some work
<u>but don't get ill</u>,
love,
L.

P.S. Do you know an Irish poem which starts something like this –

> My grief on the sea!
> How the waves of it roll
> For they come between me
> & the love of my soul . . . etc.[3]

Anyhow that's how I feel. Very un-Parisian (& unAmerican?) of me. The chief asset of the sea however is that it can be crossed. Or as Caesar said, jacta alea est, meaning To hell with the Three Gauls & I feel like dinner in Rome.[4] (I suppose you are having breakfast now; it's about time we got in step again).

1 – 'Novelettes', in *The Last Ditch* (Dublin, 1940), 21–8; *PP* (1941), 45–56; repr. in *Collected Poems, 1925–1948* (1949), excluding 'Suicide' and 'The Expert', 192–8.
2 – Oliver St John Gogarty (1878–1957), surgeon, author, celebrated wit and raconteur. Educ. Stoneyhurst; Clongowes; TCD. Wrote plays, novels, poems (*Collected Poems*, 1957) and three volumes of autobiography, including *As I Was Going Down Sackville Street* (1937).
3 – Douglas Hyde (trans.), 'My Grief on the Sea', in Quiller-Couch, *Oxford Book of English Verse: 1250–1900*.
4 – 'The die is cast' (allegedly spoken by Caesar as he crossed the Rubicon).

16 July [1939]   16A Primrose Hill Road

Darling,

I am very worried at not having heard from you for so long. I hope it is because you just don't feel like writing or have put the wrong address or something & not that you're ill. I had one letter from you just after you reached Yaddo & none since. Darling, you <u>mustn't</u> be ill or anything like that. & <u>please write</u>.

I had a crazy time in Ireland. The man I had the radio discussion with was crazy (he thinks I've sold my birthright)[1] & the Orange procession was crazy – banners depicting Samson fighting with the Lion, Christ giving water to Total Abstainers, The Storming of Jhansi, William III of course ad nauseam, Queen Victoria pretty often, Lord Beaconsfield quite a bit, plenty of local worthies, a number of local churches & also some allegoricals like Justice & Truth. All very gaudy & the bearers staggering under the weight of them.

Next day: I don't know why I stopped this. I think I went to sleep. This morning, darling, I read in the British Museum & was interested to find what appallingly bad verse Yeats wrote in his early twenties – suppressed in the later editions. Have heard a lot of good stories about Yeats lately from Gogarty & Higgins e.g. when Yeats' Spanish doctor wrote an account of his health to Gogarty which G. read out, knowing Yeats wouldn't know what it meant – 'This is an antique sclerocardiac . . .' & Yeats stopped him & rolled the word on his tongue & said 'Sclerocardiac! I'd rather have that title than be King of Lesser Egypt.'[2]

1 – Broadcast on BBC Northern Ireland (also on Scottish, Clevedon and Aberdeen stations) on 11 July (10.25–11.00 p.m.) and published as 'Tendencies in Modern Poetry: A Discussion between Prof. Higgins and Louis MacNeice' in the *Listener*, 27 July 1939. The broadcast was immediately preceded by a ten-minute broadcast entitled 'The Travelling Exhibition of the Ulster Academy of the Arts, by R. T. [*sic*] Hewitt'. The poet John Hewitt wrote to FLM next day: 'I wish heartily to congratulate you on yr. advocacy of socialist internationalism in last night's discussion with Higgins. Yr. defence of contemporary poets was an invaluable piece of work especially in a cultural Sahara such as this' (*Ms Bodleian, Ms Res, c. 589*). Frederick Robert Higgins (1896–1941), Irish poet, author of *Island Blood* (1925), *The Dark Breed* (1927), *Arable Holdings* (1933) and other works. He was a director and business manager of the Abbey Theatre. An excerpt from the discussion was later used in lieu of a preface to the *Faber Book of Contemporary Irish Poetry* (1986), ed. Paul Muldoon. Higgins appears as the character Reilly in *AS*.

2 – Gogarty told a slightly different version to Horace Reynolds: '"We have here an antique cardio-renal sclerotic of advanced years." Why! It sounds like a lord of Upper Egypt.' Gogarty to Reynolds, 14 Nov. 1936, qtd in R. F. Foster, *W. B. Yeats: A Life*, vol. II: *The Arch Poet*

Have been writing quite a lot of poetry lately – one which I think good, called Les Sylphides; I will send it to you when it is typed.[1] Had lunch today, darling, with my friend who has a job in Rumania;[2] he says any time I want it he can get me £8 a week there <u>and</u> all expenses (including drinks, cigarettes & newspapers), so if I can't raise any money in the States this year I might go to Rumania – if you will come back with me (you could give some lectures there on America, yes?)

You are very wicked, darling, not telling me when your birthday is (or was?) I expect I shan't reach the states till mine is over too.

Higgins after denouncing me for 24 hours for having de-Irishised myself asked me if I'd like to belong to the Irish Academy of Letters.[3] I said yes. But they'll probably think better of it. The Irish Academy of Letters meets once a year in Dublin's only decent restaurant & gets so drunk they have to send the waiters away. Did I by the way, darling, ever tell you the epic story about the meeting of the P.E.N. club in Dubrovnik?

O hell, I have to go out to dinner now. London is really no good for working in. I just <u>can't</u> finish my Greek play, have lost my touch, it comes out frightful. I am going to give up translating after this.

Darling, for God's sake (or Anything's sake, you believe in) write & tell me about yourself. I am not really quite so Olympianly calm as you sometimes imply & I don't like it <u>AT ALL</u> not knowing what's happening to you. Please, my darling.

Well, I suppose I must cultivate my dinner.

goodbye, darling,
be well & happy,
L.

—

(Oxford, 2003), 570, 755, n. 118. Foster notes that elsewhere Gogarty attributes the 'Upper Egypt' *bon mot* to Yeats rather than to himself, as here.

1 – 'Les Sylphides', published in *NS*, 12 Aug. 1939.

2 – Reggie Smith.

3 – Yeats established the Irish Academy of Letters in 1932, with George Bernard Shaw as president.

TO *Eleanor Clark*   MS Yale

4 September [1939]¹   c/o Abbey Theatre, Dublin

Darling,

I am back in this town which at least has some lights though neither
merry nor bright. It looks now as if I shan't be able to come before January
as the Trinity College appointment is taking longer than I thought. Also the
boats at the moment will only carry American citizens. I am afraid it is a
complicated & exasperating business & you must be sick of hearing about
it, darling. I feel that I shall be hanging about for years.

> 'Like a strange soul upon the Stygian banks
> Waiting for waftage?'²

My friends continue to write me exceedingly dismal letters from England.
As for the radio & the newspapers they diffuse together with patriotism &
horrible insipid facetiousness. One grows older every day in impotent rage
& desolation. On the chief bridge in Dublin – O'Connell Bridge – there is
a barrel organ every night which makes me very nostalgic.³ I had a nice
quarter of an hour's escapism today discussing with a Dublin poet whether
in a certain line one ought to write 'has gathered' or merely 'gathered'.
Also Dublin was very lovely in the sun. Perhaps you will come here
sometime?? Nothing but bacon & eggs to eat – over & over again with
very strong tea. In Belfast I met a young man who was wildly anti-
everything & spends his time compiling huge albums of newspaper
cuttings. Museum of human idiocy. Having previously been Trotskyite he
says he has gone Stalinist since Russia invaded Poland. Which is as logical
as anything else. My own feeling is that regular wars don't do any good but
irregular wars may. & you only get irregular wars as a byproduct of
regular wars. Which reminds me, I expect in the States you hear more
about this Indian business than we do. If they gave India her independence
I might almost reconsider my attitude but I take it they won't. My friends
in London seem to spend their time joining things like the River Police &
promptly being axed.

Do write to me, darling, & tell me something human. I am going to bed
now which is a lonely proceeding except that here people seem to talk in

1 – FLM's Irish passport is stamped 4 Sept. 1939.
2 – After Shakespeare, *Troilus and Cressida*, II.ii: 'Like a strange soul upon the Stygian banks /
Staying for waftage'.
3 – See 'O'Connell Bridge' in *Poems, 1925–1940*, PP, and CP07, 769.

the streets all night. In my bedroom last night I wrote a ballad so morbid that I frightened myself. Tomorrow I have got to think up a talk on English painting, I might as well put on a record of the Last Post. I have by the way – did I tell you – undertaken to write my first serious prose book (all my other prose has been potboiling) but my scheme is very difficult to describe. A sort of apology, perhaps, for what was not my life. I want to do it now as it seems for once in perspective.[1]

Darling, you mustn't get thrown out of gear by the mob hysteria. This is ever so important. <u>Please</u> be good & get on with your work – & write yourself. The idea of sacrifice can be overdone. & the silliest sort of sacrifice is to let oneself be distracted by something one can't do anything about merely because one's humanity distracts one.[2] I always said, of course, darling, you were too humane for your own good. Perhaps some day there will be a point in abdicating for a principle. Not at this moment. The more people go on being themselves at this moment (at least if they are people like you, darling), the better.

By the way, darling, how good a Marxist are you? Marx of course wasn't a very good one himself. Living in Eire reminds one that people are by no means exclusively governed by economic factors. It also seems to me questionable whether they ought to be. Sounds puerile put like this & I can't go into it now. No doubt it is a necessary hypothesis if anything is ever going to be done, e.g. it was the Communists in Spain who got things done & not the Anarchists. But the Anarchists had got hold of something which the C.P. are just dumb about. More things in heaven & earth . . . I'm sorry, darling, I seem to be getting awfully preachy these days. Comes from having to talk to my stepmother's aurophone.

Goodnight my darling. Bedtime story: Once there were people in a desert & they went through a sandstorm & when the storm was over they saw an oasis – palms & grass & water – & they went a mile more & a mile more & another mile all blisters & when they got up to it the palms were shady & the grass was green & the water was fresh & the whole dream thing was real. That's all. Love ever. Louis.

1–Published posthumously as *The Strings Are False* (1965). Her response was discouraging: '(Why are you doing a prose book? Why be so prolific? I suppose it's all right if you feel like it, but you're really not an old man yet darling)', EC to FLM, 29 Oct. 1939, *Ms Yale*.
2–Her response: 'Incidentally don't worry about me and sacrifice, I just don't see any gangplank to walk off at the moment and so am being quite quite alive, riding horseback and such, and if I were settled in my place I think I'd be writing furiously' (EC to FLM, 29 Oct. 1939, *Ms Yale*).

TO *T. S. Eliot*   Faber archive

14 September [1939]   Abbey Theatre, Dublin

Dear Eliot,

My plans are rather in the air at the moment. I will try & finish the Roman Smile – although I am no longer an academic by profession.

Would you by the way consent to my doing a short book of about twenty short poems for the Cuala Press here? A limited edition of about 300 copies for subscribers. Yeats had most of his poems done by them first & subsequently – in bulkier collections – by Macmillan's. It would be good Irish (&, I think, American) publicity & I should like to do it for the sake of someone connected with the press who has done a lot for me. If you preferred, there need be no copies sent out for review. They could publish it Christmasish & by late spring I could add enough new poems for a book from Faber's.

I have also a scheme for my first serious creative prose book – to be called something like Plaudits & Aspersions or Blessings & Curses.[1] Autobiographical but not in the usual way. A series of quick shots – with some more drawn-out-ones – of the significant events of my life, not so much things I have done as things I have met; the padding left out & a pattern appearing through variations on several recurring themes; some of it – the more personal parts – in disguise, possibly fantasy. Roughly, in chronological order, it would cover:- The North of Ireland, child's nightmares, Ulster mentality, Ulster religion, sadist mother's help, zany gardener, Orangemen: the last War, preparatory school in Dorset, a Dorset Powys, a 1919 Oxford aesthete : public school (Marlborough), games etc., sex fantasies, a dream about the Crucifixion,[2] public school Picasso fans : Oxford, Auden & Spender, etc., dons, drink : Jewry & marriage – treated obliquely : Birmingham, pigeon-fanciers, the Birmingham surrealists, provincial universities – maybe classical digressions : divorce treated obliquely : London from 1936, various odd travels, the Left : Barcelona New Year 1939 (a whole chapter)[3] : New York : finally Ireland again ending with news while in Galway of Germany invading Poland. This was the sort of book I mentioned to Robert Hale & they were prepared to contract for it – to be delivered within twelve months.[4] This is of course

1–Presumably this is material which became *SAF*.
2–Cf. 'Tiers and tiers of people in gala dress – bunting, rattles and paper streamers – and in the arena were the three bodies on the crosses' (*SAF*, 101).
3–*SAF*, 176–96 (ch. 35).
4–FLM had previously written to TSE on 14 Aug. about Robert Hale's offer, 'a very elastic sort of suggestion to me that I should do a book for them during the next year (travel-book

confidential but a young man on the firm told me I could get £150 advance for it. I had much rather of course that Faber's did it & should in that case be prepared to drop £50 but I <u>should</u> like £100 advance as I now have no money at all. Being an Irish citizen I am exempt from conscription, so shall no doubt have time to write it long before a year's time.

I hope you will approve the Cuala Press scheme,

Yours ever,
Louis MacNeice

P.S. Please reply to me c/o the Abbey.

TO *E. R. Dodds*　　　　　　　　　　　　　　　MS Bodleian

24 September 1939　　　　　　　Bishop's House, Malone Road,
　　　　　　　　　　　　　　　　Belfast

I was very sorry indeed to hear about your wife's operation but am very glad to hear from Margaret Gardiner that she is now recovered.[1] Do give her all my best wishes.[2]

I have been hanging around in this country communing with my conscience – such as it is – & revolving various schemes, most of them rather wild & none of them lucrative (unfortunately I need lucre because of my dependants). In the middle of this indecision I met Walter Starkie in

—

if I happen to go round America; failing that, some sort of eclectic pageant of reminiscences and aspersions)' (*Faber archive*). He said he was inclined to accept the offer since it might be lucrative – 'me being so poor at the moment'.

1 – Margaret Gardiner (1904–2005), educ. Froebel School (Hammersmith), Bedales, and Newnham College, Cambridge. An exponent of the theories of A. S. Neill, she became briefly a primary school teacher at Gamlingay (Cambridgeshire). Her circle of friends included Barbara Hepworth and Ben Nicholson and she had a son with Desmond (J. D.) Bernal. She was a founder of the anti-fascist Association of Writers for Intellectual Liberty (FIL), which FLM also joined (see next letter). A founder member of the Institute of Contemporary Arts, she gave her personal art collection to a gallery in Orkney. As Stallworthy wrote: 'She "knew everybody," had met D. H. Lawrence, climbed in Snowdonia with I. A. Richards, and known Auden in Berlin' (Stallworthy, 263–4). Auden introduced her to FLM in 1939 at 4A Keats Grove, which she recalls in 'Louis MacNeice Remembered' (*Quarto*, May 1980, repr. in *A Scatter of Memories*, 1988, 117–33.)

2 – Cf. WHA to Mrs Dodds, 27 Oct. 1939: 'How horrid about the op: I hope you are healing and that the results have been worth it; I wish you weren't always so reticent and had said exactly what it was; you make it sound like something vaguely disgraceful, Venereal Disease or something.' 'Six Letters from Auden to the Doddses', ed. Kathleen Bell, in K. Bucknell and N. Jenkins (eds), *W. H. Auden: 'The Map of All My Youth'*, Auden Studies 1 (Oxford, 1990), 105.

Dublin who asked me bang out of the blue if I would apply for the chair of English at Trinity.[1] So I said Yes. I daresay this may scandalise you as being a kind of escapism but I can't really see that I should be doing any more for civilisation by what they say the intellectuals must do – propaganda work.

Anyhow I am going to apply for it. Of course it is ridiculous as I know nothing about Eng. Lit. but Walter Starkie seems to think that doesn't matter in the least. Would you feel like writing me a testimonial sometime. There is no great hurry as the thing hasn't yet been advertised.

Failing that, I shall revert to my original scheme for this winter which is not yet impracticable. (I should like to see E. before settling down for the duration.)

Failing that, I think of plumping for something brainless. There must be plenty of people to propagand, so I have no feeling of guilt in refusing to mortify my mind.

I get so bored here, I feel all the time like running off & joining the herring fleet or something. But, although everyone around is deaf, halfbaked or superannuated, I am forcing myself to hold my hand. When I come over, I must see you & talk about the principles of it all. If there are any left by then. / hasta la vista, / Louis.

TO *Eleanor Clark*   MS Yale

24 September [1939]   Bishop's House, Malone Road,
                                              Belfast

Darling,

Here I am back again in this place with my family. A mistake – except financially – as the atmosphere is demoralising in the extreme. Every day I have to keep my head to prevent myself running off & selling my freedom in some way or other. I got your letter here, darling, sent by the Yankee Clipper; it had taken a long time to come. It is very cheering indeed to think you are still interested in me. I didn't send a cable as I had already sent one from Dublin. My request by the way in that cable still goes. I think now that it is possible I may have to come over <u>temporarily</u> by myself (which is much more feasible), try & fix up something for later, then return here & later,

1 – Walter F. Starkie (1894–1976), CMG, CBE, MA, DLitt, MRIA, FRSA, FRSL, Hon. Fellow TCD. Lecturer, later Professor of Spanish Literature, TCD; director Abbey Theatre 1927–42, director British Institute (Madrid) 1940–54. Brother of literary critic Enid Starkie (see FLM to BCM, 19 July 1963, n. 1, p. 700).

when I have a watertight reason for so doing, return with Dan. In the meantime I have been asked to apply for the Chair of English at Trinity College, Dublin.[1] If I got this (which would incidentally be an academic scandal) I should have to start work in Dublin in January, but I could then possibly come over to see you before that (provided that they don't take too long making the appointment) & almost certainly come at Easter and/or in the summer. Paradoxically this appointment while making it impossible for me to be in America except at certain times would make it much easier for me to get to America as it would square me for good with your consuls. However, if I <u>don't</u> get this job, I can still, I am pretty sure, arrange to come for a bit but I must have some prospects of paying my way. At the moment I am paying large sums to keep Dan & Miss Popper in a separate ménage in the country & I still have to pay rent for my old flat as it seems unlikely that I shall be able to sublet it. However, darling, I will stop oppressing you with these boring details. The main point is that, unless something unforeseen happens, I <u>shall</u> be able to see you in the more or less near future although I can't promise that I shall not have to keep coming and going. But if I go, I shall always go to return. My sister, who is here now on a holiday from looking after lunatics in London, is seriously shocked by my schemes & thinks I should be putting my brains at the disposal of the British Government. I got a letter to the same effect from a thing called The Association of Writers for Intellectual Liberty under the aegis of Day Lewis.[2] My point on the contrary is: Either European civilisation is doomed or it isn't doomed. If it is doomed there is no point in my prostituting my mind in its defence; if it isn't doomed, I may as well be there with an unprostituted mind to carry on with it. Of course hardly any of the English writers would agree with me; they are all for mortifying themselves. But then after all I amn't even <u>English</u>. No doubt I shall soon be a pariah in this hemisphere – excepting in Eire – but, when they tell me the situation is clear-cut, I just can't agree with them. My father fortunately thinks I am quite right. I imagine that in two or three years a lot more people will think so.

Life here is very piano & grey. The only person at all gay is Miss Popper's father, a Hungarian Jew, who is staying for a bit with my family. I talk with him in dog-German. He is mad on etymology & used to be a bank-manager. His dream is to take part in the burning of Mein Kampf in Berlin.

1 – He would learn of the rejection of his application on 6 Dec. 1939. H. O. White was the successful applicant. See FLM to ERD, 8 Dec. 1939 (*Ms Bodleian*).
2 – FLM was elected to the committee of the FIL in Dec. 1938, and took part in a number of anti-fascist marches (Stallworthy, 234).

This seems an extraordinary way to be writing to you, darling, awfully dry & stilted but I guess you know how I feel. All the time one is suffocating. There has been a lot of sun lately & the sunshine seems dead. I find it hard to go to sleep at night, so I smoke myself silly in bed, & then sleep instead in a dead way after lunch. Sometimes – very laboriously – I write a few more pages on Yeats. I hope you got the poems I sent you. I dare say you will think them slight. I don't myself, having been brought up on the Greek Anthology & Catullus, but of course they don't go blazing any trail or anything like that (I had a letter from a schoolmaster saying he expected Wystan, Stephen & me to blaze a trail for him in these troubled times). The war seems to have invested me with an odd blend of humility & arrogance – I am that I am (meaning out of touch with reality. So, admitting it may be my funeral to be out of touch with 'the facts,' it is equally the funeral of anyone who thinks these facts are everything). O hell, darling, please forgive me for dreaming along like this. It is Sunday morning now, some of the household at church, my father in bed & one little desolate bell clanging somewhere in the suburbs. This is one of the ugliest houses I know; it was built by a mid-Victorian tea merchant & is all plaster cornices & anaglypta. But they have enormous white dahlias in the garden. I have been reading a life of De Valera.[1] It is appalling to think of the amount of energy – & singlemindedness – people spend on contradictory ends.[2] My stepmother is very puzzled by the prospect of ration books. I tell her that after the rationbooks will come the Revolution but of course that makes no sense to her. The bell, thank God, has now stopped – no, darling, that is another illusion, it hasn't. The trams here are shrouded in blue; at night it is like going into a tomb. Far, far darker than Barcelona.[3] I have heard from none of my friends in England except from two women belonging, I feel, to the past. Whereas you, I feel very strongly, belong to the future. Darling, please write to me some more. Letters seem to take a time to come but they come. I am sorry, darling, this letter is so dim. I am, as I said, hopeful about <u>my own</u> prospects but that is not the whole story. No doubt one will soon become more callous. At the moment I feel vaguely wicked when I think how happy it would make me to see you. As if it were wrong for anyone ever to be happy again. Of course that is a fallacy but it soaks into one. Lots & lots of love, darling, & get on with your novel. A thousand kisses. Louis.

1 – Probably Sean O'Faolain, *De Valera* (1939).
2 – See *AJ*, XVI (1939): 'I note how a single purpose can be founded on / A jumble of opposites' (*CP07*, 138).
3 – FLM had visited Barcelona in Dec. 1938. Cf. *SAF*, 176–96.

P.S. It might be a good idea if you or anyone else sent me (alone) an invitation to stay <u>on a visit for a month</u> anytime I could manage in the near future.

TO *T. S. Eliot*   Faber archive

6 October [1939]   Bishop's House, Malone Road,
                                          Belfast

Dear Eliot,

I was glad to hear from you about the Cuala Press (they won't send any review copies outside Ireland) and also that you are willing to do the prose book.[1] Yes, I intend to be all prose. It would be convenient if, as you say, I could have the contract at once. 80,000 words will be all right. I am pleased at the prospect of writing prose for a change (it will be rather different from my pot-boiler prose), especially as in verse at the moment I can write nothing except short – almost Greek Anthologyism – lyrics.

I have been asked to apply for the Chair of English Literature at Trinity College, Dublin. Of course I don't know anything about Eng. Lit. by examination standards but I am going to put in for it. I wonder if you could send me some sort of testimonial.[2] If, as is likely, I don't get it, I still hope to try to crash America for a three months' lecturing visit starting in January. The consulates however are very difficult these days.

I am still labouring at this terrible book on Yeats[3] but I hope soon to be able to finish 'The Roman Smile' (when I can get hold of the right books) and the translation of Hippolytus.[4] One – rather grey – advantage over here is that there is nothing to do but read and write. Especially now that the Irish weather has returned to type.

Yours sincerely
Louis MacNeice

---

1 – The reference is to what eventually became *SAF*.
2 – Eliot's testimonial is dated 10 Oct. 1939 (*Faber archive*).
3 – *Poetry of W. B. Yeats*.
4 – Neither book was published.

TO *E. R. Dodds*

13 October [1939]

Belvedere Hotel, 1 Nth Gt George's
Street, Dublin [hereafter Belvedere
Hotel] [letterhead, scratched out],
as from Malone Road, Belfast

Dear E.R.D.

Thank you very much for the charming but undeserved testimonial. The
business doesn't come up for a month yet so I am hoping that by the time
I have failed to get it, I may have come to some decision about this war.
Down here one gets quite de- (or dis-) orientated. It all sounds like a
nightmare algebra which you have to change back into people being killed.
It is all very well for everyone to go on saying 'Destroy Hitlerism' but what
the hell are they going to construct? I am now falling into a sort of paradox
which is:- if the war were a rational war leading somewhere, I should want
to stay out of it in order to see where it led to: but if it is a hopeless war
leading nowhere, I feel half inclined to take the King's shilling & escape –
more likely than not – the frustration to come. The motives in each case
of course being selfish.

I still want – if possible – to go the States January to March in order to
clear myself up emotionally. Three months would solve the question of E.
one way or the other. (She has incidentally gone to a lot of trouble getting
lectures & things for me).[1] At the moment I am all at sea & even sliding
– among my own countrymen – into perhaps my rashest entanglement yet.
(If it weren't for my American fixation I should fall into it headlong). Of
course the King's shilling would solve all that too. It is difficult not to be
egotistical over here. Yet I get the impression that in England it must be
difficult to avoid wishful thinking. I would rather be quit of thinking
altogether & just let people order me about. All this boosting up
democracy – it seems to me just throwing the sand against the wind. If
democracy does survive, it won't be Anthony Eden's. But if the Anthony
Edens are to dragoon us into a crusade it seems better they should dragoon
our bodies than our minds. I feel that if one puts one's mind at their service
& sits in a civilian chair for the duration mumbling about democracy one
will just be a period piece by the time one gets to 'victory' or 'defeat'. I
wish you would tell me what you think about it as everyone one meets
just thinks from hand to mouth.

---

1 – 'Darling, it is terribly nice of you to go writing to all these institutions. I simply loathe
writing to institutions myself & I shouldn't dream of doing it, I guess, on behalf of anyone
else. You must really be a very angelic person' (FLM to EC, 3 Oct. 1939, unpublished).

It was simply lovely here in Dublin tonight with a barrelorgan on O'Connell Bridge & the wind blowing the Liffey into crinkled ink. This is a nice hotel & people talk in the street all night. I gave a talk on English Painting of all things in an exhibition here the other day. & Miss Sarah Purser, you may be pleased to hear, is still having her At Homes.[1] Plenty of Nero fiddling around here. Rather nice Neros though.

It seems to me typical that the British Govmt. should simultaneously tell you to cut out all luxuries & preen themselves on the millions that are going to come in from the new taxes on liquor & tobacco.

The four horsemen of the Apocalypse & the horses were harnessed with red tape. After which someone swallowed a book didn't he? & it was plenty to swallow.

I do hope your wife is now fully recovered. I had a letter from Mary. She is cultivating her chickens.[2]

Please tell me any news of anyone. The only letters I get from England are melancholy. Except one from an unknown thanking me for Minch & Zoo. Nice to think that the pots one boiled do the same job as the BBC's light music.

To adapt Rupert Doone: Aeschylus is static, Hitler is dynamic so f— all.[3] And now to be after a glass of milk,

Yours ever,
Louis

1 –Sarah Purser (1848–1943), Irish painter who in 1923 became the first woman to be elected to membership of the Royal Hibernian Academy. Educ. Dublin School of Art and the Académie Julian, Paris. She established a factory in Upper Pembroke St, Dublin: An Túr Gloinne (Tower of Glass) Co-Operative Stained Glass and Mosaic Works, Ltd. FLM later dubbed her 'mistress of stained glass and malice' in 'Under the Sugar Loaf' (1962), repr. SP, 246.
2 –Mary MacNeice and Charles Katzman had a poultry farm in southern New Jersey, near Egg Harbor.
3 –Concerning his 1936 production of the *Agamemnon*, Doone had remarked: 'Aeschylus was static, I am dynamic, so fuck all' (qtd in Dodds, *Missing Persons: An Autobiography*, Oxford, 1977, 132). Cf. 'Auden and MacNeice: Their Last Will and Testament': 'Item, we leave our old friend Rupert Doone / Something dynamic . . .' (*LI*, CP07, 736).

TO *Eleanor Clark* MS Yale

25 October [1939] Belvedere Hotel

Darling,

This is me again; I hope you don't dislike me after my last letter.[1] I have had no letters from you for ages but one today from Selden Rodman who says he is expecting to see me. Maybe he will but it is all on the knees of what, if one were a cynic, one might call gods. I wish you would write to me, darling, as my world is all confusion & I, though merely flowing with tides, am always finding myself guilty. I have just had this afternoon a depressing letter from a girl in England whom I became temporarily & casually involved with this summer as the result of a party.[2] She doesn't feel temporary or casual about it & says she is very unhappy, has got to see me etc. Myself I don't want to see her at all. & then there is my ex-wife writing to say she never sleeps at night. & then there is someone I used to know very well writing for consolation because her life is breaking up. & here on the spot there is the Irish girl I told you about[3] & I want to go on knowing her while at the same time I don't want to lead her up the garden. Finally there is you, darling, about whom I feel every so often terribly nostalgic – like someone in a dream fading away in ripples & you wake up & there is only an empty lake. I guess I ought to retire – either into the war or into a hermitage. I have met a terribly nice man called Ernie O'Malley[4] who says he could find me a cottage in the West.[5] Literary Dublin is very

1 – Their letters frequently crossed: 'You say I hope I don't dislike you after it, but not having gotten it of course I don't, and wouldn't anyway' (EC to FLM, 27 Nov. 1939, *Ms Yale*).

2 – Margaret Gardiner.

3 – He may have written about Eileen Phillips ('Irish girl'), but EC had not received the letter when she wrote on 27 Nov.: 'I never got it. I suppose it was where you told me about the Irish girl. Never mind – these things are sad and sometimes worse but they will straighten themselves out.' Not a great deal is known about Eileen Phillips except that she worked at Victor Waddington Publications (and Gallery), Nassau Street, Dublin. Only a few letters are extant: cf. Phillips to FLM 14 Feb. and 6 March 1942 (*Ms Bodleian, Ms Res, c. 584, Box 9*). Stallworthy writes that their friendship 'flowered to the point at which [FLM] considered asking her to marry him' (263). Cf. FLM to ERD, 6 Nov 1939, p. 364.

4 – Ernie O'Malley (1898–1957), writer and Irish republican. Author of *On Another Man's Wound* (1936), a classic account of the 1916 rising and of his career in the IRA. He later became a journalist and broadcaster. His other works include *The Singing Flame* (1978) and *Raid and Rallies* (1982). He appears as Aidan in *AS*. O'Malley lived in Dublin and at Burrishoole Lodge, Co. Mayo, where FLM stayed in 1945 (FLM to LG, 4 July 1945, pp. 455–6).

5 – EC was upset by this: 'You made it all seem so desolate this morning that I had to cable, just to feel you were somewhere on this world. But it needn't be like that, if you will only not talk about taking cottages in the West, which has overtones of a Viking funeral, and not coming here and me fading in ripples and being an empty lake etc.' (EC to FLM, 27 Nov. 1939, *Ms Yale*).

frivolous & riddled with petty spite. They all hit each other over me in a pub the other day (I am regarded here as an intruder, representative of London etc). I am writing a little – but slowly & creakingly. Have you met Wystan? I hear he is in New York. Please, my darling, write to me. I love you a lot.

Louis

TO *E. R. Dodds*

MS Bodleian

6 November [1939]   Bishop's House, Malone Road, Belfast

Dear E.R.D.,

Thank you very much for your letter. Of course I don't mind being talked to like that; in this case however I rather disagree with what you say. I am not in the habit of using my friends like prostitutes but I do feel guilty over M.G. as she is the only person I have ever had anything to do with without feeling in the slightest degree romantic about her. I don't know what account she gave you of the business but I expect you have gathered that it happened as a pure accident. I don't argue that such accidents are defensible & I don't pretend to have calculated at the time what its effects might be. If however I had done any celebration, I shouldn't have imagined that she would suffer over it. After all (1) she moves in a circle which accepts the philosophy of a famous lady doctor in London: 'It doesn't matter with whom but go to bed whenever you possibly can.' (2) Her relationship with B.,[1] which you accuse me of breaking up, was already an unholy mess both according to herself & to others. (I might – if I had thought about it – even have tended to think that a frivolous – & passing – affaire would be just the thing for her. She is terribly intense.) Anyhow she must have known that if she had anything to do with me, it must be purely ephemeral. She knew about my American fixation & other things. I don't know what I can do for her. If & when I come to England, I shall of course see her but I don't see that that can do much good. You see, I like her very much but I haven't even the beginnings of any romantic feeling for her. & if she is, as you say, empty-handed, so are most people I know, including myself.

Now about your warning to me not to start any more entanglements. I am not at the moment feeling polygamous & I shouldn't dream of starting a new affaire, in the technical sense, with anyone who was likely to build up

1 – Desmond Bernal, cf. FLM to ERD, 24 Sept. 1939, p. 355, n. 1.

a permanent attitude on it. The girl I know over here has been through the mill & is the last person to bank upon mere romantic possibilities.[1] All the same my relationship with her is strictly Platonic & will remain so unless (which is quite on the cards) I decide to marry her. You will probably be horrified by this possibility. Actually I am pretty sure that it would be a great success. The trouble is not that I may do it but that I more likely shan't. I still keep thinking about E. on whom it would be a good deal rasher to depend but who represents permanent adventure & – I suppose – the marriage of true minds. The Irish girl hasn't got a mind in the intellectual sense though she is very intelligent & has got masses of character. Nor – any more than most women – does she represent permanent adventure, her ideal not being Revolution but efficient domestic felicity.

I have just been provisionally offered a job at Cornell University in America.[2] I cabled for details, pending the decision at TCD which I don't think for a moment will come off. If I went to America, I could of course finally find out about E. (Her letters are rather equivocal & she seems to change from week to week.)

About England, I want to come over but I am told on good authority that, if I go, I shan't be allowed back to Ireland. Seeing that I shouldn't be conscripted for at least a year & that I have the hell of a lot of things to write, I would rather do my writing over here in the interim even if in the long run I am to find myself under the colours. Also it saves money staying with my family (I still have to pay rent in London & for Dan down in Co. Down).[3]

M.G. suggested visiting Belfast. I discouraged her from doing so because I thought that in that case she would go on building up this terribly mistaken thing upon me. If however you think it is a good idea, I will suggest she comes. Only I can't make out what she wants from me. She <u>knows</u> there is no question of my ever being in love with her. There are only two people in the world with whom I might tie myself up &, if I don't tie myself up with either of them, it is quite useless anyone else becoming emotionally dependent on me. This probably all sounds very unpleasant

1 – Eileen Phillips.
2 – Cf. EC to FLM, 29 Oct. 1939: 'John Chase phoned me in NY and we talked about this wonderful job he has for you at Cornell. I told him you had written about the Dublin thing but it didn't sound definite yet. What will you do? Could you take it from Feb. to June and bring your child over later?' (*Ms Yale*).
3 – Dan was probably staying in Killyleagh, Co. Down, with the family of Rev. Stanley Mann, the local Church of Ireland minister (later of St John's Church, Hillsborough, Co. Down), who had a daughter of Dan's age. He stayed for a few weeks, before being moved eventually across the border to Cavan (DM, private correspondence, 2008).

but I can't see that your <u>responsibilities of polygamy</u> can include the necessity of giving what is properly a monogamous affection to anyone one has ever slept with. I quite agree that copulation seems to affect women differently. A woman, who has had a lot of experience, told me that once she has slept with someone she ever afterwards regards them with a special affection. But that doesn't mean that she expects each of them to act towards her for ever as if they were in love with her – even if they once were (& in this case I wasn't). Obviously M.G. (because her old relationship with B. was foredoomed to failure) needs, being naturally very warm-hearted, a new one but I wish she would understand that it would be disastrous to look for anything like that with me. I am afraid you will think me very callous but over a year ago I nearly had a breakdown myself over someone & I now regard myself as well out of it.[1] Actually I am tired to death of polygamy. I should like to live somewhere monogamously & work eight hours every day. I do feel (though you probably won't believe me) very remorseful over M.G. but what can I do? If I try meeting her halfway, it would only make things worse,

Yours ever
Louis

TO *T. S. Eliot*   Faber archive

7 November [1939]   Bishop's House, Malone Road,
                                     Belfast

Dear Eliot,
    Thank you for your letter. I think the scheme for cheap selections is a good one at this moment.
    Here are my suggestions about your list of selections which I approve on the whole:-

From <u>Poems</u>: I am not so keen on 'The Individualist Speaks' & 'Circe'. I would rather have 'Train to Dublin' or – if that is too long – 'Snow' and/or 'Perseus'.
From <u>The Earth Compels</u>: If you have to cut, I suggest substituting 'Leaving Barra' for 'On Those Islands'.
From <u>Autumn Journal</u>: I would rather you didn't use either vi (about Spain) or xvi (about Ireland). Two of the sections which seem to me to stand best by themselves are ii and ix.

---

1 – Nancy Coldstream.

Lastly what about putting in – for a change – the chorus from <u>Out of the Picture</u> beginning 'Shall we remember the jingles of the morning'?

My book of poems for the Cuala Press should be out New Yearish. I can definitely promise it to you (plus quite a few additional poems) for later in the spring. Title: <u>The Last Ditch</u>. I have already thirty poems assembled.

Stewart sent me the contract for the prose book. I notice that the clause about the advance promises £100 <u>at the time of publication</u>. What I want is £50 now and the remaining £50 at the time of publication. I am writing to him about this.

Yours ever,
Louis MacNeice

TO *E. R. Dodds* MS Bodleian

19 November [1939]   Bishop's House, Malone Road, Belfast

Dear E.R.D.,

It would be nice if you would write to me again sometime. I hope you were not scandalised by my last letter?[1] I thought in retrospect that it must have read rather unpleasant but I can't pretend feelings for people I haven't got. M.G. by the way is probably coming to Belfast for a few days if she can get a permit.

However I don't want to talk about sex now as there is no logic in it. My conscience is troubling me about this fool war. I am beginning to think this may be <u>my</u> war after all. It doesn't seem any good being perfectionist like the Trotskyites & E. over in America. Obviously there is plenty wrong with the British Empire & especially India & no doubt our present Government have no intention of mending this state of affairs. However the war they are supposed to be running may mend it in spite of them. I find myself liable to use things like India or interferences with liberty at home to rationalise my own cowardice. It does however seem to be <u>clear</u> that, in this choice of evils, Mr. Chamberlain's England is preferable to Nazi Germany (& anyhow it won't if people have any sense, remain Mr. C's England). I find it natural to remain agin the government but in this case it seems quite feasible to be agin the govmt. & still support the war.

---

1 – See last but one letter.

(Just as it seems feasible to support the war & at the same time attack the people who attack the people who are anti-War). Anyhow it seems to me that the line we all took over Munich probably still holds good. (The fact that Poland was probably a bloody awful state is irrelevant.)

The tiresome corollary of this from my point of view is that, <u>if</u> it is my war, I feel I ought to get involved in it in one of the more unpleasant ways. Ignoring the argument that writers are more use writing. No doubt they are. But writers also unfortunately seem to be expected to express opinions on these subjects, & if, <u>qua</u> writer, one were to say that one was pro-War, then one ought to be prepared to accept the nastier parts of the war just as much as anyone else. Otherwise one would lapse into the false position of a cabinet minister or a fighting bishop. ('As much as anyone else' in my case would mean allowing myself to be, in my proper time, conscripted. Joining up, I think, would be over-doing it.)

I think now of coming over in the New Year (I hope I shall have finished Yeats by then). Before that I must arrange the transfer of Dan to Dungannon, where there is a good kindergarten.[1] I also have the hell of a lot of other things to write but I could do those in England. The typescript of Latin Humour is temporarily lost, owing, I think, to a muddle on the part of Elizabeth. But I guess it will be found. I am writing a whole series of verse epigrams (in the Gk. Anthology sense).[2] Did I tell you that I have also written a One Act play called Blacklegs for the Abbey – at least I hope the Abbey will do it? The set is in mid-air – steeplejacks.

<u>It is vastly boring here</u>. The only thing is that I save money; my overdraft is now enormous & no prospect of cutting it down. I go & stay in the country sometimes with a surrealist painter called McCann [*sic*] – very intelligent, fond of dogs, cats & whisky, has an enormous wife called Mercy.[3]

I hope you both flourish,

Yours ever,
Louis

1 – DM was at Maria Grey, north London, but was evacuated in 1940 to Co. Down and thence to Dungannon HS for Girls, Co. Tyrone. Cf. FLM to JFM/GBM, 16 May [1934], n. 4, pp. 240–1.

2 – Possibly 'Entered in the Minutes' (CP07, 202–3).

3 – George MacCann (1909–67), educ. RBAI and Belfast School of Art; taught at Royal School, Armagh, Belfast College of Art, and Sullivan Upper, Holywood. Captain, Inniskilling Fusiliers 1939–45 (POW). He later worked as a theatre designer and painter. Author of collection of short stories, *Sparrows Round My Brow* (Newcastle, Co. Down, 1942). Mercy MacCann (née Hunter) (1910–89), educ. schools in Toronto, BRA, Belfast College of Art, and Royal College of Art. Taught at Dungannon HS for Girls, Banbridge Academy, Armagh HS

TO *E. R. Dodds*

22 November [1939]   Belfast

Dear E.R.D.,

Just got your letter for which many thanks. I do quite agree that it (the M.G. business) was stupidity but surely there are <u>two</u> agents in anything of this kind? I thought the old neat division into seducer & seduced had been superseded. This is of course a caddish thing to say but surely, if – as you say – I don't notice people much, it's up to other people to notice themselves?

I don't know if she's going to get her permit or not. I didn't awfully want her to come over but she said she didn't expect anything & that it would cheer her up. I think (surely?) she realises that there is no prospect of a 'stable relationship' – in any very intimate sense, I mean. I am quite on for 'becoming friends' up to a reasonable point. (Didn't Groddeck say that people were much better able to be normal friends if they slept together?[1])

Yes, you need a permit just as much for (& from) Ulster as for (& from) Eire. That is why I don't want to come over until I have definitely decided to burn my boats (it being quite probable that I should be refused a permit back). I still don't know about TCD & I have just heard again from Cornell (who never got the cable I sent over 3 weeks ago). They now specify the <u>temporary</u> job which is a 'special lectureship in Prebus' (whatever that is) from February 12th – May 31st for 2000 dollars. As I am now nearly £250 overdrawn, I think I shall take this, assuming that TCD doesn't come off, & return to Europe in June. I fancy I can make another £100 there through visiting lectures, so my tottering finances would be bolstered up again.

You are all wrong about the Irish girl.[2] She isn't Ulster at all, she is Dublin (very much so) & when I say 'efficient' I don't mean tiresome, I merely mean capable of running things with a certain stability. She comes from what my stepmother would think a dubious stratum of Irish society. She would <u>not</u> be a cutter-off-from-friends.

–

and Victoria College, Belfast. MBE 1970. MacCann was introduced to FLM by Maurice James Craig at Erskine Mayne's Bookshop, Belfast, in 1938 ('Louis MacNeice in Ulster', *PRONI D/2833/D/5/21*). FLM later wrote a testimonial for him (FLM to H. M. Collins, 19 April 1960, pp. 664–5). He is Maguire in *AS*.

1 – Cf. 'Wystan lent me Groddeck's "Book of the Id" which is very exciting and uncommonly human' (FLM to Nancy Coldstream, 15 Feb. 1940, *Ms Bodleian, MacNeice and Nancy Coldstream*). See also FLM to WHA, 21 Oct. 1937, p. 304.

2 – Eileen Phillips.

1 Elizabeth and Louis MacNeice, *c.*1915

2 Rev. John Frederick MacNeice in The Rectory garden, Carrickfergus

3 Louis MacNeice in The Rectory garden, *c.*1915

4 Louis and Elizabeth MacNeice about to go mackerel fishing, Carrickfergus, *c.*1920
5 The wedding of Elizabeth MacNeice to John Nicholson, Carrickfergus, 18 October 1928, with (left to right) Mary Pilkington, Louis MacNeice, Hugh Davies, Barbara Nicholson
6 Georgina Beatrice and John Frederick MacNeice, The Rectory, Carrickfergus, 1931
7 Louis MacNeice as one of 'Guillebaud's XV', Marlborough College, *c.*1925

10 Louis and Mary MacNeice at home,
Highfield Cottage, Birmingham, c.1936

8 Anthony Blunt (left) at Cambridge, December 1929, with (left to right) Francis Warre-
Cornish, unknown, Dadie Rylands, Edward Playfair. Photograph by Lytton Strachey
9 Mary MacNeice with Betsy the borzoi, Birmingham, 1933

12 Louis MacNeice with Dan, Wickham Lodge, Hampshire, 30 August 1938

11 (top) Hedli Anderson, 1930s
13 (bottom) Hedli Anderson, New York, c.1953. Photograph by Rollie McKenna

14 John Frederick and Dan MacNeice, Cushendall, 1937

15 Louis MacNeice with students at State College, Pennsylvania, 1939
16 Louis MacNeice in 1942. Photograph by Howard Coster

17 Eleanor Clark, New York, c.1939

18 Louis and Dan
MacNeice, Bishop's House,
Malone Road, Belfast,
*c.*1937

19 Dan MacNeice, London, spring 1945. Photograph by Douglas Glass
20 Hedli, Louis and Corinna MacNeice at Corinna's christening, Dorset, 1954

21 E. R. Dodds
22 Charles Monteith, All Souls College, Oxford, early 1950s
23 Louis MacNeice with (left to right) Ted Hughes, T. S. Eliot, W. H. Auden and Stephen Spender at a Faber and Faber cocktail party, 23 June 1960. Photograph by Mark Gerson

24 Corinna MacNeice,
c.1964, in Kinsale

25 Louis MacNeice, London, c.1954.
Photograph by Lotte Meitner-Graf

I had a letter from E. today which, like many of her letters, made me enraged. Apparently she hasn't written any of the novel she has been talking about for some time; it is still all in her head. On top of which she rebukes me for being prolific, saying that I'm not an old man yet. She always seems terribly all-over-the-place in her mind.

Glad you liked the Statesman poems.[1] In 'Galway' unfortunately Venus, I find, ought to be Jupiter which is very inconvenient. & I never knew Jupiter could be so bright. The only verse I am writing now is kind-of-epigrams (did I tell you?) – 4 lines going forward, & 4 lines coming back again. I have written about 20 of these. I expect E. would think them awfully 'slight'.

Could you tell me by the way if University teaching is a reserved occupation? That might make it easier to get permits.

Dan was in Belfast yesterday. I took him to the Zoo (which has a grand view of the Lough).[2] He has a raging Co. Down accent.

I am getting near the end of the Yeats book (1st version) which is at last coming to life. I shall probably scrap nearly all that I read to you. The book is nearly all quotations (I am beginning to think the ideal lit. critic would only speak in person in footnotes). The Latin Humour typescript has been discovered but I am not sure if I have got all the Mss which contain Gk. Quotations etc. which have to be copied in. I hate this finishing of things.

With regard to America it may of course be very difficult to get (a) a visa, (b) a boat. But it would be fun if one knew one was only doing it for 3 months. As for the 'dangerous Atlantic' I had been thinking that, if I came over to England & were going to be conscripted anyway, it might be less soul-destroying to get into something on the sea. Do you know if that is possible? I don't suppose the R.N. is but there are all sorts of other things.

I suppose I must get on with Yeats, damn him. I am going to have a beautiful chronological appendix. Would you mind if I dedicated it to you?[3]

The family tempo here is impossible. No one can take in anything until one is round the corner. I thank God for the Co. Armagh surrealist.[4]

---

1 – 'Galway', NS, 21 Oct. 1939; 'September Evening', NS, 18 Nov. 1939.
2 – Belfast Zoo (originally Bellevue Pleasure Gardens), Antrim Road, Belfast.
3 – The dedication read: 'To E. R. Dodds / AN IRISHMAN, A POET, AND A SCHOLAR / WHO KNOWS MORE ABOUT IT ALL / THAN I DO'.
4 – George MacCann.

Have you heard about Connolly's new paper, 'Horizon'? I think it sounds good.[1]

I have just re-read this. The first page sounds callous again. Don't you think, however, that she may be dramatising herself a bit? I mean, even admitting a physical connection may have (on women) the effects you say, they don't usually build up a whole fixation on someone <u>without any encouragement at all</u>. (Obviously the more I write on this subject, the more debased – or irresponsible or merely ignorant – I shall appear to you.)

Please write again, Yours ever,
Louis

TO *E. R. Dodds*   MS Bodleian

28 November [1939]   Bishop's House, Malone Road,
                              Belfast

Dear E.R.D.

Many thanks indeed for your letter which has just come. I went out to see one H. O. White the other night who says he knew you very well.[2] Bryce Clark was there also – in good form. No news from T.C.D., damn them. Did I tell you about the latest offer from Cornell – for February–May? I think (Trinity failing – which it will) I shall try to make it. I had a cable from E. this morning who had just apparently received letters I wrote over a month ago. She seems to think I should take Cornell. It is all most difficult.

Yesterday I got a long essay about planetary government from someone called Robert Jordan who represents something called the Cambridge Peace Aims Group. Reads very Utopian to me but stimulating all the same. I quite agree with you about the two fronts. It is infuriating that to line up against H. you have to line up behind C[hamberlain].

Talking of Yeats, which of the neo-Platonists was it who said 'a fabulous & formless darkness'?[3]

---

1 – Cyril Connolly's legendary journal, *Horizon: A Review of Literature and Art* ran from Jan. 1940 to 1950, with circulation figures sometimes approaching 100,000 per issue. The first number carried FLM's poems, 'Cushendun' and 'The British Museum Reading Room'.
2 – See FLM to H. O. White 6 March 1941, p. 422, and footnote.
3 – Yeats, from 'Two Songs from a Play' (1928), partially reprinted in *The Resurrection* (1931). Eunapius (b. 347 AD), in his 'Life of Aedesius, the philosopher', wrote of 'a fabulous, formless darkness tyrannising over the fairest things on earth' cf. Dodds, *Missing Persons*, 60.

I am also trying to do a poem on Barcelona in terza rima, which is filthy difficult.[1]

Meals here are surrealist – my stepmother taking up everything wrong through her aurophone & old Mr. Popper, who can't speak English anyway, trying to make puns in it.

I hope to know in about a week what I shall be doing. Maybe I shall come over after Christmas. God knows how one gets to America, if one gets. I don't think that there are any boats calling at Cobh now. Perhaps one has to go via Portugal or somewhere?

I should like to meet Atkinson. It is about time for some new novelists. Now I must go back to the old Moon-phaser.[2]

With all best wishes for you both & the dogs,

Yours ever,

Louis

TO *E. R. Dodds*   MS Bodleian

8 December [1939]   Belvedere Hotel [letterhead]

Dear E.R.D.,

Things are clarifying. H. O. White has got TCD. I am definitely going to try America, shall start agitating for a permit (from the British Govmt.) next week; it seems I shall probably have to sail from Liverpool. In a British boat! In that case I can see you first. In case the Permit People query my bona fide intentions of going only for a temporary job till May 31st & then returning, might I quote you as a reference? I mean, it <u>is</u> bona fide. Whatever happens, I want to return in the summer because of Dan etc. I had a long discussion of the matter today with Eileen (she is my friend here).[3] She is probably going to London in January to get a job. (Would you like to look her up some time? I don't think she knows people there.)

I got a long letter this morning from Eleanor who is assuming I am going over. Said my last letter was dated Oct. 3rd.[4] What is one to do with these posts?

---

1 – 'Barcelona in Wartime', part one of 'Entered in the Minutes', CP07, p. 202.
2 – Yeats.
3 – Eileen Phillips.
4 – EC wrote (10 Nov.): 'It's awful, I just discovered the last letter I had from you was October 3rd, my God, you might be requisitioned or dead or a new man by now, how can we remember anything at this rate' (*Ms Yale*).

I can't do Barcelona into terza rima. Am splitting it into series of little octets (like the 2 in the Statesman this week) to be called Notes on Barcelona.[1]

It is lovely being quit of my family for a little. Have to go back on Tuesday to give a talk at Queen's.[2]

The Abbey seem favourable to my play but want adjustments.[3] Did I tell you not only have I (indirectly) designed the set but have also (accidentally) made up the tune for a song in it?

Yours ever,
Louis

1 – 'Octets', *PP*, 75–7; repr. (with addition of 'Barcelona in Wartime') as 'Entered in the Minutes' in *Collected Poems, 1925–1948*, 208–9, CP07, 202–3.
2 – Queen's University, Belfast.
3 – Negotiations seem to have reached an advanced stage, but *Blacklegs* was never performed at the Abbey.

1940

TO *E. R. Dodds*   MS Bodleian

14 January [1940]   Cunard White Star, Cunard
                                     Building, Liverpool 3 / Passengers
                                     Waiting Room [letterhead]

Dear E.R.D.,

In haste. On a separate sheet I am putting, more formally, some instructions about Dan. I am so sorry I could not get down to Oxford this week.

Will write you all the lowdown on Wystan etc.[1]

The name of the Dublin girl is Eileen Phillips. I am taking the liberty, as they say, of giving her your address in case she feels lonely in London. Actually she & I shall never be getting married or anything like that, as it dawned on me that – for fairly obvious reasons – it wouldn't work. She is one of the nicest people I have ever met & I think you would like her.

Nancy has just painted a good picture of Curigwen Lewis for a show.[2] I suppose you wouldn't like to look her (Nancy) up some time as she is very lonely in London (her address is 9 Percy Street, off Tottenham Court Road). I feel myself that it is all very well Bill going all Gauguin – the independent artist etc. – but that it is rather rough on her, especially as he chose to run off just when the War came, having refused to consider the suggestion on more feasible occasions earlier.[3] Of course it is all a very long story & they are both extremely temperamental but Bill comes out of it more comfortably as, thanks to his reputation, he now has various very

---

1–FLM may have received EC's letter of 18 Dec. 1939, in which she complains about WHA's behaviour in New York: 'Auden by the way is making himself thoroughly unpopular here. Is appallingly rude in the time-honoured [*sic*] Briton-in-America style, is pompous and condescending and whatnot, gets people to go to all sorts of trouble getting him jobs and things and then doesn't turn up. I haven't seen him but the reports from all sides are very funny . . . Incidentally he is making it all much more difficult for people like you coming over, people begin to think that all young English poets are superficial and conceited and have bad manners . . . You see I'm getting very nationalistic' (*Ms Yale*).
2–Curigwen Lewis, actress. One of the cast of thousands in 'Auden and MacNeice: Their Last Will and Testament' (see FLM to Mrs ERD, after 13 Oct. 1936, p. 274).
3–Bill Coldstream, Nancy's husband.

assured niches for himself, whereas N's friends, being also Bill's, tend to be too embarrassed to see her for fear of committing Bill in some way. I am very fond of Bill but I do think it extremely unfair the way everyone always regards him as a martyr & tends, correspondingly, to regard N. as rather wicked. I probably know more about their past history than almost anyone & I think it is high time that this opinion (which is largely founded on snobbery because the Charlotte St. gang know that Bill is on the upgrade) should be adjusted. N. may be temperamentally difficult but she is certainly one of the nicest – & one of the most interesting – personalities I have ever met & I think it extremely regrettable that she should have to live in a room by herself in London with hardly any of her friends to talk to. (Don't repeat all this.)

Well, I must get to my boat, remember me to your wife
& all best wishes to you both,

Yours ever,
Louis

P.S. If I die (which I shan't) I hope you won't find your executorship intolerable. I am very grateful to you for undertaking it.

Enclosure:

14 January 1940   As from 16A Primrose Hill Road

Dear Professor Dodds,

I am writing in haste before sailing to USA to give you as my executor a few instructions about Dan, of whom you & Mary are co-guardians. This being so, Mary can do nothing without your consent. Therefore, as you & Dan are both on the same side of the Atlantic, I think that, in the event of my death, it would be for you rather than for Mary to decide what should happen to him in the immediate future. The points I wish to make are these:-

(1) I do not wish Dan to cross the Atlantic if it is obviously dangerous – unless Great Britain & Ireland have by that time become equally dangerous. (2) If he goes to live with Mary, I do not wish the break from his present mode of life to be too abrupt; i.e. as he is devoted above everyone to Miss Popper, I feel he should be 'weaned' from her gradually. I suggest therefore that for a period he & Miss Popper should both live with my sister Elizabeth, who is eager to co-operate, & that subsequently Elizabeth (or Miss Popper) shall relinquish him to Mary, staying in the same place with Mary until he has become in turn acclimatised to her.

(3) I feel it might be preferable for Dan not to go to Mary in America until he is at least eight, when he can better understand the circumstances. I leave this to your discretion but I should myself recommend, unless unforeseen circumstances occur, that he should remain in England or Ireland until he is eight. (4) Before he goes to Mary, I think it would be desirable that you should ascertain her present mode of living. In the unlikely event of Mary being unable to provide a happy & peaceful home for Dan, I should wish him to stay with Elizabeth until Mary could do so.

I hope this is clear. As you will see, I am leaving rather a lot to your discretion. What you really have in fact is a veto over Mary's actions. I hope you won't find it a frightful nuisance (however I don't think I shall die!)

Yours ever,
F. Louis MacNeice

TO *Bennet Cerf*[1]   MS Columbia

4 February 1940   c/o Mr. & Mrs. Jessup,
                                       29 5th Avenue, New York City

Dear Mr. Cerf,
    You asked me to let you know about my visiting lectures. Here is the list to date (others are to be added):-
    Feb. 6th – Yale.
    Feb. 8th – Goucher College, Baltimore.[2]
    Feb. 11th – Bryn Mawr College, Pa.[3]
    Feb. 21st – Vassar College, Poughkeepsie.[4]

---

1 – Bennet Cerf (1898–1971), publisher. Educ. Columbia (BA 1919, BLitt 1920). Founded Random House in 1927 with his friend Donald Klopfer. Author of several books on humour, and a memoir: *At Random: The Reminiscences of Bennet Cerf* (New York, 1977).
2 – At Goucher, where he was described as 'an associate of W. H. Auden', he gave a lecture on W. B. Yeats on 5 Feb. (not 8 Feb.). Cf. 'Louis MacNiece [*sic*] Speaks On Yeats', *Goucher College Weekly*, 2 Feb. 1940.
3 – T. S. Eliot had written to Professor A. C. Sprague on 8 Nov. 1938 to arrange a lecture at Bryn Mawr the following spring (*Houghton, Ms Am 1691.3*). According to Eleanor Clark, he was very well received there: 'I hear from Bryn Mawr incidentally that they like you speaking better than Auden . . .' (EC to FLM, 23 Feb. 1940, *Ms Yale*). For a full report of his lecture on 'the Auden group', see 'Poet Defines Place of Art During War', *The College News* (Bryn Mawr), 26: 12 (14 Feb. 1940), 12.
4 – FLM gave his lecture on Eliot's influence to a large audience at the Aula auditorium, Vassar. He then read poems by Auden and Spender and closed by reading a few of his own poems: 'Snow', 'Iceland' and 'Prognosis'. See 'Poets of the '30's Bring Vitality and Conviction

Feb. 23rd – University of Buffalo.
Feb. 26th – People's Farm, Montreal.
March 8th – Hotchkiss School, Lakeville, Conn.
March 11th – Skidmore College, Saratoga Springs, N.Y.[1]

I shall be free in New York this week on Wednesday & Friday & possibly Saturday (in case of the meeting you suggested with Ralph Bates).[2]

Yours very sincerely
Louis MacNeice

TO *E. R. Dodds*   MS Bodleian

5 February 1940   116 College Street, New Haven, CT;
                                          as from: Department of English,
                                          Cornell University, Ithaca, NY

Dear E.R.D.,

Just a scrawl while I am hanging around here to let you know I made the passage successfully. I start Cornell next week, it sounds cushy. Have been in New York up till now. As soon as I saw E. everything fell back into place; I must have been merely aberrant the last six months or so.[3] Don't ask me what's going to happen next because I don't know. I think maybe it's about time I had a bout of irrationality. I feel I've been fitting myself into patterns for so long & (though you may be sceptical about 'romance'?) it is so exciting to find oneself timelessly happy; also I am going to write (at least I hope so) quite new kinds of poems. After which, no doubt, the deluge but I can't think about that now. I have never felt like

---

to Work: MacNeice Analyzes Eliot's Influence', *Vassar Miscellany News*, 24 Feb. 1940, 1, 3. EC had written to Vassar on FLM's behalf as early as July 1939: 'I wrote to Vassar . . . and I should hear soon. He says there is not much chance of a real job now, it being so late – I suggested perhaps something could be fixed for the second semester – but they will want you to lecture in any case. On the modern poetry "movement" in England or some such stuff' (EC to FLM, 22 July 1939, *Ms Yale*).

1–FLM delivered a lecture, 'Since the Victorians', at the student assembly, Skidmore College on 12 March. 'He stated the contemporary poets have not broken from the Victorians, but rather they have returned to the more normal tradition of poetry; that there is a reaction against a specialized and false view of poetry, such as the poets of the 1890's wrote when they believed in art for art's sake.' *The Saratogian* (Saratoga Springs), 13 March 1940, 3.

2–Ralph Bates (1899–2000), English novelist associated with the Spanish Civil War (author of *The Olive Tree*, 1936). Professor of English at New York University 1947–66.

3–For further elaboration, see FLM to NC, 4 Feb. 1940 (*Ms Bodleian, MacNeice and Nancy Coldstream*).

this about anyone, it pervades everything. If I had imagined ideal people for years, I couldn't have come near it.

However, this will horrify you. I saw Wystan who is very much himself & working intensely. The days here are very clear & the nights all lights. Please write to me.

All best wishes to you both,

Yours ever,
Louis

TO *Eleanor Clark* MS Yale

13 February [1940] Telluride Association, Ithaca, NY
[hereafter Ithaca, NY]

Darling, heart of my heart,

I must write to you again because I have just been wandering in falling snow in the night & am feeling very uplifted & a little arrogant for some reason, which is all to the good surely & better than feeling Ölbaumgarten.[1] Snow is an absolute too. Until it compromises & turns slushy but even then SNOW remains an absolute & the compromise, the slush, is properly something else. Which only shows one oughtn't to compromise; if one does one isn't one. My own (arrogant) belief is that you-&-me is an absolute also. Unaffected therefore by the fact that either you or I might temporarily turn slushy. On the other hand it's better we shouldn't because though snow is snow even if it isn't there at the moment, it is fun for the snow to have its moments because the Universal always longs to be concrete. Now I am beginning to sound Germanic so I must lay off because the Celtically minded don't talk about universals, they just sense them.

Darling, I am sick & tired of having the suspicion I may be bad for you, so am turning right round & deciding I am very good for you (I don't have to worry about what you are for me because that is a thing also I know through sensing). In fact darling (this will probably make you irritated), I have decided I really fulfil some curious need of yours & that if you don't recognise that, you are merely being stupid or wilful or wilfully stupid.

Another point darling. I am only too liable – if I like people (if I don't I don't adapt at all) – to adapt myself to people, go into low gear when they're in low etc. And the snow tells me (not that I didn't know it already)

1–Forsaken, like Christ in Rainer Maria Rilke's poem, 'Der Ölbaumgarten' ['The Garden of Olives'].

that that's all wrong too. If one can be running in high gear let one get on with it. That goes for either you or me. One mustn't compromise with other people – all the less if one is very fond of them. All the messy relationships are due to compromise. Supposing the ideal relationship between two people is a six-pointed star, each person being a triangle. Now a six-pointed star should have all its points shining & should be circumscribable in a circle so that the two triangles combined can roll along like a wheel. But what usually happens is that the two triangle people think they will function better together if they merge, or nearly merge, which is hooey.

Witness this:–

Whereas we ought to have this:–

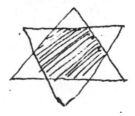

The shaded part which is the superficial unity is less but the real functioning unity is much more because the whole relationship makes a proper pattern. I hope you know what I mean, darling; this isn't really geometry. Anyway I think we should make a nice six-pointed star; the two triangles of course have to be more or less the same size & they have to be colours which don't kill each other where they meet in the middle. But I think that's all right. As I said, darling, I am feeling rather arrogant tonight &, if you want to have doubts about it, you will have to have them for two. It doesn't suit me to go round having doubts. When I was younger I had plenty of them & they never did me any good. If one had ten lives perhaps it would be salutary to have doubts – homage to Pro & Con (who are really two sides of a Janus & you have to keep running round to genuflect to each) – but seeing one has only one & it is very exciting, one might as well get on with what one knows & not contaminate it with all sorts of niggling little reasonings which anyway are mostly not reasoning proper but mere rationalisation of one's own damned panic about committing oneself. This may not be common sense but it is the voice from the tripod. (By the way if the apices of the triangles represent work etc. you see what an advantage it is to be able to roll.)

On reconsideration, darling, I think it was a good thing we met.

All my love, Louis

TO *Bennet Cerf*   MS Columbia

24 February [1940]   Buffalo, as from Ithaca, NY

Dear Bennet Cerf,

Thank you so much for your letter, which I ought to have answered before but have been running round to Vassar & Buffalo & places (am at Buffalo at the moment). No, of course I wasn't offended by that very amusing lunch-party; Liam O'F. is perhaps too dynamic for a museum but it strikes me he would do fine in a zoo. (I like zoos).[1]

By the way, a number of people at Vassar told me they couldn't get any of my books because they were all out of print, & two people at Buffalo had ordered 'Autumn Journal' from Brentano's in New York & have been told it is out of print. Is this so?[2] If it is, I have a suggestion to make to you which will horrify you, so I will keep it back for the moment.

I am enjoying Cornell very much. Everyone very friendly & the work interesting.

Thank you again for the lunch.

Yours sincerely,
Louis MacNeice

1 – In 'American Letter' FLM wrote deprecatingly about Liam O'Flaherty, 'who, like many Irish revolutionaries, wears a veneer of would-be sense over a welter of anarchic impulse', *Horizon*, 1, 7 (July 1940), 462. In an unpublished letter to Nancy Coldstream he describes meeting O'Flaherty in New York and suffering his insults (2 Feb. 1940, *Ms Bodleian, MacNeice and Nancy Coldstream*).

2 – Cerf replied on 28 Feb. that the first importation of sheets of *AJ* was 'exhausted' but that a second shipment was on order from Faber and Faber. He adds, 'I take it for granted that you have seen copies of the leading reviews. They have certainly been fine ones' (*Ms Columbia, Random House*).

TO *Mrs E. R. Dodds*   MS Bodleian

22 March [1940]   Ithaca, NY

Dear Mrs. Dodds,

Just got your letter (which was a very great pleasure) &, as I am feeling in vastly high spirits, am writing straight back. I guess Himself must be through with Hon. Mods now (or at least by the time you get this); I find London University are under the impression that I'm examining for them this summer – I'm not. It seems I may be offered a rather sympathetic combination of jobs over here next year which I shall probably take, though in any case I shall probably come back to England this summer. I am staying all the time here as a guest of this Telluride Association which is an eleemosynary institution for brilliant undergraduates.[1] Means my salary is more or less sheer profit; I benefit on the exchange too when I send money back to my inhuman bank in King's Norton. Have been running around giving lectures in Montreal & places (I don't like Canada) & am just going to have an Easter vacation in which I shall fly from New York to Chicago to utter my usual on poetry; have developed a new oratorical manner suited to the natives. Last time I saw Wystan we ate snails & Eleanor heckled him rather unkindly about his gymnastic classes.[2] My situation with E. remains v. good but v. peculiar – not at all by any of the books. What is so nice, I feel if we do have to be in different countries even for quite a long time, it won't make any essential difference – though it will be damn uncomfortable. She is still fretting about her work, has an almost Flaubertian conscience about it. Talking about work I am writing a new kind of poetry (very slight so far but will gain body, I hope) & will send you some soon, if you don't mind, to dispense to papers as you do

1 – FLM was one of several visiting academics who lived in a house with twenty-two undergraduates at the Telluride Association, Cornell University. Other residents in 1940 included Professor Victor Lange (PhD Leipzig, 1934) and Professor Maurice Barret (Director of the Institute of Research and Artistic and Technical Coordination at the Ecole Nationale des Arts Décoratifs). They appear as Viktor and André in *SAF*. Like André, Barret had a mental breakdown and was admitted on 12 July 1940 to Willard State Hospital, Willard, NY (E. M. Johnson to FLM, 5 Aug. 1940, *Ms Bodleian*).
2 – For which she later apologised: 'I'm sorry by the way to have been so silly versus Auden on the gymnastics question. I don't have many black spirits but I do have purplish ones that get hold of me occasionally' (EC to FLM, 14 Feb. 1940, *Ms Yale*). Auden had taken up 'gymnastics classes' (mainly relaxation and breathing exercises) given by his friend Tania Stern in her apartment on East 68 St. He considered it '*most* painful, but illuminating' (Carpenter, p. 281). Cf. WHA to Mrs Dodds, 29 Nov. 1939, in 'Six Letters from Auden to the Doddses', ed. Kathleen Bell, in Bucknell and Jenkins (eds), *W. H. Auden: 'The Map of All My Youth'*, 107–8. See also FLM to BCM, 5 July 1962, n. 1, p. 693.

Wystan's. Am also (this sounds terribly like Wystan too but it's all right) formulating a new attitude, the basic principle of which is that Freedom means Getting Into things & not getting Out Of them; also that one must keep making things which are <u>not oneself</u> – e.g. works of art, even personal relationships – which must be dry & not damp; as sticking cloves into an orange makes a pomander, = something NEW. Because it seems high time neither to be passive to flux nor to substitute for it, Marxist-like, a mere algebra of captions.

Later, after lunch. We get lots of food in this house though it tends to include mixtures of cream cheese & pineapple etc. I always get very sleepy in the afternoon & rather awake at night. I only have classes in the morning (Tuesdays, Thursdays & Saturdays). The students are nice though I have too many of them. Greatly to my surprise, I find I <u>enjoy teaching</u> here; this is paradoxical because I am thinking, within the not so distant future, of quitting the profession. No, I haven't had much open air life yet because the ground is so slippery one can't do anything with it. E. was very eager I should go skiing (which she is crazy about) but I hadn't the time.

Yes, I heard from Nancy she'd had flu. She is back in London now & I'm sure would like to see you if you're round there any time.

Yeats book is practically (truly, this time) finished; it is v. much better than 'Modern Poetry' though still lousy (like 99% of the world's literary criticism). I am going to write a long (indescribable) work in prose when it is finished – a fusion of gossip, apercus on art, esoteric metaphysics, dreams & bits of landscape. A fusion, though.

My sleep is coming on me so bad now that I must give up. If you know what the war stands for now I'd wish you'd tell me as it gets more & more obscure to me. It's depressing to think we may get linked up with Japan.

Later // I didn't sleep at all but finished the last chapter (not counting the conclusion) of Yeats. Am now feeling a little bored; the boys in the house are all playing poker & there is nothing but night & snow outside. The University here is on a violent hill & there are gorges & a campanile that plays 'The Harp That Once' etc. & lots of hymn tunes. (Cornell, I am told, is the place Linklater wrote about in 'Juan in America.') If the film of 'Grapes of Wrath' comes to England you must go to see it; it is v. good except for a few over-sentimental passages. Everyone is very surprised it should have come out of Hollywood. Expect to see Wystan again next week & also think of looking up Father D'Arcy. Did I tell you I met Wyndham Lewis in New York & how rude we were to each other? Erika Mann is wandering around somewhere too; she has become a pal of E's. E. gave me a party in New York for which she borrowed two large live

Picassos from some exhibition which seemed a rash thing to do as someone might have done them wrong but luckily no one did. I must stop now & think of something to discuss with the discussion groups which I have on Saturdays; the discussion groups are so large that noone can discuss except me, which is a pity as I have no ideas in my head about poetry or literature at all – only about life & pomanders.

all best wishes to yourself & himself,
Yours ever
Louis

TO *Nancy Coldstream*[1]　　　　　　　　　　　　　　　MS Bodleian

14 April 1940　　　　　　　　　　Ithaca, NY

Dearest Nancy,

You really are a pig not to write to me. If I hadn't had a letter from Stephen saying you were going to have dinner with him, I shouldn't know you were alive. I still don't know what I am doing in the summer but, like as not, I shall be seeing you; it depends on a great many factors. I had a strenuous little vacation; it was great fun flying to Chicago – they give you meals in the air on a tray on your knees & you look down on this apparently never-ending continent & every so often the plane kicks and throws you off your seat. I stayed a weekend at Mary's farm; they send over 3000 eggs to market per week now & the whole place is a circulation of poultry – Leghorns & Rhode Island Reds (M. says they are quite different in temperament – Leghorns rupture themselves if you frighten them whereas R.I.R.'s are beautifully phlegmatic.) The house was a litter & M. & Charles like navvies; meals were all cream. Their goat is going to have babies & they have two new pigs. M. is going in for some sort of Women's Cooperative Scheme; on the whole she seems gayer than last year. E. seems rather run down & weary, is possibly going down south for a change from N.Y.C. The knees of the Gods seems to apply here more than in most cases.[2] I am getting so fatalistic however that I just go along from

---

1 – The Bodleian Library holds ten letters from Nancy Coldstream to FLM (1937–8) and a few more dating from spring 1940 (*Ms MacNeice, Box 8*). In addition, the Bodleian has acquired a cache of at least nineteen letters from FLM to Nancy (including one very short note, a postcard and a telegram). The earliest letter in this series dates from spring 1938, the latest from 1942, and over half were sent from America in 1940.
2 – Cf. 'On the knees of bountiful Gods / We lived in the ease of acceptance' ('Taken for Granted', *EC*, 50, CP07, 90–1).

day to day without calculating or anticipating. I am quite convinced that, other things being equal, E. & I ought to get established but God knows if they'll ever be equal. I wish you'd write to me, pussycat, & <u>be friendly</u>. Being in Ithaca's rather like being in a desert – without any of the glamour of deserts. I don't know when I heard from you last but it was the hell of a time ago. Wystan was speaking of you very friendlily when I saw him last. I hope to ask him up here some time for a weekend if I can get someone to pay his fare. Now I have to go to a Sunday tea at a thing called the Cosmopolitan Club – designed for foreigners like me – won't write anymore therefore but will write again soon.

Lots of love, darling

L.

TO *Eleanor Clark*   MS Yale

17 April [1940]   Ithaca, NY

Darling,

Sorry my last letter was glum & that you think I have not been writing. Writing in a hurry now to catch the morning mail. I hope you are having a lovely time on the Hudson, & <u>you must do the Puerto Rico book</u>; was very impressed again by your piece in the New Republic.[1] If you go down there maybe I <u>could</u> meet you later somewhere; I want to go to Mexico. Unless I cross the Atlantic for a bit, which is possible (pros & cons of this much too complicated to discuss now). By the way, darling, what the hell do you feel guilty toward me for? I'm not the sort of person who expects to get the moon – at least not overnight. Remember the Marvell poem – 'My love is of a birth as rare . . .'?[2] All I do wish is that you could have the same sort of faith in things – I mean in the 6-pointed star[3] & things like that – that I have & then I shouldn't feel so bad if & when I go to Europe or anywhere else. There is another thing occurred to me last night in bed

---

1 – She had written: 'Am pondering the idea of doing the Puerto Rican stuff into a book and find that it does excite me. It would be [*sic*] mean going down for two or three weeks and I would like that, and it does seem rather bad to keep all that stuff packed away in notebooks' (EC to FLM, 14 April 1940, *Ms Yale*). FLM approached Eliot about publishing it with Faber, without success (see next but one letter).

2 – Andrew Marvell, from 'The Definition of Love', in *The Oxford Book of Seventeenth Century Verse*, ed. H. J. C. Grierson and G. Bullough (Oxford, 1938). Cf. FLM to EC, 6 Aug. 1941, p. 440.

3 – See FLM to EC, 13 Feb. 1940, p. 378.

which is that in the nearer [*sic*] future – though not just yet – there may be a very remarkable upheaval in England & I shall want to see that. It looks as if history will repeatedly [*illegible*] to that. I mean, darling, at the moment I'm just out of place in England but, <u>if</u> they start having some sort of revolution, it is the one place I might function at all well other than as a pure artist; I know the language there you see & I also have a right to put my spoke in – & neither of those things is true over here. Now if I felt a chain stretching from me to you, it would be all right (though uncomfortable) but that depends entirely on you & maybe <u>you</u> would feel comfortabler without it, might prefer to put me into a tapestry of past diversions. But this is all in the future; at the moment I am beginning to fret about what I am to do with my child. As he will now, being 6 in May, probably spend most of his day in school, it seems ridiculous to import a full-time Hungarian with difficult antecedents to look after him. But, as she is so important to him, it will be very tricky getting anyone else. Then, if later I go back to Europe, I shan't want to take him & where is he to go? I don't like at all the idea of dumping him for any length of time on his mother. However it can probably all be worked out by mathematics, calculation of months & miles. Talking of the moon did I tell you about the little squireen in our district in the North of Ireland who was very obliging & someone said to my father about him: 'He's a very nice fellow, he'd promise you the moon; but, mind you, he'd never deliver it.'

Went to Syracuse last night by car with the German professor & gave them my usual.[1] As the sun set the hills to the west became deep amethyst shadow – only much more opaque than anything else. I am writing again now – prosebook [*sic*] – only you trouble me there a bit too as every so often I think to myself how futile you would consider it all & that is a trifle aggravating. I have to do it, you see, darling, just to put my lands in order. As I was brooding over it the other night one of the boys came in with a huge piece of lemon meringue pie which he had stolen for me from the kitchen.

Darling, I think I ought to warn you that once in a black moon (when my black spirits are in the ascendant) I tend to say all the most unpleasant things I can think of, most of which are quite deliberate lies. If this ever comes upon me with you, you are to make allowances.

---

1 – See 'MacNeice to Speak in Maxwell Tonight: Poet-Lecturer Will Discuss Own Works' and 'MacNeice Defends Current Poetry', in *Syracuse Daily Orange*, 16 and 17 April 1940. His lecture at Maxwell Auditorium, Syracuse closely resembled the talk he gave at Bryn Mawr. Cf. Horace Eaton to FLM, 20 March 1940 (*Ms Bodleian, Ms Res, c. 590, Box 15*).

These public lectures here etc. are taking up too much of my time & I am kicking more & more against the academic pricks. I think I am due to go to Bennington May 3rd & might come on that weekend to N.Y.C.[1]

Have been reading Keats' letters. Did you know he was only five foot & half an inch high? There is a very suggestive passage about a stoat & value. As Stoat performing marvels of rhythm, grace etc. (of which itself is unaware) is to Keats watching, so Keats performing poetry is to 'a Superior Being' watching.[2] If not taken literally, this makes sense. Moral: get on with the Existence & Value will look after itself.

It having struck 10, I ought to dispose of this. Darling, do have a good time by your river & do lots of work & write me some more. & don't go feeling guilty toward me or any nonsense like that; I'd like you to feel toward me all the same.

Tomorrow am giving a public talk here mainly about Wilfred Owen. Rather depressing in the circumstances.

Am hoping the Telluride boys will put their tennis court in order soon. Playing tennis the first few times always infuriates me because I find myself so impotent but that has to be got over.

Am starting to read Malraux's book about China.[3]

Lots of love, darling,
see you in May, I hope,

1 – Bennington at that time lacked a campus paper, so there is no review of this appearance. The lecture, like others in this tour, was arranged by the Institute of International Education (2 West 44th St, New York), who sent an information sheet to Bennington with titles of lectures which FLM could deliver, including: 'The Poetry of W. B. Yeats (the subject of my book now in preparation)'; 'The Younger English Poets (Auden, Spender and myself, with readings and comments on my own stuff)'; 'The Position of T. S. Eliot in English Poetry'; and 'Since the Victorians (a general talk on the literary changes of the last fifty years)' (E. Fisher to W. Troy, 20 Nov. 1939, Ms Yale). At Bennington, FLM delivered the second of these and was paid an honorarium of twenty-five dollars plus travel expenses. Travel involved a bus from Ithaca to Syracuse, train from there to Albany, then another bus (FLM to Hendricks, 6 May 1940, Ms Yale). A week prior to FLM's arrival, Theodore Spencer of Harvard had recommended him for a job at Bennington: 'He is about 33, and a very able man. I've heard him lecture once; he does it well. But how much interest he would take in individual students & their problems, I don't know' (Spencer to Mrs Leigh, 25 April 1940, Ms Bennington College Archives). Cf. also Bennington to FLM, 30 April 1940 (Ms Bodleian, Ms Res, c. 590, Box 15).
2 – Letter to George Keats, 19 March 1818: 'I go among the fields and catch a glimpse of a stoat or a fieldmouse peeping out of the withered grass – the creature hath a purpose and its eyes are bright with it – I go amongst the buildings of a city and I see a Man hurrying along – to what?' Letters of John Keats 1814–21, ed. H. E. Rollins (2 vols, Cambridge, MA, 1958; 1972), II, 80.
3 – Probably La Condition Humaine (1936).

hope there is Spring down there (do you know a late Latin poem about Spring, the Pervigilium Veneris, with the refrain – 'Cras amet qui nunquam amavit, quique amavit cras amet.'[1])

L.

P.S. In case this doesn't appear, I am really in very good spirits.

TO *Eleanor Clark* MS Yale

[17 April 1940]   Ithaca, NY

Darling,

This is my third letter today, which must be a record.[2] It is now about midnight; have just been down town & drunk a Daiquiri to your health. This is just to say how delighted I was by your ringing up, which made a world of difference to my general mood. I am sorry if the 2nd letter I wrote today may have seemed tiresome (to use your favourite word); it was the outcome just of a particular mood & you are not to conclude from it that I am really too difficile or anything like that. To return to our 'phone conversation, darling, you know perfectly well that I would be prepared to go anywhere with you (on any terms practically) for any length of time. British reserve or no (I'm not properly British anyway or don't you know your geography?), seeing that I spend most of my time raving inwardly to be with you, it is not for you, darling, to go reproaching me with frigidity of all things; don't be a pig. As I must have suggested in my last letters, any reserve I may show is much more your doing than mine. Didn't you know that? Darling, you are so contrairy [*sic*]; here am I putting great haystacks of philosophy on my head so as not to offend you by being – vocally at any rate – over-wishful, importunate, unbalanced etc. etc & you have the face to tell me I'm British. However . . .

Enjoy yourself on the river. & write to me, darling. Don't be lonesome.

All my love,
L.

1 – 'May he love tomorrow who has never loved before, and he who has loved, let him love tomorrow.' See previous references to the Pervigilium in letters to AB (2 Oct. 1926, p. 126) and to EM (25 April 1927, p. 162). JH recalled FLM's declaiming the *Pervigilium* 'with harsh resonance and a percussive menace' (*SAF*, 244).

2 – He wrote three letters to EC on 17 April, the first and third of which are reproduced here.

TO *T. S. Eliot*   Faber archive

21 April [1940]   Ithaca, NY

Dear Eliot,

I meant to write before but have been terribly busy disseminating culture. Ithaca is a nice enough place but inaccessible & always snowing & raining. I hope to get another job over here for next session but don't know yet for certain.

To come to business:- (1) Random House want to do next spring a collected book of my poems up to date, 1926–40, though not called 'Collected Poems' as that suggests one's dead. I think that's quite a good idea for the States but not for England. Bennet Cerf said he might be writing to you to suggest that Faber's should do the same thing but I suggest they don't. On the other hand I shall have a brand new book of poems for you in the Fall, including the poems in my little Cuala Press book but more than as much again & the new ones mostly better. I could let you have the complete Mss. by about September.

(2) The Oxford University Press (N.Y.C.) are very eager to do my quasi-autobiographical book over here but tell me that Stewart told them I am tied up with Random House. This is not so, as my Random House contract only applies to verse. I should be very pleased if the O.U.P. could do it, especially if they will give me enough money. According to my contract for this book with Fabers, Fabers are to act as my American agents for a 15% commission. As the Oxford Press are very willing to give me $500 advance without any negotiation, I suggest that you earn your commission by getting $450 out of them (say $400 down & the rest on delivery of Mss). Also, if I am going to be over here, it would be obviously convenient if the money could be paid to me direct instead of going to England to pass through your hands.[1]

Sorry to be so commercial-minded. I hear you have a new poem coming out in Partisan Review (who are delighted about it) which I am looking forward to very much.[2] Talking of Partisan Review there is a friend of mine over here who writes for it, Eleanor Clark, (whom Edmund Wilson a few years ago thought one of the only two young prose-writers of genuine promise in the States) who is probably just about to do a travel

1–TSE replied on 10 May, agreeing that it was not the right time for a British edition of collected poems, and that he had nothing against the proposed arrangement with OUP. However, there was no possibility of publishing the book on Puerto Rico which FLM mentions in the next paragraph (*Faber archive*).
3–'East Coker', *PR*, 7, 3 (May–June 1940), 181.

book on Puerto Rico for an American publisher. I wondered if you would like to do it in England (N.B. this is quite unofficial; she merely mentioned the book to me & hadn't as yet considered publishing in England). She had a little piece about Puerto Rico in the New Republic for April 15th.

I got the Sesame books & think they are a nice job. Do the public like them?

Now I must go & have lunch in a fraternity.

With all best wishes,
Yours
Louis MacNeice

P.S. Have seen Wystan several times who is living a wonderful routinal life in Brooklyn; he has just written a philosophical poem in short couplets of nearly 2000 lines.[1]

TO *Eleanor Clark*   MS Yale

14 May [1940]   Ithaca, NY

Eleanor Darling,

(please notice I am using your name to please you). I would really be asleep now (had the hell of a night in a train which kept coming to pieces) if a man I met last year in State College, Pennsylvania, hadn't arrived to disturb me. Actually he disturbed me in more ways than one because that was the first place I lectured in America, which was before I met you, & it suddenly came home to me that it is quite <u>out of the question</u> (my question, I mean, I don't know about yours but you must allow me to be selfish) that I should cease to know you; at the same time it seems also out of the question that we should go on much longer in this half-way house of ours. Which being so only endorses some thoughts I was having in the train while it was coming to pieces. Before I come on to these, darling, I want to say how very much I enjoyed our weekend – especially the river – & also that I am sorry about my outburst Friday evening. I don't really misunderstand you all that much, darling; it is mainly nerves – occasioned partly by Europe & partly by jealousy. Anyway I <u>am</u> very sorry about it.

1 – 'New Year Letter', published in *Atlantic*, Jan.–Feb. 1941 (as 'Letter to Elizabeth Mayer'), *The Double Man* (1941) and *Collected Poetry* (1945).

I got back here to find some copies of 'Poetry' with my 10 poems[1] & a little article on me by Julian Symons[2] who I always thought was probably a fool but seems to have got in some palpable hits on the subject of me & my lack of belief besides quoting an embarrassing remark from my critical book[3] which I only trailed as a rag anyway to annoy the odour-of-sanctity-ists. Maybe this fits in with your remarks on my 'empiricism' but God damn it, darling, I am not contented with the way I am either, only I am not going to foist a 'belief' on to things; it has got to grow out of them.

To come back to you-&-me I want you just terribly, darling, but in case you should think this is merely 'subjective' (remember what you were saying yesterday about subject & object?) maybe I ought to remind you of what is really a truism: if A is in love with X he mightn't be in love with her if he were B but on the other hand he wouldn't be in love with her if she were Y. I can't be bothered to elaborate this, darling, as surely it is obvious. What you may not however know, darling, is that I have never yet, I think, made any serious mistake, so far as my judgment goes, about my relationships with women, i.e. I have never entered into a relationship which turned out to be less significant for either party than I expected. What I have done is that I have willed against my judgment or omitted to will, according to my judgment, against certain relationships. This being so, I am damned, darling, if when the two things come exactly together (which they never have done before) I am going to let the whole thing evaporate either through my own inertia or yours. This sounds selfish & crude & by the way judgment is not the right word, should be something more like vision, but the point is, darling, that while I feel just crazy about you, I can still see the whole thing quite sanely & clearly (you may not believe this but it is so & it is a clarity maybe acquired at a price). Listen, darling, & don't be so sceptical: I am completely convinced – i.e. as convinced as I am that there are now some leaves on the trees outside my window – that you-&-I will be all right. When I say all right I mean something very good indeed. Maybe I should copy a letter you wrote me just before I came over & put it in propositions.[4]

1 – 'Prognosis', 'Obituary', 'O'Connell Bridge', 'Entirely', 'Order to View', 'I Am that I Am', 'Three Thousand Miles', 'The British Museum Reading-Room', 'Perdita' and 'Stylite', *Poetry* (Chicago), May 1940.
2 – Julian Symons, 'Louis MacNeice: The Artist as Everyman', ibid., pp. 86–94.
3 – *MP*.
4 – 'Propositions / 1. Words are idiotic / 2. You are so far away / 3. You have been so far away so long / 4. Supposing you are in love with an Irish girl / 5. But other things matter more. / 6. Or so I tell myself / 7. Today I walked past a window where you & I once watched a poor helpless manikin being undressed, & I thought about that' (EC to FLM, 26 Dec. 1939, *Ms Yale*).

<u>Propositions</u>:-

You are not doomed.

Nor am I.

You & I <u>could</u> have a very wonderful relationship together.

Which neither of us could have with anyone else.

a relationship would <u>not</u> be bad for either of our works, might very possibly be good for them.

Such a relationship should be definite, i.e. should be intended (subject to unforeseeable circumstances) to be (a) permanent, (b) monogamous.

It is not a question of my wanting to buy your soul; all I want is to have an understanding with it.

To have an understanding with soul it is necessary to have an understanding with body.

Whatever you may <u>think</u>, this latter is perfectly feasible between you & me.

an all-round understanding is feasible.

All the above, darling, I regard as indisputable (tell me if you don't). Here are some more thoughts I had in the train which are not certainties – only probabilities.

Firstly, with regard to my child: I know very well, darling, that that might seem alarming to you but I think me-&-my child is rather a special case & not very likely to complicate (I could explain this at more length if you liked. You see I had planned out things for him before your time & it so happens that these plans would be the least likely to impinge upon you.)

Secondly, picking up what I was saying about living in a house yesterday . . . I don't think it at all established that people who have a permanent connection have got to live continuously in one house or even in one place. That depends on a lot of things, work, temperament etc.

Thirdly, I think that we ought to do something about you-&-me <u>soon</u>, darling. Partly because time seems to be moving faster than usual now. I don't believe that war makes personal relationships unimportant but it is capable of sabotaging them – I don't mean in material ways so much as by its effect on one's nerves.

Fourthly, I think it <u>would</u> be a good idea if you got a divorce because in a world getting steadily more bureaucratic it may become very inconvenient to be nominally married to someone you aren't really married to. Also possibly you & I might get to a position where it would be not only practically more convenient but psychologically more satisfactory to get married to each other.[1] As you know, I have a dread of that institution as no doubt you have too but I have no dread of <u>you</u>, darling, & the thing has one good point (which lots of people probably think its worst point) i.e. that it means committing oneself & when something is valuable it is good to commit oneself.

Of course this is all from my point of view, darling, & may horrify you over the horizon but I thought I might as well try to be explicit. I hate being explicit in this cut-&-dried way because it leaves out one's feelings but by this point, darling, you must know my feelings. Each time I leave you it cuts into me more. That doesn't mean I'm not happy, because I am – but I guess you understand, darling.

Have just been listening to the news about which there is nothing to be said; I can't bear to sit listening to people talking about the war as if it were a parlour game. Father D'Arcy produced the Catholic point of view last night – shockingly slick. By the way, I described him to you wrong. The rest of him was as I remembered but his hair instead of being crisp curls is long wires curling at the ends. & the features rather ravaged by God.

About your work, darling, I am afraid you may think you-&-me would get in the way of it. I am <u>dead certain</u> that is not so.

By the way, in case you think I am in the habit of affirming certainties like this, I have never done it before in this way – not even to my wife or to the girl I was so crazy about in London. Reason (quite simple) – that I wasn't certain with regard to them.

Now I must go to bed, darling. Will write you a nice frivolous letter next time. Tomorrow I am going to a concert by Egon Petri.[2]

Sleep well, darling, & be a good girl & work & be happy.

Lots of love,

L.

P.S. (Wednesday morning): I can't stop thinking about the war this morning. Darling, I am utterly appalled by it, feel like jumping off a bridge. Not that I shall but my whole inside feels full of panic. & desolation. It gives me two crazy impulses both of which represent sheer defeatism. One is to run away by going back to England, ceasing to be myself any more, letting things just happen to me – jumping down into the machine. The other is to run away over here by giving up entirely – I mean giving up the

1 – This seems to be as close as he comes in writing to a proposal of marriage to Eleanor Clark.
2 – Egon Petri (1881–1962), German-born classical pianist; he moved to the USA in 1939, where he taught at Cornell University and later in California.

effort to hold on to the things I think valuable – you, work, my more real (if unrealised) self – & just becoming fatalist in the worst sense, lapsing, self-doping. I don't mean to do either of these things (il gran rifiuto) but if you see me in a lunatic moment starting out in either direction you might remind me, darling, that it is sheer perversion – which it is but I might go blind to that on occasions. It hurts so to keep one's eyes open all the time. You see, dope is neither pleasure nor happiness nor a solution; dope is dope. But work & love (in spite of what some people think) & life are not dope. Dope stands for the death-wish & it is only the feebler part of me wants to quit. It would be easier with a 'belief'. I wish, darling, some time you would talk about beliefs & world-views with me & I will try to be good & not run emotionally amok (as on Friday); I feel you have got some sort of faith which is good where I have only got an instinct on the one hand & a number of intellectual recognitions on the other – the two need fusing. I think, darling, though, it is a distortion on your part to align yourself with 'Teutonic' idealism & me with British hand-to-mouthness.[1] Neither of those things, as I conceive them, is good & I don't think either you or I belong to either of them. There are other alternatives. In a sense, I think, far from being the kind of complete sceptic all the book-reviewers think me, I have always had rather more than the normal share of 'belief'; only it is a belief not properly orientated if you see what I mean. And I wish you would help me about it, darling; maybe I could repay you in kind (it takes more than one spoke to make a wheel).

What a lot about myself, you must forgive me for it. Did you ever hear about the Asiatic (I think) tree which only blossoms in a forest fire? I feel one might blossom like that any moment. Or burn. Or perhaps both. But if one really blossomed it would be worth it. The trouble (& the glory) about being in love with you is that I see you against the world.[2] Not – as so often happens – in a corner. & it is very windy. But it is good.

1 – FLM writes elsewhere, 'A world view is a Teutonic thing, which is why, no doubt, people prefer to say *Weltanschauung*. The English for better or worse – I think for better – have generally tended to be empiricist.' 'Notes on the Way [2]', *Time & Tide* 33: 28 (12 July 1952), 779–80; repr. *SP*, 180.

2 – She replied: 'You see, darling, you said one thing in your letter that rather startled me, about seeing me against the world. I don't know that I warrant that, but in any case, I don't see you that way' (EC to FLM, 20 May 1940, *Ms Yale*).

21 May [1940]   Ithaca, NY

Darling,

Your letter wasn't quite what I expected & I am really angry with you, instead of being merely upset as I thought I should be. I am now going to say a lot of things to you but, as they say, you asked for it. I thought you might accuse me of 'inhumanity' (which I shall explain about in a moment) but what in hell do you mean by telling me that I have 'an awful lack of curiosity about the world?'[1] I was curious about the world & suffering from my curiosity about it before you were born. And if you think you can judge my curiosity about the world by the fact that I don't look at newspapers when you're around, you show an appalling lack of feminine imagination. Apart from which, newspapers aren't the world anyway though one might think they were to judge from the conversation one hears at Eunice's.[2] Secondly as for 4 months before coming over I had read 2 or 3 newspapers practically from cover to cover & had also spent half the day listening to the radio – all of which led nowhere – I felt, being in America, a reaction against it. And if you think the only way the world impinges on me is through my nerves, you are – I am sorry to say, darling – a fool. When for the last week I have been feeling steam-rollers go over me all the time, that isn't just nerves; it was imagining (with my brain & also – if I may be hackneyed for want of a better word – with my heart) what this war is going to do to England & Ireland as I know them & to particular people whom I know there – & this doesn't just mean my bosom friends or ex-mistresses but it means people like my family's chauffeur (who joined the territorials) & the little electrician in Birmingham whom I probably told you about & it means people also whom I've never seen but whom I <u>know</u>

---

1 – 'You have, darling, an awful lack of curiosity about the world. Forgive me for putting this so grossly, I cant seem to beat around about it, now that your formulation makes me see it as I hadn't before: I had often had, before, a sort of half-conscious thought around the edges of my mind, something like this: that if I had ever once seen you turn back in the street to read something at a newsstand, or pick up a book that was way off from your field and become engrossed in it, I would fall really in love with you.' (EC to FLM, 20 May 1940, Ms Yale).
2 – Eunice Jessup (1911–87), née Clark (sister of Eleanor Clark), educ. Vassar College; co-founder in 1932 of the literary magazine *Housatonic*. During the 1960s she became active in the civil rights movement, helping to register black voters in the American South. M. (1) (1933) Selden Rodman (see FLM to EC 18 May 1939, n. 1, p. 339); (2) (1937) John Knox (Jack) Jessup (1907–79), educ. Yale; worked for *Time* 1935–69; *Life* 1951–69; CBS 1971–6. Author of *America and The Future* (1943), *The National Purpose* (1960), *Communism: The Nature of Your Enemy* (1962). FLM stayed with the Jessups through July (Stallworthy, 278).

much better than you obviously think I can know even the people I meet (more about 'knowing' people in a minute). As for 'curiosity,' darling, this seems rather a cheap Tu Quoque but you have in your time taken me aback by showing no interest in people I was telling you about – e.g. the German refugee [*illegible*] on the Samaria whom (in a non-sexual way) I practically fell in love with. As for looking at books 'off my field' I am no Wystan or Aldous Huxley & I don't value information for information's sake but you obviously have no knowledge of the sort of books I do look at & why; & once again you seem to forget the distracting effect sex has on one (in situations like mine at the moment) if you are judging my book-interests by what I do in your presence. Also, darling, our respective ways of looking at the world are perhaps appropriate to our branches of writing (poetry – to crib a book I have just been reading – being more concerned with internal reality – the pole of instinct – & the novel with external reality – the pole of environment) but you do seem to me every so often to distort the world by projecting ideological prejudices on to it – & one shouldn't do this even to damn an ideologist, e.g. it is all very well for you to say – if you are convinced of it – that Stalinism is horrible but, unless American Stalinists are very different from English ones, you are uttering a damned lie when you say – as you have said – that all Stalinists are horrible.[1] (& I am not thinking of fellow-travellers or dilettantes like Stephen but in particular of a 100% Stalinist I knew who would, I suspect, still be a Stalinist if he were alive). In the same way, darling – although I quite agree that you can have very good intuitions about people – you also do much too much facile labelling e.g. last year you had no use for Erika Mann & this year you think she's swell & talking of labelling, it is high time you & Eunice dropped this little pixie myth about me[2] (which means, I suppose, much the same as what you call 'automatically sheltered' in your letter) because, though no doubt superficially apt & amusing, it is completely false & if you are such the hell of an intuitive, you ought to be able to see beneath people's skin.[3] If you want a formula for me (which will also explain our discrepancy much more nearly) it is that I am a peasant who has gate-crashed culture, & when

1 – Like everyone involved with *Partisan Review*, EC was anti-Stalinist; cf. 'The Stalinist contingent is in a pitiful state, scurrying around like mice and struggling desperately to hang on to their two by four illusions' (EC to FLM, 26 Aug. 1940, *Ms Yale*).
2 – '. . . remember too that [Eunice] started to write poetry and fell on the way, partly for the very reasons that make her able to think of you, in so far as she does, as a pixie. (She doesn't exactly anyway, of course)' (EC to FLM, 7 May 1940, *Ms Yale*).
3 – '. . . there is something to me a little appalling in being as automatically sheltered, except thru the nerves, as you somehow are' (EC to FLM, 20 May 1940, *Ms Yale*).

I say that I am a peasant this isn't a figure of speech or an inverted snob romanticism, it is just a statement of fact, though very few people can see it except some people who have come from your 'lower classes' themselves &, having also gatecrashed culture, realise my curious position.[1] Not [that it?] is a bad position at all (it's why I'm able to write poetry that is not stale) but it does lead to the paradox – that one can talk better to the people one has gate-crashed on than to the people one feels more identity with. & you, darling, obviously judge my 'knowledge' of people or my 'curiosity' about them by my capacity for surface gestures towards them – which is very naïve of you. Actually, darling, you are much more 'upper class' in your attitude to people than I am just at the time when you are taking an intelligent interest & being sympathetic etc. e.g. if you & I were talking to a slum-dweller you would certainly make a much better job of the talking & the slum-dweller would think you were sympathetic & I was aloof. Because he couldn't recognise me owing to my metamorphosis. But I should recognise him &, what is more, I should be him – which you couldn't be, darling, not in a thousand years. For you he remains an external person & you feel about him; you may do much more 'feeling' than I do but I don't feel about him; I feel him plain & simple; I have an internal identity with him. This is what makes me very sceptical about all idealistic, or reformist, or humanitarian or call-it-what-you-will movements which come from 'above' – cult of the proletariat or getting to grips with 'facts'. For the upper-class mentality these remain 'facts' i.e. objective & they collect them & systematise them & try to do something about them & all the time, whether they know it or not, they are feeling superior. Even you, darling, when you say things like 'It's amazing the way these people live' are being superior. It doesn't seem to me amazing the way poor people live, though as the case may be, it may seem admirable or regrettable. There is nothing exotic in it for me, it's a stratum which is still (instinctively) intelligible to me, my relations are still living in mud-floored cottages in the West of Ireland.[2]

Now a little autobiography on the subject of 'inhumanity'. You are not the first person who has thought me inhuman though the other people didn't think my inhumanity as established & final a thing as you seem to. Again I think you are only looking at the skin – perhaps this time, a crust.

1 – Cf. 'And to my own in particular . . . I leave the credit for that which may endure / Within myself of peasant vitality' (LI, CP07, 732).
2 – Cf. FLM's tribute to his Sligo ancestors, 'above the yellow falls of Ballysodare' in 'Auden and MacNeice: Their Last Will and Testament' (LI, CP07, 731–2), and in SAF: 'Down through Ballysodare in County Sligo where my ancestors were buried under brambles to the Island of Omey where my father had been born' (SAF, 111–12).

You, darling, think I am 'automatically sheltered'. Well, <u>if</u> I am automatically sheltered, I'm sorry for the people who are not sheltered. This again you can't boil down to nerves &, if I go back to my childhood for examples, I don't do so out of self-pity or because I want you to think of me as a pathetic little boy – which is the last thing I want. The point is that by the age of 12 far from being automatically sheltered, I was extremely vulnerable to contacts with 'the world' & other people & I was vulnerable just because I was comparatively clear-sighted about them, because I could imagine myself into them whereas they couldn't imagine themselves into me. If in one's childhood one has had to act as interpreter for an idiot brother whom none of the adults could understand, if one has been kept awake half the night every night by a father moaning about his life, if one has got so that one winces in advance on behalf of one's family's reactions in any possible situation, the important effect is not the (admittedly heavy) effect on one's nerves but the terrifying, precocious development of insight. I am not exaggerating this, darling. By the time I was 12 I could sit in a classroom of little boys at my school & foresee pretty accurately what reactions <u>each</u> of them would have to anything anyone said or did; even when the foresight wasn't accurate the point was that I was imagining myself inside each of those boys, a thing which I guess they weren't doing in turn. Well, later I closed down on that, darling, because of the strain & because, in order to make myself, I couldn't keep on feeling on behalf of other people. And so I got this detachment or aloofness or whatever it should be called but if you think I am aloofness to the core & can't see behind what was only a protective crust, you are, darling, more short-sighted than I should have expected. One other point: you seem to think I have a purely aesthetic approach to the world. This is crazy of you. I suppose you think the reason I haven't got a lovely comprehensive world-view is that I amn't interested in world-views. When I was married I <u>did</u> try to do without a world-view but it was a failure & I have known for years that I must develop one & I am trying to develop one but I am damned if I am going to swallow Marx or Trotsky or anyone else lock stock & barrel unless it squares with my experience or, perhaps I should say, my feelings of internal reality. Also when you say my attitude leads to tiredness & the death-wish etc., I don't see that if I am either tired or have death-wishes at the moment, that is necessarily due to my attitude (at moments it is <u>you</u> who seem to me defeatist, especially in regard to work) but may quite understandably be due to circumstances which are not of my making at all. In the time between my two visits to America there was after all the outbreak of war, while on the private plane (though this, I suppose, was of my own making) I had (a) an absurd amount of work on hand, (b) some very exhausting personal experiences – & – talking of being interested in people – with regard to people as individuals, when you have had 3 people within as many months pour out upon you all their inmost & most horrifying secrets & when you think it on the cards that any or all of them may commit suicide, you may tend temporarily to feel surfeited with individuals & turn for a change to the bathroom tiles or, as you say, to 'thinking about airplanes & rivers'; with regard to people in the mass, if you had lived in England last year, you might feel temporarily escapist in that respect too. Anyhow, darling, if you really can only see me from the angle you took in your letter, I think it's about time we wash up – if the world situation isn't going to wash us up anyway.

Seeing you've been 'honest with yourself' I might as well – this isn't just spite though there may be spite in it (I don't pretend not to be spiteful) – be honest with yourself too. I think you think, darling, that I think you're some sort of angel but I don't & never have. I am completely in love with you but I am not, as they say, blindly infatuated. I am not blind to you either physically or any other way, e.g. I think you are astonishingly beautiful but this doesn't mean that I think you are perfect or that I forget I have seen people say with more beautiful legs. In the same way I don't think that as a character you are anything like perfect, you just happen to appeal to me very much (by the way, your complementation talk was off the mark; I didn't mean to ask you to complement me, at least not in the crude sense of atoning for my deficiencies), you may as well know what I think are your imperfections & then the air may be cleared a bit. Apart from your being upper-class (which is perhaps the most serious) I think, darling, that you are – in some respects (for God's sake don't think I mean this absolutely) – immature, soft, 'inhuman' (though not in the same way as me) &, sexually inhibited, & to some extent self-deceiving. I first realised your immaturity & perhaps also the others (except the sex one) when we were walking with your mother up Fifth Avenue last year & you came all over pathetic little girl passing the hat-shops. & your softness manifests itself dialectically in a certain intellectual arrogance & in a contempt which spreads over people instead of being concentrated on institutions, also in a perfectionist attitude to work (Flaubert surely was softer than Shakespeare). Also I think your revolutionism is partly self-deceiving, a sort of couvades[,] but that is too long to go into now. As to your sexual inhibitedness I don't say this on the strength of you & me because for all I know I am not at all your type but it comes out in a lot that you do & say & I think it is a great pity because, even if the novelist is more concerned with environment than instinct, I can't see how he can present the world at all adequately if he hasn't got <u>inside</u> knowledge of what is about the most important of the instincts. If he hasn't got that, his <u>internal</u> reality remains in a sense in the nursery.

Well, that's that, darling, for the present. I shan't be coming down this weekend though I shall probably go somewhere else than to NYC next week. You see, I don't really accept your imputations except in a very modified form. I used to have a masochistic instinct to agree with things people said against me but I have given up pretending to agree when I don't, just for the fun of playing the lost soul. I am not a lost soul (though, if your view of me were correct, I should consider myself one), neither am I a little spring lamb gambolling forever through meadows of inconsequence. That you should think of me as either makes me feel like taking the next boat for hell though even that I wouldn't do – not for that reason – because it would involve a defeat & I am prepared for you-&-me to come to nothing but I am not going to let myself come to nothing because of you.

Love, L.

TO *Bennet Cerf* MS Columbia

14 June [1940]   Ithaca, NY

Dear Bennet Cerf,

I shall be coming to New York next week and my address till further notice will be

c/o Mr. J. K. Jessup,
29 Fifth Avenue.

About this book of 'Poems 1926–40,' the contents will approximately be as follows:-

   I.   All the poems included in 'Poems' (Random House) excepting 'Insidiae', 'Trapeze' & 'Sonnet.'
   II.   At least three other very early poems. About four lyrics from 'Out of the Picture'. At least six additional poems from 'The Earth Compels' (Faber 1938), including one long Eclogue.
   III. 'Autumn Journal' (with a few changes).
   IV.   At least forty shorter poems (1938–40), not counting about ten lighter poems of epigram length.

I think these should make quite a sizable book. I will call you up about it some day next week.

Yours sincerely
Louis MacNeice

TO *Nancy Coldstream*

MS Bodleian

16 August 1940   Portsmouth Hospital, NH

Dear puss,

   You will be amused to hear that I am coming back to England after all
– by order of the British government. I am really rather pleased at having
the onus of choice removed from me. Shall probably sail sometime in
September but it depends on how I convalesce. Have been in the hospital
a month following an operation for acute appendicitis & peritonitis; they
all expected me to die when I came in.

   After the war I think I shall migrate here for good – unless there is a
social revolution in England which makes everything new. I have got v.
attached to this county & I like it being so big.

   E. & I still intend to try to make a go of it when the mess is over. She
was here till the beginning of August but had to go away then to teach a
magnate to write English.

   I am going to a v. rural spot to convalesce when I get out of here. Wystan
& his boy drove over one day a long way from Massachusetts to see me.

   Before I got ill I met Jean Connolly in New York, going round with the
most awful people but much slimmer.[1] She said she had seen you & that
you were v. vigorous & blooming.

   I am afraid, puss, this is not a v. bright letter but I am lying on my back
& feeling fragile. I have no idea what I shall do in England but hope it will
be in London. I suppose you have to be v. much on the alert now at your
ambulance station.

   Have just been correcting some proofs of the Yeats book; the bulk of
them have gone astray. Have also just received a parcel of delicacies from
a queer frustrated woman in New York whom I hardly know but who has
a crush on me. They are v. welcome as the food here is pretty dreary.

   Well, darling, I expect to see you some time. Hope things are not too
grim.

                    Lots of love,
                    Louis

P.S. The doctor has just told me that I must not sail before October.

1 – Wife of Cyril Connolly. See FLM to MM, 10 March 1937, n. 7, p. 296.

18 August 1940   Portsmouth Hospital, NH

Dear E.R.D.,

You probably have heard from Wystan that I was ordered back to England by the British Govmt & immediately afterwards got acute appendicitis (please forgive my writing – I am on my back). I have now been in this place 4½ weeks & am sick of it; had every kind of complication, due to initial peritonitis. I am now for the first time feeling on the upgrade, thanks to two days of intravenous injections.[1] Expect to get out of here in about 10 days time. The doctors say I mustn't sail for England before October, so I shall spend a month convalescing in the country (forwarding address: c/o Oxford University Press, 114 Fifth Avenue, New York City).

It is v. difficult writing to England these days. Half of me is pleased to be coming back. I should probably be altogether pleased if it weren't for Eleanor. It may be years before we see each other again. Also I don't know what to do about Dan. I <u>was</u> going to get him over here.[2]

I hear you are going to work on the land – which sounds fine. What do you think they'll make me do? By this stage I am on for doing anything – cleaning sewers or feeding machine guns, but preferably nothing too intelligent.

I met Cyril Connolly's wife in New York; she said everyone at all leftist or pink in England was under a cloud. (?)

Some of the Yeats proofs arrived here at the hospital; the bulk of them seem to have been lost.

Afraid this letter is rather dim; I am still feeling sub.

With all best wishes to both of you,
Yours, Louis

1 – Cf. 'In Portsmouth, New Hampshire, plugged with morphia . . .' ('The Messiah (*a memory of 1940*)', *Solstices*, CP07, 533).
2 – Eleanor Clark had suggested FLM might bring Dan to America, but Dodds advised FLM to let Dan remain in Ireland, thus avoiding a dangerous Atlantic crossing (ERD to FLM, 5 June 1940, *Ms Bodleian*).

TO *Bennet Cerf* MS Columbia

20 August 1940 Portsmouth Hospital, NH

Dear Bennet Cerf,

I have been in this place five weeks after an operation for acute appendicitis and have another week to run. I wonder if you could have sent to me (and charge to my account) the following books from the Modern Library –

Gibbon's Decline and Fall?

Conrad Aiken's anthology of modern American Poetry? I should be very grateful as I have nothing to read here.[1]

Second sombre piece of news:- I have been called back to England by the British Government. But I shan't sail now till October. I will let you have that volume of poems before I go. (Please forgive my handwriting)

Yours
Louis MacNeice

TO *Eleanor Clark* MS Yale

Thursday evening [29 August 1940] Old Ferry Lane, Kittery, ME

Darling,

You will be surprised to see I am still here but the air ace has not come yet because of weather.[2] (He is supposed to be fetching me tomorrow). I left hospital 11.0 Tuesday morning & everything has been a delight since. Matthiessen & Russell Cheney, both of whom I think are very nice though old maidish in general & damned bad drivers in particular, have the dream of a little wooden house at Kittery opposite Newcastle.[3] I sleep up in a

---

1–In a letter of commiseration (21 Aug.), Cerf notified FLM that he had sent the requested books, as well as 'one of our new novels for which we have particularly high hopes. It is called THE OX-BOW INCIDENT [by Walter Van Tilburg Clark], and I will be interested to hear what you think of it' (*Ms Columbia, Random House*).

2–EC's mother – Mrs Eleanor Phelps Clark – had arranged for Batch Pond, a local 'air ace', to pick up FLM at Portsmouth and bring him to Connecticut. Cf. EC to FLM, 28 Aug. 1940: '. . . mother straightened it out: she didn't hire one but simply procured a local Ace. (She can produce anything)' and Mrs Phelps Clark to FLM, also 28 Aug.: 'Mr Pond is a famous ace, lives near me, is doing this in his own plane for fun and for you and me in sheer goodwill. We can't pay him – just "thank you," prettily.'

3–F. O. Matthiessen (1902–50), educ. Yale, Harvard, Oxford (Rhodes Scholar, 1923). He taught for many years at Harvard, and was author of *The Achievement of T. S. Eliot* (1939), *American Renaissance; Art and Expression in the Age of Emerson and Whitman* (1941), and *Henry James: The Major Phase* (1944). Russell Cheney (1881–1945), educ. Yale and Arts Student League (NY), a painter, was Matthiessen's partner.

duck's egg attic in a sumptuous double bed. There are a lot of books & very fine cooking by a solid coal black negro from Hayti [*sic*] (he appeared as epigon to an earlier negro cook who died & dying sent him to take his place). There are two huge ginger & white cats who eat asparagus & melon & there is a luxuriant over-run garden sloping down to the sea; on the sea are some white boats all asleep. Cheney showed me his paintings which don't seem v. good but have a certain gusto. Poor old Matthiessen is just finishing an enormous book on Whitman, Thoreau, Emerson, Melville etc.; he types all day in a little attic study. The house seems plumb full of beds. It has enormous fireplaces & I should like to stay here in the winter. Further up the road there is a whole series of colonial houses – very attractive. Since coming here I have been amusing myself writing Ballades; I have written 4 already.[1] I thought it would be almost impossible to make them seem real & other than fretwork but now am not so sure. Today I also wrote a quite different sort of poem called Jehu.[2] I am now smoking as much as ever which makes me feel healthy though I still have a dressing.

On Tuesday I had my hair cut in Newcastle (rather short but that was nice by reaction) & bought some yellow sort of moccasin shoes made of elk which are marvellously comfortable. Yesterday I wrote you a telegram poem which I would have sent as a telegram but I thought it would have puzzled you my still being here, besides I was stingy. I will write it on the back of this. You will write to me at Roxbury, won't you, darling. I called up your mother last night to find out about the air ace & she says there is lots of cream down there. Get the maggot to take some more photos.[3]

love ever,

Louis

1 – FLM published five 'Ballades' (including 'Ballade for Mr MacLeish') in *Poems, 1925–1940* (New York, 1941), though they were later dropped from *Collected Poems, 1925–1948*. They have been reprinted in CP07, App. 5, 765–8.

2 – 'Jehu', published in *Poems, 1925–1940*, *PP*, and CP07, 198.

3 – EC was employed in a ghostwriting or editorial capacity by a man she called 'the maggot' (Charles Ward) in Northeast Harbor, Maine: 'The maggot is terrific, he works like a diesel engine and thinks he's having a vacation. So I have to be quite an engine too to keep up with him . . .' (EC to FLM, 7 Aug., *Ms Yale*) and 'the man is a dynamo and more, has decided he <u>will</u> write and by God he will' (EC to FLM, 11 Aug. 1940, *Ms Yale*).

<u>Telegram.</u>

Just left
hospital feel
beautifully real
staying by sea
with two ginger
cats golden
rod tiger
lilies to be
out is great
I eat and eat
chops lobster
ignore future
nice to think
appendix gone
for good beastly
nuisance boon
lose it lots
of love drink
my health hope
see you soon.

TO *Eleanor Clark*   MS Yale

3 September [1940]   Old Ferry Lane, Kittery, ME

My darling,

   This is becoming a farce though by no means unpleasant. Every day the
ace, whose name is Batch Pond, has been coming & then there have been
fogs or storms & your mother has sent wires calling it off. This morning
at 7.15 – only about an hour ago – Matthiessen & Cheney left in a taxi
(they are going to New Mexico) & I had decided to go with them & go to
Hartford by train but at 7.0 your mother called up & said Batch Pond
would fetch me this afternoon if the fog lifted. <u>If</u>. Anyway I am now alone
in the house which is rather fun & have eaten up the breakfast that the two
boys hadn't time for. Both of them were terribly nice to me & for a week
I have been stuffing food & drinking Alsatian wines & pouring out poems
in an unprecedented spate. I have written <u>ELEVEN</u> since coming here;
what do you think is wrong with me? Five ballades (which, in spite of all

the reasons to the contrary, seem to be alive & Matthiessen thinks so too), & a poem about the War called Jehu, & one about Picture Galleries, & an 80 line philosophical poem called Plurality[1] (difficulty of content balanced by an easy, almost-slick, metre & rhyme-scheme), & a naïve-seeming kind of little ballad with refrain called 'Autobiography',[2] & a short flat piece called 'Province' but really a comment on human beings, & a hurry of short lines about smells. Last night – but this doesn't count – some damned insects kept jumping on me in bed & I wrote v. quickly a little hymn beginning

> 'There's a home for little insects
> Above the bright blue sky . . .'

I have also been reading in a dipping & splashing kind of way M. & C's books heterogeneously – Whitman & Hemingway & Gide about Russia & Gauguin about Tahiti & Alice B. Toklas & the Declaration of Independence & Havelock Ellis on Spain & a book about Goya (some facts I need for my prosebook) & a book on Toulouse-Lautrec & the New Directions Dylan Thomas & a few poems by Frost & the whole of the New Republic supplement on Willkie (M. & C. have a pal called Davenport who is Willkie's stage manager) & Nicolas Pevsner on the birth of modern architecture;[3] also have been looking through books of reproductions of Greco & Matisse & Picasso & Zurbaran & Grosch & Piero Della Francesca (rediscovered one of my favourite pictures – Carthusians in their refectory by Zurbaran, which I saw in Seville);[4] also

1 – 'Picture Galleries' was published (with 'The Dowser') in *Kenyon Review* (Winter 1941) and *PP*; it was later dropped, but restored in CP07, 760–1. 'Plurality': *Horizon*, Jan. 1941, 10–12; *Poems, 1925–1940*, *PP*, CP66, CP07, 204.
2 – 'Autobiography', *Harpers Bazaar*, 1 Sept. 1941, 120; *PP*, *Poems, 1925–1940*, *Eighty-Five Poems*, *Selected Poems*, ed. W. H. Auden (1964), CP66, CP07, 200.
3 – A. Gide, *Return from the USSR*, trans. D. Bussy (1937); P. Gauguin, *Noa Noa*, trans. O. F. Theis (1920); G. Stein, *Autobiography of Alice B. Toklas* (1933); H. Ellis, *The Soul of Spain* (1908, repr. 1937); N. Pevsner, *Pioneers of the Modern Movement from Morris to Gropius* (1936). The Dylan Thomas is possibly *The World I Breathe* (1939) or *Portrait of the Artist as a Young Dog* (1940). Wendell Willkie (1892–1944) was a corporate lawyer and Republican Party nominee for the 1940 presidential election, and was defeated by Franklin D. Roosevelt. Bruce Bliven edited the *New Republic*'s 2 Sept. supplement, 'This Man Willkie', in which he was accused of being 'a front man and a fixer'. The supplement was massively popular, selling 38,000 copies in twenty-four hours and a further 60,000 copies in the following week ('Martyr Milton', *Time* magazine, 16 Sept. 1940).
4 – Recalling his visit to Seville in 1936, with AB, he wrote: 'Our new revelation was the painting of Zurbaran' (*SAF*, 159).

Walker Evans' photographs of America. All of which has made me all the more eager to give up teaching & cocktail parties etc. & live somewhere not too accessible. I re-read 'The Ball' in the Kenyon Review & was very impressed; I had forgotten it was so precise & it penetrated me much more this time.

Matthiessen & Cheney are slightly of a comic strip (I can't imagine either of them ever had any sex-life, I suppose they did but I can't imagine it): M. looks out of his rimless glasses under a baldish dome & with superlative mildness tells C. that he has been silly; C. is fat & red-faced with a fleshy jowl & pathetically doggy eyes – always anxious to please, he looks very well in the evening when the black man goes; is crazy about France & keeps telling you of course he's not intelligent. M. is very old maidish about his cats, takes one up to work with him every afternoon; the cats are very heavy & snore, yesterday I thought it was sounds in my stomach & was getting alarmed because they were unorthodox till I saw the cat sleeping in the bed.

Outside the house there is a thing I suppose you know but I had never seen called a smoke bush; I like it very much. There is also a honeysuckle & tigerlilies & phlox & nasturtium & hollyhocks & Queen Anne's Lace & masses of golden rod.

When I get back to New York I must go to the Metropolitan Museum to see Greco's picture of Toledo.

Some letter which came for me at the hospital last week was sent on wrong & is lost; was it yours?

The negro here makes cornbread & blueberry pies; I have to concede to you, darling, that there are more things in heaven & earth than are dreamt of under Big Ben. But I still haven't had my rhumbaba [sic].

The fog seems to be lifting; maybe Pond will come. The airport is very primitive. When we were there last week there was an old man . . . He had nothing to do with the airport, he wasn't going up in a plane, was spending the afternoon [illegible] because his son flies planes in [illegible].

Have been reading some Wallace Stevens; I can't catch on to him.[1] Have found however five poems of Dylan Thomas that survive as wholes. In Roxbury I shall stiffen myself with Dante. Anyone writing poems in English suffers from Shakespeare-legacy [sic] of swashbuckling phrases, ripeness is all & too much, chiaroscuro, self [sic].

1–Over a decade later he still clung to this view: 'Thus I myself have a blind spot for most of Wallace Stevens, but I can smell that he is trying.' 'Poetry Needs to Be Subtle and Tough', *Highlights of Modern Literature*, ed. F. Brown (New York, 1954), 158.

Darling, the sun is coming out; it looks as if the pond will come to Mahomet.

When are you leaving the maggot, damn him? Maybe you could make it for my birthday? 33 seems a pretty age; I always prefer the odd ones.

Must send some stuff around to the papers to raise some money & we can have a party. Rivers of milk & honey – for milk read cream. Love, darling, be happy.

L.

The negro has just turned up, so I shall have some lunch after all.

TO *Mary MacNeice*   MS Bodleian

4 September [1940]   Southover Farm, Roxbury, CT

My dear,

I only got here yesterday because previously the weather was too bad to fly. However yesterday's flight was a pleasure – a tiny little black plane called a Monocoupe & a very tough man piloting it. The week in between I stayed with two men I knew at Kittery, just outside Portsmouth – a little wooden house by the sea with a profusion of flowers & 2 enormous ginger & white cats; v. comfortable & beautiful cooking.

Thank you for your letters. One of them, I thought, was rather truculent. I <u>had</u> been in touch with experts – a woman attorney who has handled a lot of these cases – & I <u>had</u> also done everything required by the American Consulate in London (these requirements were reprinted by the New York Times). What you don't seem to realize is that the whole obstruction comes from the American consul in Belfast (who, I think, had his knife into me already because of my visit to him in December. I think, in that he as good as refused me a visa for my Irish passport, he imagines I pulled a fast one on him by coming to America on a British one.) I am afraid that he may keep on obstructing as long as I am in this country. However, I am trying to find out about that from Elizabeth. Incidentally I have been told that the President of Cornell could probably have fixed up for me to stay here but by this stage I rather feel like going back & having a look at history.[1]

---

1 – The President of Cornell had earlier written to the British Consul General in New York, requesting an extension of FLM's visa so he could teach at Cornell for a second year (1940–1), having already taught 'the second term of the current academic year' (7 May 1940; *Ms Bodleian, Ms Res, c. 590, Box 15*).

As to the calculation of danger – I had a letter from my old man today saying that in his opinion the sea was much more dangerous for Dan than staying in the country.[1] Of course we know what <u>his</u> opinion is worth on such matters but many other people over there seem to think the same; Dodds wrote me a letter to the same effect some time ago.[2] I think the danger of Ireland being <u>invaded</u> is wildly improbable (thanks to the British navy) & as for the I.R.A. the Germans may encourage them to do a bit of sabotage but there aren't enough of them to conduct a civil war. Bombs are more possible: I expect them to bomb Belfast sooner or later but not further west.[3] All this doesn't mean that I don't want to get Dan over but I think it possible that safer ways of transport may come about in the near future – e.g. if they would send American ships for British children to Galway. With regard to your remarks about mines & submarines, the people working on my Cunard boat definitely thought winter much safer than summer. You won't find many drifting mines in the <u>Atlantic</u> winter or summer whereas round the coasts of Ireland, England & Scotland, if you may meet drifting mines in winter, you will also meet submarines in summer. I am a bit discouraged, you see, by that boatload of British children being torpedoed the other day.[4] Anyhow, while these things are pending, there is no point in getting in a panic about the dangers over there. Naturally it sounds horrifying to hear of these raids (I <u>do</u> read the papers, you know) but I don't know if you've noticed how very few casualties there have been. In peacetime they used to kill more than that per day in road accidents. (In Portsmouth Hospital, incidentally, they reckon on several automobile casualties per week.) Maybe I've come out of hospital a bit fatalistic but I don't feel much in the way of qualms for Dan's safety at the moment & I don't feel any qualms about going back myself. In the modern world one can't keep dodging these things &, even if one does dodge them, one's just as likely to be knocked out by a germ or a train-crash or something. Understand – I'm not arguing for laissez faire:

1 – His father wrote: 'The seas now seem to be the really dangerous places. No ships, neutral or otherwise, seem to be immune from attack. I think the danger of travelling to America should be far greater than that of staying where one is. I have discussed this question with people who ought to know & they are positive that there is no safer place than an inland spot in Northern Ireland. I think so too. For the present Dan will be all right near Dungannon. It is a lovely spot in itself' (JFM to FLM, 19 Aug. 1940, *Ms Bodleian*).
2 – ERD to FLM, 5 June 1940, *Ms Bodleian*.
3 – Belfast was the main target in severely damaging air raids on 17 April and 5 May 1941. In both instances, areas further west were unharmed.
4 – On 1 Sept. 1940, the flagship of the Ellerman Line, *The City of Benares*, was torpedoed en route to Canada, but all 320 children on board were rescued and returned to Britain safely. 'Evacuee Ship Torpedoed. All the Children Safe', *The Times*, 2 Sept. 1940, 4.

my points are (1) that I'd like to get Dan here while I'm here & am trying to find out if that is possible but (2) if there's any chance of his crossing me I'd rather he stayed till I got over & (3) that in any case there's no point in getting in a panic & that conditions even in England – bar Kent & certain other places – are obviously (from the evidence of people who are there & not of Americans over here who are always alarmist) nothing like as frightful as you might think.

Above in reply to what seemed rather an attack on your part.

It is very nice here, warmer than in N.H. I can't do much except read.

Love to you both,
L.

TO *T. S. Eliot* Faber archive

24 September [1940] c/o Oxford University Press,
114 Fifth Avenue, New York City

Dear Eliot,

You may have heard that I am returning to England in November & am at the moment recovering from an operation for a ruptured appendix (+ complications). I thought I should notify you in advance about my next book of poems which will be ready for the spring; title:- PLANT AND PHANTOM (a phrase from Nietzsche describing man.) At the moment I seem to have 58 poems for it, not counting about 10 quasi-epigrams. I expect however to add one or two more – possibly a new Eclogue. There is one long poem already (300 ll.) on Freedom. A good number of the poems have been written in America. I will add a list of them here in the proper order + comments in case that will help you with a blurb, also in case the Mss. get dissipated somehow in these troubled times.[1]

Plant and Phantom.

(Note: C.P. = publ. by Cuala Press in the Last Ditch.

Am. = written in America

W. = connected with the war.

2.39 (e.g.) = February, 1939.)

---

1 – The published volume ended with the poem 'Cradle Song', unlisted in the letter. The following titles from this list were not published (although some have appeared in CP07, App. 5): 3 Love Poems, Primrose Hill, Men of Good Will, Coming from Nowhere, The Professor, The Gates of Horn, Three Thousand Miles, The Magnates, Freedom 1940, 5 Ballades, I Am that I Am, The Sense of Smell; 10 Octets were reduced to 3 Octets.

Prognosis: 5.39. C.P.
[3 Love Poems *deleted*]
Stylite: 3.40. Am.
Entirely: 3.40. Am.
Plant & Phantom: 9.40. Am.
3 Love Poems: summer 38: C.P.
Departure Platform: 7.38: C.P.
The British Museum Reading Room: 7.39: C.P.
London Rain: 7.39: C.P.
Primrose Hill: 6.39: C.P: W.
Men of Good Will: 11.39.
Picture Galleries: 8.40: Am.
The Coming of War (7 poems with Irish background) 8–9.39: C.P.: W.
Meeting Point: 4.39: C.P.
A Toast: 5.39: C.P.
Coming from Nowhere: 2.40: Am.
Order to View: 3.40: Am.
Novelettes:
    (1) The Old Story: summer 39: C.P.
    (2) Suicide: [summer] 39: C.P.
    (3) Les Sylphides: [summer] 39: C.P.
    (4) Christina: 7.39: C.P.
    (5) The Gardener: summer 39: C.P.
    (6) The Professor: 3.40: Am. W.
    (7) Provence: 9.40: Am.
    (8) The Preacher: 3.40: Am.
The Gates of Horn: 9.39. W.
Three Thousand Miles: 3.40, Am. W.
Death of an Actress: 5.40. Am. W.
Bar-room Matins: 7.40: Am. W.
Refugees: 9.40. Am.
The Magnates: 9.40. Am.
Freedom 1940: 7.40. Am. W.
Jehu: 8.40. Am. W.
5 Ballades: 8.40. Am. W.
O'Connell Bridge: 10.39
The Death Wish: 5.40. Am.
Conversation: 3.40. Am.
The Ear: 4.40. Am.
Evening in Connecticut: 9.40. Am. W.

<u>10 Octets</u> (quasi-epigrams) 10.39: (5/16 W.)
<u>Plurality</u> (80 ll. philosophical) 8.40. Am.
<u>I Am that I Am</u>: 3.40. Am.
<u>The Sense of Smell</u>: 9.40. Am.
<u>Perdita</u>: 3.40. Am.
<u>The Return</u>: 2.40. Am.
<u>The Dowser</u>: 9.40. Am.

(Technically the book has great variety.)
Hoping to see you in London,

Yours ever
Louis MacNeice

TO *Eleanor Clark* MS Yale

Late at night, Thursday morning	Portsmouth Hospital,
[10 October 1940]	New Hampshire

Darling,

 I have suddenly come all over crazily unhappy & am – very probably, I suppose – writing to you on the impulse. I guess it's the result of having to go to Egg Harbour[1] & also working out that when I get back from Ithaca it will be about the 20th. Which leaves <u>very</u> little time before I go away. You are all wrong, darling, if you think I <u>want</u> to go away. Except with some obscure part of me which I don't understand too well myself. If it wasn't for you I don't suppose I should mind much but, as it is, when I think about leaving you, it half destroys me. Especially as you seem so pessimistic about it yourself. It would be much easier if I felt you had any confidence in a future for you-&-me (I know I oughtn't to say this as it sounds as if I were blackmailing you to pretend some confidence you haven't got; but I guess you're not blackmailable). What you <u>must</u> realise, darling, is that, <u>if</u> you want me, I shall come back, taking it of course that I'm alive (& the odds are very much in favour of that). Maybe I've only got to go to Europe in order to disprove that it's necessary to go there. I don't know, darling; it's just some phantom I've got to lay. Not just nerves either. I want to <u>know</u> something which I can't get to know over here at the moment. But having to go so soon makes me feel as if I'm missing my last chances of contact with you. I don't mean sex-life; the dream character of

1–Egg Harbor, NJ, the home of Mary and Charles Katzman.

this period makes that seem for the moment almost irrelevant – I want to sleep with you <u>very much</u> but I don't know if we should achieve a harmony in the circumstances; am always willing to try of course but still that's not the point at the moment (what you said the other day, driving from Oakland, was plumb wrong; we should eventually get on all right in that way). I want you to <u>talk</u> to me. Not all the time of course but we must fit it in somewhere. Because it would be criminal if we separated now without ever having been properly articulate. It can't be done properly in writing [*illegible*] exchange of letters some time in the spring). I have quite a lot to say to you, darling, & perhaps it would be better if you let me express my confidence before you express your doubt. (There are always grounds for doubting anything & if one begins with that one tends not to get anywhere.) Incidentally I think we oughtn't to get sidetracked too much into analysing each other's 'character' (character in that sense tending to become abstracted & unreal; by the way you seem to have a view that 'character' is something very fixed – a sort of inexorable causality – which I disagree with). What is important is what we are going to <u>be</u> (something much fuller than 'character' in the static sense) & do & whether we can be & do successfully together; I think very strongly that we can. I think myself – though you will disagree with this – that this will be still more feasible when I return from Europe & as a result of having gone to Europe. This is <u>not</u> sentimentality, darling. And again not mere nerves. All the time I have been here this year I have had the feeling that, given the bloody mess that's going on, one can only get clarified through going close to it. I know there's plenty of mess here too & more of it imminent, but in my case the clarification would more naturally come against my own background. I guess you will ridicule the whole idea of clarification & I may be wrong but that can be proved one way or the other only in fact & not by argument. & at the moment I am inhibited all round by not having it tested by fact. It makes me angry, darling, when you say that I like war. What is worse than being terrified of it (which I am) is being horrified by its negativeness (which I am still more); but even negativeness is something that sometimes one has to get close to. Before being able to move on to the next positive. & I <u>am</u> going to move on, darling, even if I am all wrong about this particular clarification. I think some of your criticisms of my poetry are true. I don't imagine for a moment that going to England is going to have any direct effect on that. But one's got to see to one's life first (whoso tries to save his art – by insulating it – shall lose it). However I didn't mean to dissert on this subject on which I know you completely disagree with me. Incidentally I'm not just 'tossed by circumstances';

otherwise I shouldn't have come over here in January (a very deliberate & fairly laborious proceeding!) & we can surmount circumstances in future. But not by ignoring them. What I want to say more than all this is that I love you very much. & I can tell you more about that some time if you will talk with me. Goodnight, my darling. L.

P.S. [*illegible*] being unhappy at all. However you once told me to mention those things. Anyway I have just been studying your photographs & one of them is smiling. Thank you, darling.

from Louis MacNeice,
Portsmouth Hospital,
Portsmouth, New Hampshire.[1]

Cradle Song.[2]

Sleep, my darling, sleep;
The pity of it all
Is all we compass if
We watch disaster fall.
Put off your twenty-odd
Encumbered years and creep
Into the only heaven,
The robbers' cave of sleep.

The wild grass will whisper,
Lights of passing cars
Will streak across your dreams
And fumble at the stars;
Life will tap the window
Only too soon again,
Life will have her answer –
Do not ask her when.

P.T.O.

1–FLM's reasons for addressing the letter from Portsmouth Hospital at this stage are not clear, since he had left the hospital some weeks before. However, it seems clear from the content of the letter (including the dating of the poem and references to the author's imminent trips to Egg Harbor and Ithaca) that it was written in October 1940.
2–The final poem in *PP*, 86. Repr. as 'Cradle Song for Eleanor', *Poems, 1925–1940*, *Collected Poems 1925–1948*, 190; CP66, CP07, 209.

When the winsome bubble
Shivers, when the bough
Breaks, will be the moment
But not here or now.
Sleep and, asleep, forget
The watchers on the wall
Awake all night who know
The pity of it all.

October 1940.

F. L. MacNeice

TO *Mary MacNeice*   MS Bodleian

[Monday *deleted*] Tuesday /   7 Middagh Street,
Postmark [Monday]   Brooklyn Heights, NY[1]
28 October 1940

My dear,

Thank you for your very sympathetic letter. The air – as you suggest – seems to be a bit cleared!

It seems there is no boat till late November, so at least I shall see the election. Nobody quite understands my reasons for going back but they are really too involved & subtle to put on paper.

I had a letter from Dan (c/o Mrs. Clements, Springhill, Moneymore, Co. Tyrone) & also from Elizabeth who is in Belfast & says everything is very quiet & peaceful there & that Dan is flourishing.[2] She has at last discovered the reason for the Belfast consul's sabotage. It seems he wrote to the London Consul to ask if he had given me a visa & the latter denied

1 – FLM was staying at this address with WHA and a rich assortment of writers and artists, including novelist Carson McCullers (1917–67), dancer and actress Gypsy Rose Lee (Rose Louis Hovick) (1911–70) et al.

2 – Springhill, Moneymore; see FLM to parents, 1 July 1927, n. 3, p. 174. Diana Clements was Mina Lenox-Conyngham's daughter, hence FLM's step-first cousin. She had gone with Dan and her own children (Marcus and Catherine) for a temporary visit. Dan MacNeice remembers that Charlie Alexander (Diana's cousin) 'took us roaring down in his sidecar', down the avenue of Springhill (DM, private correspondence, 2008). Very little has survived of FLM's correspondence with Diana, but see her letters addressed to him on 10 Dec. 1941 and to EN on 28 Dec. [1941?] (*Ms Bodleian, Ms Res, c. 584*).

all knowledge of it, then found out many months later he had made a mistake. Bastards!

Elizabeth says she talked with Dan about his American prospects & he said 'Sure if I went to America I might be torpedoed,' so E. said we would only put him on a safe boat but D. said 'Sure I think it would be better to stay at home.' She says he now has a very strong Co. Tyrone accent (that's not unattractive) & that his house is surrounded by beech trees & that he shares a v. good governess with the same virtues as Miss Popper but, E. says, 'softened by her Co. Limerick origins'.

Who he? — E. says Howard was married this summer & has just been made a squadron leader & that everyone she knows who has been to London reports that the damage is surprisingly localised (her letter was by Air Mail, dated Oct. 15th). Enclosure from the stepdam saying 'I have been busy putting a strong net over the windows – it is our 2nd or 3rd attempt to protect them – but I hope it will all be found to be unnecessary – it is a troublesome job . . .' Typical, yes?

No, I'm not likely to do anything unnecessarily dangerous for <u>personal</u> reasons. That kind of hysterical reaction is something I got over before I ever came to America. I just remembered the other day that the present chief of the BBC[1] (successor to Sir John Reith) is a great fan of mine & a pal of my old man's, so maybe I shall cash in on that.

The Brooklyn household is chronically comic – all sorts of eccentrics just coming & going. A very good antidote to general worry. There is a very nice negress who cooks for us. Gypsy Rose Lee came round yesterday; very pleasant. The whole place still looks like a junkhouse – litter all over the piano etc.

Yes, maybe in the latter end (if we all survive that long!) my business will work out. In the meantime sufficient unto the day . . . But, by the way, I <u>don't</u> hold with your suicide squad idea. There are more than enough people doing the squadding already.

> Well, lots of love; will write again soon.
>
> L.

---

1 – Sir Frederick Ogilvie (1893–1949), MRIA, vice-chancellor Queen's University, Belfast 1934–8; Director General of the BBC 1938–42.

TO *E. R. Dodds*   MS Bodleian

17 November 1940.   7 Middagh Street, Brooklyn
                                            Heights, NY

Dear E.R.D.,

Am sailing about the end of this month (no boat before), will come &
see you in Oxford & should like to dump some belongings & Mss on you
(?) before going on to London.

The rest of this will be more instructions to you as my literary & general
executor (sorry to be such a bore but they say the North Atlantic is getting
hotter & hotter):-

(1) In case any mug wants to publish any of my letters (my solicitor in
London kept mentioning that possibility), I do not want any letters to my
father or stepmother to be published as they nearly always contain some
falsity. I also regret most of my undergraduate letters (esp. to Anthony
Blunt) which are nearly always v. affected & forced but I suppose they
might be amusing to social historians.

(2) Poems: I have a new book of poems which I am bringing back from
    Fabers. In case the book & I vanish, all the new poems are included
    in a collected book being done by Random House, New York, in
    the coming spring & can be extracted from that & compiled
    separately.[1]

(3) If anyone does a Collected Poems of me in England, I do not want
    any prose bound in with it.[2]

(4) With regard to prose in general I have no interest in the potboiling
    stuff being preserved. If anyone, however, gathers together the
    literary criticism (the 2 O.U.P. books & various reviews etc. – some
    of which have their points) I hope he or she will add a few notes
    giving the attendant circumstances of their writing.[3]

(5) In case any super-mug wants to do a life of me I would warn him
    against accepting, without careful scrutiny, any alleged information
    from my family (including Elizabeth). The best authorities (though
    each only from a certain angle) are Graham Shepard, Nancy
    Coldstream, yourself, Eleanor Clark. &, I suppose, Wystan. (How
    mortuary-egotistical all this sounds.)

1 – The new book of poems was *PP*, the contents of which were contained within *Poems,
1925–1940.*
2 – No prose was published in either CP66 or CP07.
3 – His two OUP books were *MP* and *The Poetry of W. B. Yeats*. Cf. Heuser (ed.), *SLC* (1987)
and *SP* (1990) (both OUP).

(6) With regard to Dan, he is, as stated already, to go to Mary in case of my decease. He has now got a visa for America but I leave the question of when & how he is to get there to you (in consultation with Elizabeth). i.e. you have a right of veto on any suggestions of Mary's. & he is not to go to Mary if, having run away from Charles (which she might) she turns out to be unable to support him properly. In that case Elizabeth had better take him over.

(7) I do not want that early novel of mine reprinted.[1]

(8) Incomplete Mss.: 'Alcestis' had better be scrapped. The Latin Humour book, except for Introduction & Conclusion (extant versions of which to be scrapped) could be published if somebody competent undertook to cut it & check it. (It should be pointed out that I wrote it mostly 1932–4.)

I guess that's about all but I hope it's a chore that won't fall to you. With very best wishes to yourself & your wife & hoping to see you soon.

Yours ever,
Louis MacNeice

TO *John Frederick and Georgina Beatrice MacNeice*

MS Bodleian

Sunday   As from 62 High St, Oxford
[postmark 16 December 1940]

OPENED BY EXAMINER 2886
Dear Daddie & Madre

Sorry not to have written before (now writing in a Post Office) but have been v. busy. Stayed 2 nights in B'ham on my way down to Oxford & have now come on to London for a day or two. Hope to come over when I have got straight what I am going to do. I feel v. well but a doctor in Oxford told me that I am not technically fit & should probably be rejected by any medical board, so think of trying to crash in on the B.B.C. In the meanwhile I want to finish a book. The journey over was uneventful except that we saw some v. pretty porpoises. Boat packed, including some survivors from the Jervis Bay.[2] Please ask Elizabeth to let me know about

1 – *RW* has not been reprinted.
2 – On 5 Nov., when thirty-eight ships came under attack from a German pocket battleship, HMS *Jervis Bay* (captained by E. S. F. Fegen) engaged with the raider, saving thirty ships in the convoy. The *Jervis Bay* was sunk with loss of life, though sixty-five survivors were boarded on merchant vessels and landed in Canada. The gallantry of the captain and his

the Highgate house, keys etc.[1] What I saw of B'ham was rather a mess but Oxford much the same as ever. I gather that the ceilings have fallen down in my old flat thanks to the anti Aircraft, & many of my haunts in Hampstead have been heavily bombed. Writing to Dan separately; v. glad to hear he flourishes. Is Miss P. in London? If so, where? It's awfully difficult to get in touch with people here. By the way, have you seen Graham Shepard (now R.N.V.R.)? If not, expect him. America was great fun; will tell you all about it later. For the last 4 months all my friends over there (both American & British) had been trying to persuade me to change my mind about coming back. However I thought I was missing History.

lots of love, Louis

---

crew was widely praised. FLM sailed on the *Samaria*, which probably picked up the *Jervis* sailors at Nova Scotia. See '29 Ships Elude Raider', 'Fight of the Jervis Bay' and '"There She Rode Like a Hero"', *The Times*, 13 and 14 Nov. 1940. Cf. Stallworthy, 286. The experience entered the poetry: see *AS*, XXIII: 'With the survivors of the *Jervis Bay* / Absorbed in silent pingpong' (CP07, 479); and from 'The Atlantic Tunnel (*a memory of 1940*)': 'So were the survivors of the Jervis Bay; / The tunnel absorbed us, made us one' (*Solstices*, CP07, 535).
1 – Occasionally he would stay with the Nicholsons at 17 North Road, Highgate.

1941

TO *Eleanor Clark*   MS Yale

24 January [1941]   London but as from c/o Professor
                                     Dodds, 62 High Street, Oxford

My darling,

This is my third letter mailed from this country. It seems very few to have written in this time but I am inhibited by the feeling that letters are so inadequate. I was delighted to get your second; it would be good, darling, if you got on Invitation to Learning.[1] I am flirting with Radio too, have just written a whimsy script (indirectly propaganda but not the kind one is ashamed of) connected with the Florrie Forde poem & with crossing the Atlantic;[2] it will be broadcast from a record; if & when I know when they are going to use it I will cable you in case you like to hear my voice albeit mechanised. My sponsor at the B.B.C. says it is the one piece of imagination they have had since the beginning of the War. Some of the effects obvious & near-cheap but it couldn't be helped. I shall maybe get a job on the B.B.C. Having to do something to live & it's not as if anyone else wanted me – being neither a technician nor particularly (as yet) able-bodied.

Darling, I hope you got some skiing, & what about a ski story, as you said? I hope it's not <u>too</u> difficult in your house when it freezes; I should feel guilty.

My sister arrived in London today, is just coming round to see me. She is v. worried about the Irish situation. I don't know what to do about Dan. There are so many dangers to be balanced.

We have had 4 nights without a raid, so everyone is frightened, suspecting that the Germans are going to spring some awful novelty.

Have done a mass of my prose book[3] but am at the moment doubtful about it – all these little gritty details are supposed to spark together but

---

1 – 'Katherine Anne [Porter] is going to try to get me on 'Invitation to Learning' some time – I don't know that I trust her altruism, much as I love her, but she may do it and it <u>would</u> be exciting' (EC to FLM, 4 Dec. 1940, Ms Yale).
2 – Florrie Forde poem: 'Death of an Actress', *Harpers Bazaar*, Dec. 1940, and *NS*, 28 Dec. 1940.
3 – *The Strings Are False*.

do they? & I ought to finish it soon because, if I get a regular job, I shall become like everyone else over here – too tired.

It is nearly time for me to black-out the windows – our evening chore. I had lunch with Stephen today; he is getting connected with something called Reconstruction for Victory or somesuch name – Julian Huxley, J. B. Priestley & Co. I want to find out more about it; <u>anyone</u> with a positive programme is worth looking into.

I have been asked to do a weekly film critique (very short) for The Spectator.[1] Not that I know anything about films but I suppose I can do it all right considering & it is money for jam & will take up very little time. Also it is nice not to have to pay for seats which in the West End cinemas are very expensive. (The movies now are the only thing almost to go to; no pictures in the picture galleries; no entertainments at all after dinner – excepting night clubs which are lousy & full of horrible people.)

Connie, our housekeeper, has just come in & is making me tea. She is really Lady Constance Something-or-Other & looks like a hard-bitten char, was once, I believe, married to a clergyman from whom she ran away – but all that is legend & she cooks very nicely. She & I & the ex-ballet dancer play Rummy nearly every evening with a great deal of bad language & recrimination. This helps to drown out the guns when they happen. Sometimes I go round to the pub & buy us a quart of stout. I have been out a great deal lately – people seem very lavish to me as if I were Lazarus come back from the dead. Here comes my tea & two rock-cakes. Elizabeth ought to be here any moment.

The Income Tax people are going to refund me £30. Isn't that nice? I am keeping pretty level financially – largely because I have lost my check [sic] book, so am living on my hand-to-mouth earnings. Being almost the only remaining FreeLance in London I can quite see myself becoming a war profiteer. Talking of profits I met a manufacturer the other night at the Dorchester – fascinatingly awful.

I would like to write lyrically to you, darling – I feel very lyrical inside – but if I let it come out, my nostalgia for you comes up to the surface too & that hurts a lot. Every so often it comes up anyway, hurts like hell. Maybe I should remember that – as you wrote in your last letter – you are all the big V's & so out of place on the war-time scene.[2] I mean you

---

1 – FLM's 'The Cinema' column appeared in the *Spectator* on 31 Jan., 14 Feb. and 21 March 1941.

2 – Clark had written: 'I had something bordering on a serious row, the nearest I've ever come to that, with Jack Jessup over Hemingway of all things. It seems I am all the big V's – vituperative, violent, venemous [sic], vehement etc – for thinking him pretty small in the Spanish thing' (EC to FLM, 4 Dec. 1940, *Ms Yale*).

couldn't be in London being 'violent' because it would be out of key. Sometimes I feel like sending you a cable saying 'Come to London' but that would be nonsense – even if you could or would. Myself I don't regret being here at all apart (& it is a very big APART) from missing you, darling. London today is very human but I wonder if it would seem that way to you or if you would think it just squalid & pathetic. I shall have to reassess this business of roots. The point is that London in present conditions has become more comprehensible – an entity instead of just a jumble or a jungle. However . . .

> Goodnight, my darling. Remember me to Martin[1] & all my best love to yourself.   Louis

P.S. 25th Jan. Darling, just had your 3rd letter. Glad you like the R.H. bk. Can't remember the foreword which I wrote bang off – I dare say you are right about it; it's a mistake to have forewords – they asked for it.[2]

P.S. (2). Hope the carols were fun, thank you for the astral stocking.[3] Enjoy the snow, darling. Am just going out to a party. Love again. L.

---

1 – Untraced.
2 – The reference is to an advance copy of *Poems, 1925–1940*, officially published on 17 Feb. 1941, but EC had received a copy from the publisher by 22 Dec., when she thanks FLM for the closing poem, 'Cradle Song': 'Thank you for the last poem. It does strange and beautiful things to me and I am so very happy that it calls itself for me . . . Two things only upset me a little, the MacLeish poem ['Ballade for Mr MacLeish'] which I'm afraid I don't think is up to you at all, and doesn't even seem to me to make sense . . . The other thing was that you don't write poetry to be smart. For God's sake darling, the foreword to such a book was no place for parlour talk, and I don't see how you could have meant it seriously: who does do anything of the kind, sing songs or make pictures or build buildings to be smart? Given, of course, any integrity at all. No, I do think that was bad of you: it sounds chichi and unserious and generally weak. But the book is wonderful and I'm sure the public will pass over the foreword even if the reviewers don't' (EC to FLM, 22 Dec. 1940, *Ms Yale*). This was the foreword which closed with the famous remark: 'And I would ask my readers not to be snobs; I write poetry not because it is smart to be a poet but because I enjoy it, as one enjoys swimming or swearing, and also because it is my road to freedom and knowledge.'
3 – 'I don't really know how you feel about Xmas, but I like it, so I will put up an imaginary stocking for you and fill it with spiritual oranges and things, and think about you very hard' (ibid.). According to EN, FLM always felt a reverence for Christmas and all his life he tried to recreate the sense of happiness at Christmas he had felt as a child (*TWA*, 12).

TO *Mrs E. R. Dodds*   MS Bodleian

10 February [1941]   c/o Rupert Doone,
                                       34 Wharton Street, London WC1

Dear Mrs. Dodds,

Thank you for your letter; I don't think I want my laundry yet – am just going off to Ireland for a fortnight, will visit Dan in Co. Cavan.[1]

Have been very busy lately; am writing a number of scripts for the B.B.C. (mainly features for Overseas – rather fun, I demand all sorts of sound effects, have just done one about the people sleeping in the underground). Have also promised articles to all those wretched Connollys & Lehmanns & am reviewing the movies (money for jam) for The Spectator.[2]

Living with Rupert is not nearly as difficult as you'd think & the food is v. good. We are in the middle of a triangle of mil. Objs.[3] [*sic*] but have still got all our glass. Only one night the bombs sounded v. near & Connie & I (R. was out) lay under the table giggling & gasping alternately. Nearest bomb was actually 200 yds or more, shattered the whole side of a square. The Fire Night (Dec. 29th) was – aesthetically – a treat; stage-lighting everywhere.[4]

Have seen Anthony off & on; he is living in Victor Rothschild's house with a special bombproof dormitory shared with 2 girls. V. hard worked.[5]

Am not <u>on</u> the B.B.C. but they seem prepared to employ me indefinitely. Rather preferable that way. A frightful institution to have to spend yr days in.

Eleanor thinks she will go West end of next summer (hopes to have finished her book by then) & start getting a divorce.

Elizabeth has come over & gone to Devonport.[6] She says Dan has built up a legend that I am a sort of super-man (world's champion runner & draughtsman) & thinks it is high time I went over & exploded it.

1–Dan was staying at Ashfield, Cootehill, Co. Cavan, at the home of Diana Clements (née Lenox-Conyngham). See FLM to parents, 1 July 1927, n. 3, p. 174, and FLM to MM, 28 Oct. 1940, n. 2, p. 413.
2–Cyril Connolly edited *Horizon*, John Lehmann *Penguin New Writing*.
3–Military objectives.
4–There was widespread fire damage in London on the night of 29 Dec. 1940, owing to enemy action with incendiaries: 'The sky over the capital was lit up by flames with the brilliance almost of daytime' ('Fire Bombs Rained on London', *The Times*, 30 Dec. 1940, 4).
5–AB shared the flat at 5 Bentinck Street with Guy Burgess, Tess Mayor and Patricia Rawdon-Smith. Its parties were legendary and it was regarded by some as 'a hotbed of spies and debauchery' (Carter, 262–3).
6–In Plymouth.

We play Rummy here every night. It occurs to me that even playing Rummy in London now is a kind of assertion of the Rights of Man, whereas in America it would be nothing but playing Rummy.

Give my love to Himself & Ernst (hope to see you all on my way back from Ireland).

Yours ever
Louis

P.S. Address for a fortnight – Bishop's House / Malone Road, / Belfast.

TO *H. O. White*[1] MS TCD

Postmark 6 March 1941 Dept of English, TCD

Dear Professor White,

I was sorry not to see you when I was in Dublin recently. I am returning to London today & am officially not supposed to re-enter Ireland for six months. Unless I have some good reason such as an invitation to lecture. I have been wondering therefore if T.C.D. would by any chance like a lecture from me about the end of May. I could then fix up for a permit with John Betjeman (at the British Representative's Office in Dublin). If you would like a lecture of any sort, perhaps you could reply to this c/o Rupert Doone, 34 Wharton Street, London W.C.1? I should of course be delighted to come.

in haste,
with best wishes,
Yours sincerely
Louis MacNeice

1 – Herbert Martyn Oliver White, MRIA (1885–1963), had formerly lectured in English Literature at Sheffield 1920–31 and QUB 1931–9 before becoming the third holder of the Chair of English Literature at TCD, which he held until his retirement in 1960. A former pupil of Edward Dowden, his chief scholarly publication was as editor of *The Works of Thomas Purney* (1933), although he also wrote, as 'Oliver Martyn', two detective novels: *The Man They Couldn't Hang* (1933) and *The Body in the Pound* (1934).

15 March [1941]   London but as from c/o Professor
                                   Dodds, 62 High Street, Oxford

My darling,

Got your postcard (ski) 2 days ago in Oxford where I spent a week on
returning from Ireland. I am so glad, darling, the skiing was good this time.
I had 3 weeks in Ireland – Belfast, Dublin & the country place where Dan
is. Dan is v. tall & impressively athletic & walked me off my legs; he has
400 acres to play in & 2 other children & he now sings all the verses of
the 3 Lovely Lassies of Banion. I got him a scooter in Dublin on which he
does the most remarkable feats.[1] (Planes & gunfire overhead as I am
writing this.)[2]

Yesterday, darling, I had an inspiration – about a mission which will
enable me to come & see you but not before about the Fall & afterwards
I shall come back here. I miss you <u>terribly</u>, darling, only I must stay here
while this thing's on – God knows why because I hate it. Like some great
inverted pyramid balanced on one's navel. I hate all this hackwork I am
doing too but I suppose it is wrong to be too squeamish about that. The
B.B.C. in particular are infuriating (I'm glad you didn't hear that thing of

1 – Dan MacNeice remembered the song and the scooter: 'Cultural life for us Upstairs children
at Ashfield Lodge, Co. Cavan was very much Downstairs led. We imbibed the maids' singing
readily, and shared their gusto for popular song in the same way they did. (A circumstance
that surely obtains in all Big House contexts.) To digress a moment, it interests me in
retrospect to recall that the Ashfield domestic staff ran also to the wartime revision of "Run,
rabbit, run" – their vigorous rendition which would have given De Valera pause, had he
heard it . . . But I admit to its wider chorusing in England itself, where I had probably first
heard it. My father was excessively concerned that bicycling led inevitably to the needless
injury of the Too Young. Thus although I had learned how to bike several years earlier when
living with the Brogden family at Dungannon, I wasn't permitted to indulge the ability until
much later – and only then rather grudgingly – when boarding school life removed it from
parental constraint. So scooters were the vehicles of choice; I had scooted around Bishop's
House on my own, and was to continue now at Ashfield in the company of Marcus and
Catherine (though, oddly, I cannot remember whether we shared the same vehicle or if each
was equipped with his or her own). It's perhaps of further interest to recall that I was well
aware of the adult (guarded) surprise at my father's restrictive views on biking, both at
Bishop's House and later at Ashfield. The attending adults didn't express themselves on the
subject out loud, of course, but . . . you know how kids are: they can sniff incredulity at 20
paces' (DM, private correspondence, 2008).
2 – The German air raids of 15 March fell heaviest on London. According to the Air Ministry
and Ministry of Home Security: 'Enemy aircraft attacked the London area on Saturday night,
but the raid, which was not on a large scale, was over shortly after midnight. In several
districts damage was done to houses, but all fires had been put out by an early hour this
morning.' See 'Bus Passengers Killed', *The Times*, 17 March 1941, 4.

mine).[1] If you ever do hear anything remember it's liable to be corrupted after it's left me. All sorts of other minor irritations – proofs going through with the most banal sentences italicised etc. All very good, no doubt, for my vanity.

In your last letter, darling, you said something about preposterousness. I think there's no likelihood at all of my being preposterous in the narrower (proper) sense – I'm too much tied to you – but I <u>am</u> having slight diversions.[2] Which you must understand (& forgive), darling, because with all this droning overhead (such as is going on at the moment) & prospect of things getting blacker for ever & ever, I do need to get close to people if only by way of a fairly surface flirtation.

In Oxford I had one wonderful evening with a Welsh corporal whom I picked up (both of us drunk) in a pub. He had that lovely singsong voice (working class) & quoted Keats & had a long technical discussion with me about Rugby Football & then about what was wrong with Karl Marx. I don't really like the Welsh but they are v. tonic & alive.

In Dublin I had one marvellous steak. The people with me explained: 'This poor fellow's going back where there's no steaks,' so the waiter said 'Ah you'd be wanting an extra big one.' & I said 'Yes – & rare' & yes & rare it was. My memory of it, darling, is lyrical. Over here they have just rationed jam – half a pound per head per <u>month</u> (including marmalade, syrup etc). Of course they <u>ought</u> to ration nearly everything & do something about the restaurants. (Nasty noises going on now; sorry to harp on them, darling, but it makes me feel better during a raid if I'm writing to you.) Incidentally, you've no idea how hard it is to write these bloody Letters for Selden; I put them off till the last moment & then have to dish up anything. I never did anything about one for Klaus.[3] Of course

1 – Presumably *Word from America* (30 min.), broadcast 15 Feb. 1941. In a previous letter he explained: 'The B.B.C. asked me, being fresh from the U.S.A. to give them a broadcast interview – you know, impressions of England on arriving as compared with impressions I got there – but we decided this would be v. stilted, so I made it quasi dramatic. Had to write it in a morning. The lines supposed to be spoken by American students were nothing to do with me & were written in by an Irish-French-Canadian who swore to me that was how American students talked though I must say I never heard anyone use such odd expressions' (FLM to EC, 9 Feb. 1941, *Ms Yale*).
2 – Clark wrote: '. . . every day there is no letter and I can only wander foolishly around all the possible reasons for that. Your preposterousness and the preposterousness of the world together are really almost too much to cope with, but I go on coping, and hoping, and you must write whatever happens' (EC to FLM, 7 Jan. [postmarks NY 14 Jan., Oxford 18 Feb.], 1941, *Ms Yale*).
3 – Klaus Mann (1906–49), German writer, son of Thomas Mann and brother-in-law to WHA. He edited the journal *Decision* in New York. Cf. previous note on Rodman (FLM to

if the Spring Hell comes up to expectations there will probably be lots of a certain kind of copy – not that I have any particular liking for Grand Guignol. I gather that John Strachey's new book – I haven't read it – is all about Christian Love.[1] What permutations & combinations; if you turn left often enough you go anti-clockwise.

Darling, there's some kind of censor (as if we hadn't enough already) works inside me now when I write to you. So that I can't expand on how plumb crazy I am about you. But I am of course. I keep meeting (& re-meeting) people who are wildly attractive but they couldn't – not in a thousand years – represent to me what you do. Whether that's good or bad I don't know but it's fact.

Droning & droning – it's like living in a mad bee-hive. For the first time since returning I'm thinking of writing a poem. But maybe I shouldn't. I was v. irritated by a notice of my Yeats book (written by Michael Roberts) censuring my 'relativistic attitude'; he's gone Christian I believe.[2] I'm sick & tired, darling, of being accused of things like relativism & empiricism (burst of guns then) because it's all a misunderstanding; & it's not that I don't believe anything, it's just that I don't think you can explain the Universe by saying $2 + 2 = 4$ or by Dialectical Materialism or by the Cross of Christ. Etc. etc. etc. Droning & droning. The cook in my professor's house at Oxford suddenly the other day began cursing Hitler Homerically – 'I'll cut out his inside & rub salt in it, I'll cut off his leg & make him look at it etc.'.

Have just ordered myself a new suit – just one to last the next epoch. V. sombre & civilised. (Crumpled gun-fire off: it makes you feel like reading Jane Austen.) My tailor in Oxford just as decadent as ever.[3] Oxford on the whole irritatingly the same as ever except that it is astonishingly over-crowded with evacuees.

Will write more v. soon, darling. & please write back. love as ever,

Louis

—

EC, 18 May 1939, n. 1, p. 339), editor of *Common Sense*, to which FLM contributed several articles ('Letters') incl. 'London Letter: Blackouts, Bureaucracy & courage' (1 Jan.), *Common Sense* 10: 2 (Feb. 1941), 46–7, and 'London Letter: Anti-Defeatism of the Man in the Street' (1 March), *Common Sense* 10: 4 (April 1941), 110–11.

1 – *The Betrayal of the Left* (1941).
2 – Michael Roberts, 'Mr MacNeice on Yeats', *Spectator*, 28 Feb. 1941, 234.
3 – Hall Bros of 94 High Street and 1 Magpie Lane, Oxford.

TO *Daniel MacNeice*   MS Bodleian

18 March [1941]   c/o Rupert Doone,
                                         34 Wharton Street, London WC1

DEAREST DAN,
   I meant to write to you before but have been terribly busy. I spent a
week in Oxford staying with Dr. Stahl whom I think you remember.
   I hope you had a nice St Patrick's Day yesterday. Nonna sent me some
shamrock but I did not see anyone else in London wearing any.[1]
   I have not seen Betsy yet but hope to see her soon.
   The weather here is lovely &, if I had time, I would go to the Zoo.
Someday, I expect, I shall go & I will write & tell you about it.
   I expect by now you have seen Elizabeth. I hope you had fun.
   How is the scooter? Give my love to Marcus & Catherine,
                                         Lots of love to yourself,
                                         DADDIE

TO *Eleanor Clark*   MS Yale

3 April [1941]   As from c/o Professor Dodds,
                                         62 High Street, Oxford

My darling,
   It seems it is quite on the cards I may – later – get myself sent on a
mission for a month or so to the USA in a kind of liaison capacity for the
BBC (would your maggot be interested in that?) Unless I get called up –
which is on the cards too but unlikely for various reasons.
   I had lunch today with a little man called Ben Robertson who is London
correspondent of P.M.; seemed nice.[2] He gave me some addresses in
Plymouth, where I am going tomorrow for a few days to stay with my
sister & look at the damage from the recent Blitz.[3] Just another of the
curious jobs I have to do now; when I get back & the full moon comes I
am going to spend a night on the dome of St. Paul's. For a fortnight now

1 – GBM had sent a sprig of shamrock each year to FLM at Sherborne and Marlborough, and
was continuing (or reviving) the tradition.
2 – The American journalist Ben Robertson (1903–43) reported on wartime England for *PM*,
a New York tabloid. Author of *Traveller's Rest* (1938), *I Saw England* (1941) and *Red Hills
and Cotton* (1942).
3 – Plymouth was heavily bombed on 20 March, and many casualties were reported.
Churches, schools and hospitals were damaged. See 'Severe Raid on Plymouth', *The Times*,
22 March 1941, 4.

London has been peaceful but I suppose it will break soon. Last raid we had here was extremely noisy – from the A.A. barrage, not from bombs: a noise like the collision of half a dozen oceans.[1]

Virginia Woolf has just drowned herself. A new novel of hers is due from the press soon. Almost the first suicide of a British intellectual in this war. Periodically she used to go crazy & it was just coming on her again.[2]

A great flutter has been caused among my acquaintances by Day Lewis (who is 37) being called up – in spite of protests by the Ministry of Information for whom he was working.[3] Of course any of us, if we chose, could get ourselves in advance into some branch of military intelligence (cushy) but I should much rather continue independent while I can & risk being plunked into the ranks (& all the boredom that entails) later. It's a gamble as usual but if I went into mil. Intelligence now, I couldn't possibly see you again for the duration. (By the way do you still want to see me, darling?) As I have finally committed myself to supporting this war, I wonder sometimes if I haven't left you behind – looking down on me in various senses – from Olympus.

To become frivolous for a moment – in spite of a bad cold & a stye in my eye I am feeling comparatively gay, had a haircut today followed by an oil shampoo followed by an eau de Cologne friction, followed by Honey & Flowers (which you don't know about in America). My hair has quite recovered itself & isn't breaking off any more. I can't say the same for my figure. Have just had an invitation to stay in the Cotswolds & ride a horse & next Wednesday I am going to a celebration of Stephen Spender's 2nd wedding (did you read the astonishing poem addressed to S.S. by George Barker – the Christ myth again)?[4] Yes, I read 'High Wind in Jamaica' a long time ago & enjoyed it immensely.[5] Haven't enough time to read now

---

1 – The previous raid had been on 15 March, as described in letter of that date to EC, pp. 423–5.
2 – Virginia Woolf drowned herself on 28 March in the River Ouse, near her home in Rodmell, Sussex. *Between the Acts* (1941) was published posthumously.
3 – Cecil Day-Lewis worked for the publications division of the Ministry of Information 1941–6.
4 – Spender married Natasha Litvin at St Pancras Register Office on 9 April, followed by lunch at the Etoile, Charlotte Street (hosted by Cyril Connolly), and then a party at the studio of Mamaine Paget. Cecil Beaton photographed the drinks party, which included Connolly and Lys Lubbock, FLM, Nancy Coldstream, Sonia Brownell, A. J. Ayer, Guy Burgess, Erno and Ursula Goldfinger, Tambimuttu, Julian and Juliette Huxley, John Lehmann and William Plomer (cf. Sutherland, 279–80). The Barker poem is 'To Stephen Spender' ('This poet with his soul upon his shoulder . . .')
5 – Richard Hughes, *A High Wind in Jamaica* (1929). Cf. 'Last night I read the Innocent Voyage or High Wind in Jamaica by Richard Hughes, which I don't seem to have heard of before. Does everyone know about it?' EC to FLM, 28 Feb., 2 March (postmark 3 March), 1941 (*Ms Yale*).

but think I shall cut out social life soon; the people left in London whom I see are all too much of a kind. Only when they are in Government jobs you can get the most astonishing low-down from them; unfortunately I can't transmit it. I suppose sooner or later the industrialists will be put in their place (Bevin had a crack at them yesterday in the Commons) but they haven't been put there yet.[1]

Darling, <u>please</u> write to me some more (I know I haven't written much lately but I don't see why you can't be better than me). Occasionally I see you through my eyelashes but on the whole you are terribly far away & letters are a great deal better than nothing. & N.B. tell me how your novel is going. Don't do too much hack-work. There are reasons why <u>I</u> should do it at the moment but for you – I feel – it would be better to run up debts. I will drink a Daiquiri to you on May 1st. Goodnight, darling, L.

TO *Eleanor Clark*   MS Yale

20 April [1941]   London, but as from c/o Professor
                                       Dodds, 62 High St, Oxford

I go on giving you the Oxford address as one never knows how long a London one will last. You heard of our 'Biggest Raid Ever' last Wednesday, did you?[2] The town next morning was incredible. & now it looks more or less normal again – seems to have an extraordinary second wind. They had a frightful mess from H.E. in the street next to ours, parallel, which we only discovered today; a water main burst & the rescue people had to <u>swim</u> into the cellars to rescue the shelterers. My household were quite unaware of that; it all sounded equally near and/or far and/or hell to us. I went out at 5.0 the next morning & walked for hours round London, began by meeting 2 people I knew in their pyjamas who'd been burnt out. Some of the fires were staggeringly beautiful in the time before the sun while the moon was still there. I could tell you a lot more about that raid but I have a feeling you may not want to hear about it. Here of course it's

---

1–In a Commons debate about war production, Minister of Labour Ernest Bevin (1881–1951) replied to a complaint that employers should be given power of dismissal of absentee workers with the remark 'a little conciliation was better than the big stick'. See 'Labour for War Effort. Mr Bevin's Reply to Criticisms', *The Times*, 3 April 1941, 4.
2–He refers to the German raid of 16 April; German newspapers claimed 'the greatest air raid of all time' was revenge for the recent bombing of Berlin. See, in *The Times*, 'Major Attack on London' (17 April 1941, 4); 'Six Bombers Destroyed in Raid on London. Greatest Indiscriminate Attack of the War' and 'Germans Gloat Over London Raid' (18 April 1941, 4, 3). Cf. FLM, 'The Morning After the Blitz', *Picture Post*, 3 May 1941, 9–12, 14.

an unavoidable topic. I must just go upstairs & get a cigarette now (it's about 4.0 a.m. but I doubt if I'll go to bed as I have to deliver an article to an extraordinary paper v. early tomorrow morning – commissioned over the phone today, which is how everything happens here now, so one just has to forget one is a 'writer'). Darling, <u>why don't you write</u> to me? Because, if you don't, we shall get awfully out of touch, what with the War & all. Or maybe you think something's happening to my soul? (your phrase, if you remember). Maybe it is but I don't know that it's necessarily bad. But what I want to hear about is <u>you</u>, darling. & are you being happy? My scheme for visiting the U.S.A. for a month or so is liable, I am told, to be frustrated, chiefly by the business of the dollar exchange. Also nearly all the space on the boats is booked up for months ahead. But I dare say with a little more graft I can manage it later. I am probably going officially soon on to the staff of the B.B.C. It's a v. 2nd rate institution & Christ, the things they do to one's work (just chop it & sugar it & cut out the points & write in their own bloody crudities) but the choice of occupations here now – unless you choose to have no choice & be clapped into uniform for ever – is just a choice of evils & the B.B.C., though deplorable, does leave some loophole for intelligence & individual decisions – which is more than can be said of most. Really, darling, living here now is about two thirds fantasy. When I'm not doing more or less hackwork I don't do any work at all – just talk to people about anything as long as it makes a noise & every so often I get drunk & insult them. (Only I <u>have</u> written one new poem which I'm pleased with & think may lead to some more; it's about all this – the War – without being about it realistically.) This looks – on reading back – rather depressed or depressing, which isn't what I meant. As we all now of us here now [*sic*] all have one plane we live on together, whatever other planes we may think on or feature ourselves on, there isn't the same need for communication any more than between animals during a forest fire (we all know where we stand & so have a kind of automatic communication which cuts across any ordinary civilised scheme of values). Maybe I'm rambling, darling, I'm feeling rather tired. Only I wish to God you would write to me.

The other week 3 of my friends, unheard of for ages, turned up one after the other. One thing about this War, I think people like each other more. I find myself getting pallier & pallier with the World in General – rather on a taproom plane, I suppose, & perhaps it's a substitute for sex. But – in this great flux – it's comparatively a solid. A <u>bad</u> thing is that I find myself beginning to think (not to say) what some other people say about America – that it loses itself in words. I mean, darling, you remember <u>your</u> diatribes against liberalism; Well, what you mean by 'liberalism' seems to me to apply v. much to a lot of people in America, at least to a lot of American intellectuals. Not orientated properly, I can't v. well set up the British intellectuals as anything better but some of them – usually in a decadent or obsolescent way no doubt – have some kind of orientation. If the B. intellectuals could be crossbred for a bit with 'the people' we might get somewhere. Whereas the American intellectuals, who oughtn't to be so removed from the people (conditions not isolating them so much), do seem to me isolated all the same & as well as spiritual cross-breeding would need the hell of a great series of spiritual aperients. To get rid of all those WORDS. Oh hell; darling, I'm expressing this awfully badly (& irritating you too?), I do mean something & it isn't personal or malicious or anything. I will try & write to you about it again when I'm in a less half-baked condition (have averaged v. little sleep since Tuesday – awake all Wednesday night from the Blitz, up all Friday night being social & kept awake a lot of last night by gunfire).

A nice thing, the town is brimming with daffodils – in the parks & the squares & on barrows in the streets. (I told you about Plymouth did I? They had daffodils there on the Hoe – you know, the place where Drake was supposed to play bowls.) The place I cabled you flowers from had its windows blown in on Wednesday but is still functioning. The same applies to the bookshop which I got to parcel up Yeats for you; all the books were blown hugger mugger, I found it odd seeing my own stuff knocked about like that by enemy action. But now they have put them all back & are waiting to get some new windows. (How long, O Lord, how long? I don't mean until the windows come, I mean until they stop having to get new ones.)

Darling, it's evidently a mistake trying to write to you tonight; my mind keeps coagulating. I'm going to try lying on the mattress on the floor here for a bit. (Rupert had arranged it here in case there was a Blitz but there isn't.) I wish some times you were here but most times I don't. Partly because you're so sensitive to sleep & this ain't no place to be sensitive to sleep in. They seem to get louder & louder guns; when I'm asleep already I sometimes sleep through them but it's almost impossible to go to sleep once they've started – especially if you're trying to keep some absurd position where you think you're safe from glass. (Another good thing about the War: it's no longer Bad Form to be frightened, nearly everyone is & far from impairing people's efficiency it seems to limber them up.) My God; darling, it's 5 a.m., I'm dropping – I suppose you might be – what with the time-lag – just about going to bed. It seems mad we've known each other 2 years, doesn't it?[1] I think I shall send you a cable on Mayday. Goodnight my love (I'm going to try the floor). April 29th: Sorry for this letter, darling; it reads a bit stupid now I take it up again. Have just been giving a lecture to people I was told were Central European refugees, so I kept saying 'In this country', 'in our country' & then it turned out they were all British.[2]

The news these days seems bloody bad but you probably get even more of that. Have been talking to people who interview German prisoners: quite horrifying – they (the prisoners) all sound conditioned to be Nazis for ever.

A Dutchman has just given me 5 packs of Chesterfields – very nostalgic. I tried to drink a Daiquiri for your sake the other day but they hadn't got the ingredients. Rupert & Connie have now gone to bed & there is nothing to be heard but the wind in the cables of the balloons – which is now one of our characteristic noises.[3] If you see John MacDonald, tell him to look out for a new M.O.I. documentary film called 'Words for Battle' made by a man I know called Humphrey Jennings – some of the effects pretty cheap (which, I guess, was inevitable) but on the whole moving & a lovely quote from Milton (in prose).[4]

The poem I wrote the other day is about to develop into a series – all about Trolls & freedom & death & concrete lining. The 2nd one is called 'Troll's Courtship' & I want one about Ygdrasil.[5] I had some kind of release lately but I haven't found the words yet.

You remember your idea about the Bird; I think that applies very much now. Some days – I mean some minutes really – I feel 100% happy – without before or after, or rather with before & after crumpled up in my hand & giving out a scent all over me.

I must go to bed now, I suppose; it's such a luxury when it's quiet. My poor sister's been having a wretched time in Plymouth with a series of bad raids. [She now has *deleted*] Hell, the censor again; half the things I'm about to write I have to cancel. Darling, my love, will you write to me? Or are you involved or something? & couldn't you write even so? & tell me

---

1 – His first letter to EC was dated 21 April 1939.
2 – FLM had given a lecture entitled 'Britain Today– Literature' at Morley College at 6.30 p.m. ('Today's Arrangments', *The Times*, 29 April 1941, 5).
3 – Barrage balloons over London.
4 – *Words for Battle* (1941), (8 min.), sponsored by the Ministry of Information. Directed by Humphrey Jennings (1907–50), produced by Ian Dalrymple, commentary spoken by Laurence Olivier.
5 – 'The Trolls *(Written after an air-raid, April 1941)*', NS, 5 July 1941, 9, and 'Troll's Courtship', *Poetry London*, May/June, 169; both in *Springboard*, CP07, 217–20.

if you would like me to visit you in the nearer future. Because, if you would, I could still v. likely make it. But apart from you, I don't want even to come & visit (being all right here – apart from you). Only I do want to see you. Be happy, darling; love. L.

TO *Frederick Dupee*[1]   MS Columbia

5 May [1941]   c/o Faber & Faber Ltd,
                                          24 Russell Square, London WC1

Dear Fred,

Thank you so much for your letter which I have just received.[2] You make N.Y. sound rather sombre – a thing which I had foreboded. But it is nice to hear that Eunice is still giving parties & that you go skating etc.[3] As for London, it is not exciting in the melodramatic sense (except once in a way as in the great Wednesday night Blitz towards the end of April which was quite fantastic) but it is rather a good place to be living in; one feels very alive.[4] I am going to spend tonight on the dome of St. Paul's (for the B.B.C. for whom I write features) which I expect will be very cold but too too picturesque;[5] we have just had our 2nd extra hour summer Time [sic], so there'll probably be an Alert about midnight.[6] Last night there was quite heavy gunfire but we haven't had bombs for some time.

---

1 – Frederick (Fred) Wilcox Dupee (1904–79), educ. University of Illinois, Yale and Columbia. Travelled in Spain, North Africa and Mexico before moving to New York where he joined the Communist Party in the mid-1930s and was literary editor of *New Masses*. A friend and Yale classmate of Dwight MacDonald, he was a founder member in 1937 of the revived, anti-Stalinist *Partisan Review*. Later he taught at Bard College and Columbia. Author of a respected study of Henry James (New York, 1951) and editor of *The Question of Henry James* (1945), James's *Autobiography* (1956) and various other books. A selection of his essays and reviews was published as *'The King of the Cats' and Other Remarks on Writers and Writing* (1965; 2nd edn Chicago, 1984). In 'The English Literary Left' (*PR*, Aug.–Sept. 1938, 11–21), Dupee associated FLM with a 'Literary Left', tied to *New Verse*, and Spender with the 'Communist Left': 'Where MacNeice, ideologically speaking, exhibits no progression whatever . . . Spender's work falls readily into a pattern' (12). Dupee had published FLM's poem 'The Preacher', in *PR*, July–Aug. 1940, 315–16.
2 – Dupee to FLM, 22 March 1941 (*Ms Bodleian, Ms Res, c. 584*).
3 – Eunice Jessup, Eleanor's sister.
4 – The raid of 16 April; see previous letter to EC.
5 – The short programme on St Paul's was broadcast on 23 June (repeat 20 Sept.) Cf. his later retrospect, 'At sea in the dome of St Paul's . . .' ('Homage to Wren (*a memory of 1941*)', *Solstices*, CP66, CP07, 536).
6 – Double summer time ran from 4 May to 10 Aug., when the clock advanced two hours of GMT. 'Double Summer Time', *The Times*, 3 May 1941, 4.

I was listening to records of bombs falling today but they don't really put it over; one's reaction – at least my reaction as I hear them coming down (a rush & a whistle) is 4/5ths appalment & 1/5th exhilaration; then when they land the whole place shudders under you & you are v. delighted to find yourself intact & then you wait for the next. I visited Plymouth lately which – in parts – is an astonishing mess;[1] unfortunately I can't tell you any of the more interesting details about raids etc., because of the censorship. The same applies – even more so – to the remarkable backstage information which I pick up here & there. There's plenty to make me v. cynical but then one remembers that History must always have worked like that & that anyone who's got anywhere has got there largely in spite of himself or of all his Alter Egos – the wishful thinking A.E., the bureaucratic A.E., the sentimental A.E. etc. One of the most obvious things a war seems to force upon people is a sort of spiritual cheapness or crudity, which (oddly) can be found side by side with an intensified emotional life & a sharper vision. So that the same person who has jettisoned half his delicacy of touch has at the same time become, in some respects, much more perceptive. I find e.g. that half the time I am saying to myself, 'Christ, what a gross mad kind of world I am living in' & yet on the whole I feel it much more satisfactory to be in London than in N.Y.C.; London seems to make more sense. With the exception of Cabinet Ministers & people like that we have at last escaped from all those great heaps of abstractions, crumbling sandcastles, which always grow up round one when one's talking about a war somewhere else. Sorry but I must go out now & meet someone for a drink before St. Paul's; will continue this tomorrow. / May 15th: Well, I went up St. P's that night & nothing happened, so I went up again last Saturday (May 10th) & everything happened – I have never seen anything so fantastic & have no notion how to describe it.[2] All the old clichés   seas of flame, palls of smoke etc – would apply in a sense but they'd be hopelessly inadequate. Up on the dome you felt the whole place shudder & it went on all night. I walked home to breakfast through blazing streets (tinkling with falling

1 – Plymouth had been severely bombed on successive nights in late April. Cf. 'Many Casualties at Plymouth', *The Times*, 1 May 1941, 2. Plymouth had already been heavily bombed on 20 March (*The Times*, 22 March 1941).
2 – During the enemy raid on London on 10 May, conducted in the light of a full moon, thirty-three German bombers were shot down by British forces, thirty-one by RAF fighters. Casualties were heavy and damaged buildings included Westminster Abbey, the British Museum and the Houses of Parliament (*The Times*, 12 May 1941, 4). Clearly, FLM was well positioned on top of St Paul's to witness much of this destruction.

glass) to find all the windows in my own street blown in & my own house full of soot & broken glass & plaster.[1] They had had the hell of a lot of damage just 100 yds away, which, being people's houses, was far more upsetting than the commercial buildings etc. burning in the City. Our street still looks like a rubbish dump with piles of litter in the gutter in front of each house. / Have just had a batch of reviews about my latest (English) vol. of poems.[2] The stock derogatory epithet applied to me here now is 'slick'. I find this irritating & it usually comes from neo-Christians. Have only written 2 poems since I have been back but I expect these to develop into a fairly closely connected series.[3] / May 20th: Have just written a feature for the B.B.C. about Westminster Abbey, plugging the Bible shamelessly – all sorts of purple bits from Isaiah & the Psalms & the Book of Revelation, ending with the bit from Ezekiel about making the dry bones live.[4] Am planning – for my own satisfaction – a new series of prose Outbursts, possibly for the Statesman; a kind of mixture of aphorisms & expletives & shots of the passing scene – plus a certain amount of renunciation but no self-flagellation (which is what most of the intellectuals here go in for now.) The intellectuals incidentally remain pretty sterile, with the exception of George Orwell (who has always been on his own) & Stephen Spender who certainly keeps going, though still – from my point of view – deplorably soft & at least as self-centred as ever. As for our 2 cultural periodicals – Horizon & New Writing – I am v. glad they exist (it is an achievement these days) but both John Lehmann & Connolly are both racketeering & cliquey & the whole thing comes from a matrix of sherry-party gossip & college-boy rivalry & at times makes one feel like rushing off & joining the Tank Corps; only the Tank Corps would be just as college-boy in another way. My own reaction is to go around with people who're outside the intelligentsia completely; one of the good things about the war is it's made us much more a nation of mixers. I still don't know what the unknown virtue (or Unknown God) is that is never more than half-emergent but that motivates people these days. Only it seems to me much more powerful – & more to be admired

1–34 Wharton Street, WC1.
2–*PP* (Faber) appeared in April 1941 and was reviewed in the *TLS* (19 April 1941, 194), *Poetry London* (May–June 1941, 199–203) and *Scrutiny* (June 1941, 103). It was a prolific year for FLM: OUP had published *The Poetry of W. B. Yeats* in February and the American edition appeared in April. *Poems, 1925–1940* had been published by Random House in New York on 17 Feb. and was widely reviewed.
3–Cf. previous letter.
4–*The Stones Cry Out*, No. 4: 'Westminster Abbey', broadcast 27 May 1941.

– than any fully emerged or formulated God or ideology. I wish you'd
write to me again.

Yours ever,
Louis

TO *Daniel MacNeice*   MS Bodleian

20 May [1941]   c/o Rupert Doone, 34 Wharton St,
                                      London WC1

DEAREST DAN,

I have just discovered that a letter I wrote you for your birthday while
I was in Oxford, was never posted. I am so sorry about this. I gather you
were in Greenore at the time; I hope you had a lovely birthday.[1] Seven
seems rather a big age.

I am hoping that perhaps I can come to Ireland next month.

In London now all the trees are very green & we hope it will soon get
warm. Your Polar Bear is waiting here till someone can take him over; I
think he needs a wash.[2]

It would be nice if you could send me a picture some time.

I am very busy as usual, writing things to be broadcast to America &
other such places. How is the scooter?

lots of love,
D.

1 – Greenore, Co. Louth, on Carlingford Lough. Dan MacNeice recalls: 'I remember the plush
curtains in the hotel bedroom and dimly wondering why they needed to be so luxurious.
What I can't remember is whether we could see the Isle of Man from their window; or
whether I now feel we should have wondered about that' (DM, private correspondence,
2008).

2 – 'While Louis was away in America in 1939 teaching for a year, Dan went with his
Hungarian nanny, Miss Popper, to live in his grandparents' house in Belfast. Louis reappeared
from time to time, bearing distinctive presents – a polar bear in an enormous Easter egg,
memorably in 1940 – and more anecdotal vignettes, those suitable for a six-year old British
recluse: "Redcap" sleeping-car porters on American trains; the food dispensers of the
"Automat"; multi-lane highways; all of them wonderfully remote and illustrative of the never-
never reality of American life' (DM, 'Louis's Son', *Ms Carrickfergus Museum*).

26 May [1941]   c/o Rupert Doone, 34 Wharton St,
                                       London WC1

Dear E.R.D.,

This is just to warn you that the B.B.C. will be writing to you for a reference re. me. Actually I am officially joining their staff today before these formalities are completed. I had rather fun last week turning down their first offer & extorting something much more lucrative.[1]

Have not been able to write up St Paul's yet, as they switched me on to Westminster Abbey which I did by plugging the Bible.[2] I have just written a light hearted thing about Madame Tussaud's.[3] I hope to wangle a 6-days trip on an ex-American destroyer soon.[4] The job – in spite of typical B.B.C. atmosphere – seems to have its possibilities.

Please thank your wife for sending me my tarpaulin – v. useful in this weather. & do let me know when you come to London next.

In haste,
Yrs ever,
Louis

1 – The terms of his contract issued on 24 May stated that 'duties will include writing scripts under the direction of the Assistant Director of Features Dept., and any other duties connected with the feature programmes, reasonably required of you by the Corporation' ('Notes on Louis MacNeice from Staff File', *Ms BBC WAC, 910 MacNeice Source File*). He was put on the official payroll on 26 May as Script Writer, Grade B1, with an annual salary of £840 (*Ms BBC WAC, L1/285/1/Left Staff*).
2 – *The Stones Cry Out*, No. 8: 'St Paul's', broadcast 23 June 1941, and No. 4: 'Westminster Abbey', broadcast 27 May 1941.
3 – *The Stones Cry Out*, No. 5: 'Madame Tussaud's', broadcast 2 June 1941.
4 – See next letter.

TO *General Establishment Officer [Robert Burns]*
(BBC internal memo) MS BBC

5 August 1941 From: Mr. Louis MacNeice,
Bedford College

Subject: H.M.S. Chelsea[1]

With regard to the Admiralty report about the behaviour of Dillon[2] and myself in H.M.S. CHELSEA, I wish to say that it came to me as a complete surprise and that I consider it a very misleading account of our behaviour. It seems in fact calculated to suggest that we gave a display not only of gross bad manners but of incredible stupidity.

We were at sea in H.M.S. CHELSEA from June 20th till June 29th, and during the whole trip we took especial trouble to fit into the ward-room life, and to be on friendly terms with the officers. Up till the last night we had taken very few drinks and had regularly gone to bed by about midnight, with the exception of one night when we sat up rather later with three or four of the officers, playing cards. By the end of the trip we were on very good terms with the officers, and we and they treated each other with easy-going informality; I should like to say that their behaviour to us throughout was courteous and pleasant in the extreme.

On the last evening (June 28/9th), the ship being due to dock about breakfast time, we got the impression that there was rather a holiday spirit in the air; as this was our last opportunity of showing our friendliness, we were very ready to sit up and have drinks with anyone who felt like it. We began by swopping stories and later there was some singing; this was what was referred to in the report as the 'terrific noise', and we quietened down on request. After the singing had stopped, it is still possible that – owing to the small size and acoustic qualities of the ward-room – the conversation

1 – The Ministry of Information had assigned to the BBC two berths aboard a US naval destroyer (one of fifty destroyers recently transferred to the Royal Navy), to do a broadcast on the subject. FLM and Jack Dillon (see below) were sent, but were upbraided for alleged misconduct (cf. Stallworthy, 299–304). The fifteen-minute programme *Freedom's Ferry: Life on an American Destroyer* was broadcast on 16 July. The US Navy had decommissioned the USS *Crowninshield* on 9 September 1940, when it was transported to Great Britain and renamed the HMS *Chelsea*. The ship's commanding officer at the time of writing was Lt. Cdr. A. F. C. Layard.
2 – Francis Edward Juan ('Jack') Dillon (1899–1982), radio producer. Educ. Nova Scotia and Jamaica; then Frimley School; Norwood Polytechnic; Bromley HS; Dr Stephenson's Academy, Yorks.; Ayr Academy. Fought for both the White Army in Russia and the Black and Tans in Ireland. West regional features producer, BBC, 1938; London Features, 1941; joined FLM on board HMS *Chelsea* and later went with him to India, 1947. He is 'Devlin' in *AS*.

and laughter between Dillon, myself and some of the officers may have been more penetrating than we realised. A younger officer did come through the ward-room and say something like 'Don't make so much noise, chaps, there are people trying to sleep!' I wish to point out, however, that if anyone had told us to shut up completely or to go to bed, we should of course have complied; we had no wish to abuse the hospitality of the ship. (Incidentally, there was always someone sleeping off the ward-room at any time of the day or night.)

Some time after the singing stopped, we settled down to playing cards and so continued for a long time, having periodical drinks (all of which were entered in the mess sheet) but making very little noise; I myself was feeling pretty sleepy, not from drink but from a series of uncomfortable nights, and did not feel in the least like raising hell. When the game broke up, I went up on the bridge to have a look out for five minutes before going to bed and also to borrow a cigarette from a junior officer who was then on watch, (I may add that for a landsman who was 'very tight' – the phrase used in the report – it would have been pretty difficult to get up the two ladders to the bridge when the ship was in motion.) After this Dillon and I went to sleep in the ward-room. I had been accustomed to sleep there every night, sleeping in my clothes, while Dillon had the use of the Doctor's cabin. On this occasion the Doctor used his own cabin and Dillon took his place in the ward-room.

The ward-room, I admit, looked pretty untidy but it had never looked tidy on any of the nights I was on board, owing to the fact that there were two men sleeping in it and that I used to wedge myself in with chairs to prevent myself being thrown on the floor. There was usually a litter of papers and of spilt ashtrays about; on this occasion there were merely a few more glasses in evidence.

Dillon and I got up before 8.0 on the morning of June 20th and after breakfast the ship put into dock. The Captain invited us both to his cabin, where we met the new Captain, who was taking over the ship, and we were offered drinks. The Captain was very friendly and asked us to look him up at his Club in London. Afterwards, in the ward-room, several of the officers offered us drinks and pressed us to stay to lunch before going ashore. Thus when we left HMS CHELSEA we had received no indication from any quarter whatsoever that we were under even the slightest kind of a cloud. Dillon and I, therefore, both find it very hard to understand why a complaint should later have been made about our conduct. If we inadvertently occasioned any trouble among the officers, we are extremely sorry, but no one at the time gave us an inkling that this was so. As far as we were concerned, we were merely sitting up late and drinking (within bounds) to commemorate an enjoyable trip and show our appreciation of the company in the ward-room. I therefore think it advisable that an enquiry should be made into the allegation against us.

Louis MacNeice

TO *Eleanor Clark* MS Yale

6 August [1941] London but as from c/o Professor
Dodds, 62 High Street, Oxford

Darling Nell,

Maybe you could write to me again soon? I am feeling, as you would say, lonesome. I saw Erika Mann the other day; it seemed odd that she could drop in here so easily & you be beyond a million iron hedges. They seem more iron than before because, owing to a recent stupidity of mine, I doubt if I shall for some time be given a mission now over to your side.[1] In fact it would probably be easier for <u>you</u> to come <u>here</u>. I am not suggesting that you would want to in the least but, <u>if</u> you ever feel like paying us a visit, let me know as I know some people who could probably fix you a temporary job (they are getting keener daily on this American liaison business).

For the last fortnight I have been attending a course giving one all the inner workings of radio. Just like being at school – sitting on hard benches – but technically fascinating though in places difficult for me with my unmechanical mind. I am not however sure that I shall be going on with this job. If I leave it, I think of joining the A.F.S.[2] That would give me time to write my own stuff.

I am going to move from my present house soon up to my sister's house in Highgate where Housman wrote The Shropshire Lad (my sister having vacated it).[3] It has so far been a much less bombed area than where I am, so with luck we may keep our windows & ceilings into the winter (the general opinion is that the Blitz will return all right).

Just lit my last cigarette, so I shall have to go to bed soon when the craving gets too much for me. I showed your photograph (the Virgin of the Rocks) to a colleague of mine the other day who, while admiring it duly,

1 – A reference to the Admiralty report on his (and Dillon's) behaviour aboard HMS *Chelsea*.
2 – Auxiliary Fire Service.
3 – A. E. Housman (1859–1936) lived at 17 North Road, Highgate N6, 1886–1905. A commemorative blue plaque was affixed to the building in 1969.

was rather appalled by the characterfulness of your jaw & even more so when he collated it with mine which he thought looked pretty difficult too.

I had a letter from Eunice the other day from her shack. I should very much like to hear all those katydids again. The summer here seems to have been & gone, it is now cold & damp & grey. I haven't even played tennis. Have however just bought myself the Oxford Book of 17th Century Verse which is a good anthology for these times, most of the poems being hard & faceted. Do you remember 'the Conjunction of the Mind / & Opposition of the Stars'?[1] It's rather what I feel like. About you. My preposterous impulses – in the stress of hack craftsmanship – seem to have abated & I find myself even brutally uninterested in the people who feel preposterously towards me. It's the first time I've ever been bored by even mock romances but it seems to me now that, unless one's in love with people, they want (a) so little & (b) too much – & on the other hand one can't be in love with people who want too much & so little.

I <u>must</u> go to bed, darling, have to attend my school in the morning. What are you doing for the Fall? Are you going West – to the baths of Ocean & that? I should love to be able to leap on a train or a plane or a dolphin & jump across all the Prohibited Areas. All I do, as it is, is take 4 taxis a day. But I <u>must</u> go to bed.

all my love, darling,
L.

P.S. Read a review of my Poems in <u>Time</u> the other day, said I had a 'flaccid heart'.[2] It ain't true but I know what they mean. If I survive this mess, it (heart) will be what it wouldn't have been otherwise – but, all the same, what it was to have been from the start.

---

1 – From Andrew Marvell, 'The Definition of Love', see FLM to EC, 17 April 1940, n. 2, p. 383.
2 – The reviewer of *Poems, 1925–1940* claimed that FLM's recent poetry 'contains humorous, tender and thoughtful patches; but for the most part it reveals an ugly picture of a man writing with a stiff, long upper lip and a flaccid heart' (*Time*, 9 June 1941).

19 August 1941 From: Mr. Louis MacNeice,
Bedford College

Subject: H.M.S. Chelsea

Having seen the quotations from the report of the Commanding Officer of
H.M.S. CHELSEA, I wish to add the following observations:-

(1) I remain very surprised that this report should have issued
from the Captain himself, for the reason I gave in my previous
statement, i.e. that, so far as we knew, we were still on
excellent terms with him when we left his ship. I can only
conjecture that <u>after</u> we had left the ship something occurred,
unknown to Dillon and myself, which caused representations
to be made to him.

(2) The Captain reports that he saw us last soon after 6.0 p.m. It
seems to me that the report on our subsequent behaviour must
have been compiled from various sources based on memory or
assumption rather than on impartial observation.

(3) The statements in this report, while very objectively worded,
seem to be emphasised in such a way as to become distortions
of what actually happened.

(4) As regards the drinks which we took before supper, I think
that Dillon and I had about four small drinks each.

(5) I did not drink anything <u>with</u> my supper.

(6) The statement that after supper we 'had the wardroom to
ourselves' is definitely misleading because it suggests (a) that
Dillon and I were alone in the ward-room and (b) that we
were having a drinking-party on our own. The fact is that we
were <u>not</u> alone and that, when after an interval, we began
ordering more drinks, several of the officers joined us. Until a
very advanced hour, Dillon and I were never alone in the
ward-room for more than five minutes, if that.

(7) About midnight I remember a Sub-lieutenant asking us and the
officers drinking with us not to make too much noise because
people were sleeping. I do not remember the First Lieutenant
'telling us tactfully to turn in'. If he did so, he must have been
so tactful that we missed his point. When I saw him, as he
came through the ward-room, he struck me as being in an
agreeable temper and not at all perturbed by anything.

(8) I mentioned the singing in my previous statement. This singing, like the drinking, was not merely a matter between Dillon and myself, and it ceased on request. After that, as I said before, we played cards and one of the officers continued to play with us for several hours until we abandoned the game. This card-playing was perfectly quiet.

(9) I deny that at 4.0 a.m. either Dillon or I was 'definitely very drunk', though, speaking for myself, I was definitely very sleepy. We had had a good deal to drink but our drinks had been spaced. Dillon and I, during the evening, had indulged off and on in a certain amount of 'Crazy Gang' dialogue with each other; this, by people who did not know us very well, may have in retrospect been wrongly attributed to drunkenness. I myself, before I became sleepy, was in high spirits but quite in control of myself.

(10) It was not Dillon but I, who went upon the Bridge. To say that I was 'turned off' strikes me as another exaggeration. I was asked if I didn't want any sleep and I replied that I certainly did, after which I returned to the ward-room. Dillon and I looked into the Doctor's cabin, where our blankets were kept, but seeing we could not extract them without disturbing the Doctor, we settled down, as we were, in the ward-room.

(11) The picture of us asleep at 7.15 a.m. with half-empty glasses still in our hands strikes me as highly coloured; the two large armchairs in the ward-room had solid arms, flat and very wide, and I suggest that we may have gone to sleep, leaving glasses resting on these arms (I cannot see that to leave a glass on an armchair is any worse than to leave an ashtray there, as was customary in the ward-room). I have already commented on the state of the wardroom and explained that the Doctor and I were accustomed to sleep there without undressing. This fact – to my mind – makes the whole question of 'turning in' rather academic as all we had to do was to go to sleep where we were.

(12) If the report were correct in describing us as in 'a drunken slumber' at 7.15, it is surprising that within half an hour we should have been up and shaving and behaving quite normally. (I may add that, on getting up, I felt very tired but I had no hangover at all.)

Louis MacNeice

1942

TO *E. R. Dodds*   MS Bodleian

25 April [1942]   17 North Road

Dear E.R.D.,

I haven't heard from you for ages. How are you both? I should like to come to Oxford in about 3 weeks time & see you.

I don't know if you heard that my father had died – suddenly – on April 14th. I went over there immediately & stayed a few days. He had been in very good form all that day & died quickly in the evening; it seemed a good way. He had just announced that he was going to retire this year & he wouldn't have liked being retired at all.

I went over the Border & saw Dan who is in excellent form & crazy about geography.[1] His estate was blazing with daffodils & they were making a home-made fishing rod for him.

My next programme is Sunday May 10th, a thing about the House of Commons (dramatised history) which I have written & shall produce myself.[2] Henry Reed turned up the other day. He is going to do some scripts for us.[3]

In haste,

> With all best wishes,
> Louis

1 – Dan was still staying with Diana Clements at Ashfield, Cootehill, Co. Cavan.
2 – 'The Debate Continues', broadcast 10 May 1942 (Coulton, 204).
3 – Henry Reed (1914–86), poet and radio dramatist. Educ. King Edward VI GS, Birmingham University. The two men met when Reed was a student at Birmingham.

TO *Nancy Coldstream*   MS Bodleian

Thursday [2 July 1942]   BBC Broadcasting House,
                                        London, W1 [hereafter BBC]

Darling,
    I am desolated I couldn't get in touch with you yesterday. Hedli & I got
fed up with the inconveniences of our status & went & got married & we
wanted you to come & drink around the place.¹ Ernst & I rang you
repeatedly, so I assume you were at the ambulance. I would have contacted
you on Tuesday but my Yugoslavia programme was so much more difficult
even than I expected, that I forgot everything.²
    Am going to country tomorrow, but will ring you on Monday &
perhaps we can arrange something gay?
                                        Lots of love
                                        Louis

TO *Mrs E. R. Dodds*   MS Bodleian

4 July [1942]   6 Maiden Lane, London WC2³

Dear Mrs. Dodds,
    This is just to say that Hedli & I got married on Wednesday. We're
hoping to go over to Ireland for my leave about July 20th & then come
back & get a house. This weekend we're down in Hedli's cottage in Sussex;
she would like to consult Himself about the gardening.

1–Hedli Anderson (1907–89), English singer and actress. Trained with Victor Beigel and
later studied at Hamburg Conservatoire, and then Berlin, where, inspired by the example of
Yvette Guilbert, she became interested in cabaret. Worked in London for the Group Theatre
and performed in *The Dance of Death* (Auden), *The Dog Beneath the Skin*, *The Ascent of
F6* (Auden and Isherwood), *The Rescue* (Eddie Sackville-West and Britten) and *The Dark
Tower* (FLM and Britten). In collaboration with Auden, Britten later composed for her his
'Cabaret Songs' (e.g. 'Funeral Blues', 'Johnny', 'Calypso', and 'Tell Me the Truth About
Love'). She took part in performances of FLM's trans. of *Agamemnon* (1936), and *Out of the
Picture* (1937). They married on 1 July 1942 (separated 1960). FLM had introduced Hedli
to the Doddses on 15 June, in Oxford (cf. FLM to Mrs E. R. Dodds, 11 June 1942, Ms
Bodleian).
2–*The Undefeated (of Yugoslavia)*, broadcast 30 June 1942.
3–Hedli had a flat at this address.

I hope Himself is better by now. Can't write any more as I have to do a programme on Hitler.[1]

> With greetings from us both,
> Yours ever,
> Louis

TO *Eleanor Clark* MS Yale

9 July [1942] 6 Maiden Lane, London WC2

Darling,

This is to tell you that I have got married – but not to anyone I had mentioned to you before.

This makes sense to me. I hope you understand?

What I said before about you & me perhaps is what really applies: we met on the top of a mountain & should leave it at that.

But I would like you to go on writing to me. Without post-mortems.

> Be happy, darling.
> Love ever,
> Louis

TO *T. S. Eliot* Faber archive

27 August 1942 BBC

Dear Eliot,

I am now back in London from Ireland and am writing to apologise for not yet having sent you the promised samples of scripts on bombed buildings. I have been pretty busy and they need a bit more tinkering with than I had thought; however, I shall see what I can do with them in the next few weeks.

---

1 – *Black Gallery*, No. 10: 'Adolf Hitler', broadcast 16 July 1942. It was rumoured at this time that FLM was leaving the Corporation: a memo of 21 July, probably by Laurence Gilliam, expresses alarm at this prospect and goes on to praise his wartime work: 'We have used MacNeice for such direct propaganda purposes as the Overseas series "The Stones Cry Out", the anti-Nazi series "Black Gallery", and for a succession of large-scale programmes which have qualified as radio art of a high order, entertainment and propaganda. I have spent several years combing the ranks of writers for radio talent, and I have absolutely no doubt that MacNeice is absolutely indispensable to our war-time feature output' (*Ms BBC, L1/285/2/Left Staff*).

Sounds more like an answer to proposed conscription?

Apart from that, I have just been reading through a long script of my own about Christopher Columbus which is going out on the air on the 12th of October. (Its transmission will take more than two hours.)[1] This script is to all intents and purposes a verse play, and it struck me today, though I may not be the person to judge, that merely on the page it would read intelligibly and effectively. Anyhow, I propose to send you a copy of it in the next few days so that you can see what you think.

Yours with best wishes,
Louis MacNeice

TO *Daniel MacNeice* MS Dan MacNeice

[Between 14 and 18 October 1942] [Essex]

Dearest Dan,

I am writing in a hurry from the cottage in the country as I have a great deal of work. Hedli & I spent the afternoon picking apples; there are a great many down here – shiny red & yellow ones. Tomorrow we have to go back to London & next week I think we shall go to Birmingham where you used to live when you were very little. We have not yet been to see the school which we think should be so nice for you but I expect we shall go soon.[2]

I was in Scotland about two weeks ago & had to come down from the Highlands by night in the guard's van on a Fish Train; it was very uncomfortable. On Monday we were in [*removed by censor but presumably Bedford*] where Hedli was singing in a programme which I wrote; it was a very long programme about Christopher Columbus. A lot of music.

I had a lovely lunch the other day in Soho (that is the Italian part of London); it was all shell-fish – first oysters & then lobster. I don't think you would like oysters though. Most people don't till they're grown up. And the oysters here are much dearer than in America.

---

1 – *Christopher Columbus*, a forty-nine character play starring Laurence Olivier and Margaret Rawlings and produced by Dallas Bower, was first broadcast on 12 Oct. 1942 (the anniversary of Columbus's landing in the Americas). The performance, with music composed by William Walton and supported by the BBC Chorus and Symphony Orchestra, was recorded at the Corn Exchange, Bedford, where the BBC Music Division was based during the war. Cf. Dallas Bower, 'Sound and Vision', *TWA*, 97–102; Stallworthy, 313–15.
2 – Dan was sent to Springfield Grange prep school, Great Missenden, Bucks, in January 1943.

Here is a picture of HEINZ[1]

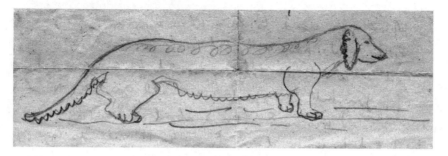

must stop now,
lots of love
DADDIE

1–I remember Heinz so well, which means he must have lived to a great age. Certainly he became completely bald all down his back. Other than that, he had a wonderful chestnut coat and the vet maintained he was the longest dachshund he had ever come across. Dreams of suffocation invariably turned out to be Heinz sitting on top of me' (BCM, private correspondence, 2010).

1943

TO *T. S. Eliot*   Faber archive

24 November 1943   BBC

Dear Eliot

Thank you for your letter of 18th November. By the way, I never made that correction in the 'Columbus' text, as someone had gone off with my spare set of proofs. If it is not too late to make further alterations, there is one other minor change which I might make, if you could send me another set of proofs.

About my new book of poems, obviously it ought not to follow 'Columbus' too quickly, but at the same time I should prefer it to appear as soon as is reasonable next year – e. g. in the summer rather than in the autumn.[1] This is partly because the bulk of the contents reflect very much a war time mood, and if by the time of publication victory in Europe has occurred or is imminent they may strike many readers as somewhat out of key.

                              Yours sincerely
                              Louis MacNeice

P.S.

Thinking it over I am not at all sure that it might not be advisable to hold up 'Columbus' till some later date and shove in the new book of poems instead, but I dare say from the publisher's point of view that would not be feasible?

1 – *Christopher Columbus* was published in March 1944; the 'new book', *Springboard*, appeared in December.

1944

TO *T. S. Eliot*   Faber archive

7 April 1944   BBC

Dear Eliot

Thank you for your letter. Here are some immediate alterations in case you can incorporate them in the typescript of my poems before you give the script to de la Mare:-

1. In 'Explorations', first verse, for 'archetypes' read 'prototypes'.
2. In 'Swing-Song', second verse, for 'where he has gone to bomb' read 'what he has gone to bomb'.
3. In 'The Kingdom' (iv), last line, for 'hand' read 'hands'.
4. In 'The Kingdom' (v), for 'that sprung Palladian dome' read 'that smooth Renaissance dome'.
5. In 'The Kingdom' (vi), at the end of the line
   'This man who flogged his brain, he was a child.'
   put a semi-colon instead of a full stop.
6. In 'The Kingdom' (viii), for 'The bogs of jargon' read 'The buzz of jargon'.[1]

Perhaps I should say that I think this will very probably be my last book of short poems for some considerable time.[2] I want in the near future to concentrate on writing a long poem, the sort of thing that will take shape slowly, probably over a space of some years. I can't tell you much about this project at the moment except (1) that the main characters will be imagined contemporary individuals, but will exist on two planes, i.e. the symbolic as well as the naturalistic. (2) That there will be some inter-shuttling of past and present (though in a much more modified way than in Ezra Pound's Cantos). (3) That the total pattern will be very complex,

---

1 – Corrections for *Springboard*: 'Explorations', 12; 'Swing-Song', 22; 'The Kingdom', 46.
2 – In fact his next volume, *Holes in the Sky* (1948) (*HS*), was a book of mainly shorter poems, although it included 'The Stygian Banks', which, like 'The Kingdom' in *Springboard*, reflected his interest in a more expansive poetic statement.

and in fact rather comparable to the 'Faerie Queen' in its interlocking of episodes, sub-plots, and digressions which aren't really digressions.[1]

Yours ever
Louis MacNeice

---

1 – Presumably this was the poem which became *Autumn Sequel*. See his remarks on *The Faerie Queene* as a structuring principle of that poem in FLM to TSE, 30 March 1954, p. 573.

1945

TO *E. R. Dodds*   MS Bodleian

21 March [1945]   10 Wellington Place, London NW8

Dear E.R.D.,

So sorry you have a chill – & also that you couldn't manage lunch. All
the same I hope to see you before you go.

About Dan's measurements, Hedli says she's sent them to Mary already.
About Dan himself, he comes to us in London on Wednesday next (28th)
so, if you have time, do come up & see him (you can always stay the night
if you fancy it). I have a completely crazy programme called The March
Hare Resigns going out from 7.25–8.10 p.m. on Thursday (29th),
originally intended for All Fools' Day.[1] I had thought of taking Dan down
to the studio to listen to it so, if you were around, you could join us?

Introductions & that:- when you see Wystan, in case he hasn't had a
letter from me by then, could you tell him I am thinking up a list of
translations for his anthology.[2]

In New York do look up Mr & Mrs. J. K. Jessup. They have changed
their address lately but it can be discovered if you ring up Time newspapers
in N.Y.C. Jessup is one of the chief editors of 'Time' itself. His wife, Eunice,
is a sister of Eleanor Clark. I used to stay with them & they are both highly
intelligent & amusing. Give them my love.

You might also look up Philip Vaudrin at the Oxford University Press in
Fifth Avenue (I think, 119 5th Ave). If so, you might explain to him that
the book I contracted to do for him in 1940 will forthcome eventually.[3]
The fact is that I had written most of it (it's the one you keep in a bread-

---

1 – In this play, the March Hare (played by Esmé Percy) tries to stop time, so that 'he will not
be ousted on 1 April'. FLM intended it to be a rather anarchic, 'crazy' show, or in his words,
'a kind of satirical fantasy which will pan around a large number of topical subjects, and
should make an agreeable catharsis for the large company of the browned off' (FLM qtd in
Coulton, 73).

2 – Auden had written: 'In a moment of madness I have undertaken to edit for Viking an
anthology of translations from the poetry of all other tongues'; he asked FLM for suggestions.
Cf. WHA to FLM, 21 Jan. 1945, Appendix 3 to this volume, pp. 721–2.

3 – *SAF*.

bin) but, as the result of living in London in war-time, I want to re-do the whole thing – very much better, I hope.

Another simpatica person is my cousin, Virginia Howell (now Mrs. Soskin) of Howell Soskin Inc., a publishing firm. She is amusing & full of information.

A mad writer you might like is James Agee (ask the Jessups about him).[1] The Jessups also know Edmund Wilson – but he is a bit heavy conversationally.

If you find yourself in Utica (N.Y. State) ring up Professor Chase (prof. of Classics) at a college just outside Utica; his son Jack Chase who might be up there, was a Rhodes Scholar at Merton in my time – a nice chap.[2] Mrs Professor would give you a very good meal. If you go to Smith College, look up the President, Herbert Davis, who was my boss at Cornell.[3]

At Harvard there is Theodore Spencer, a friend of T. S. Eliot's.[4] Also a pleasant man called Matthiesen [sic], whom I stayed with after having appendicitis.[5]

At Princeton there is Donald Stauffer (in the English Dept.) also a Rhodes Scholar from Merton.[6]

About Mary:- We may have a photo of Dan for you to take with you. If not, tell her one will be coming by mail. We are going to have him done by an excellent photographer, Douglas Glass.[7]

M. has been writing to say that she intends to leave Dan all her life interest from her deceased grandfather (which will apparently exceed

1 – James Agee (1909–55), American novelist and journalist, author of *Let Us Now Praise Famous Men* (1941). He was a film critic for *Time* magazine during the 1940s.

2 – Cf. 'Auden and MacNeice: Their Last Will and Testament': '. . . item to Jack / Chase my best regards and a case of rye' (*LI, CP07, 742*).

3 – Herbert John Davis (1893–1967), author of *Augustan Art of Conversation* (1957) and other works.

4 – Theodore Spencer (1902–49), author (with Mark van Doren) of *Studies in Metaphysical Poetry* (1939), and *Shakespeare and the Nature of Man* (1949). He had invited FLM to Harvard in spring 1939 and had also accompanied him to his appearance at Wellesley College at that time.

5 – FLM had stayed with F. O. Matthiessen at Kittery, Maine, in 1940. See FLM to EC, 29 August 1940, n. 3, p. 401.

6 – Donald Alfred Stauffer (1902–52), author of *Art of Biography in Eighteenth Century England* (1941), and *Golden Nightingale: Essays on Some Principles of Poetry in the Lyrics of William Butler Yeats* (1949).

7 – Douglas Glass (1901–78) arrived in England from his native New Zealand in 1926. He photographed the weekly 'Portrait Gallery' which appeared in the *Sunday Times*, 1949–61. His later portraits of Elizabeth Taylor, Cecil Beaton, Michael Tippett and others hang in the National Portrait Gallery.

£1000 per ann). Apart from the fact that it seems to me unjust not to leave anything to Charles (whose career has not been helped by M.)[1] I am somewhat alarmed by the thought that, if M. died, Dan at 21 might find himself rich enough not to have to work. I think ∴ that if M. is going to make a will exclusively in his favour, it would be better to appoint trustees who, according to their discretion, would let him have so much a year (= 'A') & reinvest the balance (= 'B') for the future; 'A' could perhaps be gradually increased as he grew maturer. I'm not knowledgeable in these affairs but I expect you see the sort of compromise-cum-safeguard that I mean. Perhaps you could drop a hint to M. of the desirability of this?

Two other points: do reassure M. that Dan has an ample & adequate diet (the Downs School are strong on food). Also – negatively – please be careful not to give her any handles for her old argument that Dan would be – or would have been at any time – better off in America. e.g. don't say: 'Of course he was probably a bit repressed in Ireland by all those old Church of Ireland puritans'! Mary will be lying in wait for molehills to make into mountains. Incidentally, if she trots out her (comparatively recent) thesis that it was I who broke up the marriage because I consented to a divorce, could you gently suggest that she's talking nonsense?[2]

In case I don't see you, one other thing: a charming place to eat in New York is the Lafayette, in University Place, round about 9th Street.[3] It is expensive but worth it. Eat in the outer part with marble tables which looks like a French café! There is also an excellent French restaurant – mid-town – called, I think, Les Pommes Soufflées.

Must stop – an American come in for interview! Buen viage (if I don't see you)

Yrs ever,
Louis

1 – Charles Katzman.
2 – FLM had petitioned for divorce against Mary in Dec. 1935. The divorce papers state the marriage should be dissolved 'by reason that since the celebration thereof the said Respondent [MM] has been guilty of adultery with Charles Katzman the Co-Respondent' (*Ms National Archives*). Cf. FLM to AB, 19 Nov. 1935, n. 4 and FLM to parents, 25 April 1936, n. 3, pp. 257, 262.
3 – Lafayette Hotel, University Place: by tradition a gathering place for bohemians, artists and intellectuals.

TO *Laurence Gilliam*[1]   MS BBC

17 April 1945   BBC Belfast [letterhead]

Dear Laurence,

In haste. I hope you got my memo about the recording for V-Day.[2] I do feel very strongly that this thing must be done live. When you hear the recording you will notice that the atmosphere is very inadequate, but even if this were not so I still feel that the thing would be ipso facto phoney.

About myself – the unexpected has just happened. Hedli went to a doctor yesterday and has been told that she has a very tired heart and must have a long and complete rest, e.g. she must not walk more than a hundred yards at a time, nor go up and down stairs more than once a day! You will see that this raises all sorts of difficulties. Pending the possibility that we may get a grade 'A' domestic who will really be able to cope with the house in London, we both think it best that Hedli should stay on a bit in my stepmother's house over here where they really do have facilities. This being so, I should very much like to be able to extend my own stay here, and am hoping that you may sanction this. Apart from doing research for the 'Transatlantic Call' on Northern Ireland, I find that I have various things to do here, e.g. (1) Locally – there is an excellent suggestion (as yet unofficial as Miss Ursula Eason is away) for a retrospective programme on Derry as a Naval Base during the war.[3] (It seems that in the last few weeks the Admiralty have released a lot of dope on this, and I think that, possibly with Malcolm Baker-Smith's co-operation, we might produce from this material a very good programme of the 'Flight Deck' variety);[4] (2) my old idea of a programme on 'The Dark Tower' has suddenly blossomed out and I should like to get on with writing it within the next few weeks.[5]

1 – Laurence Duval Gilliam (1907–64), OBE, radio producer. Educ. City of London School; Peterhouse, Cambridge. Joined BBC 1932; Head of Features 1936–63. He became renowned for recruiting poets and authors to write for Features. Nicknamed 'Lorenzo the Magnificent' by colleagues, he appears as Herriot in *AS*.
2 – VE Day was 8 May 1945; FLM also scripted *London Victorious*, broadcast 18 May.
3 – Londonderry/Derry was commissioned as a US naval operating base on 5 Feb. 1942, serving as a port for North Atlantic convoys, for refuelling convoy escorts and as a repair base. During the war, it had the largest US naval radio station in Europe. The base was disestablished and handed over to the British on 14 Aug. 1944, except for the radio station, which remained operational until 3 Oct. 1947. A modified version of the American naval base remained in Derry until the early 1970s. Ursula Eason was a producer at BBC Belfast.
4 – Malcolm Baker-Smith had been stage manager with the Old Vic before joining the BBC as a producer of drama.
5 – *The Dark Tower*, broadcast 21 Jan. 1946.

If you agree that the above provides good enough reason for my remaining in Northern Ireland, say an extra fortnight, I would like to point out that (a) I am prepared, if and when V-Day occurs, to return at once in order to handle my London programme (if you want it re-done live), or to give any co-operation required in the V-Day turmoil; (b) it looks as if I shall have in any case to cross over to England on the 27th April with Dan who has to get back to school, in which case I should remain in London for several days; this being so I should wish to return over here, and would like to have in advance your approval so that I could expedite the business of getting a renewed exit permit etc. etc. I shall try to arrange for a permit to return here from this end, but it may help if you could send me some little bit of paper authorising me to do so for Corporation purposes.

About the Nordahl Grieg programme, I can plan this within the next week and let Ruth Jones know what to do about it.[1] Anyhow I can cope with this if I come back to London for the weekend of the 28th to 30th April.

I hope you won't think I am being tiresome with the above requests, but as you can imagine I do find myself in rather a dilemma with this collapse of Hedli's, and I do also quite genuinely think I can get on with a number of worth while things over here.

Hoping you and your family flourish and that the prospect of V-Day isn't keeping you awake too late.

Yours ever,
Louis

TO *Laurence Gilliam*   MS BBC

4 July [1945]   c/o Burrishoole Lodge, nr Newport,
                                       Co. Mayo[2]

Dear Laurence,

I take it you're just due back from Paris, which I trust was fruitful. I wrote you a letter some weeks ago (which Stella answered) explaining my

1 – *A Voice from Norway*, broadcast BBC Home Service, 22 May 1945. Nordahl Grieg (1902–43), Norwegian poet, dramatist. Educ. University of Oslo; Wadham College, Oxford. During the war he was involved in broadcasting in London. He was killed in 1943 while serving as an observer in an Allied bombing mission.
2 – Burrishoole Lodge was the home of Ernie O'Malley. While staying here with the O'Malleys and their three children (Cathal, Etain and Cormac), FLM read the stories of Frank O'Connor (FLM to LG, 14 July 1945, *Ms BBC*).

present allergy to England. I still feel it would do me – & my work – a world of good if I could be reprieved from radio work for a short period – say till the end of August. In that case, I'd stay in Ireland & bring Dan over here for the first month of his holidays. <u>If</u> this is out of the question it won't kill me but I would like it.[1]

Anyhow I'm here at the moment – from last Saturday – on what I suppose should be called leave (as I told Ursula E.), having still a fortnight owing to me. In fact I'm finishing The Dark Tower & vetting scripts from Ulster.[2] This house is like a public library, having authoritative books on every conceivable subject (but especially on Ireland) so it would be wonderful for research – if only one were sure what one was researching on.

The amenities are good – except cigarettes which are all inferior export American. The bees have made an illicit hive above the rooms where I'm writing but they're kept down by the rats, so the ceiling is repeatedly shaken by the lurching of honey-drunk rats. Everything is nicely filmed with turf dust & there is God's plenty of butter.

Hedli is much better & Corinna[3] boisterous. There are 3 other children here – called Cathal, Etain & Cormac.

I saw David Thomson in the North (& introduced him to Rodgers) but missed Jack. David was being a bit repressed by Jimmy Mageean whose chief object in programmes seems to be to avoid any occasion of comment by anyone on anything; apart from that he's very pleasant.[4]

Hedli sends her love to you & Marianne, remember us in your prayers,

Yours,

Louis

1 – Not having received a reply, he sent a second request, informing LG that he had decided to take the leave without permission, and was renting a cottage in Achill for 21 July–21 Aug. He invited the administrators to dock his pay: 'You can tell them that I am (1) Irish & have not been in my own country for 3 years – & not for so long then – & (2) an (for lack of a better word) artist – which means that I can do some hackwork all of the time & all hackwork some of the time but not all hackwork all of the time.' (FLM to LG, 14 July 1945, Ms BBC). Another reason for remaining in Ireland was that Hedli was ill (cf. FLM to ERD, 31 July 1945, p. 459).

2 – Cf. 'I'll be sending Ruth the Dark Tower script in a few days', FLM to LG, 14 July 1945 (Ms BBC, MacNeice, Scriptwriter file 1). He sent the script on 8 August (cf. FLM to Ruth Jones, 8 Aug. 1945, below).

3 – Daughter of FLM and Hedli, b. 5 July 1943. See 15 Sept. 1961, n. 2, p. 682.

4 – On Thomson, see FLM to JL, 24 June 1954 n. 2, p. 580. On Rodgers, see FLM to Ruth Jones, 26 May 1947, n. 4, p. 466. Jack is Jack Dillon. J. R. (Jimmy) Mageean was a radio producer in Belfast and an Irish comic actor with the Group Theatre. His many film credits include The Luck of the Irish (1936), Macushla (1937), Irish and Proud of It (1938) and My Wife's Family (1956).

P.S. Apart from all questions of leave, 4 out of my 5 Northern scriptwriters haven't yet finished their labour pains.

TO *Denis Johnston*[1]

MS Bodleian

20 July [1945]   c/o Mrs Barrett, Keel, Achill,
                  Co. Mayo

Dear Denis,

Thank you for sending the package of stuff from the Corp. I have got a reprieve from that institution till the end of August.

We're delighted to hear that you, Betty & Jeremy can come here & live in our cottage of wide prospect – but a little unclear as to <u>when</u> you are coming.[2] Betty said something on the phone to H. about a Bank Holiday which didn't seem to square with her saying that you'd be a week later than Dan. So perhaps you can wire us the exact date on which you'll appear. ('Keel-Achill' will find us; they know us at the Post Office.)

Now about Dan:- We're very grateful to you for saying you'll cope with him but fear it's putting rather a chore on you. He is due to arrive in Ireland on either Tuesday 31st or Wednesday 1st – will let you know which as soon as we know. <u>But</u> the Headmaster has just wired us that the Liverpool–Dublin boats are off, so he'll have to come by Holyhead & Dun Laoghaire. I don't know what time that boat gets in but, so far as I remember, it docks opposite the train, so he ought to be able to get himself to Westland Row. Could you ∴ meet the boat-train there? If it's Tuesday maybe he could make the connection straight away to Westport (?) if it's Wednesday I understand you can hold him over till Thursday! Anyhow, once he's in the Westport part of the train (one part goes to Galway), he'll be all right as we can meet him at the terminus.

There won't be anyone to put him on the boat at Holyhead but we're trusting to God & his native wit that he'll make it all right. Perhaps you can question him carefully as to whether he's got everything with him.* He'll only have a ticket to Dublin, so could you please get him his Westport ticket out of the enclosed cheque – & bring me the residue in cash? And by the way here are some other things – any or all of which it would be nice if you could bring & we could refund you for same:-

1–On Johnston, see FLM to WHA, 21 Oct. 1937, n. 2, p. 306.
2–Johnston's second wife, Betty Chancellor (1910–84), and their son Jeremy (b.1939).

(1) 'Brideshead Revisited' by Evelyn Waugh (I need this badly for an article I'm writing).
(2) Omnibus Shakespeare or other worthy multum-in-parvo for wet days.
(3) Tea (if possible)
(4) Jam ("   )
[(5) Sugar ("   ) *deleted*]
[(6) Bathing Dresses for Hedli, me & Dan – or at least for one of us *deleted*]
(7) Bartholomew's map – Ireland sheet 3 – 'Connemara & Sligo'.
(8) old ruck-sack – or sacks.
(9) foolscap (wad of)
(10) one pair of sheets.
(11) If Betty likes to bring her bicycle (which would go on top of the Westport bus) H. says it would be very useful to her.
(12) Any old copies of the English weeklies – especially Statesman & Times Lit. – for the last month or so.
(13) SOAP. (toilet & washing).
(14) Your own ration books.

That's all we can think of for the moment. We're looking forward immensely to seeing you.

By the way, Dan's fairly easy to recognise. About average height (or a shade under) for 11, with very dark curly hair & dark eyes. We'll describe you to him anyway.

Must end this hastily.

Hasta la vista,

Louis

* He should have one trunk & one small sort of attaché case.

TO *E. R. Dodds*

<small>MS Bodleian</small>

31 July [1945]   Sandy Bank, Keel, Achill, Co. Mayo

Dear E.R.D.,

Just had your letter suggesting a meeting yesterday! I hope anyway you stayed in the house (at present occupied by my secretary). Dan was to pass through London yesterday on his way to Ireland; so maybe you saw him?

I look forward immensely to hearing about those States. Glad you liked Virginia.[1] She must be the only girl that side of the Atlantic who doesn't use lipstick.

We return to England at the beginning of September. Hedli had a sort of breakdown in April, hence our prolonged stay in the ould country.[2] But all of us are now blooming, full of eggs & ozone. During the last 2 months I have written eleven poems (after a year long lull).[3] I also reread the Bacchae in your ed., learning a lot from the notes.[4]

What do you think of the Elections? The hounds of Laski dancing the baskerville . . . ?[5]

Reggie Smith is due soon. & Wystan said he'd be back in London in August. When I saw him he seemed a shade shut up in himself.

Have you read Koestler's 'The Yogi & the Commissar'?[6] There at least is someone who's got something to say.

I wish one could either live in Ireland or feel oneself in England. It must be one of them ould antinomies.

Greetings from all to all,

Yours ever,
Louis

TO *Ruth Jones*[7]   MS Bodleian

8 August [1945]   Sandy Bank, Keel, Achill, Co. Mayo

Dear Ruth,

Here at long last is the draft script of the Dark Tower.[8] There's no great hurry for the typing – if you're working for Laurence; I'd rather not have anyone do it who's going to get my writing all wrong.

---

1 – Virginia Soskin (née Howell), FLM's cousin.
2 – See FLM to LG, 17 April 1945, above.
3 – These included 'Carrick Revisited', 'Last before America' and 'Under the Mountain' (Stallworthy, 335).
4 – Euripides, *The Bacchae*, ed. with intro. and commentary by E. R. Dodds (Oxford, 1944). Dodds's extensive commentary runs to nearly 200 pages.
5 – The Conservative Party was ousted in the 1945 elections by a landslide Labour vote. Harold Laski (1893–1950): editor of the Left Book Club, LSE political scientist, chairman of the Labour Party 1945–6.
6 – Arthur Koestler, *The Yogi and the Commissar* (1945).
7 – Ruth Winawer (née Jones), FLM's BBC secretary (1943–8). She was very loyal to FLM and later wrote to Gilliam: 'He was the only completely honest person I've ever known – I think that is why so many people find him disconcerting. I can't believe he's gone.' Ruth Winawer to LG, 17 Sept. 1963, *Ms BBC*.
8 – *The Dark Tower* was published by Faber and Faber in 1947.

I'd like a good number of carbons; please send me one & keep the top copy in office; send one carbon to Tony[1] (that is, if Laurence agrees to him composing). Tell him that, as before, I want the music done with the greatest economy – no long chunks on its own.[2] And it's v. important that the Challenge Call (trumpet or other solo instrument) should be the sort of thing that makes one's hair stand up. The Music in the Tavern Scene should of course be banal, while the Forest music should be sinister – shivering twigs & murmuring shadows.

Your letter of 1st came yesterday. Thank you very much for doing the N.Y.T. articles. 'eristics' & 'Weltanschauung' were right; the 3rd dubious word was 'static'.

Sorry that you're overworked & having to hold so many hands. Some odd hands at that. Why Rayner Heppenstall?[3]

I hope you got our wire of congratulation on Dan. H., I think, wrote you further about it. He arrived here on Friday (having stayed with Denis Johnston in Dublin) in v. good spirits & none the worse for wear. I'd never imagined his transport was going to cause so much trouble. This bottleneck is a new thing. Very clever of you in the circumstances to get him a sailing ticket. Do let me know at once if I owe you money for him.

Glad you're staying in the house till we get back. Colman R.I.P.[4]

Am just vetting 3 Northern scripts, so feel virtuous.

All best wishes,
Louis

P.T.O.

[overleaf]

P.S. I fancy Laurence will see the point of this script even as it lies on the page but, if it frightens or puzzles anyone else in the Corp., they should be told that both in Radio Times billing & in opening announcement I can easily pave the way so that the public know what to expect & don't feel

---

1 – Untraced.
2 – Benjamin Britten composed the music for the play.
3 – John Rayner Heppenstall (1911–81), broadcaster, experimental novelist and critic. Educ. local schools in Huddersfield; Collège Sophie-Berthelot, Calais; University of Leeds; University of Strasbourg. He had joined Features after the war where he worked as producer 1945–67. His novels include *The Blaze of Moon* (1939), *Lesser Infortune* (1953), *Greater Infortune* (1960) and *The Woodshed* (1962). He published also a critical study, *Raymond Roussel* (1966) and several volumes of memoirs: *Four Absentees* (1960), *The Intellectual Part* (1963) and *Portrait of the Artist as a Professional Man* (1969).
4 – Untraced.

they're being fooled. i.e. they must accept it as a play in a <u>dream</u> framework & then – in a dream way, of course – they should find it perfectly 'logical'.

With the carbon, can you return me the Mss.

TO *T. S. Eliot*   Faber archive

16 October 1945   BBC

<u>PERSONAL</u>
Dear Eliot,

Miss Grenside wrote to me on the 13th September welcoming on your behalf my offer for publication of a selection of radio plays. I herewith am sending you five pieces, namely 'The Nosebag', 'Sunbeams in his Hat', 'The March Hare Resigns', 'The Story of my Death', and 'The Dark Tower' (the last named being a draft and not word perfect), to be published in that order.[1] I am sending you the attached scripts in the form in which they were broadcast, but I should of course want to re-write the directions, supplying at least an illusion of the visual element. I should also like to add a few notes per play, and probably a general introduction. The five pieces I have selected seem to me between them to run through the whole gamut or something [sic]; here follow a few preliminary remarks about each:-

(1)   'The Nosebag'. This is based pretty closely on a traditional Russian folk tale.

(2)   'Sunbeams in his Hat'. This is based almost entirely on fact, even some of the lines having been actually uttered by Chekhov himself. One of my objects in writing this was to correct the popular conception of Chekhov as an essentially dour personality. In this as in the other scripts some of the transitions, especially in cases of flash-back, may appear to you very abrupt and perhaps confusing. I shall remedy this in my version for publication.

(3)   'The March Hare Resigns', an essentially topical programme, written in and for the spring of this year. This kind of satirical fantasy, however, seems to me to read quite well afterwards.

1 – *The Nosebag* was broadcast 13 March 1944; *Sunbeams in His Hat* 16 July 1944, rpt. 17 Aug. 1945; *The March Hare Resigns* 29 March 1945; *The Story of My Death* 8 Oct. 1943; *The Dark Tower* 21 Jan. 1946 (later broadcast on 30 Jan. 1950, rpt. 16 May 1951) (all on BBC Home Service).

(4) 'The Story of my Death', a dramatised biography of Lauro de Bosis.[1] This is the only one of the five which could be described as propaganda. It does, however, stick close to the main facts of de Bosis's life, and he does seem to me a very interesting character. Incidentally, the quotations from his own verse play are taken from the standard English translation, and are not, I think, as English very attractive. I might possibly re-write these.

(5) 'The Dark Tower', a parable or morality play. This is the only one of the five which is written in verse, or perhaps I should say off-verse. It has not yet been broadcast, and is merely a draft, but I myself think it the best of the lot. For publication, however, it will need perhaps more than the others special directions to compensate for the effects which on the air I will get by special acoustics, etc., etc.

If you fancy publishing these five in a volume, I can straight away fall to and make a readable version of them.

With best wishes

Yours

Louis MacNeice

P.S. Inspired by Eddie Sackville-West's example it has just occurred to me that it might be rather pleasant to have illustrations to such a book, i.e. one illustration per play.[2]

1 – Lauro de Bosis (1901–31), Italian poet, aviator and anti-fascist; killed when his plane, from which he had been scattering anti-Mussolini propaganda over Rome, ran out of fuel and crashed.

2 – Edward Charles Sackville-West, fifth Baron Sackville (1901–65), first cousin of the writer Vita Sackville-West. Author and critic, he joined BBC Features in 1939 and wrote regularly for the *NS*. An accomplished pianist and a close friend of Benjamin Britten's, he collaborated with him on *The Rescue* (1942). Author of *Mandrake over the Water Carrier* (1928), *Simpson: A Life* (1931), *A Flame in Sunlight: The Life and Work of Thomas De Quincey* (1936), and other books. He was co-author of *The Record Guide* (1951) with the music critic Desmond Shawe-Taylor.

1946

TO *Major Edward Lowbury*[1]

15 January 1946   BBC

Dear Major Lowbury

Thank you for your letter of the 8th December, asking about the collection of poems which you sent to Hutchinsons.[2] On referring to my files, I am very pleased to find that you were the only competitor who I thought could be properly given a prize (it was not my doing that you didn't get one).

It is a long time since I saw these poems, but I remember definitely getting a kick out of some of them. I will quote what I wrote at the time about them:-

'Lynceus

It surprised me, after reading some of the other MSS, to come across a competitor who not only interested me throughout, but on occasions also excited me. The great point about Lynceus is that he speaks with his <u>own</u> voice, being original in thought, observation and expression; he does both <u>feel</u> and <u>think</u>. At times he appears somewhat uncouth, and his rhythms are often roughish and sometimes irregular, but this I think is because he is writing <u>as himself</u> and not like most of the other competitors, derivatively, and throughout all his awkwardnesses and colloquialisms he does maintain a certain dignity. It is specially to be noted that he uses imagery functionally, and economically, instead of just sticking it in as decoration. Among the poems I particularly liked were "Ground Mist", "Language of the Dead", "Burning Question", "The Son", "Depths" and

1–Edward Joseph Lister Lowbury (1913–2007), bacteriologist and poet. Educ. University College, Oxford (Newdigate Prize, 1934); Royal London Hospital. RAMC (Maj.), Kenya (1943–6); Head of Bacteriology, Medical Research Council, Birmingham (1949–79). Author of *The Control of Hospital Infection* (1975) and volumes of poetry, including *Port Meadow* (1936), *Crossing the Line* (1947), *Metamorphoses* (1958), *Time for Sale* (1961), *New Poems* (1965), *Daylight Astronomy* (1968), *Green Magic* (1972), *Selected and New Poems, 1935–1989* (1990). Obit. *Guardian*, 15 Oct. 2007.
2–Hutchinson published Lowbury's *Crossing the Line* in 1947, the manuscript of which had been submitted for a poetry competition of which FLM was a judge.

"Reflection on Reflection", but there was hardly a poem which did not seem to me to have something to it.'

I am very glad to hear that they are being published and shall be delighted to have a copy if your sister will send me one.

From what I have heard about the place, I get your point about the dearth of 'professional opinion' in Kenya.

> With best wishes,
> Yours sincerely
> Louis MacNeice

TO *Hector MacIver*[1]   MS National Library of Scotland

5 February 1946   BBC / Reference: 03/F/LmacN [*sic*]

Dear Hector,

Thank you very much for your letter and for the additional poems by Sydney Smith. I hope to do something about his collection pretty soon.[2]

By the way, I have joined a Committee for making Rockefeller awards (approximately for about £300 for one year) to struggling writers. They want to have a sort of panel of about 40 'advisers' in different parts of the country. I have recommended you as one of the Scottish representatives (original work in Gaelic will also be considered).

Hedli and I very much enjoyed having you to stay with us, and hope you will make another visit soon.

> With best wishes,
> Yours ever
> Louis

1 – Addressed to MacIver at 26 Briarbank Terrace, Edinburgh 11.
2 – He asked TSE to look at them, as we see from the following letter. Sydney Goodsir Smith (1915–75) was a Scottish poet and playwright, often employing in his poems a variety of Scots dialect. Born in New Zealand, he attended Edinburgh University and Oriel College, Oxford. Author of *Skail Wind* (1941), *The Devil's Waltz* (1946), *Selected Poems* (1947) and other works.

5 February 1946   BBC

Dear Eliot,

A great friend of mine has handed over to me a collection of lyrics in Scottish dialect. I find them very striking, and wonder if you would like to have a look at them on behalf of Fabers. If published in book form they would almost certainly need a glossary. At the same time they are not so esoteric as Hugh MacDiarmid.

My wife and I would be delighted if you could come and have dinner with us some time towards the end of February or beginning of March. I know you are always beset with engagements, but could you let me know if you have a free evening anywhere.

Yours ever
Louis MacNeice

1947

TO *Corinna MacNeice*[1]   MS Bodleian

Postmark 9 May 1947   'ROMA – Museo Capitolino – Lupa
                                 con Romolo e Remo' [postcard]

JOLLY WOLF.
    The 2 little boys are called Romulus & Remus.
                                 Love
                                 DADDIE

TO *Ruth Jones*   MS Bodleian

26 May [1947]   Villa Bressani, Brissago[2]

Dear Ruth,
    I ought to have answered your queries before but this place is a bit lotus-
eating.
    I don't think any of those 3 Alwyn songs are right for a Northampton-
shire programme but if Bill himself wants one used, I would suggest the
Carol.[3] But I'd rather they left them alone.
    No, I don't want to take any part in the James Stephens programme. I
don't admire J.S. all that much & besides I'm sure I'd find it very difficult
speaking Iremonger narration.
    Could you ask Bertie (if he agrees) to suggest to Laurence that our great
Eire expedition should begin in good time in July rather than in August.[4]

---

1 – See FLM to BCM, 15 Sept. 1961, n. 2, p. 682.
2 – Switzerland; the home of Hedli's parents on the banks of Lake Maggiore.
3 – William Alwyn (1905–85), composer. Educ. Northampton GS, Royal Academy of Music.
Principal flautist, London Symphony Orchestra.
4 – W. R. 'Bertie' Rodgers (1910–69), poet, clergyman and broadcaster. Educ. QUB; Pres-
byterian minister in Co. Armagh until 1946, when he joined the BBC. Elected to Irish
Academy of Letters 1951. Poet in residence, Pitzer College, California, 1967–9. Author of
Awake! and Other Poems (1941), *Europa and the Bull* (1952), *Collected Poems* (1971). FLM
admired his poetry, claiming he and Robert Graves were among 'the best British poets of our
time', partly because they 'have never been plausibly classifiable' ('Poetry needs to be subtle

July will be much freer of trippers & the August date was only suggested because of Puck Fair, which I don't think we're now going to cover.

I'm delighted that my Rome project is really coming off.[1] [Foa?] calls himself George Ronald Hill in Italy & is described in the Roman press as 'il famoso direttore del B.B.C.' My address till further notice will be

c/o. G. R. Hill,

RAI, Ufficio Prosa,

Via Asiago / Roma.

Hedli & the children will be arriving back in London on Tuesday evening (29th). Could you sometime check the date of that Oxford Poetry Soc. do & let both Hedli & me know. (I put it in the diary.)

Yesterday we went up a mountain with Dan. Very gruelling but we found little white crocuses growing bang on the top of it. Spring however seems already nearly over here. The fruit blossom shoots itself off in one great salvo & that's that.

We have seen no sign of il famoso direttore e magnifico artista cinematigrafico Walter Rilla but maybe he stays in one of the many rich houses scattered along the feet of the mountains.[2] We did overhear a male German voice singing Lieder in a pension but I fancy Walter would only talk or sing Eton & Christ Church in these parts.

If Laurence wants me to do anything apart from this Window on Rome, between Italy & Ireland, could you tell him that I'm prepared to knock off an Appointment with Fear (as discussed), entitled the Golden Voice – but I would, if M.W.[3] doesn't mind, prefer to produce it myself. Which will emphasise the contrast that Martin himself said he wanted.

Well, don't do too much for Reggie; May's a bad month for breakdowns. Have you, by the way, done any research on the repeats of my programmes

—

and tough', *Highlights of Modern Literature*, ed. F. Brown, 1954, 159). He appears as Gorman in *AS*.

1 – *Portrait of Rome* (60 min.), broadcast 22 June 1947. Other than the Rome programme, FLM wrote three scripts in 1947: *The Death of Gunnar* and *The Burning of Njal*, broadcast in March, and *Grettir the Strong*, broadcast in July.

2 – Walter Rilla (1894–1980), German actor who emigrated to Britain in the 1930s, and played many secondary roles in British, German and US films, including *The Scarlet Pimpernel* (1934), *The Adventures of Tartu* (1942), *The Face of Fu Manchu* (1965) and *The Girl from Rio* (1969).

3 – Martyn C. Webster, BBC producer.

etc. last year? I shall want to do a Filthy Lucre memo to Laurence sometime.

> arrividerci a Rothwell[1]
> (sometime),
> Yours ever,
> Louis

TO *T. S. Eliot* Faber archive

12 June [1947?]   BBC, Belfast

Dear Eliot,

Thank you for your letter inquiring about my 'autobiographical work' (so long ago contracted for). I had written three quarters of this by 1941 but, thanks to my own & other people's history since, I want to redo the whole thing. It will certainly forthcome in time but N.B. it isn't strictly 'autobiographical'. I am selecting 3 or 4 contemporary themes – intercut with each other – & illustrating them from my own experience and/or observation. It will now be a much less brittle book but I hope it will make up in total pattern & meaning for what it may thus lose in surface entertainment value.

I shall probably be in Ireland for the next fortnight – if not longer. The above address should find me.

> in haste,
> with best wishes,
> Louis MacNeice

TO *T. S. Eliot* Faber archive

11 July [1947]   BBC

Dear Eliot,

Following our correspondence & conversation I am sending you the enclosed list of contents of my new book.[2] The great bulk of it is already in typescript &, <u>if</u> I have not completed the uncompleted poems, before I leave for India (August 5th), I shall send you the rest as it stands (i.e. easily enough poems to make a book).[3] Could you possibly get your people to

---

1 – Rothwell House, BBC, London.
2 – *HS* (published 7 May 1948).
3 – FLM flew to Delhi for the BBC in August to cover the transfer to independence.

provide a contract for this immediately? I have just had a startling communication from my bank which means I must raise as much money as I can during this month. As my secretary is absent ill, I can't find my last Faber's contract but I seem to remember that you gave me £50 advance. The same again would suit me admirably. If on the other hand it was only £25 last time, could you either raise it to £50 or advance me the additional £25 to be balanced against my royalties in general? (This is all due to an unfortunate synchronisation of bills – hospital, school fees, income tax etc. – all of which I settled unthinkingly!)

I'm sorry we couldn't have more talk at the Sesame yesterday & am hoping we can meet again before I fly away to the East.

Yours ever
Louis MacNeice

TO *Hedli MacNeice*   MS Bodleian

10 August [1947]   Hotel Cecil, Delhi[1]

Darling,

I hope you got the 2 cables I sent. I reached here yesterday (Saturday) evening after having made with V. Thomas a frustrated effort to get here a day earlier in time for that social do (which turns out after all not to have been so important).[2] India – so far – is not too hot & this hotel is luxurious. But, to give you a resume of our journey:-

Wednesday: Very smooth flight across France (me feeling v. upset, however, about that Gargoyle business[3] for which I hope you've forgiven me, Cat – I really didn't mean no harm) but oh I forgot; we missed the Airways bus at Victoria & had to race to London Airport in a B.B.C. car, only just making it. We didn't stop anywhere till Castel Benito (which is

1 – FLM went with Wynford Vaughan Thomas, Jack Dillon and support staff to report on the transfer to independence of India and Pakistan. On 6 August he flew to New Delhi, where he was based for the first month, also visiting Agra, Lahore and Peshawar. He visited Kashmir in September and in October he went to Calcutta, Benares, Lucknow, Madras, Trichinopoly, Madurai, Trivandrum and Cape Comorin in the south. He returned home in the second week of November (see Stallworthy, 354–66). Of a sequence of nineteen letters to Hedli, I have reproduced ten.

2 – (Lewis John) Wynford Vaughan-Thomas (1908–87) ('V.T.'). Author and broadcaster, educ. Swansea GS (a friend of Dylan Thomas) and Exeter College, Oxford. Joined the BBC in the 1930s and became a well-known war correspondent. He filed broadcasts from India in 1947. He is Evans in *AS*.

3 – Gargoyle, a club on Meard Street, Soho, founded in 1925 by David Tennant. 'Cat' was FLM's pet name for Hedli.

near Tripoli), where we had tea.[1] Got to Cairo at nearly midnight – another luxurious hotel, rather Phillips Oppenheim.[2]

Thursday: The B.B.C. chap in Cairo found there were 2 seats on a much earlier plane which we could transfer to, so after much argument V.T. & I took them, leaving Jack & Mr Graham[3] (who has confirmed our worst suspicions) behind. I was sorry not to see more of Cairo which really seems a jolly sort of Arabian Nights jumble (architecture shocking). Anyhow we soared away over a lot of desert & the Dead Sea & some very crude completely naked hills & ran into a dust storm which meant we couldn't go on to Basra but had to be diverted up north to a place called Habbaniya (about 50 miles from Bagdad [sic])[4]. This, I would say, is about the most God-awful place I've ever seen. Arid to the nth degree &, as the dust storm was on there too, we felt we were in an oven breathing grit. It's not really a civil airport at all but an R.A.F. place. We were given a filthy meal in the mess, where we eavesdropped on a conversation between an Irish R.A.F. doctor (just arrived there for 2 years, poor chap) & an elderly one-armed American who had also come in our plane & thought V.T. & I were in Standard Oil. Well, he also thought that Habbaniya was in India & when told not at all, it was in Irak [sic] near the Euphrates, said 'Ah yes, yes, the New Britain.' Seriously, you understand. And I missed this but V.T. also overheard him commenting on the Egyptian fez & saying it was the badge of the Knights of Columbus or some such American organisation & that he guessed some smart business man must have sold it to the Egyptians.[5] Seriously again, N.B. After our filthy supper we had to wait for an O.K. to proceed, so V.T. & I found a dartboard & invented a Gilliam Cup to play each other for but were unable to get a double to end our final game. So feeling v. ashamed of our darts & it then being dark & cooler & little coloured lights outside the mess on the only patch of grass in Habbaniya, we sat in deckchairs drinking rye-&-dry & looking at the bats and listening to the R.A.F. officers v. tight telling each other the worst jokes we had heard in years. But I dare say, if one lived in Habbaniya long, one's standard of wit would be nowhere. So at 2 a.m. we took the air again but, instead of going straight to Karachi as we'd hoped, had to go down to

1 – Castel Benito, airport and RAF base for Tripolitania (Libya).
2 – Edward Phillips Oppenheim (1886–1946), who wrote novels about wealthy British expatriates living on the French Riviera.
3 – Vaughan-Thomas, Jack Dillon and Sean Graham. There was tension between FLM and Graham throughout the trip.
4 – RAF Habbaniya, Iraq, which operated from 1936 to 1959.
5 – The fez is worn on certain occasions by members of the American philanthropic group, the Shriners.

Basra after all to collect a stretcher case. Got to B. in a couple of hours & had breakfast while it was still dark in the airport hotel: tomato juice, bacon & eggs. After which it all got light v. quickly & we heard what we hoped was a bulbul[1] & all the Irakians began coming v. leisurely to work, reminding one again of illustrations to the Arabian Nights, especially the women in black with pitchers on their heads etc. And lots of Arabs by the way sleeping all anywhere on the ground. By the time we got started again, we realised we'd never make the Delhi party, so resigned ourselves to staying that night (Friday night) in Karachi. Flew over some more v. savage hills to discover the first bit of India looking itself pretty pure desert. Were decanted there in the afternoon & driven into the town past lots of camels drawing huge nondescript loads. Jack & Mr. G. turned up that evening & had a good laugh at us. Karachi seemed singularly unexcited for a place which next week will become the temporary capital of a brand new country.[2] On Sat. morning we drove round it a bit in a 'garry' (horse-drawn vehicle) & really got the pell-mellness which one's always heard of as India. Thousands of people enormously varied & most of them appearing to have infinite time, some of them – like the cows – lying down on the pavements. Some v. savage faces & some v. classical (especially the bearded ones). Took off again about 2 p.m. & got to Delhi airport about 7, but that's about 10 miles from the city & we hired 2 taxis which broke down, so only got here in the 3rd where we had for dinner a v. good fish called becktie & some pretty good but too, too expensive whisky drinks. The B.B.C. 2nd string here had dinner with us & warned us that Mountbatten wants to see Jack & me shortly to tell us his views on this feature project.[3] So this morning we bought a lot of newspapers to educate ourselves & found them full of letters urging that cow slaughter shall be now made illegal throughout India. Also full of the English County Cricket scores. // Later (Monday): Have to go shortly to a cocktail party at the Viceroy's House. For which reason we went shopping this morning; plenty of clothes such as shirts etc. but no good ducks (I'm still livid about the ones I left at Tilty!)[4] We also went into the Red Fort (see 'The Legacy of India' which I'm sure must mention it in the chapter on Muslim

1 – A kind of thrush, known as the 'Persian nightingale' for its song.
2 – India would declare independence and Pakistan would be inaugurated on 14/15 Aug.
3 – Lord Louis Mountbatten (1900–79), first Earl Mountbatten of Burma, naval officer and Viceroy of India. The 'feature project' was the programme they were preparing on the transfer of power, *The Road to Independence*, India and Pakistan No. 6, broadcast 23 May 1948.
4 – The MacNeices rented Tilty Hill House, Tilty, nr Dunmow, Essex from March 1946 to the summer of 1947.

architecture).[1] The outer walls are a terrific rose-red colour & inside there are some quite staggeringly lovely buildings – much better than I'd expected but I understand there are few such. I got a v. nice letter from a pal of John Auden's[2] here but have been unable to ring him up yet as, since we've reached Delhi, the whole telephone system has been out of order; this is often the case, they say; instead of even trying to dial people just send bearers (there is no servant shortage here!)

The monsoons so far have been failing; two heavy showers since we got here but through most of India there's been v. little rain which of course may lead to disaster. // Later (Tuesday): Yesterday evening was a great success. The party at the Viceroy's House (Lutyens Odeon)[3] was a wonderful mix-up of people ranging from the Head Prefect of Marlborough in my time[4] to a poetess, Mrs Sarojini Naidu,[5] who is Governess Designate of the United Provinces & was v. disappointed to find that I had not a blue beard (somebody here must have made some crack about me which they all took literally). Anyhow old Mrs S.J. has invited me to stay with her at Lucknow. She roared into laughter when I told her how unhelpful Krishna Merrion had been to me at the Arts Theatre Club. Apparently he's just as rude to all his Congress colleagues themselves. Also present was the sister of Lys Connolly, who is married to the Viceroy's P.R.O. And there was a band playing period tunes such as Old Man River which seemed appropriate as this was one of the last functions in the <u>Viceroy's</u> House as such. Have just by the way finished re-reading Passage to India which even Indians agree is the truest picture of the country.[6]

From this party we called on Mr Sinclair (John Auden's friend) who turned out to be a charmer, v. cultivated & unexpectedly employed by Shell. Vaughan Thomas, who hadn't realised this, launched a long,

1 – Martin S. Briggs, 'Muslim Architecture in India', in G. T. Garrett (ed.), *The Legacy of India* (Oxford, 1937), 223–55. The seventeenth-century Red Fort complex (variant name Lal Quila) was built on the eastern side of Shahjahanabad, in Delhi.

2 – John Bicknell Auden (1903–91), elder brother of WHA. Educ. MC 1917–22 and Cambridge. Himalayan mountaineer and sometime president of the Presidency College, Calcutta. Engineering geologist in India 1945–51; employed by Burmah Oil Company 1956–60.

3 – Sir Edwin Landseer Lutyens (1869–1944), OM, KCIE, PRA, FRIBA, LLD, designed the Viceroy's Lodge, New Delhi (inaugurated 1931). New Delhi is sometimes called 'Lutyens' Delhi'.

4 – G. E. B. Abell, see FLM to GBM, 5 Nov. 1921, n. 3, and FLM to Eva Greer, 31 Aug. 1923, n. 1, pp. 56, 82.

5 – Sarojini Naidu (1879–1949), poet, feminist, first woman President of the Indian National Congress. Educ. Madras, KCL and Girton College, Cambridge. Known as the 'Nightingale of India'.

6 – E. M. Forster, *A Passage to India* (1924).

heartfelt & v. eloquent tirade against business men. We sat on a lawn in the dark having drinks & Sinclair said he could arrange for me to meet Dalmia who is the great Cow Champion (& also a highly successful industrialist).[1]

We left S. after midnight &, not having had any dinner, had a time looking for somewhere to eat. In the end we found a wee Muslim place, a sort of broken down robber's castle from a fairy story where we sat under the sky in a courtyard & the cooking was done on a wee platform in the corner & a chap lay irrelevantly asleep on a sort of shelf. Here we had some curry which sent V.T. off on another tirade; he considered it hell-fire.

Must stop this now, cat dearest, or it will never get posted. (I bought some better air mail paper today for future use.) If you write to me c/o B.B.C., New Delhi it will get forwarded. I shall be here till 21st & then to Agra for a couple of days, then back through Delhi & up north towards the hills. Shall leave Calcutta, Bombay & such places till later as they are much hotter than here. As regards heat the sun of course is more often than not clouded over but so far I haven't found it as walloping as during that heat wave last year in October. In fact the temperature is probably much higher but it's quite tolerable, especially with all these electric fans about.

I do hope, darling, things in London are going smartly & that Teresa will arrive soon.[2] If you want any help about the house I'm sure either Laurence or Reggie would oblige.[3] I wish you didn't have to do the move while I'm away but you can perfectly well claim compensation from Laurence for that! (Though now I'm here, I think it's good to have arrived before the 15th. Will let you know all about that occasion in my next). I miss you v.v. much, cat. <u>Do write me a lot</u>. Molti baci & all my love. And please be <u>happy</u>.

Louis

1 – Seth Ramkrishna Dalmia, 'Mr Big No. 3 of Indian Big Business'. He owned many cement factories in India, an airline, a bank and six newspapers, and called himself 'President of the Cow Protection League'. See 'Long Live Cows', *Time*, 11 Aug. 1947.
2 – Teresa Moroni, Hedli's new Italian maid. She was later replaced by a maid from Ischia called Restituta.
3 – Gilliam and Smith, respectively.

TO *Hedli MacNeice*   MS Bodleian

16 August [1947]   As from BBC, New Delhi

Dearest Cat,

I was overjoyed to get your letter (hope you have by now received my first). <u>Have</u> you found your glasses yet? If not, did you try (a) Rothwell, (b) The Stag, (c) Jack's Club (d) The Gargoyle?!

I think it's probably a good idea making the puppet boy cockney. R. Campbell <u>might</u> be some use in the business.[1] I should think with all these pending programmes etc. I'll be back on you before you notice!

Life here is pretty busy too but we've discovered it's no good relying on the B.B.C. They can't even lay on transport for one (which is essential in this v. spread-out city where there are no buses etc). Thanks to their inefficiency I missed just about 50% of the Independence Day dos I had tickets for. They've also been singularly tactless with Jarvis, the engineer attached to V. Thomas. Jarvis who's had to do all the business of his van single-handed is now, v. naturally, throwing temperament. Stimson the head chap here has only just reappeared from Karachi & is just leaving for Bombay; he appears to be only interested in his own newscasts & leaves the administration to the 2nd man, Moseley. M. is a fat young man, v. affable & not unamusing but no administrator; he is also the worst driver I've met in years. However this is all boring (through their incompetence – but don't mention it to Laurence – wastes a great deal of our time & energy). To return to India proper:-

All the Indians I've met so far have been amazingly friendly (this goes also for stray chaps in the street) – which apparently contrasts strongly with their attitude a few months ago. Mountbatten (now cheered as <u>Pandit</u> Mountbatten) is a popular hero & even the B.B.C. van, I hear, got some cheers from the crowd yesterday.[2] All the Indians on the other hand do not like each other. It seems communal differences have been getting worse rather than better. This week the road to the railway station has been cluttered with bullock carts carrying people's household goods away to Pakistan. Though among the higher-up quite a lot of the administrative types leaving are leaving under pressure <u>from Pakistan</u> which is v. short of

1 – Roy Campbell (1901–57), South African poet, who worked briefly as producer with the BBC.
2 – 'Pandit': a learned or great man. *The Times* reported: 'Scenes of jubilation and expressions of good will towards Great Britain marked the establishment in Delhi yesterday of the new Dominion of India.' 'India's First Day of Independence. Jubilant Scenes in Delhi. Public Ovation for Lord Mountbatten', *The Times*, 16 Aug. 1947, 4.

administrators & are v. sad about it as their families have been here for centuries. (Interruption at this point: 2 ladies – one English, one Indian – but both in saris & with Hindu caste marks, arrived with books for me to autograph). Re. Pakistan, there's an English girl secretary at the B.B.C. here who's married a Muslim veterinary expert who is evacuating himself to Pakistan to work for the government there. We gave them dinner the other night in this hotel, when he explained to us that the partition of India is final. Hinduism, he said, 'abhors my inside'. After which, speaking as a good vet, he bitterly attacked Dalmia the great advocate of Cow Protection (whom he represented as a racketeer; it's certainly v. odd that Dalmia, an out-&-out Hindu <u>but</u> a friend of Jinnah's,[1] should at this moment be investing lots of money in Pakistan, buying up among other things a Pakistan paper.) Well, the very next day I had the most fantastic interview with Dalmia himself in his luxury mansion (he is more or less the Henry Ford of India). (Interruption till Monday morning. People keep hectically rushing us about & we spend hours waiting for transport. Also late nights.) To return, I found myself in a v. westernised drawing room with heavy gold mouldings on the ceiling sitting on a blue silk sofa beside this extra-ordinary little man who keeps making nervous movements with his hands. Opening question from me: 'This campaign of yours for cow protection, is it primarily religious or economic?' Answer from D: 'My dear young man, you cannot separate things like that. Everything is one. Religious . . . economic . . . they are the same thing.'[2] Upon which I wondered where do we go from here. Where we went in fact was to Dalmia's scheme for world government: a benevolent autocrat (himself?) elected by a committee of all the peoples. And no more democracy, which has been disproved in the West. A decent standard of living guaranteed for all but no limits on private enterprise as it is only just & kind that a hard working man should be able to accumulate luxuries for his children (D., I'm told, has 8 wives). 'But I am a very courageous man, I follow my own ideas.' And then, returning to the cow, the cow is like your mother, only more so; she <u>goes on</u> giving you milk. And even when she's past that & v. old, she still pays her way with her dung – 'I have statistics to prove that.' All Hindu customs in brief are strictly scientific: witness our caste system – You have heard of what Krishna says in the Gita – the 4 primary divisions of mankind? Well, you have also heard of this recent scientific discovery – the 4 different kinds of blood-stream. 4 & no more. Why 4? Why 4? Tell me.

1 – Mohammed Ali Jinnah (1876–1948), leader of the All India Muslim League, founder of Pakistan. Educ. Sind Madrassa; Christian Mission HS, Karachi; Lincoln's Inn.
2 – See his notes on the Dalmia interview in 'Indian Imps', which very much resemble what he says in this letter (*Indian Diary: Ms Bodleian, Ms Res, c. 1059*).

& so on & so on & so on. I managed to survive without getting the giggles. Many Hindus consider this whole cow crusade a stunt – to divert attention from D's sharp business deals with the Muslims & to reinstal [*sic*] him as a Hindu of the Hindus. He's v. much a selfmade man & started on 10 rupees a month! 'I am uneducated but I know 6 languages & in each language I can speak to one million people at a time. & I can hold them.' But to leave Dalmia & come to more important matters:-

On Aug. 14th I went to the Midnight Session of the Constituent Assembly, where India was declaring her Independence. In an enormous circular building (Lutyens of course) rather too hygienic looking but quite impressive. Sat high up in the Press Gallery looking down on the heads of the members seen through a white whirr of revolving standard fans. The members too predominantly white – nothing gaudy about the proceedings. Atmosphere in fact rather western. President's speech about as drab in delivery as any old Labour Party M.P. Nehru sympathetic but seemed tired (can you wonder!)[1] & in English a bit 'Varsity-cum-parsonical. But one v. good & rousing speech, stressing the need for humility, realism, tolerance etc. by Radakrishnan (who is a Fellow of All Souls!) After the last stroke of midnight they were all supposed to take an oath so some musical chimes (v. western) were laid on but unfortunately, to add the Eastern touch, someone blew a great baying conch in the middle of the chimes which just made the worst of both worlds. I was a shade disappointed by this session & thought the whole Independence do was going to fall a bit flat but this was adjusted the next day, the 15th. Jack & I had tickets for the Assembly again in the morning but instead stayed outside among the crowd who were waiting for Mountbatten's state drive. Huge, heterogeneous good humoured crowd but a lot of them, I think, not quite knowing what was happening – just a nice holiday fallen out of the sky. The state drive itself was quite fun with magnificent mounted lancers. Afterwards a gun salute – v. smart gun drill. But at 6 pm there was another ceremony where the crowd really went to town. Jack & I missed it owing to the usual transport muddle but V.T. who had the van there said he'd never seen anything like it. And by the way he & his van found themselves v. popular figures – which indeed is what we've all found everywhere so far.

When it was just dark we drove up on to the 'Ridge' which overlooks Delhi to watch some alleged fireworks. The fireworks never happened but we were shown Asoka's pillar[2] (B.C. monument) by some enthusiastic

1 – Jawaharlal Nehru (1889–1964), first Prime Minister of India 1947–64. Educ. Harrow and Trinity College, Cambridge.
2 – One of several such pillars built in the third century BC by Ashoka, a king of the Mauryan Empire.

Hindus who pressed election torches into our hands & were all affability & laughter . . . After which we returned to the hotel & dressed up rather sheepishly & went to a 10.15 p.m. reception at Government House. This seemed to be attended by half India but I got out in the gardens which were romantically illuminated & was there introduced to Nehru who is really a number one charmer. I said I supposed he was tired after dealing with the milling crowds at the flag-hoisting ceremony to which he replied that he's fond of crowds & when he sees a crowd he always has an impulse to rush into it & merge in it. But sometimes, he added, I have to rush <u>at</u> it & beat it. (This is literally true. They will take anything from him). He then invited me to lunch this Sunday but yesterday it had to be cancelled as he was called out of Delhi to a conference. However I hope to meet him again in the near future. He says he wants to have a change from talking politics.

On Saturday morning we got up horribly early to go to another flag-hoisting ceremony at the Red Fort. Crowd reckoned at 300 to 400 thousand! Though we had press tickets we weren't allowed <u>into</u> the Fort which greatly amused a lot of Indian reporters & press photographers who were in the same plight. Everyone v. good humoured but not v. noisy.

On Sat evening went to Sinclair's (John Auden's friend in Burma Oil) who had a party of mixed colours, including a tiny little alcoholic Indian rather like a brown Van der Gucht,[1] v. highbrow & friend of T. S. Eliot's, & a political Indonesian girl, v. beautiful, v. sophisticated & – oddly enough – v. tall. Also a Frenchwoman with sari & caste mark. Also some old style I.C.S.[2] Anyhow a good party in a nice garden – except that they made me read poems. Afterwards, about 11 p.m., Sinclair took us to dinner in a club where Jack sang a lot of his ballads & V.T. did a comedy act. After which it was found our car was punctured, so Sinclair drove us back to his place & we sat in the garden again having drinks till about 4.30 a.m. Jack & V.T. both went to sleep. So yesterday, 17th, we were all v. tired. But a little leftist-literary Indian came & took me away to a meeting of Progressive Writers, where troops of poets were reciting – or, more often singing – poems they'd composed for Independence (it's quite usual for Indian poets to sing their own words).[3] My sponsor's wife,

1 – Michael Van der Gucht (1660–1725), Dutch portraitist and engraver.
2 – Indian Civil Service.
3 – The Progressive Writers movement in India incorporated various Urdu groups, all broadly left-wing, anti-imperialist and anti-partitionist. Sajjad Zaheer arranged the first All-India Progressive Writers' Conference in Lucknow in 1936, with the support of Nehru and Sarojini Naidu.

poetess with red paint all along her parting (a Bengali custom), & a jewel in her nose recited a poem during which we noticed that her 2 year old daughter had followed her on to the platform & was raising her dress up & down to the audience, having nothing underneath it. The chairwoman, a member of the Constituent Assembly, suddenly & unexpectedly called upon me to convey the good wishes of British writers to Indian writers. So I limped on to the platform (my leg had gone to sleep) & conveyed the good wishes of British writers to Indian writers.

After this meeting I rejoined the other boys & went to dine with a westernised Indian couple – husband Hindu in All India Radio[1] & wife half American, half Muslim. But of course when we got there (they live in a block of flats) we found there was no question of dining for hours as the two of them had organised a singing-cum-dancing performance by schoolgirls, aged 12–15, on an improvised stage in the courtyard among the flats. Schoolgirls astonishingly elegant & graceful – they dance naively with their arms, v. liquid. We tried to imagine the same sort of thing in Dolphin Square but couldn't.[2]

I'm so sorry, darling, but I've been interrupted again & have to go now – damn all these 400 millions! But I'd better send this now or I'll never get it all [sic] today. <u>I wish you were here, Cat.</u>

Please be happy – & don't get rattled over houses & anything. I'm sure the boys will help you in any emergency.[3]

&, by the way, would you like to contact Mr & Mrs NARAYANA MENON[4] (B.B.C., 200 Oxford St), the nice ones who're coming here in September? You could, among other things, discuss Indian purchases with them!

All my love, darling,
L.

---

1 – All India Radio began 1936, expanded after 1947.
2 – Dolphin Square, fashionable block of flats in sw1, built in the 1930s.
3 – The boys: Smith and Gilliam.
4 – Dr Narayana Menon (b.1911), PhD (Edinburgh), former deputy director of All India Radio and music critic of the *Indian Statesman*. Mrs Menon was a niece of the poet Tagore.

TO *Hedli MacNeice*   MS Bodleian

19 August [1947] Letter 3   Still Cecil Hotel (but as from
                                   BBC, New Delhi)

Darling,

Would you mind keeping these letters all together somewhere as they
will remind me of things & so far I haven't had time to keep a diary etc.

Have just been studying a weather table in this morning's paper. Rainfall
since June 1st is way below normal in the great majority of places.
Temperature in Delhi during last 24 hours was 95 max., 78 min. (but in
Simla 68–60 which explains why the boys used to go there). I still think it's
v. lucky I got diverted to Habbaniya as compared with that, any heat I've
met in India itself is chickenfeed e.g. I was in the open air yesterday right
over the siesta period & it was perfectly tolerable. Looking at ancient
monuments. The plain to the south of here is just littered with ruins of
forts etc. & lots of fairly well preserved tombs (these 'tombs' being quite
large, sometimes huge, domed edifices in keeping with the dignity of the
Muslim conquerors). I went up a v. famous pillar (a good deal higher than
Nelson in Trafalgar Square) called the Kubb Minor,[1] it consists of a series
of superimposed cones of red sandstone, the whole thing deeply fluted, &
from the top you get a perfectly circular horizon (as at sea) owing to the
appalling flatness of this plain. The contents of this circle a mottle of
brown & green (more green than you'd expect; for a few months now they
have <u>grass</u>) & across this snakes of darker green which are the tree-lined
roads. And, ten miles away, a spatter of white which is Delhi (identifiable,
tell Elizabeth [*sic*][2]) & all around, nearer in, these sombre domes –
pepperpot or bellpush. When built of course, a lot of them weren't so
sombre as they were covered with lapis lazuli etc. What these
immeasurable relics ram home on one is that the Muslims – & especially
of course the Moghuls – had it their own way here. Last Friday in fact was
the first time the Hindus had had the say in Delhi since the dim ages. In
keeping with this there are practically no old <u>Hindu</u> buildings around. But
I feel that, like most Westerners, I'm going to prefer Muslim architecture
anyway – especially the earlier style before it got over decorated. I saw a

1 –Kutb Minar in South Delhi, over 72 metres high, tallest brick minaret in the world.
2 –The distinctive white buildings designed by Lutyens help to make the Delhi skyline from
a distance so 'identifiable'. Elisabeth Lutyens (1906–83), his daughter, was a well-known
composer whose many works included more than 200 radio scores (some in collaboration
with FLM). Coincidentally, her first husband was an OM whom FLM knew at school,
I. H. C. Glennie (FLM to AB, 23 Oct. 1926, n. 5, p. 132).

v. fine pre-Moghul mosque yesterday which for design & proportion beats most of our Christian pieces. And the arch they use in those earlier buildings – like this [*diagram*] – not so curving, you see, as Gothic, is much preferable to the Moorish arch you find in Spain which I always thought a little Hollywood.

Well, Delhi's fascinating historically but I think it's time we left it. Too much social life & capital cityness. Jack & I are going on Thursday to Agra for a couple of days & then returning to Delhi to stay the weekend with Sinclair. After which we snap out of it all but where I'm not quite sure yet. V. Thomas is away at the moment in the Punjab but is expected back tomorrow. I find him v. good company but he is perhaps too consistently ebullient for one to want him round all the time. This is not – curiously – true of Jack who is comparatively restful. At the moment, poor fellow, he's v. bronchial.

Last night we went to dinner with Tymbyi who is Secretary of the Constituent Assembly but – surprisingly – a Muslim. V. nice, intelligent man & he gave us the best meal I've yet had in India. Lots of exotic dishes to which you help yourself standing; you'd have enjoyed it. After which we had 'pan' of which there's a description in that book with the coloured cover.[1] Among the other guests was a donnish-looking old Congressman, Diwan Chaman Lall, who used to coedit with Aldous Huxley a highbrow periodical at Oxford.[2] These people all speak v. cultured English, whereas the 2nd grade of chaps – middle-class executives of different kinds – speak v. fluently but tend to overspice it with too many 'old chaps' & rather outmoded phrases like 'What the dickens!'

A nice thing about the houses here – however elegant – is that they all have lizards hiding behind the pictures on the walls. These lizards seem to match themselves to the colour of the walls & are welcomed because they keep down the insects (which in some places make a real aura, a nebula you might say, round the lights). As regards other fauna, tell Dan I haven't seen any monkeys or elephants yet but there was a man in the street yesterday leading a bear (one of many parallels to the Middle Ages in Europe) & I'm told that jackals come regularly into the suburban gardens of New Delhi. But the most noticeable beasts are (a) the ubiquitous white cattle which being sacred can ramble around where they like except when they're harnessed to carts – the bullocks have great humps against which

---

1 – Pan usually consists of a sweet mango paste wrapped in tobacco or betel leaf.
2 – Diwan Chaman Lall (1892–1973) read Law at Oxford and later became an Indian MP. The Oxford journal was *Coterie* (1919–21).

the yoke presses & (b) the water-buffalo which are black & broad in the beam & must get a terrible neurosis in Delhi as they're always wanting to get into water (driving out to Kubb I saw a pond full of them wallowing). There are also of course lots of rather evil hawks circling around; a v. large one with a round head was perched on a tree outside my room the other morning before people were up. By the way, there's another tree outside my room which is highly flamboyant & known as the golden mohur – geranium-coloured flowers & bright green ferny leaves.[1] Beyond it is the hotel swimming pool which I've been in 2 or 3 times but find too chlorinated.

A pity you didn't read Robert Byron's 'Essay on India'[,] though I've since discovered that some of his anti-British evidence was inaccurate e.g. with great indignation he tells how he saw a British official turn an Indian clerk out of a lift.[2] Well, the official turns out to have been Sinclair who has no race prejudice whatever & who stopped the clerk getting into the lift merely because it was full; what is more, Sinclair then got out & waited with the clerk on the landing for the next lift. S. says several of Byron's stories are as shaky as this; at the same time he thinks it a v. good book. S. also says that the Blimp type has been steadily disappearing from India since 1930; I must admit I haven't met any here myself. What amuses me is what Stimson (who knows India v. well) points out that upper-class Tories often go down better here than earnest Leftists – also says that British army officers were on the whole much more popular than the I.C.S. boys because they met the Indians more half way. But he adds that the I.C.S. were consistently courteous & that the gross examples of race prejudice were usually committed by British business men.

Haven't heard any more from you, Cat, since your first. Will you keep writing to the BBC, Delhi, as they'll know where to forward. They have 2 efficient – but rather wan – secretaries. English women don't seem to look attractive out here, though there is one v. pretty American girl corres-pondent of Life in this hotel (I suppose she's not been here long enough to get dried up).[3] The Indian standard of looks among men & women is, I

1 – The Gold Mohur tree (*Delonix regia*; aka flame tree, royal poinciana), grows up to fifty feet tall and is cultivated throughout the tropics.
2 – Robert Byron (1905–41), writer, traveller, art critic, and a contemporary of FLM at Merton College, where he read Modern History. Special correspondent in India for the *Daily Express* 1929. His 'An Essay on India' (1931) was praised by the Viceroy of India, Lord Willingdon.
3 – The American 'girl correspondent' is unidentified. Robert Neville was Bureau Chief in New Delhi for *Life*, the issue of which for 18 Aug. featured a cover portrait of Mountbatten, an article, 'India Gets its Freedom', and an editorial, 'Farewell to the Raj'. Their New Delhi photographer was David Douglas Duncan.

would say, v. high. There were some young Tommies in the crowd the other day &, as Jack pointed out, they looked conspicuously low caste. & personally I do find myself ashamed of the colour of my skin. Which reminds me: I hear that J. Auden's children have dark skins & fair hair![1] Nancy didn't mention that.

Dearest Cat, do write soon & tell me all about Tilty & the new house & Moroni? & Da Fella et al et al et al.[2] I want to write a poem for you soon.[3] Must stop now & gird for more interviews. All my love ever (& to Dan & Bimba).[4]

L.

Tell Dan I'll be writing to him. Also some postcards.

TO *Hedli MacNeice* MS Bodleian

25 August [1947] As from BBC, New Delhi / Letter 4

Darling,

I don't seem to have written for about a week – though in the meantime I've written (a) to Dan, which I hope he got, & (b) to Laurence, suggesting that the B.B.C. should think again about these features on India. Tomorrow Thank God – we leave Delhi for Peshawar, whence we shall go to Cashmir.[5] I understand communications are pretty unreliable from these parts, so if there's a longish gap before you get another letter, that will be the reason. I reckon on being back in Delhi about middle of September & shall stay about a week here (probably with Sinclair) to write a Portrait of Delhi.[6] The history involved is fascinating. Yesterday (Sunday) Tyubji the nice Muslim high-up I told you about, drove us in a V8 round several of the lost cities ending up in the fantastic massive ruins of a fort called Tughlukabad outside which I saw my first monkeys.[7] Gave one a mild turn

---

1 – In 1940 John Auden married Sheila Bonnerjee (granddaughter of the first president of the Indian National Congress); they had two daughters, Anita Benedetta (b.1941), educ. St Hugh's College, Oxford, and Rita Romola (1942–2008), educ. St Anne's College, Oxford.
2 – FLM and Hedli were about to leave Tilty for a new house in Canonbury Park.
3 – 'Letter from India (To Hedli)', in *HS* (1948).
4 – Bimba was FLM's pet name for Corinna.
5 – Peshawar, near entrance to the Khyber Pass; since 1947 the capital of Pakistan's North-West Frontier Province.
6 – *Portrait of Delhi*, India and Pakistan No. 3, broadcast BBC Home Service 2 May 1948.
7 – Tughlukabad, deserted since the fourteenth century, lies approximately ten miles from Delhi.

as the trees along the road were so v. green & park-like; it was like suddenly meeting them in St James' Park. The sky went v. dramatic with slatey rainclouds when we were in the fort making the landscape for the first time not monotonous. So we all got caught in a downpour & drove home sitting in pools of water. I was really rather sorry for Tyubji's wife, a tiny little decorative thing; a sari must be v. uncomfortable when you're wet through. In the late afternoon yesterday we went to a Muslim shrine with a real live holy man (with a pretty shrewd eye on him). Here without any warning their sun-down prayers began; as there's no minaret there, the call to prayer came from ground level ten yards from us & over-modelled like mad. The ritual's enormously impressive & involves great suppleness of body (would make nice exercises for Dan). And all such conviction, one really feels this is RELIGION.

But we've really had enough of Delhi – far too many social engagements, some of which Moseley[1] laid on for us without consulting us. No time to think or digest one's experiences. The last 2 nights Jack & I have stayed with Sinclair who (like everyone well-off, I suppose) seems to have an army of servants. They pop up out of the floor & try to put your socks on for you. Both Jack & I find this embarrassing. The lawn-mower by the way is worked not by one man but by three.

However we certainly have met a fascinating assortment of people here. For instance, Dewan Chamman [sic] Lall (whom I mentioned as A. Huxley's buddy at Oxford) who has asked me to stay with him at Simla (Jack will be staying in Simla at the same time but with Sikh financier).[2] Chamman Lall is a great intimate of Nehru's & has enormous charm & culture; the British, needless to say, repeatedly imprisoned him. Then I've met Cariappa, the new Indian top general, who has to be heard to be believed – more Sandhurst than Sandhurst.[3] He told me how he used a loud speaker on the frontier when the tribesmen were sniping his troops. It was objected that a loud speaker had never been used on the frontier but he got himself obeyed & dictated what should be said. Roughly like this: 'Salaam to you, our brothers of the hills. It has been reported to me that you have fired several shots at one of my pickets. This disturbs the peace of our camp & prevents us sleeping. Salaams to you. If you continue to

1 – Assistant head of BBC, Delhi.
2 – Simla is a summer resort on the southern slopes of the Himalayas.
3 – Field Marshal Kodandera Madappa ('Kipper') Cariappa, OBE (1899–1993), first Indian Chief of Staff. Educ. Central High School, Madikeri; Presidency College, Chennai; Daly Cadet College, Indore.

disturb us we shall have to fire back & kill you. We do not wish to do this. Salaams to you. I suggest therefore that you all go away & go to bed. If any of you has any complaints let him come & see me in the morning. Goodnight, our brothers of the hills. Salaams to you.' After which, according to Cariappa, there was not a single other shot. So he's now a great believer in the mobile van. 'Shoot out the stuff to the chaps – bit of the Koran, bit of the Gita, something like that – chaps will fall for it you know, jolly good show, there you are.'

Other phenomenals we've met include Dr Wheeler,[1] head archaeologist here, who looks like a Tod Slaughter[2] villain with a curled-up moustache & a leer; he's given me introductions to several curators of museums. He & his wife (an overcharged young Australian) share a house with a dear old Indian archaeologist who's married to an Irishwoman from Carrick-on-Shannon. We met the latter in a sari & a caste-mark v. drunk at a party; she says their house is lovely, they argue from morning to night.

The other morning a nice young man from All India Radio took me to a private view of a new Indian film (which is said to be quite a new departure). Stock situation:- conflict between wicked millionaire who is real estate king & also mayor of the town & the exploited chaps in the town's most unhealthy quarter. These are organised to resist exploitation by a goodlooking young man who – as you might guess – is in love with the millionaire's beautiful daughter. Millionaire, to drain a new site for luxury flats, diverts all the filth through the poor part of the town, thereby causing an epidemic (whole series of sick beds & deathbeds). The real protagonist is the sewer; I've never seen such a vivid presentation of liquid filth. Photography on the whole v. good (cross between Russia & Orson Welles) but sound level all over the place & musical choruses vulgar westernisations of folk song. But the whole thing well worth seeing.

Talking of deaths, the funerals here are v. striking. Suddenly in the densest part of the bazaar you see a little file of people on foot chanting; the body, wrapped tightly in a gay-coloured cloth, is carried shoulder-high on a stretcher. One passed the other day when V. Thomas was doing a

---

1 – Sir (Robert Eric) Mortimer Wheeler (1890–1976), archaeologist and broadcaster. Educ. Bradford GS, UCL, Slade School of Art. Author of *Prehistoric and Roman Wales* (1925), *Maiden Castle, Dorset* (1943) and many other works. Wheeler went to India in 1944, revitalised the archaeological survey and educated a generation of Indian archaeologists. Widely admired by Indian colleagues, he founded a journal, *Ancient India*, and excavated many sites, including Taxila (1944–5), Arikamedu (1945), Harappa (1946), Brahmagiri and Chandravalli (1947).
2 – Tod Slaughter (1885–1956), screen actor, ham villain of many Victorian melodramas.

sound picture of the bazaar (but he didn't get the chanting). The van caused a great sensation & all the rag-tags of Delhi swarmed over it. Great good humour all round. I explained to one chap what we were doing. He said that was a mistake, we should do it in 10 years' time when everything (???) would be quite different.

V. Thomas came back last week from a recce in Lahore & Amritsar. He says the amount of killing & burning & still more the atrocity stories are exaggerated but recounts that the road between Lahore & Amritsar is cluttered up with 2 great rivers of pedestrian refugees, Hindus & Sikhs from the West & Muslims from the East & all of them utterly exhausted.[1] What's happened in fact is an exchange of populations – but unintended & achieved most brutally. He thinks the violence is really not committed by 'mobs' at all but by little gangs of experts who treat the whole thing as a cricket match: the scores must be kept even.

It says in the paper here today that many Englishmen in England nowadays wear even less clothes than Gandhi; in order to save their wardrobes they go about in bathing slips. Has that become true since I left?

Darling, do go on writing to Delhi (I've had 2 from you so far) even though your letters may have to wait for me in the office. I have no idea what's happened about Teresa & lots of other things.

Tell Bimba there are lots of green parrots here. They live in the pepul [sic] trees & look v. good against a red sandstone ruin. There are lots of little squirrels or (more strictly, I suppose, chipmunks, as they're striped). V. tame.

Jack is planning to go shooting in one of the princely States. I am leaving myself out of that! How on earth I'm going to fit in everything I don't know. It might help if one went about incognito. A wee fellow from the Hindustan Times interviewed me the other day. I was v. cagey & he left me with the rather crushing remark 'I will come again in September when perhaps you will have more definite ideas.' But his published interview was strictly honourable; he didn't (like any American reporter) draw on his imagination.[2]

1 – *The Times* reported, over a week later: 'More than 1,000,000 and possibly as many as 2,000,000, people – Muslims trekking west and Sikhs and Hindus trekking east – are on the move in the Punjab as a consequence of the communal massacres' ('More than 1,000,000 on the Move in Punjab', 5 Sept. 1947, 4).
2 – 'English Poet to Tour India', *Hindustan Times*, 24 Aug. 1947, 7. FLM said it would 'take some time to sort out my reactions'. He went on to make comparisons between contemporary India and Ireland: 'The present atmosphere of tension in India reminded Mr MacNeice of the situation in Ireland, where he was born, when feelings were running high between those in

Must go out, dear heart, now & collect some money. (We had to send a stiff cable to London demanding more elasticity in the money arrangements. They have no notion what things cost here – especially transport. In Delhi e.g. one has to use taxis continuously.)

All my love, Cat dearest.

& to Dan & Bimba.

L.

TO *Hedli MacNeice*   MS Bodleian

31 August [1947]   Peshawar, but as from BBC,
                                          New Delhi / Letter 5

Dearest,

I am writing this very sun-happy (having spent the day going through the Khyber pass with my head out of the roof of the recording van, à la Churchill tank), rather tight owing to the social demands of the North West Frontier hotel, & in great haste as our bête noir Grahame [*sic*] has turned up, who will take this to Delhi & post it. (The reason I've not written since Monday is that Pakistan communications are at the moment quite hopeless.)

Well, today, darling, has been our best day yet. The hills up here are a tonic after the plains & the Khyber Pass is one of those few romantic names which don't let one down. We got to the Afghan frontier & were there regaled with slices of melon & green tea. It is all beautifully arid & invigorating & the Afridis are a v. handsome & sympathetic lot of chaps.[1] We went sponsored by a wonderful Islamic professor I contacted; the Pass seems to be manned by his ex-pupils. More about him in another letter (this is really just meant to fill in an unavoidable gap).

We drove up here from Lahore through 2 v. odd landscapes – the first a great vista of tomato soup (the monsoon floods) studded with vivid green trees & pricked with rice, & the 2nd a fantasy, almost surrealist, scene – red trees eroded away into incredible shapes. Peshawar itself is a walled

---

favour of the Free State and those who did not want to separate from Great Britain. Though that was on a much smaller scale, he remembered a time when it was quite common to hear bursts of gun-fire every night. The rumours that were spread at that time were as blood-curdling as anything he had heard since. Even now newspapers representing the two points of view continued carrying on a bitter controversy.'

1 – A powerful tribe in mountainous northwest Pakistan.

city with v. lush bazaars in it – cascades of melons & pyramids of different coloured trees & people squatting in the street cooking chickens or using sewing machines. Also lots of v. nice marbled black & white goats with impertinent tails. But the politics (as one might expect) highly complicated, not to say crooked. More of that too some other time.

To go back to Lahore (where we broke our journey) I'm afraid we ran into some horrors there. The Punjab situation is utterly brutal & utterly futile. Thus on Wednesday I visited in the morning a refugee camp of Muslims from the East Punjab in an ex-Chinese Air Force barracks with, appropriately enough, a large concrete model of a bomb standing on its nose in the middle as a monument to our civilisation. 30,000 refugees in the camp – most of them dazed & with nothing but the rags they stood up – or lay down – in. More arriving every minute – the more distant ones by military truck, the nearer ones by bullock cart. I saw one bullock hauling a family of about 20.

The very same afternoon – not knowing what I was going to see – I went out with V. Thomas & the Times & Daily Telegraph correspondents (Jack didn't come) in a van belonging to the Punjab Boundary Force[1] to a place called Sheichupura [sic] which had been the scene the day before of 'communal trouble'.[2] The victims in this case (as it was <u>West</u> Punjab) were the non-Muslims, particularly the Sikhs. Quite impossible to get correct figures of casualties or a true account of how it started but I'm v. glad I've not got a sense of smell. The 1st thing we saw was the hospital, about 80 people in it v. badly injured lying on bare beds in rags, flat out & covered with flies. Just one doctor & apparently no equipment. The next thing was about 1500 of the Sikh & Hindu minority, men, women <u>&</u> children, huddled in a high school debouching into the street & waiting for precarious transport away from it all. A v. large number of these had been wounded with swords or spears & their white clothes were covered with rusty-brown dried blood. Some with their hands cut off etc. & again the hordes of flies. But hardly any moaning – just abstracted, even smiling in

---

1 – The Punjab Boundary Force was formed under the command of Major-General T. W. Rees to control violence in the region during the period of independence and partition. It was operational for only one month. Cf. 'The sober lawn / Regrets the Punjab Boundary Force / (Which, like the drinks, has been withdrawn)', 'Return to Lahore', *Visitations* (1957), CP07, 506.

2 – *The Times* reported on the massacre at Sheikhupura: 'Within 24 hours at least 800 people, nearly all Sikhs and Hindus, had been shot, stabbed, speared, slashed, clubbed, or burned to death . . . Whole areas, Muslim as well as Sikh and Hindu, had been reduced to ashes' ('Punjab Violence Growing', 29 Aug. 1947, 4g; qtd. *SP*, 165, n. 5). Cf. FLM, 'Letter from India': 'I have seen Sheikhupura High School / Fester with glaze-eyed refugees', *HS*, CP07, 296.

a horrible unreal way. We watched them pile into trucks – possibly to be ambushed on their way to the border. I won't elaborate this now, darling, but it was really a slice of death – the sort of thing one's always hearing about in the papers but ought no doubt to have encountered in the flesh – or the fester – before.[1]

Anyhow, I'm not going back to the Punjab – so don't worry about danger (not that the British are in danger anyway). From here we go to Cashmir which is sheer recreation; after which we split, I think, & I hope to stay with Chaman Lall in Simla. (He is a real charmer). So expect to hear from me from Cashmir.

Darling, I'm so glad Teresa's arrived.[2] But about the house – why put poor Bimba on the road side? I can make do perfectly in that little room.

Glad you've finished that film.[3] Any more offers by the way from the Silver Screen?

And <u>please</u>, darling, don't get the horrors about Islington. I can't see that it's worse than the World's End – & it <u>is</u> much nearer. And taxis can always be arranged (ask Judy!)

Must stop now, I fear, or Grahame will have gone to bed. Much longer letter next time.

> All my love to yourself
> & to Dan & Bimba,
> L.

P.S. If they're still around, remember me most kindly to Anna & Minky[4]

---

1 – FLM is modest about his own role in this, as recalled by Vaughan Thomas: 'I remember once driving with Louis to a little village called Shakpura. We got there to find that there'd been a terrible massacre that very morning . . . and suddenly I saw a totally different Louis, one I never imagined existed. Louis the man of action. He ordered those people into a nearby lorry, we got some sort of structure going of a way to get them out of the refugee area into something like safety and there suddenly he was ordering people about, they were obeying him – a totally different Louis I suddenly saw revealed and also a Louis that was no longer the detached observer but one deeply and profoundly involved in the human dilemma' (typescript, *Louis MacNeice: A Radio Portrait*, broadcast 7 Sept. 1966; *PRONI D/2833/D/5/21*).

2 – Teresa Moroni, the new Italian maid.

3 – Hedli played a minor character called Millicent in *Colonel Bogey* (1948), directed by Terence Fisher and produced by John Croydon.

4 – Anna Shepard and her daughter Minette.

TO *Hedli MacNeice*   MS Bodleian

5 September [1947]   Srinagar (Cashmir), but as from
                                       BBC, New Delhi / Letter 6

Darling,

I feel v. cut off from you here but am sending this with V.T.'s discs by air
to Delhi, so hope you'll get it. I hope you got my last letter from Peshawar
which I entrusted to dreary Graham. Anyhow I expect to be back in Delhi
myself next Wednesday, 10th, where at least the communications seem
reliable. Am also praying God there may be some letters from Cat in the
Delhi office.

This is a v. beautiful State (though a tour-ridden town) but am at the
moment considerably depressed. Have just been talking with an English
family who were on one of these trains attacked by Sikhs. This communal
conflict gets one down; it seems, apart from being bloody, so bloody
<u>stupid</u>. And of course it's a vicious circle. Politics in Peshawar (which is
mainly Muslim v. Muslim) though crackers, seemed comparatively clean.
We met the Khan brothers[1] who are just out of power & who told us all
about the corruption of the Muslim Leaguers & the v. same day met the
new Muslim League prime minister who told us all about the corruption
of the Khan brothers (they are the chaps who want a 'Pathanistan' – v.
Irish in their approach to things). The elder Khan brother, Dr Khan Sahib
(ex prime minister of the North West Frontier province), we found building
himself a mansion in the middle of a semidesert. The younger & more
famous brother, Khan Abdul Gaffar Khan, was also building himself a
house also in a place of wide prospect. I said to Jack, as we drove up there
in the truck over a hardly existent road, 'I bet someone's got us in his
sights' – & I bet someone had. In the verandah were retainers with rifles
& strung with bandoliers who watched us while we waited for the great
man to finish his lunch. Then we were taken into the back verandah where
K.A.G.K., a huge figure in a sort of monkish grey robe with a domineering
nose & eagle eyes, was squatting on some straw. We were told to take off
our shoes & join him. He then shot us a line of militant-cum-pseudo-
socialist-talk & all the time a man stood by with a gun. K.A.G.K. ended
by saying that if the Muslim League, i.e. the Pakistan Govmt. won't accede
to his demands, in the end 'we will do what we ought to do'.[2] Which

1–Khan Sahib (1883–1958), former PM of North-West Frontier Province, and Abdul
Ghaffar Khan (1890–1988), known as 'the Frontier Gandhi', founder of the Pathan Red Shirt
movement.
2–Regarded as hostile to Pakistan, the Khan brothers were arrested in 1948 by the new
government.

means make a revolution. K.A.G.K. is, I would say, partly out for power & partly a fanatic but he's undeniably a personality & on the Frontier, one gathers, nearly everything goes by personalities. & nearly everyone is armed. Dr Khan Sahib, a much smoother, indeed westernised figure, told us in the blandest possible way that when he was prime minister he issued arms to 'all voters'. And when V.T. & I visited the new Prime Minister that afternoon, the fellows handing round cakes (there are never any women to be seen in these establishments) were also loaded with revolvers, bandoliers etc. When leaving we were introduced to about a dozen Waziristan tribal chiefs sitting in a semi-circle on the lawn who had come 370 miles to ask the P.M. for permission to march into the Punjab to assist their fellow-Muslims (this will of course be refused).[1] One of the younger chiefs, a real charmer with a crescent & star tattooed on his fore-arm, spoke v. good English & interpreted for us. His colleagues were a wonderful collection who might have come out of Homer. Their whole mentality is sheer Border Ballad. As we were leaving, a late-comer, a great ox of a man with a great black turned-up moustache & die-hard angry eyes, stood himself plumb in front of V.T. & me & poured out a stream of rhythmical Pushto[2] (which sounds an attractive language, not like old ragbag Hindustani). This flow of eloquence was punctuated by an elegant throat-cutting gesture (all their hand movements are terrific). It turned out that he was giving the roll-call of the tribes who would go with him to Delhi & explaining what they would then do to Delhi & in fact to the whole Union of India. No more Sikhs – throat-cutting gesture! No more Hindus – throat-cutting gesture! And if the British interfere – throat-cutting gesture! And if the Russians interfere – throat-cutting gesture! Q.E.D. On the Frontier the 20th Century doesn't go.

We left Peshawar on Tuesday in the recording van – which is a godsend in lack of other transport. The snag is of course that it means us all sticking together. Jack's all right but V.T., though v. amusing, does for my taste talk rather too much & too patly & I find his interview-technique (though it certainly gets results) embarrassing at times; e.g. when talking to a Muslim Leaguer he makes a point of disparaging the Hindus. But what makes all 3 of us mad is the constant presence of Jarvis the engineer-driver – a miserable boring, bored, constantly grousing, inferiority becomplexed yet hopelessly conceited nonentity. V.T. coddles & pampers him & whenever we're invited anywhere he has to be taken too, otherwise he feels outraged.

1 – The Wazirs are a Pashtun tribe in NW Pakistan, the largest of several tribes in the region.
2 – Pushto, an Indo-Iranian language common to the region.

So all the intellectuals & statesmen & professors etc. of India are presented with this dismal face which covers no ideas, no knowledge, & no interest. I don't believe he's been moved for better or worse by a single thing he's met here. And he all but prevented us meeting Abdul Gaffer Khan as he said it would make him late for lunch! Anyhow when we get to Delhi next week I'll be parting company with him (& with the rest), I think, for a bit, as I hope to take up this invitation of Chaman's to Simla. And a little later I hope to stay on my own with Sarojini Naidu.

To return to Tuesday, we'd been invited to lunch with Sir George Cunningham, the Governor of N.W.F.P., who was away in his hill station Government House 99% out of touch with Peshawar (how anyone ever governed from there I can't imagine; it's at the top of a mountain, 7000 feet, with only one telephone line which keeps breaking down).[1] Well, we had the hell of a drive getting up there – quite staggering gradients & corners over a ravine & a v. bad surface on the road – but when you arrive you at once get an illuminating flashback to the old Raj in its glory. The difference from the plains is fantastic. It was so cool, the Governor had a large wood fire & the whole house reminded me of rich English country houses 20 years back or more; exquisite lawns outside & any amount of dahlias etc. But Sir G.C. himself a quiet old thing with far-away blue eyes & a blistered face but obviously with a grip of the problems on the Frontier. We stayed that night in the one hotel (a series of Scandinavian wooden huts) & hobnobbed with the only other guest, a young officer's wife of the Esther category who became almost hysterically talkative on meeting 4 people from England. But just too bloody ignorant of India – though she claimed of course to know all the answers. Next year there'll be an Indian Governor there – that is, if he chooses to make use of this highly artificial British pocket of luxury – so we really felt we were in on the last flicker of a falling star – or last echo of a high-pitched last mem sahib.

On Wednesday morning early I saw Nangi [sic] Parbat about 100 miles away to the North. One of the highest peaks of the Himalayas.[2] V. exciting. A long dark ridge of mountains below & a long dark ridge of clouds above & in the canal of liquid clear sky between a thing like a tiny floating lion with snow on its mane.

<hr>

1–Sir George Cunningham (1888–1963), Governor of North-West Frontier Province: Scottish, Oxford-educated, international rugby player. Joined the Indian Civil Service in 1911, and spent most of his career in the region.
2–Nanga Parbat is 8,126 m (26,600 feet) high.

From the hill station we drove here to Cashmir which is God's gift to the future as the world's playground. Mountains rather Swiss but much more palatable, roads lined with poplars & all the flowers & grass you could want. Went yesterday to see the Nishat & Shalamar gardens. Between the lake & the mountains – long series of terraces flanked by symmetrical trees & flowers with a water-course (plus chutes & fountains) as a spine down the middle. But alas, these days no water. Made me want again to know more about the Moghul civilisation. Cruel lot of chaps but at least they balanced it with beauty.

Well, Cat dearest, these are only snippets of information & I've still got mental indigestion. Individually Indians seem delightful but collectively just hell. And this hatred between Muslims & Hindus is something you can't exaggerate. As a Muslim said to me the other day, it's all v. well your top people, your Nehrus & Jinnahs getting together but that's no use at all unless the masses implement it. And the masses are conditioned to the blood feud. Most English people here by the way take sides with the Muslims – because, of course, they're more like themselves. The mem sahib whom we saw today whose train had been attacked by the Sikhs was all for the tribesmen marching at once to the boundary to cut the Sikhs to pieces. But last night we talked to Arthur Moore, ex-editor of the Indian Statesman, a liberal soul in a blimp's face, & he thinks the communal trouble <u>will</u> be solved.[1] If not, he says, it's the condemnation of the British as the one thing we could claim to have given India was a sense of unity. And he says one should discount much of the public utterances of the public figures here who are usually playing to the gallery; when on committees, he says, & really doing a job they can be the soul of reason. But Nehru he considers dangerous because he's so impulsive & gets carried away into attacking people. Gandhi on the other hand he admires enormously because 'he made India a nation; he was the first person who gave them guts'.

Cat darling, how is everything? I hope the prospective house move isn't too fret-making. And how is Teresa making out? (If by any chance – which I sincerely hope not! – the house has fallen through, I have heard of a good furnished house in Chiswick you could take for the time being. Apply Miss Maureen Bartlett, 4 Vanbrugh Road, Chiswick; say I was put on to it by her friend Mrs Patsy Dance – the Esther of the hill station.)

1 – Arthur Moore (1880–1962), native of Newry (NI), educ. Campbell College, Belfast and St John's College, Oxford. Special correspondent *The Times* 1908–14. Assistant editor *Indian Statesman* 1924–33, then managing editor 1933–42. PR Adviser, South-East Asian Command, 1944. Later, syndicated journalist for Dalmia newspapers.

I miss you shockingly, dearest; it's like being on the moon.

All my love

L.

P.S. Love to Dan & Bimba. Hope to send them both appropriate pictures some time.

TO *Hedli MacNeice* MS Bodleian

16 September [1947]   As from BBC, New Delhi / Letter 8

Well darling,

Here I come again though I only sent you a letter a couple of hours ago. I am sitting in Sinclair's v. 20th century office in Burma Shell House & it has been raining steadily. I have written a letter to Dan (at the Downs) & one to George MacCann (whose address I suddenly found) & one to Sarojini Naidu asking if I may take up her old invitation to stay with her. I'm afraid I'm too late to stay with Chaman Lall now, especially as he's kept rushing hither & thither by the present situation. Anyhow I'm not v. keen on going to Simla; it doesn't seem India & I think I can imagine it.

About that opera broadcast, it all sounds to me shockingly unprofessional. Maurice Browne is the person who should make a row over it. (Though of course there <u>would</u> be a point in doing it in Spanish).

Talking of languages, you haven't said how you converse with Teresa. Have you bought her an Italian–English pocket dictionary, phrase-book etc.?

Grant seems to have shown up v. badly. What does Mr Norris think of him? And by the way what about Peat? Any communications from him?

As for Blowers they seem to have acted with good old Essex casualness. What is the position if Peat asks you to pay damages for the walls, ceiling etc.?[1]

Am feeling a bit depressed here. Curfew still on & no taxis. Still, it's really v. good to get a rest from excessive company; I feel I've never got away from the human voice since I came to India. Especially V.T.'s voice! It's also probably good to eat more modestly for a bit; all these hotel meals have really been too lavish & Indian hospitality in various places more lavish still.

---

1 – The concern is that the landlord at Tilty will expect reparations for damage to the house which the MacNeices had occupied for the last year.

Bimba seems to be getting alarmingly sophisticated. If that new school is really too drab, can't you find another somewhere accessible? Do the Mudies know of anything?

Am reading a rather charming novel by R. K. Narayan called 'The English Teacher', about Southern India.[1] I think you'd like it. I'll bring it back with me. Have also read a v. illuminating book 'Strangers in India' by a man with the striking name of Pendrel [*sic*] Moon, who was in the I.C.S. but had to resign in 1942 for writing letters to political prisoners.[2] It clarifies a lot of shady corners; you might recommend it to Laurence as it acts as a corrective to Coupland's optimistic view of the benefits brought to India by British institutions – British law, 'democracy' etc.[3]

About Nehru, I'm not surprised you're impressed by that book. But I'm afraid his career may end in disappointment. Apart from the present mess & the misfortune of his own occasional impulsiveness, it is generally agreed that he hasn't the power in Congress & that the chaps who will really dominate are the right-wing representatives of the banias, big land-owners etc. Worse than that, it's expected that Patel, the leader of this right wing, will soon throw in his lot with the Mahasabha who are among the Hindus the real extremist reactionaries.[4]

Sept. 18th:- Just planning to leave for Calcutta in the next few days. It's really v. strange here – such a contrast with 4 weeks ago. Connaught Place, the great circular shopping centre, is half deserted – no more beggars & no

1 – Published 1945.
2 – Sir Edward Penderel Moon (1905–87), British diplomat. Educ. Winchester and New College, Oxford. Fellow of All Souls, 1927–35; 1965–72. ICS 1929–38; private secretary to the Governor of the Punjab 1938–41; deputy commissioner to Amritsar 1941–2. After enforced resignation in 1942 he returned to England, but resumed responsibilities in India in 1946, and remained after Indian independence. Author of *Strangers in India* (1944), *Warren Hastings* (1947) and *The British Conquest and Domination of India* (1989).
3 – Sir Reginald Coupland (1884–1952), Beit Professor and Professorial Fellow of All Souls 1920–48; author of *The Cripps Mission* (1942), *The Indian Problem, 1833–1935*, 3 vols (1942), *Indian Politics, 1936–1942* (1943), *The Future of India* (1943), *India: A Re-Statement* (1945) and other works. Coupland was a consultant for the BBC on their Indian programmes in 1947, but he resigned over a disagreement with the Director General about how to represent the British presence in India. As Gilliam explained to FLM, 'he, too, became convinced that any explicit celebration of the British "achievement" or "record" carried with it a great danger of a bad effect on Indian opinion. He offered to continue to work for us if the project was changed to "India in Transition" and the British achievement made implicit rather than explicit' (LG to FLM, 13 Sept. 1947, *Ms BBC*). Like MacNeice, Gilliam was clearly sympathetic to this new position and asked FLM to submit a revised proposal for a programme reflecting these views.
4 – Hindu nationalist organisation, the Akhil Bharatiya Hindu Mahasabha, founded in 1915 to oppose the Muslim League and the Indian National Congress.

more tongas (the tonga drivers being nearly all Muslim); a good few shops with broken windows or boarded up & here & there military pickets. Nearly all institutions, including All India Radio, are working with a fraction of their staff. Paringoti, the radio man who gave us dinner (with the half American wife), has quit for Bombay. Tymbyi, the Muslim who opted for India & is secretary to the Constituent Assembly, so v. important, sent his wife & children to Bombay & has had his house looted (where we had that v. delicious dinner). As someone said ironically, 'That will learn him not to go to Pakistan'. You see how mad it all is.

Got a cable from Laurence yesterday demanding a revised feature scheme 'in full'. Not easy to produce bang off – especially with Jack not here. The really hard thing is to think up 6 programmes which will make a <u>coherent series</u>.

Quite heavy rain here lately which turns everything into red mud but considerably cools the air. Sinclair's house is surrounded on all sides by an exquisite lawn which would be the envy of anyone in England. As I've probably said before, New Delhi (& astonishingly new it is) is just one grandiose super-Suburb with lots of identical tree-lined roads all connected by roundabouts & named after famous figures of Indian history (both Indian & British); the only odd note is struck by the cows & water buffalo which graze nonchalantly on the fringes of these roads.

We walked round the corner last night to call on Dr Wheeler the archaeologist who is going to lay on all sorts of exciting things for me in S. India. The gem of the collection would appear to be Sirangam, the fabulous temple city. I don't know if I'll have time to visit Narayan who's in Bangalore. Kitten (the tiny drunk poetry fan) whom I met again yesterday says 'The English Teacher' is autobiographical; Narayan really lost his wife & really thought he got in touch with her after her death.

I haven't yet been into <u>Old</u> Delhi since my return; I should guess there's a lot of charred wood there. Last night I heard machine gun fire in the distance, v. soft pop-muttering, which probably came from there. I still have plenty of exploring to do for my Portrait of Delhi but I think I'll leave it to a later visit!

I rather feel I may write a long poem re India in the latter end; but it will need a deal of digesting.

Will end this now, darling, to catch Sinclair's special mail via Karachi. (Go on writing to <u>Delhi</u> please).

All my love. L.

P.S. <u>Please</u> take things easy & be happy.

19 September 1947 BBC, New Delhi

Dear Laurence,

I received your cable and am answering in haste as I may leave Delhi tomorrow for Calcutta (but will return here within a fortnight before going South). I can't be definitive till Jack reappears so the following scheme is tentative; it may look at first sight full of gaps but you'll see below that many major themes which it would be unwise to treat directly will infiltrate easily into the programmes now suggested (all of which latter, N.B., we could undertake with a clear conscience).

The situation in India has of course drastically changed since my last letter. On both sides of the boundary talk has again sprung up about a 'British conspiracy'. I would not say that people have become again anti-British but this revival of suspicion (or scapegoatery) does mean we must be extra tactful. Some English papers, I hear have seized on the Punjab and Delhi as a pretty occasion for an I-told-you-so vindication of the British Raj; the BBC should on no account follow suit. Our objections to the old feature scheme, far from being dispelled by the present troubles, are triply reinforced. To <u>stress</u> at this moment the security, justice, good order or unity bestowed by the Raj would be surely most inopportune. Arthur Moore, very intelligent liberal, ex-Editor of the Indian Statesman, said to me – rightly, I feel – that the <u>one</u> justification of the Raj will be if India remains a unity (not necessarily implying an end of partition); if we haven't given them nationhood and self-coherence, we've given them nothing. But if chaos persists, says Moore, then <u>our</u> 'unity' was a sham and the less said about it the better.

It will clarify my scheme if I first list some subjects which should <u>not</u> be billed in the series:-

(a) <u>The Army</u>: Too invidious for a programme to itself in this series (but see my list of Subsidiaries). The old Indian Army did a good job but Moore's criticism would apply here too. Should discipline, initiative and other military virtues now fade out in India, it means that the British have failed in one most important respect and that their use of the army, however effective, will appear in retrospect mainly mercenary or selfish – a guard for their own vested interests. But a <u>subsidiary</u> programme, if tactfully done, would certainly be worth while – especially as British army officers have a far better record than say the ICS of personal relationships with

Indians. Anyhow the Army will obviously – and usually with honour – appear <u>by the way</u> in our programmes on other subjects, e.g. in Number I, II and VI.

(b) <u>Administration</u>: Ditto, Ditto. The lack of high-grade administration is painfully obvious here now especially in Pakistan. Admittedly some people think Indians <u>can't</u> make administrators but, even if this were so, it would be a grave mistake to point it by lauding British efficiency. And what <u>is</u> an established fact is that Britain gave to Indians too little and too late a share in responsible jobs. As for English <u>law</u>, some intelligent Britons out here think it more of a liability than an asset (see a most illuminating book, 'Strangers in India', by Pendrel Moon, late of the ICS). But N.B., here once again indirect and implicit tribute to the ICS and the others can be slipped in naturally in most of our programmes.

(c) '<u>Democracy</u>': No; see Moon again on e.g. the abuse of western electoral methods – confirmed here by what we've heard ourselves. But the influence of English political thinking (J. S. Mill and Co). can and should be woven in in the last three programmes.

(d) <u>Industry</u>: No. Britain deliberately prevented the growth of Indian heavy industry and, as for most Indian industrialists, as Dante says 'let us not reason of them but look and pass'. But the Tata Works etc. could be mentioned in Number I.[1]

(e) <u>Engineering</u>: No. Would be bragging again (and seeing the floods a single shower can cause on the Grand Trunk Road and in the streets of Delhi, am not sure the brag would be justified). But some bridges, dams, etc. can have honourable mention here and there.

(f) <u>Commerce and Trade</u>: Certainly not! Under the Raj almost purely, if naturally, selfish – and these boys held the record for filthy behaviour to Indians. But the glamour of the Company's early adventures could and should certainly be flashed in in retrospect.

(g) <u>Religion</u>: Hinduism and Islam must of course come in – especially in I, II, and IV – but to devote a programme to either or both would clearly be sticking one's neck out. And might appear very patronising.

(h) <u>Hindu and Muslim</u>: Ditto. Their social and economic differences are enormously important but should not be given the centre of the stage.

---

1 – Tata Steel, India's largest steel company, founded in 1907 and based in Mumbai (Bombay).

(i) <u>The Present Communal Trouble</u>: Ditto. Ditto. Ditto. Still more No! Good 'News' perhaps but a feature on this subject would tactlessly put a frame round a hideous and – it's hoped – impermanent mess and would almost certainly be unjust. But it should be just glanced at in perhaps Numbers I, II, III, and VI.

Now to become more positive. I suggest a main Series of six with a few suggestions for subsidiary features which could be put out later or betweenwhiles as self-contained pieces in the ordinary run of broadcasting. The most important and most difficult thing is to make the series a unity, self-coherent and implicitly (though not – see above – explicitly) comprehensive of all the main elements of India. I don't know what Jack would say to the following proposal as a whole but I do know that he very much wants to write all the three programmes I've put down for him.

My own Number II I thought of first as a Subsidiary (see my earlier letter) but it seems to me now it could pull its weight in the series. But, if you feel like risking it, you could make it subsidiary again and substitute for it in the Series a <u>Trial of</u> or, if you prefer the name, <u>Post Mortem on the British Raj</u>. This would make a good logical Number II and would show the listener we meant business.

N.B. The series would have to be conceived as a block and Jack and I, while not collaborating <u>in</u> writing, would need to keep in touch <u>while</u> writing, pooling our material, checking our joint impressions, avoiding unnecessary overlaps and watching the general relationship of programme to programme.

There's one important point: partition? We can't ignore it but I can't see how we can devote separate programmes to India and Pakistan. Such a radio partitioning would be (1) unfeasible and (2) just as likely to offend as if we did the natural thing and let each programme cover both.

Anyhow here's a tentative scheme but note that some of the titles are makeshift.

<u>Main Features (in the Series)</u>

I. <u>This is India</u> (Dillon to write)
Geographical-cum-historical bird's eye view. Would ram home to the listener from the start the <u>peculiarities</u> of India, physical and spiritual. Anyone hearing this should retain with him through the rest the <u>feel</u> of the country and people. And it should supply some first clues to the <u>problems</u> of India – economic, social and political.

II. <u>Portrait of Delhi</u> (MacNeice to write)[1]
Maybe start with quick flashes of other Indian cities, then track up through the Plains to the capital and try to put over (a) its physical presence, (b) its history and political significance. Would cover the Seven Cities, the Moghuls, the British Raj and the present. N.B., while capital of 'India', Delhi is dear to all Muslims, having been for centuries their centre (Witness the great Moghul buildings). This Muslim connection – like much else in these programmes – to be treated 'dialectically'. Episodes to include of course both the mutiny and the recent declaration of Independence (with maybe just a flash of the still more recent disturbances). Plenty of occasion for sidelights both on the Raj and on Indian nationalism. The picture in short will be of much more than a city and in representing the <u>public</u> life of India will lead on naturally to the private but basic life of the Village.
(Note: But, as I said, this <u>could</u> be swapped with the <u>Post Mortem</u>).

III. <u>The Indian Village</u> (Dillon to write)
For obvious reasons an essential member of the series. I write without briefing but Jack would presumably cover (a) Indian agriculture today, (b) ditto in the past, (c) prospects in the new Dominions, (d) some sketch of village traditions (folk culture) and of institutions such as the decayed but still potentially valuable <u>panchayat</u>.[2] Regional differences would of course be brought out. Dominant themes I fancy, FOOD (which Jack considers – and he's probably right – the one basic problem of India).

IV. <u>Indian Culture</u> (MacNeice to write)
By this I mean chiefly the products of the educated – philosophy and the arts – as distinct from that majority culture of crafts and customs which might be glanced at here but could also creep in in I or III or V. Dialectical treatment again perhaps – not only temple balanced against mosque but East against West. Could cover not only Gita, Buddha, Moghul architecture etc. but Tagore, Iqbal, etc. and living poets (e.g. in Urdu and Bengali) and living novelists writing in English like Narayan and Mulk Raj Anand.[3] Would touch on past influence and prospects of English language.

1–FLM wrote three scripts on India, all broadcast in 1948: *India at First Sight* (13 March); *Portrait of Delhi*, India and Pakistan No. 3 (2 May) and *The Road to Independence*, India and Pakistan No. 6 (23 May).
2–Village council.
3–Rabindranath Tagore (1861–1941), Bengali poet and educationist; educ. private tutors; Nobel Prize for Literature 1913. Mohammed Iqbal (1875–1938), Urdu and Persian poet, philosopher, known as 'the Poet of Islam'. Educ. Lahore University; Trinity College, Cambridge; University of Munich (PhD). Called to the Bar by Lincoln's Inn. Author of *Secrets of the Self* (1915, 1920); *The Message of the East* (1923), *The Call to March* (1925) and

A difficult programme but very important, I think, not only because Indian culture has declined but because the <u>West</u> has declined and a renaissance in either might (?) come from their interaction. (Such interaction has more chance now than under the Raj.)

V. <u>Education</u> (Dillon to write)

Jack has talked to Sargent and hopes to get a lot more dope from him. The programme, I assume, would largely be concerned with non-education (link-up with III here); the prospects of reducing illiteracy quickly are very poor unless they adopt some such suggestion as A. S. Bokhari made to me and conscript all college students to teach in the villages as amateurs.[1] Would cover, I suppose, not only the financial and organisational difficulties but the impediments raised by religious, social and political prejudice (e.g. the mullahs' obscurantism, the caste system and the Indian equivalents of Gaelic Leaguery). Might also touch on the minority cases of Mission Schools and of Indians who complete their education in Europe. And might well complement IV by assessing what survives of majority culture and weighing the chances of synthesis between this and Western 'enlightenment'.

VI. <u>Independence</u> (MacNeice to write)

Whatever its title (<u>The Transfer of Power</u> or what-have-you) this programme seems to me absolutely necessary. Historical resume of India's progress towards freedom, giving due recognition to such Englishmen as foresaw that aim and sympathised and also to those English writers whose ideas influenced the nationalists. N.B. This feature would be far from 100 per cent political. Could start with some sketch of the pre-British chaos, flashes of early days of Company[2] and Moghul break-up, then series of short human scenes to illustrate changing attitude of both English and Indians (due attention of course to Mutiny and its effects). Thus political issues would often be brought out implicitly rather than stated. In recent times would have to treat Congress–Muslim League rift but not over-

—

other works. Knighted, 1923; Member of Punjab Legislature, 1925–8; Hon DLitt (Punjab), 1933. R. K. Narayan (1906–2001), Indian novelist and author of *The English Teacher* (which FLM had been reading); educ. schools in Madras and Mysore and the University of Mysore. Mulk Raj Anand (1905–2004), Indian author, educ. University of the Punjab and UCL; FLM had met Anand in London in 1939 (*SAF*, 209).

1–Ahmed Shah Bokhari (1898–1958), educ. Government College, Lahore and Emmanuel College, Cambridge. Director General of All-India Radio, Delhi, 1940–7. Professor (1927–39) and later principal (1947–50) at Government College; Under-Secretary of the UN, Head of Information 1954–8.

2–The East India Company.

emphasise. Lead-up to August 15th (giving their due to British Labour Government) and end with balance of problems and hopes. Would not swallow anyone's propaganda but, with malice towards none, would aim at realistic presentation of what – in spite of all confusion – is a unique event and, on a long term view, an achievement.

Subsidiary Features (out of the Series)

Post Mortem on the Raj (MacNeice to write)
Could be handled like Jennifer Wayne's Trial of British Justice, leaving listener to draw his own conclusions.[1]

The Khyber Pass (Dillon to write)
Glamour obvious and tribute in passing to the Army. Jack saw the Khyber and was inspired by it.

Farewell to the Cantonnments [sic] or Farewell to Kipling's India (Dillon to write)
Mood and shade elegiac but could show more humour than the main features would allow.

The Moghul Empire (MacNeice to write)
Glamour again obvious, and personally it's got me.

Quite a few other suggestions will no doubt crop up later. Must end this; hope it's lucid.

Yours ever,

P.S. Just this moment had your letter. I sincerely hope you can clear, if not this exact scheme, something like it with the D.G.[2]
About timing, Jack and I were figuring on leaving for home about the first week of November (I at any rate have to be back in November for those Liverpool lectures). But we shan't, I think, want a van even as long as that. Jack thought he could record such stock sounds as we need by early October and we don't want to take a van south (it would merely be

1 – Jennifer Wayne's programme was one of fifteen outstanding radio documentary scripts specially selected by Laurence Gilliam for publication in an edited collection, *BBC Features* (1950). Other contributors included D. G. Bridson, Compton Mackenzie, FLM ('India at First Sight'), Nesta Pain, David Thomson, Terence Tiller, H. R. Trevor-Roper, Wynford Vaughan Thomas and WRR.
2 – Director-General of the BBC.

a nuisance). But Jack will confirm this when he's back here; he's still in Kashmir, I think, and we can't get a message to him!

TO *Hedli MacNeice*   MS Bodleian

3 October [1947]   'Benares – but as from the usual' /
                                     Letter 12

Well darling,

I'm delighted, as I foresaw, to find it's October & England as it were on the horizon. I've been adding some more verses to that poem for you called Letter from India. You might warn Eliot (or someone at Faber's) that I may want to add one poem to my collection in the press; it would come right at the end of the book, i.e. following The Stygian Banks, & would consist of about fifteen verses of six lines each.[1]

I travelled here from Calcutta by night train (2nd class – perfectly tolerable), much more enjoyable than flying. Lovely morning light, when I woke up, on red-roofed villages guarded by palm trees. Benares is a characterful place & I'm staying in a really romantic house with these 2 remarkable Frenchmen, one the writer on music I met in Calcutta & the other, Burnier, a photographer of sculpture.[2] They both dress Indian & have little back-knots of hair in the orthodox Hindu fashion. Their house is right at the end of the town & rises sheer from the Ganges, which is here at least a mile wide. It belongs to a Maharajah, traditional architecture with two courtyards or patios surrounded by stone galleries. You go barefoot into their drawingroom (floor all rugs) & find yourself in a beautiful long room of double height (galleries above) with a five-arched alcove (scalloped arches just over 6 foot high) filled with cushions & looking over the river; the pillars of stone, fluted with decorations at base & capital; the panels of the walls painted with floral decorations (these were covered with whitewash when they took the house 10 years ago).

1 – 'Letter from India' (dedicated to Hedli), *HS*, 58–61. The poem, dated 'October 1947', finally consisted of eighteen six-line stanzas, and was placed at the end of the volume. TSE wrote to Hedli on 31 Oct. 1947, acknowledging receipt of the poem: 'I have had the poem typed out. It is certainly a poem, and I think a good one, but I am also pretty sure that it is still a draft in the sense that Louis may want to make alterations in it so as you say he will be back so soon we shall simply hold it until we have his imprimatur' (*Faber Archive*).
2 – Raymond Burnier (1912–68), Swiss photographer, and his partner Alan Daniélou, aka 'Siva Sharan' (1907–94), scholar of Hinduism, and in 1949 appointed professor at Hindu University of Benares. Daniélou was the author of many books, including *The Way to the Labyrinth: Memories of East and West* (1987).

The Ganges is tawny at the moment & flowing fast with eddies under our walls; by moonlight you hear people singing far out in boats. Just beyond us people ablute themselves in the early morning with a lengthy ritual. And in a derelict houseboat lives an ancient sage who has himself rowed across the river morning & evening for evacuatory purposes so as not to pollute the holy shore.

There are no electric fans in the house & I've been sleeping on a first floor verandah under a mosquito net. Makes one feel v. much in the thick of Indian life – this is <u>not</u> a European quarter. This morning I went up on the flat roof about 6.0 a.m. & watched troops of rhesus monkeys jumping the narrow streets from verandah to verandah. (My hosts by the way own a giant crane about 5 foot high which wanders about in the street among the dumb oxen – & for that matter dumb bulls).

After breakfast I was rowed down river in the rain getting a diorama of the buildings on the river front, including a great number of pine cone & pepperpot temples, mostly of ugly brown stone, rising straight from the water. After which I went up a minaret of the mosque (much the highest point in the city) by a v. narrow winding stair – Laurence would hardly have made it – & got a magnificent view of the river & city & green country beyond. From above Benares looks like a Mediterranean city – predominantly white buildings all v. close upon each other with some yellow washes etc. & all flat roofs with parapets, till you notice un-Mediterranean details – not only the conical temples but monkeys on the roofs & green parrots flying around (some of them going into holes in the minarets which they compete for with the pigeons; as I went up the stair it was full of a pigeon's booming).

After this we walked through a bewildering labyrinth of v. narrow 'lanes' – canyons between high buildings which you can stretch across, paved with big flags & full of goats etc. The people here paint a little man in yellow on either side of their front door, sometimes holding a sword (I'm told this is done when one gets married). Lots of brass in the shops here, shining along these dark lanes. & Benares is well known for toys; I have bought Bimba 12 minute wooden animals & birds all different (I chose them small because of air travel).

Altogether Benares is the most fascinating town I've seen yet. Not only does its river frontage give it a sweep & a dignity but the detail in the streets is exceptionally colourful & varied. The traffic e.g. consists largely of hooded tricycle cars, coolie pedalling in front & 2 sitting behind, & of 'ekkas'(?) – a horse-drawn vehicle highly primitive & gimcrack-looking but Burnier says it's v. comfortable (perhaps because you have to squat on it). Men here put more paint on their foreheads & more women wear nose jewels. There are also a number of old men in saffron or rather orange robes which means they've retired from the world. And there are quite a few young men wearing collars or wreaths of jasmine & orange flowers just for the hell of it. I also saw a big white ox wearing a garland of flowers. And just before that a litter with a corpse wrapped in crimson silk & a heap of jasmine petals on the stomach.

We also this morning called on Radhakrishnan[1] (the man who spoke so well on Aug. 14th in the Constituent Assembly) who is Vice-Chancellor of Benares University though it seems he's hardly ever here (he's just about to leave for Oxford where he's a Fellow of All Souls & then in November goes to Mexico with an Indian delegation, then in January back to Oxford where he's asked me to visit him). We had quite a job reaching him as the students were on strike today & picketing the great gate of the University (to protest against the rising of fees)! Radhakrishnan v. depressed – not only about India (he thinks partition could have been avoided & thereby at least some of this communal trouble) but also about the world.

Came back to this Arabian Nights house (whose only snag is one bumps one's head on stone doorways) to find a young engineering student from South India who's due to go to California to study but who, unlike most English engineers, takes a great interest in Auden, Eliot & even Salvador Dali. Which reminds me: Burnier is reading Casanova which the engineer, who's v. young, considers 'an adolescent taste'. I find Casanova makes a nice complement to his caste-mark etc. I gather both these Frenchmen (the other one by the way looks rather like Lennox Berkeley[2]) were converted to Hinduism by a man called René Guénon whose books they have here (violently anti-western); I must try to read them when I get back.[3]

The Frenchmen tell me these students here have no prospects of getting good jobs – excepting in business where competition is terrible; all the professional classes are underpaid, they say. And by the way, Radhakrishnan was most disapproving of this move to oust English from the universities. Understandable, as the official language for Benares is to be Hindi which he can't speak, coming from the South. I had a similar complaint in Calcutta from Sushin Dey (who works in the Min. of

1–Sir Sarvepalli Radhakrishnan, OM (1888–1975), statesman and philosopher. Professor at Mysore, Calcutta and Oxford. Indian delegate to International Committee on Intellectual Co-operation of League of Nations 1931–9; member of Indian Assembly 1947; Ambassador to Russia, Chairman of Unesco 1949; President of India 1962–7.
2–Sir Lennox Berkeley (1903–89), English composer.
3–René Guénon (1886–1951), author of *East and West* (1941) and many other works.

Agriculture & Fisheries); the Bengal Government had just ordered all office files to be kept in Bengali. Which means, he says, getting rid of their typists; there <u>are</u> typewriters in Bengali scripts but, he says, you could write your stuff sooner (& besides some of their staff are not Bengalis themselves). But Radhakrishnan thinks, after the first gestures have been made, this provincial pride will be modified & English must survive as a 2nd language regularly used for communication between different regions.

I believe an American professor from Hawaii is coming to tea now, so I must stop, Cat dearest. Tomorrow I go to Lucknow.

All my love,
L.

P.S. Tell Bimba about the little animals.

TO *Hedli MacNeice* MS Bodleian

21 October [1947] Madras / Letter 17

Dearest Cat,

Another too short letter & in still greater haste (I expect by the time you get this you'll have had No. 16 from Wynford). Just about to leave for Tanjore after which shall be some days away from any place of air mail departure. Hence this scrawl, just to keep in touch.

The South continues terrific. Yesterday we went round Fort St. George, a bit of 18th century England with a v. simple whitewashed classical church full of white marble monuments in the Flaxman style – some comic inscriptions but the total effect pretty moving.[1] Had a chat there with the Bishop – v.v. Oxford, quite naturally as he'd been an Oxford don & knew Maurice Browne[2] & Co. After which we went sari buying & Jack & I got one each; yours appeared to be just your colour but as it was in artificial light I haven't since dared to open the parcel. After that we were dined in a 100% vegetarian restaurant by our archaeologists – lots of little hot dishes & rose sherbet (which Jack maintains tastes like a certain brand of

---

1 – Fort St George ('White Town'), British fortress founded at Madras in 1639. The simple, whitewashed church is presumably St Mary's, the oldest Anglican church in India. John Flaxman (1755–1826), English sculptor, whose work was once described as 'a T-squared world of white marble buildings inhabited by marble-white men and women exchanging lofty sentiments in heroic couplets' ('John Flaxman. A Centenary Estimate', *The Times*, 7 Dec. 1926, 19).
2 – Maurice Browne (1881–1955), author and theatre producer.

lipstick) after which we both had huge garlands of pink roses hung round our necks & were presented with a large stiff posy which we didn't quite know how to hold.

Today we started early & drove out about 60 miles to Mahabalipuram which is on the coast – quite a foamy sea (most refreshing) – where is another great collection of 8th century rock-hewn stuff – monuments, caves & temples.[1] Some of this was quite as good as Ellora & more sympathetic, having power as well as charm; in fact, the first we saw – a long frieze of slightly more than life-size figures – struck me as one of THE world's pieces of sculpture. Am ordering some photos but they are quite inadequate.

Many of these temples, as at Ellora, are to Siva who always has a lingam (phallic emblem) in his inner shrine (which usually is otherwise empty). Surprisingly (or not?) this feels truly religious. There was one temple today right by the sea & v. much weathered (which improves it) surrounded by placid stone bulls & the lingam on an axis seawards. A v. pregnant set-up. What with one thing & another, I really do intend to have a shot at that long poem. The lingam by the way is also to be noticed on humble little graves in the countryside.

I'm curious to see what the Indian Exhibition in London will be like.[2] Sculpture seems to be their forte but only for a certain period & the best sculptures are immovable – & even if you could take them out of their setting would most likely lose their impact.

Darling, I must end this; the sweepers are gathering for tips which means it's time to get cracking. We shall be all night in the train, attended by Mr. Srinivasan. Tomorrow night we sleep in Trichinopoly. I wish you could see these places. That frieze today was of rustic figures cowherds etc. but with an incredible grace added unto them; the humans in deep relief but the background was filled in, in low relief, with faces of cows – all's well with the pasture. A v. charming legend behind it all. I must try to get hold of these Hindu legends in London.

1 – Cf. 'Mahabalipuram' (1948), Collected Poems, 1925–1948, CP07, 305–7.
2 – An Exhibition of Indian Art directed by Leigh Ashton (of the V&A), opened in November 1947 at the Royal Academy, Burlington House, including exhibits selected from museums and private collections in India by Sir Richard Winstedt (RSA), Basil Gray (BM), and K. de B. Codrington (V&A), and with the co-operation of the Indian Committee, chaired by Mrs Sarojini Naidu. Cf. 'Indian Art Exhibition', The Times, 13 Feb. 1947, 3; Alfred Munnings, 'Indian Art, Winter Exhibition at Royal Academy' (letter), The Times, 15 July 1947, 5; and 'Indian Art at Burlington House, The Times, 29 Nov. 1947, 5.

And now, darling, be happy – & also well; I get appalled when I think of how much you seem to have to do. Hope Teresa is really helping you out.

all my love,

L.

P.S. One of the photos I've ordered is a monkey group for Bimba.[1] (Excepting lions, which are merely heraldic as they didn't know them, these sculptors were really brilliant on animals.)

TO *Daniel MacNeice*[2]   MS Bodleian

27 October [1947]   Trivandrum, India[3]

DEAREST DAN,

How is the term going? I'll be returning home in about a fortnight. It's just possible Hedli & I may be able to visit the Downs in November. I have to go twice to Liverpool to lecture & I might be able to work it in, coming or going.

If you'll look at the map of India you'll see that Jack Dillon & I are now in the extreme south. Tomorrow in fact we're going to drive to Cape Comorin, the southernmost point. This is a very luxuriant tropical landscape; you can't see the town of Trivandrum for coconut palms.

On our way here from Madras we visited the most famous temple cities of Southern India – Tarigore, Trichinopoly & Madura[4]. In some of these they have temple elephants, all dressed up to kill & with painted foreheads

---

1 – 'I went often with Louis to Regents Park Zoo. Amongst our favourites were seals, the sloth, ant-eaters and, of course, monkeys, which might explain the quest for the monkey photo. When he came back from India, the many gifts were unpacked in the basement at Canonbury Park. Louis was not given to coming up with presents, which is why, maybe, I remember the occasion. There were plenty of them and they seemed very exotic. Silks, saris, scarfs and materials with little round mirrors in them. In particular, there was a little bronze shiva dancing in a ring of flames that perched around the place that I was much attached to. A first taste of Asia. The trips to the zoo might also account for my insistence that he should bring a "potto" (big eyed lemur?) on his way back from South Africa (I assume). I think we were both enamoured of the word "potto" and Louis was not averse to the idea but seemed puzzled by the logistics of getting it home' (BCM, private correspondence, 2009).
2 – Addressed to DM at Downs School, Colwall, nr Malvern, Worcs.
3 – Trivandrum (now called Thiruvananthapuram), site of the temple of Vishnu on the Malabar Coast, was called by Mahatma Gandhi 'the ever-green city of India'.
4 – Trichinopoly, capital of Tiruchirapalli District in Tamil Nadu State, site of various seventh-century cave temples and a ruined seventeenth-century fort. Madura, south of Madras, is a famous pilgrimage site.

& bells; they salute you with their trunks as you enter. Jack & I were also garlanded with flowers by the priests.

Before we went to Madras we were right inland in the State of Hyderabad where we went to see the caves of Ajanta & Ellora.[1] These were carved out of the rock in the early centuries A.D. by Buddhists & Brahmins. Some of them served as temples & some as monasteries; in Ajanta there are the remains of very fine frescoes – of which I've got some picture postcards.

The biggest affair at Ellora is sheer Rider Haggard – an enormous temple hewn out of the mountain, supported by great stone elephants with colossal sculpted gods all round it – some of them with 16 hands.

In Madras we were taken round by Indian archaeologists who were also strict vegetarians. They gave us one very fine dinner of curried vegetables etc. etc. all laid out on banana leaves. And rose sherbet to drink.

Since I wrote to you last I have been in a great many places, including Benares the holy city of India, where I stayed with two eccentric Frenchmen who have turned Hindu & live in a beautiful house on the Ganges. As a pet they own a giant crane which keeps wandering into the drawing-room. They don't go in much for tables or chairs; you just lie about on cushions. Benares is also full of monkeys; in the early morning you see them jumping the streets.

However, I'll tell you a lot more about all these things when I see you. Southern India is really great fun – much more so than the North.

lots of love,
Daddie.

P.S. How is rugger? And work??

Afterthought:- I enclose eleven Hyderabad state stamps which are only used for internal post & are probably unheard of in England (in case you like to swap them, they should have a rarity value). Golconda, which appears on one of them, is an enormous old fort which we visited, conducted round by a venerable professor in a fez with a long beard & twinkling eyes. We went to another Muslim fort called Daulatabad which you ascend by a very dark spiral staircase cut in the rock.[2]

1 – System of up to thirty caves carved into sides of a ravine, near Ajanta, which contain Buddhist frescoes (650–200 BC). There are nineteen temples in Ellora – Brahman, Buddhist and Jain.
2 – Golconda Fort dates from the fourteenth century and is located seven miles west of Hyderabad. Daulatabad, near the Ellora caves, dates from the twelfth century.

TO *Hedli MacNeice*   MS Bodleian

27 October [1947]   Trivandrum / Letter 19

Well, darling,

Since my last on Saturday morning (this being Monday evening) we have undergone considerable frustration & exasperation. When I wrote to you we were expecting the local archaeologist to turn up, he being our only contact here, but after a couple of hours' wait during which we were told he was on his way to see us it turned out he was not in Trivandrum at all but out 'on circuit' miles away. So as we were relying on him to fix our visit to Cape Comorin[1] & as we had only a few rupees left & it was a Bank Holiday, we had to resign ourselves to staying put in our hotel over the weekend. This was a relaxation after our rush last week but all the same we resented it.

On Saturday evening they had a dance in the hotel which we peered at with interest. Mainly half-castes – all very odd. Jack & I came to it after trying out toddy[2] in a toddy shop down the road – sickly sour stuff of a milky colour made from coconut palms. We had just been calling on an old Belfast man who is Art Adviser to the Maharajah. He puzzled us at the time but later we saw some really shocking pictures by a man called Roerich[3] bought by the State for 20,000 rupees each (which would buy works by most living artists) & they told us . . . but perhaps this is libel. We had a long talk yesterday with a Syrian Christian who's v. cynical about the whole set-up in this far-famed Model State. What seems clear is that, since having acceded to India which meant the resignation of their former strong man the Dewan, everything's in the melting pot & no one will take any responsibility.

To return to our own troubles we went to the bank this morning hoping to find there 1000 rupees each for us in accordance with a message sent by us via Wynford to the B.B.C. in Delhi on Monday of last week. But noone had told us that Tuesday, Wednesday, Thursday, Friday & Saturday (not to mention Sunday) of last week, were all bank holidays in Delhi so that they'd just had no chance to transmit money. So Jack & I go out on the street again feeling v. cross, not even being able to hire a taxi to see the sights when who should accost us but our missing archaeologist

1 – Cape Comorin (now Kanyakumari), popular tourist destination on southernmost tip of India.
2 – A mildly alcoholic palm wine.
3 – Nicholas Roerich (1874–1947), Russian painter. Founded the theosophical Agni Yoga Society in New York and later retired to the Punjab.

Mr Poduval[1] who'd hared back to Trivandrum on hearing we were there. Mr P. was much astonished to learn we had no money & took us back to the Bank where a rather fruitless discussion ensued with the manager. After which Mr P. set about having us turned into State Guests but this sea-change has not yet occurred because no one, as I said, will take responsibility & the Dewan himself refers all such matters to the Maharajah. Anyhow we don't think we want to be State Guests as as soon as our money comes we want to leave this State & see Cochin if possible before returning North (we had planned to make a move today).[2] Sorry, Cat dearest, if this is boring – or is it possibly amusing? If the money doesn't come by Thursday morning we really are in a mess as from then on our schedule was definitely fixed.

Mr Poduval however has done one thing to compensate us for the boredom of Trivandrum; he laid on a really good dance this evening, 16 year old girl, daughter of a friend of his. Accompanied by a tambura (= tall stringed instrument), primitive drum & tiny harmonium. What this girl didn't know about rhythm would be no use to anyone. Most astonishing combination of finesse & dynamism. A little girl of 8 also appeared, to do one solo dance, with surprising finish. The most elaborate thing of all of course is their hand movements but they work pretty nearly everything, including eyes & neck. We saw this show in the girl's home – bare cement floor on which she dances in bare feet with bells round her ankles. Mr P. thinks it a great shame she shouldn't be encouraged by the high-ups here. I suspect they've had too much truck with Europeans (this small hotel is crawling with English engineers). Over a third of the population in Travancore are Indian Christians by the way. You pass several churches going down the main road – first Anglican, then R.C., & then 'Jacobite' which is a branch of Syrian-Christian.[3] Many of these Christians have taken surnames like Matthew & John & Thomas (there's a strongly believed legend that Doubting Thomas was the first missionary in India).

Mr Poduval became rather sad tonight & accused us (meaning the British) of having betrayed the Indian princes. We're getting used to being accused of having betrayed someone.

1 – R. V. Poduval (b.1894), an authority on regional archaeology, co-editor of *Arts and Crafts of Travancore* (1948).
2 – Cochin (now Kochi), large seaport in Kerala state.
3 – The Jacobite Syrian Christian Church in Kerala is a part of the Universal Syriac Orthodox Church.

Time for bed now, darling; will continue this tomorrow.

Oct. 28th: Getting on for lunch-time after which we drive to Cape Comorin. This morning we saw an alleged scientist, 'an eccentric genius' they told us, aged 85, in the Public Library. He runs something called the World Welfare Mission (fair enough?) & is v. keen on an 'organistic society' (based on a dangerous biological analogy) which appears to boil down to a revival of the caste system divorced from religion. We left him to meet the Dewan who told us that the real danger here is not communal trouble but Communism; the local communists have a slogan which appeals to the uneducated – 'Thirteen Cents & No Marriage!' Sounds pre-Soviet to me, in fact Plato.

Jack has just played the fruit machine in the hotel bar & won the highest possible. Our luck must have turned, he says. I hope it has & that our money will arrive soon; this would be a tiresome place to get stuck in. Nothing but coconut palms & caginess. Jack now wants to get back to Delhi because of the news from Kashmir (on which State he, having been marooned there, is now the B.B.C. expert).[1]

Am still perplexed as to what to buy for Dan here. India doesn't seem to produce anything up his street – I may have to fall back on an image of Ganesa.[2]

Darling, I'm afraid this is a dull, dull letter. It's partly Travancore but it's partly, I think, that I'm getting tired. High time I got home! Still, I look forward to Agra & Fatehpur Sikri if we have time to fit that in.[3] Sinclair's scheme was to stay in a bungalow in Akbar's deer park – & possibly have John Auden along.

All love – & to Bimba
(I've written to Dan from here),
L.

---

1 – On 27 October, formerly independent Kashmir had acceded to the Indian Dominion in exchange for military assistance against an all-but-overwhelming armed Muslim uprising, allegedly with Pakistani support and aid. Lord Mountbatten wrote to the ruler of Kashmir on 28 October: 'In response to the appeal for military aid, action was taken today to send troops of the Indian Army to Kashmir to help your own forces defend your territory and protect lives and property and the honour of your people.' See 'Rebellion in Kashmir: Muslim Peasants' Uprising', 'Kashmir Accession to India' and 'Kashmir Joins India: New Government To Be Formed. Rebels Repulsed', *The Times*, 27, 28 October 1947.

2 – Ganesa (Ganesh), elephant-headed, Hindu god of wisdom and art.

3 – Fatehpur Sikri, in Uttar Pradesh: a splendid sixteenth-century city built of red sandstone by the Mughal Emperor Akbar (r.1556–1605); former imperial capital, now a World Heritage site.

1948

TO *Hedli MacNeice*   MS Bodleian

19 March 1948   BBC

Darling,

Writing this – a short letter – just in case you don't leave on Sunday. It's v. sad you still have a cough. I'm missing you v. badly but – if it's a question of health – don't return prematurely.

Took Bimba & William to Highgate this morning. B. still complaining as she leaves the house, then returning to normal as if by clockwork. Odd?

V. good notice of the Indian programme in today's Statesman by 'William Salter' – who turns out to be Walter Allen.[1]

Catti, don't be cross but I did have a binge on St. Patrick's night. Not in the least disastrous or nasty but indisputably a binge & very sleepy-making. Long session at the French Club attended among others by Anna who took a great fancy to E. Lutyens.[2] Far the tightest person present was old Olwyn (?) who was too incapable for anything except to be embarrassing. I don't know how she can go on running that club if she gets like that often.[3] Speaking for myself I find these dos too tiring nowadays – don't care if I don't have another for a long time.

1 – 'It was an excellent idea to send Mr Louis MacNeice to India to observe the transfer of power and gather material for a series of features, for he is, among much else, an occasional poet in the best sense of the word, unrivalled in our day in seizing the essential spirit of a time or a place' ('William Salter', 'The Arts and Entertainment: Radio Notes', review of *India at First Sight*, BBC Third Programme, 13 March 1948, *NS*, 20 March 1948, 232–3). 'Salter' later also reviewed *Portrait of Delhi* (BBC Third Programme, 2 May 1948): '[It] was gay; it danced along; it did perfectly well what it set out to do, to give an impression of Delhi over all the centuries of its existence. And it did more than this, as was shown when Mr MacNeice came to the communal troubles following partition and the assassination of Gandhi. His rendering of these was a most moving piece of radio-writing' (*NS*, 8 May 1948, 373).
2 – Anna Shepard; Edwin Lutyens.
3 – Olwen Vaughan (1905–73), proprietor (and cook) of the Le Petit Club Français, 4 St James's Place ('The French'), which she had opened during the Blitz. Not to be confused with Gaston Berlemont's French House or York Minster on Dean Street. She also worked as a secretary at the British Film Institute (1936-45) and later helped found the New London Film society.

V. pretty pattern revealed in today's Chronicle. The News Editor of the Daily Worker has resigned in order to become a Catholic![1] It only remains for Evelyn Waugh to join the C.P.

Am now getting down to the Delhi programme.[2] Have written to the Oxford Welshman for lots of references.[3]

On Sunday morning I'm going to take Bimba to the Zoo & then to Laurence's for lunch followed by a television children's programme.[4] This will give Teresa a break.

The weather today is horrible! I hope the Primavera will return in time for your homecoming.

V. exciting about your new suit – but won't you look rather conspicuous?!

> Goodby now, cat heart,
> I love you a lot,
> L.

P.S. Just had your pretty postcard. What goings on!

1 – Douglas A. Hyde resigned from the Communist Party and from his job at the *Daily Worker* in protest against, among other aspects of Soviet foreign policy, the overthrow of Czechoslovakia. See '"Daily Worker" News Editor Resigns', *The Times*, 19 March 1948, 2. This was particularly newsworthy at a time when employees in Britain faced the possibility of losing their jobs if known to be communists, or even if seen reading the *Daily Worker* (see 'Action Against Communists', *The Times*, 27 March 1948, 6).
2 – *Portrait of Delhi*, India and Pakistan No. 3, broadcast 2 May 1948.
3 – Goronwy Rees (1909–79), novelist, journalist and university principal. Educ. Cardiff HS, New College, Oxford; Fellow of All Souls 1931. Principal, University College of Wales, Aberystwyth 1953–7, when he resigned following revelations of his early ties to the Soviet agent Guy Burgess, and inside information about AB, whom he later revealed as 'the Fourth Man'. He is Price in *AS*.
4 – Regent's Park Zoo became what BCM calls 'a focal point' for the MacNeices at this time. They were members and would sometimes eat Sunday lunch there with Laurence Gilliam and the Rawsthornes. On other occasions they walked the dog outside the Zoo's railings, peering in. They later (1952) lived nearby in Clarence Terrace, from where they could hear the seals barking at night. FLM had particular favourites among the animals, including seals, monkeys and birds: 'He was quite specific. He loved the sloth[s]. He laughed a lot when he looked at them' (BCM, private correspondence, 2008).

20 March [1948]   [Letterhead 10 Wellington Place,
                                   NW8 *deleted*]

Darling,

V. nice to hear your voice last night! I was pretty startled as I thought the Exchange said 'a call from <u>Twickenham</u>.' It's a great pity about your cough; surely there must be some responsible doctor about?

N.B. I told Teresa you probably wouldn't be back till Thursday & she says it's quite all right. I think it makes her rather proud to be holding the fort.

Still bleak weather today – but the daffodils are out in the garden. I shall take Bimba a wee comminata to the grain shop. Tonight I said I'd go to Highgate & have dinner with Elizabeth. V. exciting, yes?

No, Reggie's business was really out of Laurence's hands. However there's now been some sort of top level inquiry into his recent M.N. [*sic*] fiasco & it's been written off as a mistake, i.e. not as malice aforethought. So he's all right again pro tem. I went with him (R) to a Danny Kaye musical film yesterday. The film as a film pretty bad, ditto the music, ditto the technicolour, but D.K. himself enormously amusing at moments. I wish we'd seen him in the flesh; his season is over now.[1] The News Reel showed the King & Queen visiting Marlborough College.[2]

I've just asked Bimba to dictate you a letter but she's playing with Mrs Hepburn's little dog, so I'll have to wait.

Shall be listening in to the Grand National this afternoon; I have 10/- each way on Loyal Antrim.[3]

This scheme I mentioned re Budapest & Paris. A woman called Francesca Wilson (whom I've met, I think) rang up yesterday to say that Dodds had told her you & I wanted to give joint performances abroad, so she wants me to have lunch on Monday to meet (remeet, I think) Countess Karelyi (?), wife of the Hungarian Minister in Paris, who has just founded

---

1 – Kaye (1913–87) had recently had a triumphant season at the London Palladium. See 'Mr Danny Kaye', *The Times*, 4 Feb. 1948, 2. The film is presumably *A Song is Born* (1948), directed by Howard Hawks.

2 – The Royal visit to Marlborough was on 12 March.

3 – The Grand National at Aintree was won by Sheila's Cottage, at 50–1. Loyal Antrim cleared Becher's Brook but fell at the next fence. Eleven-year old Loyal Antrim had not been a bookies' favourite since he had been running without distinction in Ireland for several seasons. 'The Grand National. Greatest Steeplechase of the Year' and 'The Grand National. Success of Sheila's Cottage', *The Times*, 20, 22 March. 1948. In his popular history of astrology (1964) FLM wrote a section on 'How to pick the winner in horse racing by a numerological system (evolved by the British astrologer Sepharial)' (*Astrology*, 197).

a British–Hungarian Society.[1] Countess K. might be able to arrange either Budapest or Paris; Paris would be more feasible, wouldn't it? Anyhow I'm going to lunch.

Who do you think walked into my office yesterday? Diana – dressed almost the same as 2 years ago & looking both decayed & mad.[2] She said she had 'the car' outside & would I come out for tea? No, I couldn't, I said. Would she call back for me later? No, I said. I wanted to say I didn't want to see her <u>any</u> time but it seemed a bit crude in front of Ruth & Bertie. So I told her to ring next week but I think I'd better send her a note saying she's behaved so oddly both to you & me that I'd rather discontinue the acquaintance.

Bertie by the way was just about to leave by plane for Scotland. A sudden decision. He just said Marie was ill.[3]

Darling, drink in all the sun you can; there may not be much here when you get back.

Here comes Bimba – just a short letter, as I have to fetch grain & dog biscuits . . .

Letter from Bimba.

[*FLM's hand*] please, Mummy, will you bring me some chocolate if you can? Please, Mummy, don't forget to leave the Easter eggs. Can you take me a toy – it doesn't matter what you take but you must take me some things. Will you take the chocolate rabbit too; don't forget that.

I've been looking at books & Teresa's been ironing. What have you been doing?

My aeroplane's broken. I'll show it to you when you come back.

Mummy, I'll tell you a story in here. Once upon a time there was a little boy & he asked his Mummy if he can get the paper & his Mummy said Yes & then – it was a little boy called Dan – not the same Dan – & Dan went out to get a paper & when he came back he said 'Mummy, when is the lunch ready?' & Mummy said 'soon'. 'But what are we going to have for lunch?['] & his Mummy said 'Potatoes, cabbage, meat & fish' & a little boy said 'All right but can I play in my nursery?' & his Mummy said

1 – Count Mihalyi Karolyi (1875–1955), Hungarian ambassador to France 1947–9.
2 – Unidentified person, but definitely not Diana Clements, his step-first cousin (DM, private correspondence, 2008).
3 – WRR married Marie Harden Waddell (niece of the medieval scholar Helen Waddell) in 1936, and they had two daughters, Nini and Harden. Marie studied psychology and psychoanalysis in Edinburgh, but was later diagnosed as schizophrenic. She died in 1953.

'Yes, you can but you mustn't go into the drawing room which is next door for the men are painting the drawing room.' So he drawed in his nursery. Then it's finished, the story.

X That's a kiss.

X lots of love

X lots of kisses

[BCM's hand] B

TO *T. S. Eliot*   Faber archive

23 June 1948   BBC

Dear Eliot,

Thank you for your two letters of June 8th and 14th. I should have answered before had I not been away in Paris.

While I am glad to hear that the board is prepared for a new volume of radio plays, I am now swinging over to your own suggestion that I might first publish my stage play 'Eureka'.[1] I should probably want to rewrite it a bit, it being quite some time since I looked at it, but I see no point now in waiting for a stage production (though I believe it is soon to be done on Television). As I may have told you, various managers, etc. have read this play, and seem to have been put off by its content, though they have all admitted that it is perfectly 'good theatre'. In my opinion it is readable as well as produceable, and would give a nice opportunity to complain about managers, etc. in an introduction.

As regards this prose book which you refer to as my 'projected autobiography' (it was not meant to be exactly that) a long time ago I had written about fifty or sixty thousand words of this, but wartime and post-war developments both objective and subjective have made me want to start again from scratch. I still want to write this book, but cannot see myself managing it unless I get a prolonged break from other activities. I think it quite likely that I may get such a break in the moderately near future, so should be grateful if you could let the matter rest at least a little longer.

Yes, I shall be in London at the beginning of July, so I should very much like to have lunch with you and discuss the Collected Poems.[2] But what I should like to know before that is whether this collected edition is a

1 – *Eureka* was never published.
2 – *Collected Poems, 1925–1948*.

definite proposal, and if so, whether I may expect a contract (involving an advance!) in the near future.

Yours ever,
Louis MacNeice

TO *John Lehmann*   MS Bodleian

9 November 1948   [London]

Dear John,

I have now thought a bit about that proposal of yours and think that if I write it piecemeal I could eventually bring together a number of articles into a fairly coherent whole such (or roughly such) as I have outlined below. By the way I find on looking up my 1939 contract with Faber's for that prose book which I have still not produced for them, that they do there claim an option on my next prose book. I am pretty sure, however, that we could get round this, especially if I talk to Eliot about it when he returns from America.[1]

The following scheme is only approximate but will indicate the ground I should like to cover. Writing these chapters one at a time will probably mean a certain amount of overlapping; some of this I can subsequently cut but I feel there will be no harm in making some of the same points several times in different contexts. As we agreed it would be primarily a personal book drawing its evidence largely from my own experience and that of some of my friends who are working poets. This being so I would probably lay more stress than is usual on the snags and difficulties which confront the poet and on the compromises and 'second bests' which he is sometimes forced to accept.

The chapter headings I have given here are make-shift and at least three of these chapters, i.e. nos. 3, 5 and 6, should have Appendices giving more detailed or more technical illustrations of the main points made in the chapters themselves. Each such appendix could of course immediately follow the chapter to which it belongs but I think I should prefer to have all the appendices grouped together at the end of the book.

Approximate scheme

(1)   Why one does it. Evidence mainly from self and contemporaries. Attempt to reconcile personal or accidental conditioning with social function and aesthetic values.

1 – JL replied and with some enthusiasm expressed the hope that FLM could 'get round Faber' and publish the book with John Lehmann Ltd (JL to FLM, 12 Nov. 1948, *Ms Bodleian*). This did not happen.

(2) <u>The Perils of Theory</u>. Especially pertinent I think in our time. Would cover theories <u>of</u> poetry and theories, e.g. political or psychological, <u>affecting</u> poetry.

(3) <u>Wrong Models</u>. Both among the old masters and among contemporaries. Would involve a discussion of <u>period</u>. (Appendix would give examples of <u>good</u> bits of poetry both past and present and explain why they are bad models for the normal poet of our time.)

(4) <u>Intake and Output</u>. The relations, actual and ideal, between the poet's life (which includes of course his intellectual life) and his poetry. In passing would discuss the so-called 'social consciousness' of the 1930s.

(5) <u>Experiences with Images</u>. The article I sent you but expanded to include comments on certain poets past and present. (Detailed examples in appendix.)

(6) <u>The Sound Pattern</u>. Evidence mainly from self and contemporaries. A (I hope readable) discussion of functions of word rhythm with special stress on the interdependence of rhythm and other aspects of a poem. (Appendix more technical, possibly using a special notation.)

(7) <u>Poetry and Adolescence</u>. A study (1) of the 'romantic' or anarchic phase which nearly all poets seem to go through, and (2) of the experimental phase which should go with this or follow it. (Experiment in this context tending to be an end in itself.)

(8) <u>Structure</u>. This will gather up much that has gone before and in particular will make a contrast with (7), i.e. will be discussing the poem as the whole or end to which everything else must be subordinated.

(9) <u>The Discovery of Horace</u>. This and the next chapter, being detailed studies of 'classical' (i.e. structural) poets who both have affected me personally and seem to be good correctives to some of the poetic vices of our period, will follow on naturally from (8).

(10) <u>The Discovery of Herbert</u>. ditto, ditto.

(11) <u>My Present Slant</u> (or words to that effect). What I am now getting at myself, what I think others are getting at, and what I feel we should be getting at.

P.S. I might possibly do an Appendix on 'The Spoken Word', with perhaps a glance in passing at the sung word.

1949

TO *Hedli MacNeice*   MS Bodleian

22 February [1949]   The Cross House, Childe Okeford,
                                      Dorset[1]

Darling,

Just had your letter. I'm terribly sorry you & Bimba are both still feeling
wretched. In the circumstances it seems nasty to write you back a 'tu
quoque' but I think I'd better – for the sake of honesty & to get it off my
chest (you said you 'had to' write yours).

What you don't seem to understand is that, from my point of view, you
are 'not there' for weeks & weeks at a time. When you are building up for
a performance, there's an atmosphere of strain & anxiety whenever (or at
least most times) I come into the house. And the same strain-&-anxiety
comes even down the telephone into the office. This I find not only
generally depressing (I am after all, I suppose, a melancholic type) but not
at all good for my own work (which is quite strainful enough). Of course
I know how frustrated you must feel owing to the idiotic narrowness of the
music & entertainment set-ups in this country but for me this frustration
just makes me feel futile: I can't really give you much technical advice (not
being musical)[2] while I can't propaganda much for you as husbands'
propaganda is always, quite naturally, suspect.

Darling, I'm not exaggerating. It's not that you talk the greater part of
the time about your difficulties (which you do, you know) but the way
you talk about them – like a series of 'S.O.S.'s which I can do nothing
about.

As regards my 'state' at the Anglo-French, I didn't mention this before
because it sounds like a rather silly alibi, but, whatever may have been the
case on other occasions (&, apart from liking drinking, I do admit that, if

---

1 – Clifford Canning now lived at the Hanford Prep School for girls, Childe Okeford, Dorset,
which he and his wife Edith had founded in 1947.
2 – Cf. Alan Rawsthorne's remark: 'I don't think that one would call Louis a particularly
musical man in the conventional sense of the word, but on the other hand he had a very great
sense of what he wanted the music to be doing' (typescript, *Louis MacNeice: A Radio
Portrait*, BBC, 7 Sept. 1966, PRONI D2833/D/5/21).

left to myself, I would rather not be sober at these alarming dos), <u>this</u> time the 'state' was not only not intended but was a surprise to me myself; I <u>know</u> what I had had – I could give you a timetable – & it was <u>not</u> enough, in normal circumstances, to have any serious effect. I suppose the circumstances just weren't normal: (a) I'm wrought up in advance for these things, (b) I had just by the end of office hours dispatched the last remains of the Collected Poems, including the sestina, which made me both sad & tired,[1] (c) I was cooked almost crazy by sitting beside that stove & (d) I think I'd had 'flu from that morning. However, I suppose that all <u>is</u> just an alibi but I <u>am</u> truly sorry that I disappointed you.

It <u>might</u> be a good thing, darling, if you went away somewhere by yourself for a bit. I think it's quite usual for married people to get on each other's nerves even when they're not both artists (which means egocentrics!) While I'm Fausting – say, in May – I could stay in 52 with Teresa & Bimba & you could nip off abroad.[2]

Disaster about this weekend. Miss Gillett is expecting a Hanford mother which means I'll have to leave on Saturday. The mother may fall through (there <u>is</u> more mumps at the Cannings') but, if she doesn't, we might be able to stay with Eddie[3] or someone. But I'll only moot it if you want to come (& you <u>would</u> like the country here anyway); otherwise I'll come back on Saturday.

The Queen goes all right; I go walks on the hills & get ideas for her.[4]

I have dinner tonight with Coade to meet some German who knows all about Modern English Writing.[5] Alarming?

Darling, please don't be bitter with me. It makes me feel very much out on a limb.

all my love,
L.

P.S. I'd prefer you to burn this; I've burnt yours.

---

1 – 'To Hedli', a sestina, prefaced *Collected Poems, 1925–1948*.

2 – 52 Canonbury Park South, N1. FLM's translation of Goethe's *Faust* (with Ernest Stahl) appeared in 1951.

3 – Eddie Sackville-West.

4 – *The Queen of Air and Darkness* (100 min.), broadcast BBC Third Programme, 28 March 1949 (see also FLM to TSE, 26 March 1952, p. 549).

5 – Possibly F. T. Coade (1896–1963), headmaster of Bryanston School, which Daniel MacNeice had attended.

7 July 1949   BBC

Dear Tom,

   This is to introduce in advance my great friend W. R. Rodgers (of whom you know) who is proposing to ring you up probably during the last week of July when he returns from a visit to France. Rodgers is at the moment preparing a broadcast on James Joyce for the BBC Third Programme rather on the lines of one he did recently on Yeats; these programmes are a kind of jig-saw reconstruction of the personality of the man concerned, achieved mainly through the recorded voices of people who knew him.[1] Rodgers has so far contacted a number of Joyce's friends and Joyce authorities but he has not yet got hold of anyone who could give due consideration to the part played by Ezra Pound in Joyce's development. He is very much hoping that you will be prepared to fill this gap – and incidentally to discuss Pound and Yeats with a view to a second Yeats programme in the future. I am sorry that I shall not myself be able to introduce Rodgers to you as I shall be abroad then but I am confident that you will get on excellently without me!

   Something quite different: your people at Faber's may possibly be fretting because I have not yet returned the text of my play 'Eureka'. I lent this to Tyrone Guthrie some time ago in connection with some rather vague 1951 Exhibition project and he has not yet returned it.[2] I have of course other copies but, as I was proposing to make certain alterations in it anyway, I was waiting with some interest to hear his criticisms. I gather he is out of London but I am making efforts to get in touch with him and I hope to let you have a revised version in the not too distant future.

                    Yours ever,
                    Louis MacNeice

---

1 – The scripts of these broadcasts were later published by BBC Books as W. R. Rodgers, *Irish Literary Portraits: W. B. Yeats, James Joyce, George Moore, George Bernard Shaw, Oliver St John Gogarty, F. R. Higgins, AE: W. R. Rodgers's Broadcast Conversations with Those Who Knew Them* (1972).
2 – Tyrone Guthrie (1900–71), theatre director; author of *A Life in the Theatre* (1959). FLM had attended Guthrie's production of *Hamlet* at the Old Vic in 1937. Cf. FLM to MM, 10 Jan. 1937, p. 291.

TO *T. S. Eliot*   Faber archive

7 November 1949   BBC

Dear Tom,

I don't know if you have heard that I am going to Greece (as Director of the British Institute in Athens) from the next New Year for a year and a half, i.e. till the end of June 1951. I am hoping that this will enable me to write that long-delayed prose book for you!

Now an apology – about my play, Eureka. Since I last wrote to you about this, I have had two very adverse comments on the script as it stands from people whose opinion I respect. I am not normally over-susceptible to criticism but, the theatre being such a strange world (!), I have begun to suspect that in this case the critics may be right. In the last few days however I have been approached by some theatre people who are contemplating a production of this play – possibly in an altered form. In the circumstances I would like to defer the publication of the play either until it has been accepted for the stage or until, stage productions apart, I have re-written it to my own satisfaction.

As sorting out Eureka may take some time, in the meantime I should like to offer you my verse translation of Goethe's Faust (which, you may have heard, I have done for the BBC).[1] I did this this summer in collaboration with a great friend of mine, E. L. Stahl, who is Reader in German at Oxford. We undertook to make a radio version of the whole work (Parts I <u>and</u> II) but made very heavy cuts – up to nearly a third of the total (these cuts falling mainly in Part II). Even so, this version runs to between 7,000 and 8,000 lines, divided into six sections (two for Part I and four shorter ones for Part II). Though I say it, this translation is pretty faithful both to the original meaning and to the original verse pattern.

I don't think that I shall ever feel inclined or even able to translate the 3,000 odd lines which we omitted – most of which seem to me to be either irrelevant or embarrassing. Goethe himself, I understand, had declared his intention of cutting the whole thing to ribbons but never did so. I should like therefore to suggest that you might publish what I have done as 'An Abridged Version of Goethe's Faust'. I could show you the whole script (all six sections) straight away; for publication however I should wish to alter the directions and, in this respect, go back from radio to Goethe.

1 – Broadcast BBC Home Service as part of the *World Theatre* series, 30–31 Oct. 1949, rpt. BBC Third Programme, 10, 13, 17, 21 Nov. 1949. Cf. FLM, 'On Making a Radio Version of Faust', *Radio Times*, 28 Oct. 1949, 5, 7.

I shall be very interested to know what your feelings are about this proposition.

Yours ever,
(Louis MacNeice)

P.S. If your Board looks askance on the postponement of Eureka, I should be prepared to waive an advance payment on Goethe's Faust, provided I find the Faust contract acceptable in other respects.

1950

2 March [1950]   The British Institute, 17 Philikis
                               Etairias, Athens [hereafter Athens][2]

Dear Margui,

Thank you very much indeed for your most heartening letter. All
correspondence here, I should explain, has been mostly delayed &
confused by a possible strike!

I'm very glad people liked the Dark Tower; I'd heard no reactions to it
from other sources.[3] (This place is really the other end of the world.) I
suppose Blood Wedding has happened by now but if you see George Fox
again, do remember me to him.[4]

We are all well here, living part of the time Before Christ & part in 1913
A.D. Living is pleasant but the cost of it absurd. Even olives are dear –
which is a racket. But wine, I should add, is cheap – & we're getting quite
used to resin in it. Its apologists say that the Ancient Greeks resinated too.
Resinating through the ages – if you'll forgive the pun (too many late nights
have reduced my brain to that level).

I'm organising play-readings here – by the British for the Greeks. I wish
you were around to take part & make our dry bones live!

                               love from us both,
                               Yours ever,
                               Louis

1 – Marguerite Caetani (née Chapin; 1880–1963), patron of the arts and editor of the literary
magazines *Commerce* (1924–32) and *Bottteghe Oscure* (1948–60). Born in Connecticut and
educated in New York and Paris, she was a cousin of T. S. Eliot, and was married to Roffredo
Caetani, Prince of Bassiano. Cf. FLM to WRR, 12 May 1950, p. 526.
2 – FLM was Director of the British Institute in Athens 1950–2.
3 – *The Dark Tower* (75 min.), broadcast BBC Home Service, 30 Jan. 1950.
4 – A reference, presumably, to a production of Federico García Lorca's *Blood Wedding*
(1932). Fox is untraced.

TO *T. S. Eliot*   Faber archive

9 May 1950   Athens

Dear Tom,

I don't know if you have been approached by the British Council people in London about visiting Greece this autumn; anyhow I thought I might write to you on the side about it.

Everyone here is very eager to get you out as a British Council lecturer for, I suppose, from 2 to 3 weeks (visiting Salonica & possibly Patras & Corfu as well as Athens). Any time from the beginning of October. We shall be vastly disappointed if you can't manage it. They say October & November are very pleasant here & I'm sure you'd enjoy it. But could you possibly let me know soon whether it's on the cards? (The 'usual channels' waste such a lot of time).

On the whole I'm enjoying this place – but there's too much social life of a 1913 brand. Athens is also one of the noisiest towns I've visited. Partly because there's a law which exonerates a driver who's run over someone if he's blown his horn. And as for the cost of living . . . !

Am just recovering from amateur theatricals. I found myself not only producing but playing in The Playboy of the Western World. Very much bricks without straw but it's nice to have done it once.[1]

Do come here in the autumn.

Yours ever,
Louis

TO *W. R. Rodgers*   PRONI

12 May [1950]   Athens

Dear Bertie,

Have been meaning to write to you for a long time but our first 4 months here were so hectic that reading, let alone writing, seemed all but out of the question. Now, thank God, the Culture Season (which largely means smiling at a lot of old ladies) is ending & we hope fairly soon to feel human. Have just emerged from amateur theatricals &, at that, the Playboy of the W.W., which I not only produced but for lack of anyone else took part in – as Shawn Keogh, which is really pretty easy; one need just

1 – A photograph of FLM playing Shawn Keogh in the play is reproduced in Stallworthy, 377.

hang one's mouth open & hope for the worst. After which we had a great blind lying in the green corn where the locals had all relieved themselves with the Byron Professor of English at the University of Athens (a v. good man who will call on you this summer in London).[1]

Dan, as you probably know, was here for Easter & we had a week on a very appealing island where all the streets are steps & the air is all cockcrows & sheep bells.[2] We are planning to visit lots of more islands through the summer; they are a different world from Athens & a very much better one.

Hedli, Bimba & Teresa are all in great form; we live in a somewhat poshish flat but it's getting less posh daily. The Greeks have a tiresome habit of filling their homes with frosted glass doors which make one feel in a consulting room. This is counteracted by street cries from below which make one feel in a bazaar. And we have cognac in great wicker-clad containers & a mad cat who eats olives.

The Principessa Caetani has been at me about Irish writers.[3] I referred her to you (I hope you don't mind). Why not get Ernie to send her an article on early Irish sculpture?

We have heard v.v. little from London since we've been here. Do write & tell us who's dying &/or living. And what about your new book of poems?[4] (I have only written one poem since I've been here – but it is in 4 parts – called Suite for Recorders.[5] Probably no one will like it though I do – so far).

Must go home now & eat bouillabaisse which H. is making.

Love from all,

Louis

1 – William Arthur Sewell (1903–72), educ. Leeds; Queen's College, Oxford. Lectured at Cape Town and later held professorships at the Universities of Auckland, Athens, Ankara, Beirut, and Waikato. Author of *The Physiology of Beauty* (1931), *Katherine Mansfield* (1936), *A Study in Milton's Christian Doctrine* (1939) and *Character and Society in Shakespeare* (1951).
2 – DM joined his parents and they all stayed with Kevin Andrews and travel writer Patrick ('Paddy') Leigh Fermor (b.1915), at the home of the painter Nico Ghika (1906–94) on Hydra. Cf. Stallworthy, 381. Ghika is Costa in *AS*.
3 – Cf. FLM to Marguerite Caetani, 2 March 1950, p. 524, n. 1.
4 – *Europa and the Bull* (1952).
5 – 'Suite for Recorders', *World Review* (London), new ser. 20 (Oct. 1950), 8–11; *TBO, CP07*, 315.

TO *E. R. Dodds*
                                      MS Bodleian

15 May [1950]   Athens

Dear E.R.D.,

Have been meaning to write to you for a long time but the Culture Season in Athens (or rather in Kolonaki) is only just ending & culture here means burning the candle at one end with 1913 dinner parties & at the other with hack administration.

How are you both? And how did you hate America?[1] Mary keeps nattering about getting Dan out there for his summer holidays but, quite apart from M. herself (who thinks adolescence is 100% sex worry whereas with Dan it's 60% cosmic questionings), I strongly feel that America is just his wrong medicine at the moment. He was out here for Easter & he has got, potentially, European good taste. And an un-American unconcern with gadgets & success & those other things.

Our whole family flourishes – Hedli in very good voice, Bimba playing a recorder, Teresa going out with Italian hairdressers,[2] & Thompson, our tomcat, hiding under the carpets eating olives. We live in a somewhat streamlined flat full of frosted glass doors like a dentist's but the street below is full of streetcries & donkeys & fruit stalls & from our roof we get a v. good view of the Acropolis.

I am v. glad I came out here, for all Reggie's efforts to stop me. He & the boys are really talking through their hats. Of course there is injustice done (with some pretty nasty frills) but there is not complete suffocation as in Reggie's pet places due north of us.[3] Nor can everything that happens here be fitted into the stock ideological equations (any more than what happens in India); a lot of the mess & the feuds & corruptions seems to go back to the Turks.

We have not yet been out of Athens nearly as often as we should wish. Spent the Clean Monday (beginning of Lent) weekend in Aegina with octopus for lunch & the valleys smoking with almond blossom. And a week in a dream house in Hydra, an island which is like the film of Hamlet – you never stop going up steps.[4] Also a weekend in Salonica & a few day excursions to places like [*illegible*] & Aegosthena (the latter astonished

---

1 – ERD had recently returned from a visit to the University of California at Berkeley, where he gave the Sather Lectures, later published as *The Greeks and the Irrational* (1951).
2 – Teresa Moroni, Italian maid
3 – Presumably Romania, where Smith had worked for the British Council at Bucharest.
4 – *Hamlet* (1948), directed by and starring Laurence Olivier.

527

me; I'd have thought that fort was Norman).[1] But no Delphi as yet. No Mycenae. No Delos. No Olympia. For August, when Dan comes back, we plan to go to some island – possibly Andros or Icaria. Am disappointed by the Greek intelligentsia whom I'd heard much of but perhaps we haven't met the right cliques yet. The poets, of whom there are too many, all seem to think that T. S. Eliot liberated poetry from tradition(!) & that Free Verse is empress for ever. And the painters are of many styles but seem, with some notable exceptions, not only derivative but dreary. Music, Hedli thinks, is poor except for a humble little group which performs in the Byzantine tradition. Architects there seem to be none although there's an immense amount of building (walking along the streets one's nostrils get full of cement). And the University, so everyone tells me, is still quite Teutonic & opposed to all ideas. The English professor there by the way may be calling on you this summer, a v. nice chap called Arthur Sewell who is both intelligent & merry. He holds strong views (which I share) about the way we sell British culture. (Incidentally, most of what I've sold so far is Irish; we even performed The Playboy of the Western World with myself as Shawn Keogh looking as imbecile as possible).

There's a chap here (about to leave) called Hal Lidderdale who says he mooted to you that you might come out here next Easter (i.e. after April 1st when a new British Council year begins).[2] Do consider this; it would be a godsend to all of us, including those many Greeks (modern) who just cannot cope with Greek (ancient). Not that we as yet can cope with Greek (modern), at any rate as regards talking; I just haven't had time to take lessons & in Athens one can get on without it. Didn't Bachtin write some booklet on modern Greek?[3] If so, I'd like to read it. Which reminds me: could you be v. kind some time when you're in Blackwells & ask them to send me an O.U.P. Herodotus – but only if it's got that nice blue binding; I just can't read any more from those filthy clay-covered texts – & charge it to me; I'll pay them from my London account.

agreed!

1 – The Attic fortress in Aegosthena dates from 300–200 BC.
2 – Halliday ('Hal') Adair Lidderdale (1917–92), British Council officer stationed in Salonica 1952–6.
3 – Introduction to the Study of Modern Greek (Cambridge, 1935), by Nicholas Bachtin (1896–1950), educ. St Petersburg, Sorbonne; French Foreign Legion; Cambridge (PhD 1934). Brother of Mikhail Bakhtin, he was appointed in 1938 Lecturer in Classics (and later of Linguistics) at the University of Birmingham. Of Bachtin and his circle of expatriate intellectuals, Dodds wrote: 'Any group of English people needs some small foreign element to activate it; these Russians were yeast to the Birmingham dough' (Missing Persons, 113).

Must stop now & prepare to rehearse a play reading. Do write & tell us about yourself & herself & the dogs & garden & general goings on in England.

> Love to you both
> Yours ever
> Louis

P.S. Apologies for my writing; it's the sort of nib I've abominated ever since I took Common Entrance.

TO *Mary MacNeice*

MS Bodleian

16 May [1950]   Athens

Dear Mary,

Thank you for all your letters – & forgive this pen which I can only just make work.

You are obviously having hotter weather than we are; they say there's never been such a chilly May in Athens. Which is lucky as we're still having a few cultural functions. However it's the very fag-end of the season, after which there'll be nothing till October. However, I'll have to be in Athens quite a bit – damn it – till the end of July, just holding the fort which means answering correspondence or meeting any English grandee who happens to pass through. In August we plan to go to an island – we've not yet decided which – &, as you will have gathered from my last letter, we'd planned it quite a long time ago as a <u>family</u> holiday including Dan (possibly accompanied by a boy friend). He won't have the chance again & it'll be a much more exciting holiday for him than this last one most of which, alas, we had to spend in Athens[.] So you'll understand that I'd like to keep to this arrangement. Apart from which – & this is nothing to do with you – I do seriously think that he's a bit young for the impact of America. Not being an American, I mean! Since the war I've become a staunch upholder of the 'Third Force' or whatever it's called – anyway of the principle that Europeans must try (however desperate the attempt!) to escape <u>both</u> the Russian brand of communism <u>and</u> Americanisation. (There are, incidentally, some Americans who agree with me!) Which reminds me that I can't possibly agree with you in the assumption you made in one of your letters that the English intelligentsia is much <u>happier</u> than the American. The English intelligentsia has at least (with a few notable exceptions!) a sense of humour – & also a far greater tolerance of people with unorthodox opinions. I saw the hell of a lot of the New York intellectuals (all brands) & remember one particular party where Mrs. Cyril Connolly was present, having newly arrived from England. Though born an American she'd forgotten what it was like & after an hour or so's floundering in the heavy, heavy, humourless, jargon-ridden conversation, she asked me in a whisper 'Are New York parties always like this?' And I said Yes! As for the American attitude to Sex, I've strong views on that too. The English, I think, are often hypocrites about sex (though vastly less than they used to be) but most of the Americans I met struck me as being plain fools about it – & very frustrated fools at that. However, if I go on on this subject, you'll think I'm bigoted! Obviously we all depend on America now & on a long term view that may be a good thing but it doesn't alter the fact that America as a whole is still frighteningly <u>immature</u>. (As borne out by your own comments on Reno!) Ask Dodds if he doesn't agree with me.

To leave generalisations, we've had a v. nice letter from Dan from school where he's already busy with the broken down boat which his ne'er-do-well friend has.[1] He did all sorts of errands, such as delivering half bottles of Ouzo to our friends, with great efficiency in London. I dare say Margaret may have written to you about it.[2]

I see that F. O. Matthiessen, whom I stayed with in Portsmouth, New Hampshire, for a week after coming out of hospital, committed suicide the other day in Boston by jumping out of a 12th floor window. I am v. sorry about this as he was a most kindly man.[3]

Your cake for Dan sounds real Olde Worlde. We sent him back with a whacking great tin of halva but he insisted that he was going to give ½ of it to Martin in passing.

All of us here flourish. Hedli has given one concert – with great éclat – & is about to give another. Corinna is now attending <u>three</u> schools – one English, one Greek, one French (but only for a few hours each). Teresa has discovered an Italian hairdresser & Thompson is madder than ever, having lately taken (a) to eating olives & (b) to hiding under the carpets in order to jump out at people's legs. He is unrecognizable, having put on so much weight since we adopted him.

Have just been invited to a party at the British School of Archaeology – which you no doubt remember! It is now run by a nice man called Cook,

---

1 – DM had fantasised with his friend John Williams about restoring an old rowing boat to seagoing capability (DM, private correspondence, 2008). Cf. note on Williams in FLM to MM, 5 July 1950, n. 2, p. 535.
2 – Margaret Gardiner.
3 – See FLM to EC, 29 Aug. 1940, pp. 401–2. Matthiessen died on 1 April 1950, at the Hotel Manger, Boston.

an Old Marlburian & very quiet.[1] We go to play tennis there sometime[s] (Dan did twice).

love, L.

P.S. Don't overdo that weeding!

TO *T. S. Eliot* Faber archive

19 June [1950] Athens

Dear Tom,

Thank you v. much for your letter of June 13th. I am delighted to hear that, other things being equal, you would like to come to Greece in February or March.[2] I can only pray that they <u>will</u> be equal (by the way what an odd phrase that is).

Now to answer your questions:-

(1) We should want you to be in Greece <u>at least two weeks</u> – but preferably three.

(2) As well as Athens you ought to lecture in Salonica. You <u>could</u>, if you chose, lecture also in Corfu (which they say is v. attractive). You could also (but this is perhaps rather a bad fourth) throw in a lecture at Patras on your way to Corfu. But neither Corfu nor Patras should be considered <u>unless</u> you're staying a full 3 weeks.

(3) Number of lectures:- In Athens (one only elsewhere) a minimum of two lectures in English, a maximum of three. There is no need for you to give a lecture in French but the French Institute here (which is an admirable concern) would I think be delighted & honoured if you gave them one lecture. <u>If</u> you did so, then 2 lectures would be the maximum (though you need not give more than 2 in any case – if you don't want to). The French lecture by the way should be on a different subject from your English ones. But either of your English ones can be repeated in Salonica or elsewhere.

(4) Choice of subjects:- We are perfectly happy to leave this to you (you have a v. strong following in Athens who would flock to hear you on anything) but I would suggest myself that, if you're giving two lectures, one might have a reference outside literature (Writer & Society, Poet in

1–John Manuel Cook (1910–94), educ. MC 1923–9, King's College, Cambridge. He had been Director of the British School of Archaeology in Athens since 1946.
2–FLM had expressed the hope that TSE might come to Athens in 1951 and had asked him if he could finalise a date, preferably in early spring. (FLM to TSE, 2 June [1950], *Faber archive*). Eliot was interested, but he didn't go.

the Community, & all that) while the other could be more purely literary (study of a particular writer, school, tradition, genre or whatnot).

(5) Time off to look at things:- I agree with you that this is enormously important & that the British Council are often v. inconsiderate about this. But we shall not be! If you come for 3 weeks you can obviously have lots of free time but, even if you're here only a fortnight, we can guarantee you reasonable gaps. As for going in cars, you will need a car if you want to see places like Mycenae but, as I shall probably be escorting you, you can go as slowly & stop as often as you like. The B.C. will certainly have to give you one big party (to meet all the sine qua nons) but apart from that we shall soft pedal the social side to meet your requirements; there are interesting people whom you could meet gently at a small lunch party if you so wished.

(6) You didn't ask this but where would you like to stay in Athens? The Embassy will almost certainly invite you & you would find them quite human (the Ambassador used to run a picture gallery). The B.C. Representative would also invite you (though he is a bit frightened of poets!) I would invite you but, alas, have no decent spare room. There is also a decent though smarty hotel. Not that you need to decide this yet. Yours ever, Louis.

TO *Mary MacNeice*   MS Bodleian

5 July '(Bimba's birthday!)' [1950]   Athens

Dear Mary,

Thank you for your letters. This correspondence seems to be losing itself in the sands – like the rivers in Australia, supposing they were ink! You seem to be generalising a lot now – e.g. about the 'haughty' British, so I feel I must repeat again that I was not really generalising about Americans or America as such but about their 'impact' on the casual observer. Such an impact – in any country – tends to be a caricature. The impact of England is certainly so, since the real England never appears in the shop window. For this reason I doubt whether England (unlike Ireland!) would be a worth while country for a foreign adolescent to visit – unless he were going to stay a year. The only good recent bit of generalisation about England that I remember was George Orwell's pamphlet, written in 1940, 'The Lion & the Unicorn'.[1] But regarding the dangers of generalisation about national

1 – *The Lion and the Unicorn: Socialism and the English Genius* (1941).

characteristics I can't help remembering an American corporal from Virginia whom I had a long talk with in a train during the war. He was very unusually enthusiastic about England & said he would like to come back for a good spell after the war & get to know it better BUT, he added, there were some things about the English that struck him as kind of wrong, kind of immoral . . . So I asked what they were & he answered with preliminary apologies (maybe they weren't wrong really but people would think them wrong back home) that (1) the English were so shockingly easy-going, didn't seem to bother this year about making more money next year & (2) – & this is what startled me – that the English were so shockingly outspoken to strangers, told them all sorts of things that back in Virginia would be kept family secrets! See what I mean?! So personally I'd rather not be provoked into further generalisations about Americans. When e.g. your girl friend is puzzled about anti-American feeling around the globe, the reason again is v. largely 'impact' – this time the impact of the G.I.'s, some of whom (a minority of course but so conspicuous as to be taken as typical) behaved so badly, often I think because they were homesick, that they completely put off people who were ready to welcome them, even in certain countries (e.g., from my own experience, Italy & India) sending the stock of the British soaring by contrast! Now these G.I.'s were not typical of America nor, in some cases, even behaving 'like themselves'.

However, to come to England which I know more about (I didn't know much in 1935 – nor, I think, did you). Only a v. small & obsolescent minority of English people are still 'haughty'; you may have met some in your hotel in '47 but that sort of hotel is a backwater. You may have found shopgirls etc. snooty or bored but you must remember that they were probably still dead tired from the war & from the endless boredom of coupons etc. It is a regrettable, though understandable, fact that after the war ended the manners of Londoners deteriorated. But the important thing to remember is that the great vice of England, class distinctions, is rapidly disappearing (of course there are diehard exceptions). The intelligentsia for example no longer consists of people like Harold Acton;[1] it includes many chaps like an ex pupil of Mrs Dodds from the Black Country who, meaning to say that he & Mrs D. got on well, said: 'Mrs Dodds? I'm oop her arse!' And key institutions such as the B.B.C. are, contrary to common beliefs as expressed in newspaper

1 – Sir Harold Acton (1904–94), author, legendary aesthete and historian of Renaissance Italy; educ. Eton and Christ Church, Oxford. He was a friend of Lady Beazley at Oxford, whom he recalls in *Memoirs of an Aesthete* (1948), 139–41. Cf. 'Auden and MacNeice: Their Last Will and Testament': 'A Chinese goose to Harold Action we advance' (*LI*, CP07, 742). Acton had lived in China for many years. See Mendelson, vol. I, 792

cartoons, <u>not</u> – not by a long chalk – the monopoly of public school types. Admittedly many of the administrators & nearly all the announcers are public school – the latter not because of snobbery but because, owing to the extraordinary variety of the U.K., their accent is the only accent that everyone can understand, whether they like it or not; announcers with regional accents <u>have</u> been tried & drew violent protests from rival regions who failed to follow what they said! But – much more important – the people who really compile & produce the programmes are anything but uniformly 'upper class' – or uniform in any way at all. My own Department, which numbers I suppose between 20 & 30 people in London, has only 4 or 5 public school chaps in it[1] – & <u>they</u> are completely individual; the others include ex-farmers, an ex-Guards sergeant, an ex-washer-up in Bristol, an ex-Presbyterian minister (v. earthy) from Northern Ireland,[2] a girl from a Black Country slum, a complete adventurer who has bummed round the world in various illicit wars & unsuitable jobs,[3] an ex-policeman-cum-Hampshire County cricketer,[4] a C.P. type or two,[5] an ex-Manchester book clerk[6] – & so on & so on & so on. Most of these spend a lot of their time going out among the so-called 'masses' & really eliciting things from them (this is not so easy but they're picked because they can do it). Through them & the people they bring along (crossing sweepers, tomato growers, water finders, factory hands, miners, lobster fishers etc. etc. etc.) I've really had my eyes opened to the immense variety – & vitality – of the English character.

From which follows my next point. I think you assume that Hedli & I – & therefore Dan – only meet people of one kind (a nice kind perhaps but hothouse?) This is almost the opposite of the fact. A Frenchwoman (a Jewess incidentally) whom we know in London said to us recently: 'My God, how lucky Dan is! Having the chance to meet so many interesting people – & all so different from each other.'

Which again reminds me: You have built too much on my crack about pneumonia (it's a question of degree; the Irish bogs are peculiar & have

1 – For example, Laurence Gilliam (City of London), E. A. Harding (Cheltenham), FLM (MC), Eddie Sackville-West (Eton), Christopher Sykes (Downside), Terence Tiller (Latymer Upper).
2 – W. R. Rodgers had been a minister in Loughgall, Co. Armagh.
3 – Jack Dillon had served on the Western Front, in Russia, and in Ireland with the Black and Tans.
4 – John Arlott OBE (1914–91), legendary BBC cricket commentator and former police officer in Hampshire, though he was not a county cricketer. He joined the BBC in 1945, initially as Overseas Literary Producer. Arlott's many books include *Concerning Cricket* (1949) and an autobiography, *Basingstoke Boy* (1989).
5 – Reggie Smith was at this time a Communist Party member.
6 – Geoffrey Bridson had worked for Sun Life Insurance in Manchester. Cf. FLM to Terence Tiller, 21 April 1951, n. 1, p. 544.

laid low many adults!); Dan is <u>not</u>, in my opinion, cooped or coddled or allowed no initiative. After all he's not only travelled a good deal on his own but he made that expedition to Brittany in a Galway hooker (which is not exactly a luxury yacht) with an Irish couple who are two of the toughest customers you could find anywhere.[1] And I don't know if he told you about their waiting on the sailors?!

We have just had a letter from Dan who seems in roaring spirits; it's possible he may bring Williams out with him. Elizabeth has now met Williams & was impressed by him; she thinks he's 'complementary' to Dan.[2]

Today is Corinna's birthday & she is suitably boisterous. Her chief present is a minute teaset, specially made by an Olde Greeke potter.

I must stop now & write to the Egyptian Consulate about a chap who wants to go to Egypt. After which there are a number more back letters to do.

The point of this letter by the way is, while conceding that I may have been – or rather appeared – unjust about America, to point out that you appear equally (or, I would say, more!) unjust about England. To be 'a child in England' is not really cause for pity! You should just see the children in Athens; the poor ones are undernourished & the rich ones have eaten so many cakes & been subject to so many rules that they have no more spirit left or, as Mrs D. would say, 'nater'.[3]

Anyhow . . . let's stop throwing darts into straw men!

Love,
Louis

TO *Mary MacNeice*   MS Bodleian

8 July [1950]   Athens

Dear Mary,

Just a hurried appendix to my last which crossed <u>your</u> last. I am v. sorry to hear about your hand but hope that, if physical treatment is out of the question, it will find itself again on its own as it were.

---

1 – DM sailed to Brittany with Tom and Ellie (née ffrench) Agnew. Tom Agnew was 'Ben // McQuitty who lives in a ketch' in *AS*, XVI (CP07, 444). Cf. Stallworthy, 487n.

2 – 'John Herbert Spencer Williams, whose father was the rector of a parish in Cambridgeshire. They lived in a delightful Rectory that dated from the Wars of the Roses (and that had a priest's hole behind a wall), near the village of Reach; so called because it reached into the fens' (DM, private correspondence, 2008).

3 – Mrs Dodds.

But about all these politics you bring up . . . You really must stop treating personal (& sometimes hurried) letters as if they were classical texts in which every word had been weighed! When I said '3rd Force' (if that's what I said) I was not supporting the people who want neutrality at any price. All I meant was that I think western Europe & certain other countries (between them adding up to something v. considerable) should try hard to retain their right to independent opinions, e.g. should not let American big business impose its will on them regardless. The raison d'être of such an independent group would not be to stay out of war if it came (Britain, intellectuals & all, would be in it from the word Go – & would probably suffer more than most from it!) but would be to prevent it coming. You're dead right in thinking that a socialist is the Russian communist's bête noir but the really important point is that a socialist country is far the most immune to communism. If France, Italy etc. had real labour governments Russia would be in a far weaker position in Europe. (Britain is probably the only European country where they cannot count on having a decent 5th column.)

One other protest! You may harp as much as you like on the impotence (or 'isolationism') of 'intellectuals' but without intellectuals there would have been no French Revolution, no Russian revolution – & no U. S. A. – as we know them. I know that Marx himself tried to discount their influence – but look at his own influence!

If one's 'curious about the world' it's no good either trusting one's intuition or keeping one's eye fixed on the present mess. The answer, I think, is a course of solid history! Hope I don't sound pedantic?!

All well here.
Love, Louis

TO *T. S. Eliot* Faber archive

20 September [1950]   Athens

Dear Tom,

Thank you for your letter of 6th Sept. which I received on my return from a remote island. I am very sorry indeed you can't as yet commit yourself to Greece but I see your point entirely.[1]

---

1 – FLM had invited TSE to Greece on 9 May 1950, but see also letter of 19 June.

As I don't know exactly when you are leaving for America (which by the way I hope will be pleasure as well as work) I should like straight away to mention the following project. I have been working lately on a set of longish poems (averaging c. 140–150 lines), each in four sections. I call them <u>Panegyrics</u> & I think they represent what one calls 'a new development'. I have already written eight (but 4 of these still need considerable tinkering) & am about to start on a ninth. I hope to write twelve in all & with luck may have completed them by the end of this year. They should make a more integrated book than any of my earlier ones, not only because they all have the same sort of general construction (not versification – which is considerably varied) & length but because they seem to come from a common matrix & so overlap or lead on to each other. The eight so far written are, in order of writing, as follows (I have suggested very aridly in brackets what they are 'about'):-

I.   <u>Suite for Recorders</u> (the Elizabethans: violence x pastoral)
II.   <u>Areopagus</u> (the Eumenides x St. Paul)
III. <u>Cock o' the North</u> (Missolonghi x Calydon; Byron x
      Meleager)
IV.   <u>Didymus</u> (St Thomas & India)
V.   <u>In Praise of Water</u> (primal element & symbol; hot countries x
      Industrial Revolution)
VI.   <u>The Island</u> (Greek island: Homer x today)
VII. <u>Aged Forty-three</u> (birthdays: time x timeless)
VIII. <u>Day of Returning</u> (homesickness – Odysseus, Jacob,
      evangelicals: this-worldy x other-worldly).[1]

If, as I hope, you would have it so, I would like this book published next year.[2] In the meantime, should the international situation deteriorate, I think it might be provident of me to send complete <u>drafts</u> of all my <u>Panegyrics</u> up to date to Faber's for safe keeping. Perhaps you could warn someone that I may do this so that they shall realize what I'm up to! These drafts should not of course go to press until I've had a chance to revise them & complete the set.

1–See his remarks to Terence Tiller on the broadcasting of these poems: 21 April 1951, pp. 541–4.
2–*TBO* was published by Faber on 11 July 1952.

Would you have any objection to my producing (with amateurs) The Cocktail Party in the British Institute here next spring? I should treat it with due respect. I'm glad to hear you have another play coming up.[1]

With best wishes for America

Yours ever,
Louis

TO *E. R. Dodds*   MS Bodleian

15 November [1950]   Athens

Dear E.R.D.,

I am delighted to hear that a sensible compromise has now been reached between yourself & the B. Council. They are tiresome people in many ways & I hope they didn't irritate you too much. I take it you will be spreeing before you start councilling, so I'll try to keep the last week of March free to go with you to Crete &/or other places. In the 3rd week of March I'll probably be tied up with our annual amateur theatricals.

Life here is interesting but exasperating – exasperating because it could be so much more interesting if I weren't entangled in red tape & rather futile admin. During the last 2 or 3 weeks for instance I have had to spend most of my time contacting all the scout masters & girl guide mistresses in Athens in order to lay them on for Dr. A. E. Morgan.[2]

Hedli & I have, I think, only been once out of Athens since the end of September. As for our Greek, which was progressing nicely in Icaria, it has gone right backwards as, apart from taxi-drivers, cooks etc., no one in Athens would dream of speaking Greek to us. Also one hardly has time even to read a Greek newspaper. As a result of all this I'm feeling rather strongly at the moment . . . (interruption here: passage of weekend) . . . about the B.C. in general as an excellent idea which is being at least 50% wasted.

We did get out again yesterday, for lunch, to a place called Liopesi the other side of Hymettus. The country's v. beautiful now with a lot of yellow

---

1 – *The Cocktail Party* was first produced in Edinburgh in Aug. 1949 (published 1950). FLM's review of the play for the *Observer* had appeared on 7 May 1950. The other play to which he refers, *The Confidential Clerk*, was first produced in Edinburgh in Aug. 1953 (published 1954).

2 – Arthur Eustace Morgan (1886–1972), MA, Hon. LLD and a Fellow of the Royal Society of Chemistry, had been principal of University College, Hull 1926–35; principal of McGill University (Montreal) 1935–7; assistant secretary, Ministry of Labour and National Service 1941–5; and was educational controller, British Council, 1945–50.

from the faded vines. Talking of vines, did you by any chance see my poem in <u>World Review</u> for October?[1]

Am again getting long, long scattered letters from Mary. She now maintains that <u>my</u> letters make her hand better or worse according to whether they contain any critical remarks. A new & not v. pleasant form of blackmail. As it is, I've never come really clean with her over the Dan question just because she was ill & I didn't wish to hurt her feelings. America may or may not be a good place for an adolescent (personally I think not) but my real point (which I didn't tell her) was that she herself this year seemed (& not only in my opinion) in a quite unfit state to receive Dan. This goes also for the preceding period during which Charles was running away. <u>And</u> it goes also for the long time before that (at least from 1939) when she & C. were nominally getting on all right; the atmosphere in their house when I visited them in '39 & especially the things Mary said to me about C. in his presence (v. possibly by now censored in her memory) seemed so v. unhealthy & unpleasant that I couldn't have sent any child, let alone Dan, to stay with them for more than a day or two. But now I've told her that from next summer on, <u>if</u> Dan himself so chooses, he may go & stay with her a spell. (I think he should be able to stand up to it by then.) Dan by the way hasn't written to either M. or us since leaving Greece. 'A plague on both my houses' I suppose?

Am going to Turkey to lecture etc. from Dec. 4th to 16th. Unfortunately more in Ankara than Istanbul. Do you know those parts?

At the moment I'm snowed under with galleys of Faust. Can't imagine how I ever came to write all that. Ernst is vetting them too & they're all getting mixed up in the post.[2]

Hedli is in good voice & is singing a lot of nice things this week at the British Embassy. Spiritual pearls cast before literal but maybe a few of the diplos. may like them. Corinna's in good voice too, in another way. She's now no longer dumpy but lanky & v. much concerned with changing her teeth. She is also producing v. strange pictures based on a 'bone house' she found in Icaria.[3] One skull in the corner pleased her especially (hope I

---

1 – 'Suite for Recorders', *World Review* (London), new ser. 20 (Oct. 1950), 8–11.
2 – FLM and Ernst Stahl's translation of Goethe's *Faust* was published by Faber in July 1951.
3 – 'I have vivid memories of the stay in Greece: one of those childhood spans of time that remain in the memory with great clarity. As is often the case, LM is there as a continuous presence rather than on an anecdotal level. I'm fairly certain that the Greek interval was one of, if not the most, happy periods in LM's and H's time together. I remember LM in a play, put on at the British Institute in Athens. Louis had the role of a drunk playing with a piece of rope (a noose?) at the side of the stage. Of course, as a six year old, my eyes were frequently on him, but regardless it was generally acknowledged that his carrying-ons were a show

haven't told you this already?) which she said was a happy old man. Why happy? Because he was smiling. & why old? Because his head was white.

Have you noticed some correspondence in the Statesman about one Wolfgang Kordan?[1] We met him before he left Athens. An eccentric but I would say honest.

Love to her & your selves
Louis

---

stealer. i.e. he was very funny. As a break from Athens, a primitive stone house was rented on the island of Icaria. Outside the house was a very large walnut tree under which Louis and I would sit, on a daily basis, and Louis would read to me from Rex Warner's *Men and Gods*. It's a very special memory' (BCM, private correspondence, 2009).

1 – See 'Makronessos', in 'Correspondence', *NS*, 4 Nov. 1950, 409.

TO *Terence Tiller*[1]   MS Texas

21 April [1951]   Athens

Dear Terence,

In great haste; I got your letter today & I'm leaving for Crete tomorrow. Here are 6 out of 10 Panegyrics – only I'm now calling them Burnt Offerings (all 10 are all but ready & I hope the book will be out before Xmas with the title 'Ten Burnt Offerings').[2] I'm sending you 6 to leave you some margin but you obviously can't pack 6 into one programme.

You could make <u>one</u> programme out of 3 or, conceivably, out of 4 of them or <u>two</u> programmes with 3 in each. It is up to you but here are my own recommendations:-

For <u>one</u> programme of three: <u>Suite for Recorders</u>, <u>Cock o' the North</u>, <u>Didymus</u> – in that order.[3]

For <u>one</u> programme of four: <u>Suite for Recorders</u>, <u>Cock o' the North</u>, <u>Didymus</u>, <u>The Island</u>.

For <u>two</u> programmes of 3 in each:- 1st programme: <u>S. for R.</u>, <u>C. o' the N.</u>, <u>Didymus</u>. 2nd programme: <u>The Island</u>, <u>Day of Renewal</u>, <u>Day of Returning</u> – in that order.

When I wrote last year about this I had thought I might myself write some linking commentary but haven't time for that now – unless you could add such commentary later (I'll be back in Athens on May 1st). But here are some notes which someone might use as a basis for commentary (I imagine <u>some</u> commentary's needed?):-

(All six that I've sent you were written in Greece during 1950.)

---

1 – Terence Tiller (1916–87), poet and BBC radio producer (joined Features, 1946; ret. 1975). Educ. Latymer Upper School; Jesus College, Cambridge. Taught at Jesus College and Fuad I University, Cairo. As a radio producer he is remembered for successful adaptations of Chaucer, Dante and Langland. Author of six volumes of poetry published over many years, including *Poems* (1941), *Unarm, Eros* (1947) and *That Singing Mesh* (1979). Like many of FLM's friends, he kept regular drinking hours and 'went daily at twelve sharp to the BBC club bar' (*DNB*).

2 – It was not published until July 1952. Cf. FLM to TSE, 20 Sept. 1950, above.

3 – Tiller chose the simpler option, producing these three poems for broadcast on 15 Sept.

<u>Suite for Recorders</u> (No. 1 in the series):- Theme the Elizabethans: dialectic relations of pastoral & violence. Key text the caption (Touchstone) from <u>As You Like It</u> – which some say refers to the death of Marlowe.[1] See also 'The Passionate Shepherd . . .' & 'The Nymph's Reply.' Black Jenny = (of course) spinning jenny. Note play on words throughout.

<u>Cock o' the North</u> (3rd in series):- Note caption[2] – which sanctions (I hope) the bagpipe tunes in Section I & the dialect in Section IV. Note oscillation between the 2 boars which cause the death of Meleager & Adonis respectively. Byron's fear of the dark is of course factual. Missolonghi is taken from the life; Clauss' distillery is just outside Patras.[3]

<u>Didymus</u> (4th in series):- Inspired by Portuguese 'Church of the Little Mount' (ask Jack) in outskirts of Madras.[4] Big temples in south of Shiva (pertinent (a) as dancer, (b) as destroyer, (c) as lingam god). All Indian Christians think Thomas really went there.[5]

✗ ‖

<u>The Island</u> (6th in series):- Real Aegean island towards Asia Minor coast: a village up in the hills with an unusual lot of trees; camp for political prisoners (with T.B.) in the hinterland; many émigrés from here in U.S.A. Note Calypso myth.

Nkawla

<u>Day of Renewal</u> (7th in series):- More personal. Instead of high-powered myths (e.g. Meleager, Calypso) Whittington & nursery rhymes. Themistocles fortified Peiraeus.

<u>Day of Returning</u> (8th in series):- Key text from Odyssey (more or less translated in first 2 lines of section III). Counterpointing of Odysseus & Jacob, both 'practical' men – in spite of their supernatural digressions. The idea of home: variations on home proper, 'home from home', & home beyond the sky etc.

1 – '[When a man's verses cannot be understood, nor a man's good wit seconded with the forward child, understanding, *omitted*] . . . it strikes a man more dead than a great reckoning in a little room' (*As You Like It*, III.iii).
2 – Epigraph taken from Byron's *Don Juan*: 'But I am half a Scot by birth, and bred / A whole one, and my heart flies to my head'.
3 – Cf. 'Now in the heat / Missolonghi yawns and cannot close its mouth', and 'The marble bust of Clauss, benevolent distiller', 'Cock o' the North', II, *TBO*, CP66, CP07, 328.
4 – FLM visited Madras with Jack Dillon in Oct. 1947. Cf. 'Tiny and self-assured in whitewash / Stands a plain church . . . The Church of the Little Mount' ('Didymus', *TBO*, CP66, CP07, 332–7).
5 – As alluded to in FLM to Hedli, 27 Oct. 1947, p. 510.

As I said, it's up to you what you do with these but N.B. any one poem you choose must be read in toto with all its 4 sections; also don't say they were specially written for the B.B.C. – because they weren't. Suite for Recorders & Didymus have already appeared in 'World Review' & Day of Returning I have just sent to The New Statesman.[1] The others you can say (if you like) have not appeared in any medium anywhere. Faber's have not yet received the Mss. so I suppose copyright could be fixed with me directly (but they mustn't offer me less than they offer Faber's).

About the presentation of the above, I think at least 2 voices are required for poem; some might need four. Here are some tentative suggestions, made in a hurry:-

Suite for Recorders:- Perhaps 3 voices? First & third sections to be read by same voice & a brand new male voice, v. lyrical-pastoral, to be saved for section IV?

Cock o' the North:- First & fourth sections to be read by same voice, Scots (Duncan McIntyre?), unless first section is split between 2 or more Scots, taking over where the pipe tune changes. Second section: voice like Carleton Hobbes? [sic][2] Third section yet another voice – emotive, personal.

Didymus:- Three voices? Voice A., v. dark & strong, for 1st & 4th sections (?excepting the 2 little rhymed inserts in section IV)? Voice B for 2nd section & for the inserts in section IV. Voice C (= Thomas himself) for Section III? This voice, C, ideally should be not 'straight' (Duncan McI. again could do it, if you have him already in the programme).

The Island:- Three voices? One for sections I & IV, another for section II, another for section III.

Day of Renewal:- Could be done with two voices, the 1st taking I & III & the second II & IV. The first should be sombre, the second with a lilt & lift (Alan McClelland?)

Day of Returning:- Three voices? I & III could be the same but one needs a brand new one (Jacob) for IV.

1 – 'Suite for Recorders', *World Review* (London), new ser., 20 (Oct. 1950), 8–11. 'Day of returning', *NS*, 23 June 1951, 712.
2 – Actors mentioned in this list include Duncan McIntyre and Alan McClelland, both of whom worked with FLM and were in the cast of the 1950 production of *The Dark Tower*, broadcast 30 Jan. 1950, rpt. 16 May 1951 (Coulton, 114). McClelland also played in *Return to Atlantis* (1953) and *Also Among the Prophets* (1956) (Coulton, 133). Carlton Hobbs (1898–1978) is best remembered for his radio work as Sherlock Holmes during the 1950s and 1960s.

About billing these poems, please call them (if you make just one programme of them):-

Three (<u>or</u> Four) Burnt Offerings

By L.M.

but, if you make 2 programmes,

Burnt Offerings

(first group)

&

Burnt Offerings

(2nd group).

And, if you want some talk in the billing, I suggest something like this: 'These 3 (or 4 poems) [sic] are part of a series written in Greece during 1950. Each poem consists of four sections or movements each of which sections is organically related to the other three.'

Have been writing this during the siesta period, so hope it's coherent. Hope also you like at least something in this batch?

Please tell Geoffrey I'll be writing to him soon.[1] I wrote a long involved letter to Laurence & await his reply with interest. Anyhow do tell him (L) that I'm expecting him out here any time from last days of June on – the sooner the better.[2] July 1st will be Freedom Day – when I'm off the B. Council – so we'll probably have a party.

Talking of poems on the air, I recorded 20–25 mins. of my own some time in the summer or autumn of 1949. I wish, for financial reasons, someone would put them out again! I also – for the same reasons – wish Archie would rebroadcast Faust – or at least one or two stray limbs of him.[3]

greetings,

Louis

1–D. G. (Geoffrey) Bridson (1910–80), writer and broadcaster. Educ. King Edward VII School at Lytham St Anne's; worked in insurance before joining the BBC in 1935, where he worked in production for many years. Author of several books of poems (which caught the attention of Ezra Pound) and a memoir, *Prospero and Ariel: The Rise and Fall of Radio, A Personal Recollection* (1971).

2–Gilliam arrived on 29 June. Cf. FLM to WRR, 28 June 1951, below.

3–Edward Archibald Harding (1903–53), radio producer. Educ. Cheltenham and Keble College, Oxford. He joined the BBC in 1927 and was later (1948) appointed to deputy head of drama. It was he who recruited FLM to the BBC. He produced the broadcast of FLM's translation of *Faust* (21 Nov. 1949; 8 hrs.) and is portrayed as Harrap in *AS*.

TO *T. S. Eliot*   Faber archive

7 May [1951]   Athens

Dear Tom,

Here at long last is the new book of poems about which I wrote to you last autumn. It is all ready to go to press though I shall probably alter a few words here & there later. Is there any chance in these slow times of getting it out before Christmas? I should prefer it if <u>Faust</u> could be followed quickly by an original work as I don't want people to think I've died away into a hack!

I hope you'll like this new collection; it seems to me to be the most <u>homogeneous</u> book of verse I've produced so far. Yet, I trust, with enough variety?

We were all disappointed that you couldn't visit Greece this season;[1] we hope you will next but, alas, I shan't be here then as I'm coming home in September. I did declare myself ready – on certain terms – to remain here for the Council but it seems that I'm the sort of chap they consider a luxury; the Self-Administrators are No. 1 Priority.

I saw Stephen S. as he came through from India & he lectured for us on the Art of Autobiography. At the same time we had Ninette de Valois urging the Greeks to be more classical.[2]

I don't really envy you the Festival of Britain & shall make do with a village πανήγυρις here & there during the summer.[3]

All greetings
Yours ever,
Louis

TO *W. R. Rodgers*   PRONI

28 June [1951]   Athens

Dear Bertie,

In haste. Thank you very much indeed for your letter. I'm delighted that your work, both public & poetic, is prospering but sorry to hear of the sad things in the wood.

---

1 – See FLM to TSE, 9 May 1950, p. 525.
2 – Spender applied for the Byron Professorship in Athens (Sewell's post) in 1952, without success. Dame Ninette de Valois (1898–2001), the founder of the Royal Ballet, had been appointed DBE in 1951, and Chevalier de la Légion d'Honneur the year before.
3 – Village fête or festival. The Festival of Britain opened in May 1951, marking the centenary of the 1851 Great Exhibition; it was based on the South Bank and elsewhere.

7.0 a.m. tomorrow I meet Laurence at Peiraeus. The weather has turned sticky-hot so the lean earth of Attica may get a wee bit of larding.

My poems? I've done a set of Ten Burnt Offerings. That one you mention is Number Two. Number Eight, entitled <u>Day of Returning</u>, has just, I believe, appeared in <u>The Statesman</u>.[1] & Terence T. has some others if you'd like to see them in typescript.[2] Robert American Poet Lowell [*sic*] has just passed through here. Nice. Is he good as a poet? Haven't seen his book.[3]

I leave (Thank God) the B. Council, about which I've just written most rapidly a farce, on the stroke of midnight this Saturday. We're throwing a Freedom Party.

Glad you were impressed by Dan. Bimba by the way often talks of you. She is in Switzerland for the summer.

Remember me to all, especially Jack, David, Archie & Peter du Val – & thank the last v. much for sending me that pound of letters.

I return c. mid-September. Can we have a joint office again? Sorry Margaret has gone. Couldn't we get Ruth Jones back??

We both send our love,
Louis

1 – 'Day of returning', *NS*, 23 June 1951, 712.
2 – Terence Tiller (cf. FLM to Tiller, 21 April 1951, above).
3 – Robert Lowell (1917–77), American poet. FLM is referring to *The Mills of the Kavanaughs* (1951). Lowell's previous books (which FLM evidently had not read either) include *Land of Unlikeness* (1944), *Lord Weary's Castle* (1946) (which won the Pulitzer Prize) and *Poems, 1938–1949* (1950).

1952

Dear Sir,

Thank you for your letter of December 31st, criticising my radio programme 'The Golden Ass'.[2] While I know that tastes inevitably differ about any adaptation whatsoever of any classic whatsoever, I am sorry that this honest attempt on my part to give a non-classical English public some inkling of some (not all) of the virtues of Apuleius should have evoked from you such a surprising outpouring of abuse. To start with, this was not a <u>translation</u> and your phrase 'translation in dramatic form' is a contradiction in terms, the original work, apart from the question of length, being not dramatic but narrative.

Secondly, I know from considerable experience in this field (having adapted and/or translated for radio such other authors as Aristophanes, Petronius, Goethe and the writers of the Icelandic Sagas) that, using another language and another medium, there is no question whatever of giving a listener the <u>whole</u> of one's original. The only question, therefore, is to offer the listener what one oneself considers to be some essential part of the original. In the case of Apuleius, I myself think that "The Golden Ass", for all its famous stylistic mannerisms (which do not transpose into dialogue) and its element of allegory (which in fact he forgets for nine-tenths of the time), its prime virtue is that it is a fantastic comedy of low life. I accordingly produced it as such.

No, I did not hear the Third Programme version of "Candide" but I have several times heard my own version of "Cupid and Psyche", a second programme which I abstracted from The Golden Ass, and – at the risk of appearing to do a vulgar "tu quoque" – I suggest that you also might listen to this when it is next broadcast.[3] It might possibly prove to you that I can see in Apuleius his admirable poetry as well as his admirable earthiness

---

1 – Unidentified.

2 – 'The Golden Ass', first broadcast 3 Nov. 1944; FLM produced a second version, broadcast 31 Dec. 1951 (FLM to Douglas Cleverdon, 30 May 1955, pp. 592–3).

3 – *Cupid and Psyche*, broadcast BBC Third Programme, 7 Nov. 1944; rpt. 4 March 1947.

and that I try to write every script in accordance both with my own lights and the primary virtues of the subject.

Yours truly,
Louis MacNeice
Features Department

TO *T. S. Eliot* Faber archive

10 March 1952 BBC / Reference 03/F/LMN

Dear Tom,

Please forgive me for not having answered till now your letter of February 19th about <u>The Story of Ireland</u>. I am afraid I don't really feel like taking this on.

I have found another letter of yours asking about my <u>Eureka</u>. If this is ever to be published, I should wish first to rewrite it which I am (again) afraid I have not so far done.[1]

On the other hand you may remember that some years ago I showed you the script of a long radio programme I had done on Aristophanes, which included my own translation of some of the more excerptable scenes from seven of the plays.[2] Would you consider publishing this in the near future – with or without some other scripts which I have in my files and which I think suitable for readers as well as for listeners?

Lastly, thank you very much for telling the Crown Estate that I should be a suitable tenant of Elizabeth Bowen's house.[3] I haven't yet signed the lease, but expect to do so unless dry rot or something is discovered at the eleventh hour.

Yours ever
Louis MacNeice

1–He first mentioned this unpublished play to TSE on 23 June 1948.
2–*Enemy of Cant*, broadcast 3 Dec. 1946.
3–At 2 Clarence Terrace, Regent's Park, where Bowen had lived with Alan Cameron since 1935. FLM took over the lease of the house in 1952.

TO *T. S. Eliot*   Faber archive

26 March 1952   BBC / Reference 03/F/LMN

Dear Tom,

First of all in answer to your letter of March 20th, I am very interested to hear that you are planning a new series of 'Ariel Poems' and shall be pleased to write you one (for a fee of twenty guineas) and shall let you have it by the end of July this year.

Secondly, here is the Aristophanes piece which you asked to see again, plus three other radio scripts, any or all of which you could, if you chose, include in the same volume.

As to Aristophanes, on re-reading this piece, I have decided that if it were published I should wish to cut all the invented dialogue between Aristophanes and his friends and write new linking material (in fairly formal, but concentrated prose) between the excerpts from the eight plays. These excerpts, each of which I think is self-coherent, do seem to me to give a rich and varied representation of their author. With one exception they are arranged in chronological order, pretty well covering the duration of the Peloponnesian War. The exception is The Birds which ought to have come between the Peace and the Lysistrata, but which I have transposed to the end as it seems to make a good finale. My translations, by the way, (which I should like to check again) are continuously free and sometimes somewhat condensed as I omitted various jokes and topical allusions which would be caviare to a modern.

Lastly, I should like to change the title (the original title wasn't mine anyhow). What about calling it 'Brekekekex', plus a clarifying sub-title?

Of the other pieces enclosed The Queen of Air and Darkness is a sort of morality play belonging to the same category as The Dark Tower, though I don't, in fact, like it so much.[1] It's a very dour piece and tends to be too much on one note, still I think it has its points. If it were published I should re-write the directions; I might also wish to differentiate the other-world scenes (i.e. Queen and Handmaids) from the realistic ones, either by indenting or italics or some similar device.

India at First Sight is an entirely different affair, being a sort of impressionistic documentary – a treatment which I think in this case is justified by the dialectical nature of the material.[2] It is hinged on an

---

1 – *The Queen of Air and Darkness*, broadcast 28 March 1949.
2 – *India at First Sight* was broadcast on 13 March 1948; see FLM to Hedli, 19 March 1948, n. 1, p. 512.

imaginary visitor (Edward) who is accompanied round India by three or four voices in his head, or perhaps one should call them familiars. (In print these could probably be isolated in the same way as the other worldlies in <u>The Queen of Air and Darkness</u>). Unlike the other pieces, this contains some material not written by myself, e.g. translations (by W. G. Archer, I think) of Indian popular poetry. If it were published, however, I think I should wish to condense or cut some of the middle or later sections. I should also wish to add a prose introduction, making some comments, subjective and objective, on India.

Lastly, as light relief, I am sending you another dramatised fairy story, this time of a Norwegian originality.[1] Whether this is worth printing I don't know, though it seems to me to retain some of the original folk charm, while combining it with a quasi-Carroll nonsense. Another point about it is that it could conceivably (given a somewhat trick production) make a stage play for children. If it were published, I should wish to write in a number of prose inserts at the places marked in red pencil. These should make the whole thing more visual <u>and</u> three-dimensional.

I shall be interested to hear what you think about all this. I am sorry the scripts <u>look</u> so horrible, but radio scripts always do.

Yours ever
Louis MacNeice
Features Department

TO *Daniel MacNeice*   MS Texas

30 August [1952]   BBC [letterhead]

Dearest Dan,

Thank you v. much for your letter, which was a good letter & extremely understandable. After we'd seen you off at Southampton I said to H. 'Dan will never be the same again' but I must admit I didn't say it entirely cheerfully as I wasn't sure which way this visit would take you – & I'm v. glad indeed it's taken you into happiness. But to come first to your practical question : I quite see why you want to stay longer in the U.S. but the Army people have here obviously not made up their mind about you yet as they sent you a notice fixing an appointment with an oculist (which

---

1 – 'East of the Sun and West of the Moon: A Norwegian Folk Tale', published in *Persons from Porlock and Other Plays for Radio* (BBC, 1969).

appointment I've postponed).[1] It's possible that your final acceptance or rejection might depend on this but I think you ought to come back at the date arranged so that they can accept or reject you in the normal way (I v. much doubt if they'd consider a foreign oculist's verdict; if I suggested this, they'd probably just say NO – & write you down as a fly-boy into the bargain!) However, having come back, if you're accepted, you go into the British Army (which, as armies go, is probably the best of a tiresome bunch) whereas, if you're rejected, I suggest that you pull out your capital in Belfast (this will mean some delay but shouldn't take too long) & use it to return to America for a considerably longer stretch during which you can think about your future, including the possibility of opting for America for good. Personally, although I was v. sold for a time on America, partly for personal reasons & partly for its sheer novelty, that feeling completely wore off in 1940 & since then I've never wanted to live there though I'd enjoy an occasional visit. However de gustibus etc.

To change the subject, it is of course terribly unnatural for people not to know both their parents though in this case it seemed unavoidable. If M. & I had broken up later & in a different way (& I'm quite sure now that we should have broken up some time) she might well have been able to take you with her or, alternately, we might have had some fifty-fifty arrangement like the Waterhouses.[2] But once one party disappears over the Atlantic – AND a war ensues – there's nothing much to be done about it. I may be wrong but I still think that last year ('51) was the first occasion when it was both feasible & desirable for you to go there. The endless correspondence on the subject between M. & me got a bit out of hand (both irrelevant & irascible!) because, whatever their intentions, there must

---

1 – Dan MacNeice returned to Britain in 1952 to make himself available for National Service in the British Army, but was rejected on medical grounds. Returning to America, he joined his mother in New Jersey, but was later drafted into the US Army for a period of two years. DM describes himself thus, writing in the third person: 'Had it not been for his National Service obligation back in England he would have converted his visitor's visa to an immigrant one then and there in Philadelphia: an option for British subjects in those days (though now unimaginable) that he wistfully forewent. He returned dutifully to England; was rejected for military service on account of poor eyesight, and (after a 9-months legal battle with his father who opposed his retreating from life's challenges in this way), returned to the USA, there to be conscripted for military service some two years later, his poor eyesight notwithstanding. This service was hardly more arduous than a similar stint in a benign British boarding school ('Who said anything about puttin' them earflaps down?'), and Dan did better at it than his American colleagues who had never left home before in their lives' ('Louis's Son', Ms Carrickfergus Museum).
2 – John Waterhouse had married Elspeth Duxbury (1909–67) in 1937, and the couple had later separated. They had three children.

always be a scoring-off instinct between 2 people in such circumstances (which leads to a vicious circle of tit-for-tats) but I suggest you ask M. if, looking back on it, she honestly thinks it would have been a good thing – for either or both of you – if you'd gone there in 1950.

One thing I've always felt M. has exaggerated about our break-up & her own position, your position etc. is the <u>uniqueness</u> of it. No case of course is like another but the world seems to be full of divorced couples, stranded children etc. And it's not only divorces . . . I think you had a rough deal for a number of years, yet I'm not sure I wouldn't prefer it to my own upbringing. Talk about not knowing one's parents! Apart from my mother being ill &/or away for years & then dying when I was just seven, I never can remember being at ease with my father (not but what I have things in common with him, including some of the things which put me off in <u>him</u>!) until perhaps the last few years of his life. On the other hand I remember my stepmother bursting into tears at breakfast because she thought Elizabeth & I only owed allegiance to my father & were excluding her from 'the family'. Whereas some years later she was reproving us both bitterly because, she said, we always left the room whenever my father entered it. Which, I think, was true! It gave us both guilt feelings of course & I think we'd have tried to meet him half-way if he on his side had been more elastic. I only mention this to show that there are other gulfs besides the Atlantic & divorce! Not that you don't know that.

Something that I don't understand in your letter is 'that Mary's importance for good or bad has been misrepresented up to date'. So far as I can remember, I've never tried to analyse M. to you (which would anyhow only be <u>my</u> picture of her! – & a bit out of date at that!) but have confined myself to what is more or less gossip, friendly though quite often comic little anecdotes (when things are near the bone one tends to concentrate on comedy). Perhaps I should say 'friendly <u>on the whole</u>' as no doubt, even if not consciously, the tit-for-tat element may have reared its ugly head at times. But on a serious plane I never thought it a good idea to go into a lot of past history which is obviously coloured with me, as with her, by a mass of subjective elements; there are however certain basic facts known to a number of people besides M. & me which, for better or worse, are just facts & inevitably have a bearing on anything that happened afterwards. And by the way I never said that M. 'was' Lady B. but have always maintained that she was both quite different & much nicer; on the other hand, like it or not, she <u>is</u> Lady B's daughter & if she had <u>nothing</u> in common with her mother (of whom, you should remember, you have no first-hand knowledge) she would be the first person I've ever heard of of whom this is true. Anyhow every single one of M's friends in England perceives certain things in common between them & I can't believe they're all having hallucinations. Some of those things at any rate are nice, e.g. they're both v. good raconteurs – or raconteuses? – with a v. similar sort of bubbling spell-binding technique. You can tell M. this if you like – only it will make her cross!

Which brings up another point. I know that M. nowadays has swung right round & pooh-poohs the whole Jewish business but I do tend to agree with Thérèse Mayer[1] who talking of you some time ago said it would be a great mistake if you deliberately drove the Jewish side of you underground – or words to that effect. I think in fact that that adds to the illumination which you are having at the moment. Because M. is Jewish & the Jewish part of you (however large or small it is – I don't know) must find things in her that it has been lacking. As a proof of M's Jewishness (on a minor plane) I've noticed that her bubbling type of monologue, which sooner or later tends to either irritate or bore many 'Gentiles' (including some of her best friends), seems to be sure-fire with Jewish people like the Stahls. This Jewishness is of little importance of course compared with the sheer fact that she's your mother – but I think it's of some importance.[2]

Now about 'finding yourself'. I couldn't be more glad that you feel this is happening. Of course again you're not unique here; nearly everyone of your age feels lost up to a point; still I suspect you went beyond the usual point. On the other hand – if you'll forgive me for once speaking like a Heavy Father – no one ever finds himself beyond a certain point either. Not even if he has the full quota of parents, love, money, 'success', & everything else which is supposed to make for happiness. It sounds a priggish thing to say but I think it's true, if paradoxical, that (just as one cannot live by personal relationships alone) the surest way of being happy is not to go after happiness. What one goes after is another question! My father, I suppose, went after his Christian Duty, H. & I go after our respective 'work' (interpretative or creative) although, paradoxically again, both Christian Duty & 'Work' can make one at moments unhappier. On the whole however I would say that once one's got into a rhythm (the

1 – Thérèse Mayer was a close friend of Hedli's. Married to a diplomat, she owned a villa in Ménerbes, Provence, where FLM and Stahl had stayed while translating *Faust*.
2 – DM recalled being surprised by this letter at the time, since his mother was not a practising Jew and DM 'had had no exposure whatsoever to Jewish life or thought'. Regarding the Ezras and Sassoons in Mary's family background – Jewish merchants in India and Asia – FLM used to refer teasingly to 'your Old Testament relatives' (DM, private correspondence, 2008).

Christian life, art, tilling the soil, what-have-you) the more one keeps on it the happier one gets. Speaking for myself at least, from the age of 9 I led a somewhat nightmare existence, at Marlborough I was thoroughly neurotic, at Oxford I was – sometimes – near-suicidal, the next few years (largely owing to M.) were better but not really my rhythm, & it was only in my thirties that I began to feel 'at home in the world'. Not completely at home of course – I don't suppose one ever does that & perhaps, if one did, one would just sink into a coma!

Anyhow enough about that for the moment. To return to the Practicals: I know six weeks is a short visit in the circumstances but I do think, as I said, that you'd better come back as booked on the Ryndam & get the Army thing settled one way or the other.[1] After all, if they're accepting you, the sooner you get through with it the better &, if they're not, you're welcome to an interim period of further discoveries etc.

We're not going to the sea after all but may be ten days in a cottage as from next Thursday (Sept. 4th); letters will be forwarded from the BBC. Your colourful cards have arrived but Bimba hasn't had hers yet, being away with John. Many thanks for them & lots of love from H. & me.

& love to M. (you can show her this letter if you like),

D.

PS. Let's know if you go to the Races. Dollars, dollars, dollars . . .
P.P.S. [*in pencil*] Greetings from Tom who is here again, still book-casing![2]

TO *Allen Tate*[3]   MS Princeton

28 October 1952   BBC

Dear Allen,
    Have you heard that Hedli and I are coming to your country next Spring, roughly late February till mid April, to do a lecture-cum-singing-

1 – The SS *Ryndam* was a transatlantic cruise ship of the Holland–America Line, which made its maiden voyage from Southampton to New York on 17 July 1951.
2 – Tom Agnew; see FLM to MM, 5 July 1950, n. 1, p. 535.
3 – Allen Tate (1899–1979), Kentucky-born American poet, essayist, biographer and, at the time of writing, Professor of English at the University of Minnesota. Educ. Vanderbilt University. Moved to New York in 1924 and worked as freelance journalist. Associated during the thirties with the agrarian movement and the 'Fugitive Poets' such as John Crowe Ransom et al.; his best-known poem is 'Ode to the Confederate Dead' (1928). Publications include Lives of Stonewall Jackson, Jefferson Davis, and Robert E. Lee, and *Collected Poems* (1970). Tate had met FLM at Cornell in 1940. He recorded a short radio programme with the BBC on MacNeice on 6 Dec. 1963.

cum-reading tour? It's all being co-ordinated by John Malcolm Brinnin (whom I take it you know or know of), The Poetry Center, the YM and YWHA, Lexington Avenue and 92nd Street, New York 28.[1]

If you feel like inviting us to Minneapolis – and can pay for us! – could you please contact Brinnin about it?[2] What we can offer is: lectures by me, concerts by Hedli, poetry readings by me or by both of us and lastly (what I particularly recommend) our combined programme of singing and reading which I think we told you about in Paris. If, however, Hedli is to sing, you must remember that her fee should be large enough to cover fee to accompanist.

If you want more dope about the above alternatives I can easily send you some; in the meantime I enclose a rather out-of-date hand-out about Hedli.

I have just been talking to Stephen Spender on the 'phone. He is, as you probably know, going to Cincinnati in the New Year and asks if you have any influence with them as he would like to see us doing our stuff there too.[3]

In any case, even if you can't afford us, I hope we shall meet somewhere in America while we are over.

With best wishes
Yours ever
Louis MacNeice

TO *Richard Murphy*[4]   MS Bodleian [copy]

25 November 1952   BBC

Dear Mr. Murphy,

I must apologise for having been so dilatory over the poem which you sent me in September, which I herewith return. I didn't send it on to the

---

1 – John Malcolm Brinnin (1916–98), poet, man of letters, and Director of the Poetry Center, New York (originally the Young Men's/Young Women's Hebrew Association, later known as 92nd St Y). FLM met him on 6 April 1939, at a reading with Auden and Isherwood.

2 – FLM arrived in New York on 4 March and read in Minneapolis on 6 April 1953, for a fee of $150. A joint programme of poetry and song proved impossible 'because of the rigid departmental organisation of the University; that is to say, the music department like every other in the University jealously guards the expenditure of its own funds' (AT to FLM, 11 Dec. 1952, *Ms Princeton*).

3 – Spender held the Elliston Chair of English at the University of Cincinnati, spring semester, 1953.

4 – Richard Murphy (b.1927), Irish poet, educ. Wellington and Magdalen College, Oxford. Author of *The Battle of Aughrim* (1968), *High Island* (1974), *The Price of Stone* (1985),

Princess Caetani, a) because it looks as though I were not persona grata with her at the moment seeing that she has failed to answer two if not three rather urgent letters from me and b) I am sorry to say, because this poem doesn't really "get" me. I daresay I am quite wrong, but I find it in detail over-written and on the intellectual and/or moral plane not as gripping as it is intended to be. I have talked to Rodgers about this and we agree that it would be a better idea if you sent the Princess a selection of your shorter poems.

I hope you will understand my reasons for this non-co-operation over "The Deserters". I am rather forced to make it a principle not to recommend things unless they really appeal to me. Otherwise, as you can imagine, I should be sunk!

With best wishes and renewed apologies for my delay,

Yours sincerely
Louis MacNeice
Features Department

—

Collected Poems (2000) and a memoir, *The Kick* (2002). Murphy had sent FLM a copy of the first section of his poem 'The Deserters' in the hope he might forward it to *Botteghe Oscure*, the literary journal edited by the Principessa Caetani (RM to FLM, 2 Sept. 1952, *Ms Bodleian*). RM later wrote: 'But Louis MacNeice at the BBC rejected for broadcasting the long-winded epic I had been writing at Rosroe' (*The Kick*, 143).

1953

TO *James F. Mathias*[1]   MS Bodleian

12 January 1953   [London]

Dear Mr. Mathias,

I must apologise for not having previously answered your letter regarding Mr. Kevin Andrews, but unfortunately I was abroad when this letter arrived and so had to leave the matter over till the New Year.[2]

However, I have now great pleasure in returning to you the enclosed report.

Yours sincerely,
Louis MacNeice

ENCL.

During twenty months in Greece 1950–51 I saw a great deal of Mr Kevin Andrews & it repeatedly occurred to me that he was the ideal person to write a book about modern Greece or rather about the modern Greeks of whom, for a foreigner, he seems to have an almost uncanny understanding. I am therefore most genuinely delighted & excited to hear that he is proposing such a book & it seems to be exactly the sort of project which should merit a Guggenheim Fellowship.

Mr. Andrews is exceptionally well qualified to assess that 'multiplicity of contrasts' which he finds in Greece & also, since he is not only a classical scholar but has considerable knowledge of Greece during the Byzantine & succeeding periods, to set those in their historical context. I have read some sketches which he wrote while in Greece & found that they constituted a most vivid & lucid exposition of what to most foreigners would merely be a series of puzzles. He has the great advantage of being

1 – Addressed to the John Simon Guggenheim Memorial Foundation, New York.
2 – FLM met Kevin Andrews (1924–89) in Athens in 1950 and later reviewed his *Flight of Ikaros*: 'Modern Greeks', *Observer*, 1 March 1959, 19; repr. *SP*, 217–19. Andrews was born in China, educ. in schools in England and (after wartime service in the US Army) at Harvard University (BA 1947). He was later associated with the American School of Classical Studies in Athens. Apart from *Flight of Ikaros* his works include *Castles of the Morea* (1953), *Athens* (1967), *First Will and Testament* (1974) and *Greece in the Dark, 1967–1974* (1980). Cf. Andrews's memoir of Louis, 'Time and the Will Lie Sidestepped: Athens, the Interval', *TWA*, 103–9.

able to speak demotic Greek so naturally that a peasant in the Peloponnese will take him for a Greek from another district but this in itself would not gain him that peasant's confidence did he not possess in abundance certain rare human qualities which the Greek by his nature respects.

My opinion, which many people in Athens would wholeheartedly confirm, is that Mr. Andrews has not only a hawk-like gift of observation but is a most acute & conscientious collator & critic of the many things he has observed. Over & above all that he can <u>write</u>. I very much hope that you will grant him his Fellowship.

Did they?

TO *Denis Johnston*   MS Annie Johnston

28 February [1953]   c/o The Poetry Center, Lexington
                                      Ave & 92nd St, New York

Dear Denis,

H. & I have just arrived here after a lot of McCarranism[1] & engine trouble over the Atlantic. This is in haste. It seems we're to do our Double Act at Connecticut College on March 18th. Mr. R. G. C. Levens (Merton don) with whom we've been staying there has offered to drop us on you on the 19th on his way to somewhere.[2] I'm due in Cambridge on March 22nd so should like this very much. May we come anyhow & hit it up with Betty & you? At the same time & in view of this is there any chance of your reopening the question of our performing at Mt. H. (it seems wasteful to be there & not increase our tiny stock of dollars)?[2] Perhaps you

1 – McCarranism, after Senator Pat McCarran of Nevada (1876–1954): a fiercely restrictive immigration policy associated with the anti-communism of the McCarthy era.
2 – Robert G. C. Levens wrote a week later and reported that 'a young instructor', Paul Fussell (future author of *The Great War and Modern Memory*), had given a paper at Connecticut College concerning MacNeice's poetry notebooks, which FLM had deposited in the library at SUNY, Buffalo: 'From the presence in the notebook of telephone numbers, a list of poker hands in order of value, etc., he drew the inference – a sound one, I thought – that you do not keep your writing in a separate compartment from your living. I'm sure Catullus's worksheets were full of telephone numbers' (Levens to FLM, 6 March [1953], *Ms Bodleian, Ms Res, c. 590*).
3 – FLM gave a reading at Mt Holyoke on 19 March in the Kimball Lectures series (he had been preceded by T. R. Henn in February and earlier by Mario Praz and Joseph Campbell). 'Mr MacNeice, who also gave a poetry reading at Amherst College, was at Mount Holyoke for several days, as the guest of Mr and Mrs Johnston. He talked informally to a Saturday morning group of freshmen in their classroom on modern poetry and the making of poems' (*Mount Holyoke Alumnae Quarterly*, 37: 1 (May 1953), 8). In a news release of 13 March, Hildegard Zippert wrote that FLM, 'who is often associated with W. H. Auden and Stephen Spender' was influenced by T. S. Eliot, James Joyce and D. H. Lawrence (*Mount Holyoke College Archives*).

could come to some arrangement with Wystan at Smith (which is nearby, isn't it?) which would lighten the burden. I'm writing to him anyhow to say we hope to be in that direction. Anyhow (also) if you can make an offer of any sort, would you make it to Brinnin (at the P. Center) quickly & we'll give it due consideration.

We've got to do our Double Act at the P. Center next Thursday, March 5th, & after that go to Washington. We haven't got a proper address in N.Y.C. but the P. Center will find us. Anyhow we <u>must</u> see you & swap the gossip.

> Love from us both to you both
> yrs ever
> Louis

[*Hedli's hand*] Betty dear I expect you at the Po . . . C . . . [*sic*] on Thursday about 8.30

I do long to see you both. It is strange to be here. H.

TO *Ellen Borden Stevenson*[1]   MS Texas

21 March [1953]   c/o Ruthven Todd, 132 Bank Street,
                                          New York 14, NY

Dear Mrs Stevenson,

My wife & I so much enjoyed meeting you the other day & we both are very much hoping that the project of our 'Double Act' in Chicago may come to fruition on April 7th.[2]

Now as to publicity, apart from what you have in that hand-out on Hedli, I append the following, divided into two categories – Professional & Personal!

I <u>Professional</u>:-

(a) Double Act itself. We first tried this out – with great success – in the Wigmore Hall, London, some time soon after the war.[3] It was at once recognised by such members of the audience as the novelist & critic, Rose

---

1 – American agent, located at 1362 Astor Street, Chicago. The Texas archive also holds an undated Christmas card to her from the MacNeices.
2 – They performed at three venues: Poetry Center, New York (5 March); Washington DC (19 April) and Connecticut College (24 April). FLM read alone at Harvard (22 March), Minnesota (6 April) and Chicago (8 April).
3 – The Wigmore Hall premiere was on 17 Nov. 1946.

Macaulay, as something which was not only worthwhile but unique.[1] Since then we have done it in such different places as Oxford, Paris, Oslo, Athens & New York. I should add that I do a certain amount of compering in it. As I told you, the whole programme may in a sense be a patchwork but it is a patchwork <u>with a pattern</u>. No song is included in which the words themselves do not have value <u>as words</u> & this value is fully brought out by Hedli who adjusts herself, in the most chameleonic way, to the colours & mood of each. Incidentally a fair balance is kept in the programme between the light & the serious. I don't remember if that hand-out mentions it but Hedli, especially on the Continent (where she sings a good deal in French), has often been compared to Yvette Guilbert[2] – with the important qualification that H. is a much better <u>singer</u>. The <u>poems</u> in the Double Act would, for Chicago, include a good few of my own plus some very striking but hardly known ancients & moderns.

(b) Hedli. As the hand-out makes clear, she has had a most versatile career, graduating from C. B. Cochran, Noel Coward & Co.[3] to straight concert recitals (her voice has been improving ever since I knew her) & such virtuoso pieces as Schonberg's very difficult <u>Pierrot Lunaire</u>[4] which she did several times last year in London with great éclat (many Schonbergians saying it was the best rendering ever) ending up with a performance to a packed house in the Royal Festival Hall, London, & a studio broadcast on the B.B.C. Third Programme.[5] Both these were very highly praised by the London press, including the music critic of the London Times & Desmond Shawe-Taylor, who is acknowledged to be one of England's best music critics.[6]

1 – Dame Rose Macaulay (1881–1958), novelist and essayist, author of many books including *They Were Defeated* (1932), *The World my Wilderness* (1950) and *The Towers of Trebizond* (1956). FLM recalled meeting her (and her set) at parties hosted by the Lynds in Hampstead: 'They all of them had charm but, with the exception of Rose Macaulay, they talked as if the world were static' (*SAF*, 165).
2 – Yvette Guilbert (1867–1944), Parisian music-hall singer, admired by George Bernard Shaw and painted by Toulouse-Lautrec.
3 – Sir Charles Blake Cochran (1872–1951), impresario; musical partner of Coward's 1925–35.
4 – According to Hedli, her courtship with FLM had been 'conducted to the strains of the *Pierrot Lunaire* cycle composed by Arnold Schoenberg'. Furthermore, 'Louis took a great dislike to the poetry of Giraud as set by Schoenberg and, shortly after our marriage . . . casually remarked that he would write a song-cycle for me' (Introduction, *The Revenant: A Song Cycle for Hedli Anderson* (Dublin, 1975), 7.
5 – She performed the *Pierrot Lunaire* on 11 Feb. 1952 at Hampstead Town Hall prior to the RFH concert to which FLM refers. See 'Hampstead Town Hall: Pierrot Lunaire', *The Times*, 12 Feb. 1952, 2.
6 – Desmond Shawe-Taylor (1907–95), music critic for the NS 1945–58, had reviewed *Pierrot Lunaire*.

Another recent virtuoso performance: last May in the Twentieth Century Festival of the Arts in Paris she performed <u>Façade</u> by Edith Sitwell, set by Sir William Walton,[1] being I think the first person to do <u>all</u> the speaking on this herself & also getting a quite incredible variety into each of its twenty-one numbers.

Her last appearance in Europe was two recitals in Barcelona, this February, very much appreciated by the Catalans. During the War by the way (this is not in the hand-out) she was summoned to Windsor Castle hush-hush to perform before the King & Queen on the occasion of Princess Elizabeth's birthday.

I might add that among English singers, she is probably more closely connected than any other with both modern composers & poets. Thus Auden, David Gascoyne[2] & myself have all written poems specially for her while Dylan Thomas, W. R. Rodgers & others have specified her as the ideal artist to sing certain pieces by themselves. Among composers who have set songs specially for her are Benjamin Britten, Alan Rawsthorne, William Alwyn & Elizabeth Lutyens.[3]

(c) Myself. I remain, though I say it (!) one of the best known – & best selling – poets in the U.K. This in spite of the fact that I have recently had a bad press which is partly, I think, because my friends, having become successful, have largely stopped writing book reviews which have consequently fallen into the hands of the younger & as yet less successful writers (who also, I think, tend to be jealous of me in particular because I have the kind of job which they pretend to look down on but in fact would be delighted to have!)

My last book of verse is <u>Ten Burnt Offerings</u>, ten long poems all written in Greece, during 1950 & 1951, which is very shortly going to be published here by the Oxford University Press.[4] Personally I think that this

1 – Sitwell first performed *Façade* in 1923.

2 – David Gascoyne (1916–2001), English surrealist poet and translator, author of *Roman Balcony* (1932), *A Short Survey of Surrealism* (1935), *Poems, 1937–42* (illus. Graham Sutherland), *Night Thoughts* (commissioned by Douglas Cleverdon for the BBC, 1956), *Collected Poems* (1965) and other works.

3 – (Edward) Benjamin Britten (1913–76), composer. Educ. South Lodge Prep School, Lowestoft; Gresham's School; Royal College of Music. Wrote music for John Grierson's GPO film unit and collaborated with Auden on several films as well as on plays for the Group Theatre. A prolific and wide-ranging composer, his most celebrated works include the operas *Peter Grimes* (1945) and *Billy Budd* (1951, revised 1960); and *War Requiem* (1962). Alan Rawsthorne (1905–71), composer. Educ. private tutors, Liverpool University (no degree), Royal Manchester College of Music. In 1954, m. (2) Isabel Agnes Lambert (née Nicholas) (1912–92).

4 – *TBO* was published in New York by Oxford University Press in 1953.

book breaks new ground, these poems being more architectural – or perhaps I should say symphonic – than what I was doing before. My last publication before this was a verse translation (abridged) of Goethe's <u>Faust</u> Parts I & II. I am now supposed to be undertaking the <u>Iliad</u>![1] In all, not counting 'Selections', 'Collections', overlaps, verse plays & verse translations, I have published eight books of verse. Have also of course published literary criticism, travel books etc.

My official career, quickly resumed, is:-

Graduated at Oxford ('First' in 'Greats') 1930.

1930–36 Lecturer in Classics at Birmingham University.

1936–39 Lecturer in Greek at Bedford College for Women in the University of London.

1940 Special Lecturer in Poetry at Cornell University for the Spring Semester.

1941 & since, writer & director of dramatic radio pieces in the Features Department of the B.B.C. with the exception of 18 months (1950–51) when I was seconded to the British Council to be Director of the British Institute in Athens.

Personal.

(a) Hedli. Irish & Scots-Canadian parentage. Brought up largely abroad. Red hair, lots of vitality, people in England are always assuming she's foreign. Studied music in Germany. Excellent German & French. Very good cook, specialises in Continental dishes. Much travelled.

(b) Self. Irish parentage (Gaelic family). Father a Protestant bishop but a nationalist. Married for the first time on the last day of my last term at Oxford. One son by this marriage – Daniel John. Divorced 1936. Much travelled – Iceland, India, Spain etc.

(c) Joint. H. & I were married in London, during the Blitz, 1942. One daughter, Brigid Corinna, born 1943. Our base since then has been London except for the episode in Greece. Continual house-moves but landed up last year in a Regency house in Regent's Park just evacuated by Elizabeth Bowen. During the 'V-Ones' in 1944 kept our spare bed on top of a 'Morrison shelter'[2] (a sort of iron table); the writer V. S. Pritchett used

1–Never completed.

2–Officially the Table (Morrison) Indoor Shelter, designed in 1941 to provide protection during air raids in houses that lacked a cellar or a bomb shelter. It was named after Herbert Morrison, Minister for Home Security.

often to sleep on top of it & when things got bad the whole family crowded inside, the dog & cat going first.[1]

(d) Likes & dislikes. Hedli's likes include: opera, Paris, gardens, children, dachshunds, wine, skiing, bathing, spaghetti. Her dislikes include: the white-voiced concert singers, standing in pubs, English food, suburbanisation, people who are like cold fish. My likes include: Irish rain, Constantinople, watching rugby football, playing tennis, standing in pubs, large dogs (I have owned an Old English sheepdog, a Russian wolfhound & a bull-mastiff), Tintoretto, Chardin.[2] My dislikes include: the 'poetry voice', pseudo-scientific jargon, Surrealism, suburbanisation,[3] spaghetti.

I hope some of the above may be some use to you. And, as I said, we shall be delighted if you can fix a joint appearance for us. Though we shall perfectly understand if it is too late in the day for this to be feasible.

Yours sincerely
Louis MacNeice

TO *Hedli MacNeice*   MS Bodleian

10 August [1953]   BBC

Dearest,

In some haste (the climbers are on my trail again).[4] Wonderful weather here at last.[5] Had lunch yesterday in Highgate with Joan & Philip Harding,

1 – Victor S. Pritchett (1900–97), novelist, short story writer, critic. Educ. Alleyn's School, Dulwich, after which worked in a variety of professions including photography and journalism. Author of *The Spanish Virgin and Other Stories* (1930) and many other works. His *Collected Stories*, 2 vols, were published 1982–3.

2 – Cf. 'The Strand': 'White Tintoretto clouds beneath my naked feet' (*HS*, CP07, 263); 'Ravenna': 'Secondly, / That after Tintoretto's illusory depth and light / The mosaics knocked me flat' (*BP*, CP07, 589); 'Nature Morte': 'And in your Chardin the appalling unrest of the soul / Exudes from the dried fish and the brown jug and the bowl' (*Poems* (1935), CP07, 23).

3 – On suburbia, cf. 'In hundreds of chattering households where the suburb / Straggles like nervous handwriting, the margin / Blotted with smokestacks' ('Christmas Shopping', *EC*, CP07, 94).

4 – FLM was busy writing the script for the Tom Stobart film *The Conquest of Everest* and had recently met the members of the expedition at the Royal Geographical Society; he seemed particularly intrigued by Noyce, a schoolmaster at Charterhouse who wrote poems. Two days later he would write: 'Everest is right on top of me – & heavier than I'd expected' (FLM to Hedli, 6 and 12 Aug. [1953], *Ms Bodleian*).

5 – On the weekend of 8–9 Aug. temperatures reached 80 °F or more throughout England and Wales, and on the 9th thirteen hours of sunshine was recorded throughout the south and southwest. Cf. 'Warmest Day Since Whit Monday', *The Times*, 10 Aug. 1953, 6.

most of it cooked by the latter. Joan much more normal than on the last occasion. V. outspoken about Marianne & threw some (to me) new light on the Marianne-Laurence set-up.[1]

News (somewhat indeterminate, alas) of Dan. Paul Bloomfield[2] rang me up yesterday morning saying he had run into Mrs Mosbacher who was expecting Dan to lunch yesterday. So I rang up Mrs M. who turns out to have seen Dan on several occasions since he vanished. She said she had wanted to come & see me about it but that this made Dan quite desperate, so she didn't. ('Candidly,' she said, 'I am afraid you are at the moment the Ogre'.) Apparently she tried to talk sense to him (though I expect she vacillates)[;] at any rate she earned herself a stinker of a letter from Mary. It seems that Dan was in a v. bad way spiritually, till he was rejected, & also lost weight but since his rejection has picked up in both respects.[3] He'd shown her your letter (or letters?) so I said, if he brought up mine, would she please tell him it makes sense. Apparently she did (I rang her up again this morning) but Dan said he'd 'think it over' & went back again to the country, where he is living alone – & doing damn-all, I gather. Mrs. M. also told me that the lawyer had told Dan he ought not to come to No. 2.[4] I really think I should talk to someone in the Law Society. What Dan can be waiting for I don't know; I suspect that (directed by Mary) he's gone off the student's visa & maybe is hoping once again to get an immigrant's one without me. Anyhow I hope at least to <u>hear</u> from him this week. If I don't, I think I may change my tactics & write to him tearing off a strip. Both Margaret & Joan H. say I've been much too rational & that he's just a naughty child who warrants one losing one's temper.

Got the necessary material on Saturday to start the Everest script with. On Friday, in my last lull, who should turn up but Ernst & we had a v. merry wine-drinking after which I went pretty mellow to the Spenders' for dinner. From my point of view this was all to the good as the evening consisted of an autobiographical monologue from Stephen (little of which I now remember!); also present was Tom Harrison [*sic*] (the Mass Observation man from Borneo) who made no observations whatsoever.[5] Allen

1 – In autumn 1952 Laurence Gilliam's wife Marianne Helweg had left him for W. R. Rodgers.
2 – Paul Bloomfield was Mary Ezra's uncle on her mother's side.
3 – Dan had been rejected by the British Army on medical grounds (eyesight), and he had consulted a solicitor regarding his father's refusal to let him travel to America where he hoped to join his mother. See FLM to DM, 30 Aug. 1952, n. 1, p. 551.
4 – 2 Clarence Terrace.
5 – On Tom Harrisson see FLM to EC, 20 June 1939, n. 3, p. 344.

Tate's wife seems old. The Berrymans are leaving this Sunday, so will just miss you.[1]

looking forward vastly to Monday next –

Phoebe flourishes & Sue seems <u>not</u> to have mange –

all my love, darling

– L.

TO *Principal Fulton*[2]

MS Bodleian

21 November [1953]   BBC

Dear Principal Fulton,

I have just been talking to Philip Burton on the telephone &, to my great pleasure, he tells me that he is sure you would be willing to sign the enclosed letter. I need not tell you how we appreciate the weight that this would add to its appeal.

If you agree to be a signatory, could you please sign the enclosed and send it to The Editor, The Times, Printing House Square, London, E.C.4. (They insist on documentary evidence that all the signatories to such a letter have really consented to sign!) The matter is urgent as we wish to have it printed in The Times (publication in certain other papers to follow) on Wednesday next, November 25th, the day after Dylan Thomas' funeral.

I do not know how you feel about this but it might be a good idea to add in brackets after your name, 'Vice Chancellor of the University of Wales.' If you agree, perhaps you could make this clear either on the letter itself or in a covering note?

I do apologise for approaching you like this out of the blue but we do all feel that this is a most deserving cause. We should have acted sooner had we not heard that various other appeals had been launched, in particular that by the Mayor of Swansea. We have now, however, been informed that these are all more or less <u>ad hoc</u> whereas, as you will see from the enclosed, we had been thinking of an appeal on a long term basis; the most important thing about it of course being the establishment of a Trust. As the letter indicates, all the machinery for this has already been set up; we hope you will agree that there is a very strong case for putting this appeal

---

1 – FLM first met the American poet John Berryman (1914–72) on an Atlantic crossing in 1953. Cf. Stallworthy, 398.

2 – John Scott Fulton, Baron Fulton (1902–86). Principal, University College of Swansea 1947–59; vice-chancellor, University of Wales 1952–4, 1958–9; principal, University of Sussex 1959–67; vice-chairman, BBC 1966–8; chairman, British Council 1968–71.

on the widest possible basis. We all recognise that Dylan Thomas was essentially a <u>Welsh</u> poet; at the same time he had countless admirers throughout the British Isles, not to mention the USA, all of whom, we feel, should have this matter brought to their notice.

With renewed apologies for troubling you but sincerely hoping that you will agree to the above,

Yours sincerely,
Louis MacNeice

[Enclosure]¹

DYLAN THOMAS MEMORIAL FUND.

Sir,

The death of Dylan Thomas at the age of thirty-nine is an immeasurable loss to English letters. In memory of his poetic genius a fund has been started for the establishment of a Trust to assist his widow in the support and education of his three young children. This Trust will be administered in their interests by a committee which will include Messrs. Drummonds, Branch of the Royal Bank of Scotland. Subscriptions should be sent either to Messrs. Drummonds at 49 Charing Cross, London, sw1, or to A. G. Dennis, Esq., LL.M., Solicitor, 40 Berkeley Square, London w2. The latter will supply any information required either as to the means of payment or the nature of the Trust; it is hoped that subscribers, wherever possible, will enter into a deed of covenant to pay over a period of years, thereby securing for the beneficiaries a relief of income tax which would otherwise not be available. We earnestly hope that the response to this appeal will be both immediate and sustained.

T. S. Eliot, Peggy Ashcroft, Kenneth Clark, Walter de la Mare, J. S. Fulton, Graham Greene, Augustus John, Louis MacNeice, Edwin Muir, Goronwy Rees, Edith Sitwell, Osbert Sitwell, Ben Bowen Thomas, Vernon Watkins, Emlyn Williams.²

---

1 – The letter was published in *The Times*, 25 Nov. 1953, 9.
2 – Those not glossed in previous notes include Dame Peggy Ashcroft (1907–91), actress; Augustus John (1878–1961), painter; Edwin Muir (1887–1959), poet and novelist; Ben Bowen Thomas (1899–1977), Permanent Secretary to the Welsh Department of the Ministry of Education; Vernon Watkins (1906–67), poet; Emlyn Williams (1905–87), Welsh playwright and actor.

TO *John Malcolm Brinnin*

30 November [1953]   BBC

Dear John,

I am indeed grateful to you for your letter. I would have answered before but have been distracted this last fortnight, largely with helping to organize a trust fund for Dylan's family. I gather a similar fund has been started in the U.S. & we should like to enter into a liaison with them.

I went to Dylan's funeral last Tuesday in Laugharne.[1] It was a beautiful day and a very moving occasion: most of his nearest friends were there. We were all worried about Caitlin but she went through it surprisingly well. Though what she will do now God knows![2]

We are all very grateful to you for all you did for Dylan during those last terrible days. I do not see that more could have been done. I have had a very long letter from Ruthven which brings out in detail and with great emphasis the efforts you made and the sufferings you must have gone through.[3]

I must admit some of us had forebodings when Dylan left for America this time. He'd told me about the strange blackouts he'd been having this summer and I saw him have a (very short) one the day before he flew. He also seemed rather sad about leaving, which was unusual. I am surprised, however, that he went so far as to talk about suicide; I never heard him do that and it doesn't seem in character. The other thing that surprises me is that he had D.T.'s. I thought, to get those, one had to have been drinking <u>spirits</u> heavily and continually for several days and <u>without taking food</u>. Is that what he had been doing? Ruthven's letter implied that Liz had been, more or less successfully, trying to keep him on beer.[4] I only ask this out

---

1–Thomas died in New York on 9 Nov. 1953 and was buried at Laugharne, Carmarthenshire, on 24 Nov. An obituary appeared in *The Times* on 10 Nov. ('Mr Dylan Thomas: Innovation and Tradition'). See FLM, *AS*, XVIII and XX, but also 'Dylan Thomas: Memories and Appreciations' (Jan. 1954), *SLC*, 183–4; 'Round and About Milk Wood' (April 1954), *SLC*, 185–9; and 'I remember Dylan Thomas' (Dec. 1954), *SLC*, 194–9.

2–Caitlin Thomas (née Macnamara) (1913–94), writer; m. (1937) Dylan Thomas and settled in Rome after his death. Author of *Leftover Life to Kill* (1957), *Not Quite Posthumous Letter to my Daughter* (1963), and *Double Drink Story: My Life with Dylan Thomas* (1997). FLM reviewed *Leftover Life to Kill* in NS, 8 June 1957, 741. She was very grateful to FLM for his work organising the Trust Fund. See Caitlin Thomas to FLM, 13 and 31 Dec. 1953; 22 Feb. and 5 May 1954 (*Ms Bodleian, Ms Res, c. 587, Box 12*). See also Dylan Thomas to FLM, 6 Sept 1952, ibid. ('thanks for answering the SOS so quickly and so largely').

3–Ruthven Todd (1914–78), Scottish poet, novelist, Blake scholar. Cf. 'Auden and MacNeice: Their Last Will and Testament': 'And to Ruthven Todd the works of Burns entire' (*LI*, CP07, 742).

4–Elizabeth Reitall, Brinnin's assistant.

of curiosity. Obviously no one can be held responsible for failing to prevent Dylan from doing what he wanted to. It's also, I think, very probable that he had not very long to live in any case – and that he knew this himself.

With all possible feelings of sympathy and gratitude,

Yours ever,

Louis

1954

TO *Jack Loudan*[1]   MS Bodleian

18 January 1954   BBC

Dear Jack,

I have talked to Hedli about the suggestion that we should do our Double Act for you in Belfast, and, other things being equal, she is very keen on this. She says, however, that April 2nd would not be a suitable date for her as she has a big engagement in London on April 7th. The best date apparently would be towards the end of the second week of March.

We should also like to know what fees you suggest a) for Hedli, b) for myself and c) for the accompanist. I gather that both you and Mr. Sempill think it would be preferable to bring an accompanist over from London. In that case, he need only stay a couple of days in Belfast, but possibly he would require some subsistence in addition to his return fare.

I enclose a couple of sample programmes. N.B. these were intended for the American market and are capable of very great variation. Normally I would not include so many of my own poems, but the Americans wanted it that way.

I understood from Mr. Sempill that he would prefer Hedli to soft-pedal modern works, but would he be prepared to concede her space for just two or three? The Streets of Laredo, for example, is a number with an immediate impact.[2]

I greatly enjoyed meeting you again and look forward to another reunion in March, provided as I very much hope, we can all agree on the above proposition.

> With all best wishes,
> Yours ever,
> Louis MacNeice

1 – Loudan was the Organiser for CEMA (Council for the Encouragement of Music and the Arts), a forerunner to the Northern Ireland Arts Council. CEMA had previously invited FLM to do a reading on 7 Jan. 1954 with W. R. Rodgers at the Belfast Museum and Art Gallery (*Ms Bodleian, Ms Res, c. 993*).
2 – FLM, 'The Streets of Laredo' (*HS*, CP07, 253–4).

TO *T. S. Eliot*   Faber archive

20 January 1954   [BBC]

Dear Tom,

   This is just to let you know about <u>Autumn Sequel</u>. I have now finished
a complete draft of this running to twenty-six cantos, total number of lines
something over 3,500.

   It will need quite a lot of revision, but I can promise that I will let you
have it for the press by the end of March. I am assuming that if you have
it by then you will be able, as you told me, to publish next September.[1] In
that case Knopf would also be able to publish it before I arrive in America
in October for a two-months lecture tour. Which presumably would be
greatly to the advantage of all.[2]

   With all best New Year wishes,

                                        Yours ever,
                                        Louis MacNeice

TO *Miss E. Robb*[3]   MS BBC

27 January 1954   BBC

Dear Miss Robb,

   Your letter about my programme The Heartless Giant has been passed
on to me. I am so glad that on the whole you enjoyed it.[4]

   As regards the two criticisms you made in your letter, 1). I called the
hero 'Boots' because he was so-called in the translation from which I took
the story. 2). I don't follow your objection to the Princess being played
Irish. After all, she has to have some sort of voice and in a radio
programme I always like to differentiate the voice as much as possible.

---

1 – *AS* was eventually published on 12 Nov. 1954 but radio listeners had heard the poem
broadcast over six programmes on the Third Programme, 28 June to 1 Aug. 1954. The
reviewer for *The Times* declared that '*Autumn Sequel* falls clearly as well as richly on the ear
at a first hearing' ('Mr Louis MacNeice's "Autumn Sequel": New Poem Broadcast', *The
Times*, 5 July 1954, 11).
2 – Prior to submission of the manuscript of *AS*, an agreement had been reached with New
York publishing house Knopf to publish the volume simultaneously with Faber. In fact Knopf
reneged on the agreement after they received the manuscript and decided it would not appeal
to the American market. Cf. FLM to Philip Vaudrin (and footnotes), 18 Feb. 1954, below.
3 – Unidentified. Addressed to Coledale Edge, Braithwaite, Keswick, Cumberland
4 – *The Heartless Giant*, a play by FLM based on a Norwegian fairy tale, first broadcast BBC
Home Service on 13 Dec. 1946, rpt 1954. Cf. FLM, 'Dramatising a Tale of a Giant', *Radio
Times*, 1 Jan. 1954, 4.

Moreover in <u>dramatising</u> a folk story one inevitably has to give characters something additional in the way of 'character' and I just felt that this Princess in contrast both with the oafish Giant and the ingenious Prince seemed convincingly to fall into an Irish mould: there is one other reason that when I first produced this programme in 1946 I wrote the part for Betty Chancellor who happened to be Irish.[1]

But I do agree with you that this kind of material is very suitable for radio. It is certainly great fun to do!

Yours sincerely
Louis MacNeice

TO *Philip Vaudrin*[2]   MS Texas [carbon in BBC archive]

18 February 1954   BBC Reference 03/F/LMN

Dear Philip,

Thank you for your letter. I look forward to receiving the book by Randall Jarrell, which hasn't arrived yet.[3]

I completed the draft of my long poem, which is to be called <u>Autumn Sequel</u>, some time ago, and am now revising same. I have promised to let Faber and Faber have the complete revised version by the end of March, in which case they say they will be able to publish it before the end of September. When I deliver this version to them I shall send them a second copy to pass on to you. As regards a contract, this should be done through Faber's and the person to write to there is Mr. Peter du Sautoy.[4]

1–The actress Betty Chancellor married Denis Johnston, who was then employed by the BBC, in 1945.
2–Addressed to Vaudrin at Alfred A. Knopf, Inc., 501 Madison Avenue, New York.
3–Possibly *Pictures from an Institution* (1954); cf. FLM to ERD, 19 Dec. 1954, p. 582. On 29 July 1953, Vaudrin had promised to send FLM a copy of Jarrell's *Poetry and the Age* (1953) (*Ms Texas, Knopf archive*). Cf. FLM's review of this in *LM*, Sept. 1955, 71–4.
4–Peter du Sautoy (1912–95), publisher. FLM had formerly been published in America by Random House, then by OUP (*Faust*, 1952; *TBO*, 1953), but Philip Vaudrin (formerly of OUP, now at Knopf) proposed to Faber in 1953 that Knopf might add FLM to their list (Vaudrin to du Sautoy, 3 April 1953; Vaudrin to FLM, 19 May, 26 June 1953. This and the correspondence referred to below from *Ms Texas, Knopf archive*). Everyone seemed interested in this, and FLM proposed to Vaudrin (with the agreement of TSE) that Knopf might publish *AS* simultaneously with Faber, and have the option of doing a *Collected Poems* thereafter (FLM to Vaudrin, 9 and 29 Oct. 1953). Things began to unravel, however, when Knopf read the manuscript of *AS* and decided that from a marketing standpoint 'it is not too promising a prospect, chiefly because of the overwhelmingly British contemporary background, I suppose' (Vaudrin to FLM and to du Sautoy, 28 April 1954). Knopf proposed publishing the book with imported Faber sheets, which Faber (and FLM) agreed to on the condition that

I can't remember if I ever gave you much indication as to what this poem is! It consists of twenty-six Cantos all in terza-rima (and incidentally in pure rhymes throughout) totalling over 3,500 lines. It is an occasional poem and hinged to the autumn season of 1953, just as <u>Autumn Journal</u> which I wrote in 1938 was hinged to <u>that</u> autumn season. It is, however, a good deal less occasional than its predecessor and also, I think, differs from it in many other ways. There is a good deal less of sheer topicality in it, but on the other hand, there are a good many more characters, these being mainly people I know, but throughout represented under pseudonyms (they include, by the way, certain of my colleagues, such as W. H. Auden and Dylan Thomas). What I think myself should be most interesting about this work is the balance I have tried to achieve between the realistic and the contemporary on the one hand and the mythical or historical on the other. The mythical elements I have borrowed from all sorts of sources, Greek, Christian, my own dreams etc., and also even from modern science, while the real scenes portrayed include for example, Oxford, Norwich, Bath and Wales not to mention the Great Wen.[1]

When you come to doing advance publicity, I would like you somehow to bring out that, while in one way this long poem has affinities with Byron's <u>Don Juan</u>, in another way it has affinities with quite different works, say, Goethe's <u>Faust</u> or <u>The Faerie Queene</u>.

With all best wishes,

Yours ever,
Louis MacNeice

TO *Norman MacCaig*[2]   MS Bodleian

23 February 1954   [BBC]

Dear Norman,

How are you? I don't seem to have heard from or even of you for a very long time!

Knopf would publish a *Collected Poems* at a later date (du Sautoy to Vaudrin, 24 May 1954). Knopf would not meet this condition and *AS* was not published in the USA, despite the fact it was forwarded for consideration to Robert Giroux at Harcourt Brace.

1 – A disparaging nickname for London.

2 – Norman MacCaig (1910–96), OBE. Scottish poet. Educ. Royal HS, Edinburgh; Edinburgh University; Moray House (teacher training). A primary school teacher for many years, he later taught creative writing at Edinburgh and Stirling. As the letter indicates, FLM admired MacCaig's work greatly and had tried to urge John Lehmann to publish some of it: 'At a

I have been asked to compile an anthology of modern poetry for the Clarendon Press (intended primarily for schools but in order not to put off the adults this will not be made clear either in the book or on the dust jacket).[1] I told them I did not wish to attempt a 'comprehensive' anthology and am suggesting confining it to exactly a dozen poets who, between them, should provide enough variety and represent most things. The poets I propose are:

Yeats: Eliot: D. H. Lawrence: Robert Graves: Norman Cameron:
  William Empson: Auden: Henry Reed: Dylan Thomas:
  W. R. Rodgers: Laurie Lee and yourself.

I very much hope you will be willing to come in on this.

If so, could you please let me know where to get hold of your latest poems and also those which you showed me in typescript some time ago (I particularly want to include a couple of love poems from the latter).

With all greetings,
Yours ever,
Louis MacNeice

TO *T. S. Eliot* Faber archive

30 March [1954]   BBC

Dear Tom,

Herewith the typescript of <u>Autumn Sequel</u>, with a separate copy for Knopf's.

I would like each Canto to start on a separate page & I'd rather not have any line, squiggle or what-have-you at the end of a Canto.

As to blurbs etc., whenever that may arise, I'd like it brought out that I'm attempting a balance between the topical & the mythical or, putting it another way, that while A.S. may have affinities with <u>Don Juan</u> it also may have some with <u>The Faerie Queene</u>.[2]

---

time when many poets are either merely intellectual or merely physical I find that he's both – & both on a high level.' FLM to JL, 19 Nov. [1952] (*Ms Texas*).

1 – This projected anthology never appeared.

2 – The blurb did indeed point to the poem's balance between topical and mythical: 'A poem of this nature, concerned chiefly as it is with personal friendships and the events of a particular year in the life of one man, can depend too much for its interest on its topicality. But in *Autumn Sequel* the ephemeral and the topical have been transmuted into poetry which will remain permanently moving and which attains indeed something of the timelessness of myth.' On using *The Faerie Queene* as a structuring principle in a projected long poem, see

I wrote to Du Sautoy, while you were away, about Knopf's. I gather he is going to send them the second copy straightaway, at the same time fixing up about a contract.

I hope you'll like at least some of the 3,500 lines (at the moment I've reached the stage where I just can't judge it any more).

Yours ever,

Louis   P.T.O.

[overleaf]

Could the printers be instructed to stick to my punctuation?

TO *Harold Taylor*[1]   MS Sarah Lawrence

19 April [1954]   BBC

Dear Harold,

Thank you very much for your letter of April 12th, which I would have answered sooner had it not been for the intervention of Easter. Your proposition took me a little by surprise as, it being so long since we had discussed these possibilities, I had assumed the whole thing was off![2] However, I feel very honoured that the Rockefeller Foundation should consider me persona grata in the circumstances.

I am terribly busy here with a radio play, which I have written & am just about to direct, till April 27th; so will you take what follows as merely my off-the-cuff reactions to your proposition?

First of all, I definitely could not manage January & February next year. Secondly, the letter to the Rockefeller Foundation of which you sent me a copy, seems to be specifying a good deal more work (& time) on my part than you & I had envisaged when we discussed this a year ago.

—

FLM to TSE, 7 April 1944, pp. 449–50. FLM had produced a reading of *The Faerie Queene* over twelve programmes on the Third Programme, from 29 Sept. to 15 Dec. 1952. Cf. FLM, 'Spenser's Symbolic World', *Radio Times*, 26 Sept. 1952, 15.

1–Harold Taylor (1914–93), educ. University of Toronto (BA, MA, 1935, 1935) and University of London (PhD, 1938). Taught Philosophy at University of Wisconsin 1938–44; president, Sarah Lawrence College, New York, 1945–59. Author of *Students Without Teachers: The Crisis in the University* (1969), *How to Change Colleges: Notes on Radical Reform* (1971) and other works.

2–Taylor had recently invited FLM to take up a visiting position at Sarah Lawrence for spring 1955. For details of FLM at Sarah Lawrence in autumn 1954, see footnotes to next letter.

(Admittedly $2,000 dollars [sic] seems a fair price but – if I remember correctly – it is about the same that I received in 1940 (when the standard of living was much lower) from Cornell – &, at that, they allowed me much more freedom of movement (& of money-making!) than seems to be contemplated in your letter to the Foundation).

Thirdly, as you mention, there is this serious question of an overlap with Miss Janet Lauren who is arranging joint performance dates for my wife & myself during the same period.[1] It seems to me that, in so far as Miss Lauren has already committed us to certain definite engagements, we are bound to honour them. At the same time possibly some compromise might be worked out; for example I might come to you for a shorter period, or for two periods divided by an interval (during which any seeds I might have sown might be germinating?)

However, supposing all this got sorted out, I should be prepared (a) to give one course (two hours per week) in the Literature of the Theatre with emphasis on poetic drama. (b) I should be prepared to produce one play of my own on the stage, provided male cast (from Columbia or where-have-you) was also available. While I should not wish to undertake more than one stage production proper, I would be prepared to lay on two or three play-readings (a modest but potentially impressive form of which I had great experience when I was Director of the British Institute in Athens). (c) I could not cope with opera or dance drama. (d) I am not altogether happy about being farmed out to neighbouring colleges merely for my train fare.

These are my main points. I do apologise if (as is probable, this being in haste!) I've put them rather crudely.

Yours ever,   Louis MacNeice

1–Janet Lauren, American agent, of Norma Waldon Associates, 16 West 55th Street, New York. Lauren had been patient with FLM's various changes of plan to visit the States; he decided to come in the autumn to coincide with the publication of AS. Cf. FLM to Janet Lauren, 8 Oct. 1953 (Ms Bodleian).

TO *Laurence Gilliam (BBC internal memo)*   MS BBC

19 May 1954   From: Mr. Louis MacNeice,
                                     203 Rothwell [House]

Subject: PROJECTED VISIT TO THE U.S.A.

Following our conversation yesterday, I have been pondering what I could do of benefit to the B.B.C. if I were allowed to accept my double invitation to America this autumn.

First, perhaps I should recapitulate the overtures made to me from that side.

When Hedli and I were in America over a year ago, a somewhat high-brow but sympathetic woman agent suggested that she might provisionally try to fix up a short but concentrated tour for us (doing, what in conversation we call our Double Act) for the autumn of this year. She lately came through with a proposal for three weeks of such engagements starting in mid-October. Unfortunately, the total of fees involved did not seem enough to pay both our ways. Since then I have received a quite independent invitation from Harold Taylor, President of Sarah Lawrence College just outside New York (which traditionally goes in for taking on writers for a term or so at a time). The salary offered me by the President for eight weeks would put us quite definitely in the clear, provided I was able to fulfil the touring engagements as well.[1]

1 – The American tour was arranged by Janet Lauren (see previous letter). FLM's official title at Sarah Lawrence College was Visiting Professor of Poetry and Theatre, and the tax-exempt honorarium of $2,000 was made possible by a Rockefeller foundation grant (Harold Taylor to FLM, 10 Dec. 1954, *Ms Sarah Lawrence*). With Hedli he sailed from Southampton to New York (21–27 Sept.) and he stayed at Sarah Lawrence College until 15 Dec. (though absent on a reading tour from 12 Oct. to 5 Nov.). He did a poetry reading at Sarah Lawrence on 4 Oct. and the following day delivered a lecture, 'The Poet Today' (see 'Famous English Poet to Teach at SLC', *The Campus*, 26 May. 1954; 'Distinguished Poet to Teach Here', *Sarah Lawrence Alumnae Magazine* summer 1954; 'MacNeice to Direct Euripides Hippolytus', and '"The Poet Today"', by Alice Davies, *The Campus*, 13 Oct. 1954; 'Louis MacNeice Famed Poet Heralded by SLC and Faculty' by Alice Davies, *The Campus*, 20 Oct. 1954). He gave a 'play reading' course, 5 Nov. to 10 Dec., including discussion of *The Playboy of the Western World*, *The Family Reunion* and *The Dark Tower*. He offered another course, 'The Nature of Poetry', 9 Nov. to 13 Dec., in which he examined poems by Pope, Raleigh, Marvell, Donne, Herbert, Blake, Shelley, Keats, Tennyson, Browning, Yeats, Eliot, Hopkins, Lawrence, Cummings, Auden, Empson, Dylan Thomas, and his own poem, 'Day of Returning'. Finally, he directed a student production (8–10 Dec.) of *Hippolytus* (trans. P. Vellacott), assisted by student director Nicola Schenck and faculty advisers Madalyn O'Shea, Jeanne Button and Carlotta Damanda. The campus review of the play was fairly negative: see Carolyn Holmes, 'Hippolytus Revisited', *The Campus*, 15 Dec. 1954, 1. His reading tour included University of Kansas (15 Oct.), University of Iowa (18th), University

I have been having some correspondence with both the President and the agent about this, making it clear to both that my acceptance of either invitation is, of course, subject to my receiving leave of absence from the B.B.C.[1] I have had three letters from Taylor, the second and third of which unfortunately exactly crossed letters from me to him, as a result of which he seems to be getting slightly nettled and would like a definite yes or no as quickly as possible. He has already offered one considerable concession, i.e. that if I would come to Sarah Lawrence for three weeks to start with and four weeks afterwards, he would agree to my absenting myself for three weeks in between to keep the agent's touring dates. This, of course, would stretch my total period of absence to considerably more than it would have been if financially I had been able to confine myself either to Sarah Lawrence or to the tour. It would mean in fact I should have to be away for just about three months, leaving England towards the end of September. One month of this I could take as leave, but what about the other two?

You asked me to think over (supposing I go there) what places I should be visiting and what writers I might be meeting who would be likely sources of feature scripts on American subjects. Firstly, I am perfectly sure that during the Sarah Lawrence period, when I should be living in New York City, I should have plenty of time to meet writers in and around New York, while on tour I should probably not be staying long in any one place but at the same time most American colleges (and it is mainly colleges that I shall be visiting) have at least one creative writer attached to them and it would after all only take a couple of hours to proposition such.

The following are the places the agent can lay on definitely:-

Kansas and down Missouri way: Iowa: Minneapolis (where I know Allen Tate very well), and some other places in Minnesota: Wilmington, Ohio: Antioch, Ohio: Geneseo, N.Y.

Probables are:-

Boston (Harvard et al), and perhaps one or two other places in New England: Yale: Washington and Baltimore.

---

of Minnesota, Duluth (19th), Concordia College, Montreal (20th), University of Minnesota (21st), Wilmington, Ohio (25th) and Geneseo College, New York (2 Nov.). See also Stallworthy, 409–10.

1–Leave for three months' absence (including one month's leave) was granted within a fortnight and FLM wrote a letter of thanks to Lindsay Wellington on 3 June, stating, 'As the USA these days seems to be increasingly with us, I do feel it helps a Features writer to be <u>au fait</u> with the set up there' (*Ms BBC L1/285/2 Left Staff*).

I already know a great many writers in America, of whom I think the following, if persuaded into it, might very well be capable of turning out good radio scripts:-

Robert Penn Warren, who, as you know, is not only a distinguished poet but has written best-selling novels.[1] His latest work, Brother to Dragons which is generally considered a 'distinguished failure' at the same time shows that he is feeling out in the feature direction. It's a poem the length of a novel telling an historical story of inter-family violence and analysing from different angles (it is broken up among a number of character voices) the motives for and effects of that violence. He is of course a Southerner and might, I should think, do something very interesting on the problems and attitudes of the south. He is, at the moment, Professor in the Drama School at Yale, and I shall certainly be seeing him as I know him very well and also his wife Eleanor Clark.

William Alfred, much younger and so far not at all well-known, who is on the English Faculty at Harvard, and is connected with an experimental theatre group in Boston. He is a rather naïve young man, but very sensitive and imaginative and can write. The Third Programme have already seen a dramatic verse script by him on the old Agamemnon theme. Everyone, including myself, saw considerable merits in this, but thought the theme was an initial mistake. If he were allowed a poetic approach to his material, I am sure he would need little persuasion to write something for us.[2]

Howie Schoenfeld (or one of his many friends and colleagues in Greenwich Village). H.S. is rather a tough and goes in for tough writing, belonging to a group of detection and thriller writers which calls itself, I think, the Crime Club. I am told he is a very efficient craftsman, and assume that he could do effective and entertaining documentaries.[3]

1 – Robert Penn Warren (1905–89), American novelist and poet born in Kentucky. Educ. Universities of California, Yale and Harvard. Author of *All the King's Men* (1946), *Brother to Dragons: A Tale in Verse and Voices* (1953), and of the influential study, co-authored with Cleanth Brooks, *Understanding Poetry* (1938). He married Eleanor Clark in 1952.
2 – William Alfred (1922–99), educ. Harvard, where he taught Medieval Literature for many years. A poet and playwright, he was author of *Agamemnon* (trans.) (1954), *Hogan's Goat* (1966), and other works. Cf. Stallworthy, 424.
3 – Howard Schoenfeld (1915–2004), a longtime resident of Greenwich Village since 1934; he published short stories in *Ellery Queen's Mystery Magazine* and was the author of *Let Them Eat Bullets* (1954).

<u>Carson McCullers</u>. As you know, best-selling novelist, specialising in the starker side of the South. Remarkable characterisation and atmosphere. Good dialogue.[1]

<u>Theodore Roethke</u>. I don't know if he has ever written anything in dramatic form, but he is an excellent and most original poet, with a very good ear. He also has a fascinating back-ground, going back through several kinds of strange jobs to his childhood in the Middle West, where his father, a German immigrant, ran an outsize nursery gardening business. Unfortunately, he has a job in the Far West at the University of Washington, but I should be surprised if he didn't turn up in New York some time during the Fall.[2]

<u>Edmund Wilson</u>, who, as you know, has a gift for satire. Apart from his outstanding criticism and a best-selling novel, he has written three 'experimental plays' – though I am afraid I know nothing about these latter.[3]

<u>Kevin Andrews</u>, who used to be in Athens and whom you have met. At the moment he is writing a long book about Greece for Knopf. He writes extremely well and with a little schooling I think could write a fascinating feature about the Greek community in New York City or elsewhere. As you know, he speaks Greek like a native and I would suggest that he made literal translations of the dialogue of the immigrants.

Other possible are Robert Lowell, Karl Shapiro (in Chicago, which I would be passing through) Muriel Rukeyser, and Randall Jarrell. The last-named is the only one of the lot that I don't know personally, but to judge by his last book which is a very entertaining, though malicious, picture of American Academic life (with excellent dialogue)[4] he ought to be able to

1 – Carson McCullers (1917–67), American novelist, author of *The Heart Is a Lonely Hunter* (1940) and *Reflections in a Golden Eye* (1941). FLM had met McCullers while staying with WHA at Middagh Street, Brooklyn Heights, in Nov. 1940.
2 – Theodore Roethke (1908–63), American poet from Michigan who taught for many years at the University of Washington. Author of *Open House* (1941), *The Lost Son* (1948) and many other works.
3 – Edmund Wilson (1895–1972), American playwright, essayist and memoirist though chiefly known as a critic and as author of *Axel's Castle* (1931), *To the Finland Station* (1940) and *The Wound and the Bow* (1941). A photograph survives of FLM in conversation with Wilson (and Rose Macaulay) at a *London Magazine* party in 1956.
4 – Randall Jarrell, *Pictures from an Institution*, published by Knopf in 1954.

featurise some aspects of the American scene very well indeed, and with a nice grain of salt which might be lacking in some of the others.

As I explained yesterday, owing to the hustling methods of Americans, I should be very grateful to know as soon as possible whether the B.B.C. a). agree to my going at all, and b). would like me to do anything about these possible contacts.

Louis MacNeice
Features Department

TO *John Lehmann* MS Texas

24 June 1954 BBC

Dear John,

I herewith return the corrected proofs of my article on Herbert. I am so glad you like it.[1]

I have now read the book I mentioned to you, The People of the Sea by David Thomson.[2] This is professedly and primarily a book about Seal-Lore, but in my opinion it is much more than that. It is beautifully written, both in the descriptive passages and the dialogue (for which latter he has a quite exceptional ear) and, in the light it throws on the Gaeltacht seems to me to make a worthy addition to that group of writings which includes Synge's book on the Aran Islands and the two autobiographical books (originally written in Irish) which came out of the Great Blasket, so I think if you can spare the space it would be quite worth a review in the London Magazine.[3]

I have just been sent another book which you might possibly be interested in and which I should be quite prepared to review – The Death

---

1–Cf. reviews of Joseph H. Summers, *George Herbert: His Religion and His Art* and Margaret Bottrall, *George Herbert* (both 1954), *LM*, Aug. 1954, 74–6.

2–David Thomson, *The People of the Sea* (1954). FLM's review of this appeared in *LM*, Oct. 1954, 94, 96. Thomson (1914–88) worked as a radio producer and scriptwriter for the BBC, and also wrote *Woodbrook* (1974) and *Nairn in Darkness and Light* (1987). Cf. FLM to Thomson, 7 Feb. 1957.

3–J. M. Synge, *The Aran Islands* (1907); the two Blasket autobiographies were Tomás Ó Criomhthain (Thomas O'Crohan), *An tOileánach*, published in Irish in 1929, translated by Robin Flower as *The Islandman* (1951), and Muiris Ó Suileabháin (Maurice O'Sullivan), *Fiche bliain ag fás*, published in Irish in 1933 and in the same year translated by Moya Llewelyn Davies and George Thomson as *Twenty Years A-Growing*, which was praised by, among others, E. M. Forster. FLM may also have seen Robin Flower's *The Western Island, or the Great Blasket* (1944) and *Lore from the Western Island* (1956). Peig Sayers's *An Old Woman's Reflections* (trans. Seamus Ennis) appeared in 1962.

of a Town by Kay Cicellis, whom I think you know about.[1] This consists
of four pieces, the longest of which (the title piece) is a remarkable re-
creation of the great earthquake in Cephallonia last year.

> Greetings,
> Yours ever,
> Louis MacNeice

TO *Harold Taylor* MS Sarah Lawrence

5 August [1954]   BBC, c/o Mervyn Morrow, Fintragh
           Bay, Killybegs, Co. Donegal[2]

Dear Harold,

We feel very remote here, but are enjoying ourselves thoroughly. One
thing that worries me is this visa question. We were informed last year that
over in the U.S. the necessary application forms tend to linger unduly in
various In Trays & Out Trays. I wrote, before leaving London, to your
Miss Milligan asking her if she could do anything with the Immigration
people &/or the State Department to expedite matters. I don't know if she
has been able to do this. If nothing has come through by, say, August 20th,
I wonder if you could possibly write a line yourself to someone who deals
with these things?

About plays, I take it that, for discussion & readings, one need not
worry so much about the proportion of female parts as one would in the
case of a stage performance. At the moment I am still too stupefied by
the Donegal air to make any comprehensive or systematic suggestions but
the following random possibilities have occurred to me:-

Everyman

One Shakespeare (? Antony & Cleopatra or Troilus & Cressida)

The Duchess of Malfi

Goethe's Faust Part I (my own translation, publ. in U.S. by Oxford
  University Press, New York)

The Family Reunion

One contemporary French play on a classical theme (e.g. Cocteau's
  Orphée or Sartre's Huis Clos)

The Dark Tower (radio play by myself)

And, as I told you in my last letter, I'd like to do the Hippolytus & The
Playboy of the Western World. Thinking of Irish plays, there are lots of

---

1–Kay Cicellis, *Death of a Town* (1954).
2–He was on holiday in Donegal.

things one might add – among others (a short piece but all depending on the central female part) <u>The Writing on the Window Pane</u> by Yeats.[1] By the way, what about Aristophanes?

But all the above is tentative.

> Trusting you are having better
> weather & getting the best out of
> Dorset.
> Yours ever
> Louis

TO *E. R. Dodds* MS Bodleian

19 December [1954]   Cunard Line /
                       RMS *Queen Elizabeth*

Dear E.R.D.

Just a scrawl from this floating middleclass palace to wish you both a very happy Christmas & say that tomorrow we're back in England. America, as usual, made me feel Yes & No. Have you read Randall Jarrell's <u>Pictures from an Institution</u>? That's the place I was working at part of the time; I produced the Hippolytus there![2]

Dan appears to have been drafted! He sent me one quite friendly postcard from Spokane, Washington. Which is about as far as he could get from Egg Harbor. Which in itself seems a good thing! Mary now, I'm told, cuts off the telephone on anyone who says he knows me. Have you read a book called <u>The Lonely Crowd</u>, all about 'the changing American character'? Written in a horrible jargon but extremely interesting.[3] Hoping to see you both soon,

> Yours ever,
> Louis

1 – W. B. Yeats, *The Words Upon the Window Pane* (1930).
2 – Jarrell had been visiting professor at Sarah Lawrence College during the academic year 1946–7.
3 – *The Lonely Crowd: A Study of the Changing American Character*, by David Riesman in collaboration with Reuel Denney and Nathan Glazer (New Haven/London, 1950).

1955

27 February [1955]   BBC, as from c/o J. B. Auden,
                                            Geological Survey Department,
                                            PO Box 410, Khartoum, Sudan

Darling,

Moving on tonight to Khartoum.[1] Cairo is v. pleasant (temperature yesterday 84). Am staying in a modern flat (rather like Sina St.) & on my return, on March 22nd, shall be in a still more modern one with Captain Howell! (His address is 14 SHARIA EL GEZIRA, Cairo.)

Flight was v. smooth – seemed to be eating all the time, including lunch at Rome airport; they also gave one free drinks. Was met at the airport by the Holmes, my present hosts, & Norman Reed who is the BBC no. 2 (his boss, Sheringham, being away in Lebanon).

Friday morning about the first thing I saw was a v. charming procession in honour of King Hussein of Jordan who was visiting here – a lot of shaggy chaps in as it were nightshirts carrying banners & blowing primitive trumpets & wielding enormous sticks which they bang against each other (? like quarter-staff play in Robin Hood's time) twirling round or dancing backwards as they go. After which Mrs Holmes took me to join up with Cyril Connolly (his last day in Egypt!) & others to visit the Coptic museum – a lot of echoes, apparently coincidental, of Byzantine. Cyril C. wan, having had flu in Luxor, but still at moments witty.[2] I met him again in the afternoon plus 2 glam girls (one a Jewess who writes sexy poems in French) & visited 2 mosques, one about the oldest in Cairo, v. big, nice & austere. The 2nd mosque was v. hard to find being in a maze of little streets where hordes of scrappy children kept jumping on the back of the car & making loud aviary noises. At 7.30 went to have drinks at

---

1 – On assignment for a one-hour programme *The Fullness of the Nile*, broadcast 3 July 1955. Cf. FLM, 'Journey up the Nile', *Radio Times*, 1 July 1955, 5.

2 – As Connolly's obituarist wrote: 'His brilliant conversation was like a reservoir which ran out after a few months, and to refill it Connolly would set off on long, solitary travels' ('Mr Cyril Connolly', *The Times*, 30 Nov. 1974, 16). Cf. Connolly's 'Impressions of Egypt' (1955), in *Previous Convictions* (1963), 33–47.

Mrs Sheringham's (she is a very vivacious Copt) where I made a bad start by striking an Egyptian match the head of which flew off blazing enormously & landed between 2 fingers of my left hand. V. painful at the time but mended now. At Mrs S's were Sir Walter & Lady Smart,[1] Joan Rayne's friends, & a medley of people mainly European but including a British Council man, Raymond Beavan, who knows Egypt extremely well & is going to prove v. useful to me. I forgot to say that at lunch at the Holmes' there is a nice placid Egyptian whose family are landowners up the Nile in a place which they took for themselves about (?) 1000 years ago. However most of their land has now been expropriated, as there is a limit of c.200 acres (?).

Yesterday I spent most of the morning mucking about in ticket offices & the BBC but also had a profitable interview with Dr Mustapha Amer who is Director of Antiquities[2] (& genuine enthusiast) & is going to give me introductions to the Inspectors of Antiquities at Aswan, Luxor etc. Had lunch with Mrs Holmes who seems the same as ever but v. friendly – I gather there's as much protocol as in Athens. In the evening the Holmes had people in for drinks (after I'd lost £1 Egyptian to him on the Scotland–Ireland match[3]) who included Tom Stobart, the Everest cameraman,[4] who's now going round the world using his camera, & a nice Greek who spends his time diving in the Red Sea & a Norwegian woman who's been living in Oldham & an American who's adviser to Egyptian State Broadcasting, & many others. After which we ate cold chicken & went for a drive up the Mokattan hills, which lie east of Cairo & give you an excellent view of it (I'm going up there again today with Mr Beavan) – not but what the view last night was mainly strings of lights with great black patches representing 'Old Cairo' which is now all rubbish mounds & 'The City of the Dead', which I haven't been into yet.[5] These hills are completely barren; in fact the beginning of the Eastern Desert. The air rather exhilarating; stars brilliant – Orion higher in the sky than in England.

1 – Sir Walter Smart, Oriental Secretary at the British Residency, Cairo, and Amy Smart (née Nimr), a painter who studied at the Slade, unofficial patroness of struggling artists and writers in Cairo. They are the alleged models for Sir Desmond and Lady Hooper in Olivia Manning's novel *The Danger Tree* (1977).
2 – Mustapha Amer, archaeologist; head of Cairo University. A prominent figure in the Ministry of Education, he became director of the Egyptian Antiquities Authority in 1953, the first Egyptian to occupy that position.
3 – Ireland lost 3–12 to Scotland at Murrayfield on 26 Feb. 1955.
4 – Tom Stobart (1914–80), OBE, cameraman for *The Conquest of Everest*.
5 – The City of the Dead is an expanse of old Muslim cemeteries in Cairo.

Am now waiting for Mr Beavan who, apart from the Mokattan Hills, is going to take me to see the Nilometer which measured the height of the Nile & was made in 716 A.D. (no – earlier). While waiting for him I'm going to tabulate my Sudan addresses as I can see that the whole Sudan business is going to be v. rushed – Khartoum, they say, is hot at the moment but not excessive (c.93°). I'm going to leave a lot of clothes here in Cairo.

Have reluctantly agreed to give a lecture for the Council on March 24th. Creative Writing for Radio again. Most of one's audience, it seems, will be v. naïve students.

Do you like Egyptian silver ornaments? There was a woman yesterday with elaborate but, to me, attractive ear-rings which she got cheap in the market here; only she had them gilded. She also says you can buy these old Turkish cavalry belts of silver mesh which go well with almost any sort of dress.

Will finish this off this evening. Hope your throat is better, darling. Love till then, L. /

Evening: Back from the Magattan [*sic*] Hills but the view (which is the chief point of them) was spoilt by the Khamsin, the wind from the South which fills the air with sound; you could see the pyramids through it merely as phantom triangles. But we picnicked in a Pharaonic quarry, i.e. a man-made cave where you can still see all the blocking out, chisel marks etc. The pyramids are all west of the Nile but were all quarried out on the East side.

Norman Reed has just been round to deliver the Midget recorder. I'd almost decided to renounce it but he seemed so disappointed that I'm taking it. As he said, I need never use it unless occasion arises.

Hope Stella let you know I'd arrived.[1]

Must stop now, Cat, as it's getting near dinner time. Lots & lots of love – enjoy yourself – L.

TO *Hedli MacNeice*   MS Bodleian

3 March [1955]   BBC, c/o John Auden, Khartoum

Darling,

Hope you got my letter from Cairo; I left it with the Holmes to post. Have had little chance to write again till today as I've had to keep altering my plans; transport in these parts is scanty & complicated, so you have to

---

1 – Stella Hillier, Features Organiser at the BBC. See FLM to Features Organiser, 9 Jan 1956.

seize what offers. I'm going to Juba tomorrow, returning here Monday; they tell me it's no great cop but it was too late to develop a better alternative.[1] It'll be even hotter than here, which is quite hot enough!

The Audens have quite a nice house but v. barely furnished because, like nearly all the other British, they're leaving here soon – 2 v. black manservants who, they say, both pinch & drink. I'd forgotten how like John's voice was to Wystan's, also sometimes his way of putting things. Quite startling.

Khartoum v. un-glam. – as is all of the Northern Sudan I've seen so far. There's one nice avenue arched over by trees, banyam etc., along the Blue Nile. Whole town laid out by Lord Kitchener; nothing from before him. Shoes get dusted over in no time. Inhabitants mainly sullen-looking; at any rate not responsive. Had a nice meal though last night with John (Sheila was poorly) in the open air at a place called the St. James's.[2] Stuffed vine leaves & Chianti. He says it's full of Greeks (business) on Sundays. Some of the traffic notices here are printed in Greek as well as in English & Arabic.

On Tuesday I seized the opportunity to get a lift down to the Gezira cotton scheme area.[3] Bloody monotonous drive. Occasional dismal villages – just flat topped boxes of bricks or mud. And dust, dust, dust. Stayed the night with a British Block Inspector who has a Brazilian wife (from one of The Sixty Families of Brazil, as she almost at once explained to me). Both pretty soused; he's leaving in October, which is later than most. The walls of their veranda were lined with British railway posters. I slept on the verandah under a mosquito net & was shot off at 6.30 next morning by car over terrible corrugated dirt roads to a place called Medani which is the irrigation headquarters. Only colour I saw en route was a brilliant red & blue bird which turned out to be a bee-eater. Had the irrigation system explained to me for an hour, then to breakfast with my cousin Archie Burton who was confined to his house by a poisoned leg (rather sinister, as his brother died out here of something similar).[4] He struck me as more broadminded than some of his colleagues. Also present his wife & 3 small children. Then went, under the supervision of a Sudanese, a tour of the

1 – Juba, a river port on the Nile, is the regional capital of southern Sudan.
2 – John Auden's wife Sheila (née Bonnerjee).
3 – The Gezira area, situated between the Blue and White Niles, was the site of a vast agricultural irrigation scheme, begun in 1911.
4 – Archie Burton was FLM's first cousin once removed. His mother was JFM's niece, Edith Burton, daughter of Caroline Matilda Frizelle (née MacNeice). Cf. 'Auden and MacNeice: Their Last Will and Testament': 'Item to Archie Burton I leave my car . . .' (LI, CP07, 739). Archie drove a three-wheeled Baby Austin (Mendelson, vol. I, 791).

scheme – or rather of part of it (the whole thing's enormous). Scenically v. monotonous but the hierarchy of the canals is nice. It's all done by gravitation, so the canals have to be higher than the fields. Visited one of the ginning factories where the seeds are extracted from the cotton. Occasional motheaten camels wandering in, wedged between 2 great bales like the most cumbrous kind of lifejacket. I notice that in the distance a camel can look like a tortoise – supposing it had eaten one of Alice in Wonderland's pills to lengthen its legs & neck. The heaps of cotton on the side of the roads looks like dollops of cream cheese. Had lunch in a Rest House – no drinks except ginger beer – & then driven back to Khartoum by 2 of the Gezira Scheme chaps. Dustiest drive I've ever had – <u>caked</u> with dust when I got home. Had never learnt Auden's address or telephone number; we had quite a time finding his house.

Today visited University College & met my first jolly Sudanese (ex-Balliol) who's the Warden there. He took me to a place called the Cultural Centre where there were more jolly Sudaneses & some bottles of Dutch beer. They have a great do on there tonight which we're all going to (in dinner jackets, alas!); I'm going to try out the midget recorder for the first time as their international programme will include (a) something called a Sudanese Kambala sung & danced by people called Nubas from the Western Sudan & (b) a traditional local singer with trad. local accompaniment. Must in fact stop this letter now to see if the recorder still works & if I still remember how to work it.

Hope you are all right, darling. As to future addresses for me, March 10th will be 'S.S. Sudan', Asswan [*sic*], Egypt & March 12th 'S.S. Sudan,' Luxor, Egypt. Dont know after that yet. Shall feel pleased when I get on that boat – though I'm afraid the Sudan part of this trip's been v. skimped – shan't get e.g. among the Dinkas.[1]

All my love. Will send Bimba a picture postcard when I come across such a thing. Will write again Monday or Tuesday. L.

TO *Hedli MacNeice*   MS Bodleian

23 March [1955]   BBC, as from 'S.S. Sudan – still!'

Darling,

Since I wrote last, our progress has been semi-static as we seem to have spent most of our time on sandbanks; this began just below Assiot where

---

1 – Cattle-herding tribes of the southern Sudan.

we spent all Friday & Saturday on one.[1] So we are still 170 kilometres from Cairo, where we were due 10.30 a.m. on Monday, & it looks (we're now stuck on another one) as if I may miss my British Council lecture tomorrow night. (Won't the Captain be mad!) But one thing: this will obviously postpone all my other movements somewhat. However will let you know later. The Arabs say Inshallah – which means 'God willing'.

Talking of Arabs, if I were this crew I should go mad. Not only, while we're moving, do they spend hour after hour standing in the bow with long poles testing the depth but, when we stick, they spend hour after hour letting down anchors & pulling them up again & rowing them hundreds of yards away & losing them & [generally trying to *deleted*] throwing out cables to passing barges & shouting at each other & generally trying to manhandle this refractory vessel. It turns out that this is the first trip from Asswan to Cairo since the War. The bed of the river changes all the time so one just doesn't know where one is. The less fatalistic passengers (mostly Americans) have already seized the opportunity to slip ashore & take a train, the first lot at Asiout, the 2nd lot at a dismal place called Minieh where it took me 55 minutes & one cup of coffee to cash a Travellers' Cheque in the bank.

So I'm certainly getting a basinful of the Nile. I must admit, considering it's just 2 banks & a lot of water, it shows considerable variety. I had thought in advance that one would see great stretches of level sand on either side but this is all wrong. The right bank is usually desert hills which often move right sheer in on the water like cliffs, while the left bank is usually flat out green. And, as the Nile is low, it's like moving permanently between 2 friezes – donkeys, camels etc. nearly always passing in file on the edge as it were of the mantelpiece. At sunset you have the stock effect of silhouetted palm trees – hell in representation but quite attractive in reality. The brown hills go pink at sunset & the sand flats go sort of lilac. The other evening we passed, at a place called Ben Hasan, some very steep high cliffs with halfway up a horizontal row of tombs in them, just like a row of portholes.[2] Quite a few birds on the river, including hoopoes, which are v. pretty, with banded wings. Our crew drink the Nile straight without any nonsense about filtering it. Our food, by the way, is v. good (the cook, I'm told, is a Greek). The crew all come from Upper Egypt (noone round

---

1 – The city of Asyut on the western bank of the Nile, capital of the Asyut Governorate, Egypt.
2 – Grotto-tombs of Beni Hassan, eastern bank of the Nile, known for its columns which are thought to be an imitation of Greek Doric. Cf. 'A row of tombs, of portholes, stared and stared as if / They were the long dead eyes of beasts inside / Time's cage' from 'Beni Hasan' (*Visitations*, CP07, 506).

Cairo, they say, is any use for this sort of work) & wear kind of dividedblue [*sic*] skirts & turbans of course & moustaches. The captain has huge black moustaches curving downwards in a crescent. Also on board we have the manager of the line – at least that's what he appears to be – a Mr Discono who speaks v. upperclass English & could, I imagine, be described as a Levantine.

To return to the passengers, whom I now know more about. Rather belatedly, I discovered that one of the girls on board, a Miss Rolo, is Ralph Harari's niece & a daughter of the Mrs Rolo whom Mrs Harari said I should contact in Alexandria.[1] She is travelling with a young man, son of a baron, called Menashi (?) & they both speak rather drawly lady-like English through having been to v. special schools in Alexandria.[2] However they're rather nice – & even a little shy, I think – & have a sense of humour. Miss R. says her mother will drive me to Rosetta.[3] Other Jewesses on board include 2 women, one young, one middle-aged, who facially are designed v. much like Mary (though they have neither her dominant eyes nor her mean forehead); so I think that Mary's face must really be a Middle Eastern face, which must have made Max Harari feel a little bit home from home.[4] (Did I tell you I wrote to Dan from Khartoum?) All these girls speak several languages easily but give one a brittle or [ruthless *deleted*] rootless feeling. The two Marian girls are rather common.

There are a number of elderly French people on board & a solid Swiss who suddenly went crackers when some children on the shore were cheering us & began to jump up & down waving & halloing & clapping; this he did for a good 10 minutes. There was an American family of six (3 generations), v. wealthy & moving in Eisenhower circles, who got restive & left at Assiout. But the old American at my table is still with us, with an endless supply of (a) 'rough' stories, (b) tips about New York restaurants – or for that matter Rome restaurants & (c) guidebook information about the Pharaohs. But, like quite a few other people, he disappeared for a day

1 – Col. Ralph Harari (1893–1969), OBE, merchant banker and art collector. Educ. Lausanne and Pembroke College, Cambridge.
2 – The Rolo and the de Menasces families, prominent Jewish families in modern Alexandria.
3 – Rosetta is on the Mediterranean coast, about forty miles from Alexandria.
4 – While at Oxford, Max Harari had a romantic interest in Mary Beazley, whom he met at dances and at the Beazley salon at Holywell. He was very disappointed when she married FLM. Harari had once been brought before Jackie Beazley for misconduct within his college, since he was given to taking hot baths more often than the college permitted. Professor Beazley told Mary that he had had a meeting with 'your young man' (DM, private correspondence, 2008). The Hararis were a Jewish family from Cairo, as the Ezras were descended from Baghdadi Jews. Harari was later associated with the Wildenstein Gallery in London.

or two to his cabin with stomach trouble. The archaeologist American I have decided is a v. amateur or dilettante archaeologist (they say his wife finances it to give him something to do); anyhow he too got restive (& rude about the Arabs in front of them) & left at Minieh. Also leaving at Minieh were the British colonel & his aunt. He seems to enjoy himself all the time as well he might, since he lives off the Stock Exchange. He also inherited some little porcelain figures which he knew nothing about, so sent them to Christie's & they realised £35,000. Almost the only proper Egyptian among the passengers, as distinct from the Alexandrian lot, is a young doctor who works at Asswan & gave me an account of Bilharzia, the very dangerous disease one gets from wading in the canals.[1] But the best value is really the large man I told you about & his wife. He is a bit Katsimbalis-like & always cluttered up with cameras.[2] Still, at age 61, rather acts the enfant terrible. She counteracts this; great deal of poise. She wants me to ring up her son in London; they'll be coming there later this summer themselves.

Noise off, at this moment, of the winch working in the bows. But we're no longer fooled by this. Doesn't mean a thing.

I don't know <u>where</u> you are, darling, not having had any more letters, but, as I can't post this till Cairo, I'll wait to see if there's a letter. I saw the postmark on Bimba's letters was Tring. How was the school? & Devon?

The first night we were stuck below Assiout they sent six armed police on board. Just in case of thieves! The Egyptian Arabs, as you probably know, are masterly thieves & during the war used to steal Army tents when the chaps were sleeping inside them.

The last week has been pretty cool; could do with a pullover quite often (left mine in Cairo). Could also do with some more reading matter. All I have is the Guide Bleu (which one can't read for long at a stretch) & Martin Chuzzlewit which I've been reading not only forwards but backwards. Someone has now lent me the Memoirs of the Agha Khan.[3] Apart from that there is a bar but people only drink between 12.0 & 1.0 (lunchtime) & usually not before 7.30 in the evening (dinner's at 8.30). The Colonel (who's gone) was the most drink-minded & kept inventing mixtures which tasted soft but were really quite hard. The only drink-minded ones now are Miss Rolo & her friend.

1 – Bilharzia, tropical disease borne by parasitic freshwater worms.
2 – George Katsimbalis, Greek author, friend of Lawrence Durrell and Henry Miller, who called him 'the Colossus of Maroussi' in his book of that name (1941).
3 – *Memoirs of Aga Khan: World Enough and Time*, by Sultan Muhammad Shah (1954).

A felucca is now passing downstream; <u>they</u> never seem to get stuck. Miss R's friend, who is an artist, has been trying to draw them but it seems they're most difficult to draw. As they would be to describe.

Crew now chanting again. Doesn't mean a thing. Think I'll stop now, Cat darling; till something more happens. /

March 24th: Something did happen – yesterday afternoon. Sheringham of the BBC appeared out of nowhere in a motor launch & whisked me back to Cairo by car. It seems Howell had been panicking. So I shall have to give my lecture tonight after all.

Just received your letters, darling. A whole batch of them – difficult to make out (a) their order, (b) your movements! I'm terribly sorry, darling, you seem so upset. It rather surprised me because the night before I left you didn't seem particularly bitter. I suppose I don't 'give' much but I do feel I give more than some (Mercy thinks I'm exceptionally considerate!)[1] However . . . perhaps we just puzzle each other. Anyway I <u>am</u> sorry, darling.

I'd have loved to come to Zurich &/or Paris but, as you can see from this letter & the one before, it's just not possible. I <u>must</u> round things off here. I don't suppose I'll be leaving Alexandria before April 3rd after which – being late anyway (I hope Bimba can be seen to all right) – I <u>would</u> love to break my journey for 2 days in Athens. It seems so wasteful to pass by it without renewing Auld Acquaintance.

Will shoot this off now to Paris – hoping that finds you.

Lots of LOVE, darling, L.

P.S. Must now renew my permit to stay here. Red Tape. Bad as Greece!

---

1 – Indeed, Mercy MacCann was very fond of him. In private notes describing his character she wrote: 'V. orderly – lists for packing / Punctual for meals / Shy <u>and</u> standoffish / One hesitated to introduce him to new people. / Once he liked – it was forever / V. loyal / loved things to follow a pattern, duck eggs, breakfast on arrival / Could be devastating . . . Fabulous memory / hated misquotes / Housman by heart – They told me Heraclitus in Greek / George could pull his leg' (*Ms Bodleian, MacNeice Papers, Box 26*). These notes were probably compiled in preparation for the BBC interview with John Boyd recorded on 21 Aug. 1964 and broadcast as 'Louis MacNeice in Ulster' on 3 Sept. 1964 (*PRONI D/2833/D/5/21*).

TO *Laurence Gilliam (BBC internal memo)*   MS BBC

27 May 1955   From: Louis MacNeice,
                               203 Rothwell House

Subject: SUGGESTION FOR CHRISTMAS PERIOD

As I told you before, I think it would be very nice to do a panoramic
programme (BBC Home Service?) during the Christmas period making use
of Bill and Wyn Cutler, possibly with other buskers in support.[1]

The idea is to do a historical survey of travelling minstrels and other
such hand-to-mouth entertainers, starting with Homer. The historical
scenes would be divided by a spot of the Cutlers themselves, thereby
underlining the continuity of their tradition and also making a nice study
of identity in difference. The material is also of course very rich and varied
and could include people as different as the French mediaeval Goliards,
and the not yet extinct Irish wandering storyteller.

Mrs. Cutler's songs would naturally have to be carefully selected so as
to give proper lead-ins and lead-outs from the historical scenes.

I am quite sure that such a programme would be both instructive and
entertaining, and it was proved in my 'Twelve Days of Christmas' that
Wyn Cutler carries a terrific punch on the air, and especially perhaps
during the Christmas season.[2]

                               LMacN/EC
                               (Louis MacNeice)

TO *Douglas Cleverdon*[3]   MS BBC

30 May 1955   BBC

In answer to your memo requesting suggestions for repeats or new
productions of Third Programmes programmes [*sic*], I would suggest any
of the following which I put in the order of my own preference:[4]

---

1 – The Cutlers were London buskers. Wyn Cutler sang the 'lead-in' to the BBC Home Service
'From Bard to Busker', broadcast 30 Dec. 1956 (Stallworthy, 423).
2 – *Twelve Days of Christmas*, broadcast BBC Home Service, 6 Jan. 1953.
3 – Douglas Cleverdon (1903–87), radio producer, bookseller. Educ. Bristol GS and Jesus
College, Oxford. He began working part-time for the BBC in 1939 and worked in Burma as
a war correspondent in 1945; later became West Regional features producer, then overall
features producer. Author of a monograph, *The Art of Radio*; qtd in Coulton, 51–2; 196.
4 – In a memo of 25 May, Cleverdon asked his producers to compile a list of suitable
programmes to be repeated in celebration of the tenth anniversary, on 29 Sept., of the BBC's
Third Programme (*Ms BBC*).

(1) <u>One Eye Wild</u>: new production[1] Length: 75'
(2) <u>Enemy of Cant</u>: there were two separate productions of this recorded and if they still have the recording of the better one I don't think it would need a new production.[2] Esme Percy was most remarkable in it and I don't think he could better himself. Length 90'
(3) <u>The Death of Gunnar and The Burning of Njal</u> which is a sequel to the former.[3] These would need a new production and new special music. Lengths: 75', 75'
(4) <u>The Golden Ass</u>, which I have already produced twice. Recording of the second production. Length: 60'
(5) <u>The Queen of Air and Darkness</u>. New production. If accepted, I would like to re-write it and, incidentally, shorten it. Original length: 100'

Apart from the above there is always 'The Dark Tower' (which in fact came to birth before the Third Programme existed) of which I have already done two quite distinct productions, neither of which entirely satisfies me. I <u>would</u> quite like to have another go at it, the only snag being that Cyril Cusack (and I can't envisage anyone else in the leading part) may be getting a little bit old for it.[4] Length: 75'

TO *Hedli MacNeice*   MS Bodleian

30 October [1955]   BBC, Colombo[5]

Dearest Cat,

Got here yesterday. Always seem to hit these important cities on week-ends when everyone's gone off swimming. So <u>so far</u> have no engagements

1 – *One Eye Wild*, first broadcast BBC Third Programme, 9 Nov. 1952.
2 – *Enemy of Cant* (extracts from Aristophanes), first broadcast BBC Third Programme, 3 Dec. 1946.
3 – 'The Death of Gunnar' and 'The Burning of Njal' (*Icelandic Sagas*, Nos. 1 and 2), broadcast 11–12 March 1947.
4 – Cyril Cusack (1910–93), renowned Irish actor.
5 – Laurence Gilliam asked FLM to visit India, Pakistan and Ceylon to gather recorded material for a projected Christmas Day programme, *The Star We Follow*, to be co-written with Ritchie Calder. He arrived in Karachi on 21 Oct. and returned to London via Bombay on 12 Nov. During the trip he visited Lahore and Madras, and Colombo, Batticaloa and Ampara in Ceylon; he also visited the Gal Oya scheme, a government plan to dam the Gal Oya river. Of a sequence of ten numbered letters to Hedli from this trip I have reproduced three. See Stallworthy, 417–18; Coulton 147–8.

for today (it's now 11.30 a.m.). but perhaps that's not a bad thing as it's almost my first chance to relax. Except that I should go to the Telegraph Office today & send a long cable to Laurence. Friday evening I was taken by the Holroydes to the Indian International Industries Fair which was due to open next day but, owing to floods, Customs red tape, & chronic inefficiency, didn't look like opening before the New Year. However, it's a vast & ambitious affair (biggest ever in Asia) & it was fun to wander round it in the broken darkness with all the poor workers still sawing & hammering & bumping into everyone & drinking tea. Went first to the British Pavilion, the only one serving drinks – which was just as well since there was almost nothing to look at; & the pavilion itself a v. dull layout, nobody it seems would spend any money or employ designers like the Festival of Britain boys (for that sort of imagination you had to go to India's own Hand Loom pavilion – v. gay & lots of charm). The High Commissioner, Malcolm MacDonald, made a not convincing speech – it seems he hates business men anyway.[1] The only people who'd got their pavilion 100% finished were the Chinese. The Czechs had put up, entirely with Czech labour (nearly everyone else used Indians), a huge affair like a nylon Crystal Palace. The Russians had mounted a frockcoated statue of Lenin just like the worthies round Birmingham Town Hall. The East Germans had devoted a chamber of horrors to displaying the insides of East German Man. Altogether a great drive being made by the Iron Curtain countries to capture Indian trade. The Americans had their own chamber of horrors devoted to atomic energy – a monstrous machine with long arms & metal hands which, earlier in the day I was told, had been manoeuvred by a v. pretty blonde to light cigarettes & write 'Jai Hind'[2] on sheets of foolscap; the Indian onlookers had said 'Why can't she use her own hands?' – but of course the machine was really for handling isotopes or something.

Flew away from Delhi at 11.15 p.m. (lights of Delhi magnificent from the air) & landed at Nagpur c. 2.30 a.m. where (how considerate!) one had to change planes & have 'breakfast'. Got to Madras airport 7.0 a.m. where I was met by Narayana Menon who drove me to his house for a real breakfast.[3] He's a charmer & v. intelligent but he made me go at 9.15 to the broadcasting station to be interviewed & read a poem (Orientals are ruthless in that way). Back at Madras airport newly landed Indian film

1 – Malcolm John MacDonald (1901–81), Britain's High Commissioner to India 1955–60. Son of former British PM Ramsay MacDonald.
2 – Roughly, 'Long live India'.
3 – See earlier reference to Menon in FLM to Hedli, 16 Aug. 1947, n. 4, p. 478.

stars (their film industry's the 2nd largest after Hollywood) were being garlanded with the usual pink roses. In the plane read an Indian film magazine – this also v. scurrilous about Nehru & Co. Reached Colombo airport c. 4.0 p.m. met by a Mr. Wizemanne of Radio Ceylon, B.B.C.-trained, v. smooth. Arriving at hotel on seafront, was immediately interviewed by Ceylonese newspaper. In my room started to check on the Midget after its series of buffetings (it contained reel with about 1/5th still to be used) & found the tape had whipped itself into convulsions. Was just trying to cope with this when I realised I was being stared at idiotically by 4 silent but peculiarly exasperating servants. This made me break the tape & I spun out the unused fifth on the floor. As you know I've never liked spaghetti & this really made me feel like screaming. //

Sorry, darling, at that point was called away by one of Brigadier Turnbull's (see Laurence) contacts, a chap in some British engineering firm. Since then till now (dinner time) have been ginning up & pretending to be matey. The chaps I was mateying with were called Stan, Les, Mac, & Fergus. However – not uninstructive.

Cat, it looks, I'm afraid, as if I must change my schedule. (1) I've decided to go to a rather ungetattable place called Gal Oya – which may mean 2 days more in Ceylon. (2) Had a cable from Holroyde today stating that Dr. Bhabha is leaving Bombay for Delhi on Nov. 2nd. (I was flying to Bombay on Nov. 3rd in order to meet him!) This being so, I think I'll go to Bombay anyway (little in it geographically & better & quicker planes than those I came here by), spend a night with Sinclair, then to Delhi pursuing Bhabha, & then home (c. 10th–11th?).

One nice thing here is the noise of the waves outside my window. Dearest, I miss you a lot. Must now get myself ready for dinner (this hotel is a stickler for ties & jackets).

> Love (as you know) – L.

TO *Hedli MacNeice*   MS Bodleian

5 November [1955]   BBC, Colombo

Dearest my Cat! I'm still, as you see, in Ceylon. What with the Midget on one hand & Dr. Bhabha possibly not on the other hand, it's nothing but hitches & hold-ups. I'm now leaving here for Bombay on Monday; Dr. B., I was told, is expected there Wednesday but one never knows. All being well, however, I hope to leave Bombay Friday Nov 11th (though this depends on someone else cancelling his reservation – which they say is likely; otherwise there's no flight till Monday 14th) – which means I'd arrive London Airport 5.15 p.m. Saturday (Flight EM535).

Darling, thank you for 2 more letters which I got in Radio Ceylon this morning; I never knew we had printed letterheading to our (pace Miss Mitford) notepaper. By the way do you know that you make your capital 'M's quite differently on different occasions? You should ask Thérèse about that!

Darling, you do seem to be living in a social whirl! It makes the East seem tame & serious. But you <u>must</u> stop this business of waking at 3.0 a.m. Brooding – especially brooding in the small hours (the Small Bad Hours) – is no good at all, I've decided.

Now, to resume my chronicle. Tuesday evening I was picked up by Mr. Nganamuttu, the Information Officer of the Gal Oya Development Board, & we got on a night train for Batticaloa on the other, i.e. the eastern, side of the island. Mr. N. both a nice & intelligent young man but with one of those monotonous percussive voices, forced & fast, which gets one down in the long run, especially if the pronunciation makes one strain for the sense. On the train we met a nice Ceylonese engineer, a Mr. Delay (pronounced Dilly) who'd spent the War making R.A.F. airfields in Britain. We had several whiskies together & a rather poor meal. Night pitch dark – Ceylon invisible. Mr. N. went to bed in a sarong. Arrived Batticaloa 7.0 a.m. & drove off in a Landrover (frightfully bumpy) c.40 miles to Amperai, the central town in the Gal Oya valley. Passed through several oldworld villages – palm thatch, paddy thatch, & general bazaarish feeling – & by causeways over lagoons but once you get in the Scheme it's all brand new Municipal type houses with red roofs all separate from each other. Large signposts directing one to 'Site for Bachelors' Dormitory' & so on. And hundreds of tractors etc etc. After the usual hanging about in offices we went into the field & began by recording (at least I thought so!) a settler ploughing with his 2 black buffalo, chanting as he did so & smacking them with a stick & all 3 splashing & floundering through a v. wet paddy field. Then someone told us of a settler who spoke English (an almost unheard-of phenomenon), so we went to interview him, by which time, checking, I found the bloody Midget was no longer working – it seems the journey had been too much for it. So we took it back to base & handed it over to a young Canadian electrical engineer called Van der Meyden (here under the Colombo Plan) & a young Ceylonese called Shelton Silva, who took it to their electrical work shop; by ill luck, for the first time on this trip, I'd left behind in Colombo the book of instructions with the circuit diagram – which would have saved them hours of work on the thing; as it was, they didn't get it mended till 4.0 p.m. the next day, Thursday. (All honour, however, to Shelton Silva who did the donkey work.) After lunch – rice & curry – I got stuck with the Deputy Resident Manager, a Mr. Abeywardena, who, in spite of suffering from low blood pressure, seems unable to stop talking. When he stopped, it was dark & I drove off with Mr. N. to Inginiyágala, where the great main reservoir is & there's a very nice Rest House. In the Rest House we found Van der Meyden having drinks with several Ceylonese & one jolly Indian from Lucknow called Mr. Singh, who was boosting the British no end. We were joined by a Doctor Szechowycz (pronounced Shekovitch) a displaced Pole who's the Forest Officer on the Scheme. Very Polish; we all drank Double Distilled Arrack made from coconut toddy. Didn't eat till after 1.0 & got to bed c. 2.30 a.m. Dr. S. got us up at 5.30 to take us in a launch on the lake hoping to see elephant; about all we saw was pelican, sitting on the tops of drowned trees with their heads clamped down on them like lids. Then back to Amperai & also a long drive further on to buy a valve for the Midget! – more & more talk & the curry this time so hot that everyone, Ceylonese included, protested (see later). At 4.0 reappeared the Midget & I started recording interviews; they all went on for too long but it would have been tactless to curtail them. Back at the Rest House we had an early dinner – far too fancy a steak & then recorded Dr. Szechowycz & his wife Mrs. Szechowycz & his daughter Miss Szechowycz (v. young) & his brother Mr. Szechowycz & his sister-in-law Mrs. Szechowycz who is also an architect. By then it was 11.30 & I was more tired than I have been for years & was sick 4, if not 5, times during the night – presumably because my stomach was just too exhausted to digest the rich lunch & dinner. Nonetheless we got up at 6.30 Friday & drove to record some schoolchildren singing – a folk song by a group & a lullaby solo in Sinhalese. The 1st little girl to do the lullaby was so strident that I asked for another. We then went out into a Mr. Jonklaas (Ceylonese but what they call a Burgher – presumably with Dutch blood – anyhow he has almost an Oxford accent) to see some Jungle Felling which he specially laid on for us (the season is in fact practically over). This is performed by 4 great caterpillar tractors & 2 'tree-dozers' (though as this was a token performance, we only had one tree-dozer; it's called the 'Scrumhalf'[.] The tractors work tandem & pull an enormous chain (ship's anchor) in a hairpin loop which pulls over the trees; the tree-dozer lurks about behind and pushes over any [diagram] trees which are obstinate. The chain shaves through the stuff astonishingly quickly. Unfortunately, for sound effects, the machines make such a noise that they tend to drown the crashing of the trees. It's all v. ruthless & rather sad. Mr.

J. says that, when they come to the <u>end</u> of a strip of jungle, all the wild
animals dart out ahead of them one after the other – all except the mouse-
deer who's a fool & keeps running along inside the chain.[1] Returned from
jungle-felling had early lunch (boiled fish this time) & went out to find
more ploughmen which we found, but failed to find a Malayan English-
speaking settler who has 15 children, though one of his little boys took us
in search of him. Then recorded another Pole (!), a Mr. Rozwadówski,
who is town-planner to the Scheme & says it will keep him busy till he
dies. Then drove back to Batticaloa & got the night train back & here I am
– the Indian Ocean still like Belfast Lough (it's been bad weather all this
time). Went to see a Big Shot this morning, Mr. Coomaraswamy, re the
Colombo Plan. Have fixed to go out tomorrow evening, my last here,
Sunday, to record some devil-dancing. Think I'll end this now, Cat, & take
a rather late (4.15 p.m.) siesta – haven't had a siesta since leaving England.
Lots & lots of love – remember about sleeping properly. & my God! I quite
forgot to say how v.v. good about John Irwin.[2] It will need crafty selection
– but we can discuss that! L.

TO *Hedli MacNeice*   MS Bodleian

6 November [1955]   BBC, Colombo [letterhead]

Darling, Just another scribble which I'll finish this afternoon before I go
devil-dancing. Was taken out yesterday evening by a slightly depressing
elderly couple called Rankin (not that they appear particularly English in
complexion, speech or bearing; I think there must be a Middle-Asian
equivalent of the Levantine). We drank a lot of whisky in deserted clubs &
had a late Ceylonese meal, which I tackled cautiously. Today I am going
out to lunch with a chap called Bill Bergne who says he was at school with
me & who knows Goronwy; he's in Shell.[3]

All the servants etc. here say 'Master' where Indians say 'Sahib'. 'Master
not gone away yet?' A little embarrassing! But they use it also of their
posher compatriots, who in their turn shout 'Boy!' at them. There is a
strong move here for Prohibition; a 14 year old girl has just committed
suicide for the cause. The Prime Minister, I'm told, recently announced

1 – Cf. the pelican in 'Jungle Clearance Ceylon': 'looking down / Its beak in contempt of
human beings / Who had drowned a valley to found a town' (*Solstices*, CP07, 555–6).
2 – Unidentified.
3 – Villiers A'Court (Bill) Bergne (b.1910), educ. MC, 1923–7. Appointed head of Edit
Department, Shell Petrol Co., 1947. M. art critic Diana Holman-Hunt (1913–93), grand-
daughter of the painter.

publicly that, if Prohibition came in, he'd be the first to apply for an Addict's Permit.

With the Rankins last night I met an interesting Englishman called Van Geyzil (!) who's a planter & lives by himself (queer possibly) & hasn't been in England since 1928 but remains v. Cambridge & was asking all about the London Theatre (reminded me of something in Kipling). One of those big bald blondes – something like that man in the Tessin called 'Sandy'.

A disconcerting feature of the Ceylonese is that they have two ways of shaking their heads. One – as anywhere else – means No but the other, a slow shake with the head going out of the vertical & the eyes simultaneously going melancholy, appears to mean they're just thinking. Have heard Tambimuttu mentioned several times; they don't seem proud of him here.[1]

Today – so far – it's not raining & the long slow breakers are shining white. Am due to be collected at 11.0 to go to a library to mug up devil-dancing. 'Băli' is its proper name & it's an exorcism ceremony to drive out fevers, evil spirits etc. It all takes a v. long time so as I may not be back till the small hours, I'll start packing this afternoon & assembling all the bloody documents one has to carry.

About Xmas, darling, I think I ought to stay in London – if only because I feel Laurence will want me around for psych. reasons. I suppose Alan & Isabel wouldn't come?[2] We could go to Mercy for the New Year – but without Teresa, I suggest; it will only be the house in Belfast, I gathered from what they said.[3] And it does cost a lot to take so many there! Re Yorkshire or anywhere else, I can't really say till Saul's got a date.[4] Perhaps it has now?

What is the 'Show' you talk about? & <u>where</u> were 'Helen & the Boys with 80 Chinese'? Cat dear, your letters are sometimes rather elliptical. //

After lunch:- The original devil-dancing scheme's fallen through, owing to floods, but another's been cooked up only a few miles away. The Rankins, who reappeared this morning, are driving me to it. Though full, I suppose, of good intentions, they're really the most unprepossessing couple (it seems they're 'Burghers'), both of them with dirty-coloured

1 – Tambimuttu (1915–83), poet and editor. Born in Ceylon, he came to London in 1937, where he established himself in literary circles and edited *Poetry London* 1939–47. After some time in America he returned to London with the announcement: 'TAMBIMUTTU BACK IN LONDON to launch the magazine of the century. Requires finance. Partnership offered' (Personal column, *The Times*, 25 April 1969, 22).
2 – The Rawsthornes (see FLM to Ellen Borden Stevenson, 21 March 1953, n. 3, p. 561).
3 – Mercy MacCann in Belfast; Teresa Moroni was the maid in London.
4 – 'Also Among the Prophets', broadcast 5 Feb. 1956, is based on the biblical story of Saul.

nondescript eyes. Mrs. R. looks rather like a v. sallow Martha McCulloch & talks at the same tempo & with much the same (!) intonation – only a shade Orientalised – as Rose Macaulay, but much less intelligible & not at all witty.

Lunch was good. Mr. Bergne really at Marlborough in my time – though not a grey hair. Mrs. B. v. pretty but v. pregnant – just like Mrs. Holroyde in New Delhi. Mr. B. pretty cynical about this country, says they're driving towards a one-party government. There's a terrific schamozzle going on here over the language question – Tamil v. Sinhalese. They say it may end in bloodshed.

Must stop now, my dearest, & pack. Have v. little Ceylonese money left – which means careful thinking about tips. (The B.B.C. are bloody stupid the way they issue Travellers' Cheques only for £10 & £20; when crossing frontiers so quickly one needs small cheques).

Darling, I'll write you from Bombay – probably just one more letter as after that I'll be returning myself. Bhabha is returning there Wednesday. Hope Bimba's better –

all love to you both. L.

1956

TO *Features Organiser [Stella Hillier]*
  (BBC internal memo)   MS BBC

9 January 1956   From: Louis MacNeice,
                                      203 Rothwell House

Subject: PROGRAMME OUTPUT IN 1955

1955 was for me a somewhat mutilated year, as approximately half of it was taken up with two programmes i.e., 'The Nile' and Christmas, and the travel which these involved.[1]

Apart from the programmes which I wrote and/or produced myself during the year, I made the following suggestions:

1. A dramatisation by myself of Joyce Cary's 'Mr. Johnson'; accepted by Third, but postponed owing to Mr. Cary's ill-health.

2. 'Also Among the Prophets': a 90' minute [*sic*] programme to be written and produced by myself: accepted by Third and scripted: to be broadcast on February 5th.

3. A programme on Horace – a combination of biographical feature and paraphrase. A tentative suggestion, approved by Third, but conditional on my finding Horace paraphrasable. Have not yet had time to investigate this.

4. A programme on wandering entertainers through the ages (from Homer down) to be skewered together by contemporary buskers (the Cutlers); accepted but postponed since it was intended for the Christmas season.

5. A First Visit to Yorkshire (1 hour): accepted – and Yorkshire visited, but postponed.

6. A programme on Emily Dickinson, by Cecil Day Lewis: accepted by Third, but postponed owing to Day Lewis' other engagements.

---

1 – *The Fullness of the Nile*, broadcast BBC Home Service, 3 July 1955, and *The Star We Follow* (with Ritchie Calder), broadcast BBC Home Service/Light Programme, 25 Dec. 1955.

7. 'Mutiny on the Bounty' by Laurie Lee: accepted but not placed. This was one of three programme suggestions of his which I put forward.[1]

8. Themes in American Poetry, by James Gindin.[2]

As for my non air-borne work during 1955, this has included the usual routine interviewing of actors and actresses, and some would-be script-writers (the last named not being promising). I have also had to deal with the usual unsolicited scripts: here again, the year proved unfruitful.

(Louis MacNeice)

TO *Hedli MacNeice*

MS Bodleian

15 October [1956]   BBC, 'from Accra'[3]

Darling,

How are your arm & shoulder? I do hope they didn't hurt too much in Oxford. Look after yourself!

Had a very smooth trip out. Good meals & lots of free drinks but nowhere to put your legs (the place packed). Last stop before here was at Karra? Airport where at about 4.45 am I had a nice large bottle of lager. Plane was a shade early at Accra so nobody on the dot to meet me but shortly there turned up a nice chap called Hall, an information officer. The place seems to be full of these, I am staying with another one, James Moxon, a v. portly blond chap who's been here 15 years & yesterday I went to lunch with yet another one called Laycock who has a v. plump Polish wife & a double-glass-bottomed ashtray with between the 2 panes of glass a tiny china female nude who wiggles when you turn a screw (made in France, need I say). A good [*illegible*] lunch.

---

1 – *Mutiny on the Bounty* untraced, but FLM produced *Black Saturday, Red Sunday*, written by Lee, broadcast BBC Third Programme, 14 Nov. 1956.

2 – Despite FLM's support, Gindin's proposal – sent to FLM after their meeting in London – was rejected on the grounds that it was 'too academic'. James Gindin (1926–94) was Professor of English at the University of Michigan, where he taught for almost forty years.

3 – Capital of Gold Coast. Gold Coast would become independent (as Ghana) in March 1957 and FLM had flown there on 13 October in order to write scripts both for the Gold Coast Film Unit (directed by Sean Graham, see below) and for the BBC. FLM spent a week in Accra before being taken on a guided tour of the country organised by the Gold Coast Information Service (22–28 Oct.), accompanied by a young Australian guide, Bob Raymond; he also visited the Northern Territories including Bolgatonga, Tamale and Bawku (29 Oct.–1 Nov.), and finally Togoland. Of this sequence of seven numbered letters to Hedli MacNeice I have reproduced five (see Stallworthy, 422–3).

602

This town is not without appeal. In one direction there's an old Danish (!) fort called Christianborg, with dungeons below it looking out on the sea, & now occupied by the Governor; in the other there's a lighthouse & a nice tatty joint called the Seaview Hotel run by a Greek. In between there's an extraordinary mix-up of fishing village (corrugated iron) & the latest Maxwell Fry architecture.[1] There are also lots of trees – some flowering loudly. Men & women in wonderfully gaudy clothes but not wild life, except for frogs & insects at night.

Today was rather gruelling. I was made to visit the Permanent Secretaries of Health, Development, Trade & Labour, & Agriculture. Still the lesser Wet Season – sky overcast most of the time – v. humid. Sean Graham, the head of the Film Unit, turned up from somewhere on his way to somewhere else, I shan't see him again for a fortnight (!) but he gave me a list of African contacts (some amusing, some 'typical').[2]

On Friday I am to go to a Farm Festival, which sounds great fun, & on Monday 22nd shall be trekking off with a nice young bearded Australian for about a week, first west along the coast, then onto Asharith. Then back to Accra, then onto the Northern Territories (the most primitive part). Then Accra again, then to Togoland.[3] Then Accra for a final round-up, then home. Have to see gold mines, hospitals, medical field units, cocoa groves, a new harbour, a new bridge, various old castles, the fishing industry, the timber trade, a furniture shop, a veterinary farm, & lots of jolly chiefs & London University graduates.

Can't write more now, darling, because it's coming up for dinner (guests) & I have to wash & change. I feel v. sticky & the insects are chirping outside. Tomorrow sounds a still more gruelling day but hope to have more time to write on Wednesday.

Lots & lots of love
& to Bimba,
L.

P.S. Please get a press for my racquet (I forgot!).

---

1 – Maxwell Fry (1899–1987), architect who worked in the 1930s in association with Walter Gropius; became town-planning adviser after the war to the resident minister in west Africa. With Jane Drew he designed many buildings in Ghana and Nigeria, 1946–61.
2 – Sean Graham, director of Gold Coast Film Unit, asked FLM to write a script on the transition to Ghanaian independence. The result was *Freedom for Ghana*, broadcast March 1957 (Stallworthy, 422–3).
3 – Most of former Togoland became Togo; a small part went to Ghana.

TO *Hedli MacNeice*   MS Bodleian

Wednesday 17 [October 1956]   BBC, Accra

Darling,

Have got an afternoon off; next date is 6.30 for drinks at Government House (= Christianborg Castle)[1] with Sir Charles Arden-Clarke, the Governor, who appears to be a v. good man.[2] Went out this morning to Tema where they are making a huge new port (so far there's only one in the Gold Coast) which means building long breakwaters to enclose a square mile of water. On the way passed buses with big slogans painted on them: 'We See God' or 'Let Them Say'. All the way to coast a long line of surf. The fishermen are still encamped in the middle of the new fort area, seeing no reason to leave.

I am enjoying this place; it's more interesting; much more colourful, & jollier than, say, the Sudan. Some v. good looking people of both sexes. The women wear 'mammy-cloth' which is imported from Manchester, Holland or Japan but often stamped with v. riotous patterns of their own; they are usually walking about with the kitchenstove, etc. on their heads.

(This biro, which you gave me, seems bloody awful feeble but the inkpot on my table is glued together with the climate.) Yesterday morning, after seeing the usual Permanent Secretaries I went with Raymond, the nice Australian, to the SeaView [*sic*] Hotel – covered terrace with a seabreeze – where we ran into Geoffrey Byng (Bing?), friend of Kingsley Martin's, Q.C. & ex-M.P., who has a house here now & makes pots of money defending people in the Gold Coast courts.[3] He got married this year up the coast in an ancient Portuguese castle by a black man in a topi with a sword. He bought us 2 bottles of champagne.

Yesterday afternoon I visited an African, Mr. Philip Gbebo, who is a teacher at Achimota School (the most famous in the country) & also 'Chairman of the Arts Council' – though I'm told that the Arts Council

---

1 – Christianborg Castle: residence of the British Governor of Gold Coast from 1877 to 1957; later the official residence of the President of Ghana.

2 – Sir Charles Noble Arden-Clarke (1898–1962), educ. Rossall School. Machine Gun Corps 1917–20. Joined the Colonial Service 1920 and served as an administrator in Nigeria, Bechuanaland, Basutoland and Sarawak before coming in 1949 to Gold Coast, which he governed for eight years.

3 – Geoffrey Bing (1909–77), born Craigavad, Co. Down, educ. Lincoln College, Oxford; author of *John Bull's Other Island* (1950); *Reap the Whirlwind: An Account of Kwame Nkrumah's Ghana from 1950 to 1966* (1968). Kingsley Martin (1897–1969), educ. Magdalene College, Cambridge; taught at LSE; editor of *NS* from 1931. Two-vol. autobiography: *Father Figure* and *Editor* (1966, 1970).

doesn't officially exist yet.[1] He lectured me on the need for maintaining the indigenous culture, i.e. mainly drumming & dancing. After which I was shown the new 'Ambassadors Hotel' which is just being completed & is costing £750,000[.] All v. modern & streamlined but I'd hate to sleep in the bedrooms – it would be like sleeping in a laboratory.

Was told yesterday about a v. minor chief here who had engraved on his writing paper: 'Prince of Princes, King of Kings, Ruler of Rulers, & Vice-Captain of the Accra Football Club'.

One eats v. well in this house: yesterday we had ground nut soup which is delicious. I am going to dinner tonight with James Millin the B.B.C. chap who runs the radio here. Tell Laurence I have already had some Xmas ideas for him which I'll be passing on shortly. I'll be taking the Midget to the Farm Festival on Friday.[2] I have to go to the Broadcasting Station tomorrow morning to talk to the employees. One of them won't be there; after 27 years' service he's just been given 9 months for fiddling the funds.

Have continued reading the James Gunther book which I can now heartily recommend to you.[3] Have just lit a cigarette with a box of matches, entitled 'Gentleman' & picturing a Negro in a dinner jacket, white tie, gold sash & medal – Made in Sweden. Have not yet visited any of the stores here but some of the chief ones are run by Lebanese who sound like the Syrian in Graham Greene's 'The Heart of the Matter'.

My host tells me that when he first came here he was landed through the surf in a canoe & that the Gold Coasters (old style British veterans) used to start the day with 3 brandies; this custom has gone out. However, he says, they seemed to thrive on it.

Have just had the notion that tonight I might time my visit to India next year so that on my way home I could drop in here (it wouldn't be so great a diversion) for the March 6th celebrations which will really be something; anyhow they will be framing the last sequence in the film. I shall suggest this to Laurence.

Hope your arm is quite cured now darling & that you are having a gay social life. Lots of love – & look after yourself. Would Bimba like a small carved devil with batwings? L.

---

1 – The Assembly Hall of this school was the venue of the historic Achimota Conference on Ghanaian independence (16 Feb. 1956).
2 – The traditional Ohumkyrie Festival, celebrated by the Kibi people of eastern Ghana.
3 – Presumably James Gunther, *Revolution in India* (1944).

TO *Hedli MacNeice*   MS Bodleian

27 October [1956]   BBC, 'as from Accra'

Darling,

Now the 28th – which just proves what I was about to say, i.e. that it's
<u>impossible</u> to write letters on this trek (going round Yorkshire with John
Sharp was nothing), so please don't be cross about it![1] Am staying in a
circular resthouse with a thatched roof & a super-mosquito net, having
just passed one of the most exhausting weeks of my life. The Gold Coast
Information Service put out a schedule for every day – first appointment
8.0 a.m. & continuous appointments (many of them useless) from then on
at half hour intervals. Still, a lot of it has been amusing &/or interesting &
the bearded young Australian, Bob Raymond, who's been driving me
around is v. nice indeed. Since Monday morning early I've visited 3 of the
old coast forts, the earliest being a Portuguese one from the late 15th Cent.,
now occupied by the police; have had lunch with a Mr Justice Bossman[2]
who asked would we eat 'African' or cutlets & then made us eat both &
threw in a magnum of champagne with the sweet; have visited the chief
port & a boat building concern & been down a gold mine (sinister &
slippery under foot), have driven through innumerable miles of forest –
green & quite cosy, not sinister at all – have visited a handweaver where I
bought you a strip of 'Kente' cloth[3] which might do for either a scarf or a
belt & an old rogue from whom I bought an 'Ashanti gold weight', i.e. a
tiny brass figure of a [*illegible*] drummer for Bimba; have sat in, last night,
on a 'High Life' session in the Hotel de Kingsway at Kumari (capital of
Ashanti) where the cabaret featured 2 medieval dwarfs (vast applause &
coins on the floor), have been over the Kumari College of Technology
where I tried to record a musical class (too loud) & the enormous new
Kumari Hospital where I met a lady Dr Gamble who is Irish & extremely
sceptical; have been lectured, over-technically, on the mealy bug at a local
Research Institute, &, today, have been the guest of the Regional Officer
here, who is the son of the late Dean of Cashel & whom my father wanted
to make a clergyman & who seems rather like the MacNab of the Colonial
Service. This morning (it is the small hours now) I shall be off early, back
to Accra, calling on my way on quite an important chief, Nana Ofori Atta
the Second, who is the Omanhene of Akim Abuakwa[4] (after which I have

1–In 1955 FLM toured Yorkshire with the actor John Sharp (Stallworthy, 416; Coulton,
144–7).
2–Kofi Adumua Bossman, legal practitioner and member of the National Democratic Party.
3–Fabric local to Ghana, made of woven cloth strips.
4–Chief of Akyem Abuakwa, a region of Ghana.

to have lunch with a drunken Old Marlburian). Raymond & I visited a comic old chief the other day called the Bekwaihene (pronounced Bik-wye-heeny) who spoke to us through an interpreter & said that he saw 'Signs of Age' in me. However, he gave us a lot of Dutch beer. All this must sound dull, but I'll fill in the details later. I can see lots of trouble ahead over the film – it seems likely that they (the Govmt) will want it all chromium-plated & no talking drums – beat the Soviet Union at their own game etc.

By the way, darling, I think we'd better drop the meeting-in-Rome idea; I shan't have the time or the money – or the clothes – & all I'll want by then (c. 15th Nov). is to get home & recuperate. I'm being railroaded into the usual extraneous activities – broadcasting, British Council, University College, Accra Dining Club etc, – & there really are limits to one's stamina.

I must go to bed now, Cat Dearest, under the mosquito net, as it is v. late. Will finish this in Accra before I rush off again on Monday morning to the Northern Territories. //

Darling, have just woken up, so will add a word or two before my breakfast is carried over out of the green.

A few boring reminders etc.:-

Did you get a press for my racquet? & cash that expenses sheet? (The 2nd could pay for the first!)

Could you ask Eileen if she got a letter from me full of directions about Laurie's programme? If not, I'll write to her again.

Could you possibly (!) before I get back, tabulate your earnings & expenses for Income Tax year April '55–'56. And ask Eileen to get a statement from the B.B.C. of all my increments from them for the same year, making clear which had tax deducted. And ask Eileen also to get statements from the London Magazine of what they paid me in that year.

Could you tell Laurence (to whom I mean to write soon) that there is good & varied material here for a half hour or 45 min. programme but that, as Matt Halton pretty well covered the political side a year ago, I'd prefer to do a sort of colour background piece (timed for round about Independence) to show the simple British public what this odd country is like.[1] By the way, the man who suggested the name Ghana has now got together with some other opposition politicians to say it must not be called Ghana.

Corruption here is called 'dash'. You say 'dash me 2 shillings' – or, no doubt, also 2,000 pounds.

1 – Probably this became *The Birth of Ghana* (broadcast 22 Feb. 1957), 'side-product for a script for a film' (Coulton, 159). Cf. FLM, 'Ghana: The Birth of an African State', *Radio Times*, 15 Feb. 1957, 27.

More bus captions:- 'Oh Had I but known!', 'Grace of God', 'Good Time Roll', 'I know that My Redeemer Liveth', 'Honest Labour'. And in Sekondi we passed the 'In God We Trust Chop Bar'. The particular pattern of Kente cloth I got for you is known as 'The rich man has many friends'. In some bars there is a notice saying 'No Political Arguments'.

Sorry – breakfast just came. I'm to eat it in a sort of wire net cage looking out on the parkland.

[*in pencil*] Back in Accra – no ink – love –

L.

xxxxxx

TO *Hedli MacNeice*   MS Bodleian

2 November [1956]   BBC, Accra

Dearest Cat,

Am snatching some siesta time to write to you. Writing was once more not feasible on my trek in the Northern Territories; anyhow, owing to the defective postal communications, a letter from up there probably would not have reached you any sooner.

What appalling bloody news about Egypt; Eden & Co. must be off their heads[1]. I hope you are not too worried. I am now booked to fly back on Nov. 15th, reaching London Airport breakfast time Friday 16th.

Thank you v. much for your 2 letters. What a time you've been having with that AILMENT of yours! I do hope you're now back to normal.

To return to my chronicle: this time I went off on my own, without the Australian, & spent Monday night in Tamale, capital of the Northern Territories, where I had a jolly evening with an Irishman called McGiffin with whom I talked Rugger Shop. The N.T.s are quite different from the south – no forest – much drier – red dust in everything. I visited a chief in Tamale called the Gulpke-Na. More Oriental-looking than African, sitting cross-legged on a cowhide (showing his toe-rings) on a concrete dais in a corrugated iron shed ('Made in Britain' stamped all over it), in the midst of a compound of round thatched houses of red earth – horses & naked children all over the place & little bonfires of straw smoking away to keep off the flies. Also visited Tamale Market – long lines of thatched booth – funny mix-up of imported tinned foods & cottons & little piles of purple

---

1 – The British government had backed an Israeli invasion of Sinai on 29 Oct. 1956 following Egypt's nationalisation of the Suez Canal.

onions & peppers & primitive grains like millet; some in white enamel basins & some in home-made earthen pots or calabashes.

Tuesday drove north a long way to Bolgatanga & then to a village of one of the nudity tribes; the women usually, though, seem to have a leaf in front as well as behind. A few of the young ones have attractive figures but this does not make up for the others! Visited another chief there, having to climb over a 5 ft. clay wall to reach him. Spent that evening with another Irishman from T.C.D. called Burleigh, who also talked rugger shop plus juju.[1] It seems there is a great fetish healer round there who is visited – secretly – by many of the most westernised high-ups from Accra.

Wednesday I returned a roundabout way to Tamale via Bawku in the N.E. corner; here there was an old woman selling charms in the market, these consisting of hen's claws, animal bones & horse-tails. Lots of horses in the north with garishly accoutred riders. Near here found a grey-haired Central European drilling for water; he had struck granite & was only making 6 inches per hour. Further on, visited a v. important chief (illiterate) called the Naweri. An old man with a fringe of beard & Tartar features. He presented me with a bundle of yarns & a live Guinea-hen. Back in Tamale ran into Sean Graham & George Noble, his camera-man, back from location & both exhausted.

Yesterday returned to Accra just in time for the Governor's Garden Party. A fine setting: well kept lawns, people in Kente cloth togas, chiefs under umbrellas, & surf seen through the palm trees, but hardly any glam – at least not among the Europeans. It ended with the confessing of O.B.E.'s etc & an African band playing European & marching & countermarching on the green. This morning I had a 9.0 am conference with the Governor[2] – v. agreeable & with a sense of humour which by God he must need & this evening I have to dress up for the Accra Dining Club (20 Africans, 20 Europeans) & make an after-dinner speech (which I'm told must be light). Before that we are to have drinks at the Brewery.

Darling, did you do anything about Bill & Wyn Cutler? David knew them well & might take you to hear them in their pub. I want to know soon what her repertory consists of – which will give me a starting point.

Latest bus caption: SEEING IS BELIVING. [sic]

Must stop now & prepare to squeeze myself into my tight-collared evening shirt. Tomorrow I am going to the races again – but this time, I think, with Africans.

---

1 – Black magic.
2 – Sir Charles Arden-Clarke (see FLM to Hedli, 17 Oct. 1956, n. 2, p. 604).

Am looking forward v. much to coming home. (Could you get my old grey trousers cleaned please?)

lots of love – & to Bimba. L.

TO *Hedli MacNeice*   MS Bodleian

10 November [1956]   BBC, Accra (7)

Dearest Cat,

Thank you for your 2 letters which I got yesterday on returning from Togoland (my last major excursion). Yes indeed, the News . . . ! We get it here only through the radio as the local papers hardly deign to mention anything outside the Gold Coast. If I follow you correctly, I'm afraid I don't agree with you over Egypt. Whatever inside knowledge Sidney may have, our attacking Egypt at the time & in the way we did is a sheer case of 'The End Justifies the Means' – a principle which we've been denouncing for years. As many people have been saying, we've thus thrown away our greatest moral asset, which, Britain & France being now 2nd class Powers materially, is also our greatest asset, internationally. (I'm astonished to see that Gilbert Murray, of all people, came out pro-Eden.[1])

Darling, I'm distressed about your back, but hope the new treatment is now getting results. How nice of Robert B. & Bill A.[2] to jolly you along.

I'm due back, as I said, on Friday morning 16th (will add the Flight Number in a P.S. – which could you please hand on to Eileen to tell Benallick). Don't come to meet me if it's too early, or if you feel poorly. I should, however, welcome a thick scarf – & possibly a towelling rug. Not but what it's cool here today, having been raining all night.

Togoland (which used to belong to the Germans) is the nicest bit of the G.C. I've visited. Quite a few hills (looking elsewhere) – & agreeable people. I stayed at a place called Ho[3] (!) with the Regional Officer, an excellent man called Tom Meade, who's been 20 years in the country & has all the charm & sympathy of the best I.C.S. types. He's less pessimistic than most of his colleagues about what's going to happen here. He dug

---

1 – Gilbert Murray, ERD's predecessor as Professor of Greek at Oxford (see FLM to JH, 'Autumn 1928', n. 2, p. 196). FLM produced an obituary talk on Murray, broadcast BBC Pacific Service, 22 May 1957.

2 – Possibly Features producer Robert Barr and the American academic Bill Alfred, who was spending the year on sabbatical leave in London, and who lived with the MacNeices at Clarence Terrace the following spring.

3 – Ho in southern Ghana, where the language spoken is 'Ewe'.

me up some Ewe (pron. Evvy) ex-Servicemen whom I recorded singing some rather comic Army songs – in Ewe. It seems that the poor chaps from the Northern Territories who were shipped off to fight in Burma, never having seen the sea before, were all in tears because noone told them where they were going so, like Columbus' sailors, they thought they'd be at sea for ever & ever.

I also recorded a group of jolly village women singing & dancing under a big tree in their village under the leadership of a 'Mass Education' instructress (African). Her real object was to teach them about vitamins but the pill has to be sugared. Their songs were play songs, largely mimed – one nice love-song with words, in Ewe, such as 'I wish I were a river so that my lover could drink from me.'

From Ho I went to an extraordinary place called Keta, built on a narrow sand spit between the sea & an enormous lagoon, across which they come sailing in their canoes to the market – a fine variegated smelly affair (I recorded the atmo).[1] I also went sailing on the lagoon with a Polish doctor (one of the eleven Europeans in the place). Also met there an astonishing old Lebanese materfamilias called Fatima who, though illiterate, is a great business woman & owns a fleet of lorries; she was tirading about the bad times – 'I vomit for this thing! I no see nothing.' And I watched the men fishing; before the season starts they sacrifice a cow to the sea.[2] Also by the roadside we found a crowd of people dancing – waving horse-tail whisks, shaking calabash rattles etc.; it was a funeral celebration (which I recorded too); I gave £1 to the collection.

I have been asking about pidgin English. If you want to say something is excellent you say 'Fine pass Takoradi stinkfish'. 'Fine pass' means 'better than' & Takoradi is famous as a fishing port. You can also of course say 'Fine pass all'.

More lofty slogans:- 'Life is War', 'Oh God Put Me Through', 'Oh Boy! Haste Not in Life!' And, on the wall of a silversmith's little shop: 'Salutation is Not Love'.

Most of the houses round Keta are built, roof walls & all, of cocoanut [sic] palm leaves. And everywhere, looking like rubble, are great piles of cocoanut husks which are used for firewood. They sell them in the market – 4 for 3d – also brooms of cocoanut fibre at 3d each.

1 – Keta, Volta region, southeast Ghana, situated between the Atlantic to the south and the Keta lagoon to the north.
2 – 'I remember watching the fishermen at Keta (which is the end of the world) hauling on a mile-long horseshoe of seine-net . . .' ('Pleasure in Reading: Woods to Get Lost In', *The Times*, 17 Aug. 1961, 11, repr. *SLC*, 230–4).

A fascinating thing I saw near Ho was a woman making a pot without a wheel. A perfect circle; she smooths it with a large pebble & with leaves dipped in water.

Yes, Togoland was great fun but the other side of the medal is the excessive zeal of the Information Service who everywhere I've been have drawn up over-specific & often boring programmes which I have to observe so as not to offend people. All that old Little Ambassador stuff – e.g. going round District Council offices & having to shake hands with every petty official or to a school where I was shown each of six classrooms & the little man with me made an identical, & embarrassing, speech about me ('a great poet' etc.) to each of the six.

This evening I'm going to the opening of a new cinema by Nkrumah, after which we see 'Carmen Jones'.[1] Next week I've got a lot of loose ends to tie up. I think I'll be travelling back on the same plane with George Noble, the camera man, so shall pick his brains about what a camera can do. He's a fat bawdy man & is much disgusted that I want to send him down that gold mine.

My driver has now come for me. I propose to spend the morning at the Library & then to the Saturday morning (Stag-like) session at the International Club. Last Sat., did I tell you, I went to the races & was given champagne by an old Old Guard African lady called Mrs Odamintan [*sic*] (the first grande dame African I've met) who sends her daughter to Roedean & wont allow Nkrumah to call on her.[2]

Lots & lots of love, Cat. Get mended soon. Looking forward vastly to seeing you.

L.

P.S. Flight Number, arr. Friday morning, is BA 258.

---

1 – *Carmen Jones* (1954), a Hammerstein film (Dir. Otto Preminger), opened by Kwame Nkrumah (1909–72), Ghana's first prime minister (1957–60) and president (1960–6).
2 – Presumably the wife of Solomon ('Solo') Odamtten, an Accra businessman who stood against Nkrumah for the National Liberation Movement and who was characterised in pro-Nkrumah posters as 'the Machiavellian "Solo"'. Hence Mrs Odamtten won't allow Nkrumah to call on her.

1957

TO *Denis Johnston*   MS TCD

25 January 1957   ['The Character of Ireland'
                                    letterhead]

Dear Denis,

How are Betty and yourself – and when are you going to emerge from cellophane and return to us?

About this book which Bertie and I are editing, and which you have heard of before (!)[1] We have now, at long last, got most of our contributions in, but, feeling that something is still missing have decided it must be you. Having looked through our list of contents we realise that there is nothing which does justice to the peculiar qualities of Irish Conversation. This in itself might not seem to be an adequate subject for an article but we feel that you could possibly expand it (under some such title as <u>The Irish Dialectic</u>) into an analysis of typical Irish thought processes, both Northern and Southern, and the way they reveal or conceal themselves in talk. You might also throw in a digression about the Irish Law Courts (which so far have not been touched upon in this book)?

If you are interested in this and feel you could do it fairly quickly I need hardly tell you that what we would expect from you is not a heavyweight or text-book article but something vivid and provocative and packed with illustrations.

The article could be anything up to five thousand words. I am afraid the money is not much of an incentive but the Clarendon Press I think would be willing to pay you something between £25 and £30.

In case you are worried as to the company you might be keeping, our contributors include Elizabeth Bowen, Geoffrey Taylor, Frank O'Connor, Estyn Evans, Jim Phelan, Michael MacLiammoir, John Kelleher, Arland Ussher, David Greene etc etc.

We both hope very much that you will agree to do this: you can make the article as elastic as you like.

---

1 – *The Character of Ireland*, eds. FLM and WRR, projected for OUP but never completed.

Love to you both from Hedli and myself.

> Yours ever,
> Louis

TO *David Thomson*[1]   MS BBC

7 February 1957   203 Rothwell House

THE CROWN AND ANCHOR by Nesta Roberts[2]

David Thomson, 313 Rothwell House

I am rather taken by this script though it seems to me too long and would benefit from cutting. The theme is very simple, the relationship of a young man and a girl whose love affair is interrupted by World War II. The writing, both narration and dialogue, is vivid and shows a welcome blend of sophistication and genuine feeling. The most interesting thing about it is the counterpoint or dialectical pattern, especially between the pastoral-idyllic mood and the theme of war (see especially part 3).

Her physical descriptions are good and she makes an interesting use of the 'Inner Voice' (i.e. what a character is thinking juxtaposed with what she is saying). Above all, this piece seems to me produceable, though I think it should be both cut and, in places, altered: e.g. I am not very happy about the Epilogue.

(Louis MacNeice)

well, did they take it or not?

TO *T. S. Eliot*   Faber archive

25 February 1957   BBC

Dear Tom,

It has occurred to me that, apart from my memories, I have a mass of note-books that with a number of radio scripts dealing with a wide variety of foreign countries might form the basis for a not too usual kind of travel book.

The material I have includes both topography and history, but the point of this book would be to illustrate the principle – which I am sure is not peculiar to me – that in foreign travel one is much of the time searching for

---

1 – On David Thomson see FLM to JL, 24 June 1954, n. 2, p. 580.
2 – Author of various travel books including *Face of France* (1976).

the implementation of certain myths. I would, accordingly, wish to call this book 'Countries in the Air'.[1]

I attach a skeleton synopsis.

Hoping to see you soon, and with all greetings.

Yours ever
Louis MacNeice [signed]

TO *Denis Johnston*[2]

MS TCD

5 March 1957

The Character of Ireland
[letterhead]

Dear Denis,

Thank you for your letter. If you could really start a piece for us after Easter and get it done by the end of May, it would still not be too late. So I do pray and hope you'll undertake it. As I think I said before, you are welcome to approach the subject quite light-heartedly.

I saw the England–Ireland Rugby match at Lansdowne Road last month. It was a savage game and very disappointing, the most notable thing about it being that the crowd booed the referee – which I understand is unprecedented.[3]

Love to Betty and yourself,

Yours ever,
Louis

P.S My secretary has given your address to the appropriate department, so I hope your letters will reach you in future without going first to Pimlico

1 – TSE was interested in this and a contract was signed (FLM was offered an advance of £100 on delivery); FLM to TSE, 1 March 1957 (*Faber archive*). According to the enclosed synopsis FLM had planned to discuss his experiences of (in order): Ireland, Paris, Spitzbergen, the Mediterranean, Iceland, Scotland, Spain, America, Norway, Denmark, Switzerland, Rome, India and Pakistan, Ménerbes, Greece, Turkey (Istanbul and Ankara), Venice, Ravenna, the Tessin, the Nile, Rouen, Gold Coast (in relation to 'the myth of darkest Africa'), with a coda on London, 'which even now seems to me a foreign city'. On 21 Aug. he wrote: 'I have started that prose book, <u>Countries in the Air</u>; the 1st chapter has come out rather subjective' (ibid.). The book was never published.

2 – Addressed to Johnston at 10 Jewett Lane, South Hadley, MA (where he taught at Mt Holyoke).

3 – Ireland lost 0–6 to England on 9 Feb. before a record crowd of 56,000. England played with one man short for most of the match, and there were many injuries: 'there were times when the field looked like a casualty clearing station for the lightly wounded' ('England Pack Scorns Handicap', *The Times*, 11 Feb. 1957, 12).

TO *W. R. Rodgers*   PRONI

8 October 1957   [BBC]

Dear Bertie,

In haste. Have you any unpublished poems, or poems which have appeared in periodicals but not in book form since November 1st 1956, which you could let me have for New Poems 1958 (the P.E.N. Anthology)?

It is now possible that I may not be going East after all.[1] If not, we could have our session on 'The Character of Ireland' sooner.

All greetings,
(Louis MacNeice)

TO *Hedli MacNeice*   MS Bodleian

16 October [1957] (5.0 pm)   New Delhi[2]

Darling,

Now recovered from travel stupefaction & had not a bad day so far. Saw the All India Radio[3] people in the morning & had 2 good Xmas ideas. It seems the Festival of Lights is on Oct. 22nd, so shall be in Calcutta for that.

Had lunch with the British Information Officer, Jack Hughes, with whom I stayed 2 years ago. A dull mixed grill but 2 John Collinses before it. But it is v. awkward not having transport; the B.B.C. car is away with Holroyde who doesn't return till Saturday.[4] I'll be leaving for Calcutta v. early Monday morning.

(later) The British Council Representative has just rung up & offered me the use of a car tomorrow – which will be a Godsend. I'm to have dinner with him tomorrow. Tonight – any moment now – I'm dining by myself in this hotel which is full of decrepit old American ladies &

---

1 – In fact, he was in India the following week. WRR was not represented in *New Poems, 1958*.

2 – FLM had returned to India a decade after independence, arriving in Delhi on 15/16 Oct. He hoped to record material for use in a Christmas broadcast, *The Commonwealth Remembers*, although very little of what he recorded was used. During October he visited Delhi, Calcutta, Dacca, Colombo and Calcutta. He was in Singapore by 1 November, and subsequently in Kuala Lumpur and Malacca, flying home from Colombo on 17 Nov. (see Stallworthy, 426). He wrote nine, possibly ten letters to Hedli during this trip, of which I have reproduced seven.

3 – AIR began broadcasting in 1937 and grew rapidly during the decade before independence and after. Lord Reith personally ensured that close connections existed between AIR and the BBC.

4 – Derek Holroyde, BBC Delhi.

presumably correspondingly expensive. Am just having my solitary pre-dinner drink in my bedroom; you're not allowed to drink anywhere else. Nor are you supposed to buy one for anyone else. Thank God Calcutta's still what it was. How can one meet people this way?

Have finished the Aubrey Menon book.[1] V. funny – & v. clever. Wish I had something else light for the rest of the evening. Am immobilised through not having a car, & don't feel like taking a series of taxis all by myself to nowhere in particular. (Most of the chaps I wanted to see seem to have left Delhi.) Perhaps it's a mistake to come back to places where one has really enjoyed oneself?

Later. Dinner, unlike breakfast, was served in a large room called the Tavern – red plush chairs & muted lights & a small European-style band – which is approached through a large & necessarily empty bar on the wall of which is painted 'In Vino Laetitia'. There were quite a few people dining but none of them raised their voice. Afterwards I found a long terrace with innumerable tables, each with an ashtray on it, & beyond in the garden many more tables & one waiter waiting – with no one to wait on. Prohibition has killed this place. I'm now going to take a swig of cold water from the thermos provided by the management.

That wasn't v. inspiring either. I think I'll go to bed now & continue this tomorrow, Cat!

Oct 17th, after breakfast, while waiting for B.C. car. This air-conditioning, both in my bedroom & the breakfast room, has an aquarium feeling about it. The fish, as I said, are mainly American.

Am going to the Indian radio this morning to listen to effects recordings of a recent festival. Shall also try to buy a bottle of liquor.

How are you getting on, darling? How lucky you are to have access to the Gloucester Arms & the George & even the Volunteer. Caitlin & Goronwy are dead right; the lack of drink means lack of communion.[2] Sorry to harp on this!

Am now going to ring up a chap called da Costa.[3] Will write again soon, hoping I'll have met something new by then.

Look after yourself, Cat,

all my love, L.

---

1 – Possibly *Rama Retold* (1954), which had been banned by the Indian government.
2 – Caitlin Thomas: see FLM to John Malcolm Brinnin, 30 Nov. 1953, n. 2, p. 567; Goronwy Rees: see FLM to Hedli, 19 March 1948, n. 2, p. 513.
3 – Eric P. W. da Costa (1909–2003), educ. Mysore, and New College, Oxford; economist and senior civil servant in Mysore and Jaipur. He was founder and for many years director of the influential Indian Institute of Public Opinion.

19 October [1957]   BBC, New Delhi

Dearest Cat,

Since my last, things have become more interesting. Thursday afternoon I went to tea with an extraordinary little man (v. little, v. vital) called Nirad Chaudhuri – we have a book by him in the house, Autobiography of an Unknown Indian;[1] his son is studying in London University & we ought to see him some time. He lives in a v. oldfashioned house in the old city of Delhi just beside the walls on the north side near the Kashmir Gate; from his balcony you look over the walls to an expanse of trees & grass where people are laundering in filthy water. His sittingroom, as they say, is lined with books, largely on European architecture. His wife made some cakes for tea of milk & lemon, also some pastries which appeared to contain spinach & potato. We talked about Chartres, Ely, & various country houses that I'd never heard of. He put himself under a cloud with the Indian Government over his book & when he was approached the other day to do some official job, he said: 'Oh so the I. Government have raised their ban on me, have they? But I have not raised my ban on the Indian Government.' A nice man but cantankerous, they say.

7.30 p.m. that day / (Exasperating but typical interruption. Was called over to the G.P.O. by an unintelligible clerk just in order to write the word 'Collect' on a cable I'd written out to Laurence 2 hours ago. Luckily the G.P.O.'s only a minute's walk; still, you have to be patient in this country. You'd go mad here, darling. Must stop now & have a bath.)

11.15 pm. Back early from dinner with the Holroydes, who were exhausted after a fortnight on tour. (He v. angry with the B.B.C. – a shocking story which I'll tell you.) To go back: 7.30 Thursday I went with Miss Walter to a cocktail party (for which nearly everyone else was wearing a black tie) in honour of John Masters;[2] it was given by an Indian naval captain more British than the British. Masters as one would expect, & rather pleased with himself. I then dined with Croome-Johnson, the British Council Rep., who's only been here 3 weeks but he had along Khushwant Singh, well-known writer & a 'character' whom I first met in

/102/

1 – Nirad Chaudhuri (1897–1999), *Autobiography of an Unknown Indian* (1951).
2 – (Lieut. Col.) John Masters (1914–83), DSO, educ. Wellington and Sandhurst. Officer in the Indian army and novelist, author of *Bhowani Junction* (1954) and many other works.

'47; he did a sort of profile of me, + rather grim photograph, in today's Indian 'Statesman'.[1]

Yesterday I hobnobbed once more in their offices with the All India Radio people & in the afternoon went round some villages with two of them, a grizzled man whose diction was like David Wright's & a lustrous eyed woman in a white sari. Recorded an old farmer who spoke for 8 minutes off the cuff – not usable. Found one village celebrating the birth of a baby – lots of percussion, & shrieking; recorded this – quite a nice effect. Also much dust, many flies. Penetrated one compound of mud & suddenly noticed a camel, couchant in the corner pretending to be stuffed. Last night dined alone in my morgue; the waiter was very surprised when I ordered an Indian dish. Holroyde says it was a great mistake my being booked into this hotel.[2] Like Miss Reeves & Rouen.

This morning recorded a nice man in A.I.R. talking about the symbolism of Hindu festivals. He'd prepared far too much so I boiled it down for him. This afternoon called on a 'Syrian Christian' woman called Susie Verghese who's going to record for me at 9.0 am. tomorrow. Then went on my own in the Council car to see the Qutab Minar again after 10 years; it's the large rose[-]red tapering minaret 7 miles from Delhi surrounded by ruins of all sorts. Something Edwardian about it – so racked (?) & frilled & embroidered – like undies – only the embroideries come out of the Koran. And great parrots again against red stone.

Tomorrow I'm lunching with a man called Eric da Costa, editor of the 'Eastern Economist'; they say he's ebullient & he's going to take me first to the Gymkhana Club.[3] At 6.30 I've been railroaded into 'talking informally' at the National Gallery of Modern Art; this is the doing of some unknown fan of mine called Miss Bhatia.[4]

I enclose a poem which I've written – only a <u>draft</u> & I don't know yet of course whether it's any good.

Where are you darling? Switzerland? If so, all greetings to your parents. Look after yourself anyway.

Lots of love. & to Bimba. L.

---

1 – Khushwant Singh (b.1915), educ. Govt. College, Lahore; St Stephen's College, Delhi; King's College, Cambridge. Author of many books including *The Sikhs* (1953), *Mano Majra* (1956), *I Shall Not Hear the Nightingale* (1959), *History of the Sikhs* (1966), *Sex, Scotch and Scholarship* (1992) and *Death at My Doorstep* (2005).
2 – Imperial Hotel, New Delhi, opened 1939.
3 – One of the oldest and most exclusive private clubs in India, first established in 1913 when it was called the 'Imperial Delhi Gymkhana Club'.
4 – National Gallery of Modern Art, Delhi, housed in the residential palace of the Maharaja of Jaipur, inaugurated 29 March 1954.

Indian Village[1]

Whatever it is that jigs & gleams –
Darting lizard, courting bird –
For which I could not, had I even
The time to implement my dreams,
Dig out one new or juster word,
Remains a heaven this side heaven,

Viz life. Euripides was right
To say 'whatever sparks or dances',
Refuting those who mark the spot
Meticulously in black & white
And who, contemptuous of the chances,
Divorce the ever from the what.

So here, beneath this pepperpot temple
Black buffalo flounder in the pond,
The sunset purple, walls of mud,
The hard & gnarled grow smooth & simple
While hunkered peasants gaze beyond
Their hookahs towards an art of blood

Which dies, to rise another day,
A one-eyed starer with a knife,
A ranter flushed with fire & wine;
But we shall also rise & say
A small piece but our own; & life,
Whatever it is, will leap & shine.

TO *Hedli MacNeice*   MS Bodleian

23 October [1957]   BBC, Calcutta

Darling Cat,
    Where the hell are you? In Switzerland? I haven't heard a word. If you are, give all my greetings to your parents.

1 – Early unrevised draft of 'Indian Village', published in *Solstices* (1961), 53; repr. CP07, 555.

Got here Monday morning & I must say it was a relief after Delhi, though the hotel room I'm in is v. archaic in comparison with the Imperial. Calcutta altogether of course is much dirtier – & perhaps much more important.

My last day in Delhi, Sunday, I had lunch with an amusing & opulent character. Eric da Costa, Editor of the 'Eastern Economist', who told me that Sudhin was in Chicago, which rather threw me out as I was hoping to stay with him here.[1] (However I've been on to his lessee & he's undertaken to forward any letters – in case you've written there.) Then I had tea in an ultra-posh new hotel, state-established, the Ashoka,[2] with a British (Labour I gather) M.P. called Donnelly[3] just back from China – & Outer Mongolia where he had to drink fermented mare's milk – & from an interview with Nehru, who told him that when Radhakhrishnan the other day smashed his finger in China in a car door the little Chinese nurse gave him a French letter (they're now worrying about their population problem) for a finger stall; this greatly tickled both Nehru & Donnelly.[4] After that went to give an 'informal talk' at the National Gallery of Modern Art; my fan, who'd fixed it, turned out to be the plainest kind of Indian girl – I had difficulty in shedding her. The talk took place in a circular lobby, v. high – with a spiral staircase & dome – & so v. resonant; I hope no one understood what I said. The lights went out in the middle. I was glad to get away as I had to leave v. early next morning. In fact, arriving at Calcutta c. 10.30 am. I was still asleep while we were taxiing to a standstill – which has never happened to me before.

Just realised it's raining like hell outside – out of order for the season & v. annoying as I'm going out later to try to record a procession to the river where they immerse the images of the goddess Kali (she's the black or dark blue one with a necklace of skulls & her tongue sticking out). After which I put on a black tie to go to a cocktail party with the U.K. High Commissioner's people. After which I dine with a v. ebullient elderly lady. Also Padmini Sengupta, whom I met here 10 years ago & whom I recorded in her house on Monday afternoon.[5]

1 – Probably Sudhindra Ghose, author of *The Vermillion Boat* (1953) and *Folk Tales and Fairy Stories from India* (1961).
2 – The Ashok Hotel, opened 1956.
3 – Desmond Louis Donnelly (1920–74), Labour MP. Born in India, educ. Brightlands School (Glos.) and Bembridge School (Isle of Wight). Author of *The March Wind: Explorations behind the Iron Curtain* (1959) and *Struggle for the World: The Cold War from Its Origins in 1917* (1965).
4 – Sir Sarvepalli Radhakrishnan; see FLM to Hedli, 3 Oct. 1947, n. 1, p. 504.
5 – Padmini Sengupta, author of *The Story of Women of India* (New Delhi, 1974).

Yesterday I visited Jamina Roy again & bought a piece of his in his later technique (cf. Stephen's) of a woman dancing & it looks as if it was in red sandstone.[1] I had dinner with Vishnu Dey, a Bengali poet whom I also met 10 years ago.[2] He's living in the same place, i.e. v. simply (astonishingly so by English standards) in a house between a cemetery & a 'tank', i.e. reservoir where people during the day wash themselves & their clothes & the lights are reflected at night. His sitting room is like a corridor or a school study – but twice the height – books (English) all round the walls & his guests sitting opposite each other as if they were in a train; when I came in he was playing the last movement of Beethoven's 9th in order to try to drown the noise of the crackers & rockets which people outside were letting off for Kali Puja.[3] Dinner was ultra-Indian – rice, dal & sloppy things generally which they all, except one, ate with their fingers; I felt rather embarrassed, being supplied with a fork. Also of course rather sickly sweetmeats – the Bengalis are great ones for those.

Tomorrow afternoon I go to Dacca (1¼ hrs flight) & return here on 30th. To Singapore, by B.O.A.C., on 31st. Don't know when I'll move on to Ceylon but not as soon as I'd scheduled. But maybe, Ceylon being so hypocritical at the moment, I can condense my time there. Anyhow I reckon to be back in London any day from Nov. 14th to 18th. In the meantime, I hope, I'll have sent Laurence some recordings. (The trouble with <u>Indians</u>, of course, is once they start talking, they won't stop. But I'm going to have another go at Mrs Sengupta who's a natural broadcaster.)

Must stop now, darling, & snatch a siesta or I'll be in no shape for the above programme. Look after yourself. All love to Bimba.

L.

TO *Hedli MacNeice*   MS Bodleian

28 October [1957]   BBC, Dacca

Dearest Catti,

Have been here since Thursday & meeting a hell of a lot of people. Stayed one night in the hotel & am now guest of a British Information chap, a rugger fan, Lancs. Dacca not attractive except for the river; went

1 – Jamina Roy (1887–1972), Indian artist.
2 – Vishnu (or Bishnu) Dey (1909–82), author of many works in Bengali and (in English) of *Jamini Roy* (1944), *Selected Poems* (1972), *In the Sun and Rain: Essays on Aesthetics* (1972) and *History's Tragic Exultation: A Few Poems in Translation* (1973).
3 – Hindu religious ceremony, performed in the autumn.

out on it in a primitive boat. Chief characteristic of the streets: the bicycle rickshaws – aluminium body, brightly striped seats, hooped hoods with gay floral designs, & usually 2 passengers. It's at least as hard work, they say, as the old footslogging rickshaws; the coolies' expectation of life = 28 years.

My host's No. 1 has a nice wife (née Wedgwood Benn) who used to be a concert pianist but fell on the ice & ruined the nerves in her left hand.[1] They are v. sophisticated (have just lent their pictures to the Tate & the Arts Council[2]) unlike most of the British Community here; Saturday night I was taken to the Dacca Club which is a parody of a Graham Greene scene at its seediest. Jute wallahs, unhealthy bank clerks, steamship executives (I asked one who'd been here 28 years if he'd noticed any change in the Pakistanis since Independence & he said he'd never met any before Independence) & a middleaged New Zealand woman who hails everyone with 'Hi! Stonker!'

Have had great frustrations here over recording gear. I was warned in India that taking my Midget either way across the Indian–Pakistan border would cause endless waste of time & trouble so I got the B.B.C. in Delhi to ask the Pak. Information people there whether Radio Pakistan in Dacca had any portable tape recorders; they said they had, so I left mine in Calcutta, only to arrive here & discover they have nothing of the sort. I was then put on to the U.S. Information people, who have two, who said I'd be welcome to use them. So I went along there only to find their batteries were completely exhausted & they're waiting for replacements from Washington D.C., which they expect around the New Year. And so on. However, something has been rigged up (I'm keeping my fingers crossed) & we're making a recording expedition this afternoon to a village.

In the bazaar district of Dacca I saw a streamer across the street saying 'Birth-Control! etc . . . One Tablet Prevents One Year's Birth!' East Pak. is v. overpopulated but none of the Bengalis will accept invitations to migrate to West Pak. On the other hand the army here, who are all West Pak. (the Bengalis being mainly too weak for military service) greatly despise the Bengalis & resent having to protect them.[3] In every respect in fact the 2 parts of the country seem at loggerheads.

---

1 – Unidentified.

2 – The Tate mounted two exhibitions this year with the Arts Council, 'British Painting in the Eighteenth Century' (15–25 Aug. 1957) and 'Claude Monet 1840–1926' (26 Sept.–3 Nov. 1957).

3 – West Pakistani army recruiters tended to think the Bengalis were not martially inclined.

Must go now & meet my friend Faiz Ahmed Faiz, the Urdu p̧
Lahore, who arrived here yesterday.[1] I'd better mail this now as the
the day will be choc-a-bloc. As usual, I'm doing double time, being als̲
little cultural ambassador. Did my stuff for the British Council, to an
accompaniment of whirring fans in an over-resonant hall, & have to do it
all over again in the University tomorrow. Have also been beset by (a) local
Press (b) Local Poets.

Look after yourself darling.

All love to you & Bimba.

TO *Hedli MacNeice*   MS Bodleian

4 November [1957]   BBC, Singapore

Dearest Cat,

I'm afraid this won't be v. long, as I'm writing it in the B.B.C. office &
I find myself generally behind schedule. It looks now as though I shan't
arrive back in London before Mon. Nov. 18th. Could I warn you in
advance to bring me out or send me out to the airport (a) overcoat (b)
thick scarf.

Yesterday I was taken out in a motor boat, passing first through
Singapore harbour which is magnificent, to a small island where the
Chinese were conducting an annual ceremony & having a general sort of
Hampstead Heath outing.[2] From the sea you'd have thought the island
was on fire, smoking away like mad; when one landed it was like dodging
one's way through a series of immeasurable small bonfires. Everywhere
burning joss sticks & candles, & in particular they were burning heaps of
factitious paper money, printed for this purpose & only payable in heaven.
There was also lots of this 'money', floating about on the sea. Most of the
boats have 2 great round eyes, like fish eyes, painted on the prow. The
island is v. small in toto, is backed like a double-humped camel; on one
hump is a Chinese temple, all horned & tufted, on the other, the higher
one, is a <u>Malay</u> shrine, tomb of some Muslim saint, but the Chinese pay
their respects there all the same.[3] It's ascended by a steep zigzag path &,

1 – Faiz Ahmed Faiz (1911–84), influential Urdu poet ('uncrowned poet laureate of Pakistan'),
and former editor of the *Pakistan Times*. Awarded the Lenin Peace Prize for Literature in
1970.
2 – Annual ceremony on Kusu island, including paper-burning rituals to appease the spirits.
3 – According to local mythology, the island's shrine and temple were built by two men (one
Malaysian, one Chinese), saved from drowning by a turtle.

my God, what with the crowds, the ascent took time & effort. On the trees at the top were hanging straw fans – to fan away evil spirits – & also small stones, representing prayers. But the whole atmosphere was gala. Waiting down below afterwards I got badly burnt – face & arms – with the sun snapping back off the rocks & all the shade already grabbed by others. But I got a nice sarsaparilla to drink – which took me back to my childhood.

In the evening I went to a do at Sir Percy's,[1] primarily to meet a Dr. Poh who I thought might do for Laurence but I doubt it as he's a gobbler-gabbler. It was an odd do. Sir P. has just built himself a v. large & smart new house, with his mother-in-law's of course rather less than semidetached; it's in a magnificent position, ground falling away steeply below it & a fine view of the islands. But this being apparently the first time he'd had guests there – tables laid for them on a great semi-circular mosaic terrace – he had along the Bishop of S., an old Reptonian robed in purple, to conduct a little service unknown to me, the Blessing of the House.[2] Most of the Chinese grinned broadly during the responses but that, I suppose, was their politeness. Food was v. good indeed but drink rather stinted. Their kitchen is like a bloody radio cubicle – any number of dials & needles to tell you when you're overmodding [sic].[3]

Tonight I go by night train to Kuala Lumpur, which will be my main base here. Am hoping to go to one of the V.H.F. relay stations built on the top of hills in the jungle. If possible also, I'll try to find Harry Craig's twin.[4]

Must stop now, darling, & go next door to Radio Malaya where I've got to see chaps, in particular a Tony Beamish whom Rona stayed with (that visit's still reverberating), a tall craggy handsome one such as is photographed to advertise pipes & tweeds; he's related to the Irish rugger

1 – Sir Percy Alexander McElwaine (1889–1969), Chief Justice of the Peace, Singapore. Ktd 1939. Educ. Campbell College Belfast; TCD; Irish Bar; RIR. Attorney General of Fiji 1927–31; Chief Justice of the Straits Settlement 1936–46. Imprisoned by the Japanese during World War II.

2 – Henry Wolfe Baines (1905–72), educ. Repton; Balliol College, Oxford. HO 1930; Anglican Bishop of Singapore 1949–60; Bishop of Wellington (NZ) 1960–72.

3 – 'Over-modulating.'

4 – H. A. L. (Harry) Craig (1921–78), Cork native, educ. Villiers School, Limerick, Kilkenny College and TCD. Formerly assistant editor of The Bell (Dublin) he became drama critic for the New Statesman (1950–61), and worked for many years with FLM and WRR on the BBC Third Programme, for which he wrote many scripts; he later wrote screenplays (obit. in The Times, 30 Oct. 1978). His identical twin was Richard J. W. Craig, OBE, M.C., CPM (1921–99), successively a soldier, colonial policeman (Malaya 1948–64) and intelligence officer (obit. in The Times, 10 Aug. 2000). In April 1957 FLM had worked with Harry Craig on a programme about Antarctic exploration (Coulton, 163).

Beamishes (how that game does crop up in outposts of empire!).[1] I'm also going to do some editing. Did some yesterday & was a bit disappointed by some of my actualities who, at the time of recording, had struck me as better value.

Hope all goes well, dearest; enjoy yourself.

All love to you both. L.

TO *Hedli MacNeice*   MS Bodleian

5 November [1957]   BBC, Kuala Lumpur [letterhead]

Darling,

Got here this morning by night train, v. comfortable, from Singapore. Just had your letter of 31st, forwarded from Singapore, for which thank you, cat; I think I must have had all your letters by now. They are v. welcome but 2 tiny criticisms, darling! (1) They do get more & more illegible! (2) They do, every so often (& I admit it only slightly) strike a carping &/or moralising note which is all v. well in the home (where one expects it!) but is just a shade discouraging when one is thousands of miles away. To take just one example: I think Bill McAlpine[2] must have misrepresented his meeting with me in the George;[3] I <u>was</u> in the middle of I think quite an interesting shop talk when he arrived but I had a quick word with him on the assumption that he'd either be staying on there till I was free or that he'd be frequently around later. Whereas he went & vanished & never reappeared. Not that I should have thought of him as 'a new or seldom seen face'; I always think of him as an old familiar & somewhat boring face – just as you think of his co-regional, Tom A. But I'm v. glad that you think he's improved, I daresay Japan <u>would</u> help both of them to shed their most irritating complexes.

Have had a strenuous two days & tomorrow, after v. lengthy & complicated organisation, I'm getting, I hope, but only for the day, on to a real backwoods hill top where a V.H.F. relay station has been carved out of the jungle. Had a somewhat irritating cable from Laurence (not his fault

1 – Anthony Beamish (d.1983), OBE. Natural history writer, conservationist and broadcaster (employed by the BBC in 1939). Wartime experience (RUR; despatches; staff of Lord Mountbatten). Transferred to Radio Malaya (established in 1946) of which he became director. Author of *Aldabra Alone* (San Francisco, 1970). Rugby Beamishes: George R. Beamish (Coleraine, RAF, Leicester), capped 1925–33; Charles E. StJ. Beamish (also Coleraine, RAF, Leicester), capped 1933–6.
2 – Bill McAlpine was a London friend of Dylan and Caitlin Thomas.
3 – The George on Great Portland St, one of FLM's regular haunts.

though but 'Theirs'!) who seems to assume that I'll be waiting in Singapore on the end of the phone till he can have a 'circuit discussion' with me.

About my return. Your suggestion that I should stay on in Malaya till I could knock up a programme of my own is completely unpractical, darling, (a) because I <u>was</u> expected back in London by 14th (b) because to do a decent programme on this country would require at least a month's stay, working on nothing else. As it is, I've had – & am having – trouble over air bookings. I've got myself booked back from Colombo to England, plane (Flight BA 775) due London Airport 9.15 am. Monday Nov. 18th, but I haven't yet got a firm reservation from Singapore to Colombo; there are fewer flights between them than I'd imagined, which is v. irritating, as I don't want to skimp Ceylon;[1] I'm trying to find out now whether I could get there via Madras. The major airlines, you know, are interchangeable; thus I'm coming home B.O.A.C. whereas I went out to Bombay by Air India (which by the way is v. good).

About finances; don't worry. I'm surprised that Faber's didn't come through with more but I can always call on the O.U.P.

I like what I've seen of Kuala Lumpur. Nice blue mountains near by, a most refreshing change after all the fly-blown flatnesses. Am going to a party shortly to meet some of the locals – Chinese, Malay, European & Indian, after which am being taken to a Chinese restaurant[.] [L]ast night in Singapore, before catching my train, I have [sic] a v. good shark's fin soup.

I'm delighted that Peter S. is being nice & helpful about your ballad histories. But talking of work, Cat, (this is harking back to some earlier letters of yours), I'm going to put this on paper because you don't seem to take it seriously when I say it in the flesh! Your work problems & mine are entirely different; my trouble all my life, as Eleanor pointed out long ago, has been <u>over</u>-production. Therefore I have to spend a lot of time lying fallow. To which you'll probably say 'O.K. but why not spend your fallow periods reading instead of just drinking & talking?' To which I'd reply that <u>my</u> work, whether poems or plays, has <u>far</u> more relation to drinking & talking than it has to other books. When I do read, it's either self-indulgence (as with Dickens) or for a special purpose; e.g. an enormous amount of reading went into <u>Autumn Sequel</u>, a work which you, like Margaret G., tend to crab but which I still am quite proud of – & after all

1 – FLM had travelled to Colombo from Dacca on 29 October before going to Singapore two days later and thence to Kuala Lumpur on 5 November. He returned to Ceylon (via Malacca) on 13 Nov., returning to London on 18 Nov. (Stallworthy, 426).

people like Geoffrey Taylor & Norman MacCaig have been all for it.[1] But the point is: <u>I do not read like a scholar.</u> This is a chronic fallacy of yours that I'm a scholarly type; if I were, I don't think you'd like it! Enough of that though, darling.

Am hoping to see Harry Craig's twin before I leave Malaya. May meet him in Malacca which I'm told is a nice place.

I'm v. sorry about Bimba's nightmares. I suppose it's adolescence plus being highly strung to start with. But I suspect that a lot of her generation are anxious underneath, partly perhaps through the unconscious infiltration of world events, bogey Sputniks etc.

Talking of world events, Derek Holroyde the B.B.C. chap in Delhi said he so much preferred a forward-looking country like India (!) to a stagnating welfare state like Britain.

My dearest Cat must stop now & finish unpacking & clean myself. This is an air conditioned room (they seem to be multiplying in all these countries, though it seems a mixed blessing, exactly like American central heating but in reverse).[2]

Look after yourself, darling, & continue cheerful.

All love, & to Bimba, L.

TO *Hedli MacNeice* MS Bodleian

9 November [1957]   BBC, Kuala Lumpur

Darling,

This is probably my penultimate letter; I'll write to you from Singapore but it will be too late, I imagine, once I reach Ceylon. I'm leaving here tomorrow morning for Malacca, but I just managed to bag the Prime Minister before lunch today;[3] he'd been ungetable [*sic*] because, it now turns out, during the last few days the Communists in the jungle have been making overtures to him. So I've now pretty well finished in K.L., as everyone calls it; tonight I'm eating Indian with an engineer called Kirpal Singh & before that I may squeeze in (a) an exhibition round of golf by Dai

---

1 – Geoffrey Taylor reviewed *AS* in *Time and Tide* and wrote, in a private letter: 'It is your high water mark so far, and there has been no higher in a hundred years. A really great poem' (Taylor to FLM, 15 Nov. 1954, Ms *TCD*). Other reviews of *AS* included 'The Poetry of Consciousness', *TLS*, 26 Nov. 1954, 794; A. Alvarez, 'Lament for a Maker', *NS*, 11 Dec. 1954, 754; and Thomas Kinsella in *Irish Writing*, 29 (Dec. 1954), 65–7.
2 – Cf. 'Owing to central heating the American house seems like a Turkish bath to people fresh from England' (*SAF*, 202).
3 – Tengku (or Tunku) Abdul Rahman, Prime Minister of Malaysia 1957–70.

Rees[1] (tell Goronwy; by the way how wonderful about his leg!) & (b) an oriental rugger match. Singapore is going to be an alternation of social dos & hard work; by the way I <u>have</u> worked hard on this trip, e.g. most of yesterday was taken up recording telecommunications technicians, both Malay & Chinese, & then – which took even longer – editing them.

The day before yesterday I was accosted by a mad looking chap who turned out to have been at Oxford in my time & is now an Adviser on Chinese Affairs here; knows Betjeman & so on. He whisked me through two Chinese temples – v. carefree affairs, doing a trade in josssticks [*sic*], lottery tickets, paper prayers that you burn etc.; & nobody minds if you smoke in them – & a Dying House where people park themselves for their last days; down below in the street a notice says 'Office of the Cantonese Cemetery' & there's an ante-room where anyone who chooses drops in for a chat. The doors of the cubicles are mostly open & you can see the people dying with some placid old women in trousers looking on & smoking cigarettes.

That evening I was given a fabulous Chinese meal – 10 people, which is the correct number, sitting round a circular table. 8 courses, which included a [kippered?] sucking pig smiling like a Cheshire cat (in the best society, you only eat the crackling & scrap the rest of him; ditto with duck where you only should eat the skin). I sat next to a South Indian girl called Saroyini Lourdes, the 2nd name being due to the fact that she's a Catholic from Pondicherry, which was a French colony.[2] Rice only came towards the very end of the meal; this, they say, is the posh tradition – just because rice is so common. Throughout we drank whisky – or brandy – & soda. The whole meal took nearly four hours & I'm proud to say I used chopsticks.

Laurence sent me a cryptic cable, saying e.g. 'Query Good Hunting Ceylon'. Query indeed! I think I may have quite a problem there, seeing my time is so curtailed. (Till further notice my deadline for arrival in London is Nov. 18th). I imagine, as soon as I get back, Laurence will be doing his Old Man of the Sea act.[3] My own stuff incidentally will take the hell of a

---

1 – Dai Rees (1913–83), celebrated Welsh golfer and Ryder Cup hero.
2 – Pondicherry, coastal SE India, south of Madras.
3 – Whatever FLM may have meant by this, it is clear from Gilliam's annual confidential report on FLM for the BBC (22 Nov. 1957) that he was slightly disappointed in his output that year: 'Louis MacNeice has not contributed any single work of the really outstanding quality that he has often achieved in the past. He carried out an extremely difficult assignment in Ghana with diplomatic slick and professionalism, and he has just completed an Asian tour for this year's Christmas programme. I feel that MacNeice's creative gifts have not been fully exploited in the past year, partly due to the planning difficulties and the change in programme

lot of editing. (Much though I dislike the scripting of actualities, I'm not sure it shouldn't be used for Orientals.)[1]

On every one of these trips one seems to bring the wrong things. That dressing gown was not really necessary & I think I have too many shirts. On the other hand I should – as I usually do – have brought a poetry book with me. By the way they made me address the students here, or rather answer their questions, e.g. 'How essential is Woman to the inspiration of poetry?' The same day, I think, I was followed by a tout who touted in 3 phrases: (1) You want woman? (2) You want boy? (3) You want money? (The last, I suppose, meant gambling.)

Goodbye now, Cat. Go on being cheerful. See you soon –
I hope. All my love. L.

—
policy. His production standards and overall expertise remain at a high level' (*Ms BBC*, *L1/285/1/ Left staff – MacNeice*).
1 – Actualities: group of sound recordings used in news reports.

1958

TO *Philip Larkin*[1]

MS Hull

15 January [1958]   BBC

Dear Larkin,

In haste. Herewith another batch. Have just sent some others, not all of which you have seen, to B.D. I suppose we should meet again about the end of the month?

B.D. seems v. keen on Redgrove & I think we might put in <u>one</u> of his. And perhaps <u>Insomnia</u> by his wife?[2]

With best wishes
Yours
Louis MacNeice

TO *I. C. M. Maxwell*[3]

MS Bodleian

28 April 1958   [London]

<u>CONFIDENTIAL</u>
Dear Sir,

<u>Chair of English – University of Khartoum</u>

In answer to your letter of the 9th April, I can inform you that I have known Mr. J. Berryman for a number of years, both in the U.S.A. and in

---

1 – Philip Larkin (1922–85), poet, novelist, critic, librarian. Educ. King Henry VIII School, Coventry; St John's College, Oxford; sub-librarian, QUB; librarian, Hull University 1955–85. Author of *The Less Deceived* (1955), *Whitsun Weddings* (1964), *High Windows* (1974) and other works. FLM corresponded with Larkin from late 1957 to the summer of 1958, concerning their editing, with Bonamy Dobrée ('B.D.'), of the PEN Anthology, *New Poems* (1958).

2 – Peter Redgrove's poem 'The Questioner' appears in the volume, although not 'Insomnia'. In a letter to Kingsley Amis, Larkin was to sum up his experience of collaborative editing as follows: 'This is pretty well done now, thank God; each editor became more like himself as time went on – Dobrée more feather-brained and corrupt, MacNeice lazier and duller witted, and me more acutely critical and increasing in integrity.' Larkin to Amis, 24 April 1958, *Ms Hull*.

3 – I. C. M. Maxwell, assistant secretary of the Inter-University Council for Higher Education Overseas (London); author of *Universities in Partnership* (Edinburgh, 1980).

London.[1] I know that in America, in the various university posts which he held, such as in the University of Minneapolis, he was considered to be a most inspiring teacher; in my own experience, people of student age find his manner most sympathetic. He is also a very good scholar, particularly, I believe in the Shakespearean field; I myself have heard him spend two hours explaining to a well-known English Shakespearean producer the subtleties of Shakespeare's History plays.

He is also, of course, a very fine poet; his recent long poem on Anne Bradstreet was considered by the American critic Allen Tate to be one of the best books of verse published in America for years.[2]

Finally, I feel that he is essentially adaptable and, unlike many Academics, would fit speedily and admirably into the University of Khartoum.

Yours truly,
Louis MacNeice

TO *Vera Seaton-Reid*[3]

MS Bruce Arnold

26 August 1958   BBC

Dear Vera,

This is just to thank you very much indeed for mixing for me so beautifully on the Strindberg plays.[4] It must be tiresome for someone of your experience to have to cope with someone of my inexperience!

I was disappointed that you didn't turn up at the Club on Friday night to have a drink with me. Didn't I ask you (which quite possible as I was not 100% compos) or was it that you had to rush off?

Anyhow, may I ring you up some day soon when I am in Line [*sic*] Grove, and will you have a drink with me then please?

Thank you again.

Yours sincerely
Louis MacNeice

1 – FLM first met the American poet John Berryman (1914–72) on an Atlantic crossing in 1953. Cf. Stallworthy, 398.
2 – *Homage to Mistress Bradstreet* (1956).
3 – Vera Margaret Seaton-Reid (née Buyers) was a BBC sound engineer at Lime Grove studios, Shepherd's Bush, and formerly at Alexandra Palace. M. (1931) Alaster Seaton-Reid, who was killed in action with the Royal Artillery in July 1941.
4 – FLM produced two Strindberg plays for television, *Pariah*, and *The Stronger*, broadcast BBC TV on 22 Aug. 1958 ('Programmes and Broadcasts by Louis MacNeice on Sound and Television', *BBC Caversham*, R94/2/509/1: MacNeice/2908).

28 August [1958]   BBC

Dear Philip,

   Sorry to have been so long in passing on Dobree's foreword. I think it needs cutting & have square-bracketed in pencil the cuts which I myself would like to see made. I am also not happy about 'subjective,' 'the underlying pulse of poetry', & the 'technical accomplishment' sentence.

   Any suggestions?

> With best wishes
> Yours
> Louis MacNeice

1959

TO *Laurence Gilliam (BBC internal memo)*   MS BBC

20 January 1959   From: Mr. Louis MacNeice,
                                   Features, 203 Rothwell [House]

Subject: 'HERE WE COME TO COVER A MAN' BY W. R. RODGERS

I have read this script with considerable enjoyment and am sorry that so far it has not found anywhere to lay its head. I agree with H.N.I.P. that 'as a purely northern Ireland programme' it would (though he does not say so in so many words) be liable to provoke strong reactions in certain circles.[1] Apart from anything else, there are bits in it which devout Ulster Protestants and possibly Catholics might consider blasphemous. (Most of these, however, could probably be cut without injury to the whole.)

I agree with Script Editor, Features in disagreeing with H.N.I.P. about 'the Beckett influence'.[2] I also agree with her when she says that the programme is too long. I'm not aware of what length was intended, but the present script strikes me as likely to overrun the hour. If it were cut to make an hour's programme I think most of the dubious things in it could be eliminated.

I do not agree with the comments on this script by Controller, Third Programme. I think the reference to Hamlet is irrelevant and I also disagree with the remark that this piece could 'only have succeeded' if it 'had conferred on the dead man some degree of reality'. The reality in question is not that of the dead man's personality but that of the Ulster countryside. As one brought up in those parts I would like to assure anyone concerned that both the dialogue (with the exception of certain verbal pyrotechnics characteristic of this author – and these could be cut) and the content are

1–HNIP: Head of Northern Ireland Programmes.
2–FLM had attended a performance of the first English-language version of Beckett's *Waiting for Godot*, directed by Peter Hall, during its first run at the Arts Theatre, on 24 Sept. 1955 (FLM Diary: *Ms Bodleian, Ms Res, c. 979, Box 56*). In *Varieties of Parable*, he discussed Beckett as a 'parable writer'. Cf. FLM, 'Godot on TV', *NS*, 7 July 1961, 27.

only too true to the mentality of the Ulster countryman, whether Protestant or Catholic. There is, maybe, a certain lack of structure (if by structure one means plot in the old-fashioned sense, but if so, who shall be saved?) but I cannot agree that this script shows 'the lack of any real idea'.

Mr. Rodgers' basic idea is the well worn – but none the worse for that – one that in life we are in death – and vice versa. Well worn though it may be, in Northern Ireland at any rate this idea has not yet taken on the staleness of a cliché. It is a mistake to assume that the piece is intended to be merely 'sprightly', i.e. just a piece of fun and games (although I must admit I find some of it very funny indeed). The same aspersion could be passed – and indeed was passed – on all the plays by the late J. M. Synge. What must always be remembered about practically any work by any Irish dramatist, whether North or South, is the dialectic between the serious elements and the comic, not to say slapstick, elements. Anyone who has listened to any Irish countryman, North or South, gossiping on the day of a funeral will know what I mean.

The above comments do not mean that I think this script 100% good. For example, while there are some very good puns (N.B. all this dialogue must be thought of as spoken in the right kind of accent – which is what gives it its edge) there are some very bad ones; but these could easily be eliminated. What worries me more is the end, which seems to me too abrupt and also too inconclusive. It should not be difficult, however, to think up a stronger and more satisfying ending.

If the adjustments suggested above were made, I think it would be worth Third's while to reconsider this programme suggestion. It is all very well to talk about 'Beckett influence' (and Rodgers was writing this way before Beckett became the fashion), but how many other radio writers are there around who can produce dialogue of this vividness – and, I would even add, truth to life (I mean life as lived in the Six Counties)? If Third remain adamant against it, is there any chance that Home would consider it? They have taken odder things before. After all an actor like Jimmy Devlin[1] would keep this programme with its feet solidly and comprehensibly on the

1–James G. Devlin (1907–91), Northern Irish actor associated during the 1950s with the Abbey Theatre, and increasingly with film and television drama. He would appear in the film *Darby O'Gill and the Little People* (1959) and in many popular TV programmes, including *Z Cars* and *Steptoe and Son*.

earth – not but what, in every sense of the term, there is God's plenty of earth in it already and man's too – at any rate Ulster man's.

Louis MacNeice

TO *Jon Silkin*[1]   MS Leeds

21 January 1959   BBC

Dear Jon Silkin,

    I herewith return the two poems which you sent me for "New Poetry".[2] I would have liked to have got one of them in but they both seemed on the long side and also, I would say, rather difficult to follow at first hearing. Even so, I should probably have included one had it not been that you had been represented in the previous selection edited by Terence Tiller. So please don't let this discourage you from offering contributions to similar programmes in the future.

With best wishes,

Your sincerely,
Louis MacNeice

1 – Jon Silkin (1930–97), educ. Wycliffe, and Dulwich College; author of many books of poetry, including *The Peaceable Kingdom* (1954). In 1950 he founded the literary magazine *Stand*.
2 – *New Poetry* was a thirty-minute programme broadcast by the BBC 11 Jan. 1959. FLM and his co-editors had carried a poem by Silkin, 'Sacred', in *New Poems (A PEN Anthology)* (1958).

TO *John Boyd*[1]   MS Bodleian [copy]

3 February 1959   BBC

Dear John,

I am crossing over to Belfast on the night of February 12/13th as I have to give a talk or reading that evening at Queen's.[2] I shall naturally be visiting Lansdowne Road the next day and shall return that evening and stay with the MacCanns and shall probably leave again for England on Monday night.[3]

I hope to be seeing you anyhow for company's sake, but apart from that and with a view to filthy lucre, would you by any chance like me to record another little talk or reading for you? You might have ideas of your own about this, but three possibilities have just occurred to me.

1. I have just written a sequence of five poems called Notes for a Biography, my first poems for a long time, which has never been published.[4] I could read these for you with a little bit of talk woven around them.

2. I don't know if you know that last summer I wrote the script for this odd thing called Son et Lumiere at Cardiff Castle where it was performed for three months.[5] This was only the second instance of Son et Lumiere this side of the English Channel and, so they told me, broke new ground (the French apparently had it à la Racine). I could easily do a little talk for you about the problems, attractions

1–John Boyd (1912–2005), playwright, radio producer. Educ. RBAI, QUB, TCD. In 1943, founded *Lagan* magazine (Belfast). From 1947, BBC producer. Author of *The Flats* (1971), *The Street* (1977), other plays, and two memoirs: *Out of My Class* (1985) and *The Middle of My Journey* (1990). He recorded FLM's fifteen-minute talk, 'Childhood in Ulster' (later 'Autobiographical Talk'; see note overleaf), on 2 July 1963, and produced a thirty-minute programme on FLM, broadcast on the first anniversary of his death, 3 Sept. 1964 (*Louis MacNeice in Ulster*, PRONI D/2833/D/5/21). In that broadcast, Boyd states that he used to join the poet at the home of the MacCanns when he visited Belfast ('many of us used to gather to gossip and to eat and drink'). In a letter of 1961 he mentions seeing the poet at a rugby match: 'I saw you for a fleeting moment at Lansdowne Road and gave a yell at you. I was with Roy McFadden. Hence the enclosed poem' (McFadden's 'The Garryowen') (JB to FLM, 16 March 1959, *Ms BBC*).
2–The invitation to QUB came from Michael Emmerson (future director of the Belfast Festival), through Mercy MacCann: 'I told the boy that you would expect a fee' (Mercy to FLM, 5 Nov. 1962: *Ms Bodleian, Ms Res, c. 585, Box 10, Folder 2*).
3–FLM wrote about England's 3–0 victory over Ireland on 14 Feb. for the *NS*. Cf. next letter.
4–'Notes for a Biography', *LM*, April 1959, 36–9; *Solstices*, CP07, 529–32.
5–Cf. 'A Light Touch Under the Stars', *Daily Telegraph*, 9 Aug. 1958, 6; repr. *SP*, 208–13.

and snags of this peculiar medium (which of course has certain affinities with the radio Feature) and in passing discuss its future, if any (it's terribly expensive!), in Northern Ireland. The building by the way which seems to call out for it is Carrickfergus Castle![1]

3. I could do you a light-hearted talk on Lansdowne Road and All That including the trip down (or is it up) from Belfast.[2]

I shall quite understand if you can't accommodate any of the above but it would be nice, in view of the incidental and inevitable expenses of such a trip, to make a little extra money in passing!

By the way, will Sam Thompson be around as I'd like to see him?[3] He said he'd be coming to London in November and never showed up.

With best wishes,

Yours ever,
(Louis MacNeice)

TO *Kingsley Martin*   MS Bodleian [carbon copy] MS Sussex

3 February 1959   [BBC]

Dear Kingsley,

I have just had a lighthearted idea which may or may not appeal to you. On February 13th I have an engagement in Belfast, so am visiting Dublin the next day to attend the rugby football match between England and Ireland at Lansdowne Road. You may possibly remember that two years ago you agreed on the occasion of the same match to take an article by a friend of mine who had never been to Ireland before. He was all set to do this but unfortunately something cropped up that week which left him no time to write it. What I am now proposing is that I should write you an article (belonging I suppose to the Mallalieu category) centring around this

1 – Cf. 'Then, of course, there was also the Castle which was very exciting and which is, as you know, one of the best preserved Norman castles in these islands. We were only taken over it once and away, but it was a great expedition' (FLM, 'Autobiographical Talk: Childhood Memories', BBC, 1963; repr. *SP*, 271).

2 – FLM recorded a five-minute talk entitled 'A Poet at Lansdowne Road' for '*Ulster Magazine*', broadcast Feb. 1959 (*Ms BBC, R94/2, 509/1*).

3 – Sam Thompson (1916–65), Belfast playwright, author of *Over the Bridge*, first produced in Jan. 1960 at the Empire Theatre, Belfast. His other plays included *The Evangelist* and *Cemented with Love*. He began his career as a painter in the shipyards and was the subject in 1956 of a BBC documentary of his apprenticeship, *Brush in Hand*. A member of the Northern Ireland Labour Party, he stood unsuccessfully as a Labour candidate in South Down, in Oct. 1964. See also FLM to Terry Kilmartin, 13 Jan. 1960, p. 658.

particular match but spreading out to embrace such topics as the mystique of rugby football, the difference of attitude (including social attitudes) towards it in the different countries, and also, spreading out yet further and getting away from the sport itself, the contrast, as underlined by this occasion, between the atmosphere of Belfast and Dublin and also (this latter is often misunderstood) between the characters of the Northern and Southern Irishman.[1] I myself, having be [sic] brought up with a foot on either side of the Border, have always felt strongly that, in spite of politics, the Ulster-man is far nearer to the Southern Irishman than he is to the Englishman.

Perhaps, if you are interested in this suggestion, you could let me know what length of article you would like? I am returning to Belfast on the evening of February 14th and could easily write such an article on the next day, Sunday 15th.

Yours

TO *Controller, Third Programme [P. H. Newby]* *(BBC internal memo)* MS BBC

17 April 1959   From: Mr. Louis MacNeice,
                                        203 Rothwell [House]

Subject: 'THE BATTLE OF CLONTARF'

Following our conversation the other day, I would like to confirm that I am keen on doing a programme on this subject (length probably 75 mins).[2] I have discussed the possibility of special music for it with Tristram Carey [sic], who lit up to it at once. He thinks he could manage with an ensemble of about twenty. As he has his own electronics workshop, I think it would be a good idea if we also authorised him to manufacture any special sound effects that might be required, which would obviously keep these effects more in key with the music proper.[3]

---

1 – See FLM, 'Talking about Rugby', *NS*, 28 Feb. 1959, 286, 288. Repr. *SP*, 214–16.
2 – *They Met on Good Friday* (75 min.), broadcast BBC Third Programme, 8 Dec. 1959. The cast included Patrick Wymark, Denys Hawthorne, Patrick Magee, Mary Wimbush and Donal Donnelly. Cf. FLM, 'The Battle of Clontarf', *Radio Times*, 4 Dec. 1959, 6; Stallworthy, 441; Coulton, 171.
3 – Tristram Cary (1925–2008), OAM, MA (Oxon), DMus, LMus TCL, Hon RCM, composer and pioneer of electronic music. Son of novelist Joyce Cary, he founded Electronic Music Studio at the Royal College of Music (1967) and composed music for many films, including *The Ladykillers* (1955), *Quatermass and the Pit* (1967) and the BBC's *Dr Who* TV

While historians disagree about Brian Boru, it is generally admitted that Clontarf was the most shattering victory on record of the Irish over the Norsemen; the latter never really recovered from it. But what interests me more than the actual result of the battle is its implications – the clash between rival cultures and contrasted mentalities (incidentally, this clash can be emphasised by the music). I don't propose to treat it too romantically, although I shall use heightened language where I feel it is called for. There is plenty of evidence that the leaders on both sides were as much the victims of power politics as their counterparts in the 20th century. In spite of that, I should like discreetly to make use of some of the more supernatural elements – portents and omens – which legend has embroidered around this historical fact.

The actual battle would only take up a fraction of the programme time. The story, I think, should start where the most famous of the Icelandic sagas, Njal's saga, ends. A number of Icelanders who, as a result of a blood feud, had burned Njal and his family to death, finding themselves as a result of this very unpopular in Iceland, responded to an appeal from the Norse garrison in Dublin to come and help them in what both sides knew was going to be the great showdown. Having established something of the character of these Norsemen, I would do the same with the Irish and

—

series from 1963. He taught for many years at University of Adelaide and was author of an *Illustrated Compendium of Musical Technology* (1992). Cary initially worked with FLM on *East of the Sun and West of the Moon* (a Norwegian folk tale, broadcast 25 July 1959), and he recalls their association as follows: 'Louis [next] asked me to do *They Met on GF*, and we had a long historical session in which he described the circumstances of the battle. Louis said that he would be jumping the scene about from the Norse to the Irish sides, and that I should aim for a distinct instrumental signature for each side. We decided that the Irish would be represented by harp music and songs with harp, and the Norse by loud and crude brass and woodwind sounds.' The show's critics complained that FLM spent too much time on 'history lessons' and not enough on the drama of the battle: 'Louis MacNeice somehow misses the target . . . Instead of being wild and brave and calling his work *Clontarf*, which has a great, weird sound to English ears, he preferred the popularizing *They Met on Good Friday . . .* he chose a documentary form which succeeds when the subject is The General Strike but not when the subject is legendary or distantly historical' (*Listener*, 17 Dec. 1959); 'At times, the irony seems to be the inadvertent result of a clever mixture of styles, for we have early Irish lyric forms and early English alliterative verse cheek by jowl with a saga-like gruffness and an almost wisecracking colloquialism' (*The Times*, 9 Dec. 1959). Cary recalled FLM's 'tendency to procrastinate. I'd know well in advance the general outline of the proposed script and more or less where and how much music would be needed [. . .] but no script appeared [. . .] When, perhaps the weekend before the first cast rehearsal, Louis finally sat down and wrote it, there was barely time for his secretary to type up the script from his MS. On at least one occasion in *TMOGF*, Louis took a recording of some of the music home with him and timed his script to my score' (Tristram Cary, private correspondence, 2007).

gradually by repeated cross-cutting of this kind, gradually [*sic*] build up to the battle, which was fought on Good Friday 1014 A.D. The battle itself is full of obviously dramatic elements culminating in the rout of the Norsemen combined with the death of Brian, who was the only true High King of All Ireland in history and who was then very old. The aftermath, of course, is that while the Norse power in Ireland was broken, the sands were running out for the Irish also as the <u>Norman</u> invaders were very shortly to appear over the horizon. I hope to be able to convey, in some naturalistic way, this glimpse into the future.

I cannot claim that this programme can be done on the cheap. Apart from the special music, which seems to me essential to it (besides the orchestra Carey and I agree it needs a small choir), it would require a middling large cast.

(Louis MacNeice)

P.S. This is a comparatively longterm project (I could produce it towards the end of the Fourth Quarter) but in the meantime – the other possibility we discussed – I am looking for some suitable folk tale which can carry the sort of symbolism that you noticed in 'The Heartless Giant'. I have a few other ideas for the Third which I will let you know about as soon as I have got them better formulated.

FLM

TO *Hedli MacNeice*[1]

MS Bodleian

5 August [1959]

South Africa Broadcasting
Corporation [letterhead], as from
Vineyard Hotel, Protea Road,
Newlands, Cape Town

Dearest Cat,

Snatching a moment to write in somebody's office. Having made the [*illegible*] c. 11.0 a.m. Monday, found them all waiting for their 10lbs of flesh; I can cope all right but it's not exactly a picnic; my 1st class yesterday

---

1 – Addressed to Prospect Cottage, Shalcombe Quarries, Nr. Yarmouth, their holiday cottage on the Isle of Wight. FLM arrived in Cape Town on 3 Aug. and during the next four weeks he gave by his estimation no fewer than forty-seven lectures, two radio talks and one radio production (his play, *One Eye Wild*). He then spent two weeks in Johannesburg teaching at the University of Witwatersrand, and in mid-September he delivered a reading at the University College of Rhodesia and Nyasaland (Salisbury) (Stallworthy, 440–1).

consisted of 300 students (high standard of looks though, but all v. innocent, they tell me). The University has the most beautiful position of any I've seen, perched on the slopes of a mountain. My hotel is comfortable – & brandy cheap – but I don't really like doing my homework (of which there's masses) in a cretonned lounge with dimmed lights & old English ladies knitting. Got beset there yesterday evening by an astonishingly drunk retired British general who tried to lend me thousands of pounds to buy shoes with on a 10% commission. He was surprised I didn't remember all his old pals from World War I etc. After that I went to dinner (my first relaxation) with an old Euston Roader now Prof. of Art here, Rupert Shepherd & his wife; the latter used to share a flat with Hetta & hates her.[1] He asked me to remind you of Stoneham (?) whom you used to wake up coming in late in Fitzroy St., where R.S. also was living. The night before the Howarths had me to dinner – to meet 2 more <u>Australians</u>.[2] Have only met one Afrikaner so far – a nice boy who wants to get out & live in Europe. Mrs Shepherd says the Afrikaners are much nicer & more vital than the [British here *deleted*] English here. Most of the latter whom I've met seem agreeable but wet. By the way, I have to depend entirely on people fetching & delivering me in cars as there's no public transport between my hotel & the University. If you pick wild flowers here on the roadside you have your car confiscated & are fined £50. The current public joke is at the expense of the Ministry of Something or Other which put on the police to capture the call girls & all the police went to bed with all of the call girls &, when reprimanded, said they thought it was their duty. The weather was wonderful on Monday – Mediterranean – but cold since – open fires. The hotel food is poor. They say this Cape Peninsula is completely different from the rest of the country – much more attractive but now a backwater. The students want to drive me into the country – I'm wondering how many bus loads this will entail. Have just been discussing One Eye Wild with the people here; v. small

1 – Hetta Empson was married to the poet/critic William Empson (1906–84; see FLM to JH, 11 June 1934, n. 2, p. 244). Rupert Shephard (1909–92) was born in Islington and studied at the Slade where he was taught by Henry Tonks; he became associated with the 'realist' Euston Road school. He was an official war artist, and in 1948 went to the University of Cape Town as a Professor of Fine Arts. He returned to London in 1963.
2 – FLM was hosted by the Australian literary critic Robert Guy Howarth (1906–74) FRSL, and his wife Lilian Irene. Howarth had a long association with the University of Sydney, and was appointed to the Arderne Chair of English Literature at the University of Cape Town in 1955. He was editor of *Minor Poets of the 17th Century* (1931), *Letters and the Second Diary of Samuel Pepys* (1932), *Letters of George Gordon, 6th Lord Byron* (1933) and of the literary journal *Southerly*. He was co-editor of the *Penguin Book of Australian Verse* (1958).

supply of artists (amateurs) to choose from.[1] Also v. small studio. But the offices look out on the sea; in summer it seems, all the staff slip out to the beach. Politics have hardly arisen yet – but obviously will when people stop being so polite to me. I'm already getting maddened by everyone calling me 'Doctor' at least once in every sentence. Did you notice I left [*illegible*] my things behind? It doesn't really matter but, if I can afford it, I'll buy some pyjamas[.] Johannesburg I didn't like the look of at all, but I got there in the dark & left v. early; it was odd to see a lot of bare trees there. Here most of them are green & there are masses of arum lilies out. Also a white egret stalking around the hotel swimming pool. It's suggested I break my journey back for one night at Salisbury to give a lecture. Probably worth it as I shall need any extra money (there don't seem to be many extras here). Hope the island is fun. Lots of love to yourself, darling, & Bimba. Will write again soon. L.

TO *Hedli MacNeice*

MS Bodleian

7 August [1959]

University of Cape Town
[letterhead], as from Vineyard
Hotel, Newlands, Cape Town

Darling, Hope you got my first letter. Have just finished my chores for the week. This morning I was still asleep when they came to fetch me for my first lecture (8.20 for 8.45 am) but I made it – without breakfast of course. This week I have held forth 8 times; next week it will be 14 – plus radio auditions! They all, except my Professor, tell me no visiting lecturer has ever been worked so hard before; it seems the Prof. has tricked me. However, I've told him I've now closed the book – but I'll do what is scheduled, as it's a challenge. One thing: one can make one's audiences laugh, except for one class of what appear to be delinquents. Tomorrow, thank God, some of the students are taking me to a rugby match (I prefer the students to the staff who seem pompous & at the same time defeated – not a congenial combination). I want to get hold of a long poem just published by someone called Delius (unfortunately away as is the other poet, Uys Kriege [*sic*], I was told to meet) satirising the Government & all

---

1 – While in Cape Town, FLM produced his play *One Eye Wild* for radio. It had first been broadcast on the BBC's Third Programme, featuring Cécile Chevreau, on 9 Nov. 1952, and in 1955 he had expressed an interest in doing a new production (see FLM to Douglas Cleverdon, 30 May 1955, p. 592).

its works.[1] They tell me that in Johannesburg anyone building a house has steel gates put in at the bottom of the staircase! Sensational case in the papers: minister of the Reformed Dutch Church caught with an African woman & beaten up by 3 Africans; judge admitted the Reverend was 'committing an offence' but has given the 3 men 6 months for taking the law into their own hands. I v. much want to meet someone other than Anglo Saxon liberals but suppose that will come.

Darling, two practical points:- (1) Could you ask Rosemary or anyone else compos who can go to No. 2 to look in the right tophand [*sic*] drawer of my desk & send me – by airmail – my old <u>Yellow Fever</u> certificate which should be there. It's a yellow document like a menu card (& I believe mine's still valid). Without it I may not be allowed back into the U.K.! (2) I have a horrid feeling I never paid the Insurance on the <u>house</u>. Could you ask Miss Borrow about this & cope – I'll refund you. (I think after all I should show a decent profit on this tour – though I may have to spend money on mackintosh & pyjamas!). I feel v. marooned in this hotel; 2 people have offered me the loan of a car to drive myself but I don't think I'd ever find my way anywhere. (I'm out in the suburbs, you see, & all the roads play snakes & ladders with each other, doubling back on themselves round Devil's Peak (a v. attractive mountain).[)] I've hardly really seen Cape Town yet. Yesterday was a foul day; wet & cold – & snow I believe on Table Mountain – but today was springlike – wonderful views.[2] I'm to be taken a drive round the Cape Peninsula on Sunday & then to tea with a nice German professor. For the rest of today, thank God, I'm all on my own. Shall go down soon & have a brandy & soda; hope I shan't run into the drunk general again – he turns out to be a major. It seems silly to come all the way here to sit in a [*illegible*] bedroom surrounded by books nearly all of which I have at home – Collected Works of Spenser, Yeats & Aeschylus, The Allegory of Love, The 19th Century Background, Eliot's Collected Essays, Auden's anthologies, A Reading of George Herbert, my own book on Yeats & so on. The 'Doctor, Doctor' business continues; a woman who called me 'Mister' today was sharply corrected. I <u>should</u> like to meet someone impolite; no doubt that will come too. I gather in a public lecture

Waugh !

1 – Anthony Delius (1916–89), South African poet and author of *An Unknown Border* (Cape Town, 1954), *The Last Division* (Cape Town, 1959) and other works; member of editorial staff of *Cape Times*. Uys Krige (1910–87), South African poet, novelist, translator and playwright; co-edited *The Penguin Book of South African Verse* (1956).
2 – Devil's Peak (3,281ft), part of the famous, elevated background to Cape Town; Table Mountain is a sandstone mountain overlooking the bay.

yesterday I offended some Marxist students (hadn't expected there'd be any here!) by my remarks about 'Yes-Men'.

How is the island & <u>who</u> is in it?![1] How lucky you are being able to lie out in the grass. Here, when they light the fire, one really wants to huddle over it. If it weren't for the types who're liable to get there first! Better 50 years of the Needles than a cycle of the Cape.[2] Not but what, as I said, it's v. beautiful. Mrs Shepherd (see my last), though a South African herself, is obviously getting irritated with her husband for not taking her back to England – but he couldn't afford the fares, poor fellow; they have several children. I forgot to tell you he has 2 v. nice (though v. Euston Roadish) paintings; one of Dylan, & the other of Caitlin; both v. true. And yesterday the Howarths (!) played me the longplaying record of Milk Wood made in <u>New York</u> with Dylan narrating. A long way too to come for <u>that</u>! But don't think I'm depressed – I'm becoming rather proud of my stamina! Look after yourself Cat (keep MacFarlane on a tight lead – preferably a choker). Lots & lots of love – & to Bimba –

L.

TO *Hedli MacNeice* MS Bodleian

10 August [1959]   Vineyard Hotel, Newlands, Cape Town

Darling; just got your letter. Thank you. Glad the island is fun and the good weather continues. Two points of yours:- (1) It was a <u>v.</u> good thing I was tired when I left or the journey would have been still drearier than it was, (2) Your suggestion about lecturing gratis in black colleges is of no avail because there <u>are</u> no adult black colleges in either Capetown or J'berg! There are still (though I gather not for long) a number of coloured students in this University. Have just been reading the long satirical poem by Delius; at least it's good that they can publish and read these things. Saturday I had lunch with a Reverend Gregorovski, father of one of my students, after which we went to the annual rugby 'test match' between the 'Coloureds' and the 'Africans' (the latter till lately were called 'Bantu'). A vigorous game though sadly lacking in science; it seems they get no coaching. I was surprised (& pleased) that coloured chaps made merry quips to us on our way out of the ground. Yesterday I was taken a drive

1–The Isle of Wight.
2–The Needles: a rock formation in Alum Bay on the Isle of Wight.

along the coast road: wonderful bare-bone mountains & lots of wattles (imported from Australia) blazing with yellow flowers.[1] Then tea – 'Black Forest cake' – with the nice German professor, name like Rosteutscher; he had a cancer operation lately followed by months of the most extraordinary x-ray treatment which has left him half dead. Has an Afrikaans wife & a carefully tended garden; is mad about Greece which he visited 25 years ago. He also did his stint at Cambridge. Humane. This afternoon gave a reading to High School Students of all people. I could have refused but felt I ought to. The rest of the schedule grinds on relentlessly. Forgot to say that on Saturday night I went to a party given by a Mrs. Alexander, roaring old Australian Jewess whose husband was a big man in politics (not nationalist). Most people there were barristers. Also present her mother of 91 who aged 15 went out from Poland to Australia to marry someone she'd never seen. V. happy marriage, she says, but lots of lovers too. She sat out the party. Have written 3 poems. Here is the first one:-

Half Truth from Cape Town[2]

Between a smoking fire & a tolling bell
When I was young & at home I could not tell
What problems roosting ten miles to the east
Waited like vultures in their gantried nest
Till Prod should tumble Papish in the river.
I could not tell. The bell went on for ever.

Now through the swinging doors of the decades I
Confront a waste of tarmac, a roaring sky.
The Southern Cross supplants the Useful Plough –
But where are Livingstone & his lion now?
That cross was raised to mark this safe hotel
Between the gold mines & the padded cell.

In each glib airport between here & you
As the loudspeaker speaks the ants pour through,
Some going north into their past & some

1 – The Cape wattle from Western Australia, a fern-like shrub or small tree, with gold flowerheads.
2 – Broadcast BBC Third Programme, 24 Oct. 1959; published (with few variants) in *Writers Against Apartheid* (London, Spring 1960), *Solstices*, CP66, CP07, 556–7.

South to this future that may never come,
But all engrossed to that same point that good
Ants would die to get to if they could.

So here I am, with Devil's Peak above,
Between a smoking fire & a calling dove,
Its voice like a crazy clock that every ten
Minutes runs down, so must be wound again;
And who is all but come or all but gone
I cannot tell. The dove goes on, goes on.

Must stop now & do my homework (it's just like being at school). Have
to skim through I. A. Richards & Empson! Have a good time, darling, &
don't worry about me. I'm eating square, if dull, meals & there don't seem
to be any temptations to any sort of excess! lots of love, Cat. L.

Aug. 22nd (from now on you'd better write to me c/o Professor Partridge,
Dept. of English, University of Witwatersrand, Johannesburg[1]). Darling,
Thank you for your letters. So glad the Island was fun. I've been having not
a bad time here – in the chinks between public appearances. Have met a
lot of nice people now; am staying this weekend (nearer to the radio station
where I'm rehearsing One Eye Wild) with a liberal novelist in a lovely little
house with terraces bang on the v. attractive sea – white breakers on
bevelled granite rocks. Cat, your criticisms are ill-informed. (a) I couldn't
get out of most of my lectures (the University ones) because I'm being paid
for out of the pockets of the students (10/- per head per annum) so that
they have an unanswerable argument, viz. that all the students in Eng. Lit.
must have their share of me! (b) Re. lecturing to 'the Blacks', as I've told
you, there are, as yet, no separate colleges for them here or in J'berg but
anyway the idea of such colleges (= segregation) is strongly disapproved of
by their sympathisers (it's the Nationalists who're promoting them just as
they're promoting 'Bantustan' which means a group of nominally
autonomous Black 'states' carved out of the Union). On the other hand
there still are (though this is threatened soon to be done away with) quite
a number of Coloured & African students in the University of Cape Town;
I get quite a few at my lectures. And apart from the academic world (a bit
hothouse here) people are trying to arrange that I meet some of the non-

1 – Astley Cooper Partridge (b.1901), literary critic, author of *The Language of Renaissance
Poetry* (1971) and works on Shakespeare, Jonson, Donne and others.

European intelligentsia before I leave here. Ditto in J'berg. So it's a much more complicated picture than you think! / A certain amount of comic relief this week, including a dinner (I was railroaded into it by the Howarths) at the home of 2 fabulously rich old museum-piece English ladies, the Misses Holt sisters of Harold Holt. The balusters of their staircase are of cut (barleysugar-shaped) crystal, the table is cluttered with Venetian glass & the walls covered with Sir Joshua Reynolds. And of course central heating. / The rest of today I'll be rehearsing again; they're not bad – the actors – but technical facilities are lacking & the gramophone effects library lamentable. lots of love – & to Bimba. L.

P.S. What about that Yellow Fever certificate?

TO *Hedli MacNeice* MS Bodleian

15 August [1959]   Vineyard Hotel, Newlands,
Cape Town

Dearest Cat, How are you? Have scraped through my 2nd week hanging on by my eyelashes. But also have met some new & more interesting people. If it weren't so sad & stupid this country would be very funny. A coloured widow went to visit her husband's grave about 3 days after the funeral & found just a hole in the ground. Without telling her, the graveyard authorities had exhumed him because he was a European & transferred him to the European part of the graveyard where, when she dies, she won't be allowed to join him. A girl I met last night went to a Coloured beauty parade with a Coloured girl & used the phrase 'a non-European parade'. The Coloured girl said 'No, it's not non-European; there will be Africans present.' The point is that the Coloureds who are of mixed blood (often largely Malay) & who are graded higher than the 'Africans' or 'Natives' or 'Bantu' apply the term 'non-European' to themselves so that the latter would logically have to be called something lower than non-European! Till lately, just as a Coloured person with a light skin could 'try for White' (i.e. try to get himself registered as European) so a 'Native' could 'try for Coloured' & thereby get privileges such as being able to buy drink in liquor stores. By the way, no woman can enter a bar here, either as barmaid or customer. Last night I was taken to an Indian restaurant, almost the only place which admits all the races; they told me that by going there we were infringing the 'Immorality Act'. The English papers attack & ridicule all this. Just as in America one never met McCarthyites, so here I haven't met any 'Nats' (Nationalists); still, they're the ruling lot. Everyone says that the English lot are largely to blame because of their apathy & reluctance to go into politics whereas the Afrikaner politicians include many of their best brains – barristers etc. The Opposition party at the moment seems anyway to be on the verge of splitting. In the schools by the way the official policy is to segregate the Afrikaner children from the English ones. There has just been a row at the meeting of a golf club committee because one of the officials, who was bilingual[,] insisted on conducting all the business in Afrikaans to spite the President who could only speak English. And so on & so on & so on. Here is another poem:-

Solitary Travel[1]

Breakfasting alone in Karachi, Delhi, Calcutta,
Dacca, Singapore, Kuala Lumpur, Colombo, Cape Town,
But always under water or glass, I find
Such a beginning makes the day seem blind.

The hotels are all the same, it might be pawpaw
Instead of grapefruit, different flowers on the tables,
But the waiters, coffee-coloured or yellow or black,
All smile but, should you smile, give nothing back.

And taking coffee alone in the indistinguishable airports,
Though the land outside be empty or man-crammed, oven or icebox,
I feel the futility of moving on
To what, though not a conclusion, is foregone.[2]

But the Customs clamour, the stamp is raised, the passport
Like a chessgame played by mail records the latest
Move of just one square. Which is surely seen
By the black bishop & the unsleeping queen.

And so to the next hotel, to the selfsame breakfast,
Same faces of manager, waiter, fellow-traveller,
Same lounge or bar whose test-tube walls enfold
The self-indulgent disenchanted old.

1 – Published in *Solstices*, CP66, CP07, 557–8.
2 – Variant: 'stays foregone'.

Time & the will are frozen.[1] If I could only
Escape into icebox or oven, escape among people
Before tomorrow from this neutral zone
Where all tomorrows must be faced alone![2]

———

Talking of travel, please remember that Yellow Fever Certificate. If it's not to be found, let me know & I can easily be inoculated here. It looks as if I should be hitting Europe on September 16th but will let you know more precisely. Look after yourselves in that snake-ridden Island. (An old Englishman in this hotel was brought up there.) Lots of love. L.

TO *Hedli MacNeice*

MS Bodleian

1 September [1959] University Residence, Cottesloe,
Johannesburg

Dearest Cat, Thank you for your letter all about Nate. Glad Bimba & he got on. The cutting you said you were enclosing you didn't, whatever it was! Got here Sunday. Bitterly cold wind & dust from the mines. Am billeted in a converted military camp – corrugated iron & the doors don't fit. But much lighter lecturing programme than in Cape Town – & I'm going to meet some Africans, see the locations etc. Today will try to get in touch with the radio people. They say everyone gets on edge here this time of year before the rains come. Have lashings of introductions but shall only be able to take up a few of them. Some of the Cape Town people were as nice as I've come across anywhere; I gave quite a gang of them farewell drinks in my hotel (luckily the H's weren't free for it!).[3] I'll have to have a Yellow Fever injection here after all; your document was yellow but not the right one! By the way, Cat, your remarks about Alcohol & Sex were a little unkind I thought across all these many miles. You're such an old beam-&-moter (see your New Testament) that you seem quite unaware that you very often don't take up my signals. When your mind is on higher things (I wonder if Brecht by the way really is higher than Drink!) Of course a lot of drink (see Shakespeare!) doesn't help the sexual act but, if it weren't for drink (I've told you this before but it never sinks in), I'd probably have

1 – Variant: 'Time and the will lie sidestepped.'
2 – Variant: 'faced alone . . .'
3 – The Howarths, his hosts.

vanished long ago to Tahiti or somewhere.[1] My main comment however is that I don't think I'm any longer interested in Sex for Sex's Sake (how horribly sibilant!) & can't really get interested – drink or no drink – unless ones tuned in on the other wavelength. Which so often (drink or no drink) we aren't – probably because we're both such egocentrics. Please don't take any of this amiss; everyone (including me) knows that you're extraordinarily attractive for your age – it will be nice to be in bed again with you anyway. But those other things do count – as you know of course but somehow, ever since those screaming days in Mousehole, quite often – not always of course, perish the thought – our tuning apparatuses seem to go haywire. Enough of this anyway, darling. Give all my wishes, regards, etc. to your parents. And love to Bimba. & lots to yourself, Cat. Let me know your Italy schemes. L.

TO *P. H. Newby*[2]   MS BBC

5 October 1959   BBC memo, 203 Rothwell [House]

When doing a new production of <u>The Dark Tower</u> in Johannesburg the other day, I realized once again what an excellent vehicle this fable type of play is for dealing with contemporary issues which might be too hot or too delicate for a more direct treatment. I have now a very strong compulsion to write a new piece of this kind about exactly this sort of issue. Provisional title: <u>The Pin is Out</u>.[3] If this suggestion were accepted, I should like to substitute it for <u>The Battle of Clontarf</u>, which could presumably be postponed till next year.

The Pin is Out would be set in an imaginary country whose population is divided into three main groups – the Alphas, the Betas and the Helots. As I think it safer to keep colour out of this, the distinctions between these groups would be political, social or economic. The Alphas, who rule the

1 – Famously, 'It provokes the desire, but it takes away the performance. Therefore, much drink may be said to be an equivocator with lechery: it makes him, and it mars him; it sets him on, and it takes him off . . .' (*Macbeth*, II.iii.28–32).
2 – P. H. (Howard) Newby (1918–97), writer and broadcasting administrator. He had joined the BBC in 1949 as a talks producer but he became Controller of the BBC's Third Programme in 1958.
3 – In a memo written the following week, FLM expanded on his ideas set out here and suggested the programme be considered for the next quarter, thus not to interfere with the *Battle of Clontarf* production. (FLM to Controller, 13 Oct. 1959, *Ms BBC, Louis MacNeice, Scriptwriter file*). See subsequent discussion on 20 July 1960 (below). Despite interest within the Department, the subject was considered too controversial for broadcast.

country, are the political élite. The Betas, slightly fewer in number, have cornered most of the wealth; their interests in nearly every sphere are opposed to those of the Alphas and the rift between these two groups is continually widening. The Helots, who greatly outnumber the other two groups put together, are . . . well . . . Helots – hopelessly backward and deliberately kept backward.

In spite of the obvious implied morals in this set-up, this programme would <u>not</u> be just a dressed-up thesis. My imaginary country is so cut off from the rest of the world, that its more liberal-minded citizens are predisposed to welcome any stranger as if he were an angel; almost any relationship between them and him will be from the start a sentimental one. So my main story-line will be one of personal relationships between real characters. Tragic of course. [I am still working out the plot but, if required, could supply a tentative synopsis quickly. *deleted*]

Incidental material will be drawn from the more horrible contemporary spheres of air travel, advertising, the mass media, etc. Technically the programme would be experimentally simple. I propose to try and do nearly everything by words, e.g. to use an incantatory kind of lyrical writing where traditionally one would use music. [*handwritten*:] <u>Some</u> effects will be needed though.

In spite of the safety device of the timeless placeless fable, I realize that in some quarters this subject might be considered dangerous, but it <u>is</u> what I want to write about at this moment. So, if you think it worth while, I'd very much like to discuss it with you.

Louis MacNeice

P.S. I have now started writing a draft script of this and it is coming so quickly that I think, <u>if</u> there were space, I could manage to do it <u>as well as</u> Clontarf in this quarter.

I attach a tentative synopsis.

FLM

MS Frances Suzman Jowell

13 Oct. [1959]   BBC

Darling,

Your letter, which came last week, made me very happy; I'd been afraid that on reflection you might think we should begin & end in Jan Smuts Airport! I'd have answered before but the General Election happened (very unfortunate) & then we went for the weekend to the cottage we have in the Isle of Wight (I forget if I told you about it).[2] The timing couldn't have been worse; the weather at long last broke (we've been having this fabulous Indian Summer)[3] & I sat looking out at the [dripping *deleted*] drooping fuchsias & the dripping apple trees & got the 'pines' for you rather badly. Still, it's wonderful to know you exist, even if so far away, & that we're on the same wavelength. Otherwise I'd feel a bird in the wilderness; that awful little tune keeps recurring to me.

You certainly seem to have a varied world on your desk. In the cottage I was reading Hopkins & wondering about the 'terrible sonnets' which you talked about.[4] I suppose one can feel as desperate as that quite apart from Christianity but these sonnets do basically exist within a Christian framework – the same, I think, goes for S. Dedalus.[5] Do <u>you</u> feel any sort of barrier to understanding here? Not but what of course the Judaic background has its full share (!) of the Sin and Despair feelings. I feel the same problem myself about <u>Catholic</u> literature. I was also rereading the Inferno in the cottage; it always gets me but presumably it would get a

1 – Frances Suzman (1939–), daughter of anti-apartheid campaigner and South African MP, Helen Suzman (1917–2009). Frances was educated at University of Witwatersrand, Courtauld Institute, and Harvard (PhD, 1971) and is an independent art historian living in London. Author of *Thoré-Bürger and the Art of the Past* (1977) and many articles and reviews. M. (1963) Jeffrey Jowell. In 1959, while a student at Witwatersrand, she was charged with the task of chaperoning FLM during his stay. 'During these two weeks we had many long conversations about a range of different subjects (theatre, literature, personal relationships, politics etc.) and we became close friends. The letters date from two periods – my last few months in South Africa (Sept.–Nov.1959) and the six months I spent in Aix-en-Provence (Feb.–July 1960). We met several times in London in Dec.1959–Jan.1960 and after I came to London in Sept.1960' (FSJ, private correspondence, 2010). FLM wrote seven letters to FSJ.

2 – The results of the General Election were declared on 8 October and on the following day.

3 – Temperatures in excess of 70 degrees were recorded throughout southern England and Wales during the first ten days of October, leading to water shortages in many areas. The temperature at Mildenhall on 3 October was the highest in the British Isles at that date since 1921.

4 – FSJ had been writing a long essay on the 'dark sonnets' of Gerard Manley Hopkins for her degree at Witwatersrand, where she was reading English and Art History.

5 – Stephen Dedalus, protagonist of Joyce's *Stephen Hero* and *A Portrait of the Artist as a Young Man*, is a prominent character in *Ulysses*. FSJ had been studying *A Portrait* at university

Catholic rather differently. There's another parallel between us on the other side of course. Just as I was brought up, seeing it was in Ireland, v. conscious of the Catholic tradition (both sides of my family were Catholics once on a time), so I imagine you must have always been v. conscious of the Christian one. Tell me if you think I'm talking nonsense. In spite of I. A. Richards this question of belief seems to me important.[1] And it's too easy to dismiss everything as a mere 'symbol'. But I just don't know the answer. I'm afraid, in spite of occasional lapses into lecturing & Lit. Crit., I'm not very good at analysis.

To turn to synthesis, if only at a low level, having been very idle for 3 weeks, trying to get reacclimatised, I now find myself with a lot of work, including the writing & producing of a peculiar radio play about the Battle of Clontarf (which you've probably never heard of).[2] It was the great showdown between the Ancient Irish & the Norsemen. This must sound v. dull but I'm using it as a peg for a study of (a) [world *deleted*] power politics, (b) the contrast between 2 v. different mentalities & cultures (probably with some anachronism). The play I mentioned in my last letter – which no one of course may accept – is on the contrary inspired by S. Africa, though I wouldn't call it that.[3] I'd like to treat it very freely – oversimplified & some bits stylised. Meanwhile people seem to be nibbling at my stage play – the 'morality' on the Everyman theme.[4] Did I tell you about that?

Darling Frances, I forgot; here are belatedly Many Happy Returns.[5] It still staggers me that you should combine all the delightfulness of youth with that cool (& I don't mean cold!) grip of things in your head. (Or, as I said before, 'crisp'.) What irritates me about many people your age is their mushiness – nothing yet crystallised. Whereas you've crystallised so beautifully. Of course there are other people your age who've (but I wouldn't call this crystallised) already got set in their ways for ever. But as Dante says, don't let's talk about them; just look & pass on. Non ragioniam di lor ma guarda e passa.[6] A favourite quotation of mine; he uses it in fact about the Trimmers. The point is: I think life must be

---

1 – FLM had been reading the critic I. A. Richards (1893–1979) for his Cape Town lectures in August (cf. FLM to HM, 5 August 1959, p. 647). Author of *Principles of Literary Criticism* (1924), *Practical Criticism* (1929) and other influential works.
2 – *They Met on Good Friday*, broadcast on 8 December.
3 – *The Pin is Out*.
4 – *One for the Grave: A Modern Morality Play*: written 1958–9, first performed in Oct. 1966, Abbey Theatre, Dublin. The play was published in 1968 by Faber and Faber.
5 – She had turned twenty on 30 September.
6 – From *The Inferno*.

dialectical (not of course in the Marxist sense). One ought to be firm <u>&</u> able to change, active (using one's right of choice) <u>&</u> passive (Keats's 'negative capability') & so on.

Darling, you're so right about the trivial things becoming significant. I feel that all the time when I remember J'burg. But ought I to apologise for having imposed Efficiency on you? After all, if you hadn't been efficient at the time, you'd never have turned up to fetch me etc.![1] But I don't mind how inefficient you're being at the moment. And, by the way, so far as I'm concerned, you can be as 'abberant' as you like. For myself, as regards you, that's another piece of 'dialectic': while I feel as selfish as everyone does in these circumstances, I would not try to impose myself on you against your wishes, darling. Write to me soon.

With love (repeat love) – Louis.

P.S. You must come to London.

TO *Gerald Abraham*[2]

MS Bodleian [copy]

20 October 1959   [BBC]

Dear Gerald,

Please forgive me for picking your brains. I am writing a script for the BBC about the battle of Clontarf fought near Dublin between the Irish and the Norsemen in 1014 A.D. According to the records, it was fought on Good Friday and Brian Boru, the old High King of Ireland, spent the battle chanting prayers, etc. in his tent. Could you please tell me what church music was like then and whether there are any recordings that would give one at least a rough idea of it?

---

1 – FSJ recalls she had to struggle 'to ensure that he arrived on time (and reasonably sober) for his lectures. The events included an evening PEN club meeting, where he gave an interesting talk on "lyric drama", a luncheon in his honour, a symposium with Richard Church at the university, an evening reading of his poetry to an audience at the university. We went to see *Under Milkwood* . . . *Dock Brief* and *What Shall We Tell Caroline* . . . One afternoon I whisked him out of his comfortable suburban accommodation and took him (with some other friends) to visit the black townships where we ended up in a shebeen, which he hugely enjoyed. (He was unconcerned that we were breaking the apartheid laws, first by entering the township without a permit, then by drinking at an illegal shebeen). On Sunday Sept. 13, the day before he left, we went to Broadcast House for a memorable recording of *The Dark Tower*' (Private correspondence, 2010).
2 – Gerald Abraham, FBA, CBE (1904–88), musicologist, noted expert on church music and much else. Author of books on Handel, Schubert, Tchaikovsky and many others. In 1959, he was Professor of Music at the University of Liverpool. He first met FLM at the George, Great Portland Street, when deputy editor of the *Listener*.

I hear you had great times in the Island with my family while I was in South Africa. Sorry to have missed you.

With all best wishes,
Yours ever
Louis

TO *Frances Suzman* MS Frances Suzman Jowell

6 Nov. [1959]   BBC

Darling Frances,

Are you in the middle of exams? I am in the middle of retarded radio programmes – one mainly taped 'actualities' on the hackneyed subject of Youth & the other the play about poor old (wicked old really) Brian Boru.[1] I was 3 days in Oxford recording for the former & am now moving into the world of cockney delinquents. A book about this type which has made a great stir here lately is <u>Absolute Beginners</u> by Colin MacInnes, written in 1st person character in jazz argot.[2] Very striking – & they tell me it's true to life.

Darling I was v. interested by all you wrote about religion, Judaic background etc. Yes, I remember Mrs Stodel very well; I liked her.[3] Was rather puzzled that she seemed to have such a dull old husband. Littleton Powys was a very loveable man & one of the few people I know to carry their old age not only graciously but gaily.

I have been through some gloomy, or glum I should say, moods lately, largely owing to my growing dislike of my employers who are getting less & less interested in creative radio. As for the television branch, they are stuck in the rut of Trying to be Popular. Not that I'm so sold on my literary colleagues either. I went to a party two days ago given by Guinness's (the brewing people) to present their annual poetry awards. Lots of champagne – & Guinness – but too many poets, some behaving badly, most behaving boringly. Which reminds me: recently I heard my own voice on tape speaking – or trying to – when very drunk. This almost cured me of drink!

Darling, do let me know when you expect to come to London & for how long. There is going to be a very peculiar party on December 11th in honour of a colleague of mine, a notoriously wild little man, who's retiring

1 – *Mosaic of Youth* (broadcast 30 Dec.) and *They Met on Good Friday*.
2 – Published 1959.
3 – An older friend of FSJ who lived in Cape Town.

from our Department. It will take place in a Drill Hall & go on all night.[1]
There should be a remarkable assortment of people ranging from radio
'beats' to lobster fishermen & from 12-tone composers to chirruping little
actresses. I think it might amuse you.

I ought to be going now to the British Museum Reading room to mug
up my Ancient Irish – & Norse – history. I wish they didn't all have such
unpronounceable names. Have you ever been to this Reading Room? It's
one of the most peculiar places in London. Someone pointed out the other
day that you hardly ever see anyone turn a page in it.

Did I tell you I went with my daughter to see Coriolanus at Stratford on
Avon [sic]? A good production with an understudy standing in v. well for
Olivier.[2] By the way I find that I'm communicating better with my
daughter. She is very much an individual.

Yesterday I met poor old Richard Church again at a British Council
lunch for a bored – & I'm afraid boring – Indian professor from Calcutta.[3]
Our host was so dim he made even R.C. seem quite lively. I was late for
this lunch because I ran into a man I know who that morning had been
knocked about by the police for trying to make a formal protest outside
Wandsworth Prison against the hanging of Podola (did you read about
him?)[4]

Have had a fan letter from J'burg about The Dark Tower but describing
it as an 'upsetting' play. Did I tell you how & when I wrote it? In Belfast
summer of '45 when I was in a state.[5] I could never write more than a little
at a time; it was mainly, as they say, 'given' & what I was given hit me so
hard that I had to keep breaking off for a drink.

Please write when you're free of exams.

With very much love, darling,
Louis.

P.S. I forgot to say: please mark your letters 'Personal' – otherwise they
may be opened by bloody bureaucrats!

---

1 – The party, which FSJ attended, was in honour of Jack Dillon. Guests included Dominic
Behan and William Empson.
2 – On 8 October a young Albert Finney performed Coriolanus since Laurence Olivier had
slipped his knee cartilage. Cf. 'Understudy goes on for Olivier', Times, 9 Oct. 1959, 18.
3 – Richard Church (1893–1972), poet, novelist, literary journalist. Educ. Dulwich Hamlet
School; Civil Service (Customs and Excise). Author of Collected Poems (1948); three volumes
of autobiography (1957–64); London: The Flower of Cities All (1967) and other works.
4 – Guenther Fritz Podola (1929–59) was executed at Wandsworth on 5 Nov. for murdering
a London police officer.
5 – The Dark Tower was first broadcast on 21 Jan. 1946; another recording was broadcast
in Johannesburg on 13 Sept. 1959. On writing the play in Belfast, cf. FLM to LG, 5 August
1945, p. 454.

1960

TO *Terry Kilmartin*[1]   MS Bodleian [carbon copy unsigned]

13 January 1960   [BBC]

Dear Terry Kilmartin,

Would you be interested in the following?

On the 26th of this month a play called <u>Over the Bridge</u> is coming on in the Empire Theatre, Belfast. It is a first play of a man called Sam Thompson, who has spent his life as a painter in the Belfast shipyards, and it has already caused a sensation over there in that it was commissioned and then rejected by the Belfast Group Theatre, who were then promptly sued by the author (he won his case). The people who are now putting it on are, I gather, throwing everything into it – two revolves for instance and sets by the most advanced of the Belfast architects.

I have not read the text and don't know whether it is a good play or not, but am assured that the dialogue is excellent and the subject is certainly one which the author (whom I know) is only too well up in, namely religious bigotry in the shipyards. I imagine he will not have pulled his punches over this.[2]

I wondered if The Observer would like to send me over to Belfast to write a notice of this piece.[3]

Yours sincerely,
(Louis MacNeice)

1 – Terence Kilmartin (1922–91), literary editor of the *Observer* 1951–85 and Proust scholar.
2 – MacNeice later wrote to Thompson, thanking him for sending the script: 'I had to read it in rather a hurry, but think it's good, strong stuff and hope the production does it justice' (19 Jan. 1960, *Ms Bodleian*).
3 – FLM attended the performance with Hedli. Cf. FLM, 'Out of the Deadpan', review of *Over the Bridge*, *Observer*, 31 Jan. 1960, 23. See also FLM to John Boyd, 3 Feb. 1959, p. 637–8.

TO *Caitlin Thomas*[1]   MS Bodleian [copy unsigned]

18 January 1960   [BBC]

Caitlin dear,

Thank you for the two dogs – just arrived – <u>both</u> of whom I find pretty. Please forgive me for not having answered your letter, which I mislaid. By the time it re-emerged from the debris of this office, I gathered you'd already got the answers to most of your questions, viz. who was the lawyer for the Fund, how much money there was in it, etc.[2] And by now you must know that your old friend D. Higham[3] is fulfilling (admirably) a double office, i.e. (1) as an administrator of the Estate and (2), along with G. Rees and me, as a trustee of the Fund. He, G.R., and I agreed, nem. con.[4] as they say, that <u>from now on</u> the money should be made quickly get-at-able provided the object seemed reasonable. <u>Previously</u> we had held the view that, as the <u>royalties</u> were booming in a way which no one could have foreseen, the Fund money (after all there's not so much of it!) should be held in reserve till it was really needed. So I hope you're glad it's still there to be drawn on! And I gather there's still more than <u>we</u> have in the American kitty.

Are you really going to live in Italy for ever? If so, let us meet soon in the Piazza Navona – which is my favourite. Anyway you're not missing much in London. Very bleak and the people the same again.

Much love – and enjoy yourself –

TO *Frances Suzman*   MS Frances Suzman Jowell

3 March [1960]   BBC

Darling Frances,

I was delighted to hear from you. I'm glad you've got out of your tossed cork phase & that the wipers are wiping again.[5] I did feel myself that you were anticipating that phase a little in London.

1 – Addressed to Thomas at Via Musio Clementi 51, Roma, Italy.
2 – Cf. FLM to Principal Fulton, 21 Nov. 1953, pp. 565–6.
3 – David Higham (1896–1978), literary agent; worked for Curtis Brown 1925–35, then established his own agency, David Higham Associates Ltd. His memoir, *Literary Gent*, appeared posthumously.
4 – 'Without dissent'.
5 – FSJ had told FLM she sometimes felt as if she were driving a car in the rain without windscreen wipers (Private correspondence, 2010). Cf. 'The Wiper', *LM* (May 1960); *Solstices*; CP07, 562–3.

I envy you Aix. London seems to get uglier every day, my B.B.C work has been very dull lately &, as for my other work, the engine's continually stalling. My trip to Belfast made a welcome change. The play by the way was v. powerful & I gave it a wholehearted write-up in the Observer, not but what I had to write it with a hangover in a typical Belfast pub surrounded by bawdy chatter.[1]

A very attractive & gifted young Indian called Zul-Vellani has entered our lives.[2] Born in Kenya, schooled in Japan (!), done film work in India & (I imagine) eased out from there for his v. left-wing politics. He wants to get in on documentary films here. He is one of those sociable drinking Indians.

Also last week I met a Cuban journalist who told me, to my surprise, that Castro had asked him to procure for him 2 autographs in England – one mine, the other John Osborne's! (Why?) We asked him what had happened to the members of the old regime in Cuba. He said well, some are working on the land, some have fled to the U.S. & some are working the counter-revolution.

A Professor Rand, one of the people sacked from Fort Hare where he'd been Prof. of English, turned up here the other day on his way to Australia.[3] He says his successor writes all his letters in Afrikaans, so he wrote him a letter of good will in French. Another S.A. Professor, Gardiner [sic] I think, whom I didn't like, has been going round London picking people's memories for a biography of Roy Campbell.[4]

You make the boy-girl life in Aix sound somewhat banal. I must admit the (far older!) boy-girl life round here gets odder & odder. I have just had the most astonishing confidences from people I've known for years. The course of untrue love doesn't seem to run very smooth either!

Are you going to get around the rest of Provence? Did I tell you about the enchanting hill village we stayed in called Ménerbes? (Strictly speaking perhaps it's not Provence as it's north of that range of mountains). We

1 – FLM reviewed Sam Thompson's *Over the Bridge* for the *Observer*. FLM to TK, 13 Jan. 1960, p. 658, n. 3.
2 – Zul Vellani (1930–), Indian actor, scriptwriter, director. Film credits include *Spring Comes to Kashmir* (1956), *All Under Heaven By Force* (1960) and *Siddhartha* (1972).
3 – Prof. F. H. Rand, head of English at Fort Hare University College for Africans (Cape Town) was one of seven white staff members dismissed due to non-compliance with the South African Government's policy of apartheid. Cf. 'Bantu University Dismissals', *Times*, 28 Sept. 1959, 9.
4 – William Henry Gardner (1902–69), editor and scholar of Gerard Manley Hopkins. A Catholic convert, he had taught in schools for many years before entering academia. He was Professor of English at the University of Natal.

stayed in an ancient house like a castle with eyrie-like terraces & I spent the mornings translating (of all things) Goethe's Faust & the rest of the day playing (including boules & table tennis).[1]

Darling, write to me again. Your last letter was the right sort of mixed grill – introspections, observations, trivia here & there & a hint of . . . [sic] the infinite spaces? I mean the ones inside one. I think when one's 20 one's internal skin is thinner so that one's more vulnerable to one's own identity (or non-identity). Later one tends to become a makebelieve extravert.

Enjoy Aix. Much love,
Louis.

TO *Martita Hunt*[2]

MS Bodleian

9 March 1960   [BBC]

Dear Martita,

Thank you once again for a lovely evening. Hedli and I both enjoyed it enormously. I think you are very clever to have discovered such a neatly tucked-away Bower of Bliss.

Here are a few additional suggestions for the second part of your programme.[3] I don't suppose you will like all of them, but some might fit in appropriately.

> George Gascoigne: <u>Gascoigne's Lullabie</u> – to be found in many anthologies.
> Henry King: <u>The Exequy</u> – to be found in many anthologies.
> Marvell: <u>A Dialogue of Body and Soul</u> – this might make a nice parallel (and contrast) to your Yeats dialogue.
> Henry Vaughan: <u>The World</u>

---

1 – FLM had worked on *Faust* chez Thérèse Mayer in Provence. FLM to DM, 30 Aug. 1952, p. 553, n. 1.

2 – Martita Hunt (1900–69), actress who joined the Old Vic company in 1929, where she played many Shakespearean roles, but was famous for her many West End performances throughout the 1930s and 1940s. Film appearances – in which she was typecast as 'the *grande dame* or patrician grotesque' (*DNB*) – include *Anna Karenina* (1948), *Lady Windermere's Fan* (1949), *The Prince and the Showgirl* (1957), *The Brides of Dracula* (1960) and *The Unsinkable Molly Brown* (1964). Within FLM's circle she was famous for saying to TSE at a dinner party chez MacNeice, in spring 1946: 'Now, now, Mr Eliot, don't be naughty!' (Cf. Stallworthy, 345).

3 – Hunt had previously spoken to FLM about a radio programme in which she would recite a selection of verse. Cf. Hunt to FLM, 'Saturday' [March 1960] (*Ms Bodleian, Ms Res, c. 570*). Later, she had to cancel the recording, due to a throat infection (Hunt to FLM, 23 March 1960, ibid.).

Swift: <u>A Satirical elergy</u> [*sic*] <u>on the Death of a late Famous General</u>
Pope: Excerpt from Canto 5 of <u>The Rape of the Lock</u> – Clarissa's
    speech beginning 'So why our Beauties . . .' and ending '. . . Merit
    charms the Soul.'
Byron: <u>Don Juan</u> – Canto II, stanzas 176–192, though if you like it
    at all you would probably wish to drop out some of these.
 W. M. Praed: <u>A Letter of Advice</u> – for light relief. We talked about
    this the other night.
Kipling: <u>A St. Helena Lullaby</u>
Walt Whitman: <u>Out of the Cradle Endlessly Rocking</u>
What in the end did you think of <u>The Shield of Achilles</u>?[1] I think it is
much the best poem he has written of recent years. Do let me know if there
is anything else I can do in connection with your recital.

Love,
[unsigned]

TO *Martita Hunt*   MS Bodleian

16 March 1960   [BBC]

Dear Martita,
    Here are my tentative answers to your three questions:
  (1) What about <u>The Book of Thel</u>, whole or part, by Blake. I have
      always found it a very haunting piece. Or, something quite
      different, <u>The Castaway</u> by Cowper, though in this the real point
      is delayed till the last two lines.[2]
  (2) I am sure it is quite all right to start with four Shakespeare
      sonnets.
  (3) I wouldn't know which single poem to plump for, but suggest that,
      apart from Donne's Sonnets and his <u>Hymn to God the Father</u> you
      might look at George Herbert, poems like <u>Affliction (1)</u> and
      <u>Miserie</u>. Perhaps his finest is <u>The Sacrifice</u>, but it is very long –
      252 lines. I already suggested <u>The World</u> by Henry Vaughan but
      would add his <u>They Are All Gone into the World of Light</u>. Going

---

1 – W. H. Auden, *The Shield of Achilles* (1955).
2 – Hunt's first question was 'Did anyone in the eighteenth century permit themselves to write
anything serious about mortality, immortality etc? You know what I mean. Don't say Gray
my dear – I adore his elergy (as your secretary spells the word), unless you feel it might be a
stunt, but then so I suppose was Agamemnon's tomb, which I have discarded.' Hunt to FLM,
'Saturday' [March 1960] (*Ms Bodleian, Ms Res, c. 570*).

back much earlier, I think <u>Quia Amore Langueo</u> is a magnificent allegorical piece and should be excellent for reading aloud. A much simpler but very attractive later medieval poem is <u>Tomorrow Shall Be My Dancing Day</u>. Both these are to be found in many anthologies.[1]

I hope this will be some help.

Love,
[unsigned]

TO *Mary Wimbush*[2]

MS Bodleian

4 April 1960   [London]
(but do time and place matter?)

Darling Mary my darling,

I have been missing you shockingly. This is in haste; I have to go & play tennis with Johnnie D. & the Tennis Girl. We played, if that is the word, yesterday & it was agreed we should repeat the performance today so as not to be stiff for a week.

I enclose something which may not be at all good; I may tinker it [*sic*] later but it's too soon for me to judge, especially as my emotions are so mixed up in it.[3] I told you about my very nasty poem called <u>Bad Dream</u>. I had meant to write a complement to it anyway but, once I got started, inevitably I suppose, it turned out to be all about you.

I have been forlorn this weekend but <u>basically</u> happy. I do hope you've been happy too. If you're <u>not</u> coming on Wednesday, let me know. Otherwise Wednesday is all I look forward to at the moment. You <u>know</u> how I love you. L.

---

1 – This answers Hunt's third question: 'Which do you think is the greatest short religious poem that has ever been written? Try not to include Hopkins because I may find myself reading the two Echoes.' All of the authors and some of the poems FLM mentions, including 'Quia Amore Langueo' (Anon.), were, of course, part of the mental furniture of his generation, and appear in the anthology he had known best as a young man, namely Quiller-Couch, *Oxford Book of English Verse: 1250–1900*.

2 – Mary Wimbush (1924–2005), actress, played in *The Dark Tower* (1946) and *They Met on Good Friday* (1959). FLM began an affair with her in 1960 and dedicated *The Burning Perch* to her ('To Mary', CP07, 576). She had a long career in radio drama and was best known for her role as Julia Pargetter-Carmichael in *The Archers*. The Bodleian Library recently acquired five signed autograph letters by FLM to Wimbush, of which this is the earliest; the last in the series is dated 22 Sept. 1960.

3 – Enclosed is a manuscript poem on four sheets, 'Good Dream (for you darling)', later published in *Solstices* (without parenthetic address), immediately following 'Bad Dream' (CP07, 567–71.)

TO *Mary Wimbush*   MS Bodleian

Postmark 11 April 1960   [London]

Mary my <u>dearest</u>,

In more haste even than last time; the weekend (wedding + Raws-
thornes) was fun but exhausting – & I've been missing you . . . well, you
know how I've been missing you. This is really only to tell you that I love
you so much I can't tell you . . . I'm assuming you'll be in the George lunch-
time Wednesday? Darling, it's intolerable but it's wonderful.

   You are to be happy.

                                   Love (oh repeat, repeat, repeat!)
                                   Louis

TO *H. M. Collins*[1]   MS Bodleian

19 April 1960   [BBC]

Dear Sir,

   Thank you for your letter regarding Mr. George G. MacCann. I would
have answered this before but have been away on an Easter holiday.

   I have known Mr. MacCann since before the war and have on very many
occasions stayed with him in Northern Ireland. I am not technically
qualified to assess his qualities as a sculptor but very many people whose
opinion I trust, regard him as being one of the few first class sculptors that
Ireland (North and South) has produced. What I do know is that he is a
very good teacher. What makes him such is what shows in all his social
contacts, i.e. a most compelling and sympathetic personality, coupled with
an unusual eloquence or (one might say) a gift for hitting the nail on the
head.

   Mr. MacCann, when an art student in London, was, I understand, very
highly thought of by both his instructors and his colleagues. He then
became, with great success, a teacher of art in Northern Ireland but after
the outbreak of war joined the Inniskilling Fuseliers [*sic*] with whom he
served in India and Burma. This gives me occasion to point out that he is
an extremely 'good mixer' with people from all strata of society <u>and</u> of
every colour. He has also an insatiable curiosity about foreign countries
and their inhabitants.

---

1 – Addressed to Secretary to the Council for Overseas Colleges of Arts, Sciences and
Technology, 12 Lincoln's Inn Fields, London WC2.

I should add that he has a great capacity for taking pains and that, since his physique is good, he should be able to put a great deal of energy into the job in question. In sum, I think he is admirably suited for an appointment as Lecturer in Sculpture at the Nigerian College of Arts, Science and Technology.[1]

Yours truly,
(Louis MacNeice)

TO *T. S. Eliot* Faber archive

21 April 1960   BBC

Dear Tom,

This is just to let you know that I have now got nearly enough poems for a new collection. I am having a writing bout at the moment and it looks as if I shall have well over thirty poems ready within a few months time. I am not yet sure about the title but provisionally I will call it <u>The Wiper and other poems</u>.[2]

The collection could obviously be ready for next spring but perhaps you would let me know what would be your dead-line for Autumn publication.

With all best wishes to both of you,
Yours ever
Louis

TO *Peter Albyn Thorogood* MS BBC

23 June 1960   BBC

Dear Mr. Thorogood,

Please forgive me for having kept your poems so long.[3] The following of course is only one person's opinion, but there is no point in my giving it unless it is a candid one.

I am sure that in many of these poems you are trying to express something which is of importance to yourself but I am afraid that, so far

---

1 – MacCann needed three testimonials in support of his application (his other referees were Henry Moore and Anne Crookshank). The deadline for application was 31 March, as he explained in an apologetic letter to FLM of 23 March ('Sorry to be a bloody nuisance': *Ms Bodleian, Ms Res, c. 570*), over two weeks before FLM's letter to Collins.

2 – *Solstices*, which includes the poem 'The Wiper', was published in March 1961.

3 – Peter Thorogood had written to FLM on 10 June 1960 (having first sent his poems the previous Sept.).

as I am concerned, this something has just not been expressed adequately or convincingly. However valid one's original experience, unless you put it over in a way that is fresh and arresting, it will not go home to your reader. I am afraid I find nothing fresh in your diction while I find your images are far too often clichés. Some of your images also are errors of taste as in the opening couplet of 'The Continent of Death'. Also when you use words like 'sin' and 'love' they remain to me quite abstract. I should add that I did on the other hand find something refreshing in your lighter poem 'Hook, Line and Sinker'. But on the whole I am afraid I could not sincerely recommend these poems either for broadcasting or publication.

I trust you will not resent my expressing my views in this downright manner.

Yours sincerely,
Louis MacNeice

TO *Laurence Gilliam (BBC internal memo)*   MS BBC

20 July 1960   From: Mr. Louis MacNeice,
                                  5112 Main Block, T.C.[1]

Subject: 'THE PIN IS OUT'[2]

You will remember that the other day, in our conference about this script, C.T.P. maintained that it fell between two stools, i.e. that it should either have been a strictly naturalistic, factual play about South Africa (the country to be called by that name) or an out-and-out satirical fantasy, e.g. (C.T.P.'s own suggestion) 'An Insect Play'. I still think that the former

---

1 – Television Centre.
2 – Cf. initial proposal for this the previous October (FLM to P. H. Newby, 5 Oct. 1959, p. 651). On 18 July 1960, LG sent a memo to the Assistant Director of School Broadcasts and the Controller, Third Programme (Newby) supporting the proposal: 'I do not think the Union of South Africa should be identified, but that the listener should be left free to draw his own conclusions, as indeed he was with "Animal Farm" and "1984".' On 21 July, LG wrote: 'I can vouch for the general validity of the satire from personal knowledge of the Union, and I think the ventilation of these issues in dramatic form can have nothing but a healthy effect.' Nevertheless, a senior executive found the subject matter too controversial and the proposal was quashed: 'its effect must be to attack a Commonwealth Government at a particularly tricky and difficult moment in Commonwealth relations' (memo from Director of Sound Broadcasting (Lindsay Wellington), 2 Aug. 1960, *Ms BBC, MacNeice Scriptwriter file 1*). Some time earlier, perhaps anticipating the Corporation's reluctance, FLM had written to the Royal Court Theatre, asking if they would be interested in producing the play for the stage, but nothing came of it (FLM to G. Devine, 4 May 1960, *Ms Bodleian*).

would have meant too much complication and too much constriction, and that the latter would take away from the personal, <u>human</u> relationships which come to the fore in the second half of the programme. As I pointed out in an earlier memo, in <u>production</u> I would make sure that the <u>whole</u> piece was played naturalistically, thereby achieving a continuity which may not be apparent on the page and avoiding the danger of excessive cartoonery. I myself at our conference used the word 'cartoon', thinking e.g. of the Salesman on page 6, of the British Council type on page 24 following, of the drunken party on page 30 following, and of the theatre scene on page 44 following, but I disagree with C.T.P. that such radio cartoons are at a disadvantage compared with visual cartoons. On the contrary, I feel that the mere presence of human voices makes for a greater suspension of disbelief.

C.T.P. also felt (a) that the programme would be 'preaching to the converted' and (b) that the ordinary listener would find it 'a satire on the unknown' and therefore would feel all at sea. But (a) when I returned from South Africa last autumn I found that many of the nominally 'converted' were astounded by my reports of the country and (b) most people, surely, by now have <u>some</u> knowledge of what sort of place it is. In spirit I think my programme is true to South Africa, though in the letter, i.e. in certain details (see below), I have taken a few liberties which I could not have taken had I called the country South Africa.

The broader points which I wished to make are the following (in the order in which they first crop up in the programme):-

1. The casual way in which an educated but internationally ignorant Englishman (Roscoe) can travel about the world; the airports and the people passing through them are meant to underline his 'out of touchness'.
2. The doctrine of inequality.
3. Bureaucracy reaching the heights of lunacy.
4. The atmosphere of fear among the whites in a city like Johannesburg.
5. The complacency and inefficiency of most of those whites who are in opposition to the Government.
6. Corruption – passim
7. The toadying of certain Britons (Hilary) to a very unBritish regime.
8. The isolation of the liberals (Greta)
9. The paradox of oafs (the drunken Inners) championing 'culture'.

10. The ambivalent relations between white liberals (Greta) and native intellectuals (Kuluru).
11. The inevitable explosion of the natives, not only against their white oppressors but also against their white sympathisers.

As to the question whether, in detail, this programme corresponds to the facts of South African life, there are not really so many inaccuracies, but I can mention the following, the first two having been queried by C.T.P. himself:-

1. South African airlines do, in fact, serve drink, but I made them dry because there is a very strong dry faction in South Africa which has excluded women from the bars, closed the bars on Sundays, etc.
2. Africans and coloureds do not have to be cremated instead of being buried, but they do have to be buried in a different part of the cemetery from the whites.
3. Political parties in South Africa, unlike the U.S.A., do not, so far as I know, employ advertising agencies in their election campaigns, but the advertising spirit is certainly a strong element in both the main parties.
4. Nationalist orators do not make speeches to passengers arriving by air, but there is plenty of similar propaganda, e.g. in the printed handouts about the country supplied by South African airlines.
5. See page 20. All South Africa was not full of Bantu when the first Europeans got there, but here Arthur and I are, legitimately I think, over-simplifying.
6. Pastors of the Dutch Reformed Church do, I believe, sometimes drink to excess. Anyway, even if they don't, they are always being caught out in sexual scandals.

(Louis MacNeice)

TO *E. R. Dodds*   MS Bodleian

27 September [1960]   BBC

Dear E.R.D.,

In haste. My sister tells me you've very kindly suggested we have lunch together this Friday. I'd very much like to do this if you'll tell me when & where.

I gather various people have been talking to you about my break-up with Hedli. This must probably sound shockingly selfish (or silly) to you but I don't think when, after <u>years</u> of things going wrong, something appears irretrievable, it's really so selfish giving up trying to retrieve it. But I'd like to talk to you about this. The <u>positive</u> side (for me) is very good indeed; I feel it's worth having lived for. (& this is not middle-aged romanticism!)[1]

Must rush off to a playback –

Love to both of you, Louis

1 – Cf. FLM to Mary Wimbush, 11 April 1960, p. 664.

1961

TO *Dan Davin*[1]   MS Bodleian

19 January 1961   'The Character of Ireland'
                                         [letterhead]

Dear Dan,

Yes, I suggest we forget about the Old Woman and the U.N. Meanwhile here are some further notes on the book. Bertie and I agree that in a list which you sent him of suggested plates, far too many are apportioned to Maurice James Craig. We think that the following authors should all have plates going with their articles: Evans, Taylor, Wheeler, Sweeney, Simms, Bowan [*sic*], Ussher, Kelleher, Feelan [*sic*], Kuwitt [*sic*], M. J. Craig, O'Connor, MacLiammoir, Murphy, H. A. L. Craig.[2]

We also feel that in selecting the plates we should avoid having too many photographs of the stock pieces of scenery or the obvious beautiful buildings. We should prefer the emphasis to be on the human element.

Most of the articles don't seem to need much added to them. As I said I would myself write the coda to Ellis Firmor [*sic*]. We think we might ask Stewart to add a little bit about Chiefs of Staff etc. contributed by Ireland to the British Services in our own time.

The order we suggest for the whole book is as follows: Verse Prologue by L.M.[3]

1–Dan Davin (1913–90), native New Zealander, writer, publisher. Educ. Marist Brothers, Invercargill; Sacred Heart College, Auckland; Otago University, Dunedin; Balliol College, Oxford (Rhodes Scholar 1936). He worked for Oxford University Press as successively editor and academic publisher (1945–78) and commissioned the *Character of Ireland* book project – an anthology of essays, edited by FLM and WRR – which was never completed. He also wrote fiction, and a memoir, *Closing Times* (1975).
2–Other than the above-mentioned architectural historian Maurice James Craig, projected contributors for this ill-fated volume included Sam Hanna Bell (on Ulster), John Hewitt (on the visual arts), and those listed in the letter: Estyn Evans (author of *The Personality of Ireland*), Geoffrey Taylor, Mortimer Wheeler, David Greene, Máire Sweeney (née MacNeill), Katherine Simms, Elizabeth Bowen, Arland Ussher, John Kelleher, Jim Phelan, A. T. Q. Stewart, John Mogey, J. C. Beckett, Frank O'Connor, Una Ellis-Fermor, Micheal MacLiammoir, H. A. L. Craig. Verse Epilogue by Rodgers.
3–Repr. CP07, 779–82.

1) Evans : Land and People
2) Taylor : National History
3) Wheeler : Archaeology
4) Greene : The Irish Language and its Literature
5) Sweeney : Folklore
6) Simms : Ireland and Her Invaders
7) Bowen : The Big House
8) Usher : The Irish Rebel
9) a. Stewart : The Wild Geese and other Migrants
   b. Stewart : The Irish Navigator
10) O'Donnall : The Shuttle between the Emigrant and Home (this is being re-written)
11) Kelleher : The Irish in the USA
12) — : The Irish in Australia[1]
13) Davin : The Irish in New Zealand
14) Phelan : The Drifting Irish
15) Jordan : The Roman Catholic Church
16) Mogey : The Presbyterian Church
17) Beckett : The Church of Ireland
18) Inglis : Government in the Republic
19) Wallace : Government in Northern Ireland
20) — : Agriculture and Industry (author to be found for this as soon as possible)
21) Maurice James Craig: Architecture
22) O'Boyle : Folk Music
23) O'Connor : The English Language and its Literature
24) Ellis-Firmer [sic]: The Drama
25) MacLiammoir : Aspects of the Theatre
26) Murphy : The Horse
27) H. A. L. Craig : Sport
Verse Epilogue : W.R.R.

Perhaps I can talk about the book when I come to Oxford. In the meantime, to change the subject, could you please remember any nice bits of gossip in connection with the Poetry Election and also suggest some

---

1–'The Irish in Australia' was later assigned to Brian Fitzpatrick (1905–65), historian of Australia, first General Secretary, Australian Council for Civil Liberties, and radical publicist. He was commissioned on the recommendation of Clem Christensen, editor of the Melbourne literary journal *Meanjin*, and he delivered an article now preserved in the papers of Brian Fitzpatrick in the National Library of Australia.

contacts for Vicky and me.[1] I'll let you know exactly when we are coming. Looking forward to seeing you both.

Yours ever,
Louis MacNeice

P.S. Yes, if it is convenient, I think I <u>should</u> like a bed. It would probably be just for one night.

TO *Harley J. Usill*[2]   MS Bodleian [unsigned carbon]

24 January 1961   [BBC]

Dear Mr. Usill,

Regarding my selection of poems for your recording on February 1st, I have looked up the file and find that you only specify 'a selection of my poetry for a 12" long-playing record'. I should like to know exactly what overall time I should aim at and when I know this I will time the individual poems which I will select from the following list:

From <u>Eighty-Five Poems</u>, published by Faber and Faber: Conversation, The Muse, The Cyclist, Dublin, The Left-Behind, The Gone-Tomorrow, Death of an Old Lady, Bagpipe Music, The British Museum Reading Room, Les Sylphides, Christina, Slow Movement, The Sunlight on the Garden, Meeting Point, A Toast, The Merman, Prognosis, Nuts in May, Brother Fire, Prayer in Mid-Passage, Prayer Before Birth, Rites of War.

From my forthcoming book <u>Solstices</u>: Apple Blossom, Dogs in the Park, Half Truth from Cape Town, The Wiper, The Truisms.

Also possibly one section (IX I think) from Autumn Journal and possibly an excerpt of about 60 lines from Autumn Sequel.[3]

Yours sincerely
Louis MacNeice

---

1 – Election for Oxford Poetry Chair. Cf. 'That Chair of Poetry' (*NS*, 10 Feb. 1961, 210), repr. *SLC*, 225–30. Cf. FLM to John Freeman, 27 Jan. 1961, p. 674, n. 1. 'Vicky' is probably Victor Weisz (1913–66) whose cartoons appeared regularly in the *NS*.

2 – Harley Usill (1925–91), in 1951 co-founded Argo Records, which was later absorbed by Decca. FLM's recording was part of their well-known 'The Poet Speaks' series. Addressed to Argo Record Co. Ltd, 113 Fulham Road, London SW3.

3 – The final selection for *Louis MacNeice Reading His Own Poems* (Argo RG196, 1961), was as follows: 'Conversation', 'Invocation', 'Carrickfergus', 'Dublin', 'The Left-Behind', 'The Back-Again', 'The Gone-Tomorrow', 'Apple Blossom', 'The Cyclist', 'The Nurse' (i.e. 'The Muse'), 'The Truisms', 'Sunlight on the Garden', 'The British Museum Reading Room',

TO *John Freeman*[1]   MS Bodleian [carbon copy] MS Sussex

27 January 1961   [BBC]

Dear John Freeman,

I see in this week's Statesman you have a piece by John Morgan about the England–Wales rugby match that was played in Cardiff last Saturday. I found this a coincidence as I was on the point of proposing a similar article to you (I had already mentioned this to Walter Allen) hinged on to England's next international, i.e. with Ireland in Dublin on February 11th.[2] What I had thought of was 'a peripheral' treatment, e.g. possibly a cross-cutting of the Brains and Brawns of Dublin. If I went over on this occasion, I should be staying with a large farmer who once played in the second row for Ireland in a disastrous match against the South Africans; through him and others I could meet quite a lot of the Brawns. As for the Brains, they are lying about in all directions.

I could easily over a week-end run into by arrangement such people as Honor Tracy, Sean O'Faolain, Cyril Cusack (who last summer got some award in Paris for the best acting of the year), Austin Clarke (neglected poet), Patric [*sic*] Kavanagh (less neglected poet), Brendon [*sic*] Behan, Norah McGuinness (painter and protégée of the late W. B. Yeats) and the staff of Radio Eireann (which n.b. has just become a Corporation like the BBC instead of being a branch of the Post Office).

I don't know whether this will appeal to you in the least, but, if it does, what I should really like of course is the normal fee for an article of this sort <u>plus</u> something for travelling expenses.[3] If I did this I could let you have a copy on Monday February 13th.

'Bagpipe Music', *Autumn Journal* IX, 'Prognosis', 'Nuts in May', 'Brother Fire', 'Rites of War', 'Death of an Old Lady', 'Christina', 'Meeting Point', 'A Toast', 'The Merman', 'Selva Oscura', 'Prayer Before Birth'. There are errors on contents list and record label (Armitage, 110–11).

1 – John Freeman (b.1915), MBE, politician and journalist. Educ. Westminster and Brasenose College, Oxford. Joined the Labour Party in 1933; MP for Watford 1945. Assistant editor (1951), deputy editor (1958) and editor (1961–5) of the *New Statesman*. Later British High Commissioner to India and British Ambassador to Washington. FLM may have discussed this matter informally with a *NS* editor the night before, when he attended their party at 7 Albemarle Street (Diary, Jan. 1961, *Ms Bodleian, Ms Res, c. 979*).

2 – Ireland won, 11–8.

3 – Freeman offered him 20 guineas, stipulating 'the match should be used only as a peg on which to hang the Dublin gossip since the Sundays will have reported the football' (JF to FLM, 1 Feb. 1961, *Ms Bodleian*). Ultimately he didn't submit the article, claiming his driver in Ireland ran out of petrol (FLM to JF, 13 Feb. 1961, ibid.).

As regards the Oxford project, which comes up a week before that, I am told by my Oxford contacts that the two lady candidates for the Chair of Poetry, who have recently been discovered to be technically 'ineligible', will almost certainly be 'made honest women' before the election.[1] So on the assumption that the story is still wanted, I am proposing to visit Oxford on February 3rd and 4th. If by any chance they are not thus redeemed – which would mean that Graves would walk it – I suppose one could still make a quite nice (and typically Oxonian) story out of there being no story.

Yours sincerely,
Louis MacNeice

TO *John Lehmann*   MS Texas

8 February [1961]   BBC

Dear John,

This is just to thank you very much for your letter about my poem for your last number; I am so glad you like it – & remember its predecessors.[2] I'm sorry you're relinquishing that editorial chair & would like to take this opportunity to congratulate you on having filled it so well.[3]

Yes, indeed; let us meet soon. I'd like to hear what you're going to do now. I for my part am about to go half time on the B.B.C., i.e. free lance the other half of the year. A gamble!

I dare say you've heard about my new way of life. For future reference, this is a good thing & – so far as I'm concerned – permanent.

Yours ever
Louis

---

1 – Election for the Poetry Chair, Oxford. 'That Chair of Poetry' (*NS*, 10 Feb. 1961, 210), repr. *SLC*, 225–30. The 'lady candidates' were Enid Starkie and Helen Gardner. A third candidate was F. R. Leavis, but Robert Graves won the election. Freeman wrote on 9 Feb. to apologise for the fact that 'some copies' of the *NS* had attributed the Oxford article to one 'Louise' MacNeice but FLM replied reassuringly that 'This happens to be an error to which I am accustomed', claiming Louis Untermeyer had once written: 'This poetess was educated at Marlborough . . .' (FLM to JF, 10 Feb. 1961, *Ms Bodleian*).
2 – 'Sleeping Winds', *LM*, March 1961, 12; the immediately previous poems to which he refers were 'Reflections', 'Restaurant Car' and 'The Wiper' (*LM*, May 1960, 12–14), but over the years he had published many poems in the journal.
3 – JL had edited *LM* since 1954. His successor was Alan Ross.

23 March 1961   From: Mr. Louis MacNeice,
                                 Features, 1053 B.H.[1]
                                 Ext. 2957/2970

Subject: WELSH PROGRAMMES[2]

When in Cardiff last week I was unfortunately not able to see either Hywel Davies, who was just about to leave for America on a fforde [*sic*] foundation, or Aneurin Talfan, who was ill, but I had several discussions about possible programmes with other members of the Welsh Regional staff, in particular with Emyr Humphreys.[3] I still, I am glad to say, appear to be persona grata with the Welsh Region.

1. The first subject we discussed was the to-ing and fro-ing or giving and taking between the Welsh and the Irish. One of the first examples of this is the abduction of St. Patrick and there are also some nice things in the Mavinogion; in recent times there has been quite an amount of cross-immigration as shown e.g. by the names of certain rugby players in Wales such as O'Connor.[4] No-one, however, had done any research on this subject, so we did not know what it would add up to and merely agreed that it is something which might be looked into hereafter.

2. The second suggestion was very much favoured by Emyr Humphreys, who by the way is taking six months' leave of absence from the beginning of October, and pointed out that therefore it would be additionally helpful if I produced anything I wrote myself to do with

---

1 – Broadcasting House.

2 – BBC Wales began in 1964 but the BBC had been producing programmes out of a small studio in Broadway, Cardiff since the mid-1950s. The Director of Welsh programmes was Hywel Davies. There is no record of a Wales programme produced by FLM. However, he did give a short talk about Dylan Thomas on *Woman's Hour* (Light Programme, 16 Jan. 1962) and appeared on a television discussion on Thomas, 30 April 1962 (*In Wales Today*). Cf. 'Programmes and Broadcasts by Louis MacNeice on Sound and Television', *Ms BBC, R94/2.509/1/MacNeice*.

3 – Aneurin Talfan Davies (also Aneurin ap Talfan) (1909–80), Welsh poet, broadcaster; Emyr Humphreys (b.1919), Welsh novelist, poet. Author of *Hear and Forgive* (1953), *A Toy Epic* (1958) and other works.

4 – Welsh scrum-half Tony O'Connor (b.1934) was capped for Wales five times, 1960–2. His elder brother, flanker Rory O'Connor (b.1932) was capped only once for Wales, against England at Twickenham, 19 Jan. 1957. Records show that Irish names on the Welsh side were highly unusual.

Wales. This suggestion is for one or possibly two programmes (i.e. dividing Wales into North and South) consisting of a modern itinerary by a non-Welshman (myself) cross-cutting past and present and using both literary material, to be read by readers, and actuality material to be recorded on a midget. For purposes of comparison he suggested that I should make use of Geraldus Cambrensis and Pennant's tours of Wales.[1]

for a
modern
reader

One good example of the material:-

In Port Madoc there are unpublished Shelley papers which include an appeal for the building of the 'Cob' across the Estuary; this is regarded as one of the two chief engineering feats in the district, the other being an atomic station at Trawsfynydd.[2] When Shelley lived in these parts (I gather the background appears in Queen Mab) so also of course did Peacock.[3] Just to enrich the mixture, Richard Hughes who lives opposite the 'Cob' is at present engaged on a huge novel on the theme of war and peace, the first instalment of which will come out this summer.[4]

Other literary figures, who wrote or write in English and could therefore be introduced, are the following:

Landor (Monmouthshire) who could be paralleled with Shelley as while he was there, it seems, he agitated about the Poor Law.

David Jones, who comes from the same place as Landor.

Gerard Manley Hopkins (Flintshire).

William Barnes (near Abergavenny) who went for a time to Wales because his theories drove him to learn Welsh.

1 – Thomas Pennant, *A Tour in Wales*, 4 vols (1778–83). Geraldus Cambrensis or Gerald of Wales (c.1146–c.1223), archdeacon of Brecon and the author of chronicles.
2 – The twin-reactor nuclear power plant at Trawsfynydd, N. Wales, was used to generate electricity for the national grid. It was fully operational between 1965 and 1998, but has been decommissioned.
3 – Shelley rented a house in 1812 called Tan-yr-Allt, near Porthmadog, close to the village built by William Maddocks on land reclaimed from the sea: the 'cob' (dyke) protected the land from the tide. Thomas Love Peacock (1785–1866), romantic poet and novelist, had lived in the area in 1810 for a year or so, at Tan-y-Bwlch near Maentrog, Merioneth.
4 – Richard Hughes, *The Fox in the Attic* (1961).

James Hanley (Montgomery).[1]

If the idea of such itineraries appeals to anyone, I suggest that I should do a little Welsh tour first thing in October when I return to duty with the Corporation and when the weather will be still plausible. Emyr thinks that I ought to enter Wales via Tintern Abbey.

(Louis MacNeice)

TO *Charles Monteith*[2]

Faber archive

29 March 1961   BBC

Dear Charles,

It has just come into my mind to write another little children's story.[3] This is because I suddenly remembered the goats of Croaghaun in Achill.[4] Did you know that quite some time ago some domestic goats in Achill ran away and proceeded to live on the ledges of the very high cliffs at the west end of the island? Apparently, through natural selection, they have now reverted to a type of Caucasian wild goat, hence my story.

I want to follow the careers of three young goats. The first wants to become a tame goat but no-one at first will accept him as he looks uncouth. The second, hearing that he is a Caucasian type, sets out to find the Caucasus. The last stays put because he falls in love with a lady goat on the cliff.

---

1 – Walter Savage Landor (1775–1864) lived at Llanthony Abbey, Monmouthshire; David Jones (1895–1974), poet who was born in Brockley, Kent, of Welsh parentage (his father was from Flintshire, N. Wales); G. M. Hopkins (1844–89) attended the Jesuit college, St Beuno's, N. Wales during the 1870s; William Barnes (1801–86), chiefly associated with Dorset dialect; James Hanley (1897–1985) novelist and playwright, author of *Drift* (1930), *The Furys* (1935), *The Kingdom* (1978) and other works, lived in Wales for over thirty years and is buried there.

2 – Charles Montgomery Monteith (1921–95), publisher. Educ. RBAI, Magdalen College, Oxford, All Souls (Prize Fellowship); called to the Bar at Gray's Inn. Royal Inniskilling Fusiliers 1940–5; Fellow of All Souls 1948–88. Joined Faber and Faber 1953 and became a director the following year; vice-chairman 1974; chairman 1977–80. Director of Poetry Book Society 1966–81. Hon. DLitt New University of Ulster 1980 and University of Kent 1982.

3 – He had previously published *The Penny that Rolled Away* (New York, 1954), published by Faber as *The Sixpence that Rolled Away* (1956).

4 – FLM had visited Achill in 1929 and, with Hedli, Dan and the Johnstons, in 1945 (cf. FLM to Denis Johnston, 20 July 1945, pp. 457–8; to ERD, 31 July 1945, pp. 458–9; and to Ruth Jones, 8 Aug. 1945, pp. 459–60). The children's story on the goats of Croaghaun was never published.

If you would like this it obviously ought to be illustrated. If I let you have the manuscript soon, would there be any chance of getting it out for Christmas?

Yours,
Louis MacNeice

TO *James Michie*[1]   MS Bodleian [unsigned carbon]

27 April 1961   [BBC]

Dear Mr. Michie,

In haste, having had your telegram. I am sorry I have taken such a time dealing with the Fitzgerald translation of <u>The Odyssey</u> but for the last few weeks I have been very distracted by various things, including a change of contract. I could write in much more detail about this but I suppose what you primarily want to know is whether I recommend this version or not. I do.[2]

There are many ways of translating <u>The Odyssey</u> and this is one.[3] I must admit that at first sight I did not fall for it but this is probably because, if I were translating it myself, I would <u>not</u> use Fitzgerald's metre (a somewhat loose form of traditional blank verse) but would go for a longer line with more of what Gerard Manley Hopkins called 'slack' and therefore more pace. I found, however, that this version grows on one. It is very honest and, unlike T. E. Lawrence's prose translation for instance, it is thoroughly consistent.[4] The diction throughout is penny plain, yet quite often Fitzgerald can get a lift out of very ordinary words e.g. 'Rag of man that I am, is this the end of me?' A minor criticism I would make is that, where Homer has his famous stock epithets or stock lines such as the one about the Dawn, Fitzgerald seems compelled to keep varying his translation of these. But, as I said, this is a minor point. The main point is that this

1 – James Michie (1927–2007), publisher with Heinemann, translator and poet. Educ. MC, Trinity College, Oxford. With Kingsley Amis, he edited *Oxford Poetry* (1949). His translations include work by Catullus, Virgil, Ovid, Euripides, and Horace's *Odes* (1964). His poetry includes *Possible Laughter* (1959) and *Collected Poems* (1994). In 1962, he became editorial director at Bodley Head.
2 – He reviewed this translation the following year: 'Blood and Fate: *The Odyssey* translated by Robert Fitzgerald; *Patrocleia*, Book XVI of Homer's *Iliad*, adapted by Christopher Logue' (*Listener*, 4 Oct. 1962, 527), repr. *SLC*, 234–7.
3 – FLM translated part of the poem for radio later in 1961: cf. *The Odyssey*, broadcast 6 Oct.–22 Dec.
4 – *The Odyssey of Homer*, trans. T. E. Lawrence (Oxford, 1932).

version is eminently readable and could easily be swallowed and digested by the modern non-classical reader. It is quite as readable as the Penguin prose translation by E. V. Rieu but does not suffer from Rieu's recurrent bathos while on the positive side it scores over Rieu rhythmically.[1]

I am returning the proofs under separate cover.

Yours sincerely,
(Louis MacNeice)

TO *Miss J. Freeman*[2]　　　　　　　　　　　　　　　　MS Bodleian

2 May 1961　　　　　　　　　　BBC

Dear Miss Freeman,

Thank you for your letter asking me about my poem <u>Snow</u>.[3] I have never understood why people should think this a difficult poem; it is probably because they approach it from a primarily symbolical angle and so do not realise that it is almost a piece of factual reporting. In metaphysical language the theme is plurality – a theme which is present for all of us every moment of every day but which does not usually strike us with a sudden emotional impact. In this case it did!

I <u>was</u> in fact on the day which occasioned the poem sitting in my room beside an open fire eating tangerines and there <u>were</u> roses in the window and outside it did begin to snow (though I perhaps should confess that the window was not a bow window).[4] What excited me was the sudden awareness that all these things were going on at the same time <u>in their own right</u>; this was enhanced by, among other things, the colour clash between the tangerines and the pink roses and also by the hardness or sheer pippiness of the tangerine pips, of which there were only too many – but these are minor points. The major point comes in the last line, which puzzles you. There was no question of the roses and the snow ever <u>merging</u>. Each was to retain its identity for ever and in my mood at the time I was glad about this.[5]

1 – *The Odyssey*, trans. E. V. Rieu (1946).
2 – Addressed to 457, Chanterlands Avenue, Hull, Yorkshire.
3 – *Listener*, 27 March 1935, 480. *Poems* (1935), CP66, CP07, 24.
4 – Dodds recalled: '"Snow" was conceived on a winter evening at Sir Harry's Road [Birmingham]. Out of doors it was snowing, but in the study window Bet had placed a big bowl of roses from our heated green-house, "soundlessly collateral and incompatible", while we sat round the fire eating tangerines' (*Missing Persons*, 117).
5 – In fair copy draft of 'Snow', dated 'Jan. 1935', the author has altered in pencil 'things being different' to 'things being various', and 'Indomitably' becomes 'Incorrigibly' (*Ms Bodleian, Box 30, Ms Notebook*).

I hope this may throw a little light on the subject.
Best wishes.

Yours sincerely,
(Louis MacNeice)
Features Department

TO *Daniel MacNeice*   MS Texas

10 May [1961]   BBC [letterhead]

Dearest Dan,

This is just to wish you many Happy Returns etc. I don't seem to have heard from you for a very long time indeed. Someone said you were planning to teach. Is that so?

I've just gone on to a half-time contract with the BBC (shall be free-lancing the other half) but the above address will still find me (but letters to be marked Personal).[1] I think I ought to tell you that Hedli & I split up last summer; we still of course are very fond of each other but latterly had been getting on too badly. I am now living with someone else – I don't think you ever met her – called Mary Wimbush & we are very happy.

Bimba is in her last term at school – she has to do the inevitable exams this term! – & has been accepted by the Slade for the autumn. There is a problem as to where she is to live as Hedli is more or less emigrating to Kinsale in Co. Cork where she is going to run some sort of steak house.[2]

Talking of musical chairs & such, did you know that Tom Agnew, after completely vanishing from everyone's ken for a year or two, has been discovered living mysteriously in Boulogne![3] Meanwhile, Ellie, I gather, is being horsey & doggy in Co. Galway.

I have to go now to look at a flat in Bloomsbury. Do write. And look after yourself.

much love,
D.

---

1 – As from 1 July of this year, FLM would work only twenty-six weeks per year for the following three years. He had first joined the wartime staff of the BBC in May 1941.

2 – The Spinnaker, Kinsale.

3 – Tom Agnew: see FLM to MM, 5 July 1950, n. 1, p. 535.

TO *Charles Monteith*   Faber archive

15 September 1961   [BBC]

Dear Charles,

   While on my holiday in the Channel Islands I had a sudden idea to
which I should welcome your reaction.[1] As there are many people who
seem to prefer their books of verse homogeneous and as there are also
many people who go for anything to do with travel, I thought that, if you
could publish it in time for Christmas 1962 I might collect my <u>Poems of
Place</u>.

   There would be about sixty-odd of these, including excerpts from
<u>Autumn Journal</u>, and <u>Autumn Sequel</u>, also two or three complete poems
from <u>Ten Burnt Offerings</u>, also two or three unpublished poems. N.B.
many of these, possibly the bulk of the book[,] would not have been
included in my <u>Eighty Five Poems</u>.

   The territories covered would be

    I

        1. Ireland
        2. England, Scotland and Wales
        3. Iceland and the North Sea

    II

        1. France
        2. Spain
        3. Italy
        4. Greece

    III

        1. India
        2. Pakistan
        3. Ceylon
        4. Malaya

    IV

        1. Egypt
        2. Sudan
        3. Ghana
        4. Union of South Africa

    V

        1. U.S.A.

1–FLM took holidays at Sark.

If you are interested in this, I could assemble the whole thing very quickly indeed.[1]

By the way, I hope to knock off that children's story soon. Could you let me know when you would like it for when?

With best wishes.

Yours,
Louis [*signed*]

TO *Corinna MacNeice*[2]   MS Bodleian

15 September [1961?]   BBC

Dearest Bimba,

V. sorry to have just missed you in London. Kitty said you had found Italy very hot.[3] Kitty's charlady expressed alarm & despondency about that heavy exotic packing case you had left in the kitchen. Whatever was it for?!

You should by now have got what I assume are your exam results. I was tempted to open them but was prevented by principle. I hope you still have the forms I gave you so that you can fill in the lot & send them to the L.C.C.[4]

Sark was great fun but strenuous; the cliff paths gave me Charwomen's Ankles. And nobody ever seems to go to bed there; there is a midget millionaire (c. 4 ft 6?) who will buy anyone champagne at sight.

1 – Members of the Faber Board decided unanimously against this proposal (Circular report, 21 Sept. 1961, *Faber archive, Monteith file*). Monteith later wrote: 'the general reaction hasn't been a very enthusiastic one. We all rather feel that it would probably be a mistake to publish a book consisting largely of poems which have already appeared in other volumes. Indeed, the ordinary book buyer might think it rather a swizz!' (CM to FLM, 5 Oct. 1961, ibid.).

2 – Brigid Corinna MacNeice (b.1943), painter and video artist. Educ. Hanford School, Dorset; Cone Ripman Arts Educational School; Queen's College, Harley Street, and the Slade School of Fine Art. Formerly she was art designer at Sean Kenny's Design Development Studio, London; lecturer at Croydon College of Art and artistic director of the October Gallery, London. She has had a long association with the Theatre of All Possibilities, and is associate member of Wise Fool, a nonprofit theatre arts project based in New Mexico. She has exhibited her work at galleries in London, Oxford, Belfast, Dublin, Berlin, Kathmandu, Fort Worth (TX), San Francisco, San Marcos (NM) and Santa Fe (NM), where she now lives and works.

3 – Katherine (Kitty) Church (1910–99), painter. Educ. Royal Academy School; Slade. M. (1937) Anthony West (illegitimate son of H. G. Wells and Rebecca West). She lived in Tarrant Hinton, Dorset.

4 – Application forms for London County Council college grant (to attend the Slade).

I hear that Dr. Schwarz gave glowing accounts of the Kinsale cuisine.[1]

Am snowed under with work, so must really be methodical in the oncoming months.

Would you by the way like that old grey carpet of mine laid down in your room? There's nowhere else to put it & it <u>would</u> warm your room up for the winter – apart from soundproofing it a bit (Kitty mentioned that she was sensitive – in the wrong sense – to jazz!)

I must go down town now & meet Ken Tynan.[2] Have a good time & don't bark your knuckles too much on the lobster claws.

Lots of love,
D.

P.S. If you have a chance, do get as far west at least as Glengariff – preferably Kenmare.

TO *Corinna MacNeice*
MS Bodleian

20 September [1961]   BBC

Dearest Bimba,

I was v. sorry to hear about the car accident; hope everyone is now all right again. Before I forget, can you say that I have settled the telephone account for Clarence Terrace which I had sent on. The Telephone Manager couldn't wait any longer!

How were your exam results & did you have those forms to fill in & send on to the L.C.C.? I take it you'll be coming back about the end of next week? By the way, <u>could</u> you bring the <u>Oxford book of 17th Century Verse</u>, <u>Hardy</u> & <u>Trevelyan's Social History</u> with you?[3]

---

1 – Jacob ('Jake') Schwarz, an all too persistent correspondent, was formerly a Brooklyn dentist and also a dealer in authorial manuscripts (many of which ended up at HRC, Texas). He ran the Ulysses bookshop, Bloomsbury, in the late 1920s, and later had such a reputation for buying manuscripts very cheaply from impecunious writers that Samuel Beckett called him the 'Great Extractor'. Carlton Lake once said of him that 'His letters boiled down to something not much more than: "If you've got the money, I've got the stuff"' ('Ed the Collector, Jake the Dentist and Beckett: A Tale that Ends in Texas', *New York Times*, 6 Sept. 1987).

2 – Kenneth Tynan (1927–80), drama critic for the *Observer* 1954–63 and literary manager of the National Theatre 1963–9.

3 – G. M. Trevelyan, *English Social History; A Survey of Six Centuries, Chaucer to Queen Victoria* (1942).

I saw Goronwy yesterday who told me Lucy ran into you in the Sistine Chapel. And that Jenny has fallen in love with an Algerian. Both the girls, he says, are now violently opposed to everything intelligent![1]

I had lunch with the Slatterys on Sunday.[2] They say they had a wonderful week in Connemara – sunshine all the time & two bathes a day.

I seem to have the prospect of a very busy autumn, both B.B.C.wise & otherwise. Don't at the moment know where to start. I am just about to do my last bit of telly-crit for the Statesman.[3]

I read a piece in the paper about Tony O'Reilly's engagement.[4] You remember: the redheaded rugby star you failed to recognise. I gather he now has a job in Cork. I suppose, by the way, Eddie Sackville West hasn't shown up yet. They say he's living somewhere in the country.

I have joined the new club called The Establishment, to be run by the four Beyond the Fringe boys.[5] I think it opens next month.

Lots of love,
D.

P.S. Had a postcard from Dan for my birthday.

1 – Goronwy Rees (see FLM to Hedli, 19 March 1948, n. 2, p. 513) had five children, including two daughters.
2 – Jerry Slattery was FLM's family doctor. He read medicine at TCD, fought in World War II and became friends with Reggie Smith and Olivia Manning in Egypt. He had a large medical practice in Hampstead, where many of his patients were actors, writers or politicians. With his wife Johnnie he threw legendary parties at home in Belsize Park, especially when Ireland played at Twickenham. BCM remembers his robust medical advice: his recommendation for teenage insomnia was to 'read a book' (BCM, private correspondence, 2008).
3 – He is referring to 'Pins and Needles' (NS, 29 Sept. 1961, 450). FLM wrote over half a dozen TV reviews for the NS in 1961, including 'Godot on TV' (7 July, 27–8); 'Look at the Faces' (21 July, 95), 'I Got Those Cathode Blues' (4 Aug., 164), 'Roll on Reality' (18 Aug., 225), 'Snow and Rock' (1 Sept., 284) and 'Two Plays, and Spike' (15 Sept., 358).
4 – Anthony (Tony) John Francis O'Reilly (b.1936), Irish entrepreneur, industrialist and legendary rugby international. M. (1962) Susan Cameron.
5 – The 'Beyond the Fringe boys' were Peter Cook (who founded the Establishment club in 1961, with business partner Nick Luard), Alan Bennett, Jonathan Miller and Dudley Moore. Performers at the club during the early 1960s included Frankie Howerd, Lenny Bruce and many others.

TO *Corinna MacNeice*   MS Bodleian

27 September [1961]   BBC

Dearest Bimba,

In haste. Am fresh (if that's the word) from my Armenian dentist & am preparing for a tricky negotiation with the people whom the BBC, lowering their voices, describe as 'The Competitor'.[1]

Thank you for your letter. I didn't get it for some days as I was out of London, so it seems pointless now sending on the things you asked for as your Slade business starts next Monday, Oct. 2nd! It <u>would</u> help by the way if you could let me know what day you're arriving.

Do you realise that Dr Conor Cruise O'Brien, who's so much in the news these days, once visited Clarence Terrace & went for a walk in the park with Phoebe & me? A v. sympathetic man.[2]

Had a royal command yesterday to go & drink champagne informally with T. S. Eliot on his 73rd birthday. He was v. benign, though frail. I asked him if he knew Dr Schwarz & he said 'Jasus!' – or words to that effect.

It seems that it's now easier to get tickets for <u>Beyond the Fringe</u>. Would you like to go to it?

I saw Isabel Rawsthorne about two days ago. Alan was just due to come out of hospital, where he's been for 3 weeks, so they're going off to Wales to recuperate.

Has Gerald Hanley turned up yet in Kinsale?[3] He said he would.

Must now stand by for the telephone.

> Lots of love,
> D.

P.S. How is Tara? Met someone the other day who said Afghans were a doubtful-tempered breed.

---

1 – ITV (Independent Television) was launched in London as a commercial television station in Sept. 1955, and in the Midlands and the North in the spring of the following year.

2 – Dr Conor Cruise O'Brien (1917–2009), at that time UN Chief Political Representative in Katanga, DR Congo, had only days earlier been praised by senior UN officials for efforts to prevent the secession of Katanga, as a result of which he and UN officers had come under attack by the Katangese, fighting under Moise Tshombe. On 18 Sept. O'Brien narrowly escaped death when a Katanga jet fighter strafed UN headquarters in Elisabethville while he was standing outside the building, talking to journalists. ('Dr O'Brien Escapes in Katanga Air Attack', *The Times*, 19 Sept. 1961, 8; 'Dr O'Brien Praised for Action', *The Times*, 21 Sept. 1961, 12). O'Brien was the subject of further publicity in ensuing months when he resigned from the UN, divorced his wife and married poet Máire MacEntee (Máire Mhac an tSaoi, b.1922), daughter of Seán MacEntee, the Irish Deputy Prime Minister (Tanaiste).

3 – Gerald Hanley (1916–92), novelist, author of *Drinkers of Darkness* (1955) and *Journey Homeward* (1961).

TO *Daniel MacNeice*

28 September [1961]   BBC [letterhead]

Dear Dan,

I was delighted to get a card from you for my birthday – which by the way I spent in the island of Sark – remember? I enjoyed Sark but going up & down all those cliffs gave me charwomen's ankles.

Am now living in the top two floors of a house belonging to your old friend Kitty Church (Mrs Canning came to stay there one night). It's supposed to be a furnished flat but Bimba (who is still in a somewhat beat phase) began by throwing all the furniture out of her room. She's at the moment over in Co. Cork acting as a waitress & breaker up of lobsters in Hedli's restaurant but is due back in the next few days to attend the Slade. By the way I notice that Maurice Feild is still teaching there.[1]

The autumn promises to be uncomfortably busy. I have to knock off a radio play about the wicked press, to be called <u>The Press Gang</u>, & at the same time write the first part of a history of Astrology (!) – a kind of study of human weakness. But haven't yet reached the point where I can understand a horoscope.

I dare say you've been reading lately about Dr Conor Cruise O'Brien in Katanga. He's a nice man whom I once spent the afternoon drinking with – along with George MacCann – in Dublin. Someone who's just gone over to Belfast by the way reports that George is getting daily more like Gully [*sic*] Jimson in The Horse's Mouth.[2] I haven't seen him since last New Year when I spent a few days in Botanic Avenue. Mercy was as large as ever.

Of the people you know Peter Duval Smith is the luckiest; he has – God knows how – got himself a job with commercial television as a roving interviewer – £100 a week, I believe, & lavish expenses.[3] He has just come back from Brazil & his next assignment is the Irish elections. But he doesn't like going round with a gang of cameras etc. Laurence Gilliam is just back from Tanganyika where Kathleen Stahl's been helping him to interview the Chagga. And Julian Lee's mother, whom I met in a restaurant where Mary

---

1 – Maurice Feild (1905–88) had previously been Art master at the Downs School when Auden taught there in the early 1930s. William Coldstream brought him to the Slade in 1954.
2 – Gulley Jimson, painter hero of Joyce Cary's First Trilogy, book 3 of which is *The Horse's Mouth* (1944).
3 – Peter Duval Smith (1926–69), BBC producer. Born in Tanganyika and educated in South Africa, he was a friend of William Empson (and the lover of his wife, Hetta). A sociable, indeed flamboyant personality, he had visited the MacNeices in Athens in 1950. They enjoyed him immensely, even though he had once in a fit of pique thrown a half-empty bottle of brandy through their front window. He died in Saigon, on assignment.

& I were having dinner, says J. is doing well in Canada. Margaret Gardiner when she's not demonstrating in Trafalgar Square, spends a lot of time in a cottage she has in the Orkneys. And Mrs Canning is still running that school.[1]

London has changed a lot since you were here. They keep pulling down the nicer buildings & putting up great slabs of coloured ice. There is far more variety in dress, & proliferation of coffee bars & Indian restaurants, lots of West Indians conducting buses etc., an insoluble traffic problem & a boom in paper backs & long playing records. There has also been a great increase in strip tease clubs & such!

I haven't been abroad for 2 years but am hoping to go to Paris at the end of October. I hear terrible reports of what Tourism is doing to Greece – soda fountains everywhere, a face-lift for the Parthenon etc. Kevin who is living in Athens now must be hating it.[2] But I imagine that places like Icaria will still be fairly untouched. By the way Ghika (you remember – the painter) split up with his wife Tiggy & is living on Hydra with Mrs Rex Warner who was once Lady Rothschild.[3] [*vertical left hand margin:*] Have just realized it's lunch time. Please write some time.

much love, D.

TO *Allen and Isabella Tate*   MS Princeton

3 November [1961]   BBC

Dear Allen & Isabella,

Thank you very much for your letters. I had meant to answer Isabella's long ago – the one about my poems, which I much appreciated – but we went off to the Channel Islands & mislaid everything & you know how it is!

We are now in our eyrie – two floors level with the treetops & have acquired (long story) a Siamese cat. Mary is in great form & so is Bimba, my daughter, who is going to the Slade School of Art. We get more & more depressed by the world but better in ourselves.

1 – Enid Canning ran the Hanford Prep School for girls which she founded in 1947 with FLM's former teacher Clifford Canning. Corinna MacNeice attended the school.
2 – Kevin Andrews; see FLM to James F. Mathias, 12 January 1953, n. 2, p. 557.
3 – Nico Ghika; see FLM to WRR, 12 May 1950, n. 2, p. 526.

Several American men of letters (e.g. Richard Wilbur) have been over here lately but I don't seem to have seen any of them.[1] Some dubious Englishmen – and Irishmen – are thinking of going the other way. Shall I tell them to look you up or would you rather know more about them before committing yourself? (One is Dominic Behan, brother of Brendan.[2])

Our home address now is:-

10 Regent's Park Terrace,
London, N.W.1[3]

It is near the Zoo.

I am trying to do 3 or 4 heavy jobs simultaneously & am alarmingly behind with all of them.

Please write again,

Love to you both,
Louis

TO *Balliol College, Oxford*   MS Bodleian

[1961]   [BBC]

I have known Hector MacIver since 1935. My own impressions combined with the considered opinions of many people who are qualified to judge give me to think that he must be one of the most remarkable teachers of English in the United Kingdom. The academic records of his pupils at the Royal High School, Edinburgh, where he is now the Senior Master, have for many years constituted an outstanding testimony both to his efficiency and inspiration.

I have always been surprised that he has not published works of his own, as it is clear that potentially he is a creative writer (incidentally, he is a native Gaelic speaker and has made some striking translations of Gaelic poetry), but assume that this is due to his concentration on his teaching. In this latter capacity it seems abundantly clear that he has the rare gift of being able to make schoolboys consider literature, of <u>whatever</u> period, as if it were something vital <u>and</u> contemporary.

1 – Richard Wilbur (b.1921), American poet, whose most recent publication at this time was *Advice to a Prophet and Other Poems* (1961). He had won the Pulitzer Prize and the National Book Award in 1957 for *Things of This World* (1956).
2 – Dominic Behan (1928–89), songwriter, journalist, trade unionist. Author of *Teems of Times and Happy Returns* (1961), *My Brother Brendan* (1965) and other works. Cf. FLM, 'Come in, Dominic', in *NS*, 24 Nov. 1961, 795–6.
3 – FLM, Mary Wimbush and her son Charles took up occupancy of a flat at 10 Regent's Park Terrace on 19 June 1961.

His career as a teacher has on occasion involved him in a certain amount of controversy, which, in my opinion, is entirely to his credit, as he has never been one to submit to the dead-hand of any sort of moribund tradition. This independence of mind qualifies him eminently, I think, in the two fields of study which I understand he has suggested were he to be given one of your Schoolmaster Studentships.

I should like to add that in every way and, particularly intellectually, he is young for his age. In short, I sincerely believe that Balliol could give him a lot and that he could give a lot to Balliol.[1]

TO *Karl Miller*[2]

MS Bodleian [carbon copy] MS Sussex

5 December 1961   [BBC]

Dear Karl,

You may remember that you asked me if I should be interested in writing a piece for you on sport and that I said I was particularly interested in the England v. Ireland rugby match at Twickenham on, I think, February 10th.[3] The seats for these matches are disposed of a long way ahead so, if you would like such a piece, do you think you could now try to procure me a couple of tickets?

> With best wishes,
> Yours,

1 – MacIver was resident at Balliol during Hilary term 1962, on a fellowship provided for teachers of Sixth Form English.

2 – Karl Miller was literary editor for the NS 1961–7. A former pupil of Hector MacIver at the Royal HS, Edinburgh, and of Leavis at Downing College, Cambridge, Miller had been literary editor of the *Spectator* (1958–61), and would later edit the *Listener* (1967–73) and the *London Review of Books* (1979–99). He was Lord Northcliffe Professor at UCL 1974–99.

3 – He attended the match, which England won, 16–0. See 'Nine New Caps', NS, 16 Feb. 1962, 239.

1962

TO *Charles Monteith*   Faber archive

21 March 1962   BBC

Dear Charles,

Please forgive me for not having answered you sooner; I have been terribly busy with radio programmes.

About the <u>Collected Poems</u> project, I do not like the idea of calling it <u>Collected Poems 1925–1962</u> if it in fact leaves out everything I have written in the last two years. I must, by the way, have expressed myself badly as I did <u>not</u> mean to imply that these new poems "should be incorporated". What I suggest is that you should <u>either</u> incorporate them <u>or</u> (which might be better) publish the new slim volume first, either in the autumn of 1963 or spring of 1964, and postpone the <u>Collected</u> till a year or two after that.[1] Would it not indeed, number-wise, be nice to make it <u>Collected Poems 1925–1965</u>?

I suppose you would not be interested in any new radio plays? I have two or three which I think would prove quite readable if I wrote in linking bits of prose. I was always sorry that, while you have kept both <u>Christopher Columbus</u> and (God help us) <u>Out of the Picture</u> in print, you let <u>The Dark Tower</u>, which I consider much more interesting than either, go out of print. Schools and amateur theatrical societies etc. still keep asking me for permission to give readings or performances of it and I imagine the same would happen with these more recent pieces.

Yours ever,

(Louis MacNeice)

Features Department

<u>P.S.</u> I have just thought: what about omitting both <u>Autumn Journal</u> and <u>Autumn Sequel</u> and calling the book <u>Shorter Collected Poems</u>?

---

1 – Despite the poet's death in 1963, this is almost exactly what happened: *The Burning Perch* came out in 1963, *Collected Poems* in 1966.

24 May [1962]   BBC [letterhead], as from 10
                                 Regent's Park Terrace, London NW1

Dearest Dan,

I meant to write to you for your birthday but was interrupted by urgent business – had to go to the country to see a man about a house which I may be buying (it is in fact 3 v. olde cottages which would be run together).[1] Since then I've had the card from Mary – for which please thank her – plus the two photographs which, if I may say so, give a better view of the barn & the boat than of yourself!

I'm going over to Ireland in a fortnight, first to Belfast where I'll stay with the MacCanns & then to Dublin where they have a great cultural gimmick on, opening Joyce's Martello tower as a museum or shrine or what-have-you.[2] At the end of June I may have to go to Ireland again, this time to Carrickfergus where they're opening or unveiling (I don't know which as I don't know what it is) some sort of memorial to my father.[3]

Bimba is in great form though she looks v. odd; she went over to Holland in the Easter holidays & came back having chopped all her hair off. She is now having driving lessons. Our Camden Town flat is pretty crowded as it contains not only Mary & Bimba & me but Mary's son, Charles (aet. 14), who is going to a crammer's. If we get the olde cottages we shall be getting a Great Dane, just to make everything more crowded still.

Did you hear that poor Ghika's house on Hydra got burned down? He all but had a nervous breakdown over it but has since married Barbara Warner who was formerly Barbara Rothschild who was formerly . . . I forget. I haven't been abroad for ages but we may be going to Barcelona at the end of August.

Anyhow, though belated, here's many happy returns & all that jazz as they say.

                                 love,
                                 D.

1 – 39 Stocks Road, Aldbury, Herts. See FLM to DM, 9 May 1963, p. 698.

2 – Sylvia Beach formally opened the Martello Tower museum at Sandycove on 17 June, before a large audience. She was introduced by Donagh MacDonagh ('Joyce Museum Opened', *The Times*, 18 June 1962, 7). For FLM's account of this visit, see 'Under the Sugar Loaf', *NS*, 29 June 1962, 948–9; repr. *SP*, 246–52. Cf. Stallworthy, 461–2.

3 – The Choir Vestry of St Nicholas's Church was reconstructed in 1962 in memory of Bishop MacNeice.

TO *Corinna MacNeice*   MS Bodleian

5 July [1962]   BBC

Dearest Bimba,

Many happy returns etc. I propose to leave a birthday present over till
you're again in London. I hope you enjoyed Dublin. Have just heard from
George who reports that you collected those pictures. Mercy is about to
leave for Belgium with the school children & we hope to see her on her
way back.[1]

We went to see the Francis Bacon pictures on Saturday. I don't like the
very latest ones but was much impressed by all those horrible Popes.[2]

We also went with Allen Tate & his wife to Hampton Court last week
& had a very fine meal, in spite of Allen's ulcers, at the Mitre opposite.[3]
The Tates are leaving tomorrow & driving themselves to Italy. Meanwhile
Wystan Auden has arrived but I haven't seen him yet. Mike Silver has also
arrived from S. Africa; he is thinking of leaving that country.[4]

We probably shan't be going to Barcelona now as the crammer says
Charles mustn't have more than a fortnight's holiday, poor fellow. It looks
as if poor M. will never get abroad! However, she went to the Colony
Room yesterday & won the jackpot twice.[5]

Astrology is weighing heavily on me.[6] It doesn't seem the weather for the
B.M. Reading Room.[7] How is it in Kinsale? I ran into Stephen (your
cousin) yesterday who says he's not been there yet.[8] I warned him he'd
have to do a lot of washing up. Good for him.

---

1 – George and Mercy MacCann.

2 – The Francis Bacon retrospective exhibition, which included *Six Studies for a Pope*, opened
at the Tate Gallery on 24 May. Cf. 'The Horrific Vision of Mr Francis Bacon', *The Times*, 24
May 1962, 7.

3 – The Mitre, Hampton Court Road, East Molesey, Surrey. The Tates arrived in London on
21 June and were staying at the Royal Court Hotel, Sloane Square (AT to FLM, 21 May
1962, *Ms Bodleian, Ms Res, c.*).

4 – FLM had stayed with Silver in Johannesburg in 1959 (Stallworthy, 441).

5 – Mary Wimbush and her son Charles. The Colony Room, founded by Muriel Belcher, was
a club in Dean Street, then associated with Francis Bacon and his circle.

6 – *Astrology*, published 1964.

7 – The weather was not as balmy as this suggests. London had witnessed on 4 July the coolest
July day since 1948, at 57 °F (*The Times*, 5 July 1962, 6).

8 – Stephen, only son of Hedli's younger sister, Elizabeth Williams. BCM recalls: 'Yes, Stephen
came over to Kinsale, maybe in his boat. Anyway he went out boating and came back, in the
middle of the night, dragging a shark behind him. He took the tail into the Spinnaker, leaving
the shark on the road. So then in comes the garda to enquire about the shark and finds the
clientele sitting around drinking Irish coffees. Of course the restaurant at that time had no
liquor licence and there was a hell of a to do' (BCM, private correspondence, 2008).

Kitty has James & Tania Stern staying with her again.[1] We were talking about the Cannings. Mouse also present & even spoke.[2]

That cheque for 25 guineas which had been mouldering for nine months in Clarence Terrace turns out never to have been duplicated, so I'm 25 guineas up. Welcome.

Hope you're having a good time.

much love,

D.

TO *Corinna MacNeice*   MS Bodleian

13 August [1962]   [10 Regent's Park Terrace]

Dearest Bimba,

Just had my hair cut by a madman who's newly back from the suburbs of Paris where he's been studying with a Professor Roget who's an expert on the Unification of the Hair. This is just to let you know – in case you're still on for meeting me by scooter (but, if you do, you must wear a crash helmet)[3] – that I'm crossing this Friday & shall probably be spending the weekend at Ellie Ffrench's guest house – Kilcolman Castle, Kilcolman, Co. Galway (Tel. Kilcolman 12).[4] I shall try to telephone her tonight & will let you know if I'm not going there. Monday or Tuesday I'll work my way north to Sligo where I've got to give a lecture on Tuesday evening.[5] I'll

---

1 – James Stern (1904–93), Irish-born novelist and translator, and his wife Constanze ('Tania') (née Kurella, 1902–93), physical therapist and translator. They married in 1935, and collaborated on a translation of Freud. After many years in New York, they moved in 1961 to Hatch Manor, Wiltshire. FLM had met the Sterns in New York, where Tania had given gymnastics classes in her apartment in which WHA had participated, much to the amusement of EC (see FLM to Mrs E. R. Dodds, 22 March 1940, n. 2, p. 380).

2 – 'Mouse' was the daughter of Kitty Church (see FLM to BCM, 15 Sept. 1961, above) and was a schoolfriend of Corinna's at Hanford School.

3 – BCM recalls: 'I never got my scooter/motorbike that Hedli had promised me. Somehow during the interim of me getting to Kinsale she decided I was too wild. This seemed doubly unfair since it had been her idea in the first place. I do remember an occasion at Regent's Park Terrace when I was about to ride the back of Jonathan Howard's (Marghanita Laski's son) motorcycle down to Oxford without a helmet and Louis said, with a snarl, "You are too young to warrant an epitaph." He had a thing about crash helmets, I suppose' (BCM, private correspondence, 2008).

4 – Actually Kilcolgan Castle, Co. Galway. Ellie ffrench (b.1918) was the Hon. Mrs Eleanor Agnew, daughter of Sir John ffrench (1872–1946) of Castle ffrench, Ballinasloe, Co. Galway. FLM often visited Ellie (and Tom Agnew) when in Ireland. DM had once sailed to Brittany with the Agnew/ffrenches on a Galway hooker (see FLM to MM, 5 July 1950, p. 535).

5 – FLM gave a lecture, 'Is Yeats a Good Model?', at the Yeats Summer School, probably on Tuesday 21 Aug.

probably return to England Wednesday or, at the latest, Thursday. Much love, D.

TO *Corinna MacNeice*   MS Bodleian

24 September [1962]   10 Regent's Park Terrace,
                                            London NW1

Dearest Bimba, Just wondering when you're likely to return. Would it be possible for you to let me know? And could you remember to bring back Under the Volcano & the Opium Eater – & also, if you can squeeze it in, the Oxford Book of Seventeenth Century Verse.[1] We have had a deluge of Behans in London – Father Behan, Mother Behan, Brendan & all – & Dominic has got away with assaulting a taxi driver; they couldn't believe he'd hit someone twice his height.[2] The astrology people have been pestering me for their pound of flesh. Otherwise all goes well. The Sewells are about to leave, though I haven't seen them lately. Laurence is in Greece, staying on Myconos.

                        lots of love, D.

1 – Malcolm Lowry, *Under the Volcano* (1947); Thomas De Quincey, *Confessions of an English Opium Eater* (1822).
2 – Cf. 'The Two Faces of Ireland' (review of *Brendan Behan's Island*), *Observer*, 30 Sept. 1962, 29; repr. *SP*, 253–6.

1963

TO *Controller, Third Programme (BBC internal memo)*

MS BBC

7 February 1963   From: Mr. Louis MacNeice,
                                   1053 B.H. Ext. 2970

Subject: THE PORLOCK PROGRAMME[1]

I was very glad to hear that this had been accepted but am now somewhat distressed to hear that you want a different title. Do you mean a <u>quite</u> different title? I originally referred to it as 'A Person from Porlock' (which in fact was Laurence Gilliam's suggestion). This, I admit might suggest that it was going to be a programme about Coleridge or, even more specifically, about Kubla Khan. I would now like to call it 'Persons from Porlock', which seems both safer and apter, but it would break my heart if either the word 'person' or the name 'Porlock' disappeared from the title. So much of the time one makes do with make-shift titles and this seems to me to be a really functional one.

Apart from the fact that to my mind 'Persons from Porlock' is both memorable and suggestive, I want to weave in the historical reference just twice in the course of the story:-

1 Say about three-quarters of the way through where the hero, looking back on his recurrent misadventures, would actually (and I cannot see that this <u>need</u> appear 'contrived') compare himself, not altogether seriously, with Coleridge being interrupted by the Person and

2. At the very end when he is dying on the mountain shelf and hearing voices, one of which voices would be used to announce 'A person from Porlock!' i.e. Death.

---

1 – FLM's final play, *Persons from Porlock*, was broadcast 30 Aug. 1963 and later published in *Persons from Porlock and Other Plays for Radio* (1969), 107–44.

If you like, I could easily add a sub-title – something like 'A Study in 20th Century Frustration' – though, what with a blurb in the RADIO TIMES and an opening announcement on the air, I don't see that that is really necessary.[1] Anyhow I look forward to hearing what you think about this.

Dictated by Louis MacNeice and
dispatched, in his absence, by
Gillian Lewis, Secretary.

TO *Charles Monteith*   Faber archive

11 February 1963   BBC

Dear Charles,

I am just assembling these poems for you; they should be ready by Friday. I am finding it difficult to think of a title. One of the poems is called 'Round the Corner'. Do you think that would do?[2]

As regards 'The Mad Islands', to which I am planning an introduction that will range from Celtic saga via the 'Faerie Queene' to 'The Waterbabies', it has just occurred to me that you might make this a double-barrelled book, following up 'The Mad Islands' with another radio piece of mine (a copy of which I enclose) called 'The Administrator'.[3] The reason I suggest this is that both these pieces involve lavish use of dream material but are otherwise quite different. In 'The Mad Islands' the material is used 'legend-wise', i.e. as overt fantasy, whereas 'The Administrator' has a naturalistic framework and the dreams in it are presented as dreams. With the latter there would be an equal, if not a greater, need to re-write the links. NB. I should also wish to re-write the last little scene, pages 38–40. I don't really want the husband to make up his mind and should much prefer to end it with the question still open.

I think these two would make a rather nice brace but please let me know what you think.

Yours ever,
Louis

1 – Cf. 'Persons from Porlock', *Radio Times*, 22 Aug. 1963, 44.
2 – The volume was *The Burning Perch*. Other than *Round the Corner*, the title on the draft proof, suggested titles included *Stairways*, *Corners and Crossings*, *Pyres and Signposts*, *Pyres and Bellbuoys* and *Bellbuoys* (note by CM, 18 Oct. 1963, *Faber archive, Monteith file*).
3 – 'The Mad Islands', an adaptation of the Celtic legend 'The Voyage of Maelduin', was broadcast BBC Third Programme, 4 April 1962 (cf. FLM's commentary in *Radio Times*, 29 March 1962, 39). The play was published by Faber (with FLM's introduction, along with *The Administrator*) in 1964. *The Administrator* had been broadcast on 6 March 1961.

TO *Charles Monteith*   Faber archive

1 March 1963   BBC

Dear Charles,

Thank you for your letter about my new book of verse. I have not got
it with me, but so far as I remember the terms you suggested were
satisfactory. But NB. I <u>don't</u> want it to be called <u>Pyres and Bellbuoys</u> and
I agree with you that 'Round the Corner' will do, unless in the near future
we can think of something better.

I have just remembered that last August I promised to send a copy of
<u>Holes in the Sky</u> to dotty Major Freyer at the far end of Achill. Can you
possibly ask your people who deal with this to send me a copy (at
Broadcasting House); at the same time perhaps they could send me one of
<u>Dark Conceit</u> by Edwin Honig, to save me searching the bookshops for it.[1]

I enjoyed our meeting a week ago in the Irish Embassy. I found that all
that Power's Gold Label made my trip to Edinburgh much easier.[2]

                                        Yours ever,
                                        Louis

TO *Charles Monteith*   Faber archive

1 May [1963]   BBC

Dear Charles,

Am studying the proofs of my poems with a view to one or two very
slight changes, but should be able to let you have them back within about
a week. As for the title what about <u>The Burning Perch</u> (a phrase from the
poem called <u>Budgie</u>)? It seems a good deal more arresting than <u>Round the
Corner</u> & is certainly just as relevant.[3]

I notice that I forgot to put in any <u>Acknowledgments</u> but assume these
would go all right on the blank left-hand page opposite the List of
Contents.

I also notice that the list of my already published books doesn't include
either <u>Autumn Journal</u> or <u>Goethe's Faust</u> but, having just had my royalty

1 – FLM used Honig's study of allegory in his impending Clark Lectures at Cambridge
University, which were printed with minimum editorial revision as *Varieties of Parable*
(Cambridge, 1965).
2 – Powers Gold Label Irish whiskey.
3 – Monteith replied the following day, stating his satisfaction with the new title (CM to FLM,
2 May 1963, *Faber archive*).

sheets, see that they don't appear there either. Does this mean they're out of print? If so, I think it's quite absurd that something like Out of the Picture should still be in print! After all, A. Journal is still the book I get most comeback about, while Goethe's Faust is . . . Goethe's Faust.[1]

in haste, Yours ever, Louis

TO *Daniel MacNeice*   MS Texas

9 May [1963]   BBC [letterhead], as from 39 Stocks
                                      Road, Aldbury, nr Tring, Herts
                                      [hereafter 39 Stocks Road]

Dearest Dan,

In haste. This is just to send you all good wishes for your birthday. I hope to God it's warmer in Egg Harbor than here. I'm sorry for the visiting team of West Indians who're trying to play cricket around this country.[2]

I'm now living in a Hertfordshire village in a very Olde Englysshe [*sic*] house – strictly speaking, 3 cottages joined together.[3] One bumps one's head a lot & it is absurdly soporific but we have two apple trees, some broken-down pergolas (for roses), & a Great Dane puppy (6 months) who spends his time making hay of the lot.

Bimba is sharing a flat in London with girl friends but she comes down quite often for weekends, having been allotted a specially crazy room where the beams wind about like snakes. She is going through a phase in her art career doing landscapes in the form of collages (everyone, I gather, laughs at her for this).

I have just been speaking across the Irish Sea to George MacCann who only recently came out of hospital where it seems he all but died.[4] But he sounded just like himself on the telephone.

I am just off to Cambridge to give the first of six lectures: as they're supposed to be published later I have to write them out which I find a terrible chore. Bimba is coming this time with me as she wants to meet

---

1 – Faber were willing to publish *Faust* in paperback, but were unsure about *Autumn Journal*. *Out of the Picture* remained in print because it sold, albeit very slowly (CM to FLM, 8 May 1963, *Faber archive*).
2 – A West Indies side captained by F. M. Worrell began a six-month tour of England in April and had so far been faring badly.
3 – FLM and Mary Wimbush moved into 39 Stocks Road on 22 Dec. 1962.
4 – MacCann had had a colostomy three months earlier (Mercy MacCann to FLM, 14 Feb. 1963, *Ms Bodleian Ms. Res. c. 586*).

Bertie Rodgers's daughter, Harden, who after T.C.D. is doing post-graduate work in Cambridge.[1] Cambridge <u>should</u> be beautiful, this being blossom time, but last week it was bloody cold. Trinity College give me an enormous four-poster to sleep in.[2]

Anyhow, I hope Mary & you have a good summer & here's repeated birthday wishes & much love.

D.

TO *Corinna MacNeice* MS Bodleian

19 July [1963]   39 Stocks Road

Dearest Bimba,

Very glad to get your letter. Sorry I hadn't written before but I was v. behindhand with a programme & on top of that the MacCanns passed through, on their way back from the German tour with the schoolgirls. Both in good form. Another one who suddenly turned up was Mike Silver (did you ever meet him?),[3] my minor tycoon friend from Johannesburg. He was just about to tell me about Dr. S. Ward, with whom he once shared a flat, when we were interrupted.[4]

1 – Harden Rodgers and her sister Nini were daughters of WRR by his first wife, Marie Waddell.

2 – While giving the Clark Lectures he stayed at Trinity College, Cambridge.

3 – 'I met most of LM's friends chiefly through Christmas all-nighters down in the semi-basement at Clarence Terrace. It was a kitchen dining room all in one, with cats, dogs, Hedli and Restituta, the Italian help, all romping about amidst the cooking fumes. Favourite guests, for me, were Ernst and Kathleen Stahl, the Laurie Lees, Alan and Isabel Rawsthorne, Bob and Sheila Pocock, Margaret Gardiner, and sometimes Nancy Spender. It always had the feel of a hilarious reunion and gales of laughter would orchestrate the night. To me, everyone looked very glamorous and Isabel would wear her python sandals that wound all the way up her calves. An endless source of fascination. On Saturday mornings, we would habitually go from Clarence Terrace to Brewer Street to shop in the market and from there to the York Minster ("The French") on Dean Street. I, being under age, would be stationed outside the pub and friends sent out to entertain me. I was very fortunate in this as many of Louis' friends were ace storytellers. I think of Bertie Rogers – particularly in the Canonbury Park days, when he seemed to be a frequent visitor. His huge limpid dark eyes and strangely slow and fluty way of delivering words were spellbinding. Later, as an art student, I liked to meet Louis at the George or the ML [the Marie Lloyd, 17 Portland Street, W1], where he passed the time with his circle of friends (chiefly producers from the BBC and actors). Reggie Smith, Harry Craig, Jack Dillon, René Cutforth and Eric Ewins were all larger than life figures in my eyes. An especial favourite was Jackie MacGowran. Louis would occasionally bring friends back to Regents Park Terrace. On one occasion it was Gerald Hanley and Louis recited "Christina" in a thoroughly chilling fashion and later danced his extraordinary flamenco elephant dance' (BCM, private correspondence, 2008).

4 – Dr Stephen Ward (1912–63), London osteopath. Central figure in the 1963 Profumo affair.

Last Saturday I went to Lord's (1st day of Oxford v. Cambridge) where we met Enid Starkie (did you ever meet <u>her</u>? elderly Irish don from Somerville) falling about all over the place in blushing pink.[1]

It has been on the whole cold & grey here, though the garden has an almost embarrassing richesse of roses. The Greyhound has been full of shivering teenage ramblers & campers in tam o'shanters etc.[2] Sabre is v. large & still eating up everyone's shoes.[3] Charles is youth-hostelling in the Lake District with his Hungarian friend. Mary has been doing a fair amount of broadcasting.

Yesterday I want to a party at Faber's in honour of Robert Lowell, American poet.[4] Our old friend Bill Alfred was there looking as quaint as ever.[5] All sorts of people such as William Golding & Ted Hughes were there too.[6] Towards the end a gang from the Plough (Museum St). arrived, dragging with them Robert MacBryde who looked like all the water-front drunks in the world rolled into one.[7] He made a nice contrast with the Establishment types there present.

1 – On 13 July at Lord's, the match was drawn. Enid Starkie (1897–1970), CBE, FRSL, Reader in French Literature at Oxford; Fellow of Somerville College, Oxford. Born Dublin, educ. Alexandra College, RIAM, Somerville College and the Sorbonne. Author of many books, including studies of Baudelaire and Rimbaud, she had been a candidate for the Poetry Chair at Oxford in 1961, which was given to Robert Graves (see FLM to JF, 27 January 1961, n. 1, p. 674). She was considered immensely kind and learned, and was regarded as a great character.

2 – The Greyhound Inn, Aldbury.

3 – FLM's Great Dane.

4 – FLM had previously met Lowell in Athens in 1951 (FLM to WRR, 28 June 1951, p. 546). Lowell later wrote about the Faber party: 'A month from his death, we talked by Epstein's bust / of Eliot; MacNeice said, "It is better / to die at fifty than lose pleasure in fear"' (Lowell, *History*, 1973). In her memoirs the British poet Kathleen Raine recalled FLM's unexpected kiss on this occasion (*Land Unknown*, 1975, 164).

5 – William Alfred (1922–99), educated at Harvard, where he taught Medieval Literature for many years. A poet and playwright, his publications include *Agamemnon* (trans.) (1954), *Hogan's Goat* (1966), and other works. He first met the MacNeices in 1953. Cf. Stallworthy, 424.

6 – It was about this time that Ted Hughes wrote a cordial and highly informed note to FLM about French Astrology books (Hughes to FLM, undated, *Ms Bodleian, Ms Res, c. 585, Box 10, Folder 2*). See also Hughes's review of *Astrology* in the *Listener*, 2 Oct. 1964, repr. Hughes, *Winter Pollen* (1995), 51–5.

7 – Robert MacBryde (1913–66), Scottish painter and partner of Robert Colquhoun. Famously inebriate, they were permanent fixtures of Fitzrovia. FLM dedicated 'Budgie' (*Burning Perch*) to MacBryde. After FLM's death, the Scottish painter Ged Melling (1934–2007) invited MacBryde to run a summer school on painting at Kinsale, where he stayed for several months. BCM recalls: 'He arrived after a tearful farewell to London saying he would never return. And indeed, he did not. After Kinsale he went to Dublin where, some time later, he got run over and died. I was a student at the Slade at that time and he would come back

Yet another who has been about, but avoiding Martha McCulloch, is Arthur Sewell. He too was present on the Enid Starkie occasion. He drove Rene & Sheila down to the country & even drove them back again.[1] They were both very frightened.

Laurence says he's going to Ireland in August & was asking if you'd be there. I take it you'll be flying there direct from Switzerland?

It sounds kind of quiet in Brissago.[2] I like the bath towel technique. I suppose you haven't been down into Italy?

I shall now have to put off my Abu Simbel trip till the New Year, assuming they haven't started chopping the thing up by then.[3] Some time, probably after that, I'll have to go to Dublin to make recordings of Stephen Behan (the Father of the Behans). I saw him & Mother Behan on this last visit to Dublin, when Brigid Wilkinson gave a party. Next morning all sorts of people emerged from corners of the larder etc & ate bacon & eggs in relays, one of them meanwhile playing the mandoline [*sic*] & another the banjo.

Please, if you think it fitting, give my best wishes to your grandparents. Look after yourself.

Much love. D.

TO *Allen Tate* MS Princeton

2 August [1963]   39 Stocks Road

Dear Allen & Isabella,

We have been very bad & lost your card (for which thank you), so don't know where to write in the U.S. But we shall be around (above address) till the last week of August, so please let us know when you hit this little old vice-ridden capital. Have a new book of poems in proof to show you – said he egocentrically – all thumbnail nightmares.[4] Apart from that, all

---

from his wanderings with his arms full of wild flowers and grasses for me to draw, chanting "Life is a bunch of Neu-roses," in his thick Scottish accent. Laughing his gappy smile' (BCM, private correspondence, 2008).

1 – Reynolds (René) Cutforth (1909–84), well-known BBC reporter. He was Blundell in *AS*.
2 – Hedli's parents lived in Villa Bressani in Brissago, Switzerland, on the banks of Lake Maggiore. BCM visited there frequently.
3 – FLM was slated to make a radio programme, *Abu Simbel and the High Dam*. His other planned features included *Confessions of a Justified Sinner* and *The Star-Crossed Daughter* (cf. 'Third Programme Features on acceptance as at 19th August 1963', *Ms BBC R71/918/1, MacNeice Correspondence Personal, 1957–63*).
4 – *BP*.

is fine. You must come & see our new residence – too Olde Rose Cottage to be true.

> in haste,
> Much love to you both from us both,
> Louis

[*In recipient's hand*] 'My last letter from Louis MacNeice.'[1]

TO *T. S. Eliot*   Faber archive

2 August [1963]   39 Stocks Road

Dear Tom,

In haste. I had already heard about that gaffe on the part of the Daily Express. I can reassure you that you are <u>not</u> one of the trustees of the fund in question, though with about a dozen others you did sign the original letter in the Times announcing that such a fund was being created.[2]

The original trustees of <u>our</u> fund were Goronwy Rees, myself, & Wynford Vaughan Thomas, a friend of Dylan's & a well-known B.B.C. commentator. The original trustees of the Dylan Thomas <u>estate</u> were Stewart Thomas, who had been his solicitor, David Higham, his literary agent, & Dan Jones, the Welsh composer, a friend.[3] At some stage Dan Jones dropped out & Wynford Vaughan Thomas crossed, so to speak, the floor of the house to replace him. He was then replaced, on <u>our</u> fund, by V. S. Pritchett.

Now about Caitlin Thomas's house! She has behaved quite impossibly throughout. A little of the fund was drained off earlier to pay for some of the children's education but, in fact, this was hardly necessary as at that time Dylan's royalties were booming in a way which no one could have foreseen. Two of the three children were grown up, however, before we had really made an inroad in the fund, Llewellyn's education at Harvard having been paid for by a similar but considerably larger <u>American</u> fund. Caitlin then began clamouring for this house & the Americans gave her <u>half</u> the price of it (c.£3,500). We refused to follow suit, because of our

---

1 – Tate's last words to MacNeice are inscribed on a Teleflowers card, addressed to St Leonard's: 'Dear Louis – Get well as fast as you can. We miss you. Our love – Allen & Isabella' (*Ms Bodleian, MacNeice Papers, Box 11*).

2 – Cf. FLM to Principal Fulton, 21 Nov. 1953, p. 566.

3 – Daniel Jenkyn Jones (1912–93) OBE (1968), Welsh composer of classical music, and a friend of Dylan Thomas. He composed the music for the radio production of *Under Milk Wood* (1954).

terms of reference, <u>unless</u> the names of the children were associated with this purchase, i.e. unless it belonged to <u>them</u> as much as to her. She baulked at this for some time but has now given in. Which is about all I know of this rather disenchanting story.

I feel I shall be needing a fund myself soon, as owing to the fact that our joint friend Mr Percy Popkin appears to have been semi-senile for the last few years of his career during which he made quite a few mistakes in my Income Tax Returns, they ('They' in the Ed. Lear sense) have now dug up my records since 1951 (!) & are about to come down on me for thousands![1]

[*right-hand margin of page*]: Yours ever, Louis

TO *John Hilton*   MS Bodleian

6 August [1963]   39 Stocks Road

Dear John,

Thank you very much for inviting me to drinks for Moore but I fear I'll be in Yorkshire tomorrow recording effects in caves.[2] Still I'd love to see Moore sometime. If you have a car why don't you drive him down to our Olde Rose Cottage (we also have a Great Dane, nice but a bit oafish)?

I'm also probably going to Connemara but about a week later.[3] Look up Richard Murphy (young poet) at the Old Forge, Cleggan. He'll sail you across to Inishboffin in one of his Galway hookers.[4]

love,
Louis

1 – See FLM to TSE, 12 Aug 1963, p. 705.

2 – Moore Crosthwaite, an old friend from Oxford; see FLM to JH 'Autumn 1928', n. 1, p. 195.

3 – FLM had planned to fly to Dublin on 23 Aug., rent a car at Dublin airport ('a small handy car, say a mini or, failing that, something like a Ford Anglia') and stay in Ireland until 3 Sept. FLM to Gerald Ryan, 13 Aug. 1963 (*BBC R71/918/1*). Cf. George MacCann to FLM, 12 Aug. 1963: 'Delighted that you and Charles are coming over on the 25th come and stay with us' (*Ms Bodleian, Ms Res, c. 570*). The trip had to be cancelled when FLM became ill.

4 – Elizabeth Nicholson wrote: 'When in Ireland, Louis often went to stay with Ellie ffrench . . . Louis had planned to visit [Richard Murphy] as well as Ellie ffrench on that holiday which he had planned to take just as he became ill' (EN to BCM, 26 Jan. 1964, *Faber archive*). Cf. 'Louis had planned a visit to Cleggan and Inishboffin, where he had sailed on my old Galway hooker the previous summer, but his trip in 1963 had to be cancelled. On the day that he was due to return for [*sic*] that holiday to England he died in London. Richard Murphy.' Inscription in item 333 (W. H. Auden, *Louis MacNeice: A Memorial Address*), *The Library of Richard Murphy*, Maggs Bros Catalogue 1433 (2009).

8 August [1963]   BBC

Dearest Bimba,

Thank you for the card from Brissago. That all sounded v. restful & health-making. Good to get brown.

I'm just back from Yorkshire where I spent yesterday recording effects in a cave for my next programme. We got a nice underground stream, also a waterfall, also general drippings. There were lots of stalagmites & stalactites, some of the latter very delicate. By contrast we returned to Leeds for the evening where we visited an ancient music hall called the Palace of Varieties, now much invaded by strip: there was one lurid act where the girl was chased by a gorilla.[1]

I am prerecording this programme which is called <u>Persons from Porlock</u> (the central character by the way is a frustrated painter!) this Sunday: it goes out on August 30th. The final person from Porlock is Death (in a cave) & has a Somerset accent.

Jack & Mollie are about to open their long-bruited grill room, which we look forward to.[2] Mainly steaks & scampi.

Before I forget, I had a letter from the Hutchinson solicitors whom I have paid, for your share of the St Andrews flat, up to June 24th. But they say that I am <u>still</u> responsible as no replacement has turned up. I thought you said one was due almost immediately. If so, could you ask her to get in touch with Magooshe or someone?[3]

Moore Crosthwaite (whom we used to know in Greece) is around but we haven't seen him yet. And Allen Tate & Isabella are due some time this month. By the way, I saw Bill Alfred at a Faber's party in honour of the American poet Robert Lowell. He was very like himself.

I am now officially off the B.B.C. for some time but in fact have to do this leftover work. The astrology people are beginning to lift their horrible heads again & there are two more quite heavy jobs to be finished before the end of September.[4]

---

1 – City Varieties Music Hall, Leeds.

2 – Licensees of the Greyhound pub in Aldbury.

3 – Corinna shared a flat at 9 St Andrews Mansions, West Kensington, near Barons Court tube station. 'Magooshe Philips was mother of Maro Gorki (one of Ashile Gorki's daughters) with whom I shared the flat. Peggy Ashcroft's daughter, Eliza, was there briefly as was Philip Gronau, son of Carmen Gronau, the first woman director of Sotheby's. We were all students at the Slade. Matthew Spender was courting Maro at the time' (BCM, private correspondence, 2008).

4 – Aldus books had commissioned *Astrology*, published posthumously.

Was interrupted at that point & must now break off.

> Have a good time,
> lots of love,
> D

TO *T. S. Eliot*   Faber archive

12 August [1963]   BBC

Dear Tom,

Thank you very much for your letter. Please don't worry about my Inland Rev. troubles which I should not have unloaded on you: I only did so – rather mischievously – because it was you in l'entre deux guerres who first mentioned Percy Popkin to me. He was of great help to me for many years but the last period was one of decline & fall!

I am going out tonight with Allen Tate & his wife. They seem to have become regular summer visitors. I expect you will be seeing them too.

Oh I was nearly forgetting. Thank you also for suggesting a good accountant. In fact I took on a new accountant over 3 years ago: he is still trying to make head or tail of the backlog.

I was sorry not to see you at the party for Robert Lowell in Russell Square.

> With best wishes,
> Yours ever,
> Louis

P.S. Percy Popkin looked exactly like his name – his letters usually ended: 'Best wishes to the wife & I trust that both of you have been enjoying the recent fine weather.'

TO *Corinna MacNeice*   MS Bodleian

20 August [1963]   39 Stocks Rd

Dearest Bimba,

Thank you very much for your letters. Delighted to hear you got to Puck Fair.[1] Dylan Thomas went to it once but seems never to have got out of the first pub he got into.[2]

Sorry about this straggly handwriting. I'm writing in bed, which I've been confined to for several days with a mystery temperature.[3] Haven't smoked since last Thursday!

Yes, I heard Willie & Geoffrey were on their way.[4] What a lot of comings & going there seem to be round you.

Don't try to listen to my programme. It's the kind that has lots of quick transitions & needs good reception.[5] I'll be having a playback some day.

About your Egypt idea(!), I had meant to go this November but have had to postpone it till January.[6] So there's plenty of time to look into possibilities, but obviously it <u>would</u> be v. expensive (Abu Simbel is a hell of a long way inland, apart from anything else.) Couldn't you volunteer for a dig or something?

We saw Allen Tate & Isabella a week ago & went to L'Aiglon with them. Otherwise there's been no one new around. As for the Old Familiar Faces, they tend to look a bit jaded, come August.

I have just read <u>The Country Girls</u> by Edna O'Brien. Rather a good account of two convent-trained girls round Co. Clare way. It's in Penguins.

1 – Puck fair (Co. Kerry), 10–12 Aug. 'I stayed overnight at the Puck Fair (in Kerry) and the pubs had had their licence extended all night for three days. The sacrificial goat placed way up on a gaudy weather-worn stand over-looking the main street of Killorglin (?) with little bars with sawdust floors opening out on it' (BCM to FLM, Wednesday [14?] Aug. 1963, *Ms Bodleian, MacNeice Papers*).

2 – Dylan and Caitlin Thomas went with Bill and Helen McAlpine to the Puck Fair in 1946. Dylan was to write a piece for the *Picture Post*.

3 – While walking on the Yorkshire moors, FLM got soaked in a rainstorm. He developed a cough and then pneumonia.

4 – 'Eric Burdick came in + says Willie + Geoffrey Wincott (?) are staying with James – though I suppose you know that already' (BCM to FLM, Wednesday [14?] Aug. 1963, *Ms Bodleian, MacNeice Papers*). Burdick and Wincott were English actors.

5 – BCM had promised to try to listen to *Persons from Porlock* on the 30th, 'though heaven knows if I'll hear a word through the clatter of plates' (ibid.).

6 – BCM had suggested joining her father in Egypt, who had planned to go to Abu Simbel, as an 'amalgamated present' for Christmas and birthdays (BCM to FLM, postmark 9 Aug. 1963, *Ms Bodleian, MacNeice Papers*). FLM had previously visited Egypt in 1955.

(Edna O'B. is a great chum of Jerry Slattery's).[1] Have also just reread (in bed) most of Carson McCullers & <u>The Power & the Glory</u>.[2]

Aug. 23rd:- Am still not recovered & am getting v. fed up with it. Have continued with a mixed bag of reading, including early 13th century story of Tristan by one Gottfried von Strasburg, Conquest of New Spain (stout Cortes & all that) by Bernal Diaz, & a crafty grey novel by John Mortimer called <u>Like Men Betrayed</u>. Am now beginning a Mauriac![3]

Did you know there's a combined H. Moore & F. Bacon Exhibition on in London? Whenever I get back to that city, I mean to try to see it. I'd also like to look at your Battersea sculpture some time. The latter is the sort of thing the Tates would go for but next week they're going to Ireland (!), where no doubt they may ring up the Spinnaker –

Later: have now finished the Mauriac which left a nasty taste in mouth.

Red Charles is coming to stay the weekend: he now has a job in a West End jeweller's! I think his police ambitions were spiked by lack of academic qualifications. Both Charleses by the way seem now to have dropped the belles of the village, but our Charles has been showing some interest in the girls at that school (now of course on holiday).[4]

Yes, why don't you go to Oxford & have another crack at E. Bowen?[5] If there's nowhere else, you could always stay with the Davins, the <u>third</u> daughter having now got married.[6]

Lots of love, D.

1–Edna O'Brien had written to FLM on 16 Sept. 1958, before she moved to London, expressing the hope that they might meet (*Ms Bodleian, MacNeice Papers, Box 3*).

2–Graham Greene, *The Power and the Glory* (1940).

3–*Tristan* by Gottfried von Strasburg (d.c.1210), trans. A. T. Hatto (1960); Bernal Díaz del Costillo (1496–1584), *Cortez & the Conquest of Mexico by the Spaniards in 1521* (trans. from the sixteenth-century original *Historia verdadera de la conquista de la Nueva España*); John Mortimer, *Like Men Betrayed* (1953).

4–'Our Charles' was Charles Wimbush and 'Red Charles' was his red-haired friend.

5–Elizabeth Bowen had recently come to the restaurant, 'exuberant at having completed a novel + again invited me to paint her in Oxford' (BCM to FLM, Wednesday [14?] Aug. 1963, *Ms Bodleian, MacNeice Papers*). BCM later painted Bowen at the home of Major and Lady Vernon, Summercove, Kinsale. She recalls: 'I was quite daunted by her presence even though she was very friendly. Trouble was she had such a grand and somewhat severe face and I had next to no experience painting portraits' (BCM, private correspondence, 2008).

6–Davin had three daughters with his wife Winnie, but he had another daughter, Patty, with Elisabeth Berndt. Patty was raised with her half-sisters.

26 August [1963]   39 Stocks Road

Dear Charles,

Just to ask if you know any more about <u>Persons from Porlock</u>. Because, if you do want to include it in <u>The Mad Islands</u>, I'll get it in shape for you. When I prerecorded the broadcast, I had to make a lot of cuts, some [of] which were improvements.

I've been stuck here for ten days with bronchitis, temperature, etc., & the doctor has still not given me permission to come up to London. However, I hope to soon. In the meantime I can do a certain amount of work here.

This illness has stopped me going to Ireland as planned but I still hope to get over for a little in September. I have a great desire to be in on the Oyster Festival at Clarinbridge, Co. Galway. My daughter by the way has written to me from Ireland describing the great time she had at Puck Fair, Killorglin.

I like the look of <u>The B. Perch</u> but the accent seems to have hopped a bit in the title of Château Jackson![1]

Yours ever,
Louis

———————

By 27 August, Louis MacNeice was having difficulty breathing and was admitted to St Leonard's Hospital the following day. He died on 3 September 1963. Corinna MacNeice recalls (private correspondence, 2008): 'I was back in Kinsale when the decision was made to go across to London with Hedli because my father was hospitalised. Aunt Elizabeth [EN] would not let me visit him when I got there. Her reasoning was that, if I showed up at the ward, then he would know how seriously ill he was. So I did not get to see him before he took off.'

———————

1 – In the poem's title, in the first edition, the circumflex accent was transferred to the second 'a' in 'Château', which FLM indicates in this letter with an arrow. *BP* (Faber, 1963 edn), p. 16.

APPENDICES

APPENDIX I
PERSONS REFERRED TO IN THE LETTERS

Elizabeth Nicholson TO *John Hilton*   MS Dan MacNeice

30 August 1977[1]

Characters connected with Sherborne Preparatory School

Littleton Powys Headmaster. Brother of John Cowper, Llewellyn & Theodore. I think Sherborne was a very happy preparatory school compared to many others at that date. Certainly, Louis always seemed very happy there & I think that this was probably largely due to the personalities of Littleton Powys & his wife. Mr. Powys very much encouraged the boys to explore the countryside & to collect all kinds of natural objects. He wrote a charming book The Joy of It (long since out of print) about his life & the school. I had Louis' copy of this with some pencilled notes in it & much regret that I lent it to somebody who lost it. Louis used to hold his dormitory spellbound with serial stories which he invented & in the book Mr. Powys remarks that he had only known one storyteller to equal Louis & that this was one of his brothers, I think John Cowper but am not sure about this.

Louis always felt in touch with Littleton Powys until the latter died & he is the origin of the old man in Stanza II of Louis' poem The Kingdom beginning 'Take this old man with the soldierly straight back.'

Mr. Lindsay 2nd master. Mr. Lindsay came from a much respected Northern Irish family located in Portadown. Louis had been ill & so was taken over late for his first term by my father & stepmother. Mr. Lindsay had a v. marked & rather harsh Northern Ireland accent & as my parents walked along the corridor, they heard this well-known accent & Mrs. Powys said 'That is our Irish master teaching the boys. He comes from

---

1 – Hilton had borrowed FLM's letters from Elizabeth Nicholson and in response to his query about various people, she agreed to send him 'a compressed list of who people were'. The document comprises what EN calls 'a v. few paltry notes' in lieu of a longer list to be completed later.

Portadown.' And later my stepmother said to my father 'Well, we have come a long way to have Freddy taught by someone from Portadown.' Later, when my father was Bishop of Down they came to know all the Lindsays well; one of the brothers was very active in the Church of Ireland synod & a great admirer of my father & his stand for toleration & peace. His brother became Chancellor for the Diocese of Armagh & was very far from sharing the prep. school Mr. Lindsay's orange views – quite the reverse. But they were all people of integrity. Mr. Lindsay was a cousin of Lord Chief Justice Best whose son Richard Best was at the Sherborne prep. & we several times travelled home in a party consisting of Mr. Lindsay, Richard Best, Louis & myself & other Irish children from one or other of the schools. At this time, the Bests lived in Dublin but after the Treaty they moved to Belfast & my father became v. friendly with the Lord Chief Justice & Louis & I used to go to tennis parties, etc. at their house.

Mr. Lindsay became headmaster of the Sherborne Prep. when Mr Powys retired. He [Mr. Lindsay] was still living when Louis died, by then sharing the headmastership with his son, & the son came to Louis' memorial service, representing Acreman House, Sherborne. The father died a few years ago & the son is now headmaster.

The Stallards are mentioned often, usually in connection with prowess at games. There were several brothers & I think they all became fairly renowned athletes including one who was at the big school but not at the prep. & who also became a fairly renowned eye surgeon.

Family mentioned in letters from Sherborne, Marlborough & Oxford.
   Eek as you will have gathered was myself.
   The relations mentioned are almost all step-relations. I think this was because my stepmother belonged to a very clannish & devoted family many of whom lived in Northern Ireland & who constantly visited one another. She was a Carrickfergus woman. Against this, we were really 'foreigners' & at the time these letters were written we had virtually no blood relations living in the North. Also, my father belonged to a very quarrelling family; he himself kept in touch with all his brothers & sisters & their children & especially after he became a bishop & lived in large houses, first in Waterford & later in Belfast they used to come & stay with him quite a lot but this was after the period of the letters & Louis & I were both married & away. Because my father kept in touch with them all, I know practically all of them, but because of their touchiness & quarrelling lots of them don't know one another. At least, the quarrelling was mainly among my father's

siblings. The next generation are friendly enough with one another when brought together but just incline to have never met.

<u>My stepmother's relations mentioned in the letters</u>

<u>Uncle Mac</u> This was my stepmother's only brother, Thomas MacGregor Greer. He lived at Seapark, Carrickfergus & I remember going to dinner there with you [John Hilton], Louis (& I think John Nicholson?) My stepmother was brought up partly at Seapark & partly at Grove House (now Nuffield Lodge) Regents' Park. Seapark is the house described in <u>Soapsuds</u> which is an entirely literal description of the house & its joys. It still stands & was a county convalescent home, now, I think, possibly a children's home. The house was built by my stepmother's maternal grandfather John Owden an Englishman who went over to Northern Ireland & made a lot of money in the once flourishing linen firm of Richardson Sons & Owden which has now fallen on very evil days. The stuffed dog in the hall, mentioned in <u>Soapsuds</u>, was Captain, a Newfoundland & in life, he was borrowed by the sculptor of Byron's statue in Hyde Park as a model for Byron's dog. I think he had probably gone when you went there as when Uncle Mac inherited Seapark from his mother, his wife asked my stepmother's permission to have him buried.

<u>Aunt Helena</u> My stepmother's elder sister, Lady Lowry. She was married to an admiral who died in 1920 & is not, I think mentioned in the letters but her children Graham & Hope probably are. The first stanza of <u>Autumn Journal</u> is an account of a visit paid by Louis to her house at Wickham, Hampshire in 1938. My father & stepmother & Dan & his Hungarian nurse were staying there at the same time.

<u>Aunt Eva</u> My stepmother's younger sister Miss Eva Greer. She lived with her great friend Gertrude Hind at a marvellous house called Glassdrumman in the Mourne Mountains. It had a wonderful garden & a wonderful site with the mountains at the back. You mention that you went there in the appendix to <u>The Strings</u>. Aunt Eva & Miss Hind went to live there in the early twenties but before that they used to spend part of the year in Bath & they travelled with Louis to Marlborough for the Scholarship Exam.[1] Miss Hind has left a detailed account of this expedition which my stepmother kept. I don't think it is in the file which you have but it exists.

1–Cf. FLM to GBM, 5 Dec. 1920, p. 42.

Glassdrumman descended to Graham Lowry & his widow still lives there in spite of the 'troubles'.

Gertrude Hind wrote verse & 'kitchen' plays under the name of Elizabeth Shane & Louis refers to her somewhere rather unkindly as a 'folk poetess'. True enough & she was a rather difficult & very dominating personality – very anti the Oxford Louis. Aunt Eva was <u>very</u> kind to us both as children & indeed always. She was a gentle & very merry person, very shy & very much dominated by her friend, but she was very kind to children. Louis never forgot how she used to cut acorns into shapes to amuse him in very early days at Seapark & it was she who gave him the book of fairy tales inscribed 'Freddy from Keddy Bock' which I mention in <u>Time was Away</u>. Keddy Bock was a very important figure in the Mac Miss Saga.

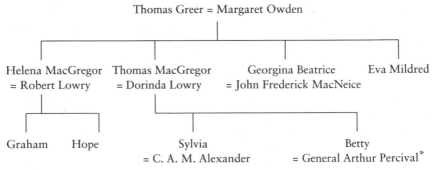

Thomas Greer = Margaret Owden

Helena MacGregor = Robert Lowry

Thomas MacGregor = Dorinda Lowry

Georgina Beatrice = John Frederick MacNeice

Eva Mildred

Graham   Hope

Sylvia = C. A. M. Alexander

Betty = General Arthur Percival[*]

[*](who lost Singapore) & was unfairly treated later.

<u>Cousin Pixie</u> This was my stepmother's first cousin, Mary Cottingham. Somewhere in the letters there is an account of a visit paid by Louis to her house in Harrow. Her maiden name was Bowen-Colthurst & they (the B-C.s) were a very erratic & rather wild Co. Cork family. Her mother was a half-sister of Thomas Greer & on the other side she was a cousin of Elizabeth Bowen. Teddy & Myrtle were Cousin Pixie's children.

<u>Robert Milliken</u> is mentioned, I think, as meeting us once or twice on the way to or from school & shepherding us between trains. He was a real old-time butler first to my stepmother's parents & later to her brother. We used to like being met by him (by then retired) as he used to take us to the Zoo etc & to tea at Buryard's & had the right kind of ideas as to our tastes. His son did extremely well in life becoming a very high-ranking Army officer.

— — — —

<u>Blood relations possibly mentioned in letters</u> (I'm not sure)

<u>Uncle Herbert & Aunt Norah</u>. Uncle Herbert was my father's younger brother & was Vicar of Melbourn in Cambridgeshire. He was quite brilliantly clever at T.C.D. but never really made great use of the brains & always gave the impression of being rather sad, cynical & disillusioned. John & I both always liked him very much & I think we were really the only relations of his own that he kept up with after my father died. He seemed to have rejected all the others & also Ireland. But he was fundamentally a most lovable man who made a very unhappy marriage – Aunt Norah was worthy, most capable & efficient, very dominant & like an iceberg.

He had a very nice son & daughter & his son who is now a vicar in Surrey (& very <u>happily</u> married) took Louis' funeral service which you were at.

Uncle Herbert lived well into the nineties & died only 8 or 9 years ago. He was one of the few relations who used to come & stay at the Rectory though I think he never revisited Ireland after my father's death.

My brother <u>Willie</u> is generally referred to as William in the letters. He came back to live at the Rectory for good about 1924, I think. Like most Mongols, he had a very kind & affectionate nature & after he went back to live in Carrickfergus after my father's death became very much beloved by everybody there. My stepmother was devoted to him.

Non-relations

<u>Hugh Davies</u> whom you probably knew at Marlborough is mentioned now & again. Louis said he used to be called 'Black Davies' there to distinguish him from someone called 'White Davies'. He was a contemporary of my husband's in the medical school at Oxford & they shared rooms in New College. He was best man at our wedding.

He became a very eminent radiologist & was on the staff at the National Hospital for Nervous Diseases, Queen Square. He must have x-rayed hundreds of cerebral tumours & as so oddly happens so often, developed the kind of disease he was interested in & died of an inoperable & fairly rare kind of cerebral tumour about ten years ago.

<u>Mrs. Wasey</u> who lived near Marlborough & whose tennis parties Louis enjoyed so much was the sister of a Carrickfergus parishioner. None of us, except Louis, ever met her, so far as I know.

Mrs. Johns lived in Carrickfergus. The Johns were a very old Carrickfergus family, what used to be called 'old residenters'. We knew them very well. Mrs. Johns was rather eccentric but a very warm-hearted character. Her son Christopher was at Cheltenham when Louis was at the prep. & is mentioned as a travelling companion. His sisters, Margaret & Nan are mentioned in some of the Oxford letters, notably Margaret who was a waitress at the Shamrock Tea Rooms while Louis was at Oxford.

I have just remembered that Seapark, the <u>Soapsuds</u> house which we used to think so romantic & glamorous had already been sold by the time you stayed at the Rectory. So that the dinner-party which you mention in your letter of 20/9/28 in <u>The Strings</u> with the 'Belfast aunt, lately engaged in gun-running' (Uncle Mac's 1st wife, Aunt Dindie) was held in a very unromantic & unglamorous villa in Belfast where they were living then. The gun-running was not very 'lately'. It refers to the Ulster gun-running of 1912 [*sic*], the year of the Ulster Covenant.[1] Many people in the Province went with their cars to Larne Harbour in the middle of the night & drove the consignments of guns (mainly, I think, from Germany) to hiding-places all over Ulster. In the case of Uncle Mac, he stored his in the cellars of Seapark.[2] He had not yet inherited this house; it belonged to his mother who though strongly Unionist in sympathy had been born & brought up a Quaker & was highly indignant when she found that her house had been used for this purpose. My father was always on very good terms with all my stepmother's relations but he did strongly disapprove of the gun-running & of the general activities of Sir Edward Carson, as he then was.

Archie White origin of the poem <u>The Gardener</u>. We knew Archie from our childhood onwards & were very attached to him. <u>The Gardener</u> describes him well enough & that poem is a great favourite with the older people in Carrickfergus.

    Apart from his own delightful character, Archie was a link with the days of our own mother & would now & again talk sadly & regretfully of 'the

1 – The Ulster Covenant was signed on 28 September 1912, but the Larne gun-running took place in April 1914.
2 – Cf. Dorinda Greer's Diary: 'Gun running at Larne // Mac & Willie [*illegible*] & W Compton started after breakfast. I put the food in Rucksack with bandgs etc. Our men were mobilized in the Green & packets in sacks. A. sat up till past 2 am. Henry stayed up all night' (24 April 1914). Next day, she recorded: '. . . spent the morning packing up ammunition in small bundles to distribute round the companies in case of a raid' (*PRONI D2339/4/8/21–23*).

ould mistress'. Incidentally, Louis says somewhere in <u>The Strings</u> that he used to speak of us as 'the bairns'. I can't remember him doing this; he called us 'the weans' (pronounced 'wains') & the latter is a much more ordinarily used term in Ulster. He may have said 'bairns' very occasionally but it was generally 'the weans'.

<u>David</u> was a rather dumb boy who drove the car.

APPENDIX 2
RELATIONS IN COUNTY SLIGO

Elizabeth Nicholson TO *Louis MacNeice*   MS Bodleian

2 August 1960

Dearest Louis,

Ever since I came back from Co. Sligo I have been intending to write &
tell you something about it, but John has had leave since then until to-day
& we have been here & there & I have not had much time.

It was a very satisfying ten days. Being 87 did not seem to affect Cousin
William's capacity for enjoying it at all. He was driven about all day &
visited many of his relations & seemed so happy to be there. After I left he
was to have a day's fishing and with any encouragement at all he would
have bathed in the sea.

I would have liked to bathe myself but did not as we were always driving
about & visiting people & the only practicable time the tide was too far
out.

We failed to get in at either Rosses Point or Ballysadare so had to stay
23 miles away from all the people we were visiting at Inniscrone, this of
course added to the time taken up in driving. The hotel at Inniscrone was
noisy & not particularly comfortable but it was kept by extremely kind,
pleasant people. One of them the mother of the proprietor was a great-
great grandmother. She was 79 & went down bathing on the yellow sands
every single day.

Just as the townland of Barrovane in the Twelve Pins is full of Mother's
cousins, so the townland of Lugawarry near Ballysadare is full of people
called Mac Neice with whom we share great-great grandparents. I was
touched to find that all these people whom Daddy scarcely knew followed
not only his career in detail with pride & sense of kinship but also your
own. Some of them both read & listen to you & it is interesting that they
have a real & intuitive appreciation of some of your work notably the Irish
poems & also one mentioned particularly 'The Dark Tower'.

We spent most time with Florrie & Hilda Mac Neice who are nieces of
Cousin William's. They were very kind & hospitable. The others were all

cousins of his but nearer to him than to us. You see, the common ancestors are Anthony & his wife Peggy Duke who flourished somewhere about 200 years ago or very nearly that. Peggy lived to be 94 & died I imagine about 1840. She must have been quite a person because there are still so many anecdotes about her & they are related as if they happened yesterday. She was one of the Dukes of New Park & ran away to marry Anthony. Of their three sons, Thomas, Ferguson & Valentine, Thomas was the eldest & I suppose had most land & it is his descendants who are still in Lugawarry & they seem largely to have stayed there or if they do go away they incline to come back. We met one who had been to America but returned & bought 3000 acres which he now farms contentedly. He is about our age. Some of them are quite prosperous. Against this, I suppose there was not much for Ferguson's two sons, our grandfather & his brother & they both left so that they have no descendant left in Lugawarry, though Aunt Alice & Aunt Margery went back & stayed there for a time in their youth. Valentine was a wanderer & a 'bad lot' but I think perhaps of parts. He is supposed to have gone to Spain & is noted for changing his religion constantly & entirely from the point of view of convenience.

They were certainly all rather queer with strongly-marked characteristics that seem to be dominant from generation to generation – both physical ones like little hands & feet & very fine skin & mental ones like the violent temper which they all talk about & seem to accept as innate & an absolutely bloody-minded unreasoning obstinacy & a queer kind of pride. I met a lot of them & there were not many I met whom I did not think above the average in intelligence but they are in many ways feckless & unpractical & the intelligence somehow goes to waste – though some are using it all right in their farming etc. It is <u>very</u> queer how scarcely any of them are good with their hands. I am especially interested in this having struggled all my life to acquire a few skills with my own which come naturally to most people & Cousin William's daughter, also a doctor, has done the same thing.

I don't know why I am so interested in all this family history. I think it is partly because it is a kind of bottled case-history which one has unique opportunities of knowing about & I am fascinated by how much these traits are carved in the genes or caused by imitation or by environment or by climate or by what have you?

I have now collected so much information & read so much old social history that it is bursting chaotically inside my head & I really must get it written down somehow for my own satisfaction. But I don't quite know how to do it or where to start. But I think there is a connecting thread in this family, as I suppose in all families, & I might be able sometime to work out a kind of cause & effect.

Any chance of meeting for coffee or tea or something & I will tell you more about it all, if you are interested.

I saw Oonagh fleetingly in Belfast.[1] She has had rheumatoid arthritis but it is rather better just at present.

This is a scrawl but I wanted to tell you how much you are thought of in Lugawarry, Ballysodare![2]

Love to H, Bimba.
Much love Elizabeth

1 – Oonagh Burton, sister of Archie Burton and first cousin, once removed, of FLM and EN.
2 – Cf. FLM's tribute to his ancestors, 'above the yellow falls of Ballysodare' ('Auden and MacNeice: Their Last Will and Testament' in *LI*, CP07, 731–2); also 'Down through Ballysodare in County Sligo where my ancestors were buried under brambles to the Island of Omey where my father had been born' (*SAF*, 111).

APPENDIX 3

W. H. Auden TO Louis MacNeice   MS Bodleian

21 January 1945[1]

Dear Louis,

I've lost your address so must send this via Faber. The <u>Springboard</u> arrived about ten days ago for which many thanks. I think <u>Prayer Before Birth</u> is probably the most beautiful lyric you have yet written, and will no doubt get into <u>all</u> the anthologies. Other favorites [*sic*] are <u>Explorations</u>, <u>Troll's Courtship</u>, <u>Prayer in Mid Passage</u>, <u>The Conscript</u>, to mention only a few. You are, I suspect, an 'anima naturaliter Christiana',[2] which means that when you try to be a Classical Humanist, as in some passages in <u>The Kingdom</u>, I imagine I detect a certain lack of conviction. I'm glad you're moving away from the elegant detail, 'the triple minor' etc to a more chastened and abstract style, not because you don't handle the former beautifully and better than any of us, but just because you can do that standing on your head.

I couldn't send you a copy of my book because, with the paper shortage, Random House sold out their copies immediately. But in April it appears again as part of my collected poems, which I will send, I hope.[3]

As you see I'm still in this place teaching co-eds and the U.S. Navy. I shall however leave in June, for what I don't yet know.

Meanwhile I need your help. In a moment of madness I have undertaken to edit for Viking an anthology of translations from the poetry of all other tongues.[4] <u>Please</u> send me soon a list of suggestions, what in fact, if you

1 – Sent from 16 Oberlin Avenue, Swarthmore, PA.
2 – 'A soul by nature Christian.'
3 – *For the Time Being* (New York, 1944); *Collected Poetry* (New York, 1945).
4 – Cf. FLM to ERD, 21 March 1945, n. 2, p. 451. FLM was privileged to receive a hand-written letter on this occasion, since WHA had sent a mimeographed form letter to several friends (including Malcolm Cowley, Aldous Huxley and AT), requesting assistance with the compilation of a list of 'best translations'. He did write personal letters, however, to FLM, TSE and Isherwood. WHA did not complete the book of translations as planned, which became instead *The Portable Greek Reader* (1948). For a fuller account, see *Complete Works of W. H. Auden, Prose*, vol. II: *1939–1948*, ed. Edward Mendelson (Princeton, 2002), 460–3.

had to do it, you would regard as essential inclusions. Have you translated anything yourself besides the Agamemnon and the Horace Ode? I would very much like you to translate some Horace and Catullus and anything else you fancy for us. We pay. Let me know soon about this.

Was down in Washington last week staying with Isiah [*sic*] Berlin. He is really <u>very</u> nice, I think.

Much love to you and Hedli, and the baby

<u>Wystan</u>

Primary Sources

ARCHIVE MATERIAL (FROM WHICH SELECTIONS HAVE BEEN MADE)

Bruce Arnold, Dublin: Letter to Vera Seaton-Reid

BBC Written Archives Centre, Caversham, Reading: Letters to Laurence Gilliam; F. L. Hetley; Stella Hillier; P. H. Newby; Gerard Ryan; Peter Albyn Thorogood; Philip Vaudrin; Lindsay Wellington; and other members of BBC staff

Beinecke Rare Book and Manuscript Library, Yale University: Letters to Eleanor Clark

Berg Collection, New York Public Library: Letters to Rupert Doone; Geoffrey Grigson

Birmingham University: Letter to Charles Grant Robertson

Bodleian Library, Oxford: Letters to Gerald Abraham; W. H. Auden; Miss J. Cleaver; E. R. Dodds; Mrs. E. R. (Betty) Dodds; John Freeman; Miss J. Freeman; Rupert Hart-Davis; John Hilton; Martita Hunt; Denis Johnston; Jack Loudan; Edward Lowbury; Norman MacCaig; Corinna MacNeice; Daniel MacNeice; Mrs Georgina Beatrice MacNeice; (Antoinette Millicent) Hedli MacNeice; John Frederick MacNeice; Mary MacNeice (née Ezra); Kingsley Martin; I. C. M. Maxwell; James Michie; Karl Miller; Richard Murphy; Elizabeth Nicholson (née MacNeice); Miss E. Robb; Caitlin Thomas; Peter Albyn Thorogood; Harley Usill; Mary Wimbush and others; and letters from Littleton Powys to John Frederick MacNeice

British Library: Letter to John Betjeman

Brotherton Library, Leeds: Letter to Jon Silkin

Buffalo, SUNY, New York: Letters to W. H. Auden; Geoffrey Grigson; Prof. C. D. Abbott and Mrs Abbott; Peter Russell; M. Wollman; and letter of Ruth Jones to Eugene Magner

Columbia University: Letters to Bennet Cerf and Fred Dupee

University of Delaware: Letters to John Malcolm Brinnin

Emory University: Letters to Basil Barr; Adrian Green-Armytage; John Lehmann; Melville Hardiment

Faber archive: Letters to T. S. Eliot; Richard De la Mare; Charles Monteith and others

Hull University: Letters to Philip Larkin

Annie Johnston, Dublin: Letter to Denis Johnston

King's College Archives, Cambridge: Letters to Anthony Blunt; Hilda Blunt; Wilfrid Blunt; letter from Graham Shepard to Anthony Blunt

Simon Kingston, London: Letter to Lady Beazley

Dan MacNeice, New Jersey: Letters to Eva Greer; Daniel MacNeice; Elizabeth MacNeice; Georgina Beatrice MacNeice; Rev. John Frederick MacNeice; Fortescue Vesey Ross; letter from Elizabeth Nicholson to John Hilton; letter from Warden of Merton to FLM; letters from Sydney Wasey and Una Parry to Georgina Beatrice MacNeice

Pierpont Morgan Library, New York: Letters to Geoffrey Grigson

National Library of Scotland: Letters to Hector MacIver

Penn State University Archives: Letters to Marguerite Caetani

Princeton University Library: Letters to Allen Tate

Public Record Office of Northern Ireland (PRONI): Letters to W. R. Rodgers

Royal Holloway and Bedford New College, London: Letters to Bedford College

Sarah Lawrence College: Letters to Harold Taylor

University of Sussex Library: Letters to the *New Statesman*

University of Texas Libraries, Harry Ransom Center: Letters to Alexie Crosthwaite; Geoffrey Grigson; John Lehmann; Dan MacNeice; Georgina Beatrice MacNeice; Rev. (later Rt Rev.) John Frederick MacNeice; Mary MacNeice (née Ezra); Mrs. Borden Stevenson; Terence Tiller; Philip Vaudrin; letters from Philip Vaudrin to Robert Giroux; Peter du Sautoy to Philip Vaudrin

Trinity College Dublin: Letters to F. R. Higgins; Denis Johnston; H. O. White

Victoria & Albert Museum, Theatre Collection: Letters to the Arts Council

Wellesley College: Letter to Elizabeth Manwaring

BOOKS BY LOUIS MACNEICE AND EDITED COLLECTIONS
(First published in London unless otherwise stated)

Blind Fireworks, Gollancz, 1929

Roundabout Way [pseud. Louis Malone], Putnam, 1932

Poems, Faber and Faber, 1935

The Agamemnon of Aeschylus, Faber and Faber, 1936
Out of the Picture, Faber and Faber, 1937
Letters from Iceland (with W. H. Auden), Faber and Faber, 1937
Poems, New York: Random House, 1937
The Earth Compels, Faber and Faber, 1938
I Crossed the Minch, Longmans, 1938
Modern Poetry: A Personal Essay, Oxford University Press, 1938
Zoo, Michael Joseph, 1938
Autumn Journal, Faber and Faber, 1939
Selected Poems, Faber and Faber, 1940
The Last Ditch, Dublin: Cuala, 1940
Poems, 1925–1940, New York: Random House, 1941
The Poetry of W. B. Yeats, Oxford University Press, 1941
Plant and Phantom, Faber and Faber, 1941
Meet the US Army, HMSO, 1943
Christopher Columbus, Faber and Faber, 1944
Springboard, Faber and Faber, 1944
The Dark Tower, Faber and Faber, 1947
Holes in the Sky, Faber and Faber, 1948
Collected Poems, 1925–1948, Faber and Faber, 1949
Goethe's Faust (with Ernst Stahl), Faber and Faber, 1951
Ten Burnt Offerings, Faber and Faber, 1952
Autumn Sequel: A Rhetorical Poem in XXVI Cantos, Faber and Faber,
　1954
Visitations, Faber and Faber, 1957
Eighty-Five Poems, Faber and Faber, 1959
Solstices, Faber and Faber, 1961
The Burning Perch, Faber and Faber, 1963
The Mad Islands and The Administrator, Faber and Faber, 1964
Astrology, Aldus, 1964
Selected Poems, ed. W. H. Auden, Faber and Faber, 1964
The Strings Are False: An Unfinished Autobiography, ed. E. R. Dodds,
　Faber and Faber, 1965
Varieties of Parable, Cambridge University Press, 1965
Collected Poems of Louis MacNeice, ed. E. R. Dodds, Faber and Faber,
　1966
One for the Grave: A Modern Morality Play, Faber and Faber, 1968
Persons from Porlock and Other Plays for Radio, BBC Books, 1969
The Revenant: A Song Cycle, Dublin: Cuala, 1975
Selected Literary Criticism, ed. Alan Heuser, Oxford: Clarendon, 1987

Louis MacNeice: Selected Poems, ed. Michael Longley, Faber and Faber, 1988

Selected Prose, ed. Alan Heuser, Oxford: Clarendon, 1990

Selected Plays of Louis MacNeice, ed. Alan Heuser and Peter McDonald, Oxford University Press, 1993

Collected Poems of Louis MacNeice, ed. Peter McDonald, Faber and Faber, 2007

INDEX OF RECIPIENTS

GENERAL INDEX

Page references in **bold** indicate a biographical note

BBC Chorus and Symphony Orchestra, 446n
BBC Features (edited collection), 501n
Beach, Sylvia, 691n
Beachcomber (John Morton), **284n**
Beadon, E., 20, 21, 24
Beadon, R., 24
Beamish, Anthony, **626n**
Beaton, Cecil, 427n
Beavan, Raymond, 584, 585
Beazley, Prof. John D. ('Jacky'), **191n**, 195n, 200, 209, 239, 589n
Beazley, Marie (neé Bloomfield), **206n**; to Greece, 191; FLM first meets, 195n; lack of servants, 200; FLM writes to from Oxford, 206–7; relations with FLM, 207–8, 209, 210; one reason for her opposition to the wedding, 212–17; interferes in the divorce, 274, 278, 279, 281n, 282, 283–4; interferes with DM's upbringing, xxi–xxii, 300, 301, 309–10, 337; in Acton's memoirs, 533; MM's likeness to, 552–3
Beazley, Mary *see* MacNeice, Giovanna Marie Thérèse Babette
Becher, G. G., **50n**
Beckett, J. C., 670, 671
Beckett, Samuel, 634, 683n
Bedford College for Women, London: overview, 265n; FLM's job at, xvii, xix, 265, 267, 285; FLM on, 276, 326; FLM granted year's leave of absence, 342
Beesley, A. H., **58n**
Behan, Brendan, 673, 688, 694
Behan, Dominic, 657, **688n**, 694
Behan, Stephen, 701
Beigel, Victor, **444n**
Bekwaihene, Chief, 607
Belcher, Muriel, 692n
Belcher, Sir Randall, 129n
Belfast, 343–4, 346, 350, 407n, 569
'Belfast', 229
Belfast Group Theatre, 658
Belfast Zoo, 369
Belgravia Restaurant, London, 66
Bell, Christopher, **132n**
Bell, Clive, 111n, 118n, 122n, 306n
Bell, Sam Hanna, 670n
Benares, 502–5
Benares University, 504, 508
'Beni Hasan', 588n
Beni Hassan, 588

Bennett, Alan, 684n
Bennett, Vivienne, 274n
Bennington, 385
Bennitt, A. J., **92n**, 129
Benson, A. Christopher, 146
Bent, W. E. L., **67n**, 68
Bergne, Diana (née Holman-Hunt), **598n**, 600
Bergne, Villiers A'Court (Bill), **598n**, 600
Berlin, Isaiah, **277n**, 722
Bernal, Desmond (J. D.), 355n, 363, 365
Berndt, Elisabeth, 707n
Berryman, John, **565n**, 631–2
Best, Rt. Hon. Richard, **40n**, 712
Best, Richard Samuel Bevington (son of the above), **40n**, 44, 46, 114, 130, 148, 164, 175, 712
Betjeman, John, **84n**; FLM meets at MC, xv; description of Oxford lodgings, 150; FLM invites to hear AB and brother giving papers, 183, 184; and Shepard, 226; works for *Architectural Review*, 241n; marries, 250n; war work, 422
Betjeman, Penelope, 250n
Betsy (dog), 232, 236, 238, 243, 245–6, 246–7, 249, 254, 271, 276, 280, 286, 288, 296, 301, 309, 337–8
Bevin, Ernest, 428
Beyond the Fringe (revue), 684, 685
Bhabha, Dr, 595, 600
Bhatia, Miss (Delhi), 619, 621
Bible, 434; *see also* New Testament
Bing, Geoffrey, **604n**
Bintley family (Carrickfergus), 67n, **161n**
Birmingham: bookshops, 98, 99, 106; Jews, 245
'Birmingham', 237n
Birmingham University Department of Classics, FLM's job at, xvii, 218–19
Birney, Mrs, **10n**
The Birth of Ghana (broadcast), 607
Black Gallery (radio series), 445n
Blackburne, K. W., **108n**
Blacklegs (play), 367, 372
Blake, William, 130, 151, 159, 175, 178, 226, 270, 576n, 662
Blavatsky, Mme, 151
Blázquez, José Martin, 329–30
Blind Fireworks, xix; 'Adam's Legacy', 180; 'Candle Poems', 145n; FLM on, 247; 'Glass Falling', 123; 'Happy Families', xxiii, 193, 198–9; 'Homo sum',

169n; preface, 193; publication, 200–1, 202, 203–4; publicity, 203, 205; 'The Twilight of the Gods', 161n; typescript, 195n, 196–8

Bliven, Bruce, 404n

'Blood and Fate: *The Odyssey* translated by Robert Fitzgerald; *Patrocleia*, Book XVI of Homer's *Iliad*, adapted by Christopher Logue', 678n

Bloomer, Rev., 116

Bloomfield, Paul, 301, 564

Bloy, C. R., 27n, 39

Blunden, Edmund, **277n**

Blunt, Anthony, **92n**; overview of FLM's letters to, xi; emotional tone of FLM's letters to, xxiv–xxv; at MC with FLM, xv, 92, 97, 103, 106, 108, 113, 114, 115; on *The Heretick*, 94n; and Anonymous Society, 97n; art activities at MC, 108, 110, 112, 118n; made prefect, 108; influences on, 111n; to Bath with FLM, 112; writes for *Marlburian*, 112, 115; on General Strike, 114n; FLM to stay in London with, 116; on Tennyson, 117n; FLM writes to from Ireland, 117–30; in Italy, 119; exhibition for BB, 119; and Poussin, 120n; on El Greco, 120n; FLM's girl's name for, 120n; aestheticism, 122n; on the Baroque, 125n; on Stein, 125n; FLM writes to from Oxford, xvi, 132–3, 135–40; crush on Robertson, 133n; visits FLM in Oxford after being rejected by boy, 135–6; FLM visits in Cambridge, 138; revisits MC, 140, 141; on Cézanne, 141n; FLM writes to from Oxford, 142–3, 150–1, 155–9; tutors sons of French art dealer in Italy, 142n, 165, 175; and BB, 143n, 155, 253; and JH, 150; visits Oxford, 151, 154, 168, 169; FLM writes to from Ireland, 159–61; FLM imagines reborn as hoopoe, 157; FLM considers holiday with, 162; on the child cult, 166; 'Ruins of Carthage' episode, 168n; on Russian Ballet and Stravinsky, 169n, 346n; antagonism to previous generation, 169n; considers trip to France with FLM and JH, 171, 173–4; exam results and courses, 172, 176; discusses FLM's future as writer, 175; stays with Canning, 175, 179; in London with FLM, 176; as model for character in *RW*, 179n; FLM writes to from Carrickfergus, 179–81; gives paper

at Oxford with brother, 182, 183–5, 186; holiday in Vienna, 186; FLM writes to from Oxford, 188–9, 202–3, 204–5; FLM writes to from Norway cruise, 191–2; FLM invites to Carrickfergus, 193–5; and MM, 203, 208, 233; unsuccessfully applies to Fitzwilliam Museum, 205n; article in *Sir Galahad*, 206–7; relationship with FLM cools, xvii, 207–8; attempts to help FLM get *RW* published, 217; FLM writes to from Birmingham, 225–6, 231–3, 236, 237–8, 241–3, 249–51, 252–4, 256–9, 263–4, 269–71; considers trip to Birmingham, 227; elected Fellow of King's, 231; and communism, 233n, 278n, 284; considers applying for professorship at Birmingham, 242, 249, 250, 251; present for DM, 243; to Spain with FLM, 257, 262, 282, 404; Burgess and other Cambridge friends, 263; transfers to King's, 283; reviews *Agamemnon*, 288; FLM dines with, 332; in *LI*, 335; on *Les Sylphides*, 346n; FLM's attitude to his adolescent letters to, 415; life in wartime London, 421; revealed as Fourth Man, 513n; *Artistic Theory in Italy 1450–1600*, 250n; other mentions, 147–8, 177, 200, 201

Blunt, Christopher, 177, 181

Blunt, Hilda Violet (AB's mother), 116, 177, 177–9, 181, 238

Blunt, Rev. Stanley Vaughan, 177n

Blunt, Wilfrid Jasper Walter, **182n**; at Haileybury, 180; reads paper at Oxford, 182, 183–4, 186; holiday in Sahara, 186, 187; FLM returns paper to, 187–8; social evening held by, 232; other mentions, 177, 178, 181

Bodkin, Thomas, **249n**, 253

Bokhari, Ahmed Shah, **500n**

Booth, Mrs (MC), 50

Boru, Brian, 640, 641, 655, 656

Bosis, Lauro de, **462n**

Bossman, Kofi Adumua, **606n**

botany, 18–19

Bottrall, Ronald, 244

Boughey, C. L. F., **53n**, 56, 78n

Bowdoin College, 341

Bowen, Elizabeth, 548, 613, 670, 671, 707, 714

Bower, Dallas, 348n, 446n

Bowle, John, 137, 143, 205

the Hudson, 383; considers Puerto Rico book, 383, 385–6; FLM writes to from Ithaca, 383–6, 388–98; FLM writes about developing their relationship, 388–91; quarrel with FLM about politics and his worldview, 393–8; FLM on her imperfections, 397–8; ghost writing for Ward, 399, 402, 405; FLM writes to about his convalescence, 401–5; FLM writes to about his leaving USA, 410–13; as authority for potential FLM biographer, 415; FLM writes to from wartime London, 418–20, 423–5, 426–32, 439–40; tries to get on Invitation to Learning, 418; plans to get divorce, 421; FLM writes to announce his marriage to Hedli, 445; marries Warren, 572n; 'Call Me Comrade', 326

Clark, Eleanor Phelps (mother of the above), 397, 401, 402, 403
Clark, Sir Kenneth, **249n**, 299, 566
Clark, Walter Van Tilburg, 401
Clark Lectures, 697n, 698–9
Clarke, Austin, 673
Clarke, Edward, **20n**, 21, 24, 33
Cleggan, Connemara, 703
Clements, Major, xxi
Clements, Diana (née Lenox-Conyngham), xxi, 421n, 443n
Cleverdon, Douglas, **592n**, 592–3
Clifton College, Bristol, 61, 64, 85, 110
Clontarf, Battle of (1014), 639–41, 651, 654, 655, 656
Clouston, Storer, 57n
Clun, Shropshire, 226
Coade, F. T., **520n**
Cochin (now Kochi), 510
Cochran, Sir Charles Blake, **560n**
'Cock o' the North', 537, 541, 542, 543
Cocteau, Jean, 258, 581
Codrington, K. de B., 506n
Coldstream, Nancy Culliford (née Sharp; later Spender), **295n**; overview of FLM's letters to, xi; FLM's relationship with, xvii, 365; FLM sends poem to, xxiii; in AJ, 295n, 321; in Hebrides with FLM, 295n, 300–1, 307n; as illustrator of I Crossed the Minch, 307; and Zoo, 308n; FLM breaks with, 317; angry with FLM for choice of portrait artist, 329; problems with husband, 373–4; communicates with FLM in USA, 379n,

381, 382–3, 399; as authority for potential FLM biographer, 415; at Spender's wedding, 427n; FLM writes to about his marriage to Hedli, 444; socialising with MacNeices, 699n
Coldstream, William, 293n, **299n**, 344n, 373–4, 686n
Coleridge, Samuel Taylor, 40n, 47, 695
Collected Poems, xxiii, 690
Collected Poems 1925–1948, 516–17, 520
Collins, H. M., 664–5
Collins, William Wilkie, 57n
Colombo, 595, 598–600
Colonel Bogey (film), 488n
'Colonel X speaks from his Coffin', 229
The Colony Room, 692
Colquhoun, Robert, 700n
Columbus, Christopher, 446, 448, 690
Colwin (at MC), 123, 136, 145, 148
Colyer, A. G. B., **72n**
'Come in, Dominic', 688n
'Coming from Nowhere', 408n, 409
'The Coming of War', 409
Common Sense (magazine), 425n
The Commonwealth Remembers (broadcast), 616n
communism, 284, 336–7, 353, 511, 529, 536
Concordia College, Montreal, 577n
Connaught House, Weymouth, 45, 46
Connecticut College, 558, 559n
Connie (housekeeper), 419, 421, 431
Connolly, Cyril, **296n**, 369, 427n, 434, 581
Connolly, Jean (née Bakewell), 296, 399, 400, 530
Connolly, Lys, 472
The Conquest of Everest (filmscript), 563, 564
'The Conscript', 721
Constable (publishers), 253
'A Contact', 235n
'Conversation', 409, 672n
Cook, John Manuel, **531n**
Cook, Peter, 684n
Coomeraswamy, Mr (Ceylon), 598
Cooper, Rosaleen (née Graves), 171
Corbett, Leonora, **290n**, 301–2
Corfield, Richard Conyngham, **63n**, 64
Cornell University: Cosmopolitan Club, 383; FLM describes campus, 381; FLM's temporary lectureship at, xviii, xx, 364, 368, 370, 376, 379, 381, 382; Telluride

737

and Joyce, 521; and FLM's *Faust* translation, 522–3; and Marguerite Caetani, 523n; invited to lecture in Greece, 525, 531–2, 536, 545; Greek poets on, 528; in USA again, 537; and *TBO*, 537, 545; FLM offers Aristophanes script to, 548, 549; FLM sends other radio scripts to, 549–50; and Dylan Thomas memorial fund, 566, 702–3; and *AS*, 570, 571n, 573–4; FLM proposes to anthologise, 573; FLM uses in poetry course, 576n; FLM considers working on with Sarah Lawrence students, 581; FLM proposes travel book to, 614–15; and Martita Hunt, 661n; and *Solstices*, 665; FLM celebrates his 73rd birthday, 685; further correspondence with FLM, 705; and WHA's anthology of translations, 721n; other mentions, 342

WORKS: 'Animula', 244; *The Cocktail Party*, 538; *The Confidential Clerk*, 538; 'East Coker', 387; *The Family Reunion*, 576n, 581; ' Fragment of an Agon', 264n; 'The Hollow Men', 158n; 'Marina', 244; 'Mr Eliot's Sunday Morning Service', 137n; *Murder in the Cathedral*, 265, 285n; *The Rock*, 241, 244; *The Waste Land*, 133n, 137n, 155n

Elizabeth II, Queen, 561
Elizabeth, Queen, the Queen Mother, 514, 561
Ellis, Havelock, 404
Ellis-Fermor, Una, 275n, 670, 671
Ellora caves, 506, 508
Emery, C. A., 71n, 73, 76
Emmerson, Michael, 637n
Empson, Hetta, 642n, 686n
Empson, William, 244, 573, 576n, 642n, 647, 686n
Enemy of Cant (broadcast), 548, 593
England, FLM on, 334, 336–7, 384, 532–4
Ennius, 197
'Entered in the Minutes', 367, 371n, 372n
'Entirely', 389n, 409
Epstein, Jacob, 121n
Erith, E. J., **69n**
Ervine, St J., 260
Establishment club, xxv, 684
Eunapius, 370n
Eureka (play), 516, 521, 522, 548
Euripides: *Alcestis* (translation started but never finished by FLM), 416; *Bacchae*,

459; *Electra*, 107; *Hecuba*, 71, 72, 76; *Hippolytus* (student production directed by FLM), 576n ; *Hippolytus* (translation started but never finished by FLM), 276, 313, 322, 330–1, 339, 348, 351, 359
Euston Road School, 642n
Eva (DM's nurse), 276, 279, 281, 282, 283
Evans, Estyn, 613, 670, 671
Evans, Walker, 405
Eveleigh, Laurence A., 547–8
'Evening in Connecticut', 409
Everest, Mount, 563, 564
'Everyman his own Pygmalion', 229
Ewing, Mary Cross, 340n
Ewins, Eric, 699n
Exhibition of Indian Art (1947), 506
'Explorations', 449, 721
Ezra, David, 203n, 206n
Ezra, Mary *see* MacNeice, Giovanna Marie Thérèse Babette

Faber & Faber: overview of FLM's letters to editors at, xi–xii, xix, xxiii; and *Poems*, 237–8, 239, 241, 245, 253; and FLM's *Agamemnon* translation, 264–5, 266, 272; and *The Rising Venus*, 265–6, 292; and *LI*, 292, 293, 297, 301n, 302; and *Out of the Picture*, 299n, 302; unhappy at FLM giving *I Crossed the Minch* to Longmans, 301; and *The Station Bell*, 302; and *AJ*, 312, 313, 321; and Harcourt, Brace, 333, 334; and 'The Roman Smile', 339, 354; and *SAF*, 354–5, 359, 366, 385, 468, 516; and *PP*, 408–10; and *Christopher Columbus*, 446, 448; and *Springboard*, 448, 449; and *AS*, 449–50; and *The Dark Tower*, 459n; and FLM's radio plays, 461–2; and *HS*, 468–9, 502; and *Collected Poems 1925–1948*, 516–17; and FLM's *Faust* translation, 522–3, 539n; and *TBO*, 537, 545; and *AS*, 570, 571, 573–4; and *One for the Grave*, 654n; and *Solstices*, 665; and *The Sixpence that Rolled Away*, 677n; rejects FLM's proposal for collection of poems of place, 681–2; keeping FLM's works in print, 690, 697–8; and *BP*, 696, 697; and *The Mad Islands*, 696; and *The Administrator*, 696; party for Lowell, 700, 705; *see also* Eliot, T. S.; Monteith, Charles
Fagan, J. B., 139n

for FLM, 85–6; gives FLM money for Oxford, 131; sends FLM cuttings about parents, 254; EN on, 713, 714

Greer, Gladys Sylvia, 58n

Greer, Helena, 713

Greer, Margaret Elizabeth Macgregor (Betty; later Percival), 58n, 163, 171

Greer, Thomas Macgregor ('Uncle Mac'), 58n–9n, 86n, 164, 171, 713, 716

Gregorovski, Rev. Paul, 645

Grenside, Miss (Faber), 461

Grettir the Strong (broadcast), 467

Gretton, H., 19, 33

Grieg, Nordahl, **455n**

Grierson, John, **254n**, 561n

Grigson, Geoffrey E. H., **233n**; overview of FLM's letters to, xii; and FLM's *NV* contributions, 233, 237, 252, 260; books edited by, 242n; own reviews for *NV*, 244n; FLM asks for work, 261–2; London flat, 275, 276, 278; other mentions, 293

Grin (cat), 81–2, 86

Groddeck, George, **304n**, 368

Gronau, Carmen, 704n

Gronau, Philip, 704n

Gropius, Walter, 603n

Grosch (artist), 404

Group Theatre, London: foundation, 291n; *Agamemnon* production, xviii, 264–5, 266, 267–8, 274, 275n, 276, 277–8, 284–5, 361n, 444n; and Britten, 561n; *The Dog Beneath the Skin* production, 261, 444n; and Hedli, 444n; *Out of the Picture* production, 285, 299, 444n; *The Rising Venus* production, 265, 292; *The Station Bell* production, 241, 253, 255, 261

Guénon, René, **504n**

Guilbert, Yvette, 444n, **560n**

Guillebaud, Hugh Lea, **50n**, 51, 55, 61, 65, 103, 115, 143, 148, 175

Guinness poetry awards, 656

Gunther, James, 605

Guthrie, Tyrone, 291n, **521n**

Habbaniya, Iraq, 470

Hadrian, Roman emperor, 129n

Haileybury school, 177, 180

Hailsham, Lord *see* Hogg, Quintin

Haldane (MC pupil), 68

Haldane, J. B. S., 125

'Half Truth from Cape Town', xxiii, 646–7

Hall, Mr (Ghana), 602

Hall, Peter, 634n

Hall Bros (tailors), 425

Halton, Matt, 607

Halward, Leslie, **326n**

Hamilton, James Alexander Stewart (Alastair), **93n**; at MC, 109, 113; at Oxford, 131, 132, 134; revisits MC, 140, 149, 151; FLM borrows book from, 150; FLM imagines reborn as canary, 157; and Morgan, 191; other mentions, 181, 185, 188

Hamilton College, 340

Hampson, John, 286n, **326n**

Hampstead Town Hall, 560n

Hampton Court, 692

Hanford Prep School for girls, 519n, 520, 687

Hanley, Gerald, **685n**, 699n

Hanley, James, **677n**

'Happy Families', xxiii, 193, 198–9

Harare (formerly Salisbury), 641n, 643

Harari, Max, 589

Harari, Col. Ralph, **589n**

Harcourt, Brace and Co., 292, 302, 333, 334, 346, 572n

Harding (at Oxford), 138

Harding, Edward Archibald (Archie), 534n, **544n**

Harding, Joan and Philip, 563–4

Hardrada, Harold, 61

Hardy, Thomas: *Jude the Obscure*, 100; *Pair of Blue Eyes*; poetry, 244; *Tess of the d'Urbervilles*, 120, 125

Harker, E., 18, 23, 28, 49

Harling, William Francis, **189n**

Harmer, John William, **189n**

Harpers Bazaar, FLM contributions, 404n, 418n

Harrisson, Tom, **344n**, 564

Harrow, 108

Harry (chauffeur), 95, 149, 161

Hart-Davis, Rupert, xii, **224n**, 224, 234

Harvard, 311, 340, 341, 348, 559n

Hauff, Wilhelm, 90

Hawk, Grace E., 340n

Hawks, Howard, 514n

Hawthorne, Nathaniel, 320, 321

Haydn, Franz Joseph, 134

The Heartless Giant (play), 570–1

Hebrides, 295, 297, 298, 299, 300–1

Holmes family (Cairo), 583, 584, 585
Holroyde, Derek, 616, 618, 619, 628
Holroyde family (Colombo), 594, 595, 600
Holroyde family (Delhi), 618
Holt (at Oxford), 134
Holt, G., 19, 21
Holt, Harold, 648
Holt, Oliver, 18n, 19, 21, 42n, 49
Holt sisters, 648
'Homage to Clichés', 260
Homer, 76, 107, 155, 160, 163; *Iliad*, 562, 678n; *Odyssey*, 542, 678–9
'Homo sum', 169n
Honig, Edwin, 697
Hook, Sidney, **336n**
Hooper, Rev. A. W., 16n
Hopkins, A. L. E., **118n**, 125
Hopkins, Gerard Manley, 252, 273, 292, 576n, 653, 676, **677n**
Horace, 601, 722
Horizon, 370, 379n, 404n, 421, 434
Horton, Dr, 281
Hotchkiss School, Connecticut, 376
Housman, A. E., 244, 273, 305, **439n**, 591n
'How to pick the winner in horse racing by a numerological system', 514n
Howard, A. S., **61n**, 64
Howarth, Lilian Irene, 642, 645, 648, 650
Howarth, Robert Guy, **642n**, 645, 648, 650
Howell, Capt. (Cairo), 583, 591
Howell, Virginia *see* Soskin, Virginia
Howells, F. G., **23n**
Howerd, Frankie, 684n
Hudson, Mr (schoolteacher), 16
Hughes, Christopher Wyndham, xv, **107n**, 112, 115, 121, 126
Hughes, Jack, 616
Hughes, Richard, 427, 676
Hughes, Ted, 700
Humphreys, Emyr, **675n**, 677
Hunt, Martita, **661n**, 661–3
Hussein, king of Jordan, 583
'Hustled by Wind', 229
Hutchinson (solicitors), 704
Hutchinson & Co. (publishers), 463
Huxley, Aldous, 133, 138–9, 144, 147, 394, 480, 721n
Huxley, Julian S., 45n, 160, 163, 419, 427n
Huxley, Juliette, 427n
Hyde, Douglas A., 513

Hydra, 526n, 527
Hyndman, Tony, 283n, 346–7

'I Am that I Am', 389n, 408n, 410
I Crossed the Minch: FLM on, 307–8; 'Or One Might Write It So', 288n; origins, 295, 297; publication, xix; research for, xviii, 298, 299, 300–1; reviews, 309
'I Got Those Cathode Blues', 684n
Ibsen, Henrik, xvi, 132, 187
Icaria, 539, 540n
Iceland, 269, 271, 282, 285
'Iceland', 375n
Icknield Street, 246
Iden Payne, Ben, 263n
'Impermanent Creativeness', 193
'In Praise of Water', 537
India: administration, 497; army, 496–7; art exhibition in London, 506; British in, 366, 481, 496–7; FLM on foreign assignment in, xxii–xxiii, 468, 469–511, 594–5, 616–22; FLM's plans for the BBC series, 496–502; FLM's programme reviewed, 512; flora and fauna, 480–1, 485; funerals in, 484–5; independence and partition, xxii, 352, 474–7, 485, 487–8, 489, 492, 498, 500–1; industry, commerce and trade, 497; lack of surviving correspondence with contacts in, xii; languages, 504–5; religion, 497; servants in, 483
India at First Sight (broadcast), 499n, 501n, 512, 549–50
Indian International Industries Fair (1955), 594
'Indian Village', 620
'The Individualist Speaks', 365
Inge, Rev. William Ralph (Dean of St Paul's Cathedral), **160n**, 164, 170, 231
'Insidiae', 398
'Invocation', 672n
Iowa, University of, 576n
Iqbal, Sir Mohammed, **499n**
IRA, 362n, 407
Iraq, 470–1
Ireland: fascist movement (Blue Shirts), 284; FLM and Irishness, xiv, xv–xvi, xvii–xviii, 117, 242; FLM on politics, 485n–6n; FLM on similarities between Northern and Southern Irish, 639; as theme for *The Station Bell*, 242; and World War II, 407; *see also* Ulster

Lindsay, Eric Mervyn, 16n
Lindsay, Frederick R., xiv, 12n, **16n**, 37, 711–12
Lindsay, Dr Mary, 16n, 30n
Lindsay, Robin, 16n
lingams, 506
Linklater, Eric, 381
The Listener, FLM contributions, 297n, 298n, 299n, 307n, 350n, 678n, 679n
Logue, Christopher, 678n
London: air raids, xx–xxi, 414, 421, 423, 427, 428, 432–4; barrage balloons over, 431; life in during the war, 419, 420; FLM on post-war changes, 687
'London Rain', 409
London Magazine, xii, 571n, 580–1, 637n, 659n, 674
London Victorious (broadcast), 454n
London Zoo, 66–7, 308, 507n, 513
Londonderry, 454
The Lonely Crowd (Riesman), 582
Longinus, 260
Longmans, xix, 297
Longus, 141, 145
'Look at the Faces', 684n
Lorca, Federico García, 524
Lord's Cricket Ground, 700
Loudan, Jack, **569n**
Louis MacNeice Reading His Own Poems (recording), 672
Lourdes, Saroyini, 629
'Love to you with tulips', 154
Lowbury, Major Edward Joseph Lister, **463n**
Lowell, Robert, **546n**, 579, 700, 705
Lowry, Dorinda *see* Greer, Dorinda
Lowry, Graham, 713, 714
Lowry, Lady Helena *see* Greer, Helena
Lowry, Hope, 713
Lowry, Malcolm, 694
Luard, Nick, 684n
Lubbock, Lys, 427n
Lucan, 251
Lucknow, 469n, 472
Ludwig, Emil, **241n**
Lutyens, Sir Edwin Landseer, **472n**, 476, 479n, 512
Lutyens, Elisabeth, **479n**, 561
Lyceum Club, **287n**
Lynd family, 560n
Lytton, Right Hon. Sir Neville Stephen Lytton, 3rd Earl of, 190

McAlpine, Bill, 626, 706n
Macaulay, Rose, **560n**, 579n
Macaulay, Thomas Babington, 225
MacBryde, Robert, **700n–1n**
MacCaig, Norman, **572n–3n**
MacCann, George, **367n**; lack of surviving correspondence with, xii; FLM stays with, 637, 691; FLM gives him testimonial for post in Nigeria, 664–5; socialising with FLM, 686; sees BCM in Dublin, 692; colostomy, 698; German tour with schoolgirls, 699; FLM's last stay with prevented by illness, xxv; other mentions, 369, 493
MacCann, Mercy (née Hunter), **367n–8n**; lack of surviving correspondence with, xii; feelings for FLM, 591; FLM stays with, 637, 686, 691; to Belgium with schoolchildren, 692; German tour with schoolgirls, 699; FLM's last stay with prevented by illness, xxv, 703n; other mentions, 599
McCarran, Senator Pat, 558n
MacCarthy, D., 25
MacCarthy, Dermod, 25
MacCarthy, Justin, 25
McCaughen, Mrs, **3n**
McClelland, Alan, **543n**
McCready, Miss, **3n**; role in FLM's life, xiii; in *SAF*, 3n, 5n, 11n; on FLM's first poetry, 6; and FLM's diary, 11n; FLM's memories of, 212; other mentions, 3, 4, 5, 6, 7, 8
McCullers, Carson, 413n, **579n**, 707
McCulloch, Martha, 701
MacDiarmid, Hugh, 162n, 244
MacDonagh, Donagh, 691n
Macdonald, Alastair, 113n, 114, 139, 143n, 151, 181, 188
MacDonald, Dwight, 330n, 333, 336, 339n, 432n
MacDonald, John, 431
MacDonald, Malcolm John, **594n**
MacDonald, Nancy (née Rodman), 339n
McDougall, William, **160n**
McElwaine, Sir Percy Alexander, **625n**
MacFarlane (dog), 645
McGiffin (Ghana), 608
MacGowran, Jackie, 699n
MacGregor, Prof. J. M., 265n
McGuinness, Norah, 673
MacInnes, Colin, 656

347, 348–9; fifth birthday, 331; boyhood bedroom, 338; whooping cough, 342, 347; in country while FLM in Ireland, 357, 364; evacuated during war, xxi, 367; visits father in Belfast, 369; ERD and MM made co-guardians in event of FLM's death on Atlantic crossing, 374–5, 416; FLM considers bringing to USA, 384, 400, 407–8; and FLM's relationship with EC, 390; prefers to stay in Ireland, 413–14; FLM worries where he will be safest, 418; FLM visits in Co. Cavan, 421, 423, 443; hero worship of FLM, 421; FLM writes to from wartime London, 426, 435, 446–7; holiday on Achill, 677n; holiday in Greenore, 435; prep school, 446; to visit FLM in London, 451; Glass takes photo, 452; MM plans to leave very wealthy in her will, 452–3; journeys home to Ireland from school, 457, 460; appearance at age eleven, 458; in Switzerland, 467; FLM writes to from India, 493, 507–8; at Bryanston School, 520n; visits FLM in Greece, 526, 528, 529, 531; adolescent interests, 527; MM's desire for him to spend summer holidays with, 527, 529, 532–5; restores rowing boat, 530; variety of social circle, 534; sails to Brittany with Agnews, 535; friendship with Williams, 535; FLM's concerns about allowing him to stay with MM, 539; and WRR, 546; goes to live with mother in USA, xxiv, 550–4; military service, 550–1, 564n, 582; eyesight, 550–1, 564n; falls out with FLM, 564; FLM writes to from Khartoum, 589; FLM writes to after long silence, 680; sends FLM birthday greetings, 684; FLM writes to from London, 686–7, 691, 698–9; other mentions, 371, 417, 455, 458, 480, 482, 483, 486, 488, 493, 511

MacNeice, Elizabeth Margaret (Lily; née Clesham; FLM's mother), 3n, 208–9, 212, 716–17

MacNeice, Frederick Louis (FLM)
ARTISTIC AND AESTHETIC THEORIES: on art theory, 120, 122, 125–6; on artificiality of art, 142; on the Baroque, 125; on flux, 120, 193n, 381; on importance of the concrete as opposed to abstractions, 169; on relationship between nature and art, 168, 170

GENERAL: aloofness, 394–7; ancestors, 172–3, 395, 718–20; attraction to multiple personalities, xvi–xvii; and belief/scepticism, 392, 425; on best authorities for potential FLM biographer, 415; black moods, 384; circle of friends, 699n; diary, 11n, 29n, 30n; dreams, 155–6, 285, 354, 696; favourite modern poets, 573; on happiness, 553–4; and Irishness, xiv, xv–xvi, xvii–xviii, 117, 242; his likes and dislikes, 563; on own lack of emotions, 122; paintings by, 96, 128; politics, xx, 296, 318–20, 321, 329, 332–3, 336–7, 343, 353, 360, 366, 394, 395–6, 536; portraits, 291, 299, 329; on reading, 627–8; and religion, 118, 135; taste in art, xv, 111, 120, 404, 563; tendency to procrastination, 640n; worldview, 393–7, 425

LETTERS: chronological overview, xiii–xxv; to editors, xi–xii; gaps, xii–xiii; on his poetry, xxiii–xxiv; scope, xi–xii; style, xxii–xxiii

LIFE: birth, 208–9, 212; childhood, xiii, 3–11, 212–13, 396, 552; at Sherborne, xiii–xiv, 12–49; mumps attack and other childhood ailments, 30n, 31n; 1919 school report, 37n; plays Gratiano in *Merchant of Venice*, 40, 41; MC scholarship exam, 42–3, 713; takes common entrance, 44–5; article published in school magazine, 49; at MC, xiv–xvi, 50–116, 533; books read in 1921, 57n, 61; trip to London with Aunt Eva, 66–7; trip to London with Milliken, 70; classics lessons, 71, 76, 80, 84, 107–8; Christmas 1923 at Carrickfergus, 85–6; verse letter, 87–9; in Greek play, 90; holiday at Ballymore, 94, 95–6; writes for *Marlburian*, 96, 112, 115; reads paper at Anonymous Society, 97; begs stepmother for holiday suit, 102–5; to Oxford for entrance exam, 105; names new Carrickfergus kittens, 113–14; golfing holiday in Portstewart, 120, 121; AB's girl's name for, 120n; visits National Gallery, Dublin, 120–1; at Oxford, xiv, xvi–xvii, 130–221, 553; visits AB in Cambridge, 138; revisits MC, 139–40, 141, 143–4, 147–8, 149, 151, 154, 155, 157, 162; walking holiday in Ireland with

on writing poetry, 517–18; on relationship between writing and money, xii; savviness about publishing, xix; on translating, 547; works proposed but never completed, xii, 179n, 227, 231, 234, 238, 241, 242, 253, 303–4, 339, 359, 416, 613–14, 614–15; on writing, 189, 258

MacNeice, Georgina Beatrice (née Greer; FLM's stepmother), 15n; overview of FLM's letters to, xi, xiii; background and family, 712, 713–14; marries JFM, 212; struggles to be accepted by his children, 552; relationship with Willie, 715; takes FLM to Sherborne, 711–12; FLM writes to from Sherborne, 15–18, 22–49; FLM writes to from MC, 50–77, 79–80, 83–5, 90–4, 96–100, 102–16; exotic dressing up, 80; house refurbishments, 82; Christmas 1923 at Carrickfergus, 85–6; FLM sends verse letter to, 87–9; FLM writes to from Oxford, xvi, 130–1, 134, 148–50, 151–3, 163–6, 185–7, 199–201, FLM writes to from Northwood, 168–77; FLM associates with the Victorians, xvi, 169; reaction to FLM's engagement, 202, 210–11, 213, 214; deafness, 202n, 371; and JH, 205, 210–11; FLM on character, 212; holiday in West of Ireland, 220; FLM writes to about taking degree and move to Birmingham, 220–2; FLM writes to about DM's birth, 240–1; comes to visit new grandson, 242; JFM's job takes them to new home in Belfast, 254; FLM writes to about his divorce, 262–3; attitude to MM, 348; description of her Belfast house, 358; and ration books, 358; FLM's attitude to his letters to, 415; FLM writes to about his return home, xx, 416–17; sends FLM shamrock for St Patrick's Day, 426; husband's death, 443; FLM and Hedli stay with, 454; other mentions, 83, 86, 163

MacNeice, Giovanna Marie Thérèse Babette (Mary; née Ezra; FLM's first wife), 203n; overview of FLM's letters to, xi, xxi; FLM meets and marries, xvii, 195n, 202–3, 213–17; and AB, 203, 208, 233; FLM on, 208, 210; health, 208; holidays in St Tropez and Achill with FLM, 209, 215, 216; FLM's parents' attitude to, 209–10; FLM's brother seen

as bar to wedding, 212–17; early domesticity, 221–2, 227; move to Birmingham, 220, 221; visits Shepard, 225–6; trip into Shropshire, 226; as model for characters in FLM's work, 231; DM born, 233, 239n, 240–1; letter to AB about DM, 243n; thank-you letter to Hiltons, 243–4; stay at Wickham, 713; encourages AB to apply for Birmingham job, 249–50; meets Katzman, 252; care of DM, 257; breakdown of marriage, xxi, 262–3, 274, 278n–9n, 453; FLM on, with hindsight, 269, 270; FLM writes to after their divorce, 278–87, 290–1, 293–7, 298, 300–2, 308–10; FLM rejects her suggestion they get together again, 293–5; FLM hopes to avoid while in USA, 348; poultry farm in New Jersey, 361, 382; still attached to FLM, 362; FLM makes co-guardian of DM in event of his death on Atlantic crossing, 373, 374–5, 416; FLM visits in USA, 382, 410; FLM writes to about return to England and DM's safety during the war, 406–8, 413–14; ERD to visit in USA, 452–3; will, 452–3; wants DM to go to USA for summer holidays, 527, 529, 532–5; FLM writes to from Greece, 529–31, 532–6; hand problems, 535; politics, 536; FLM on concerns about allowing FLM to stay with, 539; Dan goes to live with in USA, xxiv, 550–4; FLM writes to DM about, 551–3; Jewish background, 553; encourages trouble between FLM and DM, 564; bad feeling for FLM, 582; FLM on her face, 589; and Harari, 589n; sends FLM card, 691

MacNeice, Hedli see MacNeice, Antoinette Millicent Hedley

MacNeice, Herbert Henry Howell (FLM's uncle), 160, 171, 177, 186, 194n, 715

MacNeice, John Frederick (FLM's father), 3n; overview of FLM's letters to, xi, xiii; background and family, 712–13; FLM's childhood letters to, 3–5, 10–11; sees *Titanic* sail, 149n; during FLM's childhood, 212, 396; marries GBM, 212; takes FLM to Sherborne, 711–12; FLM writes to from Sherborne, 12–14, 18–21; FLM writes to from MC, 100–2, 105, 107–9; speaks at Synod, 113; FLM writes to from Oxford, xvi, 134, 173–7, 185–6;

writes to FLM at Oxford, 165; looks in vain for new comet, 178; accompanies FLM on cruise to Norway, 185, 190, 191–2; FLM on his services, 193; conducts EN's wedding service, 194n; reaction to FLM's engagement, 202, 210–11, 213, 214, 215–16; and JH, 205, 210–11; FLM writes to about DM's birth, 240–1; Bishop of Cashel and Waterford, 242n; comes to visit new grandson, 242; Bishop of Down and Connor, 254; officiates at Carson's funeral, 258; money and tax affairs, 262n; FLM writes to about his divorce, 262–3; attends George VI's coronation, 300; Mackenzie praises, 307n; health problems, 327, 328; and Irish politics, 328–9, 716; FLM writes to about US lecture tour, 340–1; attitude to MM, 348; attitude to FLM's war plans, 357; description of his Belfast house, 358; on dangers of the Atlantic, 407; FLM's attitude to his letters to, 415; FLM writes to about his return home, xx, 416–17; death, 443; Carrickfergus memorial, 691; other mentions, 8, 55, 86, 92, 105, 126–7, 172, 201, 553, 606

MacNeice, Louis *see* MacNeice, Frederick Louis

MacNeice, Mary *see* MacNeice, Giovanna Marie Thérèse Babette

MacNeice, Norah, 715

MacNeice, William Lindsay (Willie; FLM's brother), **3n**; FLM's description, 212, 213, 396; his disability seen as bar to FLM's wedding, 212–17; EN on, 715; other mentions, 3–4, 8, 86, 102, 103, 106, 109, 110, 173, 199, 201

The Mad Islands (play), 696

'Madame Tussaud's' (broadcast), 436n

Madge, Charles, 244n, 344n

Madras, 505–6, 508, 542, 594; Fort St George, 505; St Mary's church, 505

Madura, 507–8

Mageean, Jimmy, **456n**

Magnasco, Alessandro, **120n**

'The Magnates', 408n, 409

Maguire, I. J., xiv, **17n**

Mahabalipuram, 506

'Mahabalipuram', 506

'The Maiden's Song' (anon.), 330

Malaysia, 626–30

Malmesbury Abbey, 100

Malory, Sir Thomas, 57n, 107n, 118, 127

Malraux, André, 385

Mann, Erika, 285–6, 381, 394, 439

Mann, Klaus, **424n**

Mann, Rev. Stanley, xxi, 364n

Mann, Thomas, 264n, 285, **286n**

Manning, Olivia, 278n, 584n, 684n

Manson, J. B., 111n

Manwaring, Elizabeth, 311n

The March Hare Resigns (play), 451, 461

Marie Lloyd pub, Portland Street, London, 699n

Marlborough College: Adderley Library, 76; Anonymous Society, xv, 93n, 97; Bell Trophy, 74; Big Fire, 142n; C3 described, 50; cats and dogs at, 57, 60, 73, 76; chapel, 83, 154; FLM at, xiv–xvi, 50–116, 553; FLM at Old Marlburian dinners, 201, 209, 217; FLM revisits, 139–40, 141, 143–4, 147–8, 149, 151, 154, 155, 157, 162; FLM takes scholarship exam, 42–3, 713; geography round, 52; history, 55; homosexuality at, xvi; houses, 49, 54, 57; Memorial Hall, 101; Memorial Reading Room, 63–4; museum, 52–3, 77; ties, 56, 65, 69; Treacle Bolly, 69; Turner becomes Master, 110; Royal visit, 514

The Marlburian (magazine), 96, 112, 115

Marlowe, Christopher, 119n, 154

Martin, Kingsley, xii, **604n**, 638–9

Marvell, Andrew, 149, 383, 440, 576n, 661

Marx, Karl, 304, 536

Marxism, 353, 381, 645

Maskell, Miss (at Sherborne), 46

Mass Observation, 344n

Masters, John, **618n**

Mathias, James F., 557–8

Matisse, Henri, 119, 126, 169n, 404

Matthiessen, F. O., **401n**, 402, 403, 404, 405, 452, 530

Mauriac, François, 707

Mavrogordato, John George (Jack), **309n**

Maxwell, I. C. M., **631n**, 631–2

Mayer, Thérèse, **553n**, 661n

'Mayfly', 273

Mayne, Rutherford (pseud. of Samuel Waddell), **348n**

Mayor, Tess, 421n

Meade, Tom, 610–11

Medley, Robert, **291n**

of FLM broadcasts, 512; FLM at party, 673n

New Testament, 71, 295

New Verse (journal): overview of FLM's letters to editor, xii; FLM contributions, 229n, 233n, 237, 252, 260; other people's reviews, 244n; FLM's open letter to WHA about his writing, xxiv, 304–6

New Writing (journal), xii, 273, 321n, 421, 434

New York, 413, 414; Poetry Center, 559

Newby, P. H., 639–41, **651n**, 651–2

Newman, Cardinal Henry, 48

Newton, William, 101

Nganamuttu, Mr (Ceylon), 596

Nichols, Beverley, 136n

Nicholson, Ben, 259n, 355n

Nicholson, Caroline Elizabeth (née MacNeice; 'Elsie'; 'Equator'; 'Eek'), **4n**; FLM on their childhood and upbringing, 212, 213, 552; FLM writes to while she's staying in Rosnowlagh, 5–9; at Sherborne, 37, 40, 48, 49, 56; FLM to meet on way home to Ireland from school, 62; FLM sees someone who looks like, 77; at Oxford, 77–8; Aunt Eva sends books to, 80; on holiday at Carrickfergus, 80, 82–3, 86; to Switzerland, 92, 104, 105; holiday at Ballymore, 94, 95; on Oxford people, 131; visits FLM in Oxford, 135, 137, 151, 165, 187; FLM writes to from London, 161–3; engagement, 161n; on David, 161n; birthday, 163n; to go home, 166; fear of failing exams, 169; at Charing Cross Medical School, 171; on family's polyglot ancestry, 172n–3n; wedding, 191, 194; and FLM's arrest and engagement, 202; FLM nickname for her and her husband, 213n; FLM consults about whether their brother's disability might be hereditary, 214; FLM discusses his divorce with, 263; FLM stays with after his divorce, 282, 285; FLM on her vagueness, 287; helps look after DM, 297; on Virginia Soskin, 341n; reaction to FLM's plans for the war, 357; care of DM in event of FLM's death, 374, 375, 416; care of DM in FLM's absence, 413–14; as authority for potential FLM biographer, 415; visits FLM in London, 418, 419, 421; on FLM's feelings about Christmas, 420n;

visits DM in Ireland, 426; FLM visits in Plymouth, 426; experience of raids in Plymouth, 431; lends FLM her London home, 439; FLM dines with, 514; meets DM's friend Williams, 535; on FLM's Irish trips, 703n; and FLM's death, 708; holiday in Ireland, 718–20; background information supplied by, 3n, 4n, 10n, 12n, 177n, 711–20; other mentions, 4, 5, 10, 25, 36, 69, 100, 102, 175, 186, 200, 367, 406, 416–17, 669

Nicholson, Sir John: FLM socialises with, 135, 165, 171; wedding, 191, 194; FLM nickname for, 213n; attends *Agamemnon*, 276; FLM stays with after his divorce, 282, 285; other mentions, 161, 202, 213, 214

Nietzsche, Friedrich Wilhelm, 191, 192, 194, 408

Night and Day (journal), xii, 232n, 303

Nile river, 587–91

Nkrumah, Kwane, **612n**

Noble, George, 609, 612

North, R. E. G., **56n**

Northern Ireland *see* Ulster

'Northern Ireland and Her People', 328n

Norway, 185, 190, 191–2

Norwood, Dr Cyril, 56n, **59n**, 107, 108, 238

Norwood, Mrs Cyril, 175

Norwood, Miss, 56

The Nosebag (play), 461

'Notes for a Biography', 637

'Notes on the Way', 392

'Novelettes', 349, 409

'The Nurse', 672n

'Nuts in May', 673n

'Obituary', 389n

O'Brien, Conor Cruise, **685n**, 686

O'Brien, Edna, 706–7

Observer (newspaper): overview of FLM's letters to editor at, xii; article attacking FLM and other poets, 260n; FLM contributions, 538n, 658, 694n

O'Casey, Sean, 123

'O'Connell Bridge', 352n, 389n, 409

O'Connor, Frank, 455n, 613, 670, 671

O'Connor, Rory, **675n**

O'Connor, Tony, **675n**

O'Crohan, Thomas, 580n

'Octets', 372

Rilla, Walter, **467n**
The Rising Venus, 255, 261, 265–6, 292
'Rites of War', 673n
Roach, A. I., **75n**, 76
The Road to Independence (broadcast),
    471n, 499n
Robb, Miss E., 570–1
Robert Hale (publishers), 354–5
Roberts, Michael, 244, 425
Roberts, Nesta, 614
Roberts, William Paul Temple, **79n**
Robertson, Ben, **426n**
Robertson, Sir Charles Grant, 247, **256n**
Robertson, Michael, **133n**; FLM on, 135;
    FLM visits in Cambridge, 187; other
    mentions, 136, 151, 180, 185, 188, 189,
    203, 205, 238
Robinson (Birmingham), 234
Robinson (gardener), 286
Robinson, Lennox, **250n**
Robson, Dame Flora, **267n**
Rockefeller awards, 464
Rockefeller Foundation, 574
Rodgers, Harden, 699
Rodgers, Marie Harden (née Waddell),
    515n, 699n
Rodgers, Nini, 699n
Rodgers, Rev. W. R. ('Bertie'), **466n**;
    background, 534n; broadcast included
    in *BBC Features*, 501n; wife's illness,
    515; broadcasts on literary figures, 521;
    FLM writes to from Greece, 525–6,
    545–6; admiration for Hedli's singing,
    561; LG's wife leaves him for, 564n;
    reads in Belfast with FLM, 569n; FLM
    proposes to anthologise, 573; and *The
    Character of Ireland*, 613, 616, 670,
    671; Northern Ireland script, 634–6;
    daughters, 699; BCM on, 699n; *Europa
    and the Bull*, 526; other mentions, 456,
    556
Rodman, Cary Selden, xx, **339n**, 362,
    393n, 424
Roerich, Nicholas, **509n**
Roethke, Theodore, **579n**
'Roll on Reality', 684n
Rolo family, **589n**, 590
'The Roman Smile', xii, 238, 242, 253,
    339, 348, 354, 359, 367, 369, 416
Romania, 351
Roney-Dougall, R. P., 40
Rosenberg, Isaac, 273

Ross, Alan, 674n
Ross, Fortescue Eric Vesey, **79n**;
    background, xv; at MC, 84, 90, 91, 92,
    93, 94, 96, 103; FLM writes to from
    holiday, 95–6; growing religiosity, 118;
    writes to FLM, 122, 144; sends FLM
    Christmas card enquiring about plans
    for future, 181
Rossetti, Christina, **123n**
Rosteutscher, Prof., 646
Rotheram, T. A., **75n**, 78
Rothschild, Victor R., 3rd Baron, **264n**,
    421
Roundabout Way: FLM's desire never to
    be reprinted, 416; FLM's reaction to
    published version, 231; models for
    characters, 215n, 231; publication, 200,
    204, 217, 224, 226; quotes from, 144n,
    154n, 234n; writing of, 179–80, 191,
    193, 194, 197, 222
Rousseau, Henri, **128n**, 132
Roy, Jamina, **622n**
Royal Academy, London, 176, 506n
Royal Court Theatre, 666n
Royal Festival Hall, London, 560
Royal High School, Edinburgh, 688
Rozwadówski, Mr (Ceylon), 598
rugby: actual and proposed FLM articles
    about, 303, 638–9, 673, 689; All Blacks
    tour (1919), 27n; and FLM, xiii, 22,
    134, 257, 301; FLM on international
    matches, 310, 584, 615, 637n, 689; at
    MC, 82, 85; in South Africa, 645; Welsh
    players with Irish names, 675
Rukeyser, Muriel, 579
Russell, Bertrand, 246
Russell, Cicely, 278n
Russia *see* Soviet Union
Russian Ballet, 169
Rylands, George H. W. ('Dadie'), **193n**,
    227

Sabre (dog), 700
Sackville-West, Edward Charles, 444n,
    462n, 520, 534n, 684
Sadler's Wells Theatre, 241
Saffer, Charles Martin, Jr., **321n**, 323
sagas, Norse, xv, 97, 593, 640
St Bride's Well, 83
'St Paul's' (broadcast), 432, 433, 436
St Paul's Cathedral, London, 432, 433,
    436